Highlife
TIME 3

JOHN COLLINS

DAkpabli

DAKPABLI & ASSOCIATES
ACCRA

HIGHLIFE TIME 3
Copyright © John Collins 1994, 1996, 2018
All Rights Reserved
First Edition published in 1994; Second edition published in 1996 by Anansesem
Publications Limited.

ISBN for this Edition: 978-9988-2-7619-5

Editorial Team
Nana Awere Damoah
Kofi Akpabli
James Anquandah

Book Website: www.highlifetime.com

Cover design and Book Layout by multiPIXEL Limited
P O Box DC 1965, Dansoman, Accra, Ghana
Email: multipixelmails@gmail.com
Tel: +233 201 578 865 | +233 246 725 060 | +233 246 210 862

Website designed by Kojo Akoto Boateng and Divine Puplampu
(Stimuluz Technologies Limited)

Author Picture by Paul Ninson

Published by
DAkpabli & Associates
P O Box 7464, Accra North, Accra, Ghana
Tel: +233 264 339 066 | +233 244 704 250 | +233 247 896 375
Email: info@dakpabli.com

ABOUT THE AUTHOR

John Collins is a naturalised Ghanaian of British decent who has been active in the Ghanaian/West African music scene since 1969 as a guitarist, band leader, music union activist, journalist, writer, music teacher and archivist. In the 1970s he operated his Bokoor Highlife band and over the years has worked, recorded and played with numerous Ghanaian and Nigerian artists and bands such as the Jaguar Jokers, Francis Kenya, E.T. Mensah, Abladei, Fela Anikulapo-Kuti, Koo Nimo, Kwaa Mensah, Victor Uwaifo, Bob Pinodo, the Bunzus, the Black Berets, T.O. Jazz, Atongo Zimba and Aaron Bebe Sukura.

He has published ten books and scores of journalistic and academic papers on African popular music and been involved with many films on Ghanaian popular, art and traditional music.

He obtained his first degree from the University of Ghana in 1972 and his Doctorate in Ethnomusicology at the State University of New York at Buffalo in 1994. In 1982, he opened his Bokoor Recording Studio and in 1987 was made an honorary life-member of the International Association for the Study of Popular Music (IASPM). During the 1990s, Collins was Technical Director of the three-year joint Universities of Ghana/Mainz African Music Re-documentation Project, and for seven years was with the Ghana National Folklore Board of Trustees/Copyright Administration. Between 1997 and 2013, he was co-leader of the Local Dimension highlife band.

He is currently a Patron of the Musicians Union of Ghana (MUSIGA) and a Full Professor of the Music Department at the University of Ghana at Legon, where he has been teaching since 1995. He is also Chairman of the BAPMAF African Popular Music Archives NGO.

Dedication

To my late wife Dovi Helen and my son Thomas Kojo. Dovi came from the well-known musical family of traditional Ewe drummers and dancers, her father and uncle being renowned master-drummers. She had a strong voice and led the praises in her local church. Thomas has many pursuits and interests, including computer animation and graphic design. He is also interested in music, has developed into a fine trumpeter and guitarist, and currently plays in the gospel band of the First Love Church.

Unless otherwise stated, photos are from the J. Collins/BAPMAF music archives.

Summary of contents

Table
of contents

Prologue

The book starts with an up-to-date prologue which examines seventeen broad musical genres – both old and new – that the author identifies as comprising the Ghanaian musical repertoire. The newer developments include jama hiplife that, instead of using imported hip-hop beats, utilises the 'jama' rhythm, which is what the youth now call highlife and other local beats. Then there is the azonto club dance that is also based on jama beats, as well as electronic 'contemporary highlife' and R&B-influenced Afropop. Even newer with the Ghanaian youth is Jamaican dancehall and its Afro-dancehall spinoff, and a Pan African club dance known as 'afrobeats' (nb. not Fela Kuti's Afrobeat) of which the Ghanaian azonto was an early example. The prologue also delves into how the century old Ghanaian 'Highlife Imagination' has crossed into the new millennium, despite all the changing technologies, youth fashions and outside influences. Indeed, highlife music and its 'jama' beats now dominate much of Ghana's popular music – whether hiplife, local gospel dance-music, azonto/afrobeats, Afro-dancehall or 'contemporary highlife'. In short, Highlife has become 'Millennial'.

Prologue

THE CURRENT GHANAIAN MUSIC SCENE AND 'MILLENNIAL HIGHLIFE'

The main bulk of this third edition of Highlife time was completed in late 2013 and so, in this Prologue, I am bringing things up-to-date.

Firstly, Part One examines some general trends in the Ghanaian musical scene and industry. In Part Two, I look at the latest developments in the various musical genres that comprise the Ghanaian musical repertoire. Thirdly, I discuss the way highlife and the 'highlife imagination' have crossed into the new millennium.

Part One

SOME GENERAL DEVELOPMENTS IN THE GHANAIAN MUSIC SCENE AND MUSIC INDUSTRY

The general democratisation of music production in Ghana through the use of digital technology continues, with literally hundreds of recording studios now operating across the breadth of the country, many of them owned by musicians such as Sheriff Ghale, Bessa Simons, Stonebwoy and Wanluv, just to mention a few. Linked to this technology is the use of the autotuner that removes the necessity of having a trained voice, as many out-of-tune blemishes can be ironed out through this gadget. Although some believe this device artificially alters the voice, in a recent chat with Panji Anoff of Pidgin Studio, he pointed out that because the autotuner removes the need to be pitch perfect, it gives local singers the ability to place more emphasis on emotion.

Another trend related to digital technology is that the youth are moving more and more towards sharing their works on the web through social media apps like WhatsApp, with some collecting royalties through various internet music download platforms such as Menta Music, Phonophile and Mipromo. This by-passes a lot of problems connected with music promotion and distribution, such as having to bribe radio stations with 'payola' to get one's works aired, or the perennial problems that local copyright collecting agencies have in distributing royalties to musicians. Moreover, with music piracy still rampant, it is now very difficult for a young artist to find a music producer; for as soon as the CD is released, it is pirated. Internet distribution offers an alternative to CD and radio play.

In the last chapter of the 1996 version of this book, I wrote a section titled 'The Musical Ghost in the Machine' which reflected my worry – at the time – that a lot of the young artists who were influenced by electronic disco and hiphop were no longer performing live on stage with bands; but rather miming or lip-synching to studio-backing tracks. However, in this new version of the book, I mentioned a return to live musical performances by hiplife artists that began from around the year 2000 with free-styling GH rappers and artists like Sidney, Obour, Okyeame Kwame and many others. Live shows are nowadays very common, whether performed on stage by hiplifers, or by the newer generation of contemporary highlifers, rap poets, dancehall musicians; and also by Afropop divas, many of whom have been trained in church choirs.

Versatile Okyeame Kwame

This brings us onto the topic of the continuing growing importance of women singers, who not only dominate gospel music but also constitute a significant portion of current R&B-influenced Afropop and Jamaican-influenced dancehall artists. Some of these are MzVee, Ebony, Kaaki, Efya, Tiffany, Eazzy, Adoma, Adina, and Becca. Then there is Dela Hayes' group Dzesi (Women of Colour) that was formed in 2009 as the country's first all-female popular music band. It is still running and, in 2015, they released their second album that was produced by Bessa Simons, featuring the Ivorian artist Meiway. In early 2017, an eighteen-member all female police band was formed in Kumasi, called the Golden Ladies.

Yet another continuing trend is the large number of tourists who are coming to the country and, as noted in Chapter 64, they patronise a wide spectrum of Ghanaian performance, such as traditional music and dance, live popular music and street carnivals such as the Osu and Chale Wote festivals. Some also study African music and dance at the universities and the many private cultural centres that have sprung up since the 1990s. Tourism figures from 2015 show that over one million foreign visitors came into Ghana, bringing 2.7 billion dollars with them, making tourism Ghana's fourth largest foreign exchange earner after oil, gold and cocoa.

As it is estimated that tourists spend around 9% of their money on entertainment, it can be appreciated that they are providing a big boost to the local music sector. More details on this tourist impact are found in Chapter 64 of this book.

Section One of the book covers the Ghanaian highlife theatre known as the 'concert party' that goes back to the early 1900s; in its 1950s to 1970s heydays, there were around 240 such groups touring up and down the country, with some also making TV series. Although the concert party profession today has drastically shrunk, many of the actors who passed through this important Ghanaian genre have moved into the 'Kumawoood' local film industry that is based in Kumasi.

Sidney

In 2012, the Ghana Musicians Union (MUSIGA) brought in KPMG and also myself to help put together a 292-page statistical report entitled 'A Comprehensive Study of the Music Sector in Ghana' that was made available to the public in 2014. Some of the figures from this report are worth mentioning here. Firstly, it estimates that 30,000 people are working professionally in Ghana's music sector, including 13,000 musicians.

Secondly, the MUSIGA-KPMG report broke down the various categories of music being commercially produced in Ghana, arranged in descending order of recordings sales, as follows:

- Gospel (around half the total output)
- Hiplife
- Reggae
- Classic Highlife
- Contemporary Highlife
- Afro-beat/Afro-Rock/Afro-Jazz

- Traditional Music
- Jazz
- Choral
- Art-Music
- Brass Band music
- Film and video music

Moreover, in 2016, MUSIGA established its Music Academy that operates out of the NAFTI building in Accra and runs courses related to practical musicianship, music production and show business. In 2017, when the Academy went into its second session, it enrolled 140 students.

On a sadder note, since 2013, the country has lost some of its leading musical personalities, many of whom are mentioned in this book. Those who have passed include Ghana's pioneering female pop singer Charlotte Dada, the trumpeter Pa Akreshie, keyboards player Malek Crayem of the old Magic Aliens, guitarist and arranger Stan Plange, highlife composer Kojo Donkoh, the Classic Handels vocalist Ishall Kwabla Banini – and just recently Paapa Yankson and the ex-Uhuru trumpeter Kpakpo Addo.

From the concert party field are Pa Bobo (Three Axes), Patrick Yamoah, T.D.B. Adjekum (Happy Stars) and the comedians Nkomode and Bob Okala. We also lost Nana Danso Abiam of the Pan African Orchestra, the famous choreographer Francis Nii Yartey, the music producer George Prah of Gapophone, actor George Williams and singer-actor Soloman Sampah of the Arts Council's 1970s Ananse Kromian Sounds. The hiplifers Daasebre Gyamenah and Omanhene Pozo passed away, as did the young dancehall artist Vybrant Faya, with the veteran highlifer C.K. Mann and the young dancehall singer Ebony passing away in the early part of 2018. Castro has been missing since July 2014.

Just as this book was going to press (May 2018), the sad news came of the demise of the Nzema highlife singer Jewel Ackah, the Dagoni master 'gyil' xylophone player Bernard Woma and Bernard 'Solar' Quarshie, the gome player of Hewale Sounds.

Part Two

CURRENT MUSICAL POTS SINCE 2014

In the very last two chapters of the book (Chapter 64 and Coda), I present the contemporary Ghanaian musical styles as around a dozen musical pots simmering on a large artistic stove. Besides traditional and folkloric music, these pots include old-time 'classic' highlife, burger highlife, gospel music, jazz and Afro-fusion music, northern Ghanaian 'savannah' music, Afro-pop, azonto, 'contemporary highlife' and the various forms of hiplife, such as 'jama hiplife', 'GH rap' and 'ragga-life'.

I use this cooking pot analogy as it implies something dynamic rather than fixed, for each pot can be enriched with the addition of new local or foreign ingredients, whilst the various musical pots themselves can be blended together in the future to create new forms of music. Moreover, musicians themselves are not confined to one pot but can move around, during their careers, to play music from the different pots.

In this prologue, I have extended the number of Ghanaian musical pots currently cooking away in Ghana in 2017 to seventeen. We begin with old-time highlife.

MUSICAL POT ONE: OLD-TIME 'CLASSIC' HIGHLIFE

Classic highlife includes the guitar band and dance band highlife music that is played in the context of live performance by surviving old-time musicians and also by some younger artists who, as mentioned in Chapter 39, include Rex Omar, Amanzeba, Bessa Simons, Ben Brako, Paulina Oduro, Kwame Yeboah, the members of the Legon University-based Big Shots, the new Ramblers and Evergreen big-band highlife groups. Then there is Afro Moses and his 'world music' style of highlife, whilst Sly Collins released a new album in 2016. Another is Ackah Blay who got his training with F. Micah's, K.K.'s No 2, Jewel Ackah's Butterfly Six and the Western Diamonds highlife bands. In 2017 he released an album called 'Edoke' with the help of Panji Anoff's Pidgin Studio.

However, many of the old time musicians are still active and these include Koo Nimo, Gyedu Blay Ambolley, Jackson A. Adofo and his City Boys, Pat Thomas and Amakye Dede. Koo Nimo, together with his student George Ankoma Mensah 'Spratz', for instance, released an album in 2015 on the Zaria label called 'Palmwine Music in the 21st Century' that involved the engineer Francis Kwakye and producer Jonas 'Bibi' aka 'BB' Dowuona-Hammond. The following year, Bob Pinodo launched a new band called the Gold Crest. Ebo Taylor is still active and making world tours at eighty years, whilst C.K. Mann's 80th birthday was celebrated in 2016 at the +233 Jazz Club in Accra with performances by A.B. Crentsil and Smart Nkansah.

Turning a little deeper into highlife history, the British RetroAfric company released 'E.T. Mensah King of Highlife' in 2015: a two CD anthology that contains around seventy of the Tempos old 1950s/1960s hits and is accompanied by a sixty-page booklet on E.T. written by myself. Incidentally, the following year, my book 'Highlife Giants', that explores the eighty-year old relationship between Ghanaian and Nigerian Highlife, was published by Cassava Republic Press of Abuja. Still on the topic of highlife history, the Ghana Broadcasting Company held a show at its forecourt in 2015 that featured Ebo Taylor, Bob Pinodo and Efua Dorkenoo. This event celebrated the GBC's Gramophone Library that was digitized in 2008 with the help of Dr. Markus Coester and a German grant, with some of its highlife songs from 1947-1962 being released in 2012 as the double CD 'Ghana Muntie'.

MUSICAL POT TWO: BURGER HIGHLIFE

Burger highlife is still going strong and, as noted in Chapter 37, this was a form of 'disco' highlife that was first created in the early 1980s by artists in Germany such as George Darko, Lee Duodu and the Lumba Brothers. Daddy Lumba went on to release twenty five albums and a recent one released 2014 is 'Awoso' which contained the song 'Ye Nea Woho Beto Wo' that won him the Highlife Artist and Highlife Song of the Year at the 2015 Vodafone Ghana Music Awards. Another member of the original Lumba Brothers, Nana Acheampong, currently operates the Owoahene Studio in Kumasi. The burger highlife 'godfather', George Darko, continues his chiefly duties in Akropong-Akuapim, but has never put down his guitar and recently organised a performance for the chiefs of his area, with guitarists that included Koo Nimo.

POT THREE: OLD-TIME REGGAE

Many of the reggae stalwarts discussed in Chapter 36 are still active, like the roots-reggae man Black Prophet, Ghana's 'Mr. Music Man' Kojo Antwi and the US-based Rocky Dawuni whose 2015 'Branches of the Same Tree' album fuses reggae and Afrobeat into what he calls 'Afro Roots'. For this album Dawuni became, in 2016, the very first Ghanaian to be nominated for the American Grammy Awards.

Kojo Antwi continues performing his Christmas shows and releasing his Twi reggae songs in the 'Lovers Rock' style, his latest being the single 'Nyoo' (My Woman). Up to 2017, he was also Chairman of GHAMRO, Ghana's music royalty collecting body. In 2016, Black Prophet, who is a member of the Twelve Tribes of Israel Rastafari Movement, released his 'Stories of Life' reggae album. However, another reggae stalwart, the UK-based General Marcus and one-time member of the 1990s Ghanaian Kente reggae band discontinued releasing records in Ghana due to his annoyance with the country's rampant payola, that involves musicians having to bribe radio stations to play their music.

Some other current reggae-men are the northern Ghanaian artist Sheriff Ghale, who runs a recording studio in Tamale and Ahuma 'Daddy Bosco' Ocansey, who recently reformed the old S.O.S. Squad. Another is Blakk Rasta, whose 'kuchoko' reggae employs local xylophones and drums. Then there is Ras Caleb Appiah-Levi, one-time Director of MUSIGA's Reggae Department, who during the 2016 election period went on a peace tour and released a reggae album called 'Have Faith'. Another is the veteran Root Eye (Kwasi Nyarko-Ofei) who made a comeback in 2014 with his reggae single 'Heaviest Rain', and is the current director of MUSIGA's Reggae and Dancehall Department.

Many of the younger artists following the Jamaican music trend of music now play in the electronic ragga and dancehall form which is discussed later.

MUSICAL POT FOUR: HIPLIFE

As mentioned in Chapter 38, hiplife — the Ghanaian version of American electro-funk or hiphop — surfaced in the early 1990s, although the name was not coined until the mid-1990s. Reggae Rockstone is usually considered the one who coined the name, but there is evidence that it was Reggie and a group of artists and promoters, such as Panji Anoff, members of Talking Drums, BB the Virus, the American DJ Rab and some others who were meeting at Zapp Mallet's CHM Studio in 1994 that came up with the name. Whoever actually coined the name, however, it was Rockstone's 1996 album 'Makaa Maka' that contained the Twi rap song 'Tsoo Boi' that publicly launched the hiplife name. After that, hiplife developed into regional varieties rapped in Ga, Ewe, Hausa, Fanti and so on.

Reggae Rockstone

Over the last twenty years, hiplife has branched off into various forms, such as jama hiplife that draws on local Ghanaian rhythms and also free styling GH Rap. Two other forms are 'Ragga-life' that draws on Jamaican dancehall ragga and its 'toasting' deejays; and 'contemporary highlife' that draws on highlife. As these last two variants have emerged recently as separate genres, they are discussed separately later.

The hiplife mainstream comprises the original form pioneered by Reggie Rockstone and others who rap in local languages or Pidgin English over hiphop and sometimes local beats. These are sometimes known as 'GH rappers' and they often feature live 'free-styling' performances, with pioneers of this being VIP and the Mobile Boys. Current hiplife rappers include Ghana's fastest rapper Sarkodie, the 'rap doctor' Okyeame Kwame and VVIP. Then there is Hammer (Edward Nana Poku Osei) whose Last Two record company has released works by the rappers Obrafour, Tinny, Kwaw Kese, Ayigbe Edem and, from 2016, the up-and-coming artists Teephlow, Medikal, Akan and Worlasi.

Sarkodie. Beatznation.com

Some other new Ghanaian hiplife rappers are D. Black and Elom. D Black raps in English and, between 2014 and 2016, released a succession of songs from his 'Kotomoshi' album that featured the late crooner (i.e. soft romantic singer) Castro. D Black is the first Ghanaian rapper to win the Black Entertainment Television (BET) Awards. EL (Elom Adablah) is a product of the University of Ghana who surfaced musically in 2008, but by 2010/2011 was pioneering the azonto dance movement craze that is discussed later. Another hiplife outfit is the R2Bees (Refuse To Be Broke), a duo from Tema that consists of Faisal Hakeem and Rashid Mugeez who have had around twenty hit releases since 2008.

Guru is a rapper from the Brong Ahafo region who combines hiplife with highlife and dancehall. He appeared on the Ghanaian musical scene in 2008 collaborating with Sarkodie, and since 2010 has had hits like 'Lapaz Toyota', 'Pooley Swag' and then 'Booze and Boobs' for which he was nominated for the 2017 Vodafone Ghana Music Awards.

Then there is Yaa Pono who started recording from 1995 as a fast freestyle Twi rapper who often competed with Sarkodie. He became one of the best rappers in Ghana and has often travelled to perform in Nigeria, especially after joining Panji Anoff's Pidgin Studio in 2009. Like Guru, Yaa Pono is one of the new hiplifers who combines hiplife with highlife and dancehall. In his latest 2017 hit 'Gbee Naabu', he 'disses' the current 'dancehall king' Shatta Wale.

Rapper and comedian A Plus (Kwame Asare Obeng) is known for his controversial hiplife songs that deal with politics and social issues. His first album 'Freedom of Speech', released during the 2000 elections, contained the track 'Mesuro Mpo Na Merekeka Yi O' (I'm afraid but will say it anyway) that lambasted politicians, whilst his 'Letter to Parliament' won him a nomination for the Best Hiplife Song at the 2008 Ghana Music Awards. In 2016, he released another thought-provoking track titled 'Abɛn Bɛ Bom' (The Horn will Blow). More recent is the rapper Flowking Stone (Kwaku Nsiah Boamah), a KNUST graduate, who has released several hiplife songs since 2016 with his 'Go Low' becoming the best hiplife song of the year at the 2017 Ghana Music Awards. A Ghanaian hiplife rapper making waves in the United States is Blitz the Ambassador (Samuel Bazawule) who, for some of his songs, draws on Fela-style Afrobeat and the guitar band highlife of artists such as Alhaji K. Frimpong.

VVIP. Citinewsroom.com

Finally, in terms of mainstream hiplife, there is VVIP, a rap trio that consists of Prodigal (Joseph Nana Ofori), Zeal (Abdul Hamid Ibrahim) and the 'godfather' of Ghanaian hiplife, Reggie Rockstone. This band was originally a Nima-based GH rap group called Vision In Progress or VIP that consisted of Prodigal, Zeal (then called Lazzy) and Promzy. When Promzy left VIP in 2013, Rockstone stepped in. VVIP's first release was their 2014 music video 'The Book of Hiplife' that made references to many of the hiplife pioneers. This was followed in 2016 by the song 'Alhaji' that featured the Nigerian reggae and dancehall super-star Patoranking.

Mention must also be made of female highlife rap artists who, as noted in Chapter 38, are few and far between. Mzbel was still releasing singles in 2016, Tiffany gravitated into Azonto and Afropop, whilst the ragga and rap artist Abrewa Nana has, since 2016, moved fully into dancehall. Over the years, she has released songs like 'Dance Hall' and 'Mate Odo Filla'.

Triple M was Ghana's very first all-female rap group, but it broke up in 2006 after releasing its second album 'Mempe'. However, one of its members, Mildred Mark-Hansen, aka 'Sheega Styla', moved into dancehall and R&B for her 2010 releases 'Zinzima' and 'Let's Go' and her 2015 'Baawasa' (Hausa for 'it's not a joke'). Indeed, she is now considered a queen of dancehall. However, there is a new lady rapper on the block called Eno (Ruth Nana Serwaa Nyame), from Kumasi, who performs in English and Twi, as in her 2012 single 'My Love', featuring Afriyie. In her 2014 single, 'Megye

Wo Boy' (I'll Take Your Boy), that features Abrewa Nana, Eno rejects Sarkodie and Shatta Wale's claim in 'Megye Wo Girl' that they can get any girl into their corner. Eno's debut album 'Yaa Asantewa' was released in 2016 and features Medikal.

As mentioned in Chapter 38, jama hiplife emerged in the early 2000s as a result of the experiments Jeff Quaye or Jay Q was doing in digital studios such as the Virtual Studio and then, from 2002, the Hush-Hush Studio which he later bought.

Jama Hiplife pioneer at Hush-hush studio, Jay Q (Jeff Quaye)

What he was doing in these two studios was incorporating highlife, kpanlogo and other local beats into his type of hiplife, instead of the usual funk derived hiphop beats of America. Jeff Quaye is a Ga and so he called his style of hiplife 'jama'—the Ga word for a lively animated form of dance. Indeed, he is considered to be the 'king' of Jama hiplife. Earlier on, he recorded the likes of Castro, Dr. Doh, and the singer Ofori Amponsah. Another pioneering jama hiplife outfit was 4x4 made up of Captain Planet and Abortion; and also the Buk Bak duo whose first hit 'Siklitele' was made at Hush

Hush Studio in 2003. Around 2007, 4x4 went on to release albums that were in the 'crunk' hiphop style that evolved in the southern USA in the 1990s and downplayed the poetic rap voice element of hiphop , rather focusing on drum rhythms and repetitive refrains that the fans could easily dance to and chant along with. The move by 4x4 between jama hiplife and crunk was possible as both were electronic dance forms that focused on light-hearted party-time lyrics.

Other hiplifers who explored the jama vein were the Praye trio, Tic Tac, the late Daasebre Gyamenah, Adane Best and Oheneba Kissi. Yet another group functioning between 2002 and 2009 was Wuta ('fire' in the Hausa language) that consisted of Frank Kwadwo Afriyie and Daniel Morris.

Many of these jama hiplife artists are still operating, like 4x4, Samini (formerly called Batman), the R2bees and Kofi B, whilst Ofori Amponsah, K.K. Fosu and Kwabena Kwabena gravitated into what is called 'contemporary Highlife' that is discussed later.

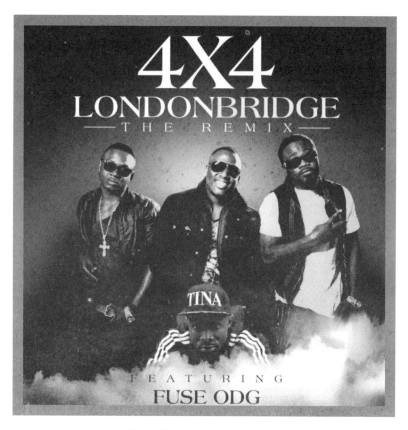

4x4. Ghxclusives.com

Jama hiplife with its local rhythms was primarily a dance music in which the rap content was reduced and singing, which was either in highlife or ragga mode, became more prominent. Indeed, some Ghanaian rappers of the early 2000s saw jama hiplife as a too light-hearted form of party-time music, and so renamed their more orthodox type of Ghanaian hiphop 'GH Rap'. Nevertheless, the jama experiments with electronic forms of local rhythms have permeated many other styles of contemporary Ghanaian music, whether it is the newer generation of mainstream hiplife rap artists like Guru and Yaa Pono, or some of the dancehall and azonto artists who are discussed below.

MUSICAL POT FIVE: CONTEMPORARY HIGHLIFE

As discussed in Chapter 38, 'contemporary highlife' is an electronic version of highlife that was initially part of the hiplife movement – and was pioneered by artists who moved away from rapping to singing, or included both singing and rapping in their songs. These included K.K. Fosu, Lucky Mensah, Oheneba Kissi, Nana Fynn, Nana Quame, Kwabena Kwabena, Daasebre Gyamenah and Adane Best. A very popular exponent of this genre was Ofori Amponsah from Agogo who began his career in 1999 when he featured on Daddy Lumba's burger highlife hit 'Wo Ho Kyere', and then had a huge hit in 2005 with his minor highlife song 'Otoolege'.

Ofori Amponsah. Graphic Online

Another is Mugeez who is a member of the previously-mentioned 2RBees rap duo and who, according to the music promoter Panji Anoff, has been an important innovator in making highlife palatable to the Ghanaian youth – and indeed Nigerian youth, as he has influenced the Nigerian Afro-hiphop/afrobeats singers Wizkid, Davido and Wande Coal who have all visited Ghana.

Contemporary highlife that features highlife rhythms, singing and guitar styles has now taken off in a big way, and as such can be treated as a separate genre from hiplife. A number of new artists play contemporary highlife and one of the most popular is the singer and record producer Bisa K'dei (Ronald Kweku) from Larteh in Ghana's Eastern Region. He cites the veteran highlife artists Nana Ampadu, J.A. Adofo, Paa Bobo, Daddy Lumba and Nana Acheampong as his musical inspirers. In 2013, he won the Ghana Music Awards Best Hiplife Song of the Year and then in 2015 released two big contemporary highlife hits 'Mansa' and 'Broda'. In both, he sings in Twi backed by jama highlife rhythms, keyboards and prominent guitar phrases played in typical guitar band highlife style.

Bisa K'dei. Photo Bisa Kdei World Facebook page

Then there is Afriyie Wutah (Frank Kwadzo Afriyie) of the old Wutah hiplife duo that broke up in 2009. Since then Afriyie has released ballads like 'Love of my Life', 'Here to Stay' and 'I Do' that are sung in English with a relaxed highlife lilt, accompanied by saxophone and acoustic guitar played by George Spratz, a student of the famous palmwine guitarist Koo Nimo.

Dobble is a duo that in 2015/2016 released the highlife songs 'Only U' and 'Christie' that are sung in Twi to the accompaniment of highlife rhythms and guitar licks, and 'Alomo' that features singer Ofori Amponsah. Two other contemporary highlifers are Vision DJ and Kumi Guitar. Vision DJ (Francis Essah Aboagye) is from Koforidua and his third album 'Grind' released in 2017 is sung in Pidgin English, Twi, Ewe and Hausa and features the rapper/singer A.I. Kumi Guitar (Nana Yaw Kumi) is a graduate of Adisadel College who broke into the music scene from 2011 with fast electronic highlife songs like 'Break into Two' followed by 'Brown Sugar' in which he sings in Twi and plays highlife guitar.

At the end of 2017, the most popular contemporary highlifer was the Fanti singer Kofi Kinaata from Takoradi who released 'Susuka' in 2015, and 'Sweetie Pie' in 2016 when he became the New Artiste of the Year at the Ghana Music Awards. In 2017, he released 'Confession' in which he begs God in Twi and Pidgin English to take over the steering wheel of his car as he is so drunk.

Like Bisa K'Dei, Dobble and Kumi Guitar, Kofi Kinaata's songs feature guitar playing in typical highlife mode and more details on the features of contemporary highlife that draw on old-time highlife are discussed at the end of this Prologue in connection with 'millennial highlife'.

MUSICAL POT SIX: GHANAIAN GOSPEL MUSIC
Gospel music is still the largest component of the Ghanaian commercial music sector and as noted earlier in this Prologue, the 2014 MUSIGA–KPMG report on the Ghanaian music industry puts the figure at 50.6% of the market.

As noted in Chapter 43, gospel music emerged in the 1970s and 1980s military era when times were hard for secular musicians who played highlife, reggae and other forms of popular music. Consequently, many brought their music into the churches which used the resulting danceable gospel music as part of their worship – following

Kofi Kinaata

the age old African practice of religious dance. Sometimes gospel music is in the syncopated 4/4 rhythms of popular dance-music styles such as reggae, R&B, disco and most types of highlife. However, gospel is also performed in polyrhythmic 6/8 time that is related to traditional forms of music, such as the adowa and kete of the Akans – as well as some forms of guitar band highlife such as the 'odonson' and 'Akan blues' variety.

The gospel bands have continued to be an important training ground for instrumentalists and singers. The following is a list of just a few of the many top gospel singers that are currently operating in the country: Joyce Blessing, Nhyira Betty, Pastor Paul, Cecilia Marfo, Rebecca Ray, Pastor Joseph Alhassan who sings Dagbani gospel, the veterans Ohemma Mercy and Grace Ashy who are still going strong and more youthful acts, such as Don D, Kingszkid, E-Rock, Cwesi Oteng and the Rock Soldiers. Some of the gospel artists given awards between 2015 and 2017 are No Tribe, the guitarist KODA, Selina Boateng, Gifty Osei, Anita Afriyie, Diana Asamoah, Emelia Arthur, Obaapa Christie (Christiana Love), Joe Mettle, Piesie Esther, Sonnie Badu, Jeshrun Okyere, Nacee, Mary Agyemang and Mabel Okyere.

As can be seen from this list, women singers still dominate gospel singing and one result of this is that the church bands and choirs have become a training ground for a new generation of secular female artists, such as the singers Efya, Becca, Adomaa, Adima and Wiyaala who all belong to the new Afropop genre discussed later.

MUSICAL POT SEVEN: FELA'S KUTI'S AFROBEAT

Afrobeat was developed in the 1970s by Nigeria's Fela Anikulapo-Kuti who, as discussed in Chapter 49, was a Nigerian highlife and jazz musician who combined these styles with soul music and traditional Yoruba music to create his danceable Afrobeat. This music was played by his large dance bands the Africa 70 and Egypt 80. Fela sang mainly songs in Pidgin English that supported the down-trodden Nigerian masses or 'sufferheads' as he called them. He preached Pan Africanism, made social commentaries and criticised the Nigerian government. His militancy resulted in many arrests and imprisonments and when he died in 1997 a million people attended his funeral in Lagos.

During his lifetime, his music became very popular in Africa and, since his death, his Afrobeat style has been taken up by many musicians across the globe. There is even a Broadway musical about him that featured the American Afrobeat band Antibalas. Fela's one hundred or so albums are constantly re-released and his birthday on October 15 is now celebrated as a 'Felebration' that is held in many African, European, American and Asian countries. The reader might check chapter 18 and 19 of my 2015 book 'Fela: Kalakuta Notes' (published by Wesleyan University Press, USA) to see more details on the spread of Fela's Afrobeat.

In Ghana, many artists have drawn inspiration from Fela's music, such as the reggae artist Rocky Dawuni, the late Nana Danso Abiam of the Pan African Orchestra, Dela Botri of the rootsy Hewale Sounds, the highlife veteran Ebo Taylor and the hiplifers Nana King, Tic Tac and Reggie Rockstone. Many Ghanaian artists have also played at the Lagos Felabrations and some of these are the Rocky Dawuni, the hiplife rappers VIP and Trigmatic, the Afropop singers Efya and Knii Lante, the Fokn Bois (Wanluv and Mensah), the guitarist Kyekyeku (a student of Koo Nimo), the free style rapper Yaa Pono and the soulish singer-songwriter Yasmeen Helwani who is daughter of Fela's long-time friend, the late Faisal Helwani.

As a sign of Felas's enduring influence in Ghana, annual Felabrations have been held at the Alliance Francaise in Accra since 2015. These have featured the highlife artists Blay Ambolley, Ebo Taylor and Akablay, the Afropop crooner Yaa Yaa Kankam, the Frafra kologo lute player Stevo Atambire, the Xtreme Volumes led by the energetic Nigerian singer Villy and Fela's ex-drummer CC Franks (Frank Siisi-Yoyo). The latter two also played at the Alliance Francaise's 7th October 2017 Felabration that I attended, as did the singer Nana Yaa who is the daughter of the singers Pat Thomas and Lola Everett.

MUSICAL POT EIGHT: AFRO-POP

As mentioned in the Coda of this book, another emerging popular dance-music style in Ghana and indeed Nigeria and other parts of Africa, is 'Afropop'. This music draws on American hiphop beats, but more importantly on the singing and crooning style of Contemporary R&B and Neo-soul of artists like Boys II Men, Mos Def, Jennifer Lopez, Beyonce, Britney Spears, Lauryn Hill, Erykah Badu and D'Angelo. In the case of Ghana, many hiplifers have experimented with R&B, beginning with Ded Buddy and Nana Kwame in the 1990s and then later artists, such as Samini, DJ Black (Kwadwo Ampofo), Nana Kwabena, K. K. Fosu and Richie Mensah.

The Afropop genre, sometimes called 'Twi-pop' when sung in that language, is now firmly established in Ghana as an independent musical category and some of its pioneering male crooners mentioned in the Coda were Chico Dawuni, Henry 'Chemphe' Agyekum and his 'urbanlife', and Khini 'Knii' Lante who won the Best Male Vocalist at the 2010/2011 Ghana Music Awards. Another is the rapper and Twi-pop singer Dr Cryme (Darlington Agyekum) whose debut album 'Finally' was released in 2011.

Some of the newer male artists who move between hiplife rapping and crooning Afropop music are Vision DJ who was discovered in 2013, and the singer/rapper Joey B who surfaced around 2013 with his hiplife songs 'Tonga' (irresistible women) that

31

Becca (Rebecca Akosua Acheampong), Photo BeccaMusic Facebook page

featured Sarkodie – but by 2016 was also singing soft romantic songs like 'U x Me'. Another is the hiplife artist Medikal (Samuel Adu Frimpong) who combines singing with rapping and rap poetry, as in his 2016 hit 'Time No Dey'.

Then there is the UK-based Ghanaian Eugy (Eugene Entsir) who first formed an R&B group with his two younger brothers, and since 2015 has released slow romantic Afropops in Ghana such as 'Dance for Me' and 'Body' featuring the soulish Nigerian afrobeats singer, Mr. Eazi.

Three other young Afropop artists are I.A., Lil Shaker and Chase. A.I. (Ayisi Ican) has recorded two hundred songs in Afropop mode since 2009 and his 'Mixtape Mayhem' released in 2013 had enormous web-play, followed by 'Making Tasha Proud' and 'Anger Management'.

Lil Shaker (Phillip Yaw Atiemo) was raised in Accra and his third Afropop release was his 2017 'Licki Licki' a slow tempo erotic song he sings in Pidgin English. Chase or Chase Forever is a UK-born Ghanaian who obtained several Ghana Music Award nominations in 2013 for his song 'Lonely' and then released 'Pull Me Down' about the problems he faced in life. His are slow bluesy type songs that he sings in Pidgin English and/or Jamaican Patois.

The previously mentioned R2Bees hiplife duo of Rashid Mugeez and Faisal Hakeem also releases some of their works in the soulish and R&B influenced Afropop style. Back in 2009, they featured on the Nigerian Afropop star Wande Coal's 'Kiss Your Hand' and in 2016 the R2Bees released the Pidgin English love songs 'Tonight' and 'More' that featured the Nigerian, Wizkid. Indeed in recent years a number of Nigerian Naija Afropop artists have visited and played in Ghana, such as P-Square, 2face Idibia, Tony Tetuila, 9ice, Bracke and Tina Savage.

As R&B is such an important component of Afropop, Britney Spears, Beyonce, Erykah Badu, Whitney Houston and other international singers have provided role remodels for African women. So Ghanaian women are very prominent in the Afropop and Twi-pop scene and they predominantly sing love songs, or songs from a woman's point of view, in English, Pidgin English, Twi and other local languages.

Some of the Ghanaian Afropop divas mentioned in the Coda of this book are Becca (Rebecca Akosua Acheampong), Jane 'Efya' Awindor, the Liberian born Jane Logan, Sala Yacubu, Lady Jaywah and Mildred 'Eazzy' Ashong. Eazzy shot to fame in 2010 with her song 'Twinkle' followed in 2013/4 by her up-tempo album 'Against the Odds'. Another is the Twi-pop crooner Bertha 'Yaa Yaa' Kankam who says she was inspired by Whitney Houston, Aretha Franklin and Celine Dion. She also studied music and drama at the University of Ghana at Legon and, in fact, was one of my students. 'Yaa Yaa' released her first song 'Faithful' in 2012 for which she received a Ghana Music Award.

Jane Awindor (Efya). www.ghanalive.tv

Some other current Afropop divas are Raquel, Tiffany, Adomaa and Adina. Raquel Naa Ayorkor Ammaha is a talented UK-born songstress, composer and actress who in 2012 won five nominations for that year's Ghana Music Awards. She sings in English, has collaborated with the rappers Sarkodie and Trigmatic and released her debut album called '@25' in 2012. She sings in Afropop or highlife mode, such as her 2014 'Cool Down' and 2015 'Lakabo' produced by Lil Shaker.

Antoinette 'Tiffany' Owusu comes from Kumasi and began her singing career in 2006 when she collaborated with Castro, the R2bees, Sarkodie, 4x4, Fuse ODG, the Afropop singers Lil Shaker and Chase and also the music producer Killbeatz (Joseph Addison). In her Afropop songs she raps and sings in English and Twi but also, since 2013, has also become one of the queens of azonto, a style that is discussed in the next section.

As her father is a bishop, the Ghanaian/Nigerian Adomaa (Joy Jasmine Adjeman) initially began singing in church choirs. She has a clear and delicate voice and shot to fame in 2015 with her 'Baafira-Adonai Mashup' and also the 'Evolution of GH Music Mashup' in which she reworks highlife and Afrorock songs by the Tempos, Osibisa, Amakye Dede and Paapa Yankson.

Adina Thembi Ndamse is a half Ghanaian/South African Afropop and soul singer who began in a church choir and then, as a youngster, joined the Ghana National Theatre's choir that performed at Kidafest and Funworld events. In 2008, Adina won the Stars of the Future singing competition for which she received a recording contract. She began releasing songs like 'Let Me Go' and 'Hamba Kahle'; followed by her 2014 'SaSa' featuring E.L. and her 2015 single 'Coastal Vibe' featuring Trigmatic. More recent is her 2016 song 'Too Late' produced by Kilbeatz, which is a sad bluesy love song in English and Twi.

A final example of a current Afropop star is Noella Wiyaala who is from Ghana's Upper West Region and so sings in English and her native Sissala language. As well as R&B and neo-soul, she sometimes draws on dancehall, rock and folk elements. She first sang in a church choir and then became a session-singer for the Echo Soundz Studio in her Region's capital, Wa – where she recorded her first song 'Tuma' (Work) in 2009. In 2011, she won the Stars of the Future Award and in 2013 went on to release the music videos 'Make Me Dance' and also 'Rock My Body' in which she featured the dancehall singer Jupitar. In 2014 she performed in Denmark alongside Ghana's Atongo Zimba and released her debut album 'Wiyaala' which won two awards at the 2015 Vodafone Ghana Music Awards. That year she also played side by side with Rocky Dawuni at the Afrikadey Festival in Calgary, Canada. In 2015 she released her ninth music video called 'Sun and Moon' about the need for peaceful co-existence and unity. Her Afropop also covers feminist themes like respect for women and love from a women's point of view, and an example is her 2014 song 'Tinambayai' (here we come) that protests the exploitation of women in Africa.

Noella Wiyaala

As can be seen women play a prominent part in the Afropop scene and so it is quite different from the more 'macho' hiplife genre that is dominated by men. One of the reasons for the feminisation of Afropop is, as already mentioned, that Ghanaian divas are inspired by foreign female R&B and neo-soul superstars. Another reason is that many of them had some sort of training in Ghanaian church choirs and gospel groups. Consequently, today Afropop and local gospel are both major avenue for professional female singers.

MUSICAL POT NINE: THE AZONTO DANCE

As mentioned briefly in the Coda of this book, azonto is an electronic dance that was created in Ghana in 2010 by a number of artists associated with the hiplife movement. It is a one or two step dance that draws some of its moves from older Ghanaian traditional dance styles like the Ga kpanlogo, as well as actions related to work and play, such as ironing clothes, washing, driving, boxing and swimming. According to the Ghanaian dance scholar Terry Bright Ofosu, it was because the azonto was created by the youth of Greater Accra, which is in the Ga Traditional Area, that this new dance drew on the local Ga kpanlogo drum-dance.

The name 'azonto' itself is a youthful slang for an erotic and wayward girl and it was pioneered by the hiplifer Gasmilla's (Odartei Milla Lamptey) song 'Aboodatoi', E.L.'s song 'Obuu Mo' and Sarkodie's 'U Go Kill Me', followed by those of Guru, Tiffany, the late Castro, Akoo Nana, Keche, 4x4, Appietus and the R2Bees. According to the US-Nicaraguan deejay and musicologist Juan Diego it was in 2012 that Nigerians began following this Ghanaian dance style; like D'banj with his 'Oliver Twist', t P-Square's 'Chop My Money' and 'Alinga', and also Wizkid who often visited Ghana and released a single called 'Azonto'.

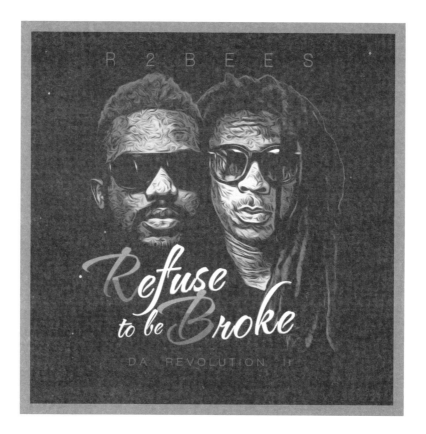

R2Bees. www.musixmatch.com

The music video that companied the Nigerian P-Square's 2012 'Alinga' used moves similar to that of azonto – and this led to some Nigerians claiming they invented azonto. But taking into account that azonto was created in Ghana as far back as 2010, and that it was only in 2012 that Wizkid had taken this dance to Nigeria, azonto has been definitely recognised as a Ghanaian creation.

Azonto not only quickly spread to Nigeria but also to other parts of Africa – and also became an international dance floor craze popularised, for instance, by the British based Ghanaian hiplifer Fuse ODG who first released his single 'Azonto' in 2011, and re-released it in 2013 when it entered the British charts. A variant of azonto called 'alkayida' appeared in Ghana in 2013 that for some reason took its name from the Al Qaeda terrorist organisation and is typified by a slower tempo than azonto, stronger upper body gestures and group routines.

The music that accompanies azonto features singers, keyboards and very prominent electronic percussion, and in some cases tuned percussion. The rhythms are the basic age-old 4/4 highlife and kpanlogo rhythms that the Ghanaian youth today call 'jama'. Indeed, Azonto can be seen as the dance that emerged to accompany the jama form of hiplife that, as already noted, was based on local beats rather than imported hiphop ones. Azonto is still going strong in Ghana and fifty azonto acts appeared at the Azonto Dance Concert held April 2017 in James Town Accra that included Heroz, NWA, The Gentlemen, Humble Stars, Footprint, Kyses, DFC, Zigi, Webbie, BBoys, I Candy and Breaking Boys.

Fuse ODG

What Ghanaians call 'azonto' is what in other parts of Africa and the world is called 'afrobeats', a word coined in Britain in 2012 by Black British DJ's for African electronic dance music that uses various local syncopated 4/4 African rhythms. And 'afrobeats' is the topic that we turn to next.

MUSICAL POT TEN: ELECTRONIC AFROBEATS

Although the name 'Afrobeat' and 'afrobeats' are similar these are quite distinct musical genres. As noted earlier Afrobeat is a live form of big band music that was developed in the 1970s by Nigeria's Fela Anikulapo-Kuti. This was a politically charged music whilst 'afrobeats' is of a more escapist nature. However both often use Pidgin English. Infact 'afrobeats' is a recently invented umbrella term for the various African forms of electronic hiphop and 'house' dance club music, that includes Ghanaian and Nigerian hiplife and azonto, Naija-rap and Afro-hiphop.

The person who is thought to have popularised the word 'afrobeats' is the young British born Ghanaian DJ Abrantee Boateng who was hosting a radio show in 2012 on the UK's Choice FM which he called 'afrobeats'. At that time the artists he was playing included UK born Ghanaian rapper and hiplifer Fuse ODG and also Nigeria's 2Face Idibia, P-Square, Tiwa Savage, Yemi Alade, Wande Coal and D'banj, whose music was then called in Nigeria 'Afro-hiphop' or 'Naija rap'.

With the surfacing of the word 'afrobeats', Fuse ODG (Nana Richard Abiona) went on to have several hits in the British record charts. As already noted, Fuse also visited Ghana around 2011 then, and discovered the azonto dance that Ghanaian youth had already created around 2010. As a result Fuse helped introduce the Ghanaian azonto to the 'afrobeats' community in Britain. He successfully re-released his 'Azonto' song and then 'Antenna' in 2013, followed the next year by the 'Million Pound Girl' that got to number five in the UK singles charts. In Nigeria the word 'afrobeats' for their electronic dance music quickly caught on but Ghanaians tended to stick rather to the word 'azonto' for their form of this electronic dance music. However, the Ghanaian impact is still felt by Nigerians, as in the case of Mr. Eazi who studied in a Ghanaian university and was influenced by the Ghanaian slowing down the tempo of later azonto variants. Consquenlty he calls his relaxed and sparse afrobeats style 'banku musik' after a favourite Ghanaian dish.

It should be noted that there has been some controversy between the older and younger generation of Anglophone West African artists over the name 'afrobeats' being so similar to the word 'Afrobeat', even though these are as different a chalk and cheese. Not surprisingly this argument was stronger in Nigeria where the word 'afrobeat' was picked up quickly and where Fela's original Afrobeat was invented This came at a head at a meeting that took place in Lagos during the October 2013 Felabration. That year I was invited to give a talk at the opening Felabration Debate on 'Fela, Nkrumah and the Ghana Connection', and this was followed a few days later by a 'Post Fela' panel discussion at Freedom Park that I was also involved with: organised by the cultural activists Jahman Oladejo Anikulapo and Theo Lawson. Speakers such as the Afrobeat artist Adu Odukoya Bantu and poet Audu Kaikori were concerned over the confusing similarity between the words Afrobeat and 'afrobeats' and decried the fact that the word 'afrobeats' itself had been coined in a foreign country. However, others like Gboyega Oyedele of the Afrologic band and Funso Ogundipe of the Ayetoro band, pointed out that by using the name 'afrobeats' the youth were paying homage to Fela Kuti.

Whatever the concerns over the name 'afrobeats' the word has come to stay – and particularly in Britain and Nigeria and even nowadays in Ghana. Consequently various Ghanaian newspaper reports since 2013 have used the word 'afrobeat' to describe a wide spectrum of local artists such as Samini, Sarkodie, Guru, Edem, Kwabena Kwabena, Okyeame Kwame, Eazzy Ashong, the R2Bees, Joey B, Guru, E.L., Stonebwoy and D-Black.

MUSICAL POT ELEVEN: DANCEHALL AND AFRO-DANCEHALL

Dancehall (or 'bashment') is a type of music that appeared in the 1970s and 80s in Jamaica and involves deejays who 'toast' in-between and over reggae music and also recordings played on sound systems; 'toasting' itself being lyrical monotone chanting in Jamaican Patois over a rhythmic beat or 'riddim'. Yellowman (Winston Foster) is one pioneer of this style. Then when in the late 1980s Jamaican music went digital and became influenced by sampling and American hiphop beats a type of electronic dancehall called 'ragga' or 'ragamuffin' appeared that was pioneered by Shaba Ranks.

The very first reggae sound system was introduced to Ghana in the 1977 by the Jamaican Ras Wolde Mikael, followed in the early 1980s by the 'Hi Power' sound-system brought by the British West Indian 'Jah Power' that featured the Ghanaian deejay's Preacher Levi, General Marcus and Wahesh Simeon. It was also at this time that the Ghanaian musician K.K. Kabobo was blending highlife and dancehall and the Jamaican reggae and dancehall deejay Yellow Man visited Ghana.

The later and more digitised 'ragga' form of dancehall was taken up in Ghana by some of the early hiplifers from the mid-1990s and early 2000s, such as the late Terry Bonchaka, Mad Fish (Raymond Frimpong), Yoggi Doggi (Samuel Twum-Barima), Samini, Bandana (now known as Shatta Wale), Abrewa Nana, Abortion, Bacteria, Natty Borax, and Slim Busterr.

Very important is Emmanuel Andrews Samini who is from the Upper West region and who was initially known as Batman. He released his single 'Linda' in 2003 and then six albums between 2004 and 2015, the first being 'Dankwasere'. He is considered as the hiplife artist who Africanized dancehall music in Ghana and, as such, he mentored dancehall and Afro-dancehall artists like Stonebwoy and Kaaki. As this ragga form of dancehall was played by Ghanaian hiplifers, this style was sometimes referred to by artists like Abrewa Nana and Yoggi Doggi back in the early 2000s as 'ragga-life' or 'rag-life'.

A pioneering radio deejay of dancehall was DJ Blakk who started his career running the Space Jam program of the University of Ghana's Radio Univers in 1997. Another was Rudeboy Sterling, aka Mr Logic, who later set up the Bad People Entertainment that today manages many dancehall artists.

The Ghanaian dancehall scene really began to take off after 2006, undoubtedly encouraged by performances in Ghana by leading Jamaican dancehall/ragga stars such as Jean Paul in 2006, Shaggy in 2007, Mcvada in 2011 and the Elephant Man Oneal Bryan in 2016.

It was in 2006 that Stonebwoy (Livingstone Etse Satekla) released his first song whilst still at school. This Accra raised rapper and baritone singer who hails from the Volta Region then moved under the wing of Samini Music through which he released his first single 'Climax' in 2008, and then his first album 'Grade 1 Album' in 2012. He has since set up his own Burniton Label and won many awards, and there is a lively public debate between him and Samini as to who is the 'king' of dancehall. Another dancehall exponent who also made his first release in 2006 is Ras Ebo (Andy Kwabena Adisi)

Stonebwoy (Livingstone Etse Satekla). Glammy News.com

By 2009/2010 more hiplife artists were moving into dancehall, such as Sugar Ranking, Jupitar (Michael Okine), the Ewe rapper Edem Hotor whose albums (first titled 'The Volta Regime') are also popular in Togo where Ewe is spoken, and the Legon University graduate Iwan (Abdul Razak Issahaku) from Ghana's Northern Region who by 2016 had released five albums, including 'Dagomba Girl'.

Award-winning dancehall artists who appeared between 2012 and 2014 are the Nyabingi Rastafarian Ras Kuuku (Kojo Kurankye), Episode (Theophilus Nii Arday Otoo) who began his career whilst still a schoolboy and, most famously, Shatta Wale who was previously known as Bandana.

Shatta Wale or Charles Nii Armah is a Ga from the Korle Gonno area of Accra who in 2004 released first his hit track 'Bandana from Ghana'. After a period of quietude, he rebranded himself Shatta Wale and in 2013 released his hugely successful album 'The Dancehall King'. Since 2014, he has released a stream of hit singles and won many national awards. In his 2017 'Hosanna' he features the Nigerian dancehall artist Burna Boy.

Shatta Wale. Photo Shatta Wale (Shatta Movement) Facebook page

Before moving onto other current male dancehall artists who have surfaced since 2014, I will first say something about some of the women involved in this genre, beginning with the pioneer rapper, singer and dancer Abrewa Nana. She began by collaborating with the Saas Squad hiplife group, and then between 2000 and 2004 released her first three rag-life albums 'Sagoa', 'African Gal' and 'Maba'. She became a judge for Nigerian Idols West Africa TV series and in 2016 released dancehall numbers like 'Dance Hall' and 'Mate Odo Filla'.

Then came the R&B and dancehall singer Grace 'Kaaki' Ocansey who began her music career as a choir girl and had her first dancehall hit 'Ewoo' in 2011. She was followed in 2014 by the dancehall, R&B and Afropop artiste Mzvee (Vera Hamenoo-Kpeda) whose first hits were the album 'Borkor' and also the singles 'Natural Girl' featuring Stonebwoy, and 'African Queen' that she did with Shatta Wale. This was followed in 2016 by 'Make I Shine' that features E.L. and 'Rewind' in 2017 that features Kuami Eugene.

Two others dancehall artistes who emerged in the 2014 are AK Songstress and 'Shegah'. AK Songstress (Akosua Kwakye) is a reggae/dancehall artist from the Ashanti region of Ghana who has released over twenty-four singles since 2014 and has collaborated with Guru and Nigeria's Patoranking. Shegah or Sheega Styla is the daughter of the highlife veteran Jerry Hansen (of the old Ramblers band) and she was a member of the all-female Triple M hiplife group. She later went solo and from 2014 gravitated towards dancehall, with her latest 2017 hit being 'Big it Up'. A very recent dancehall artiste was Ebony (Priscilla Opoku Kwarteng) who began releasing songs in 2015, and, in 2016, was recognised by the Ghana Music Awards. She collaborated with VVIP, Mugeez of the R2bees and the Ruff n Smooth Afropop duo. Unfortunately, she tragically died in a road accident in early 2018.

Ebony (Priscilla Opoku Kwarteng)

Some of the newer dancehall men who have surfaced since 2014 are Rashid Metal (Abdul Rashid Khalid) and two singers fro Nima: D Sheriff (Awuda) and Rudeboy Ranking (Mustapha Rahman) who sings in Hausa, as in his 2014 song 'Dam Banza' about the need to be self-dependent. Some others are Phinga (Jonathan Segbefia) whose family hails from the Volta Region; and Vibrant Faya, who was managed by Rudeboy Sterling (aka Mr. Logic) but who sadly died in a car accident in 2016.

Then in 2015 came the Tema based artist Bastero, followed by Konkarah who released his single 'Natural Healing' in 2016. Also in that year the musician/producer Article Wan (Bright Homenya) released his single 'Solo', and Luther whose '2016 Mix' has one song that's instrumentation is based on K. Frimpong's famous highlife song 'Kyenkyen Bi Adi M'awu'.

Before leaving this topic of dancehall it is worth noting that this genre is the fourth type of type of Jamaican music to hit Ghana since the 19th century.

First in 1800 Jamaican free 'maroon' slaves were repatriated to Freetown in Sierra Leone, from where their goombay frame-drum music spread around West Africa, arriving in Accra in the late 19th century where it became known as 'gome'. Secondly, thousands of West Indian soldiers were stationed at Cape Coast Castle during the Ashanti Wars and they brought with them Afro-Caribbean tunes and rhythms that helped Ghanaian brass band musicians develop from the 1880s the very earliest form of highlife known as 'adaha'. Thirdly, in the 1960s and 70s came the ska and reggae of Millicent Small, Jimmy Cliff and Bob Marley that resulted in the reggae-highlife of the City Boys, Kojo Antwi and Amakye Dede. Finally and fourthly comes today's dancehall and ragga.

Some today complain that dancehall is simply a copy of Jamaican music. But as noted in the above discussion about the past impact of Jamaican music, what happened in each of the three earlier cases was that Ghanaians, after a period of copying Jamaican music, mastered it, made it their own, blended it into local music and created indigenous blends such as gome, adaha, and reggae-highlife. Dancehall musicians are simply continuing this musical reconnection between Ghana and Jamaica.

This reconnection is not so surprising, considering that the skanking offbeats, backbeats and syncopations of Jamaican music themselves are partly derived from the music of West Africa, and, moreover, the ancestors of many black Jamaicans (such as the Coromantees) actually came from Ghana. Ghanaians and Jamaicans therefore not only share a common musical heritage but also a genetic one. This centuries-old Ghanaian musical love of Jamaican music, including current dancehall, may therefore be a matter of musical blood being thicker than musical water.

MUSICAL POT TWELVE: JAZZ AFRO-JAZZ AND JAZZ FUSION

The Ghanaian Jazz and Afro-jazz scene is small but strong and some of the artists mentioned in Chapter 42 who are still performing are the guitarist Cliff Eck, trumpeter Long John, drummer Frank Siisi-Yoyo, Big Wellington, the John Coltrane fan Nii Noi Nortey and reedsman Jimmy Beckley.

American jazz singer Toni Manieson is still operating her Jazz Tone Club, whilst the R&B singer Yasmeen Helwani also covers jazz numbers and in 2016 released an album called 'Music Messenger'. Another is Bibi Brew who, as mentioned in Chapter 44, became an international star in France before returning home in the early 2000s to establish her Morning Star Club in Tesano, Accra: which she still runs. A more recent addition to the Ghanaian jazz scene is the New York-born Ghanaian Ofie Kodjoe.

Mention must also be made of Elivava (Tina Mensah) who sings in English, Ga, Twi and her native Ewe language music in a style that hovers between jazz-fusion, Afrorock and Fela style Afrobeat. Her role models are the legendary American jazz singer Billie Holiday and South African's Miriam Makeba. Sometimes she sings with a 6/8 lilt, as in the 2014 song 'Agamatinga – Chameleon' that she wrote with the Canadian-based Ghanaian musician Kobena Aquaah-Harrison in 2015.

There are several jazz spots in Accra and one is Alisa Hotel's Table Bay where at one point the trumpeter and saxophonist Dela Jackson and his Sahel Breeze band were the resident group. Another is the Piano Bar at Teshie-Nungua that has featured the likes of singer Sandra Houson, the saxophonist Bernard Ayisa, and the Ivorian saxophonist and the pianist Boaz Sax.

However, the main jazz venue in Accra is still the +233 Jazz Club that was set up by a Ghanaian medical doctor in 2010 on the location of the old Jazz Optimism Club. The +233 Club hosts a range of music styles such as highlife, hiplife, Afro-rock and R&B influenced Afropop, but as its name suggests focuses on jazz and jazz-fusion. As noted in Chapter 42 this club has its own resident jazz group, the Sound Factree, which features pianist Victor Dey, bassist Phillip Acquah, Sandra Houson and trombonist Eli Amewode. The +233 Club has also featured many foreign jazz artists, like the American reed player Orin Etkin and guitarist Colter Harper. Then, in 2014, the British West Indian singer, author and TV presenter Michelle Mckinney-Hammond sang at the club at an event honouring great jazz women such as Ella Fitzgerald, Sarah

Vaughan, Billie Holiday and Nina Simone. The club also hosts local performers who like to explore jazz and jazz fusions, such as Kwame Yeboah (the Ohia Beyeya band), singer-saxophonist Blay Ambolley, guitarist Kyekyeku, the local atenteben flute wizard Dela Botri, trumpeter Paul Bilson, saxophonist Steve Bedi and singers Elivava and Brenda Joyce.

Foreign jazzists continue to stream into Ghana, often collaborating with local artists. These include the British Caribbean reed player Courtney Pine and Ghanaian-born drummer Robbie Fordjour who played together in Ghana several times. Two American visitors are the vibes played Kenny Drew Junior (son of the famous jazz pianist of that name) who did workshops in 2011 with university music students, and the jazz guitarist Earl Klugh who played in Accra in 2015 alongside Big Wellingtons local jazz group. Another American is the jazz drum 'professor' Royal Hartigan who brought his Blood Drum Spirit Ensemble on a Ghanaian tour in 2015, with Royal remaining to operate his Sunsum Jazz Quartet with a group of students from the Kwame Nkrumah University of Science and Technolgy (KNUST) at Kumasi.

The Ghana Jazz Society is still going strong since it was formed in 2004 by Sam Mensah. As a youngster he was the guitarist for Ghana's very first schoolboy jazz group, the Adisadel College Jazz Band, that was set up in 1964 and included Eddie Soga, Ricky Telfer, John Djokoto, Glenn Warren and the Canadian trumpeter Dave Godfrey. One Jazz Society event that I was personally involved with was called 'Highlife Meets Jazz' that was held at the +233 Club on the 17th December 2016, at which I gave a slide-show lecture on the long-time connection between Highlife and Jazz. This was followed by performances by Ebo Taylor, Alfred Kari Bannerman, Kojo Essah (of the Takashi Band), Victor Dey, Pat Thomas – and Koo Nimo and George Spratz in which I also featured on the asratoa/televi, a percussion instrument that I had recorded with Koo Nimo for some of his Phillips recording way back in the early 1970s.

There are also various ongoing jazz festivals that have been held in Ghana during the last few years, and one is the Afrojazz Festival held in 2013 and 2015 (with one planned for 2017) organised by Paa K. Holbrook-Smith and Kofi Amoakohene of Scratch Studio. Artists who played at these include the master drummer Okyerema Asante, the Ivorian guitarist Constant Boti, the Dzidudu Afro-rock band, Bibie Brew, Kyekyeku, and the French flotist Sabine Boyer. Since 2014 the Standik Bank has also been hosting annual Stanbic Jazz Festivals at the Accra International Conference Centre, and some of those who have played are the American jazz keyboardist Bob James and the British fusion jazz guitarist Peter White. Finally, the French Alliance Francaise hosted annual Live in Accra Jazz Festivals between 2014 and 2017 which involved the Franco-Beninois trumpeter Nicolas Genest, the Maher Beauroy Trio from Martinique, South African trumpeter Marcus Wyatt, Ivorian songstress Ruth Tafabe and the Ghanaian/Belgian flotist Esinam Dogbatse supported by Victor Dey, Dela Botri and Big Wellington.

MUSICAL POT THIRTEEN: AFRO ROCK

Some of the old-time Afro-rock artists mentioned in Chapter 42 still make occasional appearances, such as Nana Kwesi Danquah and his Dzidudu band and the US based master drummer Okyerema Asante who was originally with the 1970s Hedzoleh Sounds Afro-fusion band led by Stanley Todd.

Then there is the multi-instrumentalist Amartey Hedzoleh (Lash Laryea) who was a member of Ghana's first rock band, the Magic Aliens and also a founder member of the 1970s Hedzoleh Sounds. He later went solo and, as mentioned in Chapter 42, made several recording between 1982 and 1986 at my Bokoor Recording Studio in Accra, one of these appearing on the 'Ghana Funk' compilation album released in 2010 by Hippo Records of Amsterdam. This was followed by a full album of Amartey's songs called 'Kukuratumi' released in Holland in 2014 by Martin Van Aalst's Chop Time Music. Seven of the Afro-rock songs on this album were recorded at my Bokoor Studio and three, also recorded in the 1980s, were done by Francis Kwakye of the Ghana Films Studio.

A newer addition to the Ghanaian rock scene is Dark Suburb that surfaced around 2015 and made their debut album in 2017. The members of this alternative rock band are anonymous and they perform on stage wearing skeleton masks, with the lead guitarist playing fast rock 'shred guitar' solos with plenty of the high-gain distortion of heavy-metal rock.

MUSICAL POT FOURTEEN: THE SAHELIAN SOUNDS OF NORTHERN GHANA

As mentioned in Chapter 64, the 'Sahelian' or 'Savannah' music Ghana's Northern and Upper Regions has become an important factor in the country'a popular music since the 1990s. Particularly important for Sahelian sounds is the rise of Tamale as a hub for northern Ghanaian musicians. Many of the new artists mentioned in Chapter 64 are still operating and these include Sheriff Ghale (Yamusah Mohammad) and Sherifatu Gunu from Tamale; the reggae men Blakk Rasta (Abubakar Ahmed) and Iwan (Abdul Razak Issahaku) who are both from the Tamale-Dagbon area; and Rocky Dawuni, whose family is from Bonbonayili near Yendi, the traditional capital of Ghana's Northern Region.

Then there are the Frafra koligo lute players from Bolgatanga in the Upper East Region, Atongo Zimba, King Ayisoba and the newer Stevo Alambire. From the Upper West and Wa area comes the gyil xylophone player and leader of the Local Dimension band Aaron Bebe Sukura and the previously-mentioned Noella Wiyaala. This Afropop diva, who often sings in her Sissala language, began her musical career with the Echo Soundz Studio in her region's capital at Wa.

King Ayisoba

The importance of the 'Sahelian' factor is also reflected by a number of northern Ghanaians who are involved with the hiplife and dancehall scene, such as Faisal Hakeem and Rashid Mugeez of the R2Bees, 'Zeal' Abdul Hamid Ibrahim of VIP and VVIP, and the Hausa dancehall artist Rudeboy Ranking (Mustapha Rahman). Another is Samini who, like Wiyaala, hails from the Upper West Region. Indeed, both have helped the many younger artist now surfacing in the Upper West Region; such as the dancehall and afrobeats man Raphius Amingoes and the rapper El Twist (Elvis Wellu) who has released fifteen songs since his 'Dagara Azonto' of 2011.

As noted in Chapter 64, Tamale hosted the New Music Ghana Festival in 2013 at which the Bizung Band of the Tamale Bizung School of Music and Dance performed. A musician who helped found this music school is Mohammed Lunsi who plays the lunsi hour-glass drum of Dagbon, the Lunsi drummers being Dagomba court historians or griots who can be traced back to the 15th century Prince Bisung. So Mohammed Lunsi can trace his ancestry back to this prince. Mohammed Lunsi has travelled around the world and, in the United States, he formed a band with some Americans called the Bisung Family that in 2010 released the 'Land of Fire' album that combines lunsi drumming with reggae, 'world music' and sahelian blues. In 2015 and 2017 this band toured Ghana.

Yendi-born Sherifatu Gunu, who is also mentioned in Chapter 64, is still going strong. During her career that began in 1998, this singer worked with the likes King Ayisoba, Terry Bonchaka, Kojo Antwi, Amakye Dede, Daddy Lumba, Nana Acheampong and Sarkodie. She has made several albums and many singles in styles which range from highlife, to South African-type music and electronic versions of Fela's Afrobeat style. She sings in Dagbani, occasionally uses traditional 6/8 rhythms and sometimes adds the northern kologo and goje stringed instruments to her electronic mixes. Her music is usually in a minor pentatonic scale and so she is often called a 'soul' or 'Afro-soul' singer. Her latest 2016 single 'Salamatu' celebrates women and mothers.

MUSICAL POT FIFTEEN: THE CONTINUING RISE OF LIVE POPULAR PERFORMANCE

The live Ghanaian popular music scene suffered a set-back during the 1970s-80s military era when performing bands and night-clubs folded. As a result, the youth turned to various forms of techno-pop, such as burger highlife and then hiplife, that were recorded by studio bands and studio beat-masters for CD and music video release. When performed on stage the artists generally mimed or lip-synched to pre-recorded backing-tracks of their disco and hiphop influenced music. However, in the 1990s and with economic liberalisation and a return to democracy, music spots featuring live bands began to re-appear. This was boosted by two factors mentioned in Chapter 64, and one was the impact of Ghanaians returning home from extended stays abroad where miming is not the norm. The older returnees tended to enjoy live highlife and jazz at the various spots like the Village Inn, Baseline, Next Door and Jimmys Jazz Club. Younger returnees rather stimulated the growth of venues where live music, poetry and free-styling rap took place, like Guitars in the Park, Hypnotic, the Nebuke Foundation and Bless the Mike. Moreover, on television there was a trend away from music videos towards live performance and live music competitions such as Bands Alive, Mentor House and Music Music

Also important to the resurgence of live performance was the input of foreigners in the country. Many of the Embassy's cultural organisations like the Alliance Francaise and Goethe Institute endorsed highlife festivals, workshops and seminars, whilst visiting tourists and 'world music' fans patronised clubs where liver cultural music, reggae and highlife music were played: like the Afrikiko, Paloma, Big Millie's, the Abrantie Spot, AAMA, Bywels and the Kunta Kinte, Aliza and Regent Hotels.

M.anifest. Beatznation.com

There was also the establishment of various annual street festivals in Accra, the first being the Osu Street Carnival initiated in the early 2000s by some of the local FM radio stations in Accra. In 2011 came the 'Chale Wote Street Arts Festivals' that are held in Jamestown that involve poetry, plays, painting, music and dance. These are sponsored by the Ga Mashie Development Agency, the French Embassy, Pidgin Music and other local art organisations.

While all this was going on, from the early 2000s some hiplifers began to move from lip-synching to live performance. Early ones were Sidney, Obour and the free-styling GH rappers VIP and the Mobile Boys, followed by Kwaw Kese, Samini and Okyeame Kwame with his 'Versatile Shows' hiplife musicals.

There was also the establishment of various annual street festivals in Accra, the first being the Osu Street Carnival initiated in the early 2000s by some of the local FM radio stations in Accra. In 2011 came the 'Chale Wote Street Arts Festivals' that are held in Jamestown that involve poetry, plays, painting, music and dance. These are sponsored by the Ga Mashie Development Agency, the French Embassy, Pidgin Music and other local art organisations.

While all this was going on, from the early 2000s some hiplifers began to move from lip-synching to live performance. Early ones were Sidney, Obour and the free-styling GH rappers VIP and the Mobile Boys, followed by Kwaw Kese, Samini and Okyeame Kwame with his 'Versatile Shows' hiplife musicals.

Some artists now constitute what can be called 'rap poets', who perform live at small intimate venues like Bless the Mike, and these include M.anifest, Wanluv the Kubolor, Mutomba Da Poet and also Poetra Asantewa who in 2015 released a number of songs that expressed feminist ideas. Indeed, after many years of stage miming many of the new generation of hiplife, contemporary highlife, dancehall and Afropop artists put on live shows.

MUSICAL POT SIXTEEN: GHANAIAN CHORAL AND ART-MUSIC

Ghanaian art music began with the pioneering efforts of Dr. Ephraim Amu and the Reverends Allotey Pappoe and Otto Boateng who, in the early 1900s, composed Christian hymns, chorales and anthems sung by choirs in local languages. As noted in Chapter 41, one of the most famous of these compositions was Ephraim Amu's 'Yen Ara Asase Ni' (This Land is Ours) that has become Ghana's second national anthem.

Wanlov the Kubolor and Band

Later came Professor J.H. Kwabena Nketia, Atta Annan Mensah and Philip Gbeho who experimented with African art-music played by string quartets and full symphonies, at which their audiences sat down and listened to in a concert setting. Philip Gbeho, for instance, wrote Ghana's national anthem, whilst Professor Nketia, who is discussed in Chapter 41, helped develop the concept of 'African Pianism'. Incidentally, a film about this famous composer and musicologist called 'Nketia: The African Maestro' was released in 2015 by Roaming Akuba Films.

Some more contemporary art and choral musicians includes Kenn Kafui (famous for his 'Pentanata'), the African Pianist Gyimah Larbi, and the cellist George Dor. Some others are the choral composers Newlove Annan, Cosmas W.K Mereku, Kweku Acquaah Harrison, the late Alexander Agordoh and Clement Adom, as well as Joshua Amuah and Hilarius Wuaku of the University of Ghana's Music Department at Legon.

Turning to actual outfits that play African art-music, the first was the Ghana National Symphony Orchestra set up in 1959 on the instructions of Kwame Nkrumah and first led by Phillip Gbeho. Some of its later directors and conductors include Gyimah Larbi, Akosua Obuo Addo, George Dor, Kenn Kafui, Dinah Reindorf, Nana Danso Abiam, Oscar Sulley, Kweku Acquaah-Harrison, Mrs. Theresa Tetteh and Isaac Annoh. Since the 1980s this national ensemble has included the German violinist Thomas Woermle. In 2017, the National Symphony Orchestra released its very first album called 'Ghana Classic'.

Then, in 1988 and as mentioned in Chapter 41, Nana Danso Abiam set up his Pan African Orchestra that developed an Afrocentric system of making symphonic music. After his death in 2014 at the age of just 61 his son, Yaw Kwakye, has taken over the leadership of this world-renowned outfit.

More recently, there is Dr. Mensa Otabil and his International Central Gospel Church that in 2012 established the Accra Symphony Orchestra, to which operatic voices known as the 'Lumina' were added in 2014. Also there are the Afro Maestros which is under the management of the dynamic cultural promoter Korkor Amarteifio. This is a small classical outfit formed around 2014 that consists of two singers and twelve musicians who play piano, violins, bass, cello woodwind and brass combined with African drums. Their repertoire ranges from classical pieces, to spirituals, Ghanaian popular songs and traditional African based art-music compositions.

MUSICAL POT SEVENTEEN: TRADITIONAL AND FOLKLORIC MUSIC

As mentioned in the last chapter of this book the traditional bedrock of Ghanaian ceremonial and communal music still thrives – as does its various folkloric and neo-traditional offshoots, such as kpanlogo, borborbor, simpa and Ga 'cultural' music. This heritage is still vital for Ghana's ethnic communities and particularly those living in the rural areas. Furthermore, this traditional music also provides young Ghanaian with a resource for developing their own contemporary music, and is also attractive to the many foreign tourists, students and 'world music' fans who visit Ghana.

Although it would be impossible to list all the traditional forms of music and drum-dances of Ghana, the reader can appreciate its continuing importance from the following list that I have culled from pages 83-98 of the 2014 MUSIGA-KPMG

'Comprehensive Study of the Music Sector in Ghana'.

GREATER ACCRA REGION
The Ga Kpanlogo, Gome, Tokoe, Fume Fume, Kolomashie, Adaawa, Otofo and Kple and Kpa religious music.

ASHANTI & BRONG-AHAFO REGIONS
Akom shrine music, Adenkum, Adzewa, Adowa, Asonko, Asaadua, Atente, Sanga, Sikyi, Kete, Fontomfrom, Nnwonkoro, Bosoe, Akosua Tuntum, Mpre and Ntan.

EASTERN REGION
Apiredwa, Gyewani and also the Agbaei, Kpatsa, Klama and Dipo music of the Krobos.

NORTHERN REGION
Bamaaya, Jera, Bambaya, Gonji, Takai, Kinatsu, Nmane, Simpa, Tora and the music of the following Fetivals : Damba, Bugum, Chugul, Gobandawu (Yam), Chimsi Chugu (Ed-Il-Adha), Konyurichugu (El-Il-Fitr), Kpini Chugu (Guinea Fowl) and Sonyor Deng.

UPPER EAST REGION
Nagla, and the music of the Gologo, Fao, Paragbiele, Willa, Zumbenti, Kobina, Kakube, Feok and Builsa Festivals.

UPPER WEST REGION
Bawa, Gyil xylophone music and the music of the Kobine, Kakube, Wilaa and Zumbenti Festivals.

WESTERN REGION
Kundum and Abisa music and dance.

VOLTA REGION
Atrikpui, Atamga, Aavu, Yevevu, Kokuvu, Atsiagbekor, Adzogbo, Kinka, Gota, Gahu, Gazu, Agbadza, Tudzi, Boborbor, Gbolo, Gahu, Atimevu, Trovu, Sowu, Gadzo, Akpese, Gbedze, Atrikpui, Gabada and Egbenegba.

CENTRAL REGION
Asafo, Adzewa, Adenkum, Apatampa, Osibi, Osode and Abibindwom (Fanti Lyrics) and the Efutu Aboakyer.

The above list of over one hundred music styles is the very tip of the traditional musical ice-berg of Ghana, as distinct forms of ethnic music and dance are associated with all the different seventy-five or so ethnic/linguistic groups of the country. Moreover, many of the above traditional genres involve a collection or suite of anywhere from between two to twelve or more separate dances and accompanying rhythms. Taking this into account, as well as the fact that the above list is incomplete, one can safely assume there are at least several thousand distinct styles of traditional music and drum-dances in Ghana.

The diversity of Ghana's traditional performing arts is therefore enormous – and so it is no wonder that their dance rhythms and melodies have been and still are being incorporated into many of Ghana's popular dance-music forms: stretching from brass-band and dance band highlife, odonson highlife, sikyi highlife and osoode highlife to Afro-rock, burger highlife, jama hiplife, contemporary highlife and the current azonto craze. It is therefore likely that in the future traditional music and dance resources will continue to be an important resource for contemporary Ghanaian musicians.

Part Three

'MILLENNIAL HIGHLIFE' AND THE 'HIGHLIFE IMAGINATION'

Osibisaaba dance 1907. Photo Basel Mission Archive

Althgough, and as noted in Section One of the book, the word 'highlife' was coined in early 1920s, it actually goes back to the early Fanti adaha brass band of the 1880s and the osibisaaba 'palmwine' music of the early 1900s. By 1950 two major forms of highlife were in place, the dance band type and the more rural oriented guitar bands that become linked to concert party acting groups.

Then in the early 1970 came by various pop-music blends of highlife; such as the Afrorock of Ghana's Osibisa (see Chapter 18), the Afrobeat of Nigeria's Fela Kuti (see Chapter 49) and the reggae-highlife of guitar bands like the African Brothers, City Boys, Teacher and his Afrikana and Amakye Dede's Apollo High Kings (see Chapter 36).

All this came crashing down during the military era of the late 1970s and 80s when much of the local popular music scene was wiped out. Indeed, by the late 1980s many highlife artists thought their music was finished, which is why a number of them became interested in preserving highlife as an endangered musical species. Early examples discussed in Chapter 64 are Professor Nketia's ICAMD that included both traditional and popular music in its holdings and the BAPMAF music archives that I set up in 1990 with the help of concerned musicians such as E.T. Mensah, Kwaa Mensah and King Bruce.

Indeed, for a while it did look as if highlife was in terminal decline. But new highlife offshoots began springing up during the 1980s; namely Ghanaian gospel music that primarily draws on highlife music and rhythms (see Chapters 43 and 45) and burger highlife that combined highlife with the drum-machine and synthesizer music of disco (see Chapter 37) . This was followed in the 1990s by a resurgence of old time highlife and by hiplife ('hiphop highlife') which in its 'jama' form replaced American hiphop beats with 'jama' beats that are basically various combinations and recombinations of old 4/4 highlife rhythms. As also discussed in Chapter 38 the hiplife generation has also created an electronic version of highlife they call 'contemporary highlife' that, as discussed more fully below, draws on highlife and traditional rhythms and modes.

Even the azonto (aka afrobeats) club dance genre draws on jama beats, as does much of the Jamaican inspired dancehall or Afro-dancehall that not only uses both reggae and ragga beats but also local jama ones. Indeed there is a remarkable similarity between jama highlife rhythms and some Afro-Caribbean rhythms. For instance, the five pulse (3+2) clave or bell pattern played in 4/4 time is found on both sides of the Black Atlantic. In Ghana and West Africa it is derived from boxing up into 4/4 time the old five pulse bell pattern of traditional African polyrythmic music. Likewise, centuries ago West African slaves, who were forbidden in the Americas from playing African polyrhythms because of the link to to slave revolts, also boxed this bell or clave pattern up into 4/4 time. So this five pulse rhythm has become a 'Black Atlantic Beat ' and so is found in both West African highlife, and across the Atlantic in Latin-American and Caribbean dance music such as salsa and calypso.

The consolidation of highlife rhythms, modes and singing style into modern Ghanaian electronic music is particularly evident in the case of 'contemporary highlife' that has recently emerged out of the hiplife generation. However, before moving on to this contemporary highlife, it should be noted that young Ghanaians artists have gained a lot by passing through hiplife. Firstly, they have mastered the use of hi-technology, such as drum-machines, beat boxes, sampling, digital recording, autotuners and so on. Secondly, the hiplife focus on the super-rhythmic poetry of 'rapping' has improved the rhythmic skills of those who are moving from rapping to singing.

Contemporary highlife singers began to surface around 2005 with artist like Ofori Amponsah and Wutah, followed by Bisa K'dei, Dobble, Kofi Kinaata and others mentioned earlier. These artists naturally use highlife/jama rhythms and also the highlife guitar style. Sometimes they feature a highlife guitarist and, sometimes, they use loops from old highlife guitar band songs by Opambuos, the African Brothers, K. Frimpong and others.

As with so much of the old guitar band highlife, the contemporary highlifers also sometimes draw on old Akan scales that feature microtones such as the flattened seventh note. These exist in the cracks between the piano keys but can be easily be created using the pitch-bend wheel of a modern keyboards.

Contemporary highlifers also sometimes use the old Akan modal arrangement that are used in both traditional music and in the 'odonson' 'Kwaa' and 'sikyi' forms of guitar band highlife. In this traditional mode the melody moves or rotates between two tones centre that are full tone apart, rather than following the I-IV-V harmonic progressions of western music. Likewise, contemporary highlife singers delve into Akan style of singing in thirds [cf western 4 part harmony] and sometimes chant in age-old recitative style. Other features of both traditional Ghanaian music and highlife that they employ are polyphony, the call-and-response between singer and chorus and polyrhythmically moving between duple and triple time.

So despite the use of hi-tech gadgets, contemporary highlife artists use the rhythms, melodic flow and singing style of old-time highlife. Moreover, even young Ghanaian azonto, jama hiplife and to some extent dancehall exponents utilise the rhythmic side of highlife, which they call 'jama' beats.

This resurfacing of highlife beats and other elements in various forms of modern Ghanaian popular music is not so suprising, as highlife has been the foundation of Ghanaian popular music for over one hundred years. The music producer Panji Anoff calls the gradual move away from imported American hiphop beats to highlife and jama beats a result of the 'musical genetic memory' of the youth. Likewise, in Chapter 63 of this book that I wrote way back in the early 1990s I have a similar notion that I call the 'Highlife Imagination', which I will return to later.

However, back in mid-nineties it really did look as if burger highlife and emerging hiplife that were based on imported electronic funk, disco and hiphop beats would completely dominate the popular music of the Ghanaian youth. I metaphorically called this 'the musical ghost in the machine', which is a way of saying that the voice was becoming a spirit or 'ghost' lost in the electronic mix. Moreover, with this new techno-music came something that, up to then, was quite unheard of in Ghana: namely miming or 'lip synching' on the live stage. Indeed with so much miming the youth had to invent the word 'live music' in the 1980s for the live popular performance format. This was a strange situation, as for thousands of years and until the early 1980s all music performed in Ghana was 'live', whether popular, religious or traditional. Indeed in the past, there was no word for 'live' as compared to 'unlive' musical performance.

At this point let me quote what the veteran highlife musician King Bruce told me about the importance of live performance back in the late 1980s when electronic music, drum-machines and spinners were first coming to the fore (see Chapters 14 and 16). According to him, although drumulators and miming to backing-tracks makes stage performances more economical they also had several negative consequences:

'There can be no last minute ideas or afterthoughts incorporated into the music. Often mistakes made by a musician can be a blessing in disguise as he may, on-the-spot, come up with a better idea. Moreover, the musicians inspire one another to do their best and I have always believed that it is the actual playing in a band onstage or at rehearsals that sharpens your faculties and brings new ideas'.

I used the 'ghost in the machine' notion in the early 1990s as I was saddened by the absence of local rhythms in Ghana's emerging electronic music, by the fashion for miming and by the fact that many brilliant and skilled percussionists and hornsmen were becoming unemployed as they had been replaced by gadgets. I recall this even effected my 1980s Bokoor Recording Studio as I saw young musicians more and more insist on the use of synthesizers and the then very primitive drum-machines that could not handle the complexities of African music. So mechanical beats were replacing the live groove.

However, I also looked on the brighter side by considering this situation a temporary one, due to the 'Highlife Imagination'. This notion which I used in the 1990s version of this book is that there are rhythmic and melodic skills stored in Ghanaian culture that are passed from individuals of one generation to the next. This huge store of traditional Ghanaian musical knowledge is discussed in Chapter 27 of this book and it includes syncopations, offbeating, polyphony, swinging rhythmic space, modal scales, internalised beats, body rhythms, unplayed hidden beats and the general multi-rhythmic perspectives of players and dancers alike. Much of this was, in turn, transmitted into early forms of Ghanaian highlife.

It is this age-old ability of Ghanaian to maintain syncopated and offbeat highlife rhythms internally in their mind or dancing feet that enables them to insert these beats into any form of 4/4 popular dance music, whether disco, hiphop, or for that matter danceable gospel songs. In Chapter 63, I compare the Ghanaian 'Highlife Imagination' to the Jamaican ability to 'reggify' the rhythms of any 4/4 songs, even non Jamaican ones, with their reggae offbeat 'skank' guitar, back-beats and one-drops. It was these Jamaican ways of handling rhythm that both helped make reggae a unique global phenomenon and were continued into the electronic reggae offshoots of dancehall and ragga.

The Highlife Imagination and its rhythmic orientation has likewise enabled Ghanaians to creatively develop their own music and contribute a unique perspective to world music, even when borrowing ideas from outside. This is exactly what Fanti musicians did one hundred and twenty years ago when they turned European regimental brass band music into adaha music – or what E. T. Mensah and his Tempos band did when they created a jazzy type of dance band highlife in the 1950s. More recently, artists like Reggie Rockstone indigenised American hiphop by rapping in Twi. In each case these pioneering Ghanaian artists initially imitated Black American and Caribbean music, then mastered them and found their own voice. So by using their own unique Ghanaian musical perspective they were able to absorb these outside influences into their own local music to create new blends of Ghanaian music.

Despite all my despondent talk in the last chapter of the 1996 edition of this book about the human spirit or ghost getting lost in the musical machine, I did, however, end on an optimistic note; by saying that because of the 'highlife imagination', I doubted that in ten years or so the youth would still be playing over-processed computer music with little Ghanaian content, and so we had to give the youth a chance to 'highlife' electronic music.

Well, this has actually happened, and as we can see today highlife and its jama beats have been endorsed by the youth and dominates their electronic music. So highlife is back to stay and is now found to varying degrees in many forms of local music, whether contemporary highlife, jama hiplife, azonto, afrobeats or dancehall.

E. John Collins, Accra, May 2018

Introductory Chapter

HISTORY OF GHANAIAN HIGHLIFE: 1880s TO 1940

This Ghanaian trans-cultural popular music developed during the 19th and early 20th century as a blend of three elements: the indigenous African, the European and the New World music of the Black Diaspora. As the imported influences first came to West Africa via European and American ships, early popular music styles grew up in the coastal areas, before moving inland. Although the term 'highlife' was not coined until the 1920's it existed well before then under various names and its creation took place within three musical contexts: music coastal military-fort brass bands, the music of seamen and fishermen, and the local dance orchestras of the western-educated and christianised African elites of port towns such as Accra, Cape Coast and Winneba. Let us look at each of these contexts in turn.

Gold Coast Regimental Brass Band early 1900s

The first was the local 'adaha' brass-band music that appeared on the Fanti coast in the 1880s, triggered by the regimental bands of six thousand West Indians soldiers who were stationed at Cape Coast and El Mina Castle by the British colonialists. Adaha music subsequently spread like wildfire throughout southern Ghana. And, for those small towns and villages that could not afford expensive brass instruments, a *poor-man*'s drum-and-voice version called konkoma (or konkomba) developed in the 1930s that spread as far eastwards as Nigeria.

The second early form of highlife was Fanti 'osibisaaba' music and associated circle dance that combined local percussion instruments with the guitar and accordion of sailors. Its name stemmed from the traditional Fanti fishermen's 'osibi' recreational dance. A particularly important influence came from the Kru or Kroo seamen of Liberia who, in the early 20th century, pioneered Africanised two-finger guitar plucking techniques on the high seas.

Early Ghanaian Brass Band – from Krobo 1897-98
(photo Basel Mission Archives)

Liberian 'krooboys' rowing white lady ashore in Accra 1900

These became a seminal influence not only on Ghanaian highlife, but also on the maringa of Sierra Leone, the juju-music of western Nigeria and 'dry' Congolese guitar music of Central Africa (via the port of Mutadi).

Kwaa Mensah in cloth with guitar around 1940

Coastal Fanti *osibisaaba* percolated into the rural hinterland of Ghana where, during the 1930s, it fused with the music of the traditional Akan 'seprewa' (or seperewa) harp-lute: creating a more rootsy style of highlife called 'odonson', Akan 'blues' or 'palm-wine music'. During the 1920s to 40s, many records of these early guitar highlife styles (by Jacob Sam/Kwame Asare, George William Aingo, Mireku, Kwasi Manu, Osei Bonsu, Appiah Adjekum and others) were released by western companies such as Zonophone, Columbia, Odeon and HMV. During the early 1950s, highlife guitar bands incorporated dance-band instruments (double-bass, trap-drums) and became linked to a local Ghanaian form of popular theatre known as the 'concert party'. E.K. Nyame was the outstanding pioneer of this development and his records also became popular in Nigeria, particularly in the east.

Ghana's first ballroom dance orchestra, the Excelsior. Surviving members in 1959

The third type of highlife evolved from the large ballroom and ragtime dance orchestras formed from 1914, like the Excelsior Orchestra and Jazz Kings of Accra, the Winneba Orchestra, Professor Grave's Orchestra of Cape Coast, the Koforidua Casino Orchestra and the Ashanti Nkramo Orchestra. Indeed, the name 'highlife' was coined in this high-class context by the poor people who gathered around the elite dancing clubs whose orchestras began orchestrating local street-tunes in the 1920s. And the very first reference to this name is the 1925 program of the Cape Coast Social and Literary Society with 'highlife' being supplied by the Rag-a-jassbo Orchestra.

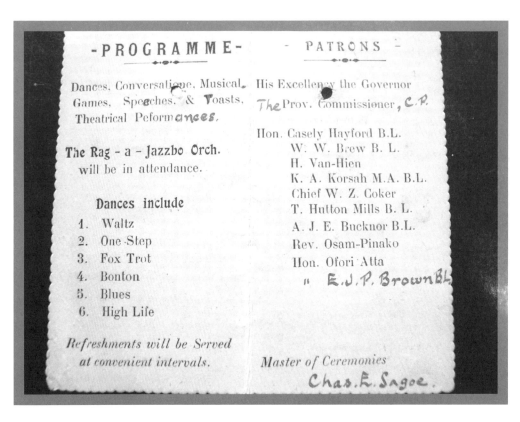

-PROGRAMME-

Dances, Conversazione, Musical, Games, Speeches, & Toasts, Theatrical Peformances,

The Rag - a - Jazzbo Orch. will be in attendance.

Dances include
1. Waltz
2. One Step
3. Fox Trot
4. Bonton
5. Blues
6. High Life

Refreshments will be Served at convenient intervals.

- PATRONS -

His Excellency the Governor
The Prov. Commissioner, C.P.

Hon. Casely Hayford B.L.
W. W. Brew B. L.
H. Van-Hien
K. A. Korsah M.A. B.L.
Chief W. Z. Coker
T. Hutton Mills B. L.
A. J. E. Bucknor B.L.
Rev. Osam-Pinako
Hon. Ofori Atta
" E.J.P. Brown BL.

Master of Ceremonies
Chas. E. Sagoe.

First reference to word highlife. Cape Coast Literary & Social Club, 1925 (courtesy Nate Plageman)

One such early 'highlife' orchestra, the Cape Coast Sugar Babies, made a sensational tour of Nigeria in 1937.

Cape Coast Sugar Babies Orchestra and fans in Enugu, Nigeria 1938

HISTORY OF HIGHLIFE: WORLD WAR II AND EARLY INDEPENDENCE TIMES

British and United States servicemen were stationed in Accra and an aircraft assembly plant was set up at Takoradi port. Indeed, if Britain had been defeated by the Germans, Ghana (then the British Gold Coast) would have become a base for a British Government in exile; like De Gaulle and his anti-Hitler Free French army in Congo Brazzaville. These British and American soldiers in Ghana loved swing and jazz and, together with Ghanaian dance orchestra musicians who could read music, they set up the Black and White Spots and the Tempos swing bands to entertain themselves. The Tempos survived the war and the departure of the foreign service-men, so it became an all-Ghanaian group which, from 1948 and under the leadership of E.T. Mensah, began to concentrate more on local highlife, but with a strong swing, jazz, calypso and Afro-Cuban touch. During the 1950s and 60s, many Ghanaian and Nigerian dance bands modelled themselves on the Tempos.

The war sped up the Ghanaian nationalist struggle, particularly after the 1948 demonstrations by Ghanaian war veterans and following lootings of European shops. As a result, Ghana obtained internal self-rule in 1952 and full independence in 1957 under the leadership of Prime Minister Kwame Nkrumah. This nationalist upsurge affected popular music. E.T. Mensah's Tempos, for instance, wrote independence songs and played at Nkrumah's Convention Peoples Party (CPP) rallies. Indeed, the Tempos type highlife dance-bands, with their then sophisticated swing-jazz line-up, reflected the spirit (zeitgeist) of the early independence era; for just as these bands that used western instruments played African music (i.e. highlife), so independence ushered in a western type nation-state, but run by Africans.

Likewise, the guitar bands and concert parties were involved in the independence struggle. One early example is that, after the Ghanaian servicemen of the wartime West African Theatre which operated in the Far East returned home to Ghana, they called themselves the Burma Jokers concert party, but renamed it the 'Ghana Trio' in 1948 in line with rising nationalist sentiments. Then, both the Axim Trio and Bob Ansah's concert parties wrote plays in favour of Nkrumah, whilst guitar bands like those of Kwaa Mensah and E.K. Nyame released pro-independence records. E.K is

Tempos L-R Grippman (trombone) ET (trumpet) and Joe Kelly (sax) (photo from Grippman family)

also important, as it was his Axim Trio that combined guitar band music with the plays of concert parties – creating a comic highlife opera format that became the model for about two hundred and fifty other concert parties that were created from the 1950s onwards.

Due to the active support highlife performers gave to the independence struggle, Nkrumah's government supported the local popular arts. In the late 1950s, his government began establishing state highlife bands and concert parties as part of its 'African personality' policy, which also led to the employment of substantial numbers of actresses, instead of the female impersonators of the earlier concert parties. Furthermore, in the sixties, concert party plays and music began appearing on state radio and later TV. Nkrumah's CPP government also directly intervened in 1965 to give the green-light to the popular Ga youth 'kpanlogo' drum-dance that was frowned upon by the elders for its inclusion of supposedly indecent dance moves borrowed from popular music idioms like rock 'n' roll and the 'twist'. The CPP government also encouraged the formation of trade unions for popular performers; one for the urban based highlife dance bands and the other for the more provincial-oriented guitar bands/concert parties. As these were both affiliated to Nkrumah's CPP, they were dissolved after the anti-Nkrumah coup of 1966. It was only after a gap of eight years that another union (MUSIGA) was formed.

1970s AND 1980s: AFRO-FUSION, ROOTS AND REGGAE MUSIC

From the mid-1960s, there were new outside influences on Ghanaian popular music. From other parts of Africa came 'Congo jazz' (later called 'soukous'), introduced live to Ghana by Ignace de Souza's Black Santiago's, and from South African came the 'phatha phatha' and township jazz introduced through the records and visits of Miriam Makeba. Then from Black America came the jazz of John Coltrane and Miles Davis, and the soul and funk music of James Brown whose 'Afro' fashions and 'black and proud' message helped spark off a period of intense Ghanaian musical 'Afro-fusion' experimentation during the early 1970s.

In 1970, the London-based Ghanaian super-group Osibisa created its internationally-acclaimed 'Afro-rock' out of highlife and rock, a fusion style quickly taken up in Ghana by Hedzoleh Sounds (that worked with South African trumpeter Hugh Masekela), the Magic Aliens, Boombaya and the Zonglo Biiz. Another fusion was created in the late sixties when Nigeria's Fela Ransome (Anikulapo) Kuti moved away from jazzy highlife towards his militant Afro-soul or 'Afrobeat', taken up in Ghana by the Big Beats, Sawaaba Sounds and the 'Afro-hili' music of Nana Ampadu's African Brothers. This musical 'doing your own thing' message was augmented by the 1971 'Soul to Soul' concert in Accra when the Latin and African-American artists Tina Turner, Wilson Pickett, Santana, Roberta Flack and the Staple Singer played in Ghana. It should be noted that the Afro-centric climate fostered by the 'back-to-roots' message of jazz and soul also encouraged the indigenisation of music by popular artists who (except for the guitar) did away with western instruments altogether. In the late 1960s, the Asante guitarist Koo Nimo became 'unplugged' (i.e. from the electric guitar) and began to recreate the old acoustic 'palmwine' style. And, in the early seventies in Accra, there was a proliferation of rootsy 'Ga cultural groups', spearheaded by Wulomei, whose leader, Nii Ashitey, had originally been a highlife dance-band musician.

Another Black Diasporic music that had an African 'roots' message, which triggered a creative Ghanaian musical explosion, was Jamaican reggae. An early form of reggae, known as 'ska', hit Ghana in the late 1960s when the recording star Millicent, or 'Millie' Small, made two African tours. This was followed in the early seventies by pioneering reggae artists like Desmond Dekker, Johnny Nash and Jimmy Cliff. Almost instantly, Ghanaian highlife guitar bands like the African Brothers and the City Boys began to create their own blends of highlife-reggae music. Then, from 1977, with the release of Bob Marley's 'Exodus' album, dread-locked Ghanaian bands and artists like the

Classic Handels and Classic Vibes appeared, doing imitative cover versions of Jamaican reggae. From the mid-eighties, and partly stimulated by the vernacular reggae of Cote d'Ivoire's Alpha Blondie, some of these imitative Ghanaian performers started to sing reggae in local languages and/or utilize traditional instruments and rhythms. These 'Afro-reggae' artists include Kojo Antwi, the Cultural Imani Group, Kente and, more recently, Rocky Dawuni.

HIGHPOINT OF GHANA MUSIC SCENE IN THE LATE 1960s AND EARLY 70s

By the early seventies, Ghana boasted about one hundred operating highlife guitar bands (cum concert parties), scores of private or state-run highlife dance bands and, literally hundreds of Afro-rock/beat bands and aspiring pop stars who performed at schoolboy 'pop chain' competitions. Catering for these were four recording studios, numerous dance-spots (sixty night-clubs in Accra alone) and two local pressing plants (Ambassador Records and the Record Manufacturers of Ghana) that produced hundreds of thousands of records a year. Furthermore, during the early seventies, two full-length musical films were produced by Ghana Film Industry Corporation (GFIC). The first, based on a concert partly play and produced in 1970, was `I Told You So', directed by Egbert Adjeso, that included the singer/actor Bob Cole and Nana Ampadu's African Brothers highlife guitar-band. Then, in 1974, came GFIC's 'Doing Their Thing', directed by Bernard Odjidja starring Charlotte Dada, the El Pollos and the Kwanyako Brass band. It was about two soul-music fanatics advised by their parents to tour the country in search of their own musical roots. This was the first colour film made in Ghana.

THE 1970s-80s: ECONOMIC COLLAPSE AND DEMISE OF LIVE POPULAR MUSIC

The economic decline of Ghana from the mid/late 70s, due to a combination of economic and political problems, led to the gradual decline of live popular music bands and their venues. This began with the general collapse of the Ghanaian economy due to the mismanagement and corruption ('kalabule') of the latter part of the Acheampong/Akuffo military regime that had come to power in 1972. As the economy crashed, so did the commercial music sector, which finally ground to a halt in the late seventies when record manufacturing almost ceased and Ghanaian artists began to leave the country in droves. In 1979, when I was on the executive of the Musicians Union of Ghana (MUSIGA), we estimated that one quarter of our members had left the country. For instance, many of the guitar bands (like Okukuseku's, Konadu's, T.O. Jazz, Conadoe, Super Seven, Eddy Maxwell's Odoyewu Internationals and Opambuas) moved to oil-rich Nigeria, particularly eastern Nigeria, where highlife was popular. Others moved to, or partially operated and recorded in, North America, Europe and Australia. Some of these were Jerry Hansen, Eddie Quansah, Bob Pinodo, Gyedu-Blay Ambolley, Pat Thomas, A.B. Crentsil, Jewel Ackah, Eric Agyeman, C.K. Mann, Amakye Dede, Ekow Savage Alabi, Aweke Yaw Glyman, Herman Asafo-Adjei, Alfred Bannerman, Kofi Adu, Kwabena Oduro Kwarteng, John Kay, Ben Brako, Nana Tsibo, Alfred Schall, Charles Amoah and Nana Yaw Boakye.

The Acheampong/Akuffo era was followed by a period of political instability (two military coups by Jerry John 'JJ' Rawlings in 1979 and 1981) and a two-and-a-half year night curfew (1982-4) that prevented night-time entertainment; not to mention the 1983 drought and sudden expulsion of over a million Ghanaians from Nigeria. This interregnum in the music industry between the late 1970s and 1984 was immediately followed by the imposition of huge duties on imported musical band equipment which were classed as 'luxuries' and so attracted a 160% import duty. As a result, bands and concert parties could not obtain equipment and so folded up. At one point (1983/4), there were only two recording studios operating in the country (Ghana Films and my own Bokoor Studio). A little later (in 1988), music education was demoted in the school curriculum when the JSS/SSS system was introduced, and so children did not get access to western band instruments.

Other factors of a technological nature also helped in the decline of live music bands. One was the appearance of cheap-to-operate mobile discos or 'spinners' in the late 1970s that gradually took over the dance floors during the 1980s. Moreover, it was during the 1980s that cheap-to-produce local video productions began in Ghana, and these, like the 'spinners', went mobile, gradually eclipsing live concert party in the rural and provincial areas. However, local video did provide work for many concert party-trained actors and actresses.

In 1987, the economy was liberalised and the country gradually began to move towards civilian rule. But, by then, many of the old-time 'classic' highlife bands and concert parties had been inadvertently wiped out by the above-mentioned political and economic problems. On the positive side, the Rawlings government recognised MUSIGA in 1982 and promulgated the 1985 Copyright Law to combat cassette piracy; as with the demise of local record manufacturing, the country had switched to music cassette production, which is easy to pirate. As a result of the demise of live popular music, two new forms of music began to emerge in the 1980s, these being disco music-influenced 'burger highlife' and local gospel dance-music. Even though these two new forms of 1980s popular dance music will be discussed in full later in the book, let me say a few introductory words about them here.

Burger highlife is a 'techno-pop' form of highlife that uses drum-machine and synthesizer horns, and so does away with the need for large numbers of musicians and instrumentalists. It was created by expatriate Ghanaian musicians who left Ghana in the 1970s and settled in Hamburg, Germany – thus the name 'burger'. When these Ghanaian musicians made records abroad, or periodically returned, they introduced this 'made in Germany' style of disco-highlife. Particularly important was George Darko's and Lee Duodu's Bus Stop band that began releasing hits like 'Akoo Tse Brofo' from 1983. Other pioneering burger highlife musicians in Europe were the Lumba Brothers, Rex Gyamfi, McGod, Charles Amoah, Sloopy Mike Gyamfi and Ben Brako.

The explosion of local gospel in the 1980s also has its roots in the economic decline of the 1970s. In southern Ghana, there was a massive move towards local brands of Christianity which, unlike western orthodox churches, allowed dancing for worship and outreach purposes. As a result, the economic slump of the 1970s/80s pushed many secular dance-music artists under church patronage. Furthermore, being charitable bodies, the churches were able to circumvent the huge taxes on the commercial music industry (import duties on instruments, entertainment tax, etc.) and so could afford to buy instruments and run bands. All this helped the country's drift from secular to sacred dance-music. Indeed many unemployed old-time highlife musicians ended up running church bands. As a result, local gospel now comprises over half the commercial recording output of Ghana's popular dance music. Furthermore, whereas in the olden days it was almost impossible for women to get on stage and maintain their respectability, local gospel has, for the first time, introduced large numbers of female artists to the Ghanaian popular music industry.

THE GHANAIAN POPULAR MUSIC SCENE: 1990s TO PRESENT

There are three important recent developments in the Ghanaian music scene that have appeared due to a combination of factors, including the liberalisation of the economy, a stable and democratic political system, the boom in tourism, the growing international interest in African and 'World Music', and the emergence of novel digital music technologies. Firstly there is newer local 'techno-pop style' that followed burger highlife, namely Ghanaian rap or 'hiplife'. Secondly, there has been a revival of highlife, sometimes called 'contemporary highlife'. Thirdly, there has been an upsurge of folkloric groups, and traditional drum and dance schools catering for the many tourists and 'World Music' fans now coming to Ghana.

Hiplife or local rap emerged in the mid-1990s, after Reggae Rockstone shot to fame and coined the name *hip-life* (i.e. hip-hop highlife). Early hiplifers like Rockstone, Nana King and Lord Kenya sang in Twi and Ga, mainly over imported American hip-hop beats. Most of the first generation hiplifers also mimed or 'lip-synched' their raps onstage to pre-recorded backing beats. Whereas these first generation hiplifers only indigenised the words of their music, the generation that followed began indigenising hiplife music with local rhythms and percussion, like Akatakyie, Okomfo Kwadee, Castro, Buk Bak, Nkasei, Tic Tac and the 'jama' sound of Wuta and K.K. Fosu. Some specialised in Hausa like VIP, FBS, and Wutah, whilst some rapped in Ewe like Ayigbe Edem and on occassion X Doe/Chicago. Also, hiplifers like Sidney (Barima), Batman-Samini and Wanluv the Kubolor began performing live rather than miming onstage. Highlife is also now becoming an important resource for younger hiplifers like Tic Tac, Adane Best, Kontihene, Akyeame, Ex Doe and Omanhene Pozo. On the other hand, Nana Quame, Daasebre, Nana Fynn, Ofori Amponsah, Barosky and Kwabena Kwabena alternate between rapping and highlife singing. Indeed, some consider this new generation of hiplifers to also be 'contemporary highlife' artists. Hiplife is also currently fusing with contemporary /urban, dance hall and house music into a new type of Afropop that is sung rather than rapped, and is being developed by the likes of Becca (Rebecca Akosua Acheampong), Jane 'Efya' Awindor, Eazzy (Mildred Ashong), Rough and Smooth, Jay Ghartey, the R2Bees, Richie, Morris de Voice (Babyface), 4X4, Echo and Bradez. Then there is Henry 'Chemphe' Agyekum who calls his hiplife/highlife/R&B fusion 'urbanlife', Dr. Cryme who calls his music 'Twi Pop' and Boy Wadon (Boateng Forson) who calls his style 'Komdigi'.

The current highlife scene consists firstly of artists and bands that play in the old-time highlife vein. There are the survivors of the 1970s/80s' down-turn in live music, such as Jewel Ackah, Paapa Yankson (recently deceased), C.K. Mann, Amakye Dede, Pat Thomas and Blay Ambolley. Moreover, a number of new 'classic' highlife big bands have been established since the 1990s, like the Marriots, Western Diamonds, Megastar

Band, Alpha Waves and new Ramblers. Secondly, there is a younger and upcoming generation of highlifers. These consist of the previously-mentioned 'contemporary highlife' hiplifers who specialise in singing, as well as young Ghanaian artists who have been influenced by old time highlife and the current international interest in 'World Music', like Felix Owusu, Smilin' Osei, Afro Moses, Nat 'Amandzeba' Brew and Rex Omar.

The third major development in the local music scene since the 1990s has been a result of a dramatic increase in tourists and 'world music' fans coming to Ghana. They not only enjoy live highlife but also the traditional music and performing arts. As a result, there has been a proliferation of folkloric and neo-traditional groups that play at private hotels and beach resorts, as well as government-sponsored festivals like PANAFEST. Indeed, some visitors are coming to Ghana to specifically learn local music and dance at the universities or the many private cultural centres and drum schools that have sprung up. Some musical 'purists' may argue that 'folklorisation' fosters less 'authentic' versions of local music. However, what is important in Ghana at the moment, taking into account the saturation of the country with foreign music, is that the tourist interest in traditional music is encouraging many Ghanaian youth to learn and preserve the artistic skills of their elders. Foreign tourists and international 'world music' fans are therefore encouraging young Ghanaian musicians to turn towards their own folk roots.

The following Diagram of a HIGHLIFE TREE will help the reader with many of the highlife and hiplife related music styles discussed in this book.

Diagram of Highlife Tree

1990 1980 1970 1960 1950 1940 1930 1920 1910 1900

Highlife Dance Bands (Almost died out)

Local Electronic Music Contemporary Highlife Jama Beats, Hiplife, Burger Highlife

Neo-Traditional Music Simpa, Kolomashie, Kpanlogo, Gome, Akpese Akyewa, Bosoe, Gahu

West African Guitar Bands. Highlife, Maringa, Makossa Concert Party Bands Reggae-Highlife, Gospel-Highlife "Cultural" Highlife

Brass Bands Now mainly linked with Masquerades & Churches

Fela Afrobeat Afrosoul/funk Afrorock Afrojazz

Highlife Dance Bands Tempos, Black Beats, Ramblers, Uhuru etc.

Ballroom Dance Orchestras Excelsior, Accra Orchestra etc.

Guitars Go Electric

Acoustic Guitar Bands

Nigerian Juju Guitar Band Music

West African Palmwine Music. Accordion & Guitar Music, Osibisaaba, Akan/Native Blues, Odonson, Asiko, Goombay

Borborbor from Konkoma + Traditional Ewe Music

Akan Konkoma Music: (Poormans' Adaha)

Akan Brass Band Adaha Music

The Term 'Highlife' Coined

Coastal African Christian Elite

Traditional Music. Particularly Social/ Recreational Music

Freed Slaves, African Sailors and Fishermen, Local Carpenters and Artisans

Colonial Coastal Regimental Bands (including West Indian ones)

Traditional Performance Background

(Syncopated and polyrhythmic, audience participation, social commentary, dance oriented, local scales and languages)

1990 1980 1970 1960 1950 1940 1930 1920 1910 1900

Diagram of Highlife Tree

This book examines the origins, leading lights and transformations of highlife dance music in detail. It mainly, but not exclusively, focuses on English-speaking West Africa, with some references to Ghana's Francophone neighbours. It also deals with the Ghanaian concert party, as this was a major medium for highlife music and dance. Information is furthermore provided on music styles that are related to highlife, or can be treated as 'cousins' of highlife, such as the maringa of Sierra Leone, the early guitar styles of Liberia, the juju-music of Nigeria and the makossa of the Cameroon. From this introduction, and as will be more fully appreciated by the end of the book, because of highlife's ramification throughout West Africa, it can almost be considered to be an ECOWAS music.

The information is largely drawn from my personal and first-hand experience in the West African music field since the late 1960s, and the numerous interviews I have done over the years. As much as possible, I have allowed the musicians to talk in their own words. I hope this book will provide an introduction to highlife and related music forms for Ghanaian school pupils, university students, visiting tourists, researchers, and for the general Ghanaian, West African and indeed African public at large.

Highlife Time consists (exluding Prologue, Introduction and Coda) of sixty-four chapters divided into ten sections.

SECTION ONE: PAMWINE HIGHLIFE, GUITAR BANDS AND CONCERT PARTIES

This deals with the origin of the guitar band variety of highlife from the so-called 'palmwine' music of the turn of the century, to how this music has become inseparably linked to the concert parties. Section One also supplies details on some of the leading personalities of the concert party-cum-guitar-band profession.

SECTION TWO: HIGHLIFE DANCE BANDS AND THEIR MUSICIANS

This turns to the more prestigious and urbanised dance-band variety of highlife that emerged after the Second World War from the earlier local dance-orchestras. This section further looks at how some dance band musicians have fused highlife with various forms of imported pop music.

SECTION THREE: INTERACTIONS BETWEEN HIGHLIFE AND TRADITION

This concerns some early drummed forms of trans-cultural West African popular music (goombay, gome and asiko). It looks at various types of local Ghanaian drum-dance styles (konkoma, borborbor, simpa and kpanlogo) that have been affected by highlife, which has resulted in what might be called new or 'neo-traditional' music. Despite modern influences, this neo-traditional music is played on drums and is performed in the communal context of a village or urban ethnic community.

SECTION FOUR: BACK TO ROOTS

This begins with a look at traditional African music and then focuses on several leading Ghanaian musicians who were trained in guitar bands and dance bands, but later decided to indigenise their music in various ways. These are Koo Nimo, Kofi Ghanaba, Kwesi Asare and Nii Ashitey.

SECTION FIVE: OUTSIDE INFLUENCES SINCE THE LATE 1950s AND RESULTING MUSICAL FUSIONS

This first turns to how jazz, rock and soul influences coming into Ghana, Nigeria, Sierra Leone, Liberia and Cote d'Ivoire since the 1950s have been blended with highlife and other West African popular music styles. It is followed by chapters on the rise of local reggae in West Africa as well as Ghanaian disco-influenced burger highlife and the more recent rap-influenced hiplife.

SECTION SIX: CURRENT HIGHLIFE, FOLKLORIC CROSSOVERS AND AFRO-FUSION

This firstly looks at the old-time highlife musicians who have survived the 1970s to 80s collapse of the Ghanaian popular music industry and who are still active. It then turns to the younger generation of current highlife musicians who have appeared on the scene. This Section also deals with various forms of current cross-overs between traditional folkloric music and highlife as well as other popular musical idioms. It then deals with the new wave Ghanaian of Afro-fusion music: Afro- rock, Afro-beat and local jazz.

SECTION SEVEN: THE GOSPEL-HIGHLIFE EXPLOSION AND WOMEN ON STAGE

This looks at the main ways the initial hostility to women operating in the Ghanaian commercial popular music scene has been overcome since the 1950s. Very important in this feminisation of popular music is the role of highlife gospel bands of the local separatist churches, which are providing a major avenue for women into Ghana's commercial music profession.

SECTION EIGHT: NIGERIAN HIGHLIFE, JUJU MUSIC, AFRO-BEAT AND APALA

This examines the palmwine ('native' blues) music, juju, apala, highlife and Afro-beat of Nigeria, as well as the makossa guitar music of neighbouring Cameroon. It also supplies biographies of some of Nigeria's leading musical stars.

SECTION NINE: THE POPULAR MUSIC OF SIERRA LEONE, LIBERIA AND FRANCOPHONE WEST AFRICA

This provides an overview of maringa and other popular music styles of Sierra Leone. Following this are some details of the early Liberian guitar styles that made a formative impact on highlife – and a number of short profiles of some of the top recording artists of Liberia during the mid-1980s. The last chapter in this section looks at Francophone West Africa and particularly the popular music scene of Ghana's close neighbours – Cote d'Ivoire, Togo and Benin.

SECTION TEN: THE AFRICAN MUSIC BUSINESS – AFTERTHOUGHTS – AND CODA

This begins with chapters on the West African recording business and the growth of Ghanaian and Nigerian musicians' unions. It also includes a look at the rise of the World Music since the 1980s that has helped open up African music to the international community. There are also chapters on five of Ghana's music producers and/or recording studio managers, some of whom have been operating since the 1950s. There is then a chapter that examines the pros and cons of computer technology on highlife and the highlife Imagination. The last chapter surveys the positive musical developments in Ghana since the 1990s when the economy was liberalised and the country returned to civilian government. The developments include the growing commercial music sector, the impact of foreign tourists and Ghanaian returnees, the revival of highlife and live popular performance spots as well as the impact of newer forms of music on the local scene such as jazz, 'world music', revamped folkloric music, 'contemporary highlife' and northern Ghanaian Sahelian sounds. The Coda updates things with references to the current state of hiplife and Afropop and their associated azonto dance – as well as the convergence of MUSIGA and the government towards a Creative Arts Industry.

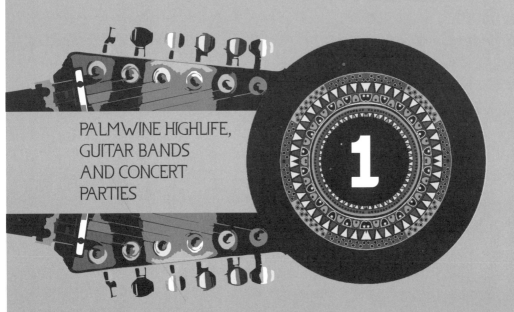

PALMWINE HIGHLIFE, GUITAR BANDS AND CONCERT PARTIES

1

Highlife TIME 3

This deals with the origin of the guitar band variety of highlife from the so-called 'palmwine' music of the turn of the century, to how this music has become inseparably linked to the concert parties. Section One also supplies details on some of the leading personalities of the concert party-cum-guitar-band profession, such as E.K. Nyame, Kwaa Mensah, Yamoah, Nana Ampadu, F .Kenya, Kakaiku and Onyina, to name a few.

Chapter 1

KWAA MENSAH AND 'SAM': THE GRAND OLD MEN OF THE PALM WINE GUITAR

The 'grand old man' of palmwine guitar music is the Fanti musician, the late Kwaa Mensah. He was born in 1920 and, up until his death in 1991, was recognised as master of the palmwine type of highlife which, in contrast to the fully electrified guitar bands like the African Brothers, utilised acoustic guitar, giant bass hand-piano, clips/claves and local hand-drums. Kwaa was actually born in Lagos where his family was temporarily located, but was brought up in his home town of Cape Coast. In Cape Coast lived his relative Kwame Asare, or Jacob 'Sam' as he was popularly known, one of the first Ghanaians guitarists to play highlife or 'osibisaaba' as it was called in those days. Sam was a goldsmith and was taught the guitar by a Liberian Kru. It was Sam who made some of the first highlife releases when he went to England in 1928 to record for Zonophone (another was the fellow Fanti, William Aingo).

Sam helped teach Kwaa the guitar and, during the 1930s, Kwaa played in a Cape Coast adaha band; adaha being a type of highlife played on flutes, fifes, and brass band instruments. Then, in the 1940s, Kwaa joined up with a konkoma (or konkomba) group, a popular highlife style of those days which specialised in complex drill-like dances performed in fancy dress. Finally, in 1950, Kwaa formed his own guitar-band and, in 1952, cut his first single for H.M.V. At that time, he received £5 cash for each number recorded, for royalties were then unheard of in Ghana. In 1955, Kwaa followed E.K. Nyame's example and added concert party opera to his band's repertoire, with Kwaa playing the lady impersonator. He called his group the 'Fanti Trio', and it was so popular with the less westernised and more rural fans that by the early '60s, Kwaa had released two hundred records.

For a long time, Kwaa's music was considered too 'bush' by more sophisticated Africans, especially by the young pop fans who were surprised when they saw him at the *Soul to Soul* concert in Accra at the Black Star Square in 1971. Some of the critics had thought that Kwaa's music was so old-fashioned that he must be dead! Fortunately, in 1975, Kwaa made a comeback, by recording an L.P. for Ambassador Records, and then going on a tour of the United States with Wulomei. In 1976, Kwaa joined up with Faisal Helwani's Afrodisia team that recorded in Lagos. The following is an interview I had with Kwaa on November 25, 1975, at Temple House in Jamestown, Accra. I should add that I met Kwaa Mensah in 1974 when I visited his house in Mankesim. We became firm friend and, over the years, he often stayed with me in Accra at my apartment at Temple House in James Town or, later, at my father's farm-house in South Ofankor (now Bokoor House). In fact, it was I who arranged for him to record for Faisal Helwani. It was primarily Kwaa who taught me to play 'palmwine' highlife guitar.

JC: How did you first come to learn to play the guitar?

MENSAH: When I reached Standard Five, my father and mother made some trouble so I had to leave my Cape Coast Elementary School just like that. I was a carpenter so I went to the Bubuaso Mines near Dunkwa-on-Offin to find business. But I didn't get some, so I went to the surveyor's department as a line-cutter (cutting lines through the bush for surveyors). When I was there, I met one of my brother-in-law's nephews called Kofi Adzei. He was a guitarist and showed me how to play. That was in 1937. Then, when my mother fetched me back to Cape Coast, I met my Uncle Sam, and he also taught me to play. I went everywhere with him. We were entertaining the soldiers during the war in Cape Coast, Kumasi and Accra. We made music and mime for the soldiers and army officers. I was the singer and clips player and he was playing the guitar, singing and changing costumes. He used to dress up sometimes as a Sierra Leonean woman, and sometimes as an Asante woman.

JC: Tell me more about your Uncle Sam (who was born in 1903).

MENSAH: Sam's father was a storekeeper who sold carpenters' tools in Cape Coast. His father played the concertina and used to take Sam, when he was very small, on his shoulders to play clips. His father played adaha, the music of the flute, fife and brass bands, and also opim or ohugua (this is Akan highlife played in 6/8 time with a bell rhythm similar to adaha, usually referred to today as Akan or Asante 'blues'). Opim was special music for the concertina (i.e. Akan 'blues' played on this instrument). Another rhythm they played was ashiko, a highlife played with a musical saw. Ashiko bands consisted of an accordion or concertina, clips and a carpenter's saw, where the saw is bent and an iron or knife is used to rattle the mouth or face of the saw. Sam later learned to play guitar against his father's wishes, who thought only ruffians played the guitar. Subsequently, Sam ran away to Kumasi and joined the T.T.C. (the Tarkwa Trading Company that ran the local Kingsway chain of stores). There, in Kumasi, he met Kwah Kanta from Elmina and H.E. Biney from Cape Coast. Kwah Kanta played wooden box, and Biney and Sam played guitar. In 1928, they went to London to make recordings. Later, when Biney died and Kanta left, Kweku Bibi came in on guitar and Kofi Lawyer on gong. Sam died around 1950.

JC: Tell me more about your early musical activities.

MENSAH: Before the war, I was in an adaha band called the Atwem Band (*atwem* means drawing, as in drawing a bow), which consisted of a sidedrum which had a string at the back, pati drums (a local version of a European military side-drum), the angle (triangle), two pieces of iron, fifes and cymbals. I didn't use any guitar in this band; I played pati and fifes. As a small boy, I had played in the small boys' section of the Atwem Band, but when I returned to Cape Coast from the mines I joined the big one. In 1939, the Silver Stars Konkoma Group was formed and I left the Atwem Band. When konkoma came, it destroyed the Atwem Band. The konkoma band had something like drums, pati drums, bass, tenor and alto tambourines (hand-held frame-drum) and thirty singers. I was the first to bring a guitar. We played adaha music, Akan adesim which is a hot music faster than highlife, Asante 'blues', rumbas, foxtrots, bumps-a-daisy, sambas, la congas, Spanish music and dagomba highlife.

JC: What do you mean by dagomba highlife? Is it from the North?

MENSAH: No, it was brought by the Kroos (or Krus of Liberia). The word possibly comes from a Kroo word, as one early Kroo dagomba highlife goes 'Dagomba wiya tangebu'.

JC: What happened after you joined the Silver Stars?

MENSAH: I went on to form my own Akote Special Konkoma Group and I left when the war finished; as when the war finished, konkoma finished. By this time, I was a master guitarist and formed the N.A.A.F.I. Franklin Band. We played highlife, ohugua, everything. N.A.A.F.I. means Navy, Army and Air Force Institute, and Franklin is a name I saw in the papers of a District Commissioner I went to see. I just liked the name. Then I formed the Navy Blues which used apremprensemma (or premprensua giant bass hand piano), pati, tambourines, cigarette pan and clips. The Navy Blues collapsed when I went back to Kumasi in 1951 and, when I came back after Christmas, I formed Kwaa Mensah's band which had the same instruments. My first recordings were with H.M.V. (His Master's Voice) and we were paid five pounds for each side. Altogether, I have made nearly 200 records! At first, I was not an actor, but the promoters forced me to be an actor, so I formed my concert party in 1955.

JC: Kwaa, I am looking at the photograph taken in 1959 of a scene from your play, 'If You Bamboozle Somebody, He Will Bamboozle You'. In this you are the good-time girl, Awurama, seated and holding a guitar. The man with the black and white minstrel face and one leg thrown over yours is Johnson, the joker or 'Bob' of the play. Behind you in top-hat is the Gentleman Sousu, and, behind Johnson, the Old Lady smoking a pipe. Could you tell me about the play?

MENSAH: Johnson was a taxi driver and, because of the lifts he gave women, he was always poor. So the owner took the taxi from him. Johnson had been taking cigarettes from some old lady's store to Awurama's shop and bossed this old lady that, 'I will marry you because I am a strong man so if anybody wants to buy cigarettes from you and they behave nonsensically, I will beat him'. The old lady liked him and always gave him money, and, as he liked to play the guitar, she went and bought a guitar. The old lady didn't take the advice of the gentleman, Mr. Sousu, who wanted also to befriend her. One day, Awurama came to the shop to buy cigarettes and she met the old lady alone and saw the guitar lying down and asked her who gets the guitar. The old lady said she bought it for her man and gave it to Awurama to play. Then Johnson appeared and he was very happy; and he thought if he could get this woman he would like it. Awurama came again, and Johnson told his wife to go and buy chop. Johnson told Awurama that he liked her, but she asked "what about your wife?" He said that she wasn't his wife, only an old lady he wants to help and the shop is for his own father. So,

Kwaa Mensah's concert party in 1959. Kwaa is dressed as a women holding a guitar

then, Awurama played the guitar and Johnson put his leg on hers. When the old lady came back, she met them like this. She exclaimed "Hey, what are you doing here? So you be (i.e. is that how you are)?" Then Johnson sacked the old lady and she took all the dresses she had given him so that only one remained. She said to him "What you have done to me, someone will do the same to you." Mr. Sousu rented out suits to anyone that wanted them so Johnson rented a suit, to make fine play with Awurama. Awurama went away, came back to find Johnson in the beautiful suit and so she thought he had more money. She told him she had two brothers who had scholarships for overseas, so he gave her all his money. When Mr. Sousu came, he asked "Where's my money?" and took the suit. When Awurama returned, she told Johnson that she wanted him to meet her mother so he should go and change his dirty old clothes. He told her that he had no suit so she abused him. At the end of the play, only Johnson is on stage and he says to the audience: "The first time I was a driver but I fell, then I saw some old lady and told her I would marry her and she agreed. But when I saw Awurama I went and called her and she took all my money; that's why I make like this. So if your wife is an old lady, or farmer, don't go and take the one with lipstick, otherwise you will fall."

JC: Kwaa, could you tell me about your future plans?

MENSAH: I don't want to make dialogue (plays) anymore. I want to make duet with the music. The musicians will speak and joke, then we will play and someone will dance. Afterwards one of us will say something again. I am going to continue with my cultural music but I don't want to use any drum like a chief's drum or fetish drum. It's not good to play the Omanhene's (chief's) drum, and we are not fetish men. I am now making new long-playing records as some of my old numbers are very good and all the old records are spoilt.

JC: What about some advice for young musicians?

MENSAH: If you are a black man and you want to play soul, you can do it; if you are white and you want to play cultural, you can play. But if you mix them it is not good. My advice to young musicians is if you want to play culture, play real culture; and if you want to play Afro, play Afro. I am not advising them to stop, but if you are playing culture, don't bring organ inside. But if you use guitar for cultural music, it is fine. You see, the guitar came from Africa and the Europeans came to imitate it.

I will finish this chapter on Kwaa Mensah by providing an update. In 1982, Kwaa was awarded a Scroll of Honour by the Ministry of Culture and Tourism, and in 1986 he was one of the winners of Ghana's Entertainment Critics and Reviewers Association (ECRAG) awards. In the late 1980s, he became Senior Research Fellow of the Music

Department of the University of Cape Coast and, then, of the School of Performing Arts at the University of Ghana at Legon. In both places, he taught the guitar. In 1990, Kwaa became an executive member of the Bokoor African Popular Music Archives Foundation (BAPMAF) and he donated a number of old shellac 78 rpm highlife records. In October 1990, he was given an award at the 'Highlife Awards Night' organised by the National Commission on Culture at the Trade Fair Site. On February 22, 1991, he died after a short illness in Cape Coast.

Chapter 2

THE YAA AMPONSAH STORY

Yaa Amponsah is Ghana's most popular highlife song; its melody and rhythm are, for Ghanaians, what the twelve-bar blues is for African-Americans, a standard chordal progression on which many differing lyrics can be based. Yaa Amponsah is traditionally associated with a class of music that is usually referred to in Ghana as 'guitar-band' or 'palmwine' music. This Ghanaian style of predominantly guitar music has its origin in the early part of this century when the West African cross-rhythmic 'two-finger' technique of plucking indigenous harp-lutes (like the Senegambian kora, Liberian Luu and Akan seprewa) was transferred to the Spanish guitar.

It was the Kru people of coastal Liberia who initially pioneered this Africanisation of the Spanish guitar. They were a famous maritime people who would often go on two-year canoe journeys along the West African long before the Europeans came and settled in West Africa. As a result, they were hired by the Portuguese as navigators. In the 18th century, Europeans began employing them as seamen on sailing ship, and, from the mid-19th century, the British and Americans hired them on steamships. They also operated as dockers and surfboat operators in many West African ports where they sometimes settled and created 'Kru towns'. The favourite Kru instruments were portable sailors' ones like the concertina, mandolin, penny-whistle harmonica, banjo and, above all, the guitar. Consequently, the Krus developed a number of guitar patterns that used the two finger plucking technique related to one of the techniques used on local West African harps and lutes.

The basic Liberian guitar style is called 'mainline' which every Ghanaian guitarist today has to master. Another is 'dagomba' which the late Kwaa Mensah told me is a shortening of the Liberian Kru expression 'dagomba wiye tangebu'. The musicologist Dr. Cynthia Schmidt told me that this refers to the Dagomba ship telegraphing or wiring (i.e. 'wiya') a seaman called Tangebu. Yet another guitar pattern is 'fireman' that takes its name from the job of stoker aboard steamships. Because the Kru people had 'Kru town' settlements in many West African coastal towns (Accra, Freetown, Porto Novo and Lagos), they spread these early African guitar styles far and wide, playing them at dockside drinking and palmwine bars where they were blended with local music. Indeed, their influence was felt down the African coast as far as Mutadi at the mouth of the River Congo, and even further south in late 19th century Namibia.

As mentioned in the previous chapter, Ghana's pioneer guitarist Jacob Sam (or Kwame Asare) was taught his instrument by a Kru. It was his 'Kumasi Trio' that made the first ever recordings of Ghanaian osibisaaba guitar music (also known as Akan 'blues' and, later in rural settings, as 'palmwine' or 'odonson'). The Kumasi Trio's recordings took place in June 1928 at Kingsway Hall in London for the Zonophone gramophone company's EZ series (some of which were re-released on CD in 1993 by Heritage Records, London). The well-known song 'Yaa Amponsah' was one of these 1928 recordings (EZ 100l) and, according to the late Beattie Casely-Hayford, this song was associated with a group of local cocoa brokers who were sent by the British merchant, S. Barnet, to Apedwa in 1918. There, they also set up the town's first modern dance club. Yaa Amponsah was the sister of one of the musicians and she taught highlife and ballroom dancing at the club. As ballroom dancing involves holding men in public, and, because she collected coins from them as dance teacher, she gained a bad but un-deserved reputation.

Kwame Asare (right) and his Kumasi Trio at a recording session at Kingsway Hall London in 1928

Whether Sam or Kwame Asare was the actual author of the song is less clear. Beattie Casely-Hayford claimed that Yaa Amponsah was composed by Asante Kwapong, whereas A.T.A. Oscarmore Ofori said that Kwapong arranged it after hearing the melody from an unknown old lady. Then, the Achimota schoolteacher W. E .Ward recalled hearing the song played in Kibi in 1924 (see *Ghana Copyright News, Issue One, 1990*); in 1927, he published an article called 'Music in the Gold Coast' that contains three different notated versions of Yaa Amponsah in the keys of G and B flat. And, on page eleven of the 1929 Zonophone Catalogue of West African Native Artists, Yaa Amponsah (record number EZ 74) is accredited to Daniel H. Acquah under the direction of George William Aingo.

Although Yaa Amponsah is therefore an Akan popular song of unknown exact origin, the Kumasi Trio's recording of it in 1928 spread it far and wide. Many later Ghanaian bands, such as those of E.K. Nyame and E. T. Mensah's Tempos (Decca WA 971) released their own versions of it. It even spread to Nigeria, where, under the name 'Yaponsa', the musicologist Chris Waterman says it became a popular guitar-pattern with Lagosian 'paImwine' musicians before the Second World War. More recent versions of the Yaa Amponsah pattern have been used by 'burger' highlife musicians George Darko and the American singer Paul Simon who wove it into his song 'Spirit Voices' that appears in his 1990 'Rhythm Of The Saints' album.

The highlife guitarists on Paul Simon's record are the Ghanaian Kofi *Electric* Addison and the Cameroonian Vincent Nguni, who was in Ghana for a number of years and, in fact, once visited my Bokoor Studio. The drummer and bass guitarist Kofi Electric or Elektric had played with a number of bands from the late 1960s and 70s, such as the Blue Monks, Prince Ali's Jets, Pat Thomas and the Sweet Beans and Mirijata. Kofi Electric was in the States in the late 1980s and was contacted by Hugh Masekela that Paul Simon needed some West African musicians, after having released his South African-influenced 'Graceland' hit. So the two musicians supplied the guitar lines for several tracks including 'Spirit Voices'. The Ghanaians in New York told Paul Simon that that 'Yaa Amponsah' was written by Kwame Asare, and so this famous American frock star sent monies to the Ghanaian Copyright Office to be passed onto him. However, with the confusion over the authorship and the fact Sam/Kwame Asare had died round 1950 and so the then 25-year copyright protection period has ended, the Yaa Amponsah composition was treated as an anonymous folkloric work. As a result, Paul Simon's royalties for Yaa Amponsah ($70,000 in all) went to help establish the National Folklore Board of Trustees, of which I had the honour of being a member between 1991 and 1997. Other founding members included the musicians Koo Nimo, Nana Ampadu and Oscarmore Ofori, the poet Professor Kofi Anyidoho, the folklorist Dr. Owusu Brempong, the governmental appointee Colonel Amuzu, and Betty Mould-lddrisu and Bernard Bosumprah of the government Copyright Administration. The fact that the foreigner Paul Simon was paying royalties for the commercialisation of a Ghanaian folkloric work was both in line with then operating PNDC 1985 Law 110, and with the United Nations linked World Intellectual Property Organisation (WIPO) recommendations to protect the folklore of Third World countries from exploitation by developed nations.

Chapter 3

THE CONCERT PARTY: POPULAR THEATRE AND COMIC HIGHLIFE OPERA

The concert parties are groups of professional performers who, since the early 1900s, have been touring up and down Ghana, performing local language shows for village people and the urban poor. Their performances involve music, stylised acting, magical acts, acrobatic dancing, fancy dress, trickster clowns, old legends, morality tales, and current news and fashions. The concert party continues a long African tradition of professional roving minstrels and troubadours, such as the griots and jalis of the Sahel region of West Africa, who are entertainers, historians and news bringers.

The concert parties also draw on traditional practices such as ritual dramas that combine music, dance, masks, body paint and costumes, found throughout the continent; and even in the New World as Jamaican carnival and African American Mardi Gras. The Akans of Ghana also have their dramatised Ananse stories, humorous morality-tales about the mischievous spider hero that has even found its way to the Caribbean as Nancy stories. All these types of indigenous African theatre were (and still are) unscripted, performed out of doors and involve active audiences who dance, clap, make interjections or become possessed. The concert parties include many of the above traditional features. They use fancy-clothes, masked figures, ananse-like tricksters and magical displays. Their shows are open-air ones that are partly improvised and involve a high degree of audience participation.

Between the 1950s and 1980s, about two hundred and fifty of these groups were operating in the country. It would be true to say that the concert party has acted as a major 'cultural powerhouse' for Ghana, providing the country with a major avenue for local singers and, more recently, TV and film actors and actresses.

Let us turn first to the concert party story in some detail. The story begins in southern Ghana around 1900, at the height of the colonial period. As the name 'concert party' suggests, it was initially based on imported western variety concerts, performed at elite locations like the Palladium Cinema and Merry Villas in Accra, and Optimism Club in Sekondi. Also important were the school concerts that were performed on stage every British Empire Day (May 24th). Church mission 'cantata' bible-stories and morality plays also helped introduce western stagecraft to Ghana. A fourth foreign influence on the early concert party came through films that began to be shown from around First World War times which starred comedians like Charlie Chaplin and the blackface minstrel actor AI Jolson. Fifthly, American vaudeville and British music-hall acts were brought to the country by visiting artists, including African-American and Caribbean ones.

The first evidence of local Ghanaian comics are the Two Macs who performed at a 'Magic Costume Ball and Concert' held at Cape Coast Castle's Great Hall in 1903 for a mixed audience of local and European ballroom dancers. Then came Ghana's first concert party actor of note, Teacher Yalley, the headmaster of a Sekondi elementary school. His career began at his School's Empire Day concerts in 1918 when he joked, sang and danced; wore fancy dress, wig and moustache, and put on the make-up of an American black-and-white minstrel. According to the Ghanaian dramatist Efua Sutherland, his three-hour shows opened with a hired brass-band campaigning around town and ending up outside the theatre. Inside, Yalley performed his comedy sketches assisted by a trap-drummer and pump harmonium player who provided a cross-section of then current popular ballroom dance tunes: ragtimes, foxtrots, quicksteps and waltzes. His shows were in English and the tickets expensive. Consequently, his audience consisted mainly of the educated black elite. The famous Fanti comedian Ishmael 'Bob' Johnson, who was a boy at the time and sneaked into some of these high-class shows, recalled that the audience consisted of local 'official people and gentlemen' and included a small number of Europeans. As will be discussed below, it was Bob Johnson who was later indigenised this elite performance genre, and took it to the urban and village poor.

Bob Johnson's own acting career started at the shows performed at his Sekondi Methodist School that took place after the Empire Day parade around town. His first group was a schoolboy affair called the Versatile Eight which, nevertheless, included the three principal stock characters of all subsequent concert parties: the Joker, the Gentleman and the Lady Impersonator. Johnson, in blackface and wearing bizarre or ragged clothes, played the joker. In fact, he did it so well that this local clown role has since become known as the 'Bob' for the concert party profession. Johnson's success was partially a result of his fusing together the character of the imported blackface minstrel with that of the mischievous Ananse-the-Spider hero of Akan folklore. This was an important early step in the Africanisation of the concert party genre that began when Johnson moved his shows from the cities to the provincial towns and villages.

Johnson told me in 1974, when I met him at his house in Nungua, that he obtained his name 'Bob' from the seamen who visited the Optimism Club opposite his house in Sekondi. He often went there to watch Liberian seamen singing sea-shanties to the accompaniment of guitar and musical saw, and African-American ones performing comedy sketches and singing foxtrots and ragtime. It was the latter who gave him the nickname 'Bob' for, as he told me, the African-American sailors of those times seemed to call everyone 'Bob'. Another African-American (or possibly Americo-Liberian) influence on Bob Johnson came through the shows performed between 1924 and 1926 by the African-American team of Glass and Grant. This comedy duo was brought from Liberia to Ghana by the local film distributor and cinema-hall owner Alfred Ocansey. Johnson saw them in Sekondi and was much impressed by the 'boldness on stage', i.e. their professionalism. Their shows, like Teacher Yalley's, were high-class affairs and began with a silent film before the comedy act. The act itself was vaudeville, with the minstrel Glass and his wife Grant joking, tap-dancing and singing ragtime. This team based themselves at Accra's Palladium Cinema where they were understudied by the Ga comedians, Williams and Marbel and the Sierra Leone ones, Williams and Nicol. When this man and wife duo left for Nigeria to continue their West African tour, the 'Accra Vaudeville' tradition continued.

The Ga concert party comedians Williams (right) and Marbel in 1923

After Johnson formed the schoolboy Versatile Eight, he went professional in 1930 when he set up the Two Bobs and their Carolina Girl that staged for villagers as well as the urban poor. It was then that the concert party tradition began to separate into two distinct varieties: the upper-class shows of Yalley and the 'Accra Vaudeville' on one hand, and Bob Johnson's sixpenny shows on the other. In a nutshell, Johnson 'hijacked' the genre from the elite, which is lucky for Ghana, as the high-class variety gradually died out. According to Efua Sutherland, the Two Bobs shows were given pre-publicity by a masked bell-ringer wearing a billboard, which was cheaper than hiring out a full brass-band. The show itself began with half-an-hour of 'Comedies', which consisted of three segments: an 'Opening Chorus' of a quickstep danced and sung by the three comedians, followed by a so-called 'In' section during which one of the Bobs sang ragtime, ending with a 'Duet' of joking by the two Bobs. Music was supplied by the group's own 'jazz' (i.e. trap or kit) drummer, with some help from a few members of a local school brass or orchestral band hired for the night. After the opening 'Comedies' came the 'Scene' or play proper. This lasted an hour and was performed in English, but with an occasional translation into Akan since their audiences were less westernised than those of their high-class counterparts. Yet another difference between the two varieties of concert was that Johnson began using an occasional highlife in his acts, in addition to popular Western songs.

The pioneering concert party comedian Bob Johnson

In 1935, Bob Johnson became the joker or 'Bob' for the Axim Trio concert party that became the prototype for all succeeding ones. E. K. Dadson played Susanna and Charlie Turpin was the Gentleman. They acted to the accompaniment of their own drummer and pump harmonium player. According to Efua Sutherland, at one point, the Trio also featured the famous early palmwine highlife guitarist Kwame Asare (Jacob Sam) who performed in drag and sang in a falsetto voice. The Axim Trio's very first major engagement was a 1937 tour of Nigeria when they hooked up with the twenty-two strong Cape Coast Sugar Babies dance-orchestra. The Axim Trio's normal practice in Ghana, however, was to supplement their two musicians with some members of a local brass band or 'konkoma' marching group that they hired for the evening's performance. Their shows consisted of an 'Opening Chorus', 'In' and 'Duet', followed by a two-hour play. The titles of some of the plays they staged up to the mid-1950s (when the group dissolved) include 'The Coronation of King George the Sixth', 'The Bond of 1844' (about the Fanti-British alliance), 'The Ten foot Man', 'The Kyibi Murder Trial', 'The Downfall of Adolph Hitler' and 'Kwame Nkrumah Will Never Die'.

Besides Nigeria, the Axim Trio made extensive tours of Ghana that included the North. They also visited Liberia, Cote d'Ivoire and Sierra Leone. According to the Nigerian writer, Ebun Clark, the performances of the Axim Trio and the Cape Coast Sugar Babies at Tinubu Square in Lagos influenced the Yoruba highlife musicians Bobby Benson who, at the time, was only playing swing-jazz and staging western variety acts.

Whereas the high-class concert parties died out during the 1930s, the Axim Trio became so popular in Ghana by the 1940s that many other groups modelled themselves on it. Bob Cole's Happy Trio, the Jovial Jokers, the Dix Covian Jokers and the West End Trio that all came from the Western Region of the country; the Saltpond Trio and Sam (i.e. Kwame Asare) and His Party from the Central Region; Y.B. Bampoe's Schoolboy Yanky Trio from the Eastern Region; and the Keta Trio from the Volta Region.

The Second World War had a direct impact on the concert profession as several performers staged shows for the visiting allied troops. Concerts were even held for the African troops in India and Burma, for between 1943 and 1946 an African Theatre was set up within the West African Frontier Force that was stationed in these countries.

The leader was Bob Vans who, together with six other Ghanaians, visited camps and hospitals, performing in 'pidgin' English to the music of the 'konkoma' variety of highlife. When Vans returned to Ghana in 1946, he and other Ghanaian ex-servicemen formed the Burma Jokers. In 1948, they renamed it the Ghana Trio due to the rising nationalist sentiments of the period. This was the year of the Christiansburg shooting of protesting unpaid local ex-serviceman and consequent lootings of European shops. It was also that year that the pioneer of Nigerian popular theatre, Hubert Ogunde, visited Ghana and whose earlier nationalist play 'Strike the Hunger' had been banned in Nigeria by the British. Ogunde made two trips to Ghana and so, for a while, adopted the ragtime-jazz music and black-and-white minstrel make-up of the Ghanaian concert parties for his own group in Lagos. Later, he began the move towards the more Yoruba format that was taken up by other subsequent travelling theatre groups; of which there were over a hundred in the 1980s, such as those of Baba John Bull, Baba Mero, Oje Lapido, Moses Olaiya and Kola Ogunmola.

Another major contribution to the indigenisation of the Ghanaian concert party profession was made by the guitarist E. K. Nyame who, in 1952, formed the Akan Trio. As will be discussed in the next chapter, the Akan Trio fully grafted local highlife music onto the concert party to produce what might be called a 'highlife opera' format. E.K.'s synthesis of guitar-band highlife music and concert acting, plus the fact that his Akan Trio was the first to perform exclusively in the Akan language, made E.K.'s group an instant success. Within a few years, most other guitar-bands followed suit. Conversely, already existing concerts expanded their small musical sections to a full guitar-band. Yet another of E.K.'s innovations was that his was the first guitar-band to use Afro-Cuban instruments (bongos and congas) and American jazz ones (trap-drums and plucked double-bass), an idea he borrowed from the highlife dance-bands of the period being pioneered by E. T. Mensah and his Tempos (see Chapter 12).

It was both the Axim Trio and the more Africanised Akan Trio that became the prototypes for most post-war Ghanaian concert parties and, indeed, Togolese ones such as the Happy Stars of Lome. Some of the most important Ghanaian concert groups of the fifties and sixties were Kakaiku's, the Jaguar Jokers, Bob Cole's, the Ghana Trio, Onyina's Royal Trio, Kwaa Mensah's, the Happy Stars (of Nsawam), I.E. Mason's, Yamoah's, 'Doctor' Gyasi's Noble Kings, the Brigade Concert Party and Nana Ampadu's African Brothers. By 1960, when the first concert party union was formed, there were about thirty groups in the country, reaching a high-point in the mid-1970s when there were seventy or more functioning groups.

Although the numbers of active concert parties have dwindled in recent years, the impact of concert parties has continued through the use of new media. There were film versions of concert plays such as 'I Told You So' that starred Bob Cole. Television concert party series began in the 1970s and these tend to have a strong moral and didactic tone, as well as providing an avenue for many concert actresses. The most popular were Jatakrom, Osofo Dadzie, the Adabraka Drama Troupe, Agbedefu, Obra and, more recently, Cantata. During the late 1970s and 80s, concert groups also had their plays photographed and put together in comic literature or 'photoplay' form. Another medium that began in the 1980s was the 'dialogue' cassette on which concert play and music are recorded on audio-cassette for the commercial market.

The enormous number of the country's current top performing artists and recording stars who have been influenced by, or actually ran concert groups, emphasises the importance of this highlife-drama to Ghana. The 'back-to-palmwine-roots' highlife guitarist Koo Nimo was once with I.E. Mason's concert party; 'golden voiced' Pat Thomas was influenced by his uncle Onyina; guitarist Eric Agyeman, drummer Thomas Frempong, trumpeter Tommy King and keyboard-player Ernest Honey were all with Doctor Gyasi's Noble Kings; the guitarist C. K. Mann who created the rootsy 'Osode' highlife beat in the seventies had been a member of the late Kakaiku's concert, as had the guitarist and singer Senior Eddie Donkor.

Other musicians influenced by the concert genre includes Smart Nkansah and Agyaaku who had formerly played with Yamoah's concert party band, the soulful singer Pozo Hayes who was first with the Vis-a-Vis guitar band, Amakye Dede who started out with the Kumapim Royals and the lady singers Mum Bea, Awura Ama and Janet Osei who came out of the Nana Ampadu's African Brothers concert band. Some of Ghana's top television comic actors and actresses have likewise passed through the concert profession. These include Adelaide Buabeng who began with the Workers Brigade Concert Party, Esi Kom who was with Efua Sutherland's Kusum Agoromma, the late Kwadwo Kwakye who was with the Osofo Dadzie concert party, and Grace Omaboe, the late Joe 'Stationmaster' Eyison and Doctor Rokoto of the Obra group.

Moreover, a large number of Ghana's most well-known 1970s/80s guitar-band musicians were also operating concert parties. The following are just a few of them: Nana Ampadu (African Brothers), Kofi Sammy (Okukuseku's), Jackson Adofo (City Boys), Alex Konadu, F. Kenya (Riches Big Sound), Akwasi Ampofo Adjei (Kumapim

Royals), Amakye Dede (Apollo High Kings), Senior Eddie Donkor (Simple Seven), Osei Kofi (Heroes), Eric Agyeman's (Kokroko), A. K. Yeboah's (K. K.'s Number Two), F. Micah (F. Micah's concert party), Alhaji Frempong (Cubanos Fiesta) and Paa Bobo (Three Axes). Although A. B. Crentsil (Ahenfo) and Jewel Ackah (Butterfly Six) run dance-bands, when they toured Ghana during the 1980s, especially the rural areas, they usually operated with a concert party.

Mention must also be made of those who have performed at the National Theatre's long-running concert party shows sponsored by Unilever/Keysoap that began in November 1994. These include concert parties like Abibiman, Anokyekrom, Christ for All Missions, Krabehwe, Kristo Asafo, Obeye Yie, Nyame Nti's Agrobessa and Adikanfo Efiritete, as well as the concert comedians Bob Okala, Nkomode, the late Santo, Ice Kenkey, Bob Cedi, Cocoa Tea, Kwame Alhaji and Agya Koo (Kofi Adu).

Chapter 4

THE CONCERT PARTY MUSICIAN E.K. NYAME

E.K Nyame was born in the Kwahu area of Ghana in 1927 and went into the guitar-band music field in the late 1940s, when a flourishing record market for this music was starting up after the break in record production during the Second World War. This guitar music was supplied by Akan artists such as Appiah Adjekum, Kwaa Mensah and Otoo Larte, and Ga ones like Obiba T.K. Adjekum (an Akan resident in Accra) whose his group's instruments consisted of bass, treble and tenor frame-drums (known also as 'konkoma' or 'gome' drums), finger bell, two acoustic guitars and an accordion. The Accra-based Obiba T.K. was recording songs in the konkoma highlife vein using guitars and mandolins. Kwaa Mensah, on the other hand, was based at Cape Coast, where in 1949 he formed a group similar to Adjekum's in composition, but it also included a premprensua bass hand-piano. During these times, the most popular highlife styles with all these bands were the Akan odonson (more love) or 'Asanti blues' style of guitar highlife, the Akan marching style of 'konkoma' highlife and a Ga street music related to konkoma highlife known as 'kolomashie'.

As noted in the previous chapter, the concert party stems from quite a different origin than the guitar-bands, although both spread throughout the Akan hinterland during the inter-war period. It was during this time that the high-class coastal vaudeville style of concert party gave way to trios, like Bob Johnson's and the Axim Trio, that played to less-educated and more provincial audiences. As mentioned in the previous chapter, the music for these early travelling concert trios was supplied by a trap drummer and harmonium player who played ballroom numbers and ragtime.

However, today it is the highlife guitar band that has become closely linked with concert, and the first to combine these two distinct art forms was E.K. Nyame. From 1948, he was a guitarist and singer for Appiah Adjekum's band, and then, with falsetto singer Kobina Okine (or Okai), left in 1950 to form his own E.K.'s guitar-band which also added instruments (like the double bass and Afro-Cuban percussion) from the contemporary dance bands of the period. Finally, in 1952, E.K. formed a concert group and merged it with his guitar band, naming the new combined group the Akan Trio. His synthesis of guitar band highlife and comic opera was such a success that, within a few years, other guitar bands like those of Kwaa Mensah, Onyina and Kakaiku followed suit. Conversely, concerts already in existence enlarged their small musical section to a full-scale guitar band.

E.K.'s guitar band around 1950. E.K. is sitting holding a clarinet and Kobina Okai is sitting on his right

Below is a conversation I had with E.K. at his house in Jamestown, Accra, on May 25, 1975. I began by asking him about the Akan Trio's early days.

NYAME: It was derived from the band, to give us our daily bread and let everyone know about the efforts we were making in our music. We staged in English, but there were parts of it when a character came in and spoke our dialect (Akan). Because we minded the colonial ideology and British mind, whatever we did in those days was in English. However, by 1957, we were using Twi. We were the first concert to use guitar band and the first to use Spanish bongos, playing highlifes, ragtimes and calypsos in rare cases. I played the Gentleman and Bob. The lady impersonator was Mr. Baidoo, and Okine was the lady in cloth or native attire; but Baidoo was in modern dress and hat. We three introduced the show, but we had our own way: an opening chorus which was a quickstep sung in English. In the early days, we started the concert by eight-thirty; but gradually, later on, the time was moved to around ten or eleven o'clock. So, between eight and eleven we would play records. The play would then last two hours; we were using highlifes, blues (Akan) and Christian songs.

JC: You were originally with Appiah Adjekum's band. What was that like?

NYAME: I was a clerk at the time. It was an amateur group, and if anyone wanted to make some out-dooring or function that needed music, we would go there. You know Appiah Adjekum is the originator of these modern (guitar) bands. As for Sam (Kwame Asare), I can say it was folk music but not on the line of modernization. I played the fundamental (rhythm) guitar and Adjekum played the Hawaiian guitar. There were three oblong tambourines covered in vellum and about five to eight inches in size. They were treble, tenor and bass; the bass one was sat on (i.e. a gome). We also had a 'four corner' (concertina) with 48 keys and castanets or claves. Sometimes Adjekum's (Liberian) wife played the guitar.

JC: Why did you leave Adjekum's band?

NYAME: I was having the idea of modernising the music, to use staff notation and raise the standard. At first we used tambourines, guitar and clips; but we made a change in 1951, and replaced the tambourines with bongos (treble), jazz drums (tenor) and fiddle bass (bass).

JC: From where did you get the ideas for your stories? Could you describe one?

NYAME: When we create a very good highlife number on the market, it's out of this we build our concert story; because the whole nation has the feeling that they want to see us performing what we have done on the recording side. We just narrate the story, then everybody will choose their part and just act. If you act well, we let you stay. If not, we fetch another person. We have so many plays that I can't mention (all of them). One we had was 'Wo Sum Brodea Sum Kwadu', which means 'When You Support Plantain You Have to Support Push Banana' (i.e. you have to treat everyone equally). It is about when you have a child who does not come from your family and you neglect the child and keep supporting yours, not knowing that the child you neglected is rather to your interest and will come to your aid. It's just like these lotto (lottery) numbers, you don't know which number is going to win. It (the play) is about a man who has married two wives and he loves the one (more) than the other and the son (of the less-loved wife) got to know the father had become poor and wretched, and so he brought the father up again.

JC: You mentioned before that you sometimes used Christian music for your plays. So what is the difference between your concert and church cantata?

NYAME: With cantata you have a complete cast, but in our trio there were only three people who did everything. Cantata is older than concert and many tribes do it (especially the Ewes). They use their own cultural music and combine it with Christian hymns. They always do these Christian doctrine and Bible Stories, but we used modern stories.

JC: Nkrumah liked what you were going and you went to Liberia with him for the inauguration of President Tubman. Tell me about this.

NYAME: We went to Monrovia with the then Prime Minister, Kwame Nkrumah, for one week in 1953. When there was any function, we would play for them at places like the Executive Mansion. They had no concerts there (in Liberia) and no idea about them. What they did have was (Classical) music for piano and singer. We also met the Regimental Police Band which played wedding music, swing and any other type of music, provided the sheet was laid in front of them.

JC: Since you first started recording in 1951, you have made about four hundred singles for record companies like Decca, Queenophone and H.M.V. What are some of your favourite numbers?

NYAME: One was 'Minni Agya, Minni Na' (I Have No Father, No Mother), which is about an orphan who is in trouble and nobody will come to his rescue. Another was 'Mane Meoo Made Ye Mobo' (Help Me As I Am Melancholic), which is a plea to the ghost of my mother to help me from the grave. A very popular number was 'Maye Maye Meni Aye' (I Do Something Good and He Repays Me with Ingratitude); even the Whites from the University liked it. One of our first popular numbers was 'Onim Deefo Kukudurufu Kwame Nkrumah' (Honourable Man and Hero Kwame Nkrumah) which we did in 1950 to welcome Nkrumah back from prison (he had been imprisoned by the British).

JC: At the moment you are busy with a series of L.P.s which you are going to release under the title of 'Sankofa' (Go Back and Retrieve). These are recordings of your old numbers. Why are you doing this?

NYAME: Formerly our records were on the breakable 78's and the songs are so good that we want to leave them for the next generation, so any time they play our old songs so much will be reflected. You can't write this dance music, it's never written. I'm worried about this and that is why we are releasing our old numbers. If we don't, it will be something like a lost thing. Besides, the public kept telling me they want our old songs. Financially, we are not so much disturbed, but just to put the record down so that when we are dead and gone, they'll still be able to hear us. Highlife is important because, all over West Africa, Ghanaian highlife is supreme. It's out of this that the Nigerians have their Afro-beat.

JC: What are your other plans for the future?

NYAME: I intend to balance the whole musical trend and create a different sound that will suit the present epoch. Mine will be a developed highlife, with changed rhythms and I will use the pati, which is like the tenor drum on a jazz drum and has a very high tune. I will use this gombe (or gome) idea instead of bass guitar. We changed over from bass fiddle to bass guitar in 1968. I will also use three tambourines, castanets and acoustic guitar. We will use a two-four beat; it will come near to Afro-beat.

107

In the mid-1970s, Nyame began to re-release his old highlife hits on a record album series called 'Sankofa' (go back and retrieve). Unfortunately he died in 1977. His body was laid out on a golden bed covered in guitars and he was given a state funeral attended by ten thousand people, for over the years his music and records had touched the hearts of many Ghanaians and indeed Nigeria.

As evidence of E.K.'s fame in Nigeria I will narrate an incident that happened at Faisal Helwani's Napoleon club in 1976. I had invited E.K. to meet Faisal to discuss the possibility of him being included (with Kwaa Mensah and others) on Faisal's Afro-disia promotions project. Coincidentally, Fela Anikulapo-Kuti turned up to discuss the pre-planning of his Black President film (see Chapter 49). Later, as I was leaving with E.K., I suddenly remembered that Fela had often mentioned the influence of E.K.'s records on Nigerian musicians. So I turned and told Fela whom I was leaving with. Much to my and E.K.' surprise, Fela rushed up to E.K. and kneeled down in front of him to pay homage.

Chapter 5

THE FALSETTO SINGER KOBINA OKAI (OKINE)

On Friday, May 24, 1985, the wake-keeping took place of sixty-three year old Kobina Okai (or Okine), falsetto singer of E. K. Nyame's legendary Akan Trio that recorded and released over four hundred hit songs. After a long illness of diabetes and hypertension, Okai finally succumbed on May 12, 1985, following his band-leader, E.K. who died in 1977. Okai was buried at the Osu cemetery in Accra on Saturday, May 25, 1985, leaving behind a wife and four children.

Like E.K.'s wake, Okine's too was a massive affair, almost a state funeral, at which many of Ghana's musicians paid homage in a marathon twelve-hour music session. They included Kofi Sammy, Kakaiku, Koo Nimo (then President of the Musicians Union), Bob Cole, Pat Thomas, Ambolley, Eddie Donkor, A.B. Crentsil, Smart Nkansah, Kofi Ani Johnson, Jerry James Lartey, Joe Eyison, Jewel Ackah, Kojo Brake, Efua Dokenu, Paapa Yankson, Nana Ampadu, K. Frimpong, Akwasi Ampofo Adjei and many others. In front of the stage, the body of Okai was laid out on a silver bed, wearing a kente cloth given him by a previous Head of State. Around the bed were wreaths donated by the Ministry of Culture and Tourism, the Musician's Union of Ghana, the Osofo Dadzie group, the Kusum Agoromba group, the Ghana Drama Society and the Church Mission.

Kobina Okai was born in Dunkwa in the Central Region of Ghana and first became interested in music when he was thirteen years old, joining the 'See There' konkoma band in 1940. Konkoma was a local dance and drumming craze that swept Ghana in the 1930s and 40s which evolved out of the local syncopated adaha brass band tradition. In those days, music was considered to be a 'useless' profession for a young man, and so Okai's elder brother, attempting to divert him away from a musical career, sent Okai down to Accra to study tailoring with a friend called Appiah Adjekum. Unfortunately for the brother (but luckily for Ghana), Adjekum played the Hawaiian guitar and had just started his own guitar band in Accra. So within a short time Okai became a member.

Then in 1948, guitarist and singer E.K. Nyame joined Adjekum's group. Two years later, E.K. and Okai left Adjekum to form E.K.'s band. As mentioned in the previous chapter, this group did away with the gome drum and tambourines of Adjekum's band and replaced them with the jazz (trap) drums, double bass and bongos. Kobina Okai sang in a falsetto voice for E.K. and it was from 1951 that E.K.'s band first began to make records, with the help of a Syrian called Mr. Taymani. Their first hit was 'Small Boy Nye Emi Bia' released by Decca (WA 001), followed by 'Tetteh Quarshie', 'Car Bi Reba' and 'Nokware Asa'.

Then, in 1952, the band expanded into the Akan Trio concert party with Kobina Okai acting as a lady impersonator in traditional cloth. As already mentioned, the Akan Trio revolutionised Ghanaian show business by merging highlife and comic concert party acting. From its inception, the Akan Trio supported Ghana's independence struggle and played at C. P. P. (Convention People's Party) rallies. In 1953, they accompanied Prime Minister Nkrumah to Liberia to meet President Tubman and, later, in 1963, they and some other concert party artists ('Lord' Bob Cole, Kakaiku and Dr. K. Gyasi) accompanied President Nkrumah on a state visit to Eastern Europe and North Africa. To quote from the Ghanaian magazine, *Positive Joy* (volume 31, 1985, page 8), 'Some freedom fighters fight their wars of liberation with guns and academic degrees, Kobina Okai fought and helped build Ghana with his voice'.

The 1970s was a period of decline for E.K.'s band, culminating in E.K.'s death in 1977. However, Kobina Okai was re-discovered in 1980 by a Ghanaian-Lebanese music promoter, Faisal Helwani, who took the singer to his Studio One recording studio at the Napoleon nightclub in Accra and recorded Okai with the Edikanfo band. Later, when Okai fell sick, it was Faisal who took him to the hospital and helped look after him; for Faisal was planning a comeback for him, starting with a West African tour by this grand old singer. Unfortunately, this never was to be, and Kobina Okai's last public performance was at the Star Hotel in Accra on February 9, 1985, when he was given an award by ECRAG, the Entertainment's Critics and Reviewers Association of Ghana.

One of my own most vivid impressions of Okai was at E.K. Nyame's wake in James Town, Accra in 1977. For as E.K. had no wife to mourn him, Okai dressed up in the lady's traditional cloth that he so often wore onstage and played the part of E.K.'s distraught and wailing wife, whom we mourners had to come up to and try and console.

Chapter 6

THE JAGUAR JOKERS CONCERT PARTY

The Jaguar Jokers (or J.J.'s) was formed by Mr. Y.B. Bampoe in 1954 and was operating up until the 1980s. This concert party was on the road for over thirty years, performing fifteen to twenty shows a month, with each show lasting over six hours. This means that the J.J.'s must surely have been one of the hardest working groups in Ghanaian show business. I first got to know them in 1969 when I went to meet my father's Ghanaian wife and step-mother (who I affectionately called Auntie) Amma Adowaa, at the house my dad had built for her in Adoagyiri. Luckily, Mr. Bampoe was a tenant in her house and, as I was holding a guitar, he invited me to come on 'trek' with them to the rural areas. So I joined them as a guitarist for almost three weeks and lost seven pounds weight in the process. Though I found the life on the road exhilarating, playing at a different venue every night was extremely tiring. (For more details on my on the road experiences, see *West African Popular Theatre* by Karin Barber et al.)

The group used to make twelve treks a year, touring the towns and villages of Ghana; always starting at the end of the month (pay day) when people have money in their pockets. They first sent their 'pioneer man' ahead of them who booked the gigs, put advertisements in the newspapers and hung posters all over the place. When the band

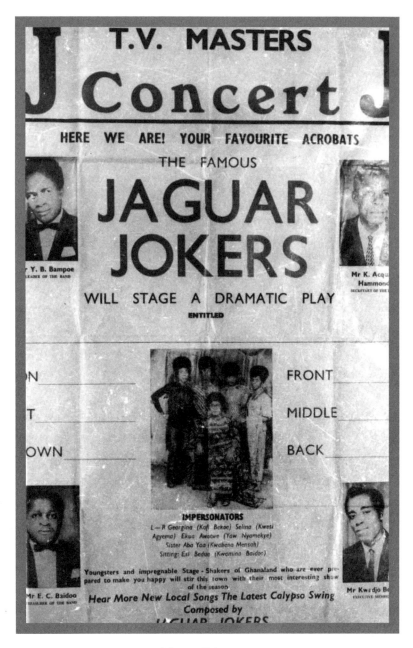

A Jaguar Jokers poster

hit a village, the twenty actors and musicians unloaded the minibus and set up their equipment, including a portable generator for places without electricity. There were usually no cinemas and clubs in the villages so the J.J.'s hired compound houses and put up a make-shift stage constructed of wooden boards and concrete blocks.

Some of the musicians were released from this work as they had to go out to 'campaign' with a speaker on the roof of the bus. Paintings called 'cartoons' of scenes from the night's show were slung on the sides of the vehicle. Whenever I was with them, they would feature me on these campaigns as a crowd puller, playing fast pachangas and Congo jazz guitar with the band's conga player. Hordes of children would follow us as we drove slowly through the dusty streets. Everyone in sight would stop what they were doing and start to dance. Women with buckets on their heads and children on their backs would start to sway. Old people would get up from their chairs and do a turn to our music. When we returned, everything would be set up for the night's show and the 'cartoons' (painted by Mark Anthony of Swedru) were put outside the theatre to pull in the crowd.

Once, while passing through Swedru in southern Ghana, I had the good fortune to meet the artist who did these paintings for the J.J.'s and for many of the concert parties. Mark Anthony started out as a bar artist, painting murals to attract customers. Later, he began to do pictures for the spiritual churches and concert parties. He was so much demand that he could rattle off a twenty-square-foot painting in just a couple of days.

A typical J.J.'s show in the early seventies started at about eight in the evening with the band playing the 'inside rhythm' which was the name they gave to the music their band played right at the beginning of the program when people began to trickle in. Nobody ever comes in before they heard something going on inside, they just hung around the gate until they heard the first few notes of the music. This warming-up music included a selection of all the then current popular music, like local top highlifes, soul, reggae, Afro-beats, Congo jazz, their own version of the Afro-Cuban pachanga and 'smoochie' numbers. The band stopped playing when the place was full and then the musicians who accompanied the actors played a few of the J.J.s' own best-loved highlife compositions. Anytime between ten and eleven, the play itself started. First, there was an 'opening chorus' when Bampoc, supported by K.A. Hammond and the lady impersonator E. C. Baidoo in wig and spectacles, sang and danced ragtimes and foxtrots, just like the Ghanaian concert parties of the 1920s and 1930s. As all female parts were performed by men; there were no women in the J.J.s. This was typical of most Ghanaian concert parties of the time, although a few did employ women and two concert parties were even led by women; namely Vida Rose's concert party and Efua Sutherland's Kusum Agoromma. The hard life of the road and having to sleep on the floor after a performance did not make this profession attractive to women.

114

Furthermore, the public looked down on concert people, making it particularly difficult for women to break into this profession.

After the opening chorus, the three principal actors retired to the changing room called an 'ante-room'. When not actually performing, the busy ante-room was somehow used for cat-napping by the actors, who had the uncanny ability to wake up at exactly the right moment they were to appear on stage. After the opening chorus, the audience was entertained by a comic 'Bob', complete with black-face make-up. Then, by midnight at the latest, the three-hour play was under way. The J.J.'s had dozens of plays, but normally stuck to one play on any single trek. There were involved stories about orphans and wicked step-parents, the problems of having too many wives, money matters, and the clash between the old and new. The very first play the J.J.'s ever performed was about a latrine worker who wasn't being paid for his onerous duties of collecting the night soil from a certain house. So he went on strike and started throwing excrement from a bucket at his debtors (on stage he used mud).

Bampoe used to get incensed when people claimed that concert plays are a corrupting influence. In spite of the slapstick, he believes that they are educational and uplifting. This derogatory attitude toward concert parties gradually began to change in the sixties when Nkrumah established state concert parties. And, in 1973, Colonel Acheampong's government initiated the First National Festival of Concert Parties.

Mr. Bampoe started his acting career in 1946 at the age of eleven when he performed Ananse and Bible Stories in his elementary school plays. At the same time, he was influenced by the Axim Trio, who regularly lodged at his home in Suhum, a town forty miles north of Accra. As a result, Bampoe and some of his school friends formed the Yanky Trio. As Mr. Bampoe describes, their families were initially not too happy about this:

> My senior uncle disagreed that a schoolboy should adopt this habit and we were told not to make concert again; but we were so stubborn, you see. We used to go secretly and stage somewhere, and, when we came home, we would be beaten severely. This went on until, after one holiday, after a longish tour, I showed my uncle some sandals I had bought with the money I earned. This took him by surprise and so he advised me that if I could make money out of the concert during my holidays, he had no objection.

After completing elementary school, and a short period in tailoring, he joined the City Trio, and then, in 1954, formed the Jaguar Jokers. As he explains, he used this name because "a jaguar is a wild animal – you can't make it laugh – but we can. In those days we had jaguar cars and to be 'Jagwah' meant to be fine or modern and to be a 'Jagwah' man or woman was high class."

Off stage, Bampoe is the quietest of individuals, but, in the limelight, he literally gets possessed by his bouncy, compact and energetic stage character, Opia. Opia is usually a servant in the play, a greedy and mischievous imp whom the audience loves to hate and who always ends up helping the hero and heroine of the plot. The character of Opia is, like other concert 'Bobs', an updated version of Ananse-the-spider. The difference between them is that the Bob character wears the make-up of a black and white minstrel, whereas Opia puts on only dark pancake. Mr. Bampoe originally used to make up as a minstrel but later cut out the white around the eyes and lips altogether. When I asked him why even bothered with the black face-powder, as that is the colour of his skin already, he told me he did not want people to recognise him off-stage in public places.

The Jaguar Jokers campaign bus in 1974. Slung on the side is a 'cartoon' painting by Mark Anthony of the J.J.'s play 'Awisia Yi Wo Ani'

116

All sorts of other characters crop up in the plays: 'good-time' girls played by the more slender actors, Hausa corporals, rural farmers and town slicks, lawyers, teachers, as well as masked ghosts, 'mammy waters', forest devils and angels. The lanky Mr. Hammond always plays Mr. Johnson and, with his deep and sonorous voice and 'big English', gives the poetic or sung moral at the end of the night's tale. Throughout the play the actors keep bursting into highlife song, the lyrics of which are integrated into the play. This music is therefore not just mere background or incidental music for the plays; which is why it is quite correct to call them 'highlife operas'. Furthermore, all the stage action is accompanied by a guitarist, trap-drummer, hand-drummer and clip (calves) player who, besides highlifes, also occasionally provide pop music, Christian hymns and 'fetish' music depending on the plot of the play. Even though no scenery is used, the crowd really gets into the story and joins in by singing, clapping and commenting loudly. I often saw people weeping and, if they really empathised with an actor or musician, they would dance up to the stage and 'spray' or stick money on the performer's forehead. Sometimes it is the other way around, such as Opia jumping into the crowd, chasing or being chased by someone or something.

The fact that concert parties involve the audience to such a degree and combine music, acting, dance, poetry and painting, illustrates a traditional African multi-media approach toward art. This is quite different from European arts that fragmented into separate spheres, such as poetry, drama, painting, religious and secular art, literature, ballet, masked mimes, instrumental music and so on. Concert parties, however, have re-combined the different facets of western art they have absorbed, creating something more in tune with the traditionally integrated art-forms of Africa: combining music, dance and drama, conjuring, masquerade and graphic art ('cartoons') and even comic 'photoplay' literature. Furthermore, whereas western theatres prevent audiences from interacting with the actors (by using a pit or proscenium arch), the concert party encourages audience participation; again a feature of traditional performance. The plays are also performed in the local languages and, unlike western plays, are unscripted. So a show can be lengthened or shortened at will, depending on the size and response of the crowd. There is therefore a great deal of improvisation.

Below is a synopsis of one of the J.J.'s plays performed in December 1973 called 'Awisia Yi Wo Ani' (Orphan Don't Glance Enviously). The entire play contained forty songs of various styles: mainly highlifes plus a Fanti funeral song, two quicksteps, four local hymns, one rock 'n' roll, one Congo jazz and two soul numbers.

Mr. Johnson is a building contractor who works away from home most of the time. He has three children, one by his dead wife, and two by his domineering second wife, Comfort. Whenever he is away, Comfort favours her own children – the arrogant King Sam and the 'hightime' daughter Dansowa – over the unfortunate and humble orphan, Kofi Antobam. Opia is brought to the house as a servant, but the wife Comfort feeds neither him nor Kofi. Finally, she decides to remove Kofi altogether by sending an evil spirit to him, but he is saved by three angels singing apostolic hymns. Mr. Johnson is so disturbed by his wife's behaviour that he sends Kofi to Kumasi to complete his education out of harm's way. Some years pass, and while Dansowa and King Sam are wasting their lives in beer bars listening to pop music, Kofi is working hard at school and is rewarded by passing the Common Entrance Exam. He becomes a postmaster, marries and travels home to introduce his wife to the family. He arrives to find King Sam harassed by women and expelled from school. Kofi's wife gives advice to girls about the way they should go about looking for husbands. The couple then distributes presents to everyone and promises to help King Sam continue his education, if he mends his ways. Mr. Johnson sings the closing highlife, in which he points out the problems of having children by different wives, especially preferential treatment by stepmothers. He also advises young people to respect their elders, and suggests that, if they are not succeeding in life, they should move on and try their luck somewhere else.

From the 1970s, when things began to get economically difficult in Ghana, the J.J.'s began going farther afield, to Cote d'Ivoire and Liberia in order to obtain precious foreign exchange needed for repairs and new equipment. Then, in September 1982, tragedy struck the J.J.'s when their lorry was involved in an accident in the Aburi Hills. Mr. Baidoo was killed, as were guitarist Kwadwo Doku and percussionist Kwadwo Amankwah. Both Bampoe and Hammond were injured. Somehow they managed to pick up the pieces and put the band together, and in the mid-1980s the two of them made a trip to Britain to perform comedy sketches alongside the musician A.B. Crentsil. Although both Mr. Bampoe and Hammond have retired in the town of Adoagyiri, they are still both active members of the Concert Party Union and also occasionally featured at the National Theatre's concert show program that began in 1994 and which is broadcast on television. Moreover, an educational film was made about the J.J.'s in 2001 called 'The Stage Shakers' by the American Director Kwame Braun in association with Indiana University Press.

Chapter 7

THE NIGERIAN MUSICAL CLOWN AND GHANA STATE COMEDIAN AJAX BUKANA

Ajax Bukana is a real trickster and it is difficult to place him. He is a musician and a clown, a Ghanaian and a Nigerian. He also has one foot in the dance bands and another in the concert party, for he looks exactly like a concert party 'Bob'. Ajax is a Yoruba whose real name is James Kehinde (meaning twin) Ajayi. He was born in Lagos in 1920, the son of a policeman. After leaving an elementary school in 1950, he joined Bobby Benson's band (see his picture with Benson in Chapter 47) and then, in 1952, came to Ghana and became a naturalised Ghanaian citizen in 1961. He was very popular with late President Kwame Nkrumah. In January 1988, the Provisional National Defence Council (PNDC) government sent him a letter recognising him as a 'State comedian' and put him on a monthly salary.

I first encountered Ajax at film shows where he would cleverly pick a quiet moment to sneeze extraordinarily loud, whereupon everyone would shout 'A-Jax'. In the early 1970s, I got to know him better at the Napoleon Club in Accra, where I was playing guitar and harmonica for the resident Bunzu band, and Ajax was doubling as club doorman and comic. I also had a beautiful grey top-hat for his stage-acts which I had brought back with me from Canada.

In 1988, I interviewed Ajax at the Presidential Hotel Annex in Accra, where he often hung out. The first question I asked him was why he decided to become a dance-band musician and comedian.

AJAX: I was very interested in jazz and Bobby Benson was playing plenty of jazz, as well as rumbas, highlifes, and quicksteps. So I started with maracas, then from maracas to congas; from congas, I started to learn string bass (double bass) and then I qualified. Anytime we had a show, we would make a concert and Bobby Benson would give me a part. He used to make some funny top hats and tails for us; I painted my face white and had a walking-stick. I used to make short comedies just like in Louis Armstrong's shows (who visited Nigeria in 1960/61). I used to dance jazz and do tap-dancing. It was Bobby Benson who gave me the name 'Ajax Bukana', and I registered that new name on my passport when we were coming to Ghana.

JC: How was it you all went to Ghana? And which band did you join?

AJAX: E. T. Mensah came to Nigeria in 1950 and his Tempos band played side-by-side with us. Then, in 1952, he invited Bobby Benson to come to Ghana. At that time, there was a night-club in Accra called the Weekend-in-Havana, in James Town, and there E. T. used to play. So he invited us to that place for two weeks. Then I said I am not going back to Nigeria. I look [at] all the bandsmen (in Ghana) and don't like the way they don't play jazz, they don't respect their leaders, and they don't dress neatly. So I said no I won't join any band. Then I try to make one-man shows and go to night-clubs to display. Only, sometimes, when they have a police or army band, they would ask me to go with them and gave me a chance to play some numbers on the string bass.

JC: You very quickly came to the attention of the then Prime Minister Kwame Nkrumah. How did this happen?

AJAX: I first met him at Kumasi as I was doing show business at the Hotel de Kingsway – afternoon jumps (shows) on Saturdays and Sundays. At that time, Kwame Nkrumah was coming to Kumasi to address the CPP (Convention People's Party) and we went to the airport to meet him. I dressed myself fine and started to roll myself around. He looked at me and asked "who is that man?" They told him I was a Nigerian man. He then asked what I was doing here and they said I was making a show here. He then asked where I was working and they said I didn't work. Nkrumah then said:

"What! You should send him to Accra to come and see me". So he gave me work at the Guinea Press (later called New Times) and I started working there as a paper-packer and later as chief canvasser. They even gave me a motor-bike.

JC: I've been told that you were very free with Kwame Nkrumah?

AJAX: Yes, I could go to Flagstaff House-or the Castle and sit down with him. Then he would ask me if I wanted to chop and he would tell them to give me a plate and I would chop with him. He loved me too much.

JC: I believe you also worked with the Afro-American jazz trumpeter, Louis Armstrong. When did you meet him?

Ajax Bukana and Louis Armstrong 1956

AJAX: I first met him when he came to Ghana in 1956[1], when we all went to the airport. At the airport, E. T. Mensah and all Ghanaian trumpeters lined up and I was in

[1]For another photo of Ajax with Armstrong in 1956, see Chapter 33.

the crowd. I stood on top of a car with my painted face and big belly. And when Satchmo was coming down from the plane, he saw me, pointed out and said he wanted to see that man. The policemen brought me down to him. When he came again around 1960, he asked President Kwame Nkrumah that he wanted to take me on an African tour for two weeks with his band, as a comedian. So, from Ghana, we went to Lagos and Kano in Nigeria, then we went to the Congo. But when we reached the Congo, there was a war (the civil war), so we slept in a hotel and on the second day, we left for Lome in Togo. After we finished at Lome, Satchmo gave me money and I came back to Ghana. He flew on straight to Sierra Leone. (For Ajax with Armstrong see photo in Chapter 33).

JC: You also met the British Queen the same year you played with Louis Armstrong.

AJAX: That's right. When the Queen came, President Kwame Nkrumah sent a Minister to ask me to entertain her at a parade in Black Star Square. Dr. Nkrumah said I should make the Queen laugh. So the Queen sat down, the Duke of Edinburgh also sat down and the whole place was full of big people. I was told that the time they were marching, the Queen didn't laugh. I was the last man to display and when I came everyone was shouting and as soon as I reached my point to perform, I started to roll myself and threw my shoes and hat up. The Queen started to laugh and wanted to fall down. Afterwards, I was told that the Queen asked Dr. Nkrumah who I was and later told him to send me overseas for training. The government sent me to Russia for three years – and I still speak Russian alright. I was at the Moscow State Circus School and was trained there in balancing, juggling and acrobatics. That was from 1961 to 1963, and I had my certificate as a professor. I even appeared on television in Russia. I was the first African at that school and I met the Queen again too. It was when I left Russia and went back home through London. Our High Commissioner there met me at the airport and took me to the Queen's house at Buckingham Palace, as the Queen said she wanted to see me. I put on my tail coat and walking stick and she and her children sat down. They played a gramophone record for me and I joked and danced for just thirty minutes. Then I drank tea and the Queen presented me with a shirt, a pair of trousers and a coat.

JC: You said that Kwame Nkrumah helped you get a job at Guinea Press. What happened when he was overthrown?

AJAX: When the coup against Kwame Nkrumah took place in 1966, it was the CPP people who were working at Guinea Press – so as all of us there were close to Nkrumah, we were all sacked. And the police came, arrested me and took me to the CID headquarters. They arrested all of the CPP security people and myself, as some CID people asked me if I was an informant and I said no. Then they looked through a list of all Nkrumah's security people, but my name was not among them and they left me. But I stayed in the cells for three days.

JC: What did you do after this?

AJAX: I worked with a private pressman and continued entertaining at night-clubs, like the Star Hotel, for instance. I also worked with Faisal Helwani for three years at his Napoleon Club and sometimes would go with his bands; like when he took his bands to play for the prisoners at Nsawam and Ussher Fort Prisons.

JC: Faisal was also helping to organise the Musician's Union (MUSIGA) at the time. Was it through him that you became involved in the Union's march for official recognition in May 1979?

AJAX: Yes, and I was also a member. I was with them carrying a placard and went with them all the way to the Castle.

JC: What are you up to these days? And what are your future plans?

AJAX: I made advertising films for Wiseway Laundries and Club Beer, and was also filmed for the Ghanaian Spear photo-comic magazine. The comic was called "The Case of the Hunchback Craze". I was a judge. Osofo Dadzie and the comedian Bob Cole were also in it. And every Saturday and Sunday, I display at the Ambassador Hotel. I want to go to New York next summer for two weeks as a friend of mine is there. I met him when I went to New York in 1977 as guest artist with a band from Kumasi called Dr. Gyasi's. That time I stayed for three months and visited eleven States. Then, just now the Moscow State Circus School has written to the PNDC (Provisional National Defence Council) government for me to go to Russia on 15 March for two weeks of celebration, for all the school's old students from all around the world.

Sadly Ajax and his famous sneeze are no longer with us as he died in March 2006 in Accra at the age of 86.

Chapter 8

YAMOAH, NANA AMPADU, EDDIE DONKOR AND OSEI KOFI

P.K. YAMOAH

Patrick Yamoah was born in 1932 in Agona Nyakrom and learnt music early as his step-father was a church organist. As a schoolboy he was a member of one of the town's 'singing bands', Christian local language four-part harmony choirs that proliferated in southern Ghana during from the 1930s, that were sometimes backed by light percussion and later in the 1950s the instruments of guitar bands. Yamoah bought his first guitar at the music shop in Accra of the Argentinian Mr. Chebib, and learnt the instrument with the aid of a tutorial book. Around 1950 Yamoah moved to Accra where he joined Gyak's guitar band for a number of years that released records on the Basel UTC label. This was the Swiss Union Trading Company of Basel that between 1931 and 1957 released 728 Ghanaian and Nigerian titles, at first recording out of Zonophone in London and then, after the Second World War, using their own mobile studio. From Gyak's band Yamoah moved on in the mid-fifties to form his own Yamoah's guitar band. This became one of the most important guitar bands of the period that released a string of songs on the Senofone and Decca labels in the fifties and sixties: such as 'Odonamkoma Wu', 'Comfort Mensu', 'Abrebese Bebrebe', 'Adufude Ade', 'S.K. Abebrese Part 2', 'Bata Bone', 'Sika Mpe', 'Obra Twa Wuo', 'Fa Asem Kye', 'Nkrabea' and 'Wosewose W'Adwum Asei'.

Yamoah's band became so popular that it was even invited to play at the university's African Music Society evenings held in the late-fifties and early-sixties at the Achimota Junior Common Room. This venue featured guitar bands like E.K.'s, Happy Stars and Onyina and was patronised by lecturers such as Professor J.H.K. Nketia, Professor Atta Annan Mensah, Dr. Ephraim Amu, E.F. Collins (author's father), Robert Sprigge, as well as a few students like Kwadwo Donkoh (later an Ambassador) and J. E. Owiredu (later a philosophy professor). However, in general, the students did not patronise guitar bands at that time as they considered them too 'bush' and preferred to hire the more prestigious Tempos and Black Beats highlife dance bands for their end-of-term dances. Fortunately, we still have the live sounds of some of these guitar bands of the Junior Common Room as Professor Nketia recorded them on a portable reel-reel tape-machines, including Yamoah's band playing their 'cocoa song' in 1957. This recording and others by Onyina are part of the six hundred hours of 1950s/60s traditional and popular Ghanaian music archives now lodged at the university's Institute of African Studies. Incidentally, my father, E.F. Collins of the university's Philosophy Department, occasionally used to accompany Yamoah's band in the late-fifties, supplying electricity from his car for the bands amplifier.

Yamoah's guitar band in 1957. Yamoah is on the right with guitar. John Collins's father, E.F. Collins, is on the left and his step-mother, Auntie Amma, is the middle seated lady

Yamoah has now retired to the town of Nyakrom, but his old hits have been recently released on cassette and he comes to Accra from time to time in connection with various activities. For instance in the early 2000s he was an Executive member of the Ghana Old Music and Artists Welfare Association (GOMAWA).

Many musicians were influenced or passed through Yamoah's band; for instance, guitarist Smart Nkansah and soprano singer Agyaaku (Nana Kweku Addai). The late Agyaaku (died 2010) was with Yamoah for thirteen years and so sang on Yamoah hits like 'Serwaa Okoto', 'To Wo Botom', 'Otan Hunu Ye Ya' and 'Saman Me', He and Smart Nkansah then moved onto the A.B. Crentsil's Sweet Talks and, in 1977, Agyaaku was with Smart Nkansah when he formed the Black Hustlers and later Sunsum. When Sunsum broke up, Agyaaku joined to form Big Three (with Eric Agyeman and Thomas Frimpong) and then formed his own Agyaaku International Band that toured UK where Agyaaku stayed for many years. Yet another Yamoah graduate was the young Nana Ampadu, who was with Yamoah's band in 1962/3. This leads us on to the topic of this important musician and leader of the top league African Brothers guitar band.

NANA AMPADU AND THE AFRICAN BROTHERS

Nana Kwame Ampadu was born and raised in the town of Obo in the hilly Kwahu area of Ghana's Eastern Region. In 1960 and, at just fifteen years old, he joined Yamoah's band where he played 'clips' (i.e. claves) and learn to play the acoustic or 'box' guitar. In 1963, the African Brothers was formed by Nana Ampadu, his older brother Rover Amo Kofi Ampadu, Eddie Donkor, Kwame Anim, Yaw Asante and Kwadwo Ofori – with the bass player 'Joe Dee' Kwabena Appiah and singer Kofi Oppong Kyekyeku coming in a bit later. It was an amateur group of teenage musicians and they chose the name in appreciation of President Nkrumah's efforts in forming the Organisation of African Unity. Also being impressed at the time by the English rock 'n' roll guitarist Tommy Steel, Ampadu began to call himself 'Paa Steel'.

Between 1964 and 1966, Ampadu wrote compositions for Jerry Hansen's Ramblers Band and then in 1966, through Joe Eyison, he released two hit singles for Phillips West Africa Limited called 'Agyanka Dabere' and 'Maye Sominaso Ntonko'. In 1966 the African Brothers went professional when his band became the resident band of the Ambassador Gardens Hotel in Kumasi and they began recording songs for GFIC (Ghana films Corporation) and more importantly Mr. A. K. Badu's Ambassador

Records Manufacturing Company in Kumasi. Some of Ampadu's big hits then were 'Okwaduo', 'Nkran Abrabo' and particularly 'Ebi Tie Ye' released in 1967. The theme of 'Ebi Tie Ye' or 'Some Sit Well' is the growing division of modern society into rich and poor, but couched in traditional African fashion as a proverb concerning the big forest animals pushing smaller ones away from the warmth of the campfire.

Then in 1968 the music promoter D. K. Nyarko got the African Brothers to relocate to Accra, where Ampadu added a concert party section to his guitar band. Some of the actors who passed through this group are Bob Santo, Bob Okala and the comedian (not musician) Koo Nimo. From 1968 to early 70s, and with Nyarko as his producer, Ampadu recorded numerous singles, many of a philosophical or topical nature. Just a few of these are 'Okunpa', 'Sika Anibere', 'Obiba Broke', 'Kofi Nkrabea', 'Emelia', 'Ankoma Boafo', 'Article 204', 'Anomaa A Wokoyi', 'Sensam',' Okunpa', 'Betumi Yen', 'Ena Eye A Mane Me', 'Yaw Berko', 'Maame Adwoa' and 'Aku Sika'. The group made its first trips abroad to the UK in 1971 and 1973; it was after the first trip that they released their first LP album (in 1972), recorded at the Pye studio in London, and which included songs like 'Baabi A Odo Wo' and 'Gyae Su'. In 1973, the band recorded three more LP albums: 'Yaa Amanua', 'Yaa Amponsah' and 'Odo Paa'.

In the seventies, the music section of the African Brothers concert party consisted of trap-drums, congas, maracas and clips, with four guitars setting-up a scintillating network of cross-rhythms, boosted by the distinctive touch of 'Ancient' Amuah on keyboards. Ampadu was then a lightly built man who oozed energy, but he did not dominate the stage like a European superstar. Rather he held back and then suddenly broke in with a little guitar riff or solo, sending the music of the band to a new and higher level of intensity. The African brothers did not only play and record top-quality highlife, as Ampadu was always experimenting with new dance beats for his numerous fans. In the mid-seventies there was the funky-highlife 'locomotive', then the 'Afro-hili' that combined highlife with Afro-beat, and later a beautiful blend of reggae and highlife. In 1976, the African Brothers together with the concert comedian Bob Cole toured North America and recorded two LP albums in the U.S that included popular tracks 'Yeka Menu A Brofo Baako' and 'Amma'.

Amapadu, like so many concert musicians of the time, found it difficult to operate in Ghana during the early/mid 1980s with its military curfews and economic hardships. However, he managed to record albums like 'Ene Eye Mane Me' and 'Agatha', and often played outside of Ghana. His band toured the Cote d'Ivoire, Nigeria and also undertook several European tours. It also appeared in one of the episodes of the British Third Eye film 'Repercussion' released in 1984 on the British Channel-Four TV. In addition to all this recording and touring Ampadu also managed to find time in the 1980s to be the Vice-President and later General-Secretary of the Musicians' Union of Ghana. Then in the 1990s he set up a recording studio and became a trustee of the Ghana National Folklore Board. I was also a member and as we both had recording/mastering equipment we co-produced a promotional CD for the Folklore Board that consisted of digitalised versions of some of the original tracks (including 'Yaa Amponsah') of the 1928 Zonphone recording by the Kumasi Trio.

Ampadu is currently a church evangelist and continues running a recording studio at La Paz in Accra that re-releases many of his old hits. Over the years Ampadu released about four hundred songs on one hundred and fifty singles and sixty or so albums. He has also won many awards. Some of these include the Rex Image Awards, the ACRAG Award, the National Commission on Culture Award and most importantly, in 1997, the Grand Medal of the Volta Civil Division Award. His most recent album released in 2010 is 'Mmofra Monko Besa Npayin.'

Many musicians have passed through the African Brothers. One is the vocalist Captain Newman who was with the African Brothers for two years before forming the Gay Brothers guitar band in 1971. Another was Sam Derchie who left in 1971/2 to lead the Saints band in Accra. Yet another was Teacher Boateng who left in 1973 to form his Afrikana band. The guitarist Anthony Scorpion Entsie also broke away in 1973 to form the Beach Scorpions. Then, in 1983, 'Prince' Osei Kofi, who had been with Ampadu from 1974, went on to form the African Heroes which is still operating today and has released seventeen albums. Many women, like Akosua Amoam, Akosua Agyepong and Yaa Oforiwa have also sung for the African Brothers. The very first was Mum Bea (Beatrice) who was actually married to Ampadu between 1977 and 1980 when she recorded sixteen songs with his band. A very important member of the African Brothers was Eddie Donkor to whom we now turn.

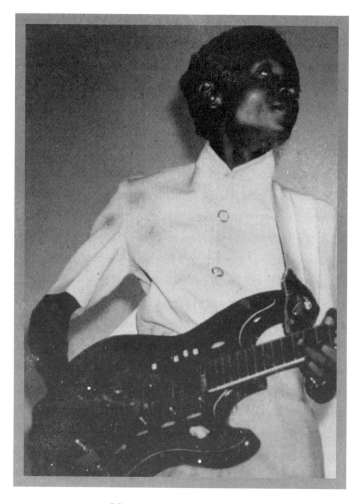

Nana Ampadu in the 1980s

'SENIOR' EDDIE DONKOR

The master guitarist and singer Eddie Donkor was one of the founding members of the African Brother in 1963 and stayed with this band until the mid-seventies when he went on to form his own group. Eddie Donkor (Kwasi Boahene) was born in Suhum in 1951. His father was a traditional drummer at the Okuapemhene's Palace. After he left Ampadu, Eddie formed his own band and concert party called the Asiko Internationals based at Abeka in Accra, which went on to release a number of top selling record singles and albums; such as 'Maye Ho', 'Kwesi Amankwa', 'Asiko Darling', 'Na Who Cause Am' and 'Menom Koo'. It was then that Eddie was given the title 'Senior', as he was an expert in playing and developing new highlife rhythms on guitar. Due to the busy schedule of his own group he set up a second one of younger musicians called the Simple Seven. This included the drummer Captain Moro and guitarist Sloopy Mike Gyamfi who formed Adinkra in 1982 and then went to Holland. Eddie Donkor's daughter Abena Nyanteh became a well-known singer through working with her father's bands. Eddie Donkor was an active member of the Musician's Union until his death in April 1995. He was buried in Akropong in 1996 after a wake-keeping in the town's Opare Theatre attended by hundreds of musicians.

ALEX KONADU AND HIS BAND

Alex Kwabena Konadu was born in 1948 in Adwumakase Kese in the Kwabere Number Three District of Ashanti. He completed middle-school in Kumasi in 1964 and as a youth formed a group that played bosoe, a then popular Akan neo-traditional drum-dance. The first guitar band-cum concert party he joined was Akwaboah's band, which he remained with for three years. He then became the lead vocalist for the Nsawam based Happy Brothers Band in 1963 that consisted of Annin, and also L(Nortey, the guitarist T.D.B. Adjekum and singer E.O. Frimpong who had all been with E.K.'s Number Two Band. Alex Konadu recorded songs like 'Aboa Aponkye' and Adwoa Bruwaa'with them. However, he only stayed with the groups for two years as in the early 1970s he went solo for a while, until he met the Accra-based record shop owner and producer Mr. A.K. Brobbey who helped him release a number of popular highlife hit songs like 'Asem Bi Adi Bone', 'Agyata Wuyo', 'Asranawa Mewua Didi', 'Si Dweso', Pay Day', 'Aweie' and 'A Good One There'. As a result, Brobey helped him financially start up his own band, aptly named after Konadu himself, which included Nana Tuffour, Charles Amoah. Kojo Bass and Kwame Owusu.

Konadu's Band soon established itself as a top guitar band and, with its associated concert party, travelled the length and breadth of Ghana. Due to his ability to sing, play guitar, dance and act he became known as 'One Man Thousand'. Konadu's released a number of albums in the 1970s such as 'Abiba Na Goodey', 'Kunkonuhunu' and 'Odo Ma Yenka Nkam Okafo Didi' and 'Asase'. Indeed, he became so successful that in 1976, the Artists/Entertainment Critics and Reviewers Association of Ghana (ACRAG/ECRAG) judged Alex Konadu 'Best Guitarist of the Year'. However, by the late seventies things were becoming tough with the economic decline in Ghana during the Acheampong/Akuffo military regime. As a result, Konadu's Band had to start touring and recording in nearby African countries like Nigeria and the Cote d'Ivoire. In fact, one of his top albums of the early 1980s 'Mewu Ama Wo' was recorded in Abidjan. Konadu's Band often travelled to Nigeria and it was during these visits that Konadu lost some of his musicians when Big Boy Robert Danso split away in 1979 to form his own Canadoes group that had several hits in Nigeria for the Rogers All Stars company in Onitsha.

Despite his various African tours Konadu's band continued to release numerous albums in Ghana in the 1980s, such as 'Dance Band of Ghana', 'Obi Aba Wuo' and 'Yere Wo Ato Mu Ate Ebi Awe'. Because of the growing interest in African music by World Music fans the band also began to make international tours. In 1987 Konadu's Band played in the UK and their 'One Man Thousand Live in London' was released by the London based World Circuit label. Then in 1989/1990 Konadu's toured Canada and released 'One Man Thousand in Toronto' that was recorded in Canada and engineered by the Ghanaian musician/producer Ricky Telfer. Konadu's band members at this time were the bass player Ray Opoku, lead guitarist Kojo Bass, keyboardist Francis Baidoo, percussionists Akwesi Ntim and Victor Nketia and backing vocalist Yaw Amoh. Other musicians Konadu worked with were Nana Tuffour, Charles Amoah and Kwame Owusu. Since 2000, Konadu has released several of his songs for World Music companies. In 2001 there were the tracks 'Mafe Wo' and 'Medan Wo' on the' Highlife All Stars: Sankofa' CD released in Germany by Network Medien and in 2002 'W'awu Do Ho No' on the 'Ghana Sounds' CD of the UK Soundways label. In January 2011, he was planning to team up with his good friend, the gospel singer Kofi Abraham, to play a mixed gospel and highlife show in Sunyani – but sadly Konadu fell sick and died in Kumasi on the 18th January 2011. He is survived by his wife and twelve children.

Chapter 9

ADOM PROFESSIONALS – THE BLIND CONCERT PARTY BAND

The Adom Professionals guitar band in the 1980s

In 1988, I recorded fifteen songs in my Bokoor Studio Accra by the only fully professional blind band in Ghana, the **Adom Professionals** (Adom means Grace in Twi) who were based at Nsawam-Adoagyiri, twenty miles north of Accra. The band moved around the country on tour with a concert party, and whilst the musicians are blind, the actors could see and so help guide the nine blind bandsmen. The Adom Professionals first came together as schoolboys in one of Ghana's two institutes for the blind, the Elementary School and Vocational Training Centre for the blind at Akropong on the Aburi Hills (the other institute being at Wa, in the north-west of the country).

After the 1988 recording, I interviewed two of the blind members of the band, the thirty year old leader singer and lead guitarist Nti Agyeman who comes from a village in the Ashanti Region, and the twenty-eight year old drummer Foster Oppon comes from the Brong-Ahafo Region and became blind when he was a child as a result of measles. The seven other members of the band are the bass guitarist Paa Willie from Akwapim; the conga player Anthony Mensah from the Western Region; keyboardist Albert Mensah from the Ashanti Region; the rhythm guitarist and singer Prince Muhamma who is from Tamale; the percussionist Mark Awotwe from Elmina and a second bassist Clement Kaba from Navrongo in the Upper Region who also sings in Grushi. The group's sax player Ampadu Asiama was not on the recording, as he had travelled at the time. I first asked them how they first got together.

NTI AGYEMAN: We had a set of instruments in the Akropong Elementary School for the Blind for those who were interested in music. So we nine blind members of Adom got our training in this school band, for the school had always had a band. We played reggaes, highlifes and funky numbers.

JC: Were you at all influenced by blind black American musicians, like Ray Charles or Stevie Wonder?

NTI AGYEMAN: They did help inspire us at school, but we nine just liked music, anyway.

JC: When did you form your first professional band?

NTI AGYEMAN: After we had all completed school at Akropong, a certain Fanti man called Mr. H.G. Ward gave us some instruments in Takoradi, and so we started there in 1979 and were with him up to 1981. It was purely a dance band and was called the Mighty Echoes. Later we wrote to a charitable organisation in West Germany called C.B.M. (Christofen Blinden Mission) and they sent instruments to us through the Ghana Society for the Blind in 1983.

JC: Was that when you moved to Nsawam-Adoagyiri?

NTI AGYEMAN: No, we didn't move there until 1985. What happened was that from 1981 to 1983 we scattered into different bands. I played for Obrempong's concert party, then for the Royal Stars in Kumasi and then for Akonoba J.K.'s band.

FOSTER OPPON: I played for two bands. The Black Scorpions which was another band that belonged to Mr. Ward and then Obrempong's band.

JC: What about your other members?

NTI AGYEMAN: Some played with the Black Scorpions after the Mighty Echoes had broken up. Paa Willie played in the same bands as myself, but Prince Muhamma, after playing with the Royal Stars went into the teaching crafts. You know when someone finishes their three-year vocational crafts course at either the Akropong or the Wa blind schools they are appointed to teach crafts in the Middle Schools. When the German instruments came we stayed at various places but always together in the same house. First at Achimota and Abeka in Accra, and from there we came to Nsawam as we had a very big problem with accommodation in Accra. In 1983, straight after we got our German instruments, we brought in about fourteen actors, like the one who led us here today, Kofi Sarkodie. And also we have a manager who pioneers (sets up tours) for us and his name is Mr. Ammishetai Oppon-Kwakye.

JC: What problems as blind people going up and down the country do you meet?

NTI AGYEMAN: We find it difficult sometimes because at the place we play for the night, we don't rest, so we become too exhausted and because of this we cannot work as happily as we feel like. Sometimes, you know, we go on trek for up to forty days at a time.

JC: This is your first recording I believe? But why have you put all these songs into the northern Dagbani, Grushi and Gonja languages rather than say Fanti or Twi?

NTI AGYEMAN: We have never recorded before and we are financing it ourselves. Our plan is to sell the cassettes as we move around the country. We have decided to go north on our next trek at the end of March and there we can sell these cassettes. When we get enough money, we will come back and record in Twi for when we tour the Ashanti Region.

JC: Are any of your songs and plays about the problems of being blind?

NTI AGYEMAN: No, each song has a different meaning but not about blindness. We do not want to sing anything sad as we want to make people happy. We don't make plays about our handicap. In fact, our most popular story, Abusua Bone (Bad Family) is about witchcraft. It is about two sisters and one wants her son to be a chief. But the head of the family decides that the other sister's son should be the chief and so the first sister spoils the man who becomes a chief.

JC: Do you think that music is a good business for blind people to be in?

NTI AGYEMAN: Yes, and this is one of our prime aim in forming this band. You see, we wanted to create a chance for the blind in this country as in our days, after completing at the school for the blind, you either had to be a typist or crafts teacher. It is only quite recently that the government has made it possible for some blind people to go to university and become lawyers. But formerly there were only the two channels. We also want to portray the capability of the disabled and blind to people. Some people think that when you are blind or disabled you just become useless. Our second aim is to raise funds to assist other disabled persons and their institutions to educate and train them. And I would like to make this appeal to individuals and organisations throughout the world. When they get any disabled person in their family, I beg them to send them to school to learn something and become useful in the future. Then I would like to appeal to anyone who wants to promote Adom Professionals in any foreign country to do so. We want to go abroad to show people what we are doing here in Ghana and to let them know what the blind can do.

Chapter 10

T.O. JAZZ AND HIS FRIEND S.K. OPPONG

T.O Jazz (left with guitar) and his guitar band around 1970

T.O. JAZZ

Thomas Osei Ampoumah was born in 1932 in the town of Obomeng in the mountainous Akan Kwahu region between Accra and Kumasi. He started learning guitar when he was fifteen years old in the town of Nkawkaw, first from Kwaku Oppong and then Mr. Ahima at his evening school. He was also inspired by seeing a performance by Ghana's leading guitarist Jacob Sam (Kwame Asare) which he saw when he was fifteen years old in the town of Mpraeso. T.O. told me that on that occasion 'Sam and His Party' came with a second guitarist and three other musicians who played 'adakam' wooden box, clips (claves) and the small 'abia' conga-drum. They toured by train and therefore came to Mpraeso via Nkawkaw on the Accra-Kumasi line. When they arrived at Mpraeso (or any town for that matter) they would find a spot in a lorry park and make a circle of ash in which to perform, with the audience seated outside around it on chairs or on the ground. According to T.O. Sam would dress up as a lady, or perform in blackface with a velvet turban. He would make comedy sketches and the group played highlifes such as 'Lumley Number One' and Liberian 'dagomba' songs such as 'Rekpete'. Money was collected in a brass basin placed within this temporary theatre-in-the–round.

T.O himself began playing in public in 1950 when he was just eighteen years old. He formed his Ampoumah's guitar band in Mpraeso in 1952 with Kwabena Amoah (vocals), Kwaku Gyima (second guitar) and Edmund Kye (congas). T.O. made his first recordings with a Ghana Broadcasting mobile van unit in 1954. These were the two songs 'Ko-Ko Sika' (Cocoa Money) and 'Medofo Bra' (My Lover Come). Later he recorded other songs, like 'Adwoa Nyarko' (a lady's name) for the Swizz United Africa Company (UAC) that had small recording studios in Accra and Nsawam. In those days he was paid eight pounds per recording (i.e. two songs). T.O told me that it was in the UAC studio in Nsawam that he met the infamous guitarist Kwasi Manu who was also recording his UAC 'Akan blues' song 'Ma Ka Na Wa'. Kwasi Manu had been deported from his home-town of Kumasi by the traditional authorities to Adeiso (near Nsawam) for composing rude songs. But after many years of exile, 'Ma Ka Na Wa' that means 'slip of the tongue' was taken as a musical apology and gained Kwesi a pardon from the King of Asante, Nana Prempeh.

In 1957/58 T.O. Ampoumah's guitar band was on tour of Burkina Faso (then called Upper Volta) where he met the Congolese band the Bantus Africana, who invited T.O. and three of his musicians to Zaire (now the Democratic Republic of the Congo) where they played highlife numbers for the Bantus who were fascinated by this music but could not play it. The Bantus band, in turn, taught the Ghanaians to play local 'Congo jazz' (later called soukous) and Lingala versions of the rumba, chachacha, meringue, pachanga and bolero. T.O. also met Franco the leader of the Congo's top band O.K. Jazz, and as a result changed the name of his Ampoumah's guitar band to 'T.O. Jazz'.

T.O. returned to Ghana in 1961 and his newly named T.O. Jazz band specialized in highlifes and Akan renditions of the rumba and chachacha. It was with this band that T.O. recorded his 1968 hit song 'Aware Bone Agu Manim Ase' (Bad Marriage Has Disgraced Me) that was released as a 45 RPM on the Phillips label. For this T.O. was, in 1970, awarded the first Phillips West African Golden Disc, and he went on to record a total of 127 songs. So by the mid-70s T.O Jazz was a household name in Ghana. important musician who passed through T.O.'s band was Kingsley Dankwa who later formed the All Brothers guitar band.

I first met T.O. in the late 1970s as he was living in James Town, near Temple House where I was running my Bokoor Band. However, due to the economic problems in Ghana at that time T.O. packed his bags and with three of his musicians settled in Nigeria for almost two years. He stayed in Onitsha with the famous Nigerian Igbo highlife musician Stephen Osadebe, who put the Ghanaians up at the FESTAC Hotel there and supplied T.O. with four additional musicians to perform with. It was whilst there that, in 1980, T.O. released the Nigerian 'top ten' album 'Ojukwu Welcome' (produced by Chris Robbin). It was dedicated to the reconciliation and return from a long exile in Abidjan of the leader of the attempted break-away state of Biafra that had been the cause of a civil war in Nigeria in the late 1960s.

In 1986 that T.O Jazz did his first recording at my Bokoor Studio. But T.O. was still finding it difficult to run his band due to Ghana's economic situation at the time, so he began to work with local gospel music and also doing other business ventures. This is how I met T.O. again. He came to my Bokoor House in 1996 to make inquiries about obtaining the waste material from a nearby saw-mill for a stove that he had invented that ran on sawdust rather than charcoal. I then asked T.O. and his long-time singer, Kojo Menu, to join my university based Local Dimension highlife band that I run with Aaron Bebe Sukura. I also got T.O. a job teaching 'palmwine highlife' at the Music Department of the University of Ghana where I work. T.O and the Local Dimension played at venues such as the National Theatre, University functions, Alliance Francaise and Paloma and appeared on local television on several occasions. At this time T.O also brought his friend S.K. Oppong to meet and interact with the university students (see below).

It was in 1996 than I recorded T.O. for the second time, on this occasion as an acoustic outfit rather than an electric guitar band. These 'palmwine' songs use acoustic guitar, 'clips' (Kojo Menu) and the giant premprensua hand-piano (university student Nana Seben) instead of bass guitar. They were released locally in Ghana, with the assistance of the UNESCO Ghana Director Bruno Lefevre, under the title 'T.O. Jazz is Back Again'. At the same time T.O. was involved with the university he was helping run the Ghana Music Pioneers Association that was working alongside the then currently active Ghana Old Musicians and Artists Welfare Association, GOMOWA. Both these organizations were mutual self-help organisations trying to obtain musical equipment and a venue to play the live classic style (rather than computerized) highlife. Here is T.O. lamenting on the fate of some top old-time musicians who have died prematurely because of lack of poverty and medical attention.

> *'E.K. Nyame died in two days of jaundice of which there is a medical application. Bob Cole the comedian knighted by Queen Elizabeth died from lack of nutrition and not having a better place to stay. Kakaiku, a man who sings very beautifully in proverbs, died after three days of tetanus. If all these people passed away in this way, then something must be done, because it's not natural.'*

T.O himself died in 2001 after a short illness and is survived by his wife Lydia and daughter Grace. His funeral was attended by many of the surviving local guitar bands.

S.K. OPPONG

Samuel Kwasi Opong was born in Tekyiman, Brong Ahafo in 1939. His father was a palmwine guitarist but did not want S.K. to follow in his footsteps. However, S.K.'s brother, Kwaku Boa, taught him how to play the guitar and premprensua. So S.K. went on to join Kwese Krah's Brong-Ahafo-based guitar band in 1956, and then Bob Thompson's Accra Trio in 1958 as lady impersonator. On a trip to Kumasi, and whilst playing at the Town Hall, he caught the attention of A. K. Badu, the manager of Ambassador Records, and so Oppong with Kwesi Krah's band recorded for him. Then, in 1959, S.K. set up his own Oppong's Guitar Band that over ten years released many songs on single 45 rpm and full length album records for Ambassador Records; like 'Daben Na Mehu Wo', 'Se Menya Wuo O', 'Ahwene Pa Nkasa' and 'Densu Do Odo Ko'. Oppong's Guitar Band was based in Accra but also toured all over Ghana and as far as Togo and the Cote D'Ivoire. Its members included Frimpong Manso, Fred Addae, Akua Boahemma, Beatrice Kissi and Super O.D (Asonoba Kweku Darko). In 1972, S.K. worked with C.K. Mann's Carousel Seven and he went on a London tour with them. On his return, he was contacted by one of the GBC bosses, Kobina Taylor, as well as Nana Bosompra and Joris Wartenberg, then respectively producing and writing the newly-started Osofo Dadzie concert party series for GBC Television. So, for sixteen years Oppong's Guitar Band provided the music for this popular drama series which featured the actors Super O.D, Beatrice Kissi and Florence Mensah. In the 1990s, Oppong and his band's aforementioned members worked again with Nana Bosompra, this time acting in the Cantata concert TV series which also included actors Agyeman Baidoo, Beatrice Adjei and guitarist Kofi Twum.

Around 2000, I was introduced to S.K. by T.O. Jazz and, subsequently, invited this well-known television personality to the university to interact with the Legon university music students, when he also played with the university-based Local Dimension highlife band, then jointly run by Aaron Bebe Sukura, T.O. Jazz and myself. S.K played with us at the Alliance Francaise and appeared on TV. Sadly, S.K. Oppong died in 2002.

The concert party actor and singer S.K. Oppong in 1981

Chapter 11

SOME MORE GREATS: KAKAIKU, GYASI, ONYINA, ADJEKUM, F. KENYA, YEBOAH AND ANI JOHNSON

Kakaiku's (second left) guitar band with C.K. Mann on guitar and
I. K. Amissah on sax. (Picture courtesy of Amissah/Catherine Cole's 2001 book)

KAKAIKU

Kakaiku was born in 1916 at Aboso near Tarkwa in the Western Region as Kweku Moses Oppong – and was educated at the Aboso Methodist Middle School. At fourteen, he embarked on a musical career, starting off with a local konkoma highlife band. He then ran his first guitar band between 1941 and 1942 which he called the Tempos (not to be confused with E.T. Mensah's famous dance band). However this was only a part-time job as Moses Oppong was also a blacksmith and winch operator in the Tarkwa-Aboso goldmines. Moreover, he was also a fearsome goal-keeper for the local Aboso soccer team, and because of this he was given the nick-name 'Kakaiku' by Nigerians working in Aboso. Kakaiku was influenced by the concert parties of Bob Johnson and Kwame Asare (Jacob Sam) who often came to Aboso to play at the mining club. So, in 1952, he formed his Kakaiku's guitar band and concert party and then released his first record 'Mempe Maa'. Others soon followed: like 'Baako Ankonam', 'Ma Yenka Ntam', 'Me Wo Adze Oye', 'Ebuagye', 'Darling Money No Dey' – all on HMV; and 'Sika Na Nyimpa', 'Ene A Mennye Bi Ntsi', 'Wua Mo Nsu Me' and 'Ohoara He Me Neho' on the Odeon label. Then between1965 and 1975 Kakaiku released seventy songs for Ambassador Records.

Besides releasing in all over three hundred songs on record, Kakaiku also enlarged the number of actors in his concert party from the handful usual in a typical trio. Furthermore, a number of concert musicians and actors passed through his group including C.K. Mann, Eddie Donkor and A.K. Yeboah (see below). Due to age, Kakaiku's oldest son, Moses Oppong Junior, took over his band in 1979 and Kakaiaku died in 1986 after contracting tetanus from being scratched by the sharp spike of a palm-tree in his farm.

DR K. GYASI AND HIS NOBLE KINGS

Kwame Gyasi was born 1929 in Ankaase in the Ashanti Region. Although Gyasi's father was not happy, in the late 1940s his uncle taught him how to play the 'odonson' style of palmwine guitar highlife, as well as imported calypso music then all the rage in Ghana. Gyasi also learnt a lot from the Accra based Appiah Adjekum. K. Gyasi began composing in 1952 when he recorded his very first song for Phillips entitled 'Me Dua Koo A Na Mmoa Awe' (the seed I planted have been destroyed). This was followed by other hits like 'Abena Boakyewaa', 'Mmobo', 'Medofo San Bra' and 'Wofa Kwasi'. During the Nkrumah era he traveled extensively throughout western and eastern Europe. On one occasion in 1963 he travelled with President Nkrumah to North

Africa and the USSR. However, he did get into trouble with Nkrumah for one of his songs. This was `Agyimah Mansah' released in 1964 about a ghost mother lamenting the plight of her children. President Nkrumah personally questioned Gyasi about the lyrics, and although the composer claimed these were based on a dream and were not a political reflection by `Mother Ghana' on the sorry state of the nation, the song was banned from the radio.

Gyasi's Noble Kings was both a guitar band and concert party and was the first of this genre to use electronic keyboards, played initially by Ernest Honey (or Honney). Then in 1974 Gyasi released his outstanding 'Sikyi-highlife' album (on the Esseibons label) of almost an hour of his own non-stop minor highlifes. The personnel of this fabulous album, now a collector's item, included Eric Agyeman on guitar, Thomas Frempong on drums, with Tommy King on trumpet, Atta Kennedy on alto sax, Yaw Kusi in keyboards and Ralph Karikari on bass guitar. Karikari went on to play with various dance bands, like the Super Complex Band, Eredecs, Sweet Talks, Sunsum, Starlites, Soronko and George Darko's Fontomfrom.

Gyasi was given the title 'Dr' by his fans and, over the years, several prominent guitar band musicians also passed though his group. F. Micah was his guitarist for some years, before forming his own group in 1961. Kwabena Akwaboah was singer in Gyasi's band from 1961-3 when he split to form his own Akwaboah's band that had numerous hits, including almost a hundred for Ambassador Records alone. Singer Kofi Sammy was on and off with Gyasi in the 1960s, until forming Okukuseku's in 1970. After passing through Oko's guitar band, K. Frimpong (born 1939 in Ashanti-Akim) worked with Gyasi for almost seven years before forming his Cubana Fiesta in the seventies which released famous hits like 'Nku Me Fie', 'Amanfo Mo Kyiri Me', 'Kyenkyen Bi Adi M'Awu' and 'Hwehwe Mu Na Yi Wo Mpena'. In later life, Dr. Gyasi was residing in Kumasi and was making occasional appearances on stage, until he died in 2012.

'KING' KWABENA ONYINA

Onyina was born 1932 in Agona Swedru. His father was a lorry driver and guitarist and his mother a chorister. When his mother and then his father died, Onyina's uncle, Opanin Kofi Obeng, brought the young orphan to Koforidua as an apprentice shoe-maker, where he was also taught guitar by Kwame Boafo. Onyina loved the guitar so much that he became an itinerant musician entertaining friends around town, and was twice arrested in 1949 for disturbing the public peace.

Onyina's first concert guitar group was called the Coolers Band, formed in Koforidua in 1951. Then he moved to Kumasi in 1953 and, with financial assistance from a businessman called Daniel Kyei, formed Onyina's Guitar Band. Its members included the Nigerian Bandele as second guitarist, Nana Atakora Manu on congas and co-singers Kwame Ampong and Afro Boateng. T.D.B. Agyekum joined later and encouraged Onyina to form his National Trio concert party. From 1953 this group released a string of popular songs for Decca like 'Ohia Asomawo', 'Wiase Nsem Adoso', 'Odo Ye Owu', 'Lumumba', 'Nanti Yie'', 'Ohia Asoma Wo', 'Menim Nea Maye' and the 'Destiny of Africa' (about the formation of the OAU in Accra). All of this helped him win the National Guitar Band contest in 1961 organised by the Arts Council and GBC. Another reason Onyina won this competition and became known as 'King Onyina' was that he introduced diminished, augmented and passing jazz chords into guitar highlife. In this, he was influenced by Professor J. E. Owiredu, who was a philosophy student in the late 1950s and early 60s, and so attended the Legon university African Music Society meetings that featured guitar-band music. Owiredu had a large collection of jazz guitar records of Barney Kessel, Tal Farlow and Kenny Burrell which he lent to Onyina to broaden his guitar skills. In all Onyina released about three hundred songs.

In 1963 Onyina accompanied President Nkrumah on a state visit to Mali, Tunisia, Poland and the Soviet Union, together with other artist like K. Gyasi, E.K. Nyame, Kobina Okai, Bob Cole, Kakaiku and the Broadway Band. In 1964 he was invited to Britain by the Decca Record Company and whilst there he performed at Battersea Town Hall with the Black Star Band run by Ebo Taylor, Joe Aikins and Teddy Osei. In 1973 Onyina became a Buddhist. In 1984 he was installed as Barima Kwame Onyina, Chief of the Oyoko Abusua in Agona Ashanti. In 1990 Onyina received a 'Pioneer of Highlife Award' from the National Commission on Culture and also became leader of the GPRTU Melodious Group that featured the ex-Sweet Beans singer, Lady Heidi Talata. Onyina's nephew is Pat Thomas, who has sometimes played with his uncle's band. Onyina considers his best friend to be the fellow Kumasi-based guitarist, Koo Nimo. From 1982-1990 he was Regional Chairman of the Ashanti Branch of the Musicians Union of Ghana, MUSIGA. He then retired in Kumasi and passed away on the 27th May 2010 aged 78 years.

T.D.B. ADJEKUM OF THE HAPPY STARS

Singer Theophilus Daniel Benson 'Skido' Adjekum was born in 1934 in Akim-Wenchi in Ghana's Eastern Region. At his Awisa Presbyterian Middle School he showed an interest in music and became a singing prefect. After obtaining his Middle School Leaving Certificate he became a driver. But against his father's advice he left this profession to join Willie's National Trio concert party. At the same time he composed songs for K. Gyasi's guitar band. He later left Willie's group and joined E.K'.s No. 1 and then No. 2 groups. He finally ended up with Onyina's guitar band and National Trio concert party in Kumasi. After financial assistance from Daniel Kyei and Mr. Larbi who bought instruments, Adjekum formed the Happy Stars together with co-singers C.N 'Love' Nortey (born in 1935 in Asamankese) and E.O. Frempong. Their first recordings were 'Wiase Afede' and 'Anopa Bosue'. The Happy Stars guitar band and concert party operated out of Nsawam in the 1960s and 70s and is famous in recording some early gospel highlifes such as the local apostolic church hymn 'Onyame Tie M'Asem' and in 1972 their highlife 'Mesi Me Dan Wo Obotan So' (I will put my house on a rock). From as early as the 1950s Adjekum had become interested in old-songs and was tutored by the musicologist Professor Nketia of the University of Ghana and an old lady and bard of folk-songs and poems called Maame Yaa Brayie. Indeed he was invited to play at the university African Music Society evenings that featured guitar bands such as those of E.K. Nyame, Yamoah and Onyina, which as mentioed in a previous chapter was patronised by lecturers such as Professor Nketia, Professor Atta Annan Mensah, Dr. Ephraim Amu, E.F. Collins and Robert Sprigge.

In the 1990s Adjekum was an active member of the Ghana Concert Party Union, of MUSIGA and also the Ghana Old Musicians and Artists Welfare Association GOMOWA that included fellow concert musicians T.O. Jazz and Yamoah. Some of the popular highlifes and folk influenced recording by Adjekum includes 'Senketenkete', 'Kwadede', 'Agyemang Onoa', 'Damirifa Due', 'Nhwiren', 'Hyiame Nonum', 'Auntie Leticia', 'Agustina', 'Adaye Wu', 'Ahoma' and 'African Unity.'

'DOCTOR' F. KENYA AND HIS GUITAR BAND

The concert party guitarist, 'Bob' and lady impersonator James Francis Kenya was born in 1934 in the Nzima town of Esiama on the Western Region, near the border with the Cote D'Ivoire. He learnt the guitar from his father, Nana Kenya Boa Akay, a chief of the town. Francis was also a young singer in local cultural groups that played at events such as the Kuntum Festival. At the age of twelve he was sent to Bibiani to become an apprentice goldsmith and shortly after joined his first concert party group, the Ghana Youngsters. He then moved to the gold-mining town of Tarkwa-Aboso where he stayed for many years and became a member of Bob Vans Trio de All Stars, Ahamano's and then Kakaiku's. He moved to Kumasi and joined Appiah Kubi's concert party. It was in Abidjan in 1956 that Francis finally got the money to form his own Riches Big Sound, which then became based in Accra.

Many important concert actors and musicians passed through this group, including Frempong Manso (Osofo Dadzie), Waterproof, Santo, Kofi Sammy, the lady impersonator Nartey and guitarist Agyekum who later led the Simple Seven. I met Francis and played with his group when we lived in the same house together in Madina near Accra in 1971. He has released many records, including the famous 'Power House' series on the Essiebons label, as well as those recorded at my Bokoor Studio between 1982 and 1985, four of which were released on the 'Guitar and Gun' (Cherry Red/Sterns) and 'Electric Highlife' (Naxos) albums. Artist with him on these Bokoor recording were Nyame, Sammy Kenya (Francis's eldest son), singer Papa Agya Kojo Menu (now with the Local Dimension band) and the wizard highlife guitarist Samuel Paa Gyimah who sadly died in 1987 after returning from Nigeria. For a while during the 1980s and 90s Francis located his band in Abidjan where he played gospel highlife. On returning to Ghana, he and his musical sons put his the band together, with the financial help of Francis's nephew, Meiway, one of the Cote d'Ivoire' top musicians. In the early-mid 2000s the group has made several treks into the rural areas and also played at the Dubois Centre and the Alliance Francaise. He then began planning on releasing forty new songs, including one dedicated to Kwame Nkrumah (himself an Nzima) and some gospel dance-tunes in the Nzima language – all recorded at Studio Three in Accra run by his old guitarist Agyeman. He retired to his home town in the late 2000s. His is a musical family and, besides Meiway and Sammy, there is his younger son Francis who is a bass player, and the hiplife artist Lord Kenya who is F. Kenya's nephew. Sadly, F Kenya died in 2012 after a short illness.

A.K. YEBOAH AND HIS K.K.'S NUMBER TWO BAND

Anthony Kwabena Yeboah was born in 1948 in Wasa Akropong in the Western Region. In 1958 and, as a schoolboy, he joined, as part-time soprano singer and lady impersonator, the Bayaa Jokers of Aboso-Tarkwa and then Kwesi Efuah's Band at Tarkwa. After finishing school he tried teaching but decided to go back into music; first with Sampson's Band in Abura Dunkwa, then the Nzima Trio, and finally in 1961

Advertising poster for F. Kenya's concert party. It is in French because Kenya is an Nzima from western Ghana and therefore often toured neighbouring Cote d'Ivoire

he became the lady impersonator for the band and concert of Appiah Adjekum, whose Liberian wife Auntie K.K. taught Yeboah the guitar. In 1963 Yeboah joined the band of Appiah Kumi (an ex-Kakaiku musician) when he got his first taste of recording, releasing with them his first record 'Ewusiaba' for A.K Brobbey of Ambassador Records. He then joined Ahamono's guitar band and recorded 'Nde Yen Da' (Asona Records) with them.

In 1964, due to Yeboah's recording successes, Moses Oppong, the leader of Kakaiku's guitar band, gave Yeboah some instruments to form K.K.'s Number Two (named after Kakaiku) that included Kwesi Manu and G.K. Akandoh. In 1985 this band made a UK tour and over the years K.K.'s No.Two has released about twenty albums and a hundred-and-fifty singles, including the songs 'Odo Fever' (Essieibons label) and more recently gospel highlifes such as 'Kronkron Ne Awurade'. A. K. Yeboah has been an active member of the Musicians Union of Ghana MUSIGA since 1979, becoming its Welfare Officer. He is currently one of its top executive members. Incidentally, A.K. Yeboah's son, Kwame Yeboah, is a top-rate recording engineer and multi-instrumentalist who is in high demand at home and abroad as a guitarist and keyboardist session-man.

KOFI ANI JOHNSON AND THE PARROTS

The late Ani Johnson was born in Obosomase Akuapem in the Eastern Region around 1940 and started work in 1956 as an agricultural labourer near Asamankese; then in 1960 he went to the Agricultural School at Bunso. In 1964, he joined the Police Service as a vocalist and composed songs for them like 'Shuulege', 'Yen Sempa', 'Osagyefo Kwame Nkrumah', 'Floyd Robertson' and 'Calypso International Trade Fair'. He also wrote highifes that were released on records by other bands: such as 'Woma Wonko', 'Brodo Kokoo' and 'Akokonini Abankwaa Wu' for Jerry Hansen's Ramblers; 'Asem Ato Me' and 'Augustina' for Ignace de Souza's Black Santiagos; and 'Odofo Bra', 'Madamfo Hiani' and 'Mani Agyina' for E.T. Mensah's Tempos.

Ani Johnson resigned from the Police Force with the rank of Sergeant in 1970 and formed his Parrots (Nkoo) guitar band in Nsawam in 1971. With his band he released a number of singles such as 'Anka Wiase Nnye', 'Den Koraa', 'Obaatan', 'Akuafo Kusa Wo Bankye' and 'Odo Ye Owu'. This was followed by his most famous hit 'Madamfo Paa' which appeared on a record album released by Ambassador Records in the mid-1970s. This album also includes the early gospel highlife 'Yesu Wo Kyen Na Metene'. With the collapse of the live recording scene from the mid-1970s to 80s, Ani Johnson switched from secular highlife to playing and recording local gospel music.

GHANAIAN HIGHLIFE DANCE BANDS AND THEIR MUSICIANS

2

Highlife
TIME 3

This turns to the origins of the name highlife and the more urbanised dance-band variety of highlife that emerged after the Second World War from the earlier local dance-orchestras, pioneered by the likes of E.T. Mensah, King Bruce, Stan Plange and Jerry Hansen. This section also looks at how some dance band musicians fused highlife in the 1970s with various forms of imported rock and funk music, such as Ebo Taylor, Blay Ambolley and the members of Osibisa.

Chapter 12

E.T. MENSAH, THE KING OF DANCE-BAND HIGH LIFE

I first got to know E.T. Mensah through one of the vocalists in his Tempos band, Jacob Awuletey or 'Obi' with whom I played in a student band in 1969/70 that included Charles Easmon and Salah and Ramzi Jebeile. Then in 1973 I stayed with Obi for six months in Osu, Accra and he introduced me to E.T. whom I began visiting at his Mamprobi house where I met his wife, family and musical sons, Chris Nii Noi and Edmund Mensah. Subsequently, E.T. and I decided to put out heads together to write his biography. I interviewed E.T. on several occasions and then, between July and August 1973, E.T. took me around town to interview important local musical personalities such as Yeboah Mensah, Joe Kelly, Horace Djoleto, Frank Torto, Squire Addo, Amoo Dodoo, Kofi Ghanaba (Guy Warren), Dan Acquaye, Kweikumah Stevens and Adolf Doku. The resulting book was entitled 'E.T. Mensah the King of Highlife' and, after many years of languishing at the Ghana State Publishing Corporation, was finally published by Off The Record Press in London in 1986 and then republished in 1996 by Anansesem Press in Accra.

Shortly after, I wrote this book I moved into Temple House in Jamestown downtown Accra, not too far from Mamprobi, so sometimes E.T .Mensah and I visited one another. Temple House itself was originally a fine story building built by the prominent Ghanaian lawyer Thomas Hutton-Mills around 1900.

151

Temple House 1970s. Venue for early elite ballroom dance parties

On one occasion when E. T. came to the house he told me he remembered coming to the place as a boy with Teacher Lamptey's Accra Orchestra and still felt uncomfortable at the house where as a child he played for Ghanaian 'big people' wearing top hats and tail at balls and soirees held in the old tennis court at the back of the house (later a factory). Oddly enough, the percussionist Kofi Ayivor also lived in Temple House in the 1960s, and after 1 left the house in 1979. Kris Bediako, the leader of A Band Named Bediako and the Third Eye group, moved into my flat. This house was built around 1900 by the Ghanaian lawyer Thomas Hutton-Mills who sponsored the balls that E.T. recalled. His daughter, Violet, was a brilliant classical pianist who reluctantly had to give up a professional musical career to become her father's secretary. So over the years Temple House maintained a strong connection with music until it was demolished in the 1990s.After I left Temple House and moved into my father's house (now Bokoor House) I continued to see E.T. from time to time and in 1990 he became one of the trustees of the BAPMAF music archives, an NGO that I established to

I

E.T. Mensah, was born in Accra in 1919 and it was his Tempos band that pioneered the urban dance-bands highlife of the 1950s. E.T. started his musical career when, as a small boy, he joined the Accra Orchestra as a flute player for the Accra Orchestra formed by Teacher Lamptey around 1930, that grew out of an earlier schoolboy brass band. Teacher Lamptey, the music and sports teacher of a James Town elementary school had been a member of one of the first dance orchestras in Ghana, the Jazz Kings formed in 1916. But it was his Accra Orchestra that became the best-known pre-war orchestra before the Second World War and many of Ghana's top musicians played in it, including E.T. his older brother Yebuah Mensah, Joe Kelly, and Tommy Grippman.

*Teacher Lamptey (middle with trumpet) and his Accra Orchestra in 1930.
Eleven year old E.T. Mensah is in second row from the front, second from right*

Yebuah Mensah went on to form the Accra Rhythmic Orchestra, which E.T. joined and which won the Lambeth Walk Dance Competition in 1939 at the King George Memorial Hall (present-day Parliament House). Here is what Yeboah told me in 1973 about comments on the origin of the term 'highlife'.

During the early twenties, during my childhood, the term 'highlife' was created by people who gathered around the dancing clubs such as the Rodger Club (built in 1904) to watch and listen to the couples enjoying themselves. Highlife started as a catch-name for the indigenous songs played at these clubs by such early bands as the Jazz Kings, the Cape Coast Sugar Babies, the Sekondi Nanshamang and later the Accra Orchestra. The people outside called it "highlife" as they did not reach the class of the couples going inside, who not only had to pay a then relatively high entrance fee of 7s 6d., but also had to wear full evening dress including top-hats.

During World War Two American and British troops were stationed in Ghana and they brought in jazz and swing. Nightclubs were opened that catered for them like the Metropole, Basshoun, Kit-Kat, Weekend-in-Havana and the New York Bar. The Allied soldiers also set up dance combos and played with local musicians. The first such was the Black and White Spots, set up by Sergeant Leopard. E.T. left his brother's orchestra and joined up with Leopard's jazz combo as sax player in 1940. Sergeant Leopard, a Scot, had been a professional saxophonist in England and according E.T:

It was Sergeant Leopard who taught us the correct methods of intonation, vibrato, tongueing, and breath control, which contributed to place us above the average standard in the town.

Just after the war, E. T. joined the Tempos, set up by Ghanaian pianist Adolf Doku and English engineer Arthur Harriman. At first the band included some white soldiers but after the war, when they left, the band became completely African and E.T. ultimately became its leader. It was a seven-piece band with E.T. doubling on trumpet and sax, Joe Kelly on tenor sax, and Guy Warren (later known as Kofi Ghanaba) on drums. Guy Warren made an important contribution as he had been playing Afro-Cuban music and calypsos in England. So the Tempos not only played with a jazz touch, but incorporated calypsos into their repertoire and added the bongos and maracas to the line-up. It was the Tempos style of highlife that became all the rage; by the early 1950s and through West Africa tours and recording for Decca, E.T. (who was a trained pharmacist) was able to go fully professional for a while. It was during the 1950s that E.T. was acclaimed the 'king of highlife' throughout West Africa.

The Tempos had a profound impact on Nigeria from their tours that began in 1950. At that time Nigerian dance bands such as those of Bobby Benson, Sammy Akpabot and E.C. Arinze whose bands were based at prestigious spots like the Empire Hotel, only played imported swing and ballroom music. But E. T.'s highlife soon began to influence them and which created a whole new generation of Nigerian highlife dance-

154

E.T. Mensah (seated with saxophone) and his Tempos band in the early 1950s

band musicians; like the three mentioned above as well as Victor Olaiya, Eddie Okunta, Rex Lawson, Charles Iwegbue, Victor Chukwu, Chief Billy Friday, Enyang Hensaw, King Kennytone and Roy Chicago. The Tempos influenced not only these mature Nigerian dance-band musicians, but also the young Victor Uwaifo. Victor Uwaifo corroborates this story:

> *I used to see E.T. Mensah and his Tempos play whenever they were in Benin city (in Nigeria) and I went to see their guitarist, Dizzy Acquaye, to put me through a few chords. I had a guitar book but I didn't understand the chord drawings. Dizzy helped me.*

Many Ghanaian musicians were also influenced by the Tempos, some of whom passed through the band: like Joe Kelly, Tommy Grippman, Saka Acquaye, Spike Anyankor, Ray Ellis, and the first female vocalists Juliana Okine and Agnes Aryitey. The Nigerians Zeal Onyia and Babyface Paul Osamade were also at one point members of the Tempos.

I first met E.T. Mensah in 1973 when I was staying at the Osu house of one of his singers called Obi 'King' Aluway. It was then that E.T. and I discussed writing his biography 'E.T. the King of Highlife' which was first published, in 1986, by the UK Off the Record Press, in 1986 and later republished in 1996 by Anansesem Press. When I moved to Temple House in James Town in 1974, E. T. and I continued visiting each other, as we were still tracking down and interviewing elderly Ga performers for the book, like Squire Addo, Mr. Williams, Frank Torto and E.T.'s brother, Yebuah. E.T. told me he remembered coming to the Temple House as a small boy with Teacher Lamptey's Accra Orchestra, which played at evening soirees there for Ghanaian 'big people' with top hats and tails, held in the old tennis courts at the back of the house (later a factory). Because of this the house still made E.T. nervous. Oddly enough percussionist Kofi Ayivor also lived there in the 1960s, and when I left Kris Bediako's Band and the Third Eye group moved into my flat. So the house has a strong connection with music. The house was built around 1900 by a Ghanaian lawyer named Thomas Hutton-Mills who sponsored the soirees and balls. His daughter Violet was a brilliant classical pianist who reluctantly had to give up a professional musical career to become her father's secretary. She died in 1971 and it was her son and daughter-in-law, Tom and Balbil Wittacker who told me the house's history.

In the 1970s E.T. retired as a professional musician and returned to his pharmacy profession. However, in 1974 he became active in the formation of the Musicians Union, MUSIGA, and was part of Faisal Helwani's Afro-disia project in 1976 when some of E.T.'s old hits were re-recorded in Lagos. Later and again in Lagos he recorded and released an album with his old friend and protégé Victor Olaiya. This occurred during the Christmas/New Year period of 1983/4 when E.T. spent a month playing at Olaiya's the Papingo Club and recording together their joint album 'Highlife Giants of Africa' that was released in 1984 by Polygram (POLP 102)

Then from the late 1980s the British based Sterns African Music Company released two CD's of old Tempos recordings (digitally re-mastered) called 'All For You' and 'Day by Day'. The launching of the first CD included a trip in which E.T. Mensah played in London organised by Sterns, extended with my assistance to Amsterdam through some of my Dutch music journalist friends (like Stan Rijven and Henk Tummers). After the show Stan Rijven, arranged a sight-seeing trip of Amsterdam for E.T his daughter him and myself.

E.T. Mensah and Victor Olaiya on their Polygram album cover, 1984

Sadly, E.T. passed away in July 1996 after a long incapacitating illness and was given a State Funeral. He is musically survived by his sons, the most-well known being the trumpeter Edmund Narku Mensah (see his photo with Ghanaba in Chapter 30) who, of course, began in his dad's band. Edmund was with the National Symphony Orchestra from 1986 to 1991 and the Ghana Armed Forces Band for many years – as well as playing with numerous other highlife bands such as the Black Beats, Diplomats, Ambassadors, Sweet Talks and Alpha Waves.

Chapter 13

THE TEMPOS TRAVELS IN WEST AFRICA

Here I will deal with E.T.'s extensive travelling around West Africa in the 1950s, excluding the Cote d'Ivoire that I discuss in Chapter 55. The country he most often visited was Nigeria and the Tempos first trip there was one week in Lagos in 1951, when Joe Kelly and Guy Warren were in his band. His next trip was in 1953, just after Tommy Grippman had left, and the band had been reorganised with Spike Anyankor. That year the whole band drove to Lagos and stayed for two weeks, living at Bobby Benson's brother's house. However, instead of going straight of the back to Ghana, a last minute change in arrangements was made and the band went on to Ibadan and the mid-west states (Warri and Sapelle). The band returned to Nigeria again that year, this time for three months and travelled as far as the then Eastern Region covering Enugu, Onitsha, Port Harcourt and Calabar. E. T. found that on both of these early trips his band received tremendous welcome. The reason for this was that although highlife was beginning to become popular in Nigeria through records, there were no dance bands in Nigeria playing this type of music.

E.T.Mensah and Bobby Benson in Lagos 1951

So from 1953 the Tempos began making regular trips to Nigeria, travelling once or twice a year by station wagon, usually stopping off along the way at Lome in Togo, and Cotonou and Porto Novo in Dahomey (now the Republic of Benin). They stayed for up to three months at a stretch since there was a ninety-day limit on the time they could spend in the country without infringing Nigerian immigration laws. These trips proved very successful financially for E. T., while the musicians were happy with the tips they received. In fact it was the Nigerian trips, which enabled the band to turn professional in 1953, for there weren't enough engagements then in Ghana to make it worthwhile. Because of the frequency of these trips E. T. decided to set up his second band in 1954, called the Star Rockets, to carry on at home while he was away.

When E.T. first went to Nigeria in 1950, highlife was hardly known outside the boundaries of Ghana. Even by 1953 and although Nigerians were developing an interest in the music, here were no bands playing highlifes to any marked degree. At that time, Nigerian dance bands such as Sammy Akpabot's Band and Bobby Benson's Band were playing mostly swing, calypsos and ballroom music. There were, however, varieties of westernised indigenous music being developed by Nigerian guitar bands, similar in some ways to highlife guitar bands. These were juju music, native blues and palmwine music, but they were never played then at respectable nightclubs and hotels.

By the mid-1950s the Tempos continual touring in Nigeria was beginning to influence dance orchestras there and they started to incorporate highlife into their repertoire. Victor Olaiya, originally a trumpeter with Bobby Benson, was one of the first Nigerian musicians to play highlife when he formed his Cool Cats. Eddie Okunta, also formerly with Bobby Benson, followed suit when he formed the Lido Band. Rex Lawson and E.C. Arinze both split from the Empire Band to form their own highlife bands. In fact Rex Lawson used one of E.T.'s numbers as his signature tune and Dan Acquaye, vocalist for the Tempos, was his idol. Nigerian musicians would sometimes come to the Tempos for tuition and Dan Acquaye told me something about this when I interviewed him in 1974:

> *Agu Norris, leading the Empire Band, always used to visit us, taking lessons from E. T. on the trumpet. In Benin City Victor Uwaifo, then a schoolboy, would rush down to our Hotel after school to watch my cousin, Dizzy Acquaye, on the guitar. He was determined to play the guitar and used to help Dizzy pack and clean his instrument.*

However, the relationship between the Tempos and the Nigerian dance bands was not entirely one way and when the Nigerian bands started to write their own highlifes, E. T. brought some of them back to Ghana; for instance the Yoruba highlifes 'Nike Nike' and 'Okamo'. Although the Tempos made an enormous impact on Nigerian dance bands, and made many friends there, it was not all plain sailing. In this context it is worth quoting Dan Acquaye again.

> *If we make a record, after the recording we often improve the song and sing it better. To the Nigerian audience, even if we sang better they didn't like it; if we made a mistake in the recording they expected us to make the same mistake in the performance. Some of the Nigerian musicians were very jealous as when we went there we captured the market and all the fans would follow us. They (the musicians) used to put it around that we could only play highlife; they wanted to distract the attention of the people from us. Once when we were playing a man from the floor told us not to play highlife as some people were suggesting that we couldn't play western numbers. This man was annoyed by the musicians who had suggested this, and wanted us to show the audience that we could play all types of music. So I sang 'Unchained Melody' and 'Answer Me' and the audience was so impressed that they wanted more. At this point the man got up and shouted out that the band should not play anymore western numbers as some Nigerians were putting around that we could only play highlife; the man was trying to publicly shame the musicians. Another incident was in*

Lagos in 1958 (during the grand tour of West Africa) when the Musicians Union officers rushed down to the place we were going to play. There was a row and they actually prevented us from playing. I remember that one of the officers was actually from Ghana and was then on the Union's Executive Committee. He was also a member of Bill Friday's Band at the Ambassador Hotel in Lagos. At first Bobby Benson wasn't with them but later he sided with them. It didn't entirely stop us from playing on that tour but it was their way of showing their resentment.

Bobby Benson was, in fact, the President of the Nigerian Union and had been a long-time friend of the Tempos, but even he was unable to prevent the Union from making a ruling to keep the Tempos out of Nigeria. Consequently, from 1958 onwards, the band had to stop their regular tours to Nigeria and never went there again apart from one visit in 1964 at the invitation of the students at the University of Lagos. Things had been becoming more difficult for some years for the Tempos in Nigeria, partly due to the increased competition from local dance bands and partly due to the diminishing returns form these trips. E.T. remembers that.

I was getting into financial difficulties. At first bar owners would give their places to me for say one third of the profits. The next time I went conditions would have changed to the owners benefit. Things were becoming tougher.

The most extensive tour the Tempos ever made of West Africa was the Grand Tour they made from October 1958 to February 1959. The nine-piece band first travelled to Nigeria in their Morris station wagon. At that time the band consisted of E.T. and his two vocalists, Christiana and Dan Acquaye; Joe Ransford, Tom Tom, Dizzy Acquaye and Rex Ofosu, plus two new musicians who had come into the band called A.P. Mensah on trombone and Alex Martey on congas. They stayed for three weeks in Lagos playing at many of the leading nightclubs, the Lido, Ambassador, Lagos Arcade, Chez Peter's, Savoy Hotel and Caban Bamboo (Bobby Benson's place). It was during this trip that the trouble with the Nigerian Musician's Union occurred.

From Lagos the band then took a boat to Freetown, the capital of Sierra Leone, where at first they had some difficulty in finding a hotel. Fortunately, they met a Lebanese who owned a nightclub at Juba, the army residential area just outside the town, who provided the band with an entire house to stay in and they played at his club every weekend. Then at a private party the band met the Prime Minister of Sierra Leone, Dr.

Margai and also a fellow Ghanaian, Judge Okai who had married one of Margai's daughters. At the party the idea of a free concert was discussed and this was later organised by the Municipal Council of Freetown to take place at Victoria Park. On the day almost the entire population of Freetown packed into the park, the band playing under a pavilion. As the band did not have sufficiently powerful amplifiers, the crowd surged forwards practically mobbing the Tempos. After a while they were forced to stop playing, though by the time the show ended everybody agreed that it had been a great success. The band stayed in Freetown for about six weeks, except for a short tour to Be Kenema in the interior, and a week-long visit to Guinea. E.T.'s impressions of Sierra Leone and Guinea are vivid. He was particularly struck by the town of Freetown itself.

The houses of Freetown were made of wood and zinc so we could see a lot of roofs. It was something peculiar to my eyes, like a slum or shanty town. Not an impressive place at all. However, at Juba, the residential area, we saw a lot of good houses. Another peculiar thing we saw was a very small passenger train that ran right through Freetown's main market. When the market people heard the train whistle they quickly got their things off the rails and the train would move slowly so that they could move their things. After the train had passed they would put their stalls back. There was much grumbling over the trade depression caused by the stoppage of local people pinching diamonds. Sierra Leone is very rich in diamonds and there was a time when these were being openly black-marketed. At that time they didn't have self-government so the rulers, or imperialists, made stringent laws to forbid this black-marketeering. For instance, if you were living in a diamond area and wanted to build a house, you weren't permitted to dig more than three feet down for the foundations. There was a greater number of Lebanese in Sierra Leone, right inside the small villages, than we could see in Ghana. In small villages we could see Syrians living there just because of diamonds. They were shop-keepers and traders but really they were dealing in diamonds. There were no dance bands in Sierra Leone and at the clubs they danced to gramophone records. Highlife was there but not under that name. Another thing we noticed during our stay was that there was a class distinction between personalities. The upper class consisted of lawyers and doctors who would not like to mix with the working class. If we wanted this upper class to attend our dances we had to raise our entrance fee, or charge two separate fees and provide two separate dance floors to accommodate the two classes of dance fans. They didn't like the free mixture, as it was in Ghana or Nigeria; so if we called a dance and charged 7/6 the upper class would not like to come; they would prefer to pay £3 double.

The Tempos spent the New Year in Guinea and as the road was pretty rough two of them flew to Conakry and the rest went by car. Dan Acquaye and Alex Martey, the two who flew, arrived first. Dan takes up the story.

Alex spoke a little French so he told a man at the airport that we were musicians, an international word, and the man took us by taxi to a restaurant. The restaurant manager phoned the Parliamentary Secretary to the Minister of Information who came round and gave instructions that we should be fed. He then took us to the Ghana Embassy which had just opened in Guinea. The late Mr. Welbeck, the Ghanaian Minister of State, and Mr. E.K. Dadson a Parliamentary Secretary were there. They questioned us, thinking we had taken advantage of the Guinea-Ghana Union and that we had turned up without proper notice. I told him that we didn't normally do this and that we were expecting E.T. any time from that moment. I told him that it was an official visit as Sekou Toure was in the know. Welbeck asked me where we were going to sleep and I told him that I would rather be a dog occupying the house of my God than dwell in the tents of wickedness, meaning that I would like to lie down on his veranda. Actually, the way he was putting questions to us was just as if we were ruffians and didn't know what we were in Guinea for. They took us to a military camp where we could sleep, but on the way we saw E.T. in the station wagon. I told Welbeck to stop and E.T. showed him the papers and cables concerning the trip. This seemed to satisfy everyone and we were all taken to the Hotel De France for the first night on the instructions of Sekou Toure himself.

E.T. continues the story.

When we first reached the border we were very well received as they hadn't seen people from Ghana come that way before. The swish road wasn't so good and we were passing through savannah, but when we got to about sixty miles from Conakry we found a first class road. Six miles from the town the way was lit by an array of lights; it was getting dark at the time. Luckily we met the boys we had sent by air. At that time there were certain Ghanaian Ministers on holiday in Guinea, including Mr. Welbeck and Mr. Dadson. They took us to the house of one of the Guinean 'big men', a Mr. Dlallo Telli, who got in touch with Sekou Toure by telephone. It was arranged that we should stay at the very posh Hotel De France for the night and on the following day they fixed up a school for us to stay. They got in beds and we were well cared for. They even arranged where we could have our meals, so in the morning people would come and take us to a restaurant where we could eat.

The Tempos had arrived in Guinea at a critical time. The Guineans had said 'No' to De Gaulle's September referendum that gave Guinea the option of remaining with France or going it alone, and so and had been given independence in October 1958. But before they pulled out the French had made a thorough job of attempting to wreck the new state. E.T.'s immediate impressions of Conakry reflect the state of affairs stemming from France's spiteful reaction to the referendum.

The city, like all French West African cities, was first class; however when independence was given to them overnight, the French took all the guns from the police and army and dumped them in a river. They also took all files form the secretariat and burnt them so there could be no identifications. So the Guineans were left just like that, and we happened to arrive just at that very time. The whole town was very strange; people were sweeping the streets without any pay and some of the army people were using bulldozers to clear certain unfinished work, again without pay. They were doing this sacrificial work until we heard that Kwame Nkrumah had given them a loan; so we were there when they got fresh money. Sekou Toure personally gave us a 33,000 Franc dash (about £55) because of this. When we went to the harbour we could only see just one bunch of bananas in the whole place, we were very sorry; nothing inside and the workers roaming around. At the Secretariat, although the people were dressed for work, they were also roaming around as there was no work for them. The French, they were not diplomatic in training the Guineans to a level and then handing over to them in a way they could carry on. No, they were asking the people of Guinea that did they want independence or did they want to go with the French; they went to the polls and opted for independence. So straight away the French seized all the files and the guns. Also all the wages for government employees up to then had been sent each month from Dakar. This was stopped and all the French officials were flown out of the country. There was great confusion, as when the French left, local people had to take over immediately. For instance the young man who was serving his master at the airport had to suddenly take over immigration and didn't know what to do. So what he was doing at the time we arrived was to collect the passports from those coming by plane, who would then be given a small note and they had to come back after three days to collect their passports. All the relevant documents had been dumped by the French. When we went to collect Dan's and Alex's passports the boy was hesitating as he wasn't used to the position he was in.

Dan Acquaye's comments run in a similar vein.

My impression of the town was that the people were determined. They were working for months without pay. Although food was being supplied, the army and civil servants were working without pay and we couldn't see any sign of grievance. Stealing had actually disappeared for if anyone stole, it was serious, because the country had been left naked and the little that someone had, if you stole, you were a saboteur.

E.T. and his bandsmen spent most of their visit touring the city and the only time they played was on New Year's Eve. They first of all played at a private party at the residence of the Minister of Defence and afterwards at a large dance organised by the Worker's Union, of which Sekou Toure had been president. Tom Tom got so drunk at the party that when the band opened with their signature tune at the Union dance he fell off his seat and Dan had to take over. This was the last straw as far as E. T. was concerned and he brought in another drummer called Edoh when they reached Liberia. Tom Tom had his fare paid and was sent back to Accra. The popular music in Conakry at the time was the chachacha, the bolero and the samba. However Dan and E.T. don't remember seeing any dance bands with African musicians, although they did see several European bands playing in the nightclubs. Dan comments on this. (For more on Guinean music scene see chapter 55).

We saw nightclubs with white musicians playing. You know Guinea and these French West African states; they mix up with the whites. When a team from the Ivory Coast comes to play in Ghana you don't expect to see only white footballers. No, there is a mixture of black and white. When you go to Abidjan you don't only expect to see blacks driving buses and taxis. So we found white bands at the clubs in Conakry, playing French music.

The Tempos returned to Sierra Leone the way they had arrived and stayed in Freetown for a week while arranging for a boat to take them to Liberia. On arrival in Monrovia they went straight to an old school friend of E.T.'s, Ayi McCarthy, who owned a night-club there. He put them up and the band started making dollars at the clubs in the town. It is interesting to compare E.T.'s impressions of Monrovia with those of Freetown.

The town is similar to Freetown with houses made of wood and zinc, many of them storied. Many of the roads are un-tarred and some of the houses are put on stones so that when it

rains, the water goes underneath. Outside Monrovia is a sister town of fine houses where the
rich live; whereas in Freetown the rich live in the town itself. The cost of living is very high
(in Monrovia) and they have extremely rich people there. Class distinction in Monrovia is
based just on money, so that even a poor man can move freely. In Freetown, however, the
class distinction is different. There the respectable rich class looks down on certain classes of
people and don't like to mix with them. They have first class nightclubs in Monrovia but no
bands; music such as swing and jazz is played on hi-fi amplifiers.

As E. T. points out, the popular music was American, but the Americo-Liberian ruling elite did have their own dance called the quadrille. This was originally creole music brought to Liberia from the southern USA and when the Tempos were in Monrovia they learnt to play it. The band stayed in the town six weeks, but before leaving they played at a function at which President Tubman was present. He told the bandsmen that he would invite them over for the inauguration of the next President. The Tempos returned to Accra by boat and on arrival received the following cablegram from Tubman. 'I am pleased to note that you and your band have safely arrived in Accra. We enjoyed the melody, rhythm and tempo of your band and this telegram constitutes an invitation to you and your band to return for the Inauguration.'

So a year later E.T. and the Tempos made their return visit to Liberia for Tubman's inauguration for a second term of office. This time things were made easy for them, as the Liberian government supplied the band with a three storey house and provided free food. In fact things were so good, with money flowing in, that the band stayed for three months, long after the ceremonies were over. President Tubman wielded enormous power in the country and was well known for his paternalistic method of governing. E.T. comments on this.

Tubman was doing all the work which you could expect to be done by his ministers and
secretaries. If you wanted to hire chairs for a large function you could go and see the
President and hire chairs from his mansion. We wanted to service our car so we needed
another one; we were told to go and see the President at his executive mansion. We went
there and saw his secretary who told us to go and sit in his waiting room. You could meet all
sorts of people there going to see the President over some personal matter or another, and he
would tell them what to do. You could meet old women from the town who were having
troubles with their husbands or households and so on. They all took their problems to the
President who would solve the problem by meeting them one by one. His word was law. My

problem was that I wanted a car to use, he took me down to a compound full of brand new unlicensed cars and told me to choose one. I chose one and drove it away. Another incident occurred when we were about to leave and were finding difficulty because no passenger boats were passing through; there were only cargo boats. They only had a few places for passengers and I wanted the whole band, and the instruments and the car to be taken home at once. So we saw the President and he somehow fixed it up personally for us all to go as deck passengers on one of the cargo ships that was passing through to Ghana.

POSTSCRIPT ON THE TEMPOS IMPACT ON GUINEA

Although E.T.Mensah knew that the *Tempos* had made a deep impact on Nigerian popular music, he had never realised that he had also made a deep lasting impression on Guinea. I discovered this during a trip to Mali in October 2011 when I spoke at a Colloquium on Modern African Music organised by the Institut Francaise in Bamako. There the Australian music journalist/musicologist Graeme Counsel alerted me to an interview by Gérald Arnaud[2] with Achken Kaba, the trumpeter and music director of the famous Guinean band Bembeya Jazz. According to Kaba it was the combined effect of the 1958 trip by Nkrumah to support the newly independent country and the presence of the Tempos band playing African music on western dance band instruments that convinced President Sekou Toure to jump-start the country's local popular music by setting up Bembeya Jazz, the Syli National Orchestra, Les Amazons and other state bands to develop a new Afro-Manding sound. And this idea was subsequently picked up by President Keita of Mali who likewise established many state and regional dance bands when that country became independent in 1960.

[2] *See Arnaud's 'Bembeya Se Réveille' at Africultures at www.africulturers.com*

Chapter 14

KING BRUCE, THE BLACK BEATS AND SAKA ACQUAYE

This chapter looks at the careers of both King Bruce and Saka Acquaye who, together, created the famous Black Beats band in 1952. We begin with the story of King Bruce.

My first contact with the late King Bruce was in the mid-1970s when I used to hire equipment from him for my own Bokoor Band, for I was living at Temple House in James Town not far from Bruce's house. At that time, King Bruce was running seven 'BB' bands and therefore used to hire amplifiers and instruments to those who needed them. For a while, in the late 1970s, we were also both on the executive board of the Musician's Union of Ghana (MUSIGA), with Bruce becoming at one point 2nd Vice President. We were, therefore, both involved in organising the MUSIGA march for government recognition in 1979, to the Seat of Government at Christiansborg Castle. Later, I interacted with Bruce in August 1987 when he gave a number of interesting presentations at the Accra conference of the International Association for the Study of Popular Music (IASPM) on 'Africa in the World of Popular Music' of which I was on the local organising committee.

Shortly after this conference I recorded four songs for him at my Bokoor studio in 1987 entitled 'Esheo Heko' (There Comes a Time), 'Onyiemo Feo Mi Feo' (Your Walk is Beautiful), 'Ekole' (Perhaps) and 'Tsutsu Tsosemo' (Old time Training) that King released locally on cassette. 'Tsutsu Tsosemo' was later released in 2002 on the 'Electric Highlife' CD on the US/Hong Kong Naxos Label. For the 1987 recording Desmond Adabio was the keyboard player, Nat was the road manager, Big Daniel Tetteh Tagoe the maracas player (and band driver) and Small Nelson was on congas. King also pulled in some of his long-time musicians: singer Lewis Wadawa, guitarist Jerry Bampoe and drummer George Annor. It was after the 1987 IASPM conference that King and I spent two years working on his biography (with editorial and discographical assistance from Flemming Harrev) – from which the quoted material in this chapter is extracted.

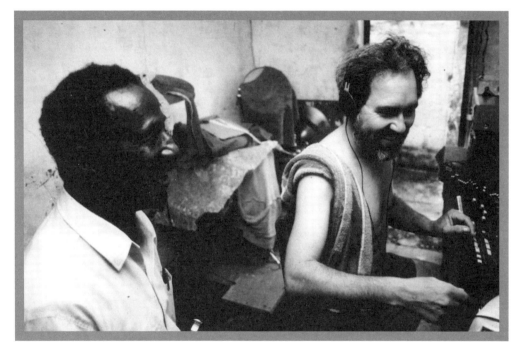

King Bruce recording at John Collins' Bokoor Studio in Accra, 1987

King Bruce was a Ga born in James Town, Accra in 1922 and his musical experiences started early and were varied. His mother belonged to a traditional women's singing group called Etsi Penfo. His eldest brother Kpakpo Thompson taught him piano. Another brother, Eddie Bruce, played palm-wine guitar-styles like 'fireman' and 'dagomba wire' in a group of seamen called Canteen. At the same time, and much against his parent's wishes, King was a keen follower of the Accra street music, such as the alaha (adaha), kolomashie, tsibode, koyin and other popular dance-styles played by the local Ga drumming groups. At the prestigious Achimota College King continued to be inspired by music, particularly by some of the teachers who taught there. These included Phillip Gbeho who composed Ghana's national anthem, and Doctor Ephraim Amu. As King explains:

Ephraim Amu was my housemaster as well as my music teacher and taught us his Twi and Ewe songs. He had come to Achimota after he lost his appointment as a teacher at the Akropong Training College because of his strong African tendencies. He didn't believe in the idea of going to classes or church in Western-style suits, but always wore traditional kente cloth or batakari. He had these strong feelings about African culture as far back as the 1930s and was welcomed at Achimota, as the founders of the school – Guggisberg, Fraser, and Aggrey – were strongly interested in promoting African ways.

It was at the end of his schooldays at Achimota that King developed a taste for swing and dance-band music. King reflects on this period:

These were the war years and we had British and American army units stationed here. They had bands for their entertainment and so ballroom music progressed very much. The airport was virtually taken over by the Americans and one wing of Achimota College itself was taken over by the British resident minister, who was taking care of the British war effort here. So this was the time of musicians like Glenn Miller, Benny Goodman, and Artie Shaw; so by the time I left Achimota, I had a definite liking for jazz and swing.

King did not actually start playing in a dance-band, however, until he had spent a couple of years in England studying to be a civil servant with the Posts and Telegraphs and learnt to play the trumpet. On returning to Accra in 1950, he hung around for a while with top musicians like Adolf Doku, E.T. Mensah, Kofi Ghanaba (Guy Warren), Joe Kelly, and Papa Hughes. He occasionally played clips (claves) for Ghana's leading highlife dance-band, the Tempos. When King felt he was ready to go on stage with his trumpet he joined Teacher Lamptey's Accra Orchestra.

King stayed with this group until 1952, when he and tenor saxist Saka Acquaye formed the Black Beats band. This name, according to King, just came out spontaneously.

One evening when we were coming home from rehearsals Saka asked me what name we were going to use. Without hesitation I said Black Beats. The reason was that Doctor Amu at Achimota had impressed on us the necessity for doing things African. At the same time, as a group we were very much enamoured with jazz, swing, and music with a beat. So we

170

were all interested in playing good dance-band music, but keen on giving everything a recognisable African beat.

Unlike the other Ghanaian dance-bands, the Black Beats vocalists the 'Black Birds' (Lewis Wadawa and Frank Barnes) dominated the instrumental line-up, and in this they were influenced by the currently popular swing and 'jump' music of African American Louis Jordan. It was with this format that the Black Beats began to release a string of high life hits for HMV, Senophone and Decca composed by King: like 'Teemon Sane' (A Confidential Matter), 'Laimomo' (Old Lover), 'Nkuse Mbaa Dong' (I'll Never

King Bruce (seated left with trumpet) and his Black Beats in the early 1950s

In 1961 disaster struck the band. Alto saxist Jerry Hansen and nine musicians left the semi-professional Black Beats to form the fully-professional Ramblers dance-band. Nevertheless, within a few months King had reorganised his band and with this second-generation Black Beats began releasing more hits for Decca: like 'Se Nea Woti Ara' (I Love You Just as You Are). 'Kwemo Ni Okagbi' (Take Care You Don't Dry Up), 'Odo Fofor' (New Love), and 'Nkase Din' (I Am Quietly Poised). During the whole period when King was running the Black Beats he was slowly working his way up the civil service ladder, but getting a lot of criticism from his superiors for playing on stage. As King comments:

At first the opposition from my employers came in hints. Then in 1967 the opposition came in black and white as a result of a letter I received from the government. It was from the head of the Administrative Civil Service and they told me that I had now got to the stage where I was due for promotion from assistant to full principal secretary, and that the only thing that stood in my way was my dance-band playing. So I had to decide whether to continue playing or accept promotion. I replied that I had commitments to play up to Easter 1968, but that from April and thereafter I would comply with the undertaking and wouldn't play in public anymore. I was very much annoyed because I had always believed that it was the actual playing in a band that sharpens your faculties and brings new ideas. When you sit down doing nothing you don't create new music. So the ban on my playing hurt me very much as I had to sacrifice a lot to play music and had always wanted to pursue it and make something out of it.

To keep his band running, King handed the Black Beats' leadership to Sammy Odoh (see Chapter 22). Instead of playing, King started managing the band, plus others that became based at his house in James Town. By the mid-1970s he was running eight 'B.B.' bands: the Black Beats, Barbecues, Barons, Bonafides, Barristers, Boulders, 'B' Soyaaya and Blessed Apostles. Besides being a senior civil servant, composer, band leader, manager and teacher of the hundred or so musicians who have passed through his groups, King Bruce has also found time to help organise all three of Ghana's music unions: the 1950s Gold Coast Association of Musicians, the short-lived (1960-1966) Ghana Musicians Union, and the present-day MUSIGA.

In 1977 King Bruce retired from the civil service but still actively pursued his musical career. He ran two 'BB' bands (the Black Beats and Barristers) and began to re-record some of his old hits. As an executive member of MUSIGA he was also involved getting the 1985 copyright law established that made infringement and piracy an offence. (For Kings' views on copyright and the Ghanaian recording business in general see Chapter 60)

In April 1988, King Brucc received an award from the Entertainment Critics and Reviewers Association of Ghana (ECRAG) at the Star Hotel in Accra for his 'immense contribution to the development of Ghanaian arts and culture in the field of highlife music'. From 1989 to 1991 he was the manager of the sixteen-track Essiebons/Phonogram Elephant Walk recording studio in Kaneshie, Accra. Then in 1990 King helped me set up the Bokoor African Popular Music Archives Foundation

(BAPMAF), an NGO to preserve and disseminate Ghanaian popular music created by a group of local musician and musicologists concerned about the decline in live band highlife. Infact it was King who assisted in sorting out some of the initial BAPMAF documentation with the Department of Social Welfare and he later donated materials to BAPMAF. He also became involved with BAPMAF projects, such as the joint BAPMAF/Goethe Institute Highlife Month in February 1996. In 1995 and with the help of his son Eddie, King launched a very successful double cassette album on the local market of old Black Beats, for which I helped with the sleeve-notes. It was entitled 'Original Highlife Golden Classics' and was also released in London on CD by the Retroafrik label.

King Bruce died in September 1997 and many bands played at his wake-keeping at the Arts Council Accra on 18th October, including the university-based Local Dimension highlife band that I run with Aaron Bebe Sukura. In 2007, and ten years after King Bruce's his death, his son Eddie Bruce released the 'Golden Highlife Classics Volume Two' (Arflag label) and also made a music-video featuring his father's 1961 Decca song the 'Queens Visit', about a visit to Ghana by Britain's Queen Elizabeth. Finally, I should mention that, in connection with the prominence that King Bruce always gave to the Black Beats lyrics, particularly his own Ga ones, in 2000 the late Gloria Akutu Vondee of the English Department of the University Ghana at Legon wrote an M.A. thesis on him. It was entitled 'The Highlife Musician as an Oral Poet: A Case Study of King Bruce's Lyrics'. It analysed King Bruce's lyrics in terms of his contribution to Ga poetry.

SAKA ACQUAYE: GHANAIAN MUSICIAN, DRAMATIST AND ARTIST

Saka Acquaye is a well-known Ghanaian saxophonist, sculptor and dramatist who was born on 2 November, 1923. During the 1950s to early 60s he played with or ran a number of highlife dance bands. The first was Teacher Lamptey's Accra Orchestra and then he was briefly with E.T. Mensah's Tempos before going on to help King Bruce set up the Black Beats in 1952. Acquaye then left for the United States to do further art studies and whilst in Philadelphia he formed his African Ensemble band that made record albums and also played for Nkrumah on an American visit. Saka returned to Ghana in 1959, became an Exhibitions Officer in the Ghana Information Department and also formed the African Tones dance band and dance group that he operated until 1963 and with which, in 1961, he toured Russia. After 1963 he diverted away from dance band music into administrative cultural work and writing plays and folk opera's such as the 'Lost Fisherman'. As director of the Ghana Art Council he was involved in the 'Soul to Soul' concert held in Accra in 1971. He also helped promote the famous

Scene from Saka Acquaye's folk opera 'The Lost Fisherman' (photo Drum Magazine, November 1963)

The following interview took place at Acquaye's house at Nanka Bruce Road in Mamprobi, Accra on 14March 2004. Also present were the American film-maker John Dansey who was recording and filming the interview. Saka's daughter, Aku Sika, occasionally popped in and out to check on him during the interview, as towards the end of his life the late Saka Acquaye went completely blind. I have put my own comments within Saka's text in bracketed italics and also have added some footnotes. I began the interview by asking him about his early life.

SAKA ACQUAYE: I was born at Korle Gonno (now called just 'Gonno') – that was my father's house where I lived. Both my mother (a trader) and father never went to school, but they were visionaries and wanted me to become a teacher. At that time I didn't know anything about music except that my father used to play a concertina before we went to bed[3]. I would be sitting down on the ground with my head against his thighs whilst he played and I would be looking up to the sky at all the stars. So immediately he played it went into my head and linked with all the stars.

[1] According to James Gibbs in his 2007 obituary of Saka Acquaye and quoting W. B. Hagan, Saka's father, John Acquayefio, played on the concertina hymns, highlifes, Ga traditional songs and tunes he had learnt from his travels as a carpenter in Nigeria and the Congo.

JC: What sort music do you remember as a child?

SA: On Saturdays they had flutes and this big bass drum at the Light House [*at the beach in Jamestown*]. As a little boy some of us who got there early enough, they would give the drum to us to hold at the sides. And we would play it all away along the road to the Palladium Cinema, which we got to by eight o'clock when it was almost ready to start the film. The daily shows on Mondays to Fridays was what were called 'small films', but Saturdays were for 'big films' like 'Charlie Chaplin' and 'Madagascar Madness'. I didn't have money, so sometimes by helping hold the drum I was able to get into the entrance. What we call the 'kolomashie' and 'okpeyi' music was played by these sorts of [street] bands. But frankly speaking, I went to the beach to go and steal fish, as my mind was then not cohesive (i.e. fully formed).

JC: Tell me more of your early schooling and how you got to Achimota College

SA: I was in the Elementary Methodist School and we then moved to Adabraka near the YMCA [Young Men's Christian Association] Hostel. Then, almost all the good schools had bands. But ours was not very attractive at all and I started looking around and became a member of the Accra Royal School as I had a friend there called Tommy Grippman. My mother's house was near his family house so we used to see each other and he was then playing the flute. So I went to the Accra Royal School to join the school band. At the same time the teacher in charge of the band was the same person in charge of football. So he knew me more as a footballer and he got me in and I was doing both [football and music]. I was there for a year or two, but I felt the band was not good compared to the Government Boys School band whose attire was very military. So When I was in Standard Seven I went to that school (i.e. the Government Boys School in Kinbu) and joined their brass band, playing flute and then becoming assistant leader. The flute had a very big effect on my musical the mind. It was also there that I met some Achimota teachers who occasionally came there and they spotted me as an artist. So it was from there that I worked hard and got into Achimota Teachers Training College [on a Cadbury's Scholarship from 1943-6]. The teacher was an Ewe art teacher called Willie Tamakloe (another was Ephraim Amu). When I finished the Achimota Teachers Training Course [1946] I taught at the Government Junior School in Adabraka. And it was then that I began with the Accra Orchestra, before going back to Achimota. You see I went back to Achimota again for three years [from 1947- 1949/50] to do the art course. Professor A.M.Opoku was one of the art-course teachers who taught me there.

JC: Tell me more about the Accra Orchestra and its famous music man Teacher Lamptey.

SA: It was when I was at the Government Junior School opposite Kingsway Stores in Adabraka. So every day after 4 o'clock I could walk quickly to the Accra Orchestra and rehearse on alto saxophone. When you are from Korle Bu going to the Post Office and cross the rail line across Korle Lagoon, you then take the second turning where you have a street light. The corner house was Teacher Lamptey's family house – and they rehearsed upstairs.

JC: Many years ago E.T. Mensah described Teacher Lamptey to me as he was in the 1930s. So what was Lamptey and his Accra Orchestra like in the late 1940s when you joined them?

SA: He was a teacher, a goal keeper and music director, and he taught at the Government Boys School near the PWD [Public Works Department] in Ussher Town. His was a full orchestra with three saxophones two alto and one tenor, and a couple of trombones. I'm not sure if there was a guitar. There was also double bass, but no violins. I got on well with the saxophone and King Bruce was there, but I didn't know him then. In my case it took me less than one year to get ready with them. We copied some of the western sounds and popular songs from abroad and that's what Teacher Lamptey helped me with.

JC: When did you first think about taking up music more seriously? Was it after joining the Accra Orchestra?

SA; No it was after I finished the three year Achimota art course that I had the idea to form an orchestra. Actually after Achimota I was teaching art at St Augustine's Training College in Cape Coast [1950-2] and some of the students there were very good at guitar. Then around 1950 or 1951 I went to Britain to do athletics as I was a runner and a hurdler and eight of us were selected to take a tour of Britain[4]. It was when I got back that my mind went off teaching. So when I had been at St. Augustine's for two years, I decided to resign and I started looking around for some musicians and had the opportunity of leading a band – before King Bruce.

JC: Where was this band located?

[4]James Gibbs (2007) says that Saka was a gifted footballer and when he left Achimota, he was among the foremost athletes in the country and represented the Gold Coast as a hurdler in the UK and captained the national team.

SA: In Accra, as I was then working for the Kingsway Store on High Street. I formed a band that rehearsed at Farisco House in Adabraka and the owner of the instruments played the clarinet and I played the tenor sax. I'll tell you a story. The tubaphone player used to fall asleep so the clarinettist would then use the microphone to make a bass sound – it was very effective. Jerry Hansen was playing the alto sax and he was a funny guy. As I mentioned I was working at Kingsway and Jerry Hansen was working nearby, and if I didn't stand outside of the gate early before he came out, he would run away. When he saw me waiting he couldn't run away. And then we got King Bruce who had started trumpet from Britain. Because King Bruce had a car he helped us a lot travelling around and we began rehearsing at his house in Korle Woko. His sound was not very firm or convincing – but gradually improved. However his compositions were pretty good. He was more of a poet.

JC: So when was the name the Black Beats given to the band?

SA: We asked ourselves what name. I am not sure if it were me or him. I think it must have been King Bruce more so than me. We were looking for the kind of name that would suit us, as we were looking for an African expression. When I left in 1953 he took over. He had wonderful ideas and they sent me one of his records and I was highly impressed by the sound.

JC: I believe you went to Philadelphia in 1953 to study fine arts[5]. Tell me about your musical activities then.

SA: When I got to America the bongos had become very popular throughout the world and I met a group of African Americans drummers who had never met an African. So we started a band and they were very hard working and I taught them traditional music, not highlife. One of them was called Garvine Masseaux and another Bobby Crowder who later came to Ghana. We started with drummers and we later expanded into an orchestra called the African Ensemble. This man picked bass, this man picked vibes and this one guitar. It was a tremendous orchestra and we recorded an album called 'Gold Coast Saturday Night'[6]. Also I was teaching African dance in Philadelphia[7].

[5]According to James Gibbs (2007) Saka studied art, sculpture and industrial design at the Pennsylvania Academy of Fine Arts in Philadelphia, (1953-6), and then Advertising and Public Relations at the Charles Morris Price School (1957-9).
[6]This album was recorded by 'Saka Acquaye and His African Ensemble from Ghana' and was released in the USA around 1959 by Elektra (ELK 167).
[7]It was there that Acaquaye established the West African Cultural Society to infuse African art-forms into American culture. One of his graduates between 1952 and 1955 was the well-known African American choreographer, the late Arhur Hall.

JC: I understand that you came back to Ghana in 1959 and then formed a dance band here?

SA: Yes, I immediately set up the African Tones, a full sixteen-piece dance band that took me a year to set up. We made our debut for the Nkrumah Trust Fund and after that I set up a dance troupe of boys and girls with the band backing it. And [in 1965] I wrote a dance-play called 'Obadzeng Goes to Town'. It was sponsored by Coca-Cola and we performed it for three weeks at a cinema near the Post Office. Immediately we finished Nkrumah sent for me and wanted a command performance. He was so impressed that he said he was taking it to the Soviet Union. So in 1961 we went for six weeks. They gave us a plane all to ourselves as the group was big, and the stewardess was a West Indian called Ms. Warren provided for us by our government.

JC: Tell me more about the Africa Tones members which I believe you operated up until 1963.

SA: The leader was the trumpeter Amartey Laryea, and then we had Nii Oscar Tei. My point was to refine and lift things up, as some highlifes are raw and from the gutter. You see when I was in L.A. I went to see an English music group from Britain. Then one of the players began running in and out of the group and another one was going to grab him and he dodged. I burst out laughing and the audience, which was white, were all looking at me – as they were all coolly sitting down. This [i.e. dramatic and humorous novelty] is what we need to grab and pull our people out. So this is the way we have to organise things and move somewhere. Just look at how well this Osibisa group did in London. This is also the way I planned Wulomei's stage movements when I took then to the States the first time, when it was sponsored by the Smithsonian and Ken Holiday was the stage manager[8]. There were two big drums, the stage was open and the audience was expecting the group to come from behind [i.e. the stage]. But suddenly they were coming from here and there – and 'boom boom' [i.e. a dramatic entrance from the front and sides].

JC: How did Nkrumah's coming to power in 1957 effect you?

SA: I was not in this country in 1957, I was in Philadelphia. However, Nkrumah and his entourage came to the States in 1958 when my band was functioning well, so we were

[8]This was in June/July 1975, when the Wulomei, accompanied by the Kwaa Mensah Group and Salisu Mahama's Gonje Group made a forty-five day tour of America, which began at the Festival of American Folklore held in Washington, D.C.

asked to come to New York. Nkrumah was giving a reception at Carnegie Hall and my band played there. Jimmy [James] Moxon was also there. He was then the Minister of Information[9]. Afterwards he called me aside and said he had got the word from Nkrumah that I should come. So in 1959 I came home to become the Exhibitions Officer for the Ghana Information Department on the High Street with Jimmy Moxon as the boss.

James Moxon with bow-tie standing behind seated Kwame and Fatia Nkrumah and the American photographer Willis 'Bill" Bell (Information Service photo via the late Moxon)

JC: As you had an important governmental position, why then did you leave Ghana again in 1964?

SA: When I came back Madam Dubois[10] was in charge of the construction of television and I met her one night at a cocktail. She told me that I had been ear-marked to head the arts section of the television when it was ready. But she said she had heard that I was planning to go back to the States. I said 'oh yes' but just for a short while to

[9] James Moxon, the British ex-colonial District Commissioner who had stayed on in Ghana after independence to become Nkrumah's first Minister of Information and also a government gazetted chief in Aburi. In the 1960s Saka also made a bust of this colourful character.
[10] She was the wife of the African American thinker W.E.B. DuBois who, in 1961, had been invited to settle in Ghana by Nkrumah to head the Encyclopaedia Africana project.

study folk opera. I told her that whenever I used to go to the office [the Information Department] I did nothing, as some people there had blocked my goals and sabotaged me. Then one Monday morning there was a call from Nkrumah's office that I should go and see him at 12 o'clock. When I got there he told me that I was going to be the guy for theatre. I don't know what Nkrumah had been told, but he was annoyed that I was leaving the country. He said he didn't want me to go and what help did I need from him to stay. I said the best help would be to let me go, and he burst out laughing as I explained to him that I had failed to produce this folk-opera thing in the way I wanted. I gave him the background on it and told him if we could do it properly the country would move forward. He was looking at me with eyes wide open. He picked the telephone and called, I'm not sure if it or were Mr. Oku or Mr. Mpreh, and told them to let me go. So I went to the States in 1964.

According to James Gibbs, it was a Fulbright Scholarship that enabled Saka Acquaye to return to America in 1964 where he spent two years at UCLA studying opera and theatre. He also reformed his African Ensemble that recorded a number of albums on the Elektra, Nonesuch and Asylum labels. The Nonsuch recording (72026) called 'Saka Acquaye: Highlife and Other Popular Music' was released in 1969 and was later re-released on CD in 2002. According to this record's sleeve-notes Saka Acquaye played drums, flute, tenor saxophone and the album explored a fusion of highlife and free jazz. Some of the other musicians included were the previously mentioned Robert or Bobby Crowder and Garvine Masseaux, as well as the free jazz saxophonist Charles Earland and the Ghanaian drummer Joseph Acquaye.

As Saka Acquaye was in the States running his African Ensemble and studying folk-opera between 1964-8, he was there in 1966 when Nkrumah was overthrown in 1966. Two years late Acquaye returned 1968 when he was appointed as Head of the Ghana Arts Council from 1968-72. This was when his musical play 'The Lost Fisherman' was produced and the popular Saturday matinee Anansekrom programs initiated. As mentioned in the introduction, in the early 1970s Saka Acquaye helped promote the 'Ga cultural' group Wulomei and he and producer Kojo Donkor helped produce some of their first recording ('Walatu Walasa' and Wulome in Drum Conference'). Saka Acquaye was also the principal local organizer of the 'Soul to Soul' concert held at

Independence (then called Black Star) Square in 1971 that brought to Ghana many top American acts, like Wilson Picket, Roberta Flack, Ike and Tina Turner, the Voices of East Harlem, Les McCann, Eddie Harris and Santana. Although Saka died aged eight-three on February 27th 2007 his enduring sculptural works are still visible in Greater Accra as the J.B. Danquah monument at Danquah Circle, the Guggisberg monument at Korle Bu Hospital and the horn playing figures at the entrance of the old African Studies building and School of Performing Arts at the University of Ghana at Legon.

In 2011, The Lost Fisherman was re- enacted at the National Theatre by the Saka Acquaye Memorial Theatre Group. It was directed by Nii Addokwei Moffat, George Dzikunu and Moses Dortey and stage designer David Amoo. It starred Soloman Sampa and Nii Odoi Mensah and was sponsored by the National Theatre and the Danish Ghana Cultural Fund. The play will tour Ghana and abroad.

Chapter 15

THE BENIN REPUBLIC'S IGNACE DE SOUZA AND HIS BLACK SANTIAGOS IN GHANA

Ignace de Souza was born in 1937 in the Republic of Benin (formerly called Dahomey) and was brought up in its capital city, Cotonou. He played trumpet and sax in Alfa Jazz, the country's first professional dance band, and later moved to Ghana where he first joined Spike Anyankor's Rhythm Aces, the Shambros Band and finally in 1964 formed his own Black Santiagos. Ignace was the first musician to play Congo jazz music onstage in Ghana, where he stayed until 1970. He then returned to Cotonou and then to Lagos, where his band became the resident group at the Ritz Hotel. I met Ignace in Benin City, Nigeria, during the latter part of 1975 when he was playing at Victor Uwaifo's Club 400 during the Black Santiagos' Christmas tour of east and midwest Nigeria. His band was composed of Nigerian and Dahomean musicians and featured a Senegalese singer on Congo numbers and the Ghanaian Picket (McGod) as the soul singer. Below is an interview I had with him on the 27th of December 1975 in Benin City and first question I asked him was how did he first become interested in music.

DE SOUZA: When I was young I learned music in the cultural way (i.e. traditional Fon music). From school I never liked music first of all, but after schooling I had a friend in Cotonou who kept forcing me to do music for two years. Then one morning in 1953 we went to the place that someone (a local man) had opened as he was wanting to form a band. He had brought instruments and asked me what type I wanted to play. I saw many instruments and there were two trumpets and I said I would like one because I saw only three valves and thought it would be simple to play. They laughed and gave me an alto sax and showed me how to play it. The band was called Alfa Jazz, and the man told us after everything was going on we would be paid and would have a salary. We had a tenor player from Paris. He worked at the bank and every day he came in to teach us the theoretical part of the music and played with our group on Saturdays. Later on, the manager brought in two musicians from Nigeria: one was Babyface Paul on tenor sax, and the other, Zeal Onyia, on trumpet. When Paul came he was pushing me on the sax, but when Zeal came I enjoyed the way he played better, so I switched to trumpet. So Zeal started teaching me the trumpet and I abandoned the sax. Since then I've concentrated on the trumpet. We played dance music, like quicksteps, highlifes and boleros. At that time E.T. Mensah was reigning so we used to do some of his songs. It was a professional band and there were ten people in it.

JC: Were there any other bands in the Benin at that time?

DE SOUZA: We had an orchestra formed by the police and the soldiers. By then you know it was the French who were ruling the country and they didn't encourage any (dance band) music, only the military orchestras. E. T. Mensah and others used to play, as we had some nightclub owners who went to Ghana to bring them, but there were no guitar bands, although in some of the villages there were brass bands.

JC: Why did you leave Alfa Jazz? And what did you do afterwards?

DE SOUZA: After everything was going nicely with the Alfa Jazz, the manager stopped paying us, so everybody had to find his way and I chose to go to Ghana in 1955. There I joined a band called the Rhythm Aces. Zeal and Paul Babyface had left Cotonou to join the Rhythm Aces before me, but by the time I arrived they had left for Lagos. I played in the Rhythm Aces until 1956 when I went to the Lido Nightclub (Accra), playing in a band called the Shambros, run by the Shahim Brothers who were Lebanese. These Lebanese people were making a hell of a lot of money and at the end of every month they wouldn't pay us. All the time we were pocketless (i.e. broke). I advised my musicians that we should start a bank account so that after one or two years we should have enough money to buy our own instruments, because these people were making fools of us. The secret leaked out and they stopped me playing for three months. But when people saw my absence, the band didn't go too well because during those days the French music (i.e. rumbas etc.) was making money. So the brothers brought me back and I told them that if they wanted me to work, 'number one' I would like to be paid more than the £9 a month I had been earning, and I would always like to have my pay at the end of the month; 'number two', as there was no day off, I would like the band to have a rest every week on Mondays. So we signed the contract and I started getting £15 a month I always kept £10 and saved it. Between 1954 and 1960 I started buying the instruments bit by bit. Then in 1961, I composed the chacha number 'Paulina' and on the other side the highlife number 'Patience is Best'. The record became a hit and I used the Shambros (i.e. band members with Bill Hesse on guitar) in the recording but changed the name to the 'Melody Aces.'

I had the contract with Decca, and after the recording I paid the boys and kept what remained. I was lucky the record was a success and I made £700 in royalties, so I persuaded the man from Decca to sell me a set of instruments instead of paying me the money. I bought two tenor saxophones, one alto, one trumpet, one guitar and I already had the drums and the other instruments. The man from Decca balanced me the rest, which was £350. I even bought materials for uniforms for whenever I would need it. I kept the instruments under my bed because I didn't want anyone to see them. By 1964, all my instruments were complete and I was finding a way to get out of the Shambros when there was trouble between the proprietor and the Minister of the Interior. The Lido was locked up and I had to run to the T.U.C. (Trade Union Council), where I made a report and we fought it out. They subsequently paid all that was due. I got a reasonable amount, went back to Cotonou and had my passport done. When I was there, I thought of what sort of music I should introduce in Ghana; because at that time, dance bands like the Ramblers, the Armed Forces Band and the Black Beats were in top form. At that time there was nothing like African Brothers (i.e., guitar bands operating in the urban night-clubs) and, in fact, Ampadu (leader of the African Brothers) was working under me during the Lido times. Everyone used to come to me as I taught the theoretical part of music. When I thought about which music to introduce, I knew that there was nothing like Congo music in Ghana, so I brought a bass player from Dahomey and went to Togoland to join with two boys who sang Congo music. I also brought many Congo records with me and we learned them nicely in Accra. I formed the Black Santiagos and I made big posters, hand bills and radio announcements for our out-dooring which was on the 11th of July, 1964 at the Metropole, where we played side by side with the Ramblers. That day there was a big turnout and many big men came, including some from the Dahomean Consulate, and I made almost £500 from the gate.

Ignace de Souza (standing in suit with trumpet)
and his Black Santiagos in Accra in 1962

JC: Did you travel much with the band?

DE SOUZA: The band used to travel all over Ghana, but we didn't travel outside until Fela Anikulapo-Kuti started coming to Ghana around 1968. He used to play at the Ringway Hotel, which I had started to rent in 1965. Many bands played there. On Fridays the Uhuru or the Ramblers used to play, and when Geraldo Pino (and the Heartbeats) was around in 1967 I kept him and his boys at the Hotel. When Fela became a good friend he said that we should come to Nigeria for a few weeks. In 1968 we played our first show with him at the Glover Memorial Hall in Lagos and the next day we played at the Surulere Night Club (Fela's first Africa Shrine) and there was a big turnout. After that we went to Lagos from time to time. During the Nigerian Civil War we toured all the Northern States and played at Cotonou and Lome on the way back to Ghana. We often used to play at Lome as it is only 120 miles from Accra.

JC: When did you leave Ghana?

DE SOUZA: I left Ghana in 1970 because of the Aliens Order and I had to go as I was seeing my people being molested. Many of my musicians were Nigerians, and my organist was a professional Italian musician called Franco. So I went back to Cotonou. I was doing music there, but not like before; there it's not like Ghana where people patronize show business. There it's a bit boring.

JC: What were the most popular bands in Cotonou and Lome ten years ago – and today?

DE SOUZA: In Dahomey we had the Jonas Pedro Dance Band and Elrigo and his Los Commandos, all playing Latin American rhythms and Congo music. In Togo there was Erico Jazz, the Los Muchachos and the Melo Togo Dance Orchestra. At the moment in Cotonou we have Jonas Pedro, Elrigo, the Poly Rhythmic Orchestra, the Les Astronauts, Disc Afrique and my own band. In Lome things are a bit better because the type of politics our people are doing in Dahomey will not permit bands to do anything good. Musicians have to play from seven to eleven in the evening and then close up because of the curfew. At the moment in Lome there is the Wilkomen Band and bands at nightclubs like the Le Reve and Marquilla Noka. The bands that play soul music have boys from Ghana. There are many Ghanaians in Togo.

JC: What are the main differences in the dance music of the English and French-speaking countries?

DE SOUZA: In the French countries right now they like Congo type of music, which is purely African, and they like a variety of music. Anything you play they will dance to. But here in the English-speaking countries they don't seem to like African music; they like copyright and soul and others which are not our fruit. In the French-speaking countries you can't keep on playing one way all the time, and if you play African music they like it.

JC: What are your plans?

DE SOUZA: We are based in Cotonou, but we are now on tour of Nigeria (in fact the band remained in Nigeria, after this interview). In the east they like highlife, but in the mid-west they don't; they like funk and soul. You know, in Nigeria, Victor Uwaifo and the juju bands are playing good African music. Fela has his own type of music. His arrangements are very good musically and theoretically, but I feel that it's still European because the background is jazzy, and jazz is not our music. In Ghana, they have many chances of improving African music, but the musicians there just play soul, soul, soul. If we don't take care, African music will be lost and our children will suffer. If we push the African music it will be good.

After this 1975 interview Ignace spent quite a while in Nigeria, but finally went back to the Benin Republic and during the rest of the 1970s and early 1980s where his Black Santiagos were based in Cotonou. In 1976, they backed the Cameroonian makossa music star Sam Fan Thomas in his album 'Funky New Bell'. Then in the late seventies Ignace and his Black Santiagos collaborated in albums like 'Dou Dagbe We' with Honoré Avolonto, one of Benin's most prolific composers. Ignace also lent a helping hand to talented musicians. For instance he was so impressed by the Ghanaian borborbor highlife musician Abebe (Jonathan Kakraba) who visited Cotonou in 1978 that Ignace employed him in his group and helped find a producer for Abebe's first solo album 'Mawu Ana.' This is what Abebe told me in June 2010 about this: the first of twenty-five albums that he and his Bantus Band released over the years. .

> I went to Benin to look for a producer for my 'Mawu Ana' recording and I ended up lodging with Ignace's musicians as some of them were Ghanaians; like the bassist the late Kwesi Kari Kari, the drummer Osei and a guitarist who is now in Germany. At that time a girl called Georgillia from Cotonou, who was a singer and composer, was working with Ignace to help him launch one of his albums. She had a show and was rehearsing with the Black Santiagos and I contacted her that I would provide some dancers for her. So I trained three girls and danced with them and the Black Santiagos backed us. It was through this that Ignace got to know me well. Later I even jammed with his Black Santiagos. Also Ignace helped me to get a producer when he introduced me to an Alhaji Siaka who paid the entire cost of the 'Mawu Ana' album.

As there was not enough work for a band in the relatively small country of Benin, Ignace decided to relocate his group. So in the mid-eighties he moved permanently to Lagos, but sometimes worked with visiting singers. For instance, in 1988 Ignace played trumpet on the first LP of the Ghanaian singer Pozo Hayes entitled 'Looking over There.'

During Ignace's recording career he released highlifes, pop songs, Afro-beats, Afro-Cuban cha-chas and Congo jazz style songs sung in a variety of language. These included the Ghanaian Akan dialects of Fanti and Twi, the Ga language of Accra, the Yoruba language of western Nigeria, his native Fon language, the Ewe language of

Ghana and neighbouring Togo, as well as Pidgin English. The following are details of some of these recordings:

With the Shambros band Ignace in the late 1950s released the highlife 'Ma Aya Nwet'. Then in 1962, and with exactly the same bandsmen but using the recording name 'Melody Aces', Ignace released several songs for Decca. There was the Yoruba highlife 'Suru lo Dara' and the Fanti 'twist' called 'Asaw Fofor' as Chubby Checker's music was beginning to become popular in West Africa by this time. However, and as he mentions in his interview, the biggest hit of this recording session was the Fanti cha-cha 'Paulina'.

After Ignace formed his Black Santiagos in 1964 he continued releasing a string of hits between 1965 and 1969 with the earliest being the Ewe cha-cha 'My Cherie', the Fanti highlife 'Anyenko' and the Twi highlifes 'Asem Alo Me' and 'Augustina'. There were also two 'cara-cara' songs[11] sung in Ewe and entitled 'Caroline Bateau' and 'Mayape'. A Beatles type 'twist and shake' pop-song he released in 1966 was 'Pretty Little Angel'. Later songs by the Black Santiagos included the Ewe highlife 'Papa Kou Maman', the Fon highlife 'Adan Egbomi' and the Pidgin English one 'Monkey No Fine'. Around 1968/9, Ignace also began experimenting with Afro-soul (or what later became called 'Afro-beat') in releases such as 'Ole' sung in Yoruba and 'Bani Wo Dzo' sung in Ga. To enable him to produce songs in these multiple language and styles, Ignace used a combination of Ghanaian as well as some Nigerian, Togolese and Beninoise musicians. For some of the Fanti highlifes he collaborated with Julius Croffie and for the Ewe ones with Willie Dohnu and Theodore Foli. For the Twi highlifes he collaborated with E.K Asare and also Ani Johnson who at the time was with the Ghana Police Dance Band and was writing compositions for them as well as for the Ramblers and Tempos[12].

Although Ignace was killed in a car crash in 1988, from the early 1990s some of Ignace's top hits became available on the international market. These were through two CD's released by John Storm Roberts American based Original Music Company. These are 'Giants of Dance Band Highlife' (OMCD 011) and 'The Great Unknowns: Ignace de Souza' (OMCD 026) released in 1994.

[11]'Cara-cara' (or 'kara-kara') is another name for Congo jazz
[12]In 1971 Johnson went on to form his famous Nsawam based Parrots (Nkoo) guitar-band.

Chapter 16

STAN PLANGE OF THE BROADWAY AND UHURU DANCE-BANDS

Stan Plange (standing third left) and the Uhuru band in 1968. Faisal Helwani is in front of Stan, Mac Tontoh (seated right), Eddie Ntreh (extreme right) and Potato (right with pork-pie hat)

Stan Plange is an Accra-born musician who has been playing guitar in dance bands for many years. In the late fifties he was with the Downbeats, Comets and Stargazers, and was treasurer of the Nigerian Union of Musicians between 1958 and 1961. It was then that Stan first met his good friend Fela-Kuti who had just finished high school in Abeokuta, but used to come to Lagos to play trumpet with Victor Olaiya's Cool Cats highlife band. On returning from Nigeria Stan joined the Broadway Band which was renamed Uhuru in late 1963. In 1965 Stan became leader of the Uhuru, arranged their music and recordings and travelled with them abroad several times. He left the group in 1972 to lead the Black Star Line dance band. Then in 1973, he teamed up with Faisal Helwani 'F' Promotions to launch the Obibini record company and help produce records for Hedzoleh, Basa-Basa and the Bunzus. The following is an interview I had with Stan Plange at the Napoleon Club in Osu on the 15th of February, 1977. I first asked Stan about his childhood and early musical influences on him.

PLANGE: I was born in April 1937 and although I am a Ga, my family originally came from Elmina. I was in the school choir in elementary school at Achimota, but I wouldn't say this was the reason I became interested in music as I tried to run away when there was singing practice. Our singing master claimed that I was a good tenor singer, so anytime I wasn't in he noticed. Later, I did music when I was attending secondary school at the Ghana College in Winneba. My father, was a trumpet player in the old Accra Orchestra of Teacher Lamptey. More important was when I used to see a group called the Rhythm Aces when we were staying near the Kit-Kat Club at Adabraka opposite the Rodger Cinema. We used to go and stand outside behind the wall, and it was they who moved me to learn an instrument. Spike Anyankor was the leader, with Zeal Onyia and Babyface Paul from Nigeria. Ray Ellis was on piano, Glen Cofie on trombone, Aggrey on guitar and Jimmy Wee Shall on double bass. They all came out of the Tempos except Freddy Tetteh, now with the Continentals and Buddy Squire who came from the Hotshots and is now with the Eden Church Band. The Rhythm Aces came out with a unique sound compared to the Tempos, Joe Kelly's band, the Red Spots and the Hot Shots. In those days the Rhythm Aces was the best and had a big influence on me. So I had to learn an instrument and forced myself into the Downbeats.

JC: The Downbeats was your first band'?

PLANGE: Yes, I joined them in 1957, although I was practically playing nothing. I had left school by then and had worked with the Ghana Bank for a time. The Downbeats was led by Bill Friday who is dead now and who graduated from Bobby Benson's band. He was an Igbo. I learned to play a bit of (double) bass and congas. Unfortunately, two days before my first engagement at the Premier Hotel, Akim Oda, Eddie Quansah came down from Kumasi to come and play. So I lost the bass. Then, after we returned, Eddie said he was going to Kumasi to collect some things, but never came back. So, I went back to the bass and played it for one year. Then our guitarist Okyere left. So, Oscarmore, who's now in London, came in. We had an engagement in Lome which was meant to be for the week-end, but after the promoter asked us to stay. Oscar said he had to go back to Ghana, so I had to take up the guitar. That year we toured the whole of Togoland as at that time there were no bands in Togo, and for all engagements they used to get bands from Ghana.

JC: What happened when you returned?

PLANGE: I left the Downbeats and joined a new group that had been formed at the Tip-Toe, called the Comets, second band to the resident band, the Rakers. It was formed by Ray Ellis, our pianist and leader with myself on guitar, Prince Boateng on trumpet (later with the National Orchestra and the Continentals), Lex King on alto sax, and Adlib Young Anim on trombone (later with the Uhuru), plus Tom Price on drums. Just three months after the band collapsed and we all thought Ray Ellis was to blame. The rest of us went to form a band called Zenith. It was financed by the Kwahu Union in Accra who had first formed the Kwahu Union Orchestra led by Anima, but it had disintegrated and the instruments were left around, which we used. After forming the Zenith we wanted a leader, since we didn't think we were ripe to lead a band. We saw (Pete) Vandepuie but he wasn't ready to lead. He's now in London and has played with Eddie Quansah and Johnny Nash. We saw George Lee – the same! So, we were forced to go back and call Ray Ellis again. Again, after three months the band collapsed. Then all of us left for Kumasi to play at the Wilben Hotel and then went on to join the Stargazers. That was in 1958. The original leader was Glen Cofie but he left us and Eddie Quansah took over. The same year I left for Lagos to re-join the Downbeats since Bill Friday had moved back to Lagos; he sent for me and I stayed there until 1961. At first we played at a club called Nad's Club de Paris but the attendance wasn't good so we went to the Ambassador Hotel in Lagos for two-and-a-half years. We played highlifes and there were only four Nigerians in the group, the rest were Ghanaians.

191

Later one of the Nigerians left and was replaced by the Ghanaian trombonist Pete Kwetey, now with the Armed Forces Band. When I was in Lagos I was also playing with the Nigerian Broadcasting Orchestra as guitarist and arranger.

JC: Tell me more about what it was like in Nigeria.

PLANGE: The Nigerian music scene was very low. Except for the horn players, the Nigerian musicians weren't really good; the guitarists nil. Juju music wasn't recognized at that time. Nobody wanted to hear juju, it was played in backyards. Highlife was the most popular music then and the most popular band was E.C. Arinze and his Empire Orchestra. In the Downbeats, I was the arranger and second leader, Joe Mensah was inside as a singer, George Emissah who is now leading the Uhuru on alto sax, Nat Hammond (Lee Ampoumah) on bongos and Akwei 'I Zero' on congas. He now plays alto sax for the Black Star Line Band. Joe Mensah and George Emissah went on leave and never returned as they joined the Broadway dance band, run by the management of the Zenith Hotel in Takoradi and led by Sammy Obot. At that time, Broadway was being regarded as a national band in Ghana as I had been travelling with the late Kwame Nkrumah, and when Ghana Airways was being inaugurated the band was going to Khartoum, Beirut, and so on. So we began to think there were better opportunities back in Ghana rather than in Nigeria. Fortunately, the Stargazers band was being reformed by the present chairman of the Kumasi Youngsters Club and timber contractor, Collins Kusi, or D.K.C. as he is popularly known. He sent for me and I played under the leadership of Adlib Young. From the Stargazers I left to join the Broadway in Takoradi around 1964 or 1965.

JC: Up to that time had you done any recordings?

PLANGE: Yes, I made recordings with the Stargazers. I did the arrangements. Then when I was in Lagos with the Downbeats we did a couple of recordings at Hubert Ogunde's studio in Lagos for Philips, with a group called the Harmonaires. I arranged the band and we did two singles that did very well. They were highlifes with guitars, drums and vocals, but no horns.

JC: How did the name Broadway get changed to the Uhuru dance band?

PLANGE: What happened was that we (Broadway) came down to Accra for the Arts Centre course in traditional drumming and dancing. We stayed for three months and were housed at the Puppet Theatre near the Drama Studio. Our group, George Lee's Messengers and the Farmers Council Band took advantage of the course. It was free for musicians. When we returned, there was some trouble about our salary so we decided that we would work with the management on a percentage basis. But the percentage they wanted was too much, taking into account the old state of the instruments. So, we left and within two months we got E.K. Dadson and Krobo Edusei to buy us instruments. In those days the whole set cost £1,600. Later Dadson paid back Krobo Edusei his share, so the band became Dadson's property. We continued to use the name Broadway as the manager of the Zenith hadn't registered it; in fact we registered it. However, Edusei took us to court saying that the name belonged to him and he sued us £26,000 for the thirteen of us. He lost, but kept the name and was awarded £75 costs. So, we chose the name Uhuru (Swahili for 'freedom'). This was in 1964 [actually late 1963]. Sammy Obot was leader until 1965 when I took over. We then went to Moscow for about six weeks when Ghana Airways inaugurated its first flight to Moscow. In fact this was when we were still called Broadway, and we played on television, at Lumumba University and at the Metropole Hotel, We went together with Bob Cole, K. Gyasi, Onyina and Sampson the comedian. In 1966 or 1967 we went to Nigeria on tour with Chubby Checker, went back to Ghana and returned just about when the Nigerian civil war was about to start. We left Nsukka and three days later the Biafran war started. We used to like the east best, as we had a lot of fans there and made a lot of money. The east was always the best market for Ghanaian music. In the late '60s we made an LP for Phillips and in 1970 made an L.P. for Decca in London. At that time the band had three trumpets, three trombones and five saxes in the front line

JC: What about the East Africa trip you made in 1968?

PLANGE: Faisal Helwani was the promoter and the trip was sponsored by the East Africa Airways. We were on the programme together with the Rolling Beats dance-troupe led by Jackie Mensah as well as Guy Warren and Willie Cheetham. When we were leaving, over half of my band didn't go. What happened was that the manager of the Uhurus, E.K. Dadson, said Faisal must pay half the money before going, but by the night before we were meant to leave he hadn't come to pay. So by eight in the evening Mr. Dadson told the secretary, who had most of our passports, to go home.

Uhuru Dance Band in 1966 – Chubby Checker and on his left and right
Stan Plange and Charlotte Dada. (Photo Teddy Addo standing third from left)

He left, thinking we wouldn't be travelling the following day. But after he left Faisal came to pay the amount and it didn't occur to Mr. Dadson that our passports were with his secretary. The following day we were expecting this secretary to come to the airport with the rest of our passports. We waited and waited, so in the end I rushed down to the office but the secretary wasn't there. I finally managed to get the passports but by the time I got back to the airport the plane had gone with Faisal, the Rolling Beats, Willie Cheetham and four of my boys. Guy Warren didn't go either, even though Faisal sent someone to call him; he was annoyed or something. So 70% of my boys, Guy Warren and myself had to wait a week before going. We met up with the rest in Kampala where we played a couple of nightclubs there and also on television. From there, we came down to Mombasa and then to Nairobi. We spent about five weeks in East Africa altogether. We met one band from the Congo there. In fact the local groups in East Africa play a type of Congo music sung in Swahili. They didn't play any highlife.

JC: You left the Uhurus in 1972. Why did you leave, and what happened afterwards?

PLANGE: I had trouble with the management. You see, what happened was that I was the artist and the repertoire representative for E.M.I. in Lagos. I got the Uhurus and Hedzoleh to record there. In fact, I was the first man to get a group from Ghana to the eight-track E.M.I. studio. I went back in 1972 to help in the re-mixing of the Hedzoleh and Uhuru recordings and after I returned there was some problem between myself and the Uhuru management, and I had to resign. After this I teamed up with Faisal to form a record company called Obibini Records. We decided we weren't going to give the Hedzoleh recordings to E.M.I. and we released two singles on our own label and intended to release an L.P. as well. After I had done the recordings I left with the tapes for Italy to negotiate for the songs to be on the sound-track of the film 'Contact'. Around this time Hugh Masekela came and when I was in Italy Hedzoleh and Hugh went to Nigeria to record the numbers again for the L.P. 'Introducing Hedzoleh'. Most of the titles on that recording were the same as the first recordings, but with Hugh Masekela on trumpet. After my association with Faisal, we couldn't go on due to financial problems and I went to the Black Star Line as Musical Director of the band. I was there for nearly two years and I left because I thought I was wasting my time there. After playing with private bands I realized that the musicians in the government or corporation bands differed from the ones in private groups. In government and corporation bands the musicians know at the end of every month they will get their salary whatever comes, so they don't care if they make mistakes or don't learn their assignments properly. In the private groups you know that if you don't play well, or don't get any engagements, at the end of the month you'll be wondering where your salary is coming from. I tried to make changes in the bureaucracy of the Black Star Line Band but some of the musicians had been there 12 or 15 years; so in the end, I left.

JC: Could you tell me about some of the recordings you did with the Uhurus?

PLANGE: I started doing experimental recordings with the Uhurus. My first was I 'Eno Brebre', which was all about advising a woman to be patient if she quarrels with her husband and not to wash her dirty linen in public. In those days, dance band musicians looked down on guitar-band musicians as they thought they were an inferior. Nevertheless I tried to bring the two together and used dance band and guitar-band musicians at the recording. From the guitar-bands I used Frempong Manso as singer – he is now known as Osofo Dadzie. For the guitarist, I used S.K. Oppong who is now the guitarist for the Osofo Dadzie concert party. In fact, the reverse side of the record was Frempong Manso's composition 'O Mama Beka Akwantumu' which said that if any trouble happens to a person the cause is bound to be another person. The other musicians were from the Uhuru dance band; like the vocalist Ed Ntreh, the drummer Rim Obeng, who's in the States now, and the Krobo singer Charlotte Dada who was with the Uhuru at that time. Later on, we did two more recordings and in these we used the same vocal group, plus Pat Thomas. The records were released on my own record label Nats Egnalp (Stan Plange backwards) Music Publishers.

JC: What were your most successful recordings?

PLANGE: The ones I did with Oppong and also another I composed with Joe Mensah called 'Uhuru Special'. But in fact, I didn't do so many compositions as arrangements.

JC: Uhuru also used to play some beebop, isn't that so?

PLANGE: The Uhuru itself played big-band jazz but a small group within the Uhuru was playing beebop and appearing on television. It was called the Bogarte Sounds, with Ebo Dadson on tenor sax and Rim Obeng on drums [also Mac Tontoh]. It was produced by this man who started Osofo Dadzie, Nana Bosompra. In fact it was I who introduced them to Nana. It was in 1969, and they started a television program called 'Jatakrom' which later was called Osofo Dadzie.

Due to the collapse of the Ghanaian music industry in the late 1970s, Stan went to Nigeria to do business and returned home in 1996 to become the director of the GBC (Ghana Broadcasting Company) Band. In 1998 he became the arranger and co-producer of a big-band highlife CD called 'Crabs in a Bucket' (Asante/Oyigbo label) with the internationally famous Ghanaian percussionist Okyerema Asante (of Hedzoleh and Paul Simon's Graceland tour fame) and American vibes player Nick Robertson (one-time Head of USIS in Ghana). Bassist for this group was a long-time friend of Stan, Slim 'Bright' Amoako. Slim began his career on double-bass with the Casino Orchestra of Koforidua in 1954 and then moved on to Broadway, and from

1972-2003 the GBC Combo. He then moved onto to the National Symphony Orchestra.

Stan became Acting Chairman of the Songwriters Association of Ghana and the Treasurer of the now defunct Ghana Old Musicians and Artists Welfare Association (GOMAWA). He was involved with the early negotiations I initiated, after I went in Washington DC in 2000, to notify interested Ghanaian parties of the World Bank project to assist the African music industry. Then, the February 2005 US Embassy sponsored Black History Month, in which I was involved, gave out a number of Cultural Ambassador Awards at a ceremony at the Du Bois Centre – of which Stan was a recipient. A few years later, he retired to Kaneshie but set up a music website for his EGNALP publishing company. He also occasionally made public appearances; for instance, he attended Ghanaba's wake-keeping in 2008 and the celebration of the collaboration between the Goethe Institute and the BAPMAF Highlife Institute at Bokoor House in Accra in 2009. On the latter occasion, he came with his old Uhuru colleague Kpakpo Addo and the two of them donated some photos to the BAPMAF Archives. Because of Stan's vast knowledge of big-band highlife arrangement and his open and helpful nature, I also sent a number of my Legon University music students to his house in Kaneshie to interview him for their various dissertations. Sadly, Stan died in 2015 and, after knowing and working with him for over 40 years, his absence is deeply felt.

(For more on the Broadway and Uhuru see chapter sixteen of my book Highlife Giants: West African Dance Band Pioneers, published in 2016 by Cassava Republic Press, Abuja, Nigeria.)

Chapter 17

HIGHLIFE PIONEERS: JERRY HANSEN, TOMMY GRIPPMAN, RAY ELLIS AND GEORGE LEE

JERRY HANSEN AND THE RAMBLERS

This famous Ghanaian highlife saxophonist was born in Bekwai in 1927 and went to Achimota in 1941 where he was taught music by Phillip Gbeho. He then became a student at the Accra Academy for six years, during which time Hansen became attracted to music through the American films of Glen Miller and Duke Ellington. In 1950 he joined Teacher Lamptey's Accra Orchestra and when this old band (goes back to 1930) broke up, Hansen moved to the Black Beats highlife band just established in 1952 by King Bruce and Saka Acquaye (and included Frank Crofie) as the resident group of the Weekend-in-Havanna. In 1961 Hansen left the Black Beats to form his own Ramblers highlife big-band helped by Habib Zakar, the Lebanese owner of Metropole Club in Accra. The Ramblers travelled to Gambia, Sierra Leone, Togo and Benin in the mid-sixties. It was around this time that the band began to release some of their famous songs on the Decca label like 'Work and Happiness', 'Awuraaba Artificial', 'Ama Bonsu' and 'Okonini Abankaba'.

Jerry Hansen (standing middle in open shirt) and the Ramblers in 1962

In 1965 Hansen set up his own music and optical repair shop, as he had gained experience in retailing from working between 1948 and 1965 as assistant manager for the United African Company. From 1967 the Ramblers began visiting London and their first trip was arranged by Ghana's Foreign Minister, Victor Owusu. On this occasion the band played for the BBC, the first live Ghanaian band to do so since the Gold Coast Police Band visited the UK in 1948. It was on their second 1968 London trip that the Ramblers recorded their first stereo record album for Decca 'The Sounds of the Ramblers'. Then in 1972 they made an East African trip during which they played for Kenya's President, Jomo Kenyatta. In 1973 the Ramblers teamed up with Professor A. M. Opoku and the Ghana University Dance Ensemble for a US tour.

In 1975, Hansen was elected the first President of the newly formed Musicians Union of Ghana MUSIGA and this is what he told Will Magib in 2006 (one of my American Ghana University music students) about unions in Ghana.

> *We the musicians were never given ample payments and as a result suffered. We didn't have control of our own royalties and we didn't have any form of retirement. It was a problem,*

especially for the government employed musicians who should have been taken care of. The first attempt to form a union was in 1961 under Kwame Nkrumah's regime. [In those days] if you were able to sell fifty records in a day you would still make very little. We went on a strike and decided not to record. After one year we went to the conference table. I told those there that we wanted the type of royalty contract that Bing Crosby could get. We got better deals worked out, but none of us were ever as rich as Bing Crosby. But [this union] had a very dangerous flirtation with the CPP government, as back then it was a rather socialist thing. We were given offices, but the party controlled everything. Eventually the regime was toppled and under the second regime MUSIGA was formed in 1974 and worked much better.

In 1984, Hansen moved to Washington DC for sixteen years. However he was able to keep the Ramblers going in Ghana through a younger generation of musicians he had trained, led by Felix Amenuda and more recently Peter Marfo. Hansen then came back to Ghana and in February 2005 he was given a Lifetime Award at the African American History/Heritage Month organised by the US Embassy Public Affairs Section and BAPMAF. The same year Sunshine Arts and Music gave him the Kanrewa Award and in 2007 two of the Ramblers songs ('Ama Bonsu' and 'Auntie Christie') were selected for the Ghana Telecom/One Touch company's promotional CD 'The Best of Ghanaian Highlife Music' made to commemorate Ghana's 50th independence celebrations. During this period of national celebration Hansen also received a Music Merit Award from the Ghana@50 Secretariat. In 2008 Hansen was given the prestigious Ghanaian ACRAG Award and the same year became a Patron of the Ghana Musicians Union, MUSIGA.

TOMMY GRIPPMAN AND THE RED SPOTS

Alfred Adotei 'Tommy' Grippman was born in 1923 in Accra and became interested in music when he was at the Government Senior Boy's School in James Town where he was supervised by the school's music and sports teacher, Joe Lamptey. As a result, in 1939 the young Grippman he became a trombonist in Teacher Lamptey's Accra Orchestra that had been formed in 1930 and through which many Ghanaian highlife luminaries had passed, including E.T. and Yebuah Mensah, Joe Kelly, Moi Buckman and George Bruce. Grippman then joined the Tempos which, by that time, was being led by E.T. Mensah. Then in 1953 he moved on to form the Red Spots with Lex Brown and Serious Amarfo (older brother of Sol Amarfo of Osibisa). The Red Spots recorded many Akan and Ga highlifes for Decca in the 1950s and early 60s; including

'Onua Kae Me', 'Metamfo Mayeo Den', ' Mara Manoma', 'Anoma Masem Yeyao', 'Alaba', 'Kae Da Bi', ' Bra Me Jolly', 'Odo Handkerchief, 'Adoma', 'Boafo Yena', 'Gye Me Ma Onka', 'She Adesa Gyebei', 'Bo Hwe Mee' and the Nkrumah song 'Wu Onu Tsulu'. In 1959 his band also did some recordings with the English pianist Robert Sprigge, who was on the staff of the History Department of the University of Ghana. Sprigge composed the melody of the song 'Agyanka' with Joss Aikins singing and supplying the lyrics.

Tommy Grippman's (trombone) Red Spots in 1952 (Mr. Vanderpuie photo)

The Red Spot band was awarded a certificate by the Ministry of Social Welfare for popularising highlife music and in 1960 was amongst those on the short-list to play in honour of the visiting Duke of York, who was representing the British Queen for the country's Republic Celebrations. During all the years of playing Grippman worked at the Post Office, the Attorney General's Office and then the Stool Land Boundaries Settlement Commission. He retired in 1978 and became a Commissioner of Oaths near Parliament House, where on several occasion I met him. During the 1980s he occasionally played with an All Stars band of veteran highlife musicians at venues such as the Arts Council and up until quite recently was Chairman of the Greater Accra Musicians Welfare Association. He died in 2004 aged 81 years.

HIGHLIFE PIANIST RAY ELLIS

The famous Fanti highlife pianist Kwamena Ray Ellis (or Ellis Kinnah) was born in 1931 and brought up in a Sekondi house where, luckily, J.B. Amoah lived. Amoah had been the pianist/harmonium player for the Axim Trio concert party of the 1930's and was a piano tuner and repairer. So recognising Ray's talent he encouraged Ray on the piano even though Ray's father thought learning this instrument a waste of time. Ray was also exposed to jazz, as in the twin port-town of Sekondi-Takoradi the wartime British and American seamen were bringing their honky-tonk and boogie-woogie jazz piano records that they would play in the local bars. Ray's first public appearance was in 1944 when, with the help of Ben Eghan Senior, he was allowed to play at the Casino Night-club in Takoradi during an intermission of the Tempos dance band. E.T. and Kofi Ghanaba (Guy Warren) were so impressed by Ray's piano skills that they allowed this schoolboy to jam with them, and some years later Ray regularly played with this famous highlife band. In 1951-3 Ray moved to Kumasi to play with guitarist Scorpion Mensah's seven-piece resident band at the Wilben Hotel. Then he moved to Accra to join Spike Anyankor's Rhythm Aces and composed the song 'Aketesia' for them. During the late-fifties Ray formed his short-lived Zenith band and Comets (not to be confused with Teddy Osei's Comets), then worked for some years with the GBC Orchestra. During this time he was also resident pianist at the Ambassador State Hotel (1958-62), and in 1965 joined the Brigade Band and went on European tour with them. Between1969-71 he was the leader of Meridian Hotel band in Tema. In 1973/4 he recorded an album at Ghana Film Studio for Kwadwo Donkor's Agoro label entitled 'Keyboard Africa: Highlife 'n' Piano by Kwamena Ray Ellis', a medley of popular old highlife tunes such as Yaa Amponsah, Sasabonsum, Ashewu and Adoma, etc. Ray kept up his connections with GBC by featuring in radio programs such as 'Melody' (with the GBC Combo) in the 1970s and 'The Ray Ellis Trio' in 1980s. In the 1990's Ray Ellis and his Quartet (that included Nat Buckle) was the resident group at the Novotel in Accra. Ray died in February 1999.

TENOR SAXIST GEORGE LEE

George Lee Larnyoh was born in 1938 in Takoradi, got his first training as a vocalist with Tricky Johnson's Palmcourt Band and then the Accra based Delta Dandies and Downbeats run by the Nigerians Jibral Isa and Roy Chicago. In 1956 he formed his Star Aces and then his Messengers dance band which specialised in highlife and the bebop style of modern jazz. This dance band was based at the Ambassador State Hotel in Accra. In the early sixties Nkrumah was encouraging dance band to utilise more traditional musical resources by arranging for some of these to undertake three month courses in traditional drumming and dancing the Arts Council in Accra, lodging them at Puppet Theatre near the Ghana Drama Studio. These bands included George Lee's Messengers as well as the personnel of Broadway, the Brigade Band, the Globemasters and the Farmers Council Band.

George Lee circa 1960

After the Messengers had completed their three month crash course in drumming they were sent by the government as Ghana's musical ambassadors to the Berlin World Fair in 1962. In fact, George Lee Larnyoh stayed on in Europe after that trip, relocating quickly to London where he worked as a session musician with Johnny Nash, Cat Stevens, Chris McGregor and Bob Marley. George Lee is one of the saxist on Marley's album 'Natty Dread'. He also toured with Toots & the Maytals and Johnny Nash. It was in London in the late 1970s that I first met George through Ghanaian music promoter Charles Eassmon.

In 1984 George Lee toured Mozambique and on his return to London formed his band 'Anansi' that released the song 'Sea Shell' that became theme tune of British TV 'Ebony' arts-series program. In the 1980's George Lee moved to Swaziland where he worked at Hugh Masekela's recording studio. He also tutored the South African musician Jimmy Dhludlu. In 1990 George moved to Johannesburg when I again met up with him – and his wife Andrea Larnyoh. At the time he was involved with Conrad Mhlongo and others in a cultural NGO called CIDA. I met him one more time when he visited Ghana in the mid-2000s – but sadly he died in 2008.

Chapter 18

OSIBISA: FROM DANCE BAND HIGHLIFE TO AFRO-ROCK

Osibisa's Mac Tontoh, Sol Amarfio and Teddy Osei (back row). Percussionist Potato is in foreground

Rock music from Elvis to the Beatles became popular with the youth of Africa during the 1960s, and this was followed by the 'progressive rock' or 'psychedelic' rock of Santana, Cream, Jimi Hendrix and Sly and the Family Stone. At first, young African musicians simply copied rock music, but later they began to fuse it with local music. This is no surprise because, after all, rock 'n' roll is based on African American 'rhythm and blues', the city version of the even earlier blues, hollas and work-songs of the American south with their roots in Africa.

Osibisa is the first and foremost of the Afro-rock bands and became internationally famous in the early 1970s for their dance rhythms, that became a craze with blacks and whites alike, before the disco and reggae dance manias of the mid-1970s. This London-based African band ended up making a million pounds for the British taxman, for which they were awarded the Medal of the British Empire (MBE). This extraordinary development started in Ghana with two Asante brothers from the Kumasi area, Teddy Osei and the younger Mac Tontoh, and also the Ga drummer from Accra, Sol Amarfio.

As a young boy Teddy had already learned to play Ashanti percussion instruments such as the Ashanti atumpan and fontomfrom drums, and at school played drums for his school brass-band. Then he studied the sax and flute and joined Glen Cofie and Eddie Quansah's Stargazers, which also included the Sol Amarfio who had begun his musical training at sixteen with Spike Anyankor's Rhythm Ace. In 1958 Teddy and Sol formed the Comets band in Kumasi and brought in Mac Tontoh who had been playing for the Broadway Band established in 1958 in Takoradi and led by the Nigerian trumpeter Sammy Obot. Besides trumpet (and later flugelhorn), Mac had also knew traditional percussion and the northern Ghanaian Lobi xylophone that he had learnt from the musicians who had settled in his village in Asante. With the three key members, Teddy, Mac and Sol, the Comets scored many hit singles throughout West Africa in the late 1950s, with 'Pete Pete' being simultaneously number one in Ghana, Nigeria, and Sierra Leone.

After a while Teddy became fed up with the local scene and so in 1962 he decided to go to London. He found that it was not easy to start playing music there and he had to wash dishes whilst trying to put a band of African musicians together. Luckily the Nkrumah government gave Teddy a scholarship to study music at a London school. He then set up his the Cats Paws group which veered toward pop music as a means of getting work. After a residency in Zurich's Beat Club and a three-month exposure at a 1969 festival in Tunis, Cats Paws returned to London and Teddy brought Mac Tontoh and Sol Amarfio over. Whilst Teddy had been in London, Mac had spent one year with a military dance-band and then joined the Uhuru big-band (formed in 1963/4 as a successor to Broadway) that played everything from highlife to the music of Glen Miller and Charlie Parker.

When playing for white rock fans in London, the Cats Paw members had noticed that if they performed a rock rendition of traditional Ghanaian rhythms such as the agbadza, adowa or highlife, the dancing crowd would go wild. So after an offer to record a sound-track for a film set in Africa, Teddy, Mac and Sol began to work on the Osibisa sound, or as they call it 'criss-cross rhythms that explode with happiness'. For this they recruited four other West Africans and three West Indians. The group's Pan African musical formula was a big success with western dance fans. As Teddy later commented, 'soul and reggae derive from Africa, so why don't people recognise the original first?' As a result the group decided to exclusively focus on their new 'Afro-rock' sound and changed the name Cat's Paw to Osibisa, a name is derived from the old Fanti name for highlife 'Osibisaaba'. In 1970 Osibisa took off by releasing their first single 'Music for Gong-Gong' and playing at London clubs like Ronnie Scott's, the Roundhouse and the Country Club. From 1971 (on the MCA and then Bronze label) they released a string of hits albums like 'Osibisa', 'Heads', 'Happy Children', 'Welcome, and 'Black Magic Night'. Some of their singles, like 'Sunshine; Day', 'Dance the Body Music' and the 'Coffee Song', got into the British Top Ten.

A number of musicians passed through the group after it inception. These included the tenor/baritone saxist Lofty Lasisi Amao and bass guitarists Fred Coker and Mike Odumosu (all from Nigeria), the conga player Kofi Ayivor and the young keyboard prodigy Kiki Gyan from Ghana, and from the West Indies Spartacus R from Grenada on bass guitar, Wendell Richardson from Antigua on lead guitar and Trinidadian vocalist and the keyboard player Robert Bailey.

In mid-1970s England, with the decline of rock music and the appearance of disco and reggae, Osibisa's danceable Afro-rock also suffered. So the band packed their bags and spent most of their time outside Britain on international tours of Australia, the East, Europe and Africa where they had massive followings. In Ghana they became a source of inspiration for the youth and even in the villages their music was a success, especially their 'Music for Gong-Gong' which became a standard among the rural guitar-bands.

They put on big shows in Ghana, like the one they did at the El Wak Stadium in Accra in 1977. They also played at the Black Arts Festival, FESTAC, held in Nigeria in 1977 and three year later were invited to the Zimbabwe independence celebrations and played to a crowd of 25,000 people in the newly named capital, Harare. The success of Osibisa inspired many African Afro-rock outfits all over Africa in the 1970s like Hedzoleh and Boombaya of Ghana; BLO, Mono-Mono, the Funkees and Ofege of Nigeria; the Super Combo and Godfathers of Sierra Leone; Kapingbdi and Kabassa of Liberia; and Harare, Javuka and Savuka of southern Africa.

In 1980 Osibisa set up their own Flying Elephant label and released a version of the old South African hit 'Phata-Phata'. This was followed in 1982 by a tour of India where they played to an estimated 350,000 fans. Whilst in Calcutta, they recruited the Indian percussionist Pandit Dinesh and their performance in Bombay was released as an album called 'Osibisa Unleashed' which was the first ever western act to ever reach a gold record sale in India. Then In 1983 German and British audiences were given a special treat when Osibisa teamed up for a six gig tour with the Highlife Stars band that combined two streams of highlife music: big-band highlife played by Osibisa members and four musicians who had passed through or worked with Ghana's concert party highlife guitar-bands. The resulting ten-man super group consisted of the Osibisa personnel with four musicians especially brought from Ghana for the summer tour. These were A.B. Crentsil of the Ahenfo band that often toured Ghana in the 1980s with a concert party and three members of the Kumasi-based band Kokroko, Eric Agyeman, Thomas Frempong and Tommy King, who had all been members of Dr. K. Gyasi's guitar band.

These four musicians helped make a remarkable break-through, as they linked the two quite distinct branches of highlife: that of the urban dance bands and that of the more rural oriented guitar bands. The gap between these two varieties of highlife was so great that for many years it was impossible to form a single musicians' union, catering to both types of players. In fact, it was only in the late 1970s that the guitar-band musicians joined their dance-band brethren in the united Musicians' Union of Ghana (MUSIGA), with two leading guitar-band musicians heading the union: its President Koo Nimo and Vice-President Nana Ampadu of the African Brothers. What was anticipated by this fusion of music organisations in Ghana, finally surfaced musically on stage in 1983 in Europe with the Highlife Stars. Everybody enjoyed their music; what most people did not realise was that highlife history was being made.

208

Osibisa still continued playing well into the nineties when its line-up included Teddy, Mac and Sol, although Sol Amarfio was sometimes replaced by Mac's son, Frank. Other Ghanaians included Daku Potato on congas, the keyboard player Emmanuel Rentoz, the bass player Martin Owusu (ex-Adam's Apple), Alfred 'Kari' Bannerman (ex Boombaya) on lead guitar and the Nigerian trombonist Remi Ala who also played with Tony Allen, Fela Kuti's former drummer. Sadly, Potato died in Ghana in the mid-nineties whilst playing in front of an audience. Ten years later, Kiki Gyan died in Ghana after losing a long battle with drug addiction.

Teddy and Sol are still in Britain, whereas Mac Tontoh returned to Ghana in 2001 and became a member of the National Commission on Culture. He ran a band called the Osibisa Kete Warriors, and set up a recording studio in his house in Accra and established the 'Mac and his Kids Project' to teach African music in schools. Sadly, Mac Tontoh died at 69 years old in August 2010, at Korle Bu Hospital in Accra.

A huge tribute for him was organised by Dr. Kwesi Owusu's Creative Storm at the Alliance Francaise in Accra in September 2010 at which many musicians played – and the following is what I wrote for the funeral brochure.

As a musician in Ghana, during the early 1970s, I knew of Mac Tontoh and the famous Osibisa Afro-rock band. In fact it was this band, as well as the music of Santana and Fela Kuti, that inspired a legion of Afro-fusion bands of the time. However, I never got to know Mac personally until after he permanently returned home from the UK in 1992. It was then that he set up a recording studio, was briefly an Executive of MUSIGA and then, from 2001, a member of the National Commission on Culture. As a result, I often bumped into Mac at various musical events, radio talk shows and at Guy Warren's house. I recall vividly seeing Mac play his flugal horn with a battery of kete-drum playing 'Warriors' at a funeral in Accra. So in the late 1990s, when I began running the University Music Department Process of Arts student music-industry outreach program, I invited Mac to Legon to interact with our students. Later on, I sent several teams of Process of Arts students to interview him on his career and the state of the Ghanaian music scene – and Mac's house in Dzorwulu was always open to them. Sadly, a student team was actually arranging to do a series of interviews with him when he fell sick earlier this year. As I knew that Mac had been a member of Uhuru band that so much influenced the young Fela Kuti I also interviewed Mac about this famous creator of Afrobeat in 2001 for my 'Fela: Kaluta Notes' book that was published in 2009. Mac's comments on this

Nigerian star makes interesting and revealing reading. Not only did Mac have a vast repository of information on African music and was helping our university students, he was also running several projects encouraging school children to appreciate and learn local music. So although he has left us a huge legacy through Osibisa, the musical knowledge he was currently in the process of imparting to our youth will be greatly missed.

Chapter 19

KOFI AYIVOR: FROM HIGHLIFE TO HIGH-TENSION FUNK

The Ewe master-drummer Kofi Ayivor in 1981

For the last forty years Kofi Ayivor's drumming has been heard all over the world, even in the Arctic Circle. Kofi has backed many top musicians and groups such as E.T. Mensah, Miles Davis, Eddy Grant, Alexis Korner, Osibisa and even a Turkish band. In fact, Kofi is so well travelled that at one point he has fifteen passports. He presently lives in The Netherlands with his Surinamese wife, where he teaches drum to school-children and musicians and runs his own Ivory Records record company. But let's go back to the start of Kofi's chequered musical career. One of Kofi's parents was Ghanaian, the other Togolese and he spent the first ten years in the town of Gusau in Nigeria's Sokoto State. In 1949 his family returned to Denu in Ghana, on the border with Togo. It was here in the Ewe region of West Africa so famous for its knowledge of cross-rhythms that Kofi first started on drums. His uncle, the master-drummer of Denu, was his first teacher. It was on this solid foundation that he was able to master over forty-five drumming styles. Kofi's father, who was a retailer, hated the idea of his son becoming a drummer, as he wanted him to be a doctor. But Kofi was so eager to play drums that he would walk a twenty-mile round trip to see top Ghanaian bands, like the Black Beats and E.T. Mensah's Tempos, play in the neighbouring town of Lome. And of course, as he told me in 1980, he would join in. 'Sometimes I would play the maracas. If the maracas player was in love with some girl and he was gone, I would take over.'

When he finished school in 1959, Kofi went to Accra and got a job as a lift operator and decided to try his luck by going to see E. T. Mensah at his pharmacy on Zion Street.

> *Fortunately E.T.'s wife, who is from Calabar, knew my father as she used to buy things from his shop. In fact she started to cry and said my dad was a real human being and a beautiful person – always helping people. So she told E. T. he had to take me. So E. T. had to buy me some heavy clothes, for in those days musicians had to wear trousers, white shirts and bow-ties.*

Kofi became the youngest member of the Tempos, playing bongos for them and being their 'gungadin' (packer or road manager). He toured the whole of West Africa with this band and fondly remembers the help E.T. or the 'old man' as he affectionately calls him, gave him at the start of his career. In 1961 Kofi was offered a job as conga player by Tommy Grippman, the leader of the Red Spots dance-band. This was a busy time for Kofi as he was so much in demand that he played with many bands, including the Gagarin Band set up by the Ghana TUC and named after the Russian cosmonaut Yuri Gagarin.

Gagarin dance band 1962 that at one point included congaist Kofi Ayivor

He also teamed up with four Italian musicians belonging to Silvio Cambert's group which played Latin-American music at cabaret spots in town. They got on so well that in 1963 the Italians decided to take the band home on tour, and asked Kofi to choose three more Ghanaian musicians to accompany them. The eight-piece band stayed three months in Italy. Then they drove a Fiat to Yugoslavia, Greece, Turkey, and all the way to Baghdad. In fact they got lost for a time in the desert on Christmas Day but as they got lucky as Kofi explains:

> *By the grace of God we met one of these camel drivers. They can just look at the sun and tell us exactly which direction to go. So we got to Baghdad and played at the Ali-Baba Club. We were a big success, as Cuban music was popular there.*

Trouble eventually arose between the Italian and Ghanaian band members over the problem of playing Turkish music. The Italians had been having trouble with the highlifes, but the Turkish music completely floored them.

> *The Turkish music was in 6/8, 9/8, and 12/8 time. The Italians couldn't play it as their syncopations were never there. Then Princess Amina, a Turkish dancer, came to join us*

and after twelve days the Italians couldn't play for her. We, the Ghanaians, were playing it within three minutes. This led to friction and the band scattered.

Kofi stayed with Princess Amina for four years and toured the Far East, Europe, and West Africa with her, finally parting company in Sweden. In Sweden Kofi taught music and rhythm at the National Ballet School, and also put together a band called the Modern Sounds with some West Indian friends and toured all over Scandinavia. This band used steel drums, congas, trap-drums, piano, guitars, and played every kind of music, including classical pieces by Bach, Beethoven and Strauss. Kofi also composed several songs for them based on the traditional Ewe agbadza beat. These were played on Swedish television, and one song, 'Otinku' was recorded in 1969 by EMI. Between gigs and teaching, the ever dynamic Kofi also played with the Swedish Symphony Orchestra as percussionist. He also worked with jazz musicians who visited the country, like Duke Ellington, Jack McDuff, Miles Davis, Alexis Komer and Sarah Vaughan. In 1973 and after a jam-session in Oslo, he was invited to join the Osibisa Afro-rock band whose leaders he knew well from Ghana.

> *When I joined Osibisa it was the same old travelling business. The first record I made with them was Superfly TNT, which was the soundtrack of a film about a black American guy going to East Africa. After that we got signed on to Warner Brothers and I did 'Happy Children' and 'Osibi Rock' for them. Then the band signed up with Bronze in 1975 and we made 'Welcome Home.'*

Two other of Osibisa's successful songs were written by Kofi; namely 'Somaja' and 'Kilele'. But as Kofi explains, he left Osibisa as he had 'met a lovely woman and decided to be a family man and give up the travelling and living out of a suitcase.'

One of the first things he did after leaving Osibisa was to release a disco album on the Bronze label with Kiki Gyan, who left Osibisa at the same time. Then he went into producing records himself. He started by producing a record with the reggae band called Tradition and then started to help High Tension, a funk band made up of young West Indians living in London, whom Kofi already knew.

> *When they were young kids they used to come around to see me and sing and I taught them to play drums. Then I got a deal for them on Island Records, as Chris Blackwell is a good friend of mine. I co-produced them with Alex Sadkin, Bob Marley's engineer. Then they*

hit the charts. The song 'Hi Tension' made it to number thirteen in the British charts and the follow-up, 'British Hustle' made it to number eight.

In 1980 Kofi decided to take a short break from family life and went on a tour of the States and the Caribbean with Jimmy Cliff and recorded a few tracks with him. His last project in England, before going off to the Netherlands was his very first solo album 'Kofi' released on the CBS label. This was partly recorded at Eddy Grant's Coach House Studios in London and partly at Phonodisc near Ibadan in Nigeria. This album boasted many top West Indian and West African musicians: Ed Bentley (Ghana), Louis Becket (Antigua) and Kiki Gyan (Ghana) on keyboards, Eddy Grant (Guyana) on traps and guitar, Jimmy Hynes (Barbados) on bass, Jake Solo (Nigeria) on guitar, Papa Mensah (Ghana) on drums, Mike Odumosu (Nigeria) and Torkuboh Shortade (Nigeria) on bass, Keith Mackintosh (West Indies) on moog synthesiser, Ray Allen (Ghana) and Lloyd Clarke (Jamaica) on sax, Hershall (West Indies) on trumpet, Amoa (Nigeria) on talking-drums, with Uwandile (Zimbabwe) and Dora lfudu (Nigeria) as vocalists.

In 2004 Kofi Ayivor released the 'Rhythmology' CD on the Dutch Otrabanda label, and it reflected his vast musical range: traditional African drumming, big-band highlife, middle-eastern music, Afro-rock and Black British funk. It is collection of recording done at different times by Kofi and for the more recent songs on the CD he worked with the Ghanaian bassist Chi-Kin-Chi, the Greek drummer Nikos Touliatos and Hungarian sax player Tony Lakatos.

Chapter 20

THE HIGHLIFE COMPOSERS; OSCARMORE, EBO TAYLOR, JOE EYISON, KWADWO DONKOH AND JOE MENSAH

OSCARMORE OFORI: PROLIFIC HIGHLIFE, COMPOSER AND FOLKLORIST

'Oscarmore' was one of the most prolific dance band highlife composers in the 1950s and 60s. 'Oscar' (his nick-name) was born in 1930 in Odumasi Krobo and was the son of Nana K.T.A Ofori of the royal Ntahera stool of New Juaben. By 1945 he was a drummer in the 'Akro' band of his Old Juaben Senior School and was studying as choirboy and guitarist under Kwesi Baiden, the school's music master. He began to study draughtsmanship, but in 1953 he joined the Koforidua Royal Orchestra, then Satchmo Korley's Ralchers and finally Joe Kelly's Band in Accra with whom he released his first highlife record hit 'Sanbra'. In 1956 Oscarmore became Ghana Repertoire Manager for Decca Records. During this time he also composed for many other bands: Spike Anyankor's Rhythm Aces, Tommy Grippman's Red Spots and Teddy Osei's Comets with whom Oscar went to Nigeria. Some of his many hit compositions were 'Agoogyi', 'Si Abotoar' and 'Enya Wo Dofo' (with the Black Beats Band); 'Gyae Su', 'Nkae' and 'Bonsu' (Broadway Band); 'Gbe Bleoo' and 'Hwe Ye' (Tempos); and 'Akai Man' and 'Me Sere Ham' (Stargazers). It was after a motor accident in 1958 that he released one of his most well-known highlifes 'Anyanko-goro'. It was his popularity as guitarist and bass player onstage that gave him the nickname 'Oscarmore' as the dance fans would shout 'Oscar, Oscar more, more'.

Oscarmore Ofori on double-bass in late 1950s

After winning a scholarship to study music in Europe in 1960 he met and worked under the Hungarian art-composer Zoltan Kodaly and then, in London, under Sir Malcolm Sergeant at the Curwen Memorial College of Music. He became a member of the Royal Institute of Anthropology studying Folk Music and worked for a while at Oregon University in the US. In the 1980s Oscar came back home to work as a cultural officer for the Ghana Arts Council (in Koforidua). In 1991 he became a member of both the National Folklore Board of Trustees and the Copyright Administration. He was also a resource person for both Professor Kwabena Nketia's International Centre for African Music and Dance at Legon and the BAPMAF Highlife Institute at South Ofankor, Accra. In the 1990s he also founded the Kete Cultural Troupe and became the chief atenteben (bamboo flute) player and horn player of the traditional court orchestra the Omanhene of New Juaben. By then Oscar he preferred to be known by the name Akora Agyare T.A. Ofori. Oscar or Akora also played a vital role in introducing traditional culture into the liturgy of the Anglican Church under Rt. Rev. Dr. Robert Okine, the retired Archbishop of West Africa. In February 2005 he was awarded a Lifetime Achievement Award at the African American History/Heritage Month at the DuBois Centre, organised by BAPMAF and the U.S. Embassy's Public Affairs Section. After a protracted illness Oscar passed away on the 25th October 2005 and was buried at Odumase Krobo.

EBO TAYLOR: HIGHLIFE COMPOSER AND TEACHER

Ebo Delroy Taylor is an ace guitarist and important composers of favourite highlife songs like 'Nsamanfo', 'Odo Ye Wu', 'Ghana Be Ye Yie', 'Twer Nyame'. He was born in Saltpond in 1936 and began learning organ at nine years old as his father was leader of a local church choir at his secondary school Saint Augustine's College. Whilst a schoolboy he also began learning guitar. He learnt to play the local 'palmwine' style of highlife popularised by two important local acoustic guitarists in his area, Kwame Asare and Kwaa Mensah. He was particularly influenced by Eddie Johnson of the Tempos, Frank Crofi of Spike Anyankor's Rhythm Aces and Kwamina Kofi of the Black Beats. Whilst still at school he joined Dan Tackie's Havana Dance Band and in 1957 moved to Kumasi to play with the Stargazers Band with whom he released his first compositions 'Mensu', 'Onyimpa Neber Ara Nyi' and 'Dance Highlife Hits.' Then in 1961 Ebo moved south to Takoradi to join the Broadway Band led by the Nigerian trumpeter Sammy Obot. Ebo became the band's arranger and also composed highlifes for them like 'Beye Bu Beye Ba' (whatever you do you'll die), 'Wofa Nunu' (there he goes), 'Nsamanfo', 'Dance Marriage' and 'Megya Wo Do' (Fatherly love).

In 1962 Ebo obtained a scholarship from Kwame Nkrumah to study music at the Eric Guilder School of Music in London, and also formed the Black Star Band with Eddie Quansah, Oscarmore Ofori, George Aikins, Sol Amarfio and Teddy Osei. Whilst in the UK Ebo was exposed to the jazz music. Whilst there he played at Ronnie Scott's jazz club in London and was exposed to the jazz music of Miles Davis, John Coltrane and Charlie Parker and also the jazz guitar styles of Kenny Burell, Wes Montgomery and Jim Hall. So when he returned to Ghana and joined Uhuru band, Ebo helped introduce advanced jazz chords to them.

In 1968 Ebo went to Sekondi to play with the Sammy Lartey's Railway Band and in 1972 he moved onto the Blue Monks. This group featured the singer Pat Thomas and singer/guitarist Bob Pinodo and was managed by two of Ghana's leading radio disc-jockeys, Mike Eghan and Carl Bannerman, Around 1974 Ebo became the leader of the Apagya Show Band, the brain-child of the music producer Dick Essilfie-Bondzie. This ten-piece band included the Uhuru saxist Ebo Dadson, the keyboard player Ernest Honey (Honney), Bob Pinodo and singers Joanna Okang and Gyedu-Blay Ambolley. Also as A&R man for the Essiebons Company he produced and arranged records by Pat Thomas ('My Love of Music' and 'Nsamanfo'), C.K. Mann ('Funky Highlife'), Blay Ambolley ('Simigwado'), Jewel Ackah and Paapa Yankson . After leaving the Apagya Show Band Ebo Taylor formed his Asase Ase (Underground) band in the mid-seventies that delved into rootsy Fanti music and proverbial lyrics.

Ebo Taylor in 2006 (photo from Titus Ofori Arko)

With the military government and accompanying curfews the 1980s was a difficult time for Ebo and other Ghanaian musicians. Nevertheless in the 1990's Ebo became involved with the small and evolving Accra jazz scene. Together with George Amissah he played with the Village Five at the Village Inn – and around 2000 he teamed up with saxophonist Ray Allen to run an Afro-jazz combo called Unconditional Love. In 2002 and after a successful interaction at the Legon campus between Ebo and the music students of the University of Ghana that I organized as part of the Music Department's 'Process of Art' program, Ebo became artist-in-residence, teaching guitar and helping run the Music Department pop band. Between 2002 and 2005, some of his compositions were released on the U.K. Soundway Label. In 2005 Ebo was awarded a Lifetime Achievement Award at the African American History/Heritage Month. In 2006, Ebo and Gyedu-Blay Ambolley jammed with the Palace Musicians of Nana Kobina Nketia at the Eastern Region's Centre for National Culture. The same year Ebo celebrated his seventieth birthday with a musical bash organized by the Alliance Francaise in Accra.

In 2009 Ebo released (on the Essiebons label) his seventeenth album called 'Abenkwan Puchaa' to coincide with the one hundredth anniversary of Kwame Nkrumah's birth. This album launched the birth of Ebo's new band he called 'Bonze Konkoma' that explores fusions of jazz, funk, Afrobeat and highlife with local asafo, agbadza, konkoma and adzewa drum rhythms. In fact, In fact the group features the old Fanti konkoma frame-drums. In late 2010 Ebo and his Bonze Konkoma went on an extended European tour and also released 'Love and Death' (Strut Records, UK) recorded with the German based Afrobeat Assembly. In 20210 he also played at festivals in Germany and Holland. Now in his mid-seventies Ebo is still (2011) on European tour with his Bonze Konkoma band that includes trumpeter Osei Tutu, trombonist Eli Amewode and three of Ebo's sons. One of them is the keyboards player Ebo Taylor Jr. who, in the late 1970s, played with Smart Nkansah, the Dutch Benglos and Tommy Darling's Wantu Wazuri.

Joe Eyison from his Old Hits album

Joe Eyison is best known as the character 'Station Master' of the GBC's 'Keteke' and 'Obra' TV concert party series – and also as an actor in local films such as 'Juju', 'Heritage Africa', 'Dede' and 'Six Lovers of Melody'. However, Joe was also a prolific highlife composer in the 1960s and 1970s. He was born in Moree in the Central Region in 1933 and educated in Cape Coast and Takoradi. He then became a trade unionist and worked his way up to be the First General Secretary of the Musicians Union of the TUC that was dissolved in the 1966 anti-Nkrumah coup. Before this, Nkrumah had asked Joe to help with the Visual Aids Department of the Ghana Farmers Council in helping set up a national drama troupe. Joe Eyison was one of the founding members of the Musicians Union of Ghana, MUSIGA and from 1974 was one of its Executive members up until his death in 2002. Some of the songs he recorded with various highlife bands (mainly of the dance band variety) are listed below:

Tempos: 'Meye Metutu Ha Nom', 'Ado Tse Se Ankuma' and 'Obaa Dzeseefo'
Red Spots: 'Moondie Man Die'

The Armed Forces Band: 'I Cry'

Ramblers: 'Auntie Christie', 'Ewuraba Artificial', 'Nyimpa Dasanyi', 'Obra Rehwe Me', 'Kosor Kopo' and 'Abonsam Fireman'

EK.'s Band: 'Oba Adeseefo' (Prodigal Son), 'Wonnkyere Abofra Nyame' (No one Teaches a Child About God), the dirge 'Meko Jerusalem' and 'Ponko Abodam' (also recorded by the Ramblers and then by Kojo Antwi for his 'Groovy' album)

C.K. Mann's Carousel Seven: 'Yefun Ye Unbeez' and 'Yebo Ommbo'

Western Diamonds: Its 1993 'Diamonds are Forever' album includes Joe's songs 'Obra Nye' and 'Woara Abo' sung by Paapa Yankson and Ekua Danquah.

KWADWO DONKOH: DIPLOMAT HIGHLIFE PIANIST AND COMPOSER

GBC Band led by bespectacled Kwadwo Donkoh on left

The Ghanaian pianist and highlife composer Kwadwo Donkoh has produced twenty albums and numerous singles since 1958 with his APEMCO recording label and ABIBIRAM publishing company. He was born in Ashanti in 1934 and went to Cape Coast's prestigious Mfantsipim School where, incidentally, he was Kofi Annan's house-prefect. Between 1956 and 1959 he studied history at the University of Ghana and was encouraged to use his piano skills for highlife by a group of university lecturers who had formed the Achimota African Music Society (J.H.K. Nketia, Robert Sprigge, Ephraim Amu and E.F. Collins). From 1958 Kwadwo branched out into productions of highlife singles by guitar-bands such as those of E.K Nyame, Kwabena Okai, the Kumasi Youngsters and Kofi Djan, and also by the dance bands like E.T. Mensah's Tempos and King Bruce's Black Beats. In the sixties Kwadwo wrote many songs for the Uhuru band such as 'Time For Highlife', 'Go Slow', 'Wobeku Me', 'Wobetumi No', 'No Parking' and 'Skin Pain. He later released a full album of his own compositions with this big band called 'The Sounds of Africa', with George Amissah (or Emissah) on sax, Kwesi Baiden on keyboards, Max Hammond on drums and vocalist Eddie Ntreh. In the late sixties Kwadwo was also running a dance band called the Hugas Extraordinaire. Kwadwo Donkoh did all this despite having a career in the Ghanaian diplomatic service.

Kwadwo also made important releases in the 1970s. He made a live album of the 1972 National Brass Band Competition. The same year (and with his assistant Nana Ofori) his Ogyataana Show Band (formed 1971) won the National Dance Band Competition and began releasing hit tunes like 'Obra Mu M'Asem' and 'Ebe Nie Ye', followed in 1975 by their 'Yerefrefre' album. Then came an album of highlife piano medleys called 'Ray Ellis Plays Highlife'. During this period Kwadwo also produced a number of 'Ga Cultural Groups' that play local Accra folk-tunes and street highlifes. One was Wulomei whom he (with Saka Acquaye) helped release their album 'Walatu Walasa'. Another he was involved with was Dzadzeloi and their 'Two Paddy Follow One Girl' hit. Kwadwo also used the Uhuru band to back the flotist Oscar Sulley Braima with singer Eddie Ntreh in an Afro-beat/rock album entitled 'Oscar Sulley and the Nzele Afrikana'. In the mid-1980's Kwadwo set up his Abokyi Parts highlife dance band with which he has made three albums. In 2000 Kwadwo became a Trustee of the newly established Ghana Association of Phonographic Industries.

JOE MENSAH

Joe Mensah was a Ghanaian highlife singer and composer who released eleven record albums and several singles. He began his musical career in the 1950's with Eddie Quansah's Stargazers and then the Broadway band. This was very much against his parents' wishes, so as a teenager he left Ghana for Lagos where in 1958 he joined Bill Friday's Downbeat highlife band that was the resident group at Nat's Club de Paris. At this time Joe became a close friend of the juju musician Ebenezer Obey – and as he explains also of the young Fela Anikulapo-Kuti.

The Club de Paris was at number 80 Ojuelegba Road in Surulere, not far from Fela's family house. One evening we played our usual gig. At the end of one of the songs I sang I saw somebody come on stage, put his head between my legs and carry me on his shoulders. He took me through the audience and was saying to the crowd 'you people, have you heard any voice as great as this one? And you just sit down and don't show any appreciation'. So people began throwing money to us on the floor. After he put me back on stage and collected all the money and brought it to the band. That was Fela! From that day on my day would never be complete if I didn't see him and he would not go out without seeing me. We became very close even though he was about twenty years old and quite a few years older than me. I would spend a lot of time at his house, but I never met his mother until one day I went there and she was washing clothes. Fela had told his mother a lot about me and she said that how is it possible that I look so much like her children. Like we're related. She also said that I'm too young for my mother to have allowed me to leave Ghana and stay in Nigeria, so from that time I should consider her my mother, call her 'ma' and when I need consolation, food or whatever, I should always go there. (See my 2009 book 'Fela: Kalakuta Notes' published by the Dutch Royal Tropical Institute, pp. 23/3).

Joe returned home after staying in Lagos for three years later and re-joined Broadway (renamed Uhuru in 1963/4). At that time he recorded his famous 'Uhuru Special/Bose' song in Lagos with the Uhuru members under the name 'Big Beats'. In 1964 he left for the United States to study civil engineering and pursue his musical career. However, he made many trips to West Africa and, for instance, in the early 1970's' and with the help of Fela's horn section, he recorded songs like 'Africa Is Home' and 'Cry Laughter' in Lagos with the Ghanaian Sweet Talks. He returned to Ghana in 1992 when he became President of the Musician Union of Ghana, MUSIGA – and Artist and Repertoire man for the Ghanaian Megastar company. Joe died at his home in Tema in 2003.

Chapter 21

GYEDU BLAY-AMBOLLEY BLENDS HIGHLIFE AND FUNK

The highlife singer Gyedu-Blay Ambolley

Gyedu-Blay Ambolley is one of Ghana's leading experimenters in the highlife field with a strong charismatic stage personality. he is a singer and tenor sax player and he is not only famous Ghana but has become currently well-known internationally with World Music fans even amongst the black youth of the coastal Cartagena Region of Colombia whose 'champeta' music has been influenced through the records of Ambolley and other African musicians introduced by visiting seamen since the 1970s.

Ambolley hails from Nzema (or Nzima) in western Ghana, the birthplace of the late President Kwame Nkrumah and an area with a rich highlife tradition that spreads into neighbouring Cote d'Ivoire. Ambolley, however, was not born there but in Sekondi-Takoradi. His first musical influences were two-fold: the military music of his father who had been a soldier during the Second World War and played the flute, and highlife music of local dance-bands like Broadway. He learnt to play drums and guitar and then in 1963 at fifteen joined his first band as a vocalist. This was Tricky Johnson's Sextet based in Sekondi, the leader of which was the one time guitarist of the Tempos dance-band. From this Sextet Ambolley joined another band in the locality, the Railway Band run by Sammy Lartey (who was later with the GBC band). It was another member of the Railway Band, Ebo Taylor, who taught Ambolley the bass guitar. In 1968 Ambolley left for Accra and joined a dance band called Hugh's (actually Hugas) Extraordinaire that was run by Kodjo Donkoh and played highlife and Latin music. But at this point I will let Ambolley himself take up the story from an interview I did with him in Accra in 1982.

> I then had the chance to play with some musicians from the Meridian Band based in Tema and we were able to play without any rehearsals. There was Ray Allen on alto sax, the late Ebo Aggrey on guitar and Ray Ellis on keyboards. From there I went to the Uhuru dance band and with them I made my first record in 1973, a single called 'Simigwa Do' under the band name the 'Steneboofs.

I asked Ambolley to go into more detail about this record as it became very controversial and was banned from being played on the radio.

> Some believe 'Simigwa Do' is profane, but in Fanti it is a proverbial phrase which means the sort of composed dance done by a chief or well established person. He is sitting on a chair with so much pride as if he has achieved something and is in a happy mood, then an inner feeling makes him get up for a moment and dance. People thought it meant "let's go and have

sex' but it wasn't like that. One thing that pained me was that this record was assessed at Broadcasting House and I wasn't called upon to analyse the phrase. But they just decided to ban the record. I tried to explain on television and so on but with no result. Then I shifted to the Apagya Show Band run by Ebo Taylor. We recorded some 45's for Essiebons Productions, the manager of which was the brain behind the Apagya Show Band. Also in the group were Ebo Dadson on sax and Bob Pinodo on vocals.

I saw this band playing at the Orion Cinema in Accra around 1977 and remember being surprised to see Bob Pinodo on stage with Ambolley, as I hadn't seen Bob since 1973 when we were running Szaabu Sounds together. Since then he had been in West Germany. However, both Bob and Ambolley blended well on stage as they are experts in combining highlife and pop. Ambolley goes on to describe his sound.

It was an experimental group and we had our own sound. I saw that reggae originated from highlife so I combined them. The disco and funk is the same, it originated here, as what James Brown is doing is that sort of northern music. There's a beat inside some of his tunes like 'Give It Up or Turn It Loose' that is the same beat as the Bamaya dance of the Dagarti people of north-eastern Ghana. We wanted in the Apagya Band to bring all this music back to its roots.

Ambolley then went on to join the Super Complex Band run by the Tema Food Complex where he made his first album called 'Simigwa', but which didn't include his first controversial hit. He has some comments on this album.

It was highlife with a funky feeling as I want the Americans, West Indians and South Americans to understand my music. Also some of the songs are reggae highlifes and smoochie highlifes. One song is called 'Akokoba', mean little chickens who make more noise than their mothers. It's a proverb similar to 'empty barrels make the most noise.'

The cover of this album has the most amazing picture of Ambolley. He is dressed up as a small boy and he has twisted his mouth at right angles to the normal position. I asked him what this meant and he said it means something like 'take it or leave it'. In 1979 Ambolley finally got around to forming his own band called Zantoda, the name coming from the initials of his birth-place and those of his two partners. 'Z' stands for Nzema, 'ant' for the town of Antoa and 'oda' for the town of Oda. His two partners were based in England and sent him the instruments from there, and so in 1980

227

decided to take the whole ten-man band to England and released a Disco 45 there on the Orbitone label. After his bandsmen split or returned to Ghana, Ambolley stayed on in London where, in 1982, he formed Zantada II. Then with the help of Osibisa, he released an album. As Ambolley comments:

> *Unfortunately, for us there was a confusion and we had to stay in our rooms without working, taking a holiday for two months. After the matter had been solved we had to book everything again. So we finally played around London, at the Venue, Africa Centre and Fulham Town Hall. Then we travelled to Manchester and Birmingham. We also did some recordings at the Chalk Farm Studio run by a West Indian company called Orbitone. After my group returned I stayed on. By that time I had met Teddy Osei and Mac Tontoh and they advised me to get some musicians from England to change my sound and they helped me with the recordings, a collection of funky highlifes and disco-calypsos on the Owu Siwa label. There was Ray Allen on alto sax, George Lee on tenor, Alfred Bannerman on guitar, Daku Potato on congas, Papa Mensah on drums plus a Jamaican drummer on three tracks and Emmanuel Rentoz on keyboards for one track. There were some Jamaican girls who did some singing and Teddy and Mac also featured on flute and trumpet.*

I asked Ambolley about the British music scene, what it has to offer Africa and what the attitude to African music in Britain is.

> *English music I really can't describe, but mostly I didn't like it. It doesn't come out of feelings, it comes out of machines and electronics. I saw some of these noisy bands like White Snake and Adam Ant who paints himself like a cat. I don't think (their) funk has anything to offer us. The only type of music that does is American type funk, disco and Caribbean reggae as they appeal to Africans. There's a long struggle ahead. The Whiteman accepts our rhythms but ignores our music. The black man is a second-class citizen and so anything coming out of him is also thought to be second-class. But inwardly they know it is first-class and they are dancing to it.*

I mentioned to Ambolley at this point that some English musicians are using African influences. For instance Mick Fleetwood, the English leader of American-based Fleetwood Mac, came over to Ghana to get some inspiration. When I mentioned Fleetwood's 1980 trip to Ghana, Ambolley became quite irate.

When I was in London I heard Fleetwood's record 'The Visitor' on the air. I couldn't see what he was trying to portray because from the look of things he came here to get involved in African sounds and make use of them, but he couldn't see what he was trying to portray. If you have an African rhythm you can add a bass line, guitars and so on to colour up the basic rhythm. But Fleetwood didn't do this, he took a piece of African music and played it for a short time and joined this to his own sound. To play a bit of African music and then a bit of his, that's no combination. He couldn't exploit our sound. Fleetwood has jived us as he couldn't do what he came here to do. If he had exploited our music the way I'm saying he could have made our music to be accepted and that would open the way for American musicians to come.

In the 1980s, Ambolley was involved with the Musicians Union of Ghana and was on its Executive. It was in this capacity that I first met him, during the events that led up the musician's march for recognition in 1979. However due to the decline of live band music in Ghana Ambolley spent a lot of time in the 1980s and 90s travelling between Ghana, Europe and the States. He spent some time in the States where he formed his Afrikan Hi-Life band with which he released his album 'Hi-Life jazz in America' As mentioned earlier his and other African popular music has also become much loved by Afro-Colombians and has influenced their 'champeta' music stars like Viviano Torres, Luis Towers and Justo Valdez.

Ambolley then returned home and is incredibly active in Ghana and often makes guest appearances. For instance, in 2006, I saw him jam with Ebo Taylor and the University highlife band, both on the Legon campus and at a garden party in honour of the late Ali Faka Toure, thrown by the musical World Bank Ghana Country Director, Matts Karlsson. Because of the interest of World Music fans in Ambolley's music some of his songs have been re-released since 2000. These are 'Take Am So' recorded in London with Mac Tontoh, Alfred Bannerman and the Zantoda Mark III Band ('Afrobeat' CD on the UK Shrine Label), and the 1973 Steneboofs recording of 'Simigwado' arranged by Ebo Taylor[13]. In 2010-2011 Ambolley played at the Alliance Francaise, the Music of Ghanaian Origin (MOGO) awards night and Solidarity Night with Haiti (after the 2010 earthquake), and regularly appears at the +233 Jazz Club in Accra. In 2011 he worked with the lady singer Eazzy on a track of a CD by launched by Lynx Entertainment that experiments with collaborations between Afro-pop artists and hiplife artists like, Richie, O.J. Black, Sonny Bali and Jay Ghartey.

---

[13]'Ghana Sounds' CD on Soundway, UK.

In fact, Ambolley's use of rhythmic slang over a steady funky highlife beat has been an inspiration to many young hiplifers. Indeed, Ambolley claims to be the very first Ghanaian rapper, twenty years before Reggie Rockstone coined the name 'hiplife' for local rap and hip-hop in the mid-1990s. Whether this is true or not, Ambolley's funky 'simigwido' style of highlife has inspired many current hiplife acts, such as Tinny, Kwaku T and Trigmatic – and in 2010 the hiplife duo of Zed Ay Kay and Ziggi released a rap version of Ambolley's music called 'Simi Rap Remix'. Ambolley has therefore crossed the boundaries between the older highlife and younger hiplife generation.

Chapter 22

SAMMY ODOH: CHAMPION OF GHANA MUSICIANS

Sammy Odoh (in suit with guitar) and Black Beats 1970s

S ammy Owusu 'Odoh', was the dynamic National Organiser of the 4,000 strong
musicians union of Ghana (MUSIGA) in the early 1980s and was involved in
setting up the union in the early seventies. He has been active in the Ghanaian

music scene right back to the fifties and has played with every type of highlife band: kombomba groups, guitar-bands and dance bands. For fourteen years he ran King Bruce's old highlife band the Black Beats. Sammy's musical activities started almost at the birth as his father was a palm-wine guitarist and accordionist who played with Kwasi Manu and Kwasi Peprah during the 1940s. The first band Sammy joined was his school band in which he played the side-drum, but being so small he kept tripping over his instruments on parades. When he was about ten or eleven he joined one of the many konkomba (or konkoma) street bands in Accra that used a combination of African and European percussion instruments. At first, being so small, they only gave him the triangle to play, but as he explained to me in 1982 he soon sorted that out.

All the time I was thinking how to get into the group more effectively, though there was no chance as all the instruments were filled up. Then I saw a magazine with a photo of some bongos and showed it to a blacksmith and asked him to make one for me. He made it free for me as he was within the group and liked the way I followed them. So when the group was playing no one asked me to play but I would mix up with them and so they became interested as at that time no konkomba group was using bongos. So any time they went to play they would call me, as people began to ask for me. My mother said 'no' as in those days if you are a musician you are out of the family — and also she didn't like me following the grown-ups. So the group had to beg her. Finally, to make me a good boy she sent me to learn tailoring at my uncles in Kwahu. But there I met Asare's Guitar Band and as they hadn't seen bongos before I began to play for them for one-and-a-half years. Then I was sent to stay with my aunt in Tafo and it was there that I joined F.K. Mensah's concert group and played bongos, congas and jazz drums for almost a year.

Within a few years Sammy's musical travels took him out of Ghana altogether, with disastrous results — as he describes.

I had a chance to go to Ivory Coast and Liberia in 1959 with the Koforidua Rockies dance band, but we got broken down in Monrovia. At that time they didn't have live music, they listened to records and weren't used to dance bands. We ran out of money and it was everyone for himself and God for us all! We all had to find our ways home and I had it tough. All my clothes got worn out and I was walking about like a mad man. I was eating raw cassava and coconut which you can buy a lot for one cent. Finally a Ga man got me back to Accra after almost two years in Liberia.

By the time Sammy finally got back, his band, the Rockies, had become the Brigade Dance Band, part of the Workers Brigades that President Nkrumah had set up. There was no room for Sammy in the band but the Brigade Authorities agreed to accept him as a sportsman rather than as a musician. As Sammy relates, he was diverted from music for a couple of years.

> *They initiated me into the Brigade but not in the band. They told me there's no chance for me in the band, so I became a boxer in the brigade. My boxing name was 'Bob Tuntuluntu' and I was the flyweight champion of Ghana for 1961 and 1962. Then we were all to go to the Olympic Games so the sportsmen were all brought down to Accra for training and it was there that I made my arrangements with Spike Anyankor, Associate Director of Music of the Workers Brigade, to be transferred from the boxing side to join the Brigade guitar-band. I gave up boxing completely and went back to music and finally ended up with the Brigade Band as conga player and drummer for a couple of years.*

By this time Sammy not only played the drums but the guitar as well. Then his 'brain was opened' as he says when he and eight other Brigade members were sent to learn music theory at Achimota College for nine months. There Sammy learnt to play piano and flute and it was after he finished these studies that he got at long last into the Brigade Dance Band. During this time (1963) he also formed a number of Sharbo-Sharbo bands on the side. Sharbo-Sharbo is Pidgin English for 'share and share' as these bands are one-off affairs that are just put together for the occasional show or recording, with all monies being divided equally afterwards. One of Sammy's Sharbo-Sharbo groups he was involved with was Ignace de Souza's Melody Aces with which he recorded popular songs like 'Paulina' and 'Sulu Ajola'. Another was Bakare Yalu's band based in Accra's Nima area. Yet another was the Ragtime Dance Band and, as Sammy explains, it was this band that took him to King Bruce's Black Beats.

> *We had an engagement side-by-side with the Black Beats at the Christmas-in-Egypt club. The way I played my guitar turned King Bruce on and he asked me to play in his band, especially when he found out that I was a master-blaster and could play many instruments. By that time I was also playing flute and saxophone. So I played part time with his band but still lived at the Brigade camp. King Bruce was by then fed-up with his band because the musicians were inconsistent. New musicians were brought in to revive the band and I was made assistant leader. At first we only had one amplifier, but it was effective. I became the leader of the group from 1969 until 1977. I changed the music to Congo jazz and pop as well as our normal highlife.*

In 1972 Sammy and the Black Beats toured the UK and had to first negotiate with the British Musicians Union. It was there that he saw how important a strong music union was. This convinced Sammy his colleague Dan Quarcoo of setting up a union in Ghana, beginning with the fifty or so members of King Bruce's B.B. bands. Within a short time they linked up with the Faisal Helwani of the Napoleon Night-club and founding father of the Musicians Union of Ghana (MUSIGA).

> *About this time Faisal had formed Hedzoleh and Hugh Masekela had taken them from him to America, so Faisal too wanted the union to stop these things happening. Then one day when we were playing at The Prisons Canteen with another of Faisal's bands, called Basa Basa, and the promoter ran away with all the gate money. So it was then that we seriously talked about forming a union and we came together. I would organise everything and Faisal would finance it.*

It was MUSIGA that organised the Great March of Musicians in Accra in 1979 for government recognition, for as Sammy put it back in 1982 'the government should stop thinking always about diamonds, gold and cocoa, and understand that countries like the United States, Sweden and Britain have music as a major export. So our government too can make a hell of a lot of money'. Sadly the countries live popular music scene continued to go into decline at the time and due to the problems of running a live band in the 1980s and 90s Sammy spent many years moving between Ghana and the Cote D'Ivoire. He has continued travelling a lot; but when in Accra, he lives at his family house in Osu, from where he used to manage local bands, advised up-and-coming musicians and at one point was teaching highlife guitar to both local and foreign students.

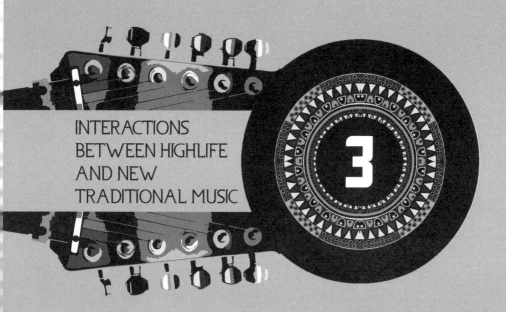

INTERACTIONS BETWEEN HIGHLIFE AND NEW TRADITIONAL MUSIC

3

Highlife
TIME 3

This concerns some early drummed forms of trans-cultural West African popular music (goombay, gome and asiko). It also looks at various types of modernised local Ghanaian drum-dance styles, one being konkoma that evolved in the 1930s as a poorman's Africanised form of regimental brass band music. Some other 20th century drum dances that have been affected by highlife are Ewe borborbor music, the simpa of Dagbon and the kpanlogo of the Ga. These are what might be called new or 'neo-traditional' music as, despite modern influences, these drum-dances are performed in the communal context of a village or urban ethnic community.

Chapter 23

GOOMBAY, GOME AND ASIKO

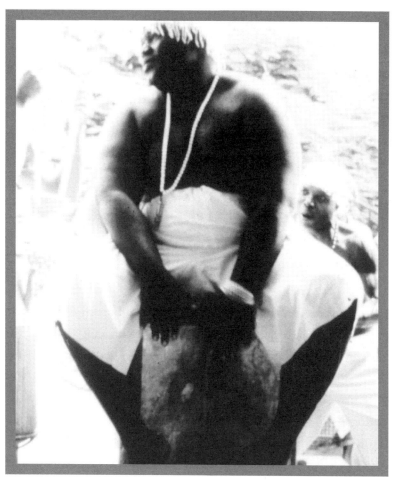

Big Boy of the Ga group Wulomei group sitting on a gome drum in 1970s

A popular Ghanaian drum-dance that goes back over one hundred years and which is particularly associated with the Ga people is gome. This music, sung in Ga and Pidgin English, is played on a large bass frame-drum tightened with a metal screw; with the musician sitting on it, and using his hands and feet to beat out syncopated 4/4 rhythms. There are also an assortment of other percussion instruments, including smaller (alto and tenor) hand-held tambourine like frame-drums called 'tamarins' or 'tamales'; or, sometimes, 'konkoma' drums, as they were associated with the konkoma highlife groups of the 1930s and 40s. Gome, gombe or goombay drums have also influenced other Ghanaian drum-dance music which, because of their recent origin, can be called new or 'neo-traditional' music styles – like the simpa music of the Dagomba people of northern Ghana which will be discussed in Chapter 25.

Another neo-traditional drum dance is gahu or (agahu) which, according to Professors Kobla Ladzekpo and Alan Eder, was created before the Second World War by some Egun speaking people of the Republic of Benin who had been playing gome. When they modified gome, they changed the name to 'agahu' or iron vehicle when they saw their first aeroplane. This music subsequently spread to the Badagry area of Nigerian where Ewe migrant fishermen adapted it. It was brought to Ghana by Kofi Dey in 1950. Gome is found in many West African countries, with its African country of origin being Sierra Leone. However, its ultimate source is surprisingly in Jamaica. So we have a complete round trip. Slaves took West African drums and rhythms to Jamaica; then, because traditional hand-carved drums were suppressed by the British, the slaves began using the modernised goombay ones, which then found their way back to Africa.

Let us look at this trans-Atlantic story in more detail.

Goombay (also gumbe, gumbay or gumbia) is a Jamaican drum-dance associated with recreational activities and the neo-African myalism healing cult of the descendants of runaway black slaves known as 'maroons'. In Jamaica it is played on the European bass and snare drum and the large square goombay frame-drum. The first reference to goombay in Jamaica is in 1774. There is evidence that it spread quickly to other Caribbean countries and even the southern United States. In 1800, it was also taken to West Africa onboard ships. This followed the maroon rebellion of 1795 when, because of white fears of a Haitian-type black revolution in Jamaica, the British signed a peace deal with the Jamaican maroons which included taking some of them to

Sierra Leone Freetown Goombay group with musical saw, 1970s
(photo from Cootje van Oven's book – see bibliography)

Freetown, to join other groups of freed slaves who had begun to settle in the newly-established British colony of Sierra Leone. The first Freetown references to goombay are from the 1820s and 1830s. Indeed, by 1858, this maroon drumming had so scandalised elements of the Krio (i.e. Creole) elite that the local church Mission Society published a newspaper article warning people that 'Gumbay is the cause of many vices'. Despite this opposition, goombay drumming and dancing continued to flourish in Freetown and spread to many parts of West and Central Africa.

The Ga musician, Squire Addo, told me that 'gome' (as it is called by Ga's) was first introduced to the country around the turn of the century by Ga carpenters and blacksmiths returning from the Belgian Congo, where they had been working for 'big firms'. In fact, the Ga's were working alongside Sierra Leone carpenters, blacksmiths and clerks, as these two groups of skilled West African workers were employed from 1885 in building the Matadi docks of the then Congo Free State, the ruthlessly-run private domain of King Leopold of Belgium who had trained no local Africans to do such work. These Sierra Leonians and Ghanaians artisans were part of the five thousand 'coastmen' from English-speaking West Africa that King Leopold employed until 1908, when the Belgium government confiscated the country from him. Besides these Ga artisans returning from the Congo, a later wave of gome music was introduced to Accra in the 1940s from Fernando Po by Ga migrant fishermen. One of these fishermen's groups – the Kpehe Gome Group – is still in existence. But even Fernando Po has a Sierra Leonian connection, as Freetown people had been settled on this island by the British who ruled there for most of the 19th century.

According to the music historian Flemming Harrev, goombay frame-drum music is found in seventeen West African countries. In western Nigeria, a 'gombe' drum is played by some juju music ensembles, most probably introduced there by 'Saro' (i.e. Sierra Leone) people. These are the descendants of Yoruba recaptured slaves who had been liberated to Freetown in the early 19th century by British anti-slavery navy patrols, returning home to Nigeria later that century. I was shown such a gombe drum in 1974 when I visited the juju musician Ebenezer Obey at his house in Lagos. In this case it was not a frame-drum, but a traditional carved hand-drum surmounted by a Western-type side drum, complete with metal screws for tightening the head. Although not a typical goombay frame-drum, it did share one of its common characteristics: it is a West African drum that possesses modern features of carpentry and joinery. 'Gumbe' or 'gube' was also popular in the Malian capital Bamako between the 1930s and 1950s where it gave its name to multi-ethnic associations of young people. Likewise, 'Le goumbe' was connected with the urban multi-ethnic youth associations of Abidjan in the Cote d'Ivoire immediately after the Second World War. It is also played in the Senegalese island of Morre. Flemming Harrev has told me that information on a 1904 cylindrical record of 'Gumbe' music made in German Togoland has recently surfaced.

Goombay, of course, is still played in Sierra Leone's capital Freetown, where it is used to accompany masked dancers and sometimes features the 'musical saw'. A variant of goombay music that evolved in Freetown around the turn of the century is called 'asiko' or 'ashiko'. Shortly after, it became popular in Ghana and Nigeria. Asiko musicians used a small hand-held goombay type frame-drum called an 'asiko' (or sometimes in Lagos a 'samba') drum. Also featured in asiko is a carpenter's musical saw and a tapped bottle, with the music being accompanied by a dance that resembled a quickstep or foxtrot. Influences from asiko found their way into both Ghanaian highlife and Nigerian juju music. Asiko may have been initially associated with the 'Aku' people of Freetown, the descendants of freed Yoruba slaves who settled and stayed there; for, as the musicologist Fleming Harrev points out, the word 'asiko' in Yoruba means 'time'. It is therefore possible that this is a borrowed word from Yoruba that refers to the role of the asiko drum as a 'timekeeper'.

In Ghana, the gome drum and music are still alive and kicking. The bass gome drum is included in many traditional Ga groups as, over the years, gome has been turned into a fully local Accra drum dance sung in Ga (see the gome drum in the Agbafoi group photo, Chapter 31). And there are still actual gome groups that perform the older type of gome music that is sung in Pidgin English, like the songs 'Mr Jacob, Iron (i.e. chisel) Cut My Finger' and 'Wata (tears) Run My Eyes O'. Equally old is the humorous gome dance that involves a man in a suit, holding a wooden carpenters box and flirting with a woman with a huge backside bustle. In 2003, there was a gome competition in Accra[14] that featured the Oblaboloi Cultural Troupe, the Sankofa Dance Theatre, the Dromo Dance Ensemble, the Shidaa Cultural Troupe, Folkloric Salemta, the Opense Cultural Troupe and Agawaso Manshie Kweloi. Several other local gome competitions have followed. The gome drums are also used in some bands like Takashi, Local Dimension and Hewale Sounds.

Goombay, gombe or gome represents the first 'homecoming' of a Black Diasporic music to Africa, having been created by African slaves in the Caribbean and then brought to Africa in 1800. As such, it is a musical icon for the re-connection of Africa and the Black Americas. So it would be fitting if a festival could be organised to bring together African, Caribbean and American musicians and musicologists to study, celebrate and play this remarkable product of Africa and its Black Diaspora.

[14]Organised by the Centre for National Culture and Skylife Tours

Chapter 24

AKAN KONKOMA AND EWE BORBORBOR

Konkoma (sometimes called konkomba) is an important early form of highlife that evolved in southern Ghana and spread far and wide up until the 1950s, when its popularity declined. It crystallised as a distinct style in the early 1930s and is associated with coastal Fanti people. Dr. Chrys Sackey traces konkoma's origin to the town of Mumford or Dwanba situated between the ports of Winneba and Cape Coast. Dr. Sackey and Professor A.M. Opoku state that konkoma was created by 'school drop-outs' and 'ruffian boys' and was influenced by the Akan brass bands that had spread adaha music from Fanti-land throughout the whole of southern Ghana by this time. Konkoma can, therefore, be treated as a "poorman's" copy of local adaha brass band music as it did away with most of the expensive imported brass instruments, substituting these with voices for the melody line and local rattles, bells and hand-held 'konkoma drums' (frame-drums) for the rhythm (for a photo of a konkoma like frame-drums see next chapter on simpa).

The few instruments that konkoma groups did borrow from brass-bands were the small double-headed metal 'pati', a local version of the European military side-drum and, occasionally, according to Kwaa Mensah, the regimental bass-drum. The repertoire of konkoma groups were basically the same highlifes, 'blues' and imported dance songs of the contemporary local adaha brass bands. Also like the brass bands, the konkoma groups often featured western-type synchronised marching to the European military 'oom pah oom pah' 2/4 and 4/4 tempo that emphasise the first or the first and third beat of the measure.

The association of military-type marching with konkoma is probably one of the reasons why the British colonial government adopted konkoma songs for recruiting and for army route marches. Professor K.N. Bame, who was a schoolboy member of the Kpandu Konkoma Group in the late 1930s and early 40s, told me that the members actually marched to the performance venue where the musicians formed a semi-circle for the dancers. Professor A.M. Opoku told me that konkoma groups also put on formation and team dances. The instrumentalists and dancers, according to Dr. Sackey, wore uniforms modelled on those of the military, police, fire-brigade and railway workers. Professor Opoku describes these as chequered shirts, shorts with 'many secret pockets' into which were put silk handkerchiefs. There were also peaked caps with tassels of varying colours, depending on the particular konkoma group; for these groups were highly competitive.

This rivalry was expressed by the use of all sorts of eye catchers. Professor Opoku mentioned that the baton-wielding conductor of a konkoma group would, for dramatic effect, pass the baton 'under his thigh and catch it with his left hand – and as soon as it came down, the drumming would start'. This competitiveness was also reflected in the dancing itself, for performers would try and knock each other. Again, Professor Opoku told me that, although the word 'konkoma' is a nonsense one, it is part of the Akan expression 'me twa konkoma ma bo f m' (I cut konkoma and I fall down), which was used when the dancers purposely bumped into each other and pretended to fall down on the phrase 'ko' of konkoma.

The connection between konkoma and youth groups also suggests that it evolved through westernising influences being absorbed into the Akan recreational music of the generational age-set of the early to mid-1930s. Indeed it was this particular youthful age-group of the 1930s that was of interest to the British Army during the Second World War, which explains why so many konkoma songs sung in the Akan language began to be used at this time in Ghana for route marches. Prior to this, the local marching music in Ghana or Gold Coast had been mainly in Hausa.

Whether treated as an indigenised "poorman's" version of brass bands or as a continuation, albeit westernised, of youthful Akan recreational music, konkoma spread like wildfire throughout the Akan area of southern Ghana. Moreover, just as konkoma was influenced by the brass bands, so konkoma itself affected other acculturated performance style, such as the post-war Akan 'akyewa' or 'aways' recreational music.

Konkoma also spread eastwards and became popular in western Nigeria during the late thirties and forties where it exerted an influence on Yoruba highlife, agidigbo (i.e. hand-piano) music and juju groups.

Although konkoma has largely died out in its birthplace Ghana, it is still played in certain parts of the Volta Region in the south-eastern part of the country. For instance, and according to Senyoh Adzei (one of my graduate music students at the University of Ghana Music Department), there is still such a group in Tsito Awudome where it was introduced by the local man Dzikum Kwesi in 1947, after returning from working as a fisherman in Cape Coast for seven years.

Uniformed member of a Tsito konkoma group circa early 1950s (photo Senyoh Adzei)

In its spread eastwards, konkoma was also taken up in the Ewe region of eastern Ghana and Togo. For, in the early 1950s and in the inland Ghanaian town of Kpandu, a regional recreational drum-dance called 'borborbor' emerged that fused the local Akpese recreational music with konkoma. In borborbor groups, the barrel drums favoured by Ewe replaced the konkoma frame-drums. Nevertheless, the adaha and konkoma influence is still felt by the presence of pati side-drum and bugle. The first borborbor group in Kpandu became known as 'Nkrumah's Own Borborbor Group' and was put together by policeman F.C. Nuatro and other young people who identified with the CPP independence party. This Ewe recreational music is accompanied by a ring dance in which the dancers shuffle anti-clockwise waving handkerchiefs and bend down from time to time; thus the name 'borborbor' or bend down. The music is associated with formal clubs that have treasurers and secretaries, and act for their members as mutual benefit societies and funeral clubs. Amongst the northern Ewe, borborbor has became the favourite new or neo-traditional recreational music, including for those who have migrated to the urban areas. Borborbor music is played in 4/4 and march-time time, and its bell rhythm is reminiscent of highlife. In a way fitting to its distant and indirect link with the highlife brass bands, the borborbor bugler or trumpeter includes, from time-to-time, bursts of syncopated military reveilles type phrases over the dense drumming.

Kpandu Borborbor group in the 1980s. Note the local Ewe barrel drums and 'pati' (bottom left), a local version of a military side drum

245

Chapter 25

THE SIMPA MUSIC OF DAGBON

*The Wait and See Simpa group of Yendi in 1974. The tambourine or
'tamale' frame-drums are identical to earlier gome and konkoma drums*

Simpa music grew out of a combination of traditional Dagomba and Hausa music with Western and particularly Western-influenced African styles, such as highlife and gome (gombe). This type of acculturation is also found in the music of other ethnic groups in Ghana; for instance, Ewe borborbor, Akan akyewa (pronounced ashewa) and Ga kpanlogo, all of which are new or new-traditional styles influenced by highlife. As we have already seen, highlife spread from the coast into the hinterland through the medium of records, brass bands and guitar-bands. By the 1930s, it had reached Dagbon, where it was transformed into simpa. A clue to this southern root of simpa is the name 'simpa' itself, for this is the local name for Winneba (i.e. 'Windy Bay'), one of the Fanti port towns in which highlife was born.

Today, there are scores of simpa groups scattered around the Dagomba traditional area of northern Ghana. It is predominantly a recreational music, played for and by young people, but is also played at weddings, funerals and out-doorings. In April 1974, when I visited Yendi, the capital of the Dagomba state, there were twelve groups, the two most important being the 'Wait and See' and 'Real Unity Stars' simpa groups. I watched performances of both these bands. In each case, the show took place in an open space in the town illuminated by kerosene lamps, starting at about nine in the evening and ending at one in the morning. The bands consisted of six or seven young male musicians and a chorus of girls between the ages of ten and sixteen. Fifty to one hundred spectators surrounded the bands and some of the girls present danced together 'flesh to flesh'. Below is a more detailed description of the two bands and their songs. I should add that the repertoires are larger than normally played, as I asked them to play as wide a selection as possible.

WAIT AND SEE SIMPA GROUP

There was one male and two female singers with six accompanying musicians playing a set of Tamale-made metal conga drums, three square frame 'tamale' (i.e. tambourine) drums (bass, second, and solo), a bell and a metal rattle made from an empty tin can. Although not used that night, the group sometimes uses a Hausa donno, a pressure drum or hour-glass drum. Below is a list of the songs played which is short as the group did not play long due to competition from another simpa group that was playing that night.

(1) a long period of warming up by the drummers playing traditional Dagomba drumming

(2) An instrumental highlife

(3) A Congo jazz number called 'Sopato' by O.K. Jazz in which the words were in Hausa

(4) An instrumental number based on the James Brown soul beat. The girls danced soul.

(5) A traditional Dagomba dance sung in Dagbani and translated as 'Shake Your Waist'.

THE REAL UNITY STARS SIMPA GROUP

In this group, there were seven musicians playing metal congas, two frame drums (bass and second), a set of Tamale-made trap drums (a snare and two side drums), a bell, metal rattles and a trumpet played by the group's leader, Halaru Sayiba. The group was accompanied by an ever-changing group of female singers.

The band was formed by Halaru Sayibu in 1967 after he left the Yendi brass band. He is, therefore, much older than the other musicians. He told me that his simpa group travelled extensively around Dagbon. Below is a list of the songs (all of which were danced to by the spectators):

(1) 'I Can't Stand It', a soul number by James Brown; however, the words were sang in Dagbani and translated as 'a monkey carries a baby on its back'.

(2) 'Hip City', a soul number by the Champs. Sang in Dagbani, the title translates as 'Fufu Is More Delicious than Konkonte'.

(3) 'Nimpa Rebrɛ' a highlife composed by C.K. Mann and sang in Akan.

(4) A traditional Dagomba dance, the lyrics of which translate as 'if I were a fish I would stay deep down in the water where nothing can harm me'.

(5) 'Sava Omo', a Congo jazz number sang in French and Lingala.

(6) A traditional Dagomba dance, the lyrics of which, when translated mean, 'if a man insults me and then buys something for me, it is a double insult'.

(7) 'Let's Do The Twist' by Chubby Checker but sang in Dagbani.

(8) A kpanlogo by Otoo Lincoln called 'ABCD'.

(9) 'Everybody Likes Saturday Night' an old highlife sung in English.

I mentioned that simpa appeared in the Dagomba traditional area during the 1930s. It was, in fact, the third of three genres of recreational dance music that appeared during this time. The first was gombe music, which was brought from Prang in Brong Ahafo (120 miles south of Yendi). According to Shani Abraham, who was one of the six Dagombas who introduced this music to Yendi, gombe was being played in Brong Ahafo by Hausas and Kotokolis, and they utilized the full set of frame-drums from the small tambourines to the large bass drum. A second style that appeared about the same time was amidziro music that was played on large kerosene cans and local congas. It was introduced to Yendi by Hausas from Salaga (seventy miles south of Yendi) and the word 'amidziro' is the Ewe word for stranger. Simpa music, which first appeared in Yendi and then spread throughout Dagbon, was a local development that drew on both these earlier-imported southern styles.

Shani Abraham recalls that the name 'gombe' was changed to simpa in the twelfth year of Na Abdallah's reign (1932), whereas Issaca-Bukari who helped organise the first simpa group, put the time in the early reign of Na Muhammad (1938-1948). Mr. Bukari pointed out to me that simpa in its early days was greatly influenced by gramophone records; so, besides traditional Dagomba music, the groups played Akan highlifes and European waltzes, foxtrots, and quicksteps. Other influences on simpa were from the concert parties, the first to tour the Northern Region (according to Efua Sutherland) being the Axim Trio in 1936. Yet another southern Ghanaian influence was from the brass bands with their adaha highlifes, marches and imported ballroom music. According to Halaru Sayibu, two brass bands were formed in Yendi during the 1950s, one of which lasted until 1965. Later, simpa groups incorporated into their repertoires Western pop music heard on the radio, or from records or through touring Ghanaian bands.

Simpa music is relevant to social tensions found within Dagomba society. This informal recreational music has always been associated with gatherings of young people and so was generally frowned upon by the older generation, who consider simpa performances as improper for young people to frequent. This is reminiscent of the attitude of the older generation in the West towards pop bands and pop festivals.

Simpa music has also played a role in traditional political divisions within Dagomba society that have emerged since independence. During the colonial times, the British administration 'froze' the traditional system of chiefly succession in which the Royal Skin was rotated between the two royal families, by establishing a single family dynasty. With independence, bottled-up tensions erupted in conflict between the

249

Abdallah/Abudu House supported by the British, and the Andani House that was suppressed by the British and therefore became linked to Nkrumah's Convention Peoples Party (CPP). This political division came to a head in 1969 when the Busia government expelled the Andani Regent from the palace in Yendi and replaced him with an Abdallah Ya Na (chief). The simpa groups took sides in the dispute and made up songs about the conflict that were considered so inflammatory that a six-month police ban was placed on their performances.

In August 1994, I visited Tamale with members of MUSIGA, the Copyright Administration and the Folkloric Board of Trustees. Although I didn't make it to Yendi, I discovered simpa was still alive and well in Tamale where there were then sixteen active groups.

According to the Tamale reggae artist and recording engineer Sheriff Ghale who wrote a report on the Tamale music industry in 2013, when he was one of my University of Ghana M.Phil music students, simpa music is still found in the Dagbon area with some of its artists, like Yakubu Gowan and Yakubu Salifu, recording and releasing their music in the fledgeling music industry that has emerged in Tamale since the late 1980s.

Chapter 26

OTOO LINCOLN THE INVENTOR OF THE GA KPANLOGO

Otoo Lincoln's (left) kpanlogo group in 1965. Mustapha Tettey Addy is on atumpan talking-drums, his brothers Obo and Emmanuel are on bell and hand drum

Just as Europe has its anonymous folk music (the famous and prolific 'anon'), so too in Ghana and other African countries there is a vast tradition of ethnic music, so old that its creators have been forgotten and their legacy has become part of the national heritage. This old folkloric music, sometimes referred to in Ghana as 'cultural' music, is often the basis for other types of new or neo-traditional music. This includes traditional recreational music styles that have been influenced by highlife and other forms of popular music, like the previously mentioned konkoma, simpa and borborbor. This can occur because Ghana has a living folklore that co-exists with a westernised popular music, and so they have a circular relationship with one another. Thus, urban popular music draws on traditional-based African performance styles, whilst these in turn can be affected by popular idioms.

In this chapter, we will turn to another neo-traditional recreational music, this time the kpanlogo (pronounced 'palogo') drum-dance of the Ga people of Accra that was invented in the early 1960s by Otoo Lincoln and a group of youth in the Bukom area from a combination of pre-existing local Ga drumming with highlife and imported rock 'n' roll. Kpanlogo is, in fact, the most recent of a succession of Ga recreational drumming styles that have drawn on outside influences; such as the Ga version of gome that evolved in the early 1900s, the processional kolomashie of the 1930s and 40s that was affected by colonial marching bands (thus the possible origin of the word 'kolo-mashie'), followed in the 1950s by the guitar and local hand-piano 'something' music of Ga fishermen, and oge drumming influenced by visiting Liberian Kru seamen

When, in 1983, I met the 'inventor' of kpanlogo, the Accra-born Otoo Lincoln (and his manager Godwin Abbey), the first thing I asked was the actual meaning of the word 'kpanlogo'.

OTOO LINCOLN: It was from a folk story my grandfather told me and the name 'kpanlogo' is the imaginary name of a girl. You see, there were three girl triplets called Kpanlogo, Mma Mma and Alogodzan. Their father, who was the chief of the town, said that the man who would guess the three girls' names could take all three and marry them. A difficult challenge, as they were always kept in the house, didn't come out and didn't socialise much. So one man went to the house dressed as a madman and met Mma Mma in the yard, who shouted to her two sisters to come and see someone dancing. As they called each other, the man learned the three names. To remember

252

them he kept on singing to himself, 'Kpanlogo, Alogodzan, Kpanlogo Mma Mma'. He was always singing this song, until the meeting the chief had called for the public to come and guess the girls' names. But if you come and can't show the correct name they kill you. Some people came and they were not fit so the chief cleared them out. But when the man came, the chief gave him his daughters.

JC: Your grandfather told you this?

OTOO LINCOLN: He told me [this story] in 1956 when I was fifteen and living at Korle Wokon, in Accra. It was what we call an Adesa or Ananse Story, and when he told it to me me, he didn't know I would make it into music. It was when I used to tell the story to my brothers, sisters and friends at our family house in Bukom, central Accra, and I used to dance and sing 'Kpanlogo, Alogodzan, Kpanlogo Mma Mma'. Some friends started to drum as they liked my kpanlogo dance, which is my own version of highlife. The drummers were Okule Foes and Ayitey Sugar. It was around 1962.

JC: Then what is the origin of the kpanlogo beat?

OTOO LINCOLN: In our house, our fathers were playing oge introduced by Liberian Kru seamen and popular in Accra during the 1950s. It's like a slow kpanlogo played on one drum, clips and a saw and nail to scrape it. Kpanlogo is really a mixture of different dances like highlife and oge, there's even rock and roll in it, as I used to dance rock and roll around 1960 with Frank Lane at the Black Eagles Club.

OTOO LINCOLN: Can you name a few of the early kpanlogos that came out of your Kpanlogo Special Band?

OTOO LINCOLN: One, of course, was the original 'Kpanlogo Alogodzan' and another was the 'ABC Kpanlogo' which I made when I acted like a teacher teaching children. And we had another popular song called 'Ayinye Momobiye' which means 'Ayine hold pickin as I am going to dance the kpanlogo'.

JC: I believe there was some opposition to kpanlogo at first?

OTOO LINCOLN: The Arts Council called me and I wouldn't go and one of the directors there started to spoil the name of kpanlogo. He called me and said my dance was no good as one of the beats in the dance makes the body move in an indecent way. I told him maybe someone is making the dance like that, but not me. So I had to make a demonstration at the Arts Council and they said it was okay. That was in 1964.

JC: But the real out-dooring was in 1965?

OTOO LINCOLN: Yes, when Mr. G.W. Amarteifio called me to perform for the big men (including President Nkrumah) at the stadium near Black Star Square. There were fifty kpanlogo groups that performed, all of whom copied my Bukom-based band. For instance, Okule Foes, Koto Lincoln and Frank Lane formed their groups from mine.

JC: Did you go professional?

OTOO LINCOLN: The Ga Mantse (Chief) made a group called Obuade with Tetteh Addy and his three brothers, Mustapha, Obo and Emmanuel and called me in to show them kpanlogo in 1967. I stayed with them [for] two years and made shows at places like Bukom Night Club, the Ambassador and Continental Hotel. Now I concentrate on my carpentry, but whenever there is a funeral or out-dooring we still play.

We can see some of the original kpanlogo players like Otoo Lincoln, Frank Lane and the others on video, as the BBC/Third Eye production team included these originators of kpanlogo in a seven-part BBC Channel 4 television series on black music called 'Repercussions' made in 1983. Master drummer Mustapha Tettey Addy of the Obuade group also released a string of recording during the 1970s and 80s that include kpanlogo songs, the most famous being 'Kpanlogo Party' released by the British Tangent company.

After the djembe drum and pressure drum, the kpanlogo drum and drumming is perhaps the most popular and widespread West African drum style played internationally. Because it is atraditional type drum-dance music, many think that it is an ancient style whose composer is anonymous. This probably explains the fact that, except for a small copyright payment made to him in the 1990s, Otoo never really received the financial rewards for having created what has become Ghana's most internationally-acclaimed drumming style. However, a year before his death in 2006, he was given a lifetime achievement award in the February 2005 African American History/Heritage month organized by the Public Affairs Section of the US Embassy and the local Bokoor African Popular Music Archives Foundation, BAPMAF.

To bring things up to date, and as will be discussed in this book's Coda, some of the kpanlogo moves have been incorporated into the new 'azonto' dance craze that swept Ghana since 2010 and is associated with electronic rather than acoustic drum music.

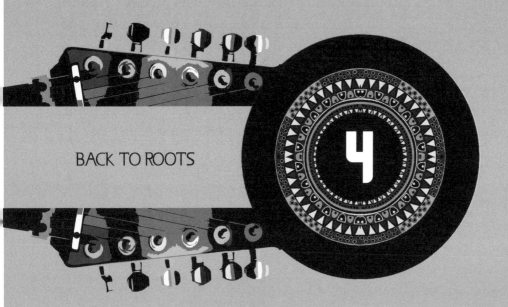

BACK TO ROOTS

4

Highlife
TIME 3

This begins with a look at some of the key features of traditional African music and then focuses on several leading Ghanaian musicians who were trained in guitar bands and dance bands, but later decided to indigenise their music in various ways. These are the folk guitarist Koo Nimo, Nii Ashitey who founded the Wulomei group and the Afro-jazzist Kofi Ghanaba (Guy Warren). Another is the jazzist and master drummer Kwesi Asare.

Chapter 27

THE TRADITIONAL MUSICAL BACKGROUND

The profusion of music and dance styles of Africa and its diaspora in the Americas have provided the world with the nearest thing we have in the modern age to global folk music. It began from the late 19ᵗʰ century with ragtime, jazz, blues, calypsos, the samba and other Latin-American ball-room dance crazes. Then came swing, Afro-Cuban rumbas, cha chas and mambos. This was followed in the 1960s by a succession of black 'pop music' styles like rock 'n' roll (partly derived from African American rhythm 'n' blues), soul, funk, disco, reggae, hip hop and rap. Since the rise of 'World Music' in the mid-1980s, these waves of black dance music have been augmented the popular music of Africa itself.

So what is it in the African approach to music that has enabled black music to cross all frontiers to become, directly or indirectly, a major force in international music? Or the question could be put in a different way: why hasn't European Classical/Romantic art-music (unlike its technology) become the dominant form of the twenty-first century? In fact, the two questions are linked. The waning of Classical/Romantic art-music from the beginning of the 20ᵗʰ century with the emergence of 'modern' atonalism and serialism corresponds exactly in time with the waxing of popular dance music styles like jazz and the samba that contain seminal black influences.

One could say that the latter filled a vacuum left by Western art-music that had become too cerebral and elitist. But more positive reasons than this can also be found, and probably the most important is the flexibility and adaptability of African music. Indeed, this is exactly how African slaves in the Americas were able to overcome the problem of having to play and copy the music of their white masters. They syncopated it by playing around the 'square' European meter and rather emphasized the gaps, off-beats and back-beats largely ignored in white tempo. This created a significant space or 'swing' for African-Americans and, as time has proved, for millions of others in the world as well. Unlike rigid European music with its score-sheets, baton-wielding conductors and passive audiences, black music involved the spontaneity of the players and movement of the dancers. The black African-derived influence has therefore had a balancing result on white western music. It has evened up the cerebral tendency of art-music with footwork and funk, the on-beat with the off-beat, the performers with their audiences, the mechanical and metronomic with soul.

TRADITIONAL AFRICAN MUSIC DYNAMICS

African music was often depicted by westerns in the past as 'primitive' or frozen in time. As is well recognised now, this notion that African music is static and archaic was part of a broader negative colonial view that saw Africa as a 'Dark Continent' that had no history. The fact that there had been numerous African nations and empires with their own historical dynamics was quite ignored. Indeed, these became relegated to mere 'tribes' and 'simple' village systems that had to be guided and civilised. Likewise, the comparative musicologists of the period considered 'authentic' African performing arts to be primeval and unchanging.

This was, however, far from the truth and as Professor J. H. K. Nketia (1971 and 1981) discusses in the case of Ghana, there was musical blending or syncretism going on between the Hausa, Dagomba, Akans, Ewe and Ga people through trade, migration and war long before European contact. Another form of traditional musical dynamic was generational change. For example, youthful age-sets, secret initiation societies and warrior associations could, through innovative performance, ridicule members of the older generation, question priests and even overthrow chiefs. Likewise, the youth continually modified recreational drum-dance styles which were often initially frowned upon by elders; thus each successive style acted as an identifier for the particular generation. Again, I refer to Professor Nketia who, in his 1973 book on Folksongs of Ghana, provides a long sequence of traditional recreational music styles of the Akan of Ghana. In the previous chapter on Ga music, we noted a similar type of sequence for their recreational drum-dances, from the gome and kolomashie of the early 20th century to the kpanlogo of the 1960s youth. Hence, each young generation re-models old musical genres and so invents new and distinct styles that distance themselves from the elders. But the youth, in turn, grow old and the process continues from generation to generation. This is very much the way popular dance-music styles in the West mark out the waxing and waning of their youthful sub-cultures, from those of jazz-age and roaring twenties to swing and its 'zoot suits', to the be-boppers and beatniks, followed by the rockers, rastas and rappers of today.

Although traditional African music was never static, there were some forms, like ritual and court performances, that were conservative and relatively slow-changing. However, informal recreational performance changed faster by the just-discussed rotation of generations. This is why so much of Ghana's early forms of popular music evolved out of traditional recreational music rather than ritual music, as recreational forms quickly incorporated novelty during the 19th and 20th centuries from outside as well as internal African influences. It could be rightly claimed therefore that much of contemporary Ghanaian, and indeed African popular dance music, is a direct continuation of ever-changing traditional youth-oriented recreational music, albeit with the novel elements no longer coming from just within Africa, but also from Europe, the Americas, India and the Islamic world.

Next we turn to the rhythmic structure of African rhythms through the prism of one particular Ghanaian rhythm or rather poly-rhythm, the agbadza drum-dance of the southern Ewe people of Ghana's Volta Region and neighbouring Togo. It is a contemporary social or recreational dance of the Ewe but was born out of a much faster traditional war-dance known as atrikpui. Although it is associated with traditional Ewe drum ensembles, the agbadza is also occasionally used by highlife and Afro-rock bands.

AN IN-DEPTH LOOK AT THE AGBADZA RHYTHM

The bell (or gong, or clave) pattern is the central time-keeper of much of Africa's poly-rhythmic drumming. In the case of the agbadza the bell rhythm is a variation of the wide-spread African rhythm that the musicologist, A.M. Jones (1959) calls the 'African signature tune'. This is written either as:

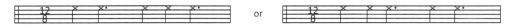

Figure 1

The basic agbadza claves or cow-bell 'time-line' pattern goes as follows:

Figure 2

ONE – THE RHYTHMIC PARTS OR SUB-RHYTHMS (THE 'HOT' ASPECT)

African music is mostly polyrhythmic, being composed of multiple rhythms stacked upon each other. It is the permutational possibilities or 'friction' between these criss-crossing strands of rhythm that generates the acoustic energy or heat. However, the first stage in learning to play African music is to acquire the discipline of the separate rhythms, and training starts in infancy on the dancing mother's back and from a myriad of children's rhythmic games and toys that abound on the continent.

For the agbadza, the simplest of the individual rhythms are those of the feet and hand followed by those of the claves/bell and the support drums, the kidi and the kagan. These five sub-rhythms are depicted below; but, rather than using the conventional notation, I have graphically or spatially separated out the individual pulses of each rhythm on twelve time divisions or intervals. Musicologists call this the Time Unit Box System.

ONE PHRASE OF THE AGBADZA INVOLVING FIVE SEPARATE SUB-RHYTHMS

Time Interval	1	2	3	4	5	6	7	8	9	10	11	12
feet	□			□			□					
hand-claps	C						c			c		
cow-bell	x		x		x	x		x		x		x
kagan	m	0	0	m	0	0	m	0	0	M	0	0
kidi	m	0	0	0	m	m	m	0	0	0	m	m

Figure Three

1. The feet and hands are played evenly four times.

2. The kagan is played with two sticks and its rhythm is made up of groups of three notes. The right stick strikes the open drum twice; then the left is played once but with the skin muted by pressure from the right stick. This results in two open high notes followed by a low muted one.

3. The kidi is a hand drum and its simplest rhythm is made by the right, left, then right hands striking the perimeter of the drum-skin, so producing three open notes. Then three muted notes are played in a likewise fashion, but on the centre of the drum-skin.

4. The claves or bell (called gankogui in Ewe) pattern is made up of seven pulses and, if a double-headed bell is used, the very first pulse is played on the low pitched bell.

A simple way for a non-African to learn to play the cow-bell rhythm is to equate it with the spacing of the seven notes of the major melodic scale on the twelve semi-tone intervals, as in the following diagram:

DIAGRAM OF THE TONIC SOL-FA OCTAVE AND BELL PATTERN COMPARED

Time Interval	1	2	3	4	5	6	7	8	9	10	11	12
cow-bell	x		x		x	x		x		x		z
sol-fa	do		re		mi	fa		so		la		ti

Figure Four

Of interest here is that the octave scale is thought to have been developed by the 6th century BC Greek mathematician and musician Pythagoras. His name comes from the sacred python and priestesses (pythia) of the Delphic Oracle, a snake-cult of which he was a member, imported into ancient pre-Achaean Greece from North Africa. Pythagoras actually studied in Egypt for over twenty years, from whence came many of his geometrical theorems. If his musical theories also came from Egypt, then there is an intriguing fact that Africa has provided the same musical structure twice over: once in melodic and once in rhythmic form.

TWO – RHYTHMIC SPACING (THE 'SILENT' ASPECT)

Besides being poly-rhythmic, another feature of African music is the importance given to the silent gaps in between the individual pulses of a rhythm; i.e. between the striking of the drum and bell, the clapping of the hands or the downward movement of the feet. This trait was noted by one of the first European musicologists (and gestalt psychologist) to become interested in African music, E.M. von Hornbostel. He divided each stroke of a drum into two components: an 'acoustic' down-beat (the note itself) and a silent 'motor' up-beat (when the hand is raised to strike). He believed that, whereas Europeans focus on the sounded aspects, Africans put equal emphasis on both components: the heard and the un-heard. This German musicologist's idea that a critical component of African music making is the motor or kinetic one can be extended from the movement of the player to that of dance; and, as is well known, dance is a vital part of African performance.

In the case of the agbadza rhythm, this even-handed stress, on down and up-strokes alike, can be illustrated by the way the maracas (called axatse in Ewe) are played. For, in the very simplest version of its rhythm, the instrument is held in the right hand and beaten on the knee in time with the bell. But instead of leaving the up-stroke silent (as with the bell), the up-beat of the maracas is rather accentuated by striking it against the left hand which is held above the instrument. This creates a slightly different sound from the down stroke, in a rhythm that is the exact opposite of the cowbell pattern, as in the following:

DIAGRAM OF THE SIMPLEST MARACAS RHYTHM

	1	2	3	4	5	6	7	8	9	10	11	12
upbeat		x		x			x		x		x	
downbeat	x		x		x	x		x		x		x

Figure Five

The complimentary aspects of the two rhythms of the maracas can be clearly seen in the above diagram: each punctuating the others space. Interestingly, the upward rhythmic complement is itself one of the versions of the A.M. Jones so-called 'African Signature Tune' that was scored out earlier in the chapter.

This ability to flip at will from the positive to negative aspect of rhythm is vital to the appreciation of African music, so much of which is based on call-and-response, and rhythmic dialogue. A visual analogy that may help the reader here is the famous figure-and-ground illusion of Gestalt Psychology: the face and vase which is depicted below:

Figure Six

If the reader can imagine the above picture rhythmically, then the faces (figure) could be the 'acoustic' sounds, and the vase (ground) the silent 'motor' gaps in between. Whereas the Europeans focus on only one aspect (i.e. the figure), African musicians are experts at 'seeing' the rhythmic boundary or contour from both points of view simultaneously; the hot sounds and the cool space. And it is precisely this skill that was utilized by black slaves in the New World, when they were forced to play in strict European time, to turn European music inside-out and syncopate it. This became the basis of the 'ragging', 'jazzing', 'skanking' and 'back-beating' by Black Americans and Caribbeans who 'colonised' the musical beats and accents the westerners ignored.

Quite another expression of spacing in African music concerns its time signature; in the case of the previous agbadza diagrams the twelve interval lines. However, it should be noted that these evenly-spaced lines, that are spatial equivalents to the exact ticks of a metronome or chronometer, are only imaginary constructs of the diagram. No drum or instrument actually plays out this rigid common denominator (the kagan comes closest in the agbadza). So, in subsequent diagrams, dotted interval lines will be used to emphasise this imaginary quality.

Taking this into account, let's take the example of the kidi rhythm, pictured earlier as:

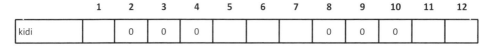

		1	2	3	4	5	6	7	8	9	10	11	12
kidi			0	0	0				0	0	0		

Figure Seven

In the above, the kidi is seen to be beaten exactly in the centre of the imaginary interval lines. However, in actuality, it is never continuously beaten in this rather dull and mechanical fashion; as the musician sometimes moves the down-stroke about in the gap between the dotted lines, by anticipating or delaying it in time.

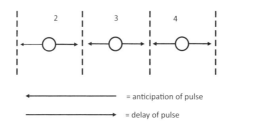

Figure Seven

These variations have an overall effect on the kidi rhythm in relation to the other. If the percussive down-stroke is anticipated slightly, the result, vis-a-vis the other rhythms, is perceived as time compression; and, if fractionally delayed, one of time dilation. The drummer of course can use any combination of these in varying degrees, so creating all sorts of what might be called 'auditory illusions'. This use of time compression and dilation is occasionally found in western music as 'rubato', or one melodic note 'robbing' the time from another. However, African musicians constantly use rhythmic rubatos and this heightened awareness of time, or what the musicologist (and jazz player) Richard Waterman called the 'subjective metronome sense', is one of the components of 'swing' in African music. And swing was an additional technique used by black slaves in the New World to circumvent the rigid on-beat metre of European music. They simply swung in the spaces between the rigid western beats.

Before moving on to the third feature of African rhythm, I will take on non-musical examples of a silent rhythm from the African kitchen! In West Africa, there is a favourite dish known as 'fufu' usually prepared by two people; one to pound the cooled starches with a pestle and the other to turn it in wooden mortar. To non-Africans, the man or woman who turns the dough have the amazing ability to always just remove their fingers from the descending pestle in time. A non-African European attempting this perilous operation would probably first put their hand where the pestle is not; a double mental procedure that can easily lead to confusion and crushed fingers. The African adept simply puts the hand directly into the silent space between the strokes – in a single mental operation that is much safer on the fingers!

THREE – THE SUMMATION OF THE SUB-RHYTHMS (THE BALANCED 'COOL' ASPECT)

The individual rhythmic patterns that constitute a particular style of African music are not fragmentary, but knit together into a total sound or acoustic gestalt that I will refer to as the 'Beat' of the piece in question (beat with a small 'b' means an individual stroke or rhythm). This rhythmic totality manifests itself in two ways. The most obvious is that the music moves in cycles, the shortest of which revolves around one key instrument, usually the bell (as in the case of the agbadza). Secondly, the pulses of the various sub-rhythms, being sound waves, cancel and reinforce each other to create an interference pattern or standing wave. A property of all wave-forms, as depicted below:

TWO WAVE FORMS AND THEIR RESULTANT INTERFERENCE PATTERN

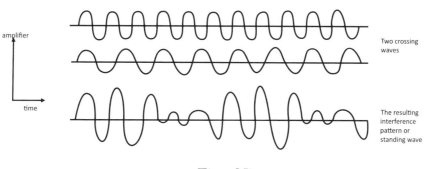

Figure Nine

As can be seen, the sum of the two wave patterns produces a third or standing wave. Precisely the same thing happens in poly-rhythmic music, although in a more complicated way as many more than two rhythms are involved. As a result, the positive and negative interferences between the various sub-rhythms creates a third rhythm that no-one actually plays and yet has a rhythmic life of its own. The sum is greater than the parts and this inherent rhythm helps hold the Beat together. I have heard

Ghanaian musicians call this the 'inside rhythm' and musicologists like John Chernoff (1979), Kofi Agawu (1986), Simha Arom (1991) and Gerhard Kubik 1962) have also noticed it, calling them 'unarticulated', 'implied' or 'inherent' rhythms.

All the individual cross rhythms, including their resultant 'inside rhythms' move, as mentioned previously, in cycles of time. So it is quite useful to depict the linear rhythmic diagrams shown earlier in circular form; for, then, the beginnings and ends of the rhythmic phrases become proximate, which they are in actual practice.

In the following diagram, I have applied this circular depiction to the five agbadza rhythms already dealt with; plus I have added the simplest resting rhythms of the sogo and atsimevu master drums as well. But, before discussing the features of the circular rhythmic diagram, I should point out some of its drawbacks. First is that this circular diagram only involves one cycle of the bell pattern, whereas in practice some of the master-drum and dance-step patterns contain many cycles, which would involve a three-dimensional spiral diagram. In fact, the musicologist Willie Anku (2002) has worked out a way of depicting these bigger cycles on paper as a series of successive circles sprouting off the primary. A second problem of the cyclical depictions below is that in all the rhythms (except the bell and maracas), those depicted are the very simplest of the many variations. Thirdly, the drum tones are only differentiated into open, muted, low, high and very high, whereas there are many more (nineteen according to the musicologist John Chernoff). Finally, the twelve imaginary interval lines cannot do justice to the more complex drum phrases. Indeed, A.M. Jones had to use seventy-two of them before he could even begin to accommodate some of the more advanced nuances of the Ewe master-drummer, Desmond Tei, that he recorded in the 1950s on graph paper!

Taking these limitations into account, this circular type diagram clearly presents several notable characteristics. The most obvious is that its six rhythmic phases do not all start at the same time, but are staggered or out of phase with each other, rather in the fashion of a musical round or canon fugue. The feet, bell and maracas open on the first of the twelve intervals, the kidi on the eighth, the sogo on the tenth, the claps on the seventh and the long atsimevu drum on the third. One can, therefore, understand why African musicians call the most European music 'one way', as its players all take off together with the fall of the conductor's baton.

Although I have asterisked the beginnings of the six phases in the diagram, of equal importance are their endings. Where one finishes, another takes its place; constituting a rhythmic dialogue between the instruments. One case is the kidi drum whose first open note phrase ends on interval ten where the sogo makes its debut. Another is the rhythmic conversation going on between the feet and the kagan's open notes. Yet another is the atsimevu phrase that closes on interval one where the cycle commences; for, paradoxically, the most important ending of all is at the very start of the fundamental Beat at interval one, where the feet, bell and maracas take their cue. This is confusing for non-Africans who find difficulty in conceiving an ending as a beginning. This proneness to unify the tempo of a rhythm on the last beat is a common feature in African music and explains the 'percussive attack' of so much black-American music, whose rhythms seem to have a pushing quality as they move towards resolution.

CYCLE OF THE FUNDAMENTAL AGBADZA BEAT
(AN ACOUSTIC GESTALT)

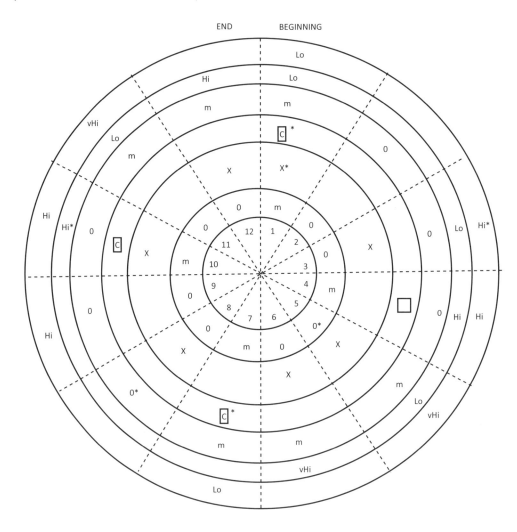

Figure Ten

TABLE:

Central Ring – The twelve imaginary time divisions or intervals

Second Ring – The kagan drum

Third Ring – The bell and the down-stroke of the maracas (the basic time-line)

Fourth Ring – The feet (squares) and the hand-claps (C)

Fifth Ring – The kidi drum

Sixth Ring – The sogo drum

Seventh Ring – The atsimevu drum

* Starting point of each particular phase.

With so many differing beginnings and endings, one of the skills of African master musicians is the ability to jump anywhere into the beat and through various rhythmic tricks always, like the proverbial cat, manage to land on their feet. This aptitude that completely by-passes the existential problem of how to initiate a creative act; a hesitancy musically equivalent to 'writer's cramp' that can occur if too much emphasis is put on starting correctly. The African approach of having multiple starting points evades this block and thus enhances spontaneity and the free flow of creative energy.

Besides depicting staggered beginnings and important endings, a third feature of African music that can be clearly seen in the circular diagram is the silent side of rhythm. The complimentary aspects of the maracas and bell pattern have already been discussed. Another is hand clapping, for although the claps follow the four-time dance-steps, they are not continuous like those of the feet, due to the gap at interval four. And it is precisely this quiet space that supplies a crucial anchoring or reference point in what would otherwise be a bewildering and sustained round of hand-clap rhythm. Two other examples are the gaps at interval two and seven that neatly bisects the atsimevu rhythm, and the kidi's three muted notes between the triple open ones that, within the cyclical Beat, creates matching negatives to the open drum pattern.

So the African master-musician has to be as much aware of the spaces within the scaffolding of sounds as is an architect of the living-room he's building from materials like brick and wood; neither is trying to fill everything in. To illustrate the spacey nature of the above four rhythmic cycles (bell, claps, atsimevu and kidi), I am portraying them below in a simplified way so that each note or pulse is totally filling up its time-interval; not such a liberty when one recalls that these intervals are potential spaces for the notes to move or 'swing' in.

SIMPLIFIED DIAGRAMS OF FOUR RHYTHMS DEPICTING SOUND
AND SILENCE

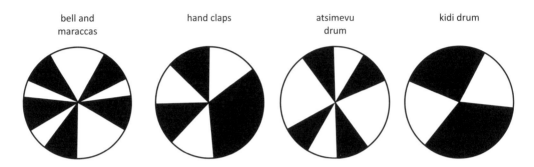

| bell and maraccas | hand claps | atsimevu drum | kidi drum |

Figure Ten

Black = silent gaps, intervals or muted notes
White = sounded intervals

To summarise; the complex web of African cross-beats with their staggered entries
and inherent patterns produce a confusing system of rhythmic relativity that only
begins to make sense when seen or heard as part of the unifying gestalt; the
fundamental one being the 'Beat' based on the bell cycle's time-line. And as the
following diagrams depict way, within the Beat, one's position can be gauged instantly
and 'at a glance' from the pattern of sounds and silences. This gestalt awareness and
ability to operate within the multiple rhythmic sounds and spaces is the basis of the
'cool', centred and balanced approach of the master musician or dancer.

Many of the ideas discussed in this chapter have been developed more fully in my book
'African Muscial Symbolism' that I had published in Germany in 2004 and which I
provide a brief synopsis of below.

AFRICAN MUSICAL SYMBOLISM IN CONTEMPORARY PERSPECTIVE: ROOTS, RHYTHMS AND RELATIVITY

This book is difficult to categorize as it dwells on African musicology, history and
anthropology, as well as the new developments and discoveries in the western hard
sciences, mathematics, psychology and philosophy. For instance, the book makes
metaphorical links between quantum physics and the old rhythmic wisdom of Africa,
in much the same way as these scientific discoveries have been symbolically related to
ancient eastern philosophy in such books as Fritjof Capra's 'The Tao of Physics'.

The book's first section, 'Ancient African Wisdom', deals with the symbolic knowledge and intuitions of sub-Saharan Africa embedded in its music and traditional world-views. Its poly-rhythms and poly-theisms. Its offbeat breaks inside rhythmic and ritual order. Its musical rounds, reincarnations and social cycles. Its audience participation and corresponding communion with nature, rather than domination over it. And at the heart of things are the poised master musicians, dancers and sages who coolly orchestrate sound and silence, beginnings and ends, improvisation and ceremonial order.

The book's second section 'The Space and Information Age', examines how some areas of recent scientific research have moved away from the mechanistic and deterministic ethos of industrialism towards relativistic, holistic, circular, and participatory ideas that are, surprisingly, in tune with the old African symbols discussed in the book's first section. Indeed, in section two of the book, these traditional symbols are used to metaphorically examine and re-appraise recent scientific discoveries. Many areas of science and philosophy no longer treat mind and matter as made up of isolated components operating within linear time and fixed hierarchical structures. Rather, today, we have the relativistic models of psychological archetypes and complexes and the fragmentation of the solid atom into ever-multiplying particles and insubstantial quarks. Circular paradigms are also back in scientific fashion, like feedback loops, eco-systems and a curved cosmos. Holism has re-surfaced as gestalt thinking, laser holograms and Einstein's multi-dimensional space-time. Flexibility and play are added to these new non-mechanistic paradigms through subconscious shadows, existential freedom, mathematical incompleteness, quantum gaps, and the 'dance' of sub-atomic particles. And it is scientific 'uncertainty principles' and 'observer effects' that have proven that everybody, including supposedly the detached scientific researcher, is inseparable from nature.

In short, the old insights and musical wisdom of Africa and its Diaspora are helping provide our contemporary age with the means of harmonizing our heads and feet, balancing our inner and outer, uniting mind and matter and generally putting breathing-space and 'swing' into a regimented and material world.

There are many explanations for the international explosion of Black and Africa music since the early 20th century. One is the 'primitivist' argument, that African music is full of wild emotions and improvised energy that is attractive to inhibited westerners.

However, although there are plenty of hot and spontaneous rhythms in African music, this explanation is far from the whole truth. Rather, as this book attempts to demonstrate, African music contains highly developed symbols and insights that resonate with the paradigm shifts going on in the western philosophy and sciences as they move beyond a mechanistic vision. African music is therefore not the just the roots music of the past; it is also the music of the future.

For those interested in this book (ISBN Number 3-938262-15-X)
It can be obtained via Amazon www.book-on-demand.de or www.pro-business.com
Alternatively it can be downloaded from the following website: www.scientific-african.org
or www.bapmaf.com

Chapter 28

KOO NIMO: GHANA'S BARD OF FOLK HIGHLIFE GUITAR

Koo Nimo in 1998 (photo by John Carson)

I first met Koo Nimo (Dan Amponsah) in 1973 at his home on the campus of the Kwame Nkrumah University of Science and Technology (KNUST) in Kumasi, where he worked as a biochemist technician. I had wanted to meet him for several years, since being bowled over by his music in 1970, which I first heard on a tape-recording done by a British music photographer friend of mine called Jak Kilby. Koo Nimo's style of highlife, which is based on the old palmwine playing that grew up in the Akan areas in the 1920s and 1930s, led me to expect an old guitarist, but the first thing that struck me about Dan was his youthful appearance. We played some music together; then I interviewed him and arranged to meet the following week at the Phillips recording studio in Kaneshie where he and his group were going to record six singles. The seven-man group consisted of Koo Nimo on classical acoustic guitar; Little Noah, his twelve-year-old adopted son on talking drums (atumpan); and George Kusi and Yaw Nimo on the apremprensemma (premprensua), a large variety of hand piano on which the musician sits and supplies the bass line. Finally, there was Nyamekye who played the long thin gyama drum and Bawuah who furnished the gong patterns. On four of the recorded numbers (including 'Densu') I played a small gourd rhythm instrument called the 'asratoa' (in Akan) or 'televi' (in Ewe).

Below is an interview I had on August 1, 1973, with Koo Nimo, starting with his life story and ending up with some of his ideas and plans. I began by asking him about his early musical experiences.

KOO NIMO: I was born in 1934 at Fuase eleven miles north of Kumasi and my first experience with music was through my father who was a guitarist and trumpeter in the village brass band. One thing that was interesting about him was that he lost some of his fingers cutting cola nuts in a tree and was therefore similar to Django Reinhardt (the internationally famous mid-20th century gypsy jazz guitarist who also lost some fingers). I started school there in 1939, and there was a catechist called D.K. Sam who suggested to the Methodist community that they needed an organ. So I started lessons on this when I was five and when I was six or seven I was playing in chapel. In 1940, I went to live with my sister and her husband, Mr. Lawrence Osei Kwame Bonsu, brother of the King of the Ashanti. He sent me to the Presbyterian school in Kumasi where I was taught music. I was forced to spend hours listening to Bach and Beethoven as there were some German missionaries there who liked this sort of thing. The German missionaries were militant and they detected something musical in me and felt they should help me.

274

JC: What was their attitude to traditional Ghanaian music? And then what did you do?

KOO NIMO: They were not interested, except for Twi hymns. They were rather rigid and their music lessons were terrible for us in the school, although I did like the fantastic harmonies of the hymns and Bach type of music. Then I went to Adisadel College in Cape Coast from 1949 to 1952 and I was still playing organ. We also formed the Adisadel Highlife Band consisting of drums, guitar and me on piano. I had a friend at the school called Harry Opoku, now a doctor; one day I saw him playing an E.K. Nyame tune on the guitar, for at that time E.K. was reigning. We were rivals and everything Harry could do I wanted to do better, so I picked up the guitar. After finishing school, I taught in my village (Fuase) as a primary school teacher where I was the music master, so I organised groups of school children to perform some of Doctor Amu's songs on the radio. There was also a brass band in the village so I learned to play the trombone, euphonium and tuba. I left there for the Medical Research Institute in Accra to do laboratory work, graduated in 1955 and went back to Kumasi where I started playing the guitar again and joined my first group called Antobre. We played pop and highlifes and used an amplifier. I was on guitar, Fred Akuffo was the alto singer, Ansong the treble singer, Yaw Gyawu on congas, Kwese Kramo on bongos and finally Boakye on maracas. This was a rival band to Onyina's which was then reigning in Kumasi. However, he did influence me very much. Then in 1957, I met the Head of Programmes of Radio Ghana and joined a group of entertainers on a programme called 'Enne yɛ Anigye Da' (today is a happy day). There were three of us: myself on guitar, T.G.B. Adjekum of Onyina's Band as alto singer and K. Quainoo of E.K.'s Band as first singer. About 1958 or 1959, I met Professor Laing, a pathologist, and I would say he has been my godfather. He bought me a £60 Spanish guitar and I started lessons on the classical guitar, taught by Mr. Opoku Manwere (Professor A.M. Opoku). In 1960, I started working at the Chemistry Department of the University of Science and Technology and then got a scholarship to London to do further studies in chemistry techniques at the Paddington Technical College.

JC: How did you get the name Koo Nimo?

KOO NIMO: It means 'Kofi who takes the blame for something he hasn't done'. It was the name people gave to T.G.B. Adjekum, who was my uncle. We were only paid seven and sixpence per show and it was never regular due to red tape. So Adjekum left in 1958 and I took his name.

JC: When did you make your first recordings?

KOO NIMO: The first time ever was in May 1955, when I was at the Medical Research Institute in Accra. I got interested in I. E. Mason's band and recorded one song with them, a dagomba (highlife) number called 'Go Inside'. My first recordings for the Ghana Film Industry were the 'Driver's Lament' and 'Owusu se Mamma' which I recorded with Doctor Kwame Gyasi in 1966. Then, in 1968, I met J. L. Latham from Salford University in the United Kingdom and he opened a fresh page in my life. He suggested that I translate my songs into English (as the booklet 'Ashanti Ballads'), as many of the listeners at the private performances I gave were Europeans. These were translations of traditional ballads, some of which I have put to music and recorded. In 1969, I won a scholarship to Salford University to study laboratory techniques in biochemistry. But before I went, I met a friend called Van Spaal, a lecturer in engineering, and he recorded myself, Kwao Sarfo on apremprensemma and Bawuah on percussion. We sent the tapes to Mike Eghan who was running the radio show 'African Beat' and they were played on the BBC External Service. When I was in Britain, I met Mike and made some more recordings for the BBC – a programme called 'London Line'. In 1970, I came back to Ghana and recorded four songs for Essiebons, with myself and Doctor Gyasi on guitars, Yaw Nimo on aprempresemma – he's fantastic – and a donno (squeeze drum) player. The songs were 'Farmers do Farm', 'Mammy where is my Daddy?', 'I've Worked in Vain' and 'Akosua Give me a Helping Hand'.

JC: The music you play is a traditional sort of highlife, the style developed by Sam before the War and by Kwaa Mensah, E.K. Nyame and Appiah Adjekum afterwards. Yet you have incorporated many foreign ideas. Tell me about some of these influences.

KOO NIMO: I find the classical musicians, the ones I was forced to listen to as a child at school, like Bach, Beethoven and Sibelius, tremendous. My Spanish influences are from Carulli, Carcassi, John Williams (whom I once met) and Julian Bream, especially his lute playing. I also like dixieland and New Orleans jazz – I saw Louis Armstrong when he came over to Kumasi (his second visit to Ghana in 1960). My two trips to the United Kingdom also helped. Kurt Anderson (Duke Ellington's first trumpeter) became a great friend of mine. I met Count Basie's guitarist, Freddie Green. I met Charlie Bird who influenced me a lot, and I met the prolific composer Jack Duarte who's got a wonderful record library. For guitar, my influences were Django

Reinhardt, Charlie Christian, Wes Montgomery and Jim Hall. Professor Laing has also exposed me to Dizzy Gillespie, Thelonius Monk and Miles Davis. I also liked oriental Indian music I saw in Manchester, especially the thing that was something like a calabash (the tabla drums). In Manchester, I got to know the Indian community, as I liked their peppers and used to practice yoga.

JC: What is your attitude towards modern Afro-beat and pop music?

KOO NIMO: I like the beat but it's repetitive. I don't get the challenge since I hate boredom in music, and I think things should move. Some of the numbers also sound as if they are out of tune, and I hate this. Jimi Hendrix is often too loud, but I like his ambitious solo work. Reggae I like best, it pulsates and pushes me. I prefer bossanova to all this.

JC: In spite of all these influences, your music is still like the old palm style.

KOO NIMO: Yes it is, and in fact one woman told me that she thought my music was too 'colo' (colonial or old-fashioned). Another person once remarked that when he first heard my music he thought I was an old illiterate running a store in a village. He thought I sounded like a 'bush' man, somebody with no literary training at all. But I'm trying to experiment with the indigenous rhythms. You see, I don't like expensive instruments. I use the apremprensemma because it is cheap. I don't like amplifiers as I don't like to play in large halls that need them. My music isn't really dance music but is for listening to. I don't try to play pure traditional music as I like to move with the times and be experimental, for stagnant waters breed mosquitoes and this applies to music. I feel we should move but be guided by what we have, and feed this like rivulets feed a stream.

JC: Have you ever tried playing electric guitar?

KOO NIMO: I've done a single recording on electric guitar. It was a record we did for the late Robert Mensah (a famous Ghanaian footballer killed in 1971). That was an experiment towards bossanova.

JC: The modern-day guitar-bands and concerts are using electric guitars, rather than acoustic guitars and apremprensemma. What's your attitude to these bands?

KOO NIMO: I don't like the way they are going for two reasons. Firstly, it is cheap music in the sense that the lyrics aren't well thought-out; and also the language isn't decent. It should be sifted. There is some language the Akans won't tolerate, like "m'alomo" (a slang word for 'my girlfriend'). It is necessary for musicians to sit down and think about balancing the lyrics and get the right thought. I don't like the use of common talk, for Akan music dwells on philosophy and the socially significant, whereas in European music, love reigns supreme. Love is the thing, blah, blah, blah. In the Ghanaian songs that are concerned with love, some words should be given euphemisms. For example, in the highlife song 'Koforidua' about a young man who spells his own doom because he follows women and drink, people may think that when you go to Koforidua you are engulfed in this sort of thing. The second reason I don't like the modern guitar bands is that they are all monotonous. I like the African Brothers – I like the singer and sometimes I like the beat, but the accompaniment of guitars and so on is too monotonous. Also, although I like C.K. Mann's singing, his work is not true osode, it's too commercialised. Listen to C.K. Mann and you will find it is all in E flat and F. Why is this so? It doesn't give any colour. I know a story about an Indian who remarked to a Ghanaian audience in London who were enjoying the highlife, "Kofi, do you have only one style of music?" because they were using the same harmonies all along.

JC: How do you think these problems can be overcome?

KOO NIMO: We all have to learn music seriously. I interviewed about forty people this morning for a band here in Kumasi, and not a single one of them could read music. Well, Django Reinhardt couldn't read music, West Montgomery couldn't read music, but they were geniuses of their time and if there is a legacy of written music from which you can draw, why not make use of it. Because, let's face it, we have been – and are being – exposed to Western music. Now, if we want to sell Ghanaian music abroad, we must get the thing well-organised and you can't organise without getting the basics or rudiments. Jack Duarte wrote a guitar book and gave me a signed copy, saying that he hoped I was going to bring the classical guitar to Ghana. The inscription has always been at the back of my mind. I've decided to expose Ghanaians to the guitar and classical techniques and set up a sort of institute for it here in Kumasi. In fact, I have been teaching the guitar since 1957 and one of my pupils who has come out is Mike Ofori, leader and guitarist of the Dominoes highlife band.

JC: What are your future plans in music?

KOO NIMO: From my corner, I would like to develop percussion, then insert heavy chords into highlife, rhythmic chords that will enrich the harmony. I'm going to marry the traditional highlife guitar with Spanish and Latin American music; an Afro-Spanish style using traditional rhythm and arpeggios – for I always use finger-picking, never the plectrum. Also, I want to develop an Afro-jazz and use Wes Montgomery and Charlie Christian type chords in it. I'm thinking of bringing the European flute and the durugya, which is an Akan horn played when the old chief dies. It has very low tones and is very melancholy. My interest at the present is towards drumming and I've got a little boy whom I have adopted, called Little Noah, and he will be featured in our recording (of 11th August, 1973). I picked him up when he was nine and he's going to revolutionize my band. He plays the talking drums. At this recording, I'm going to use kete rhythms (a traditional Akan court music). The interesting thing about kete is you sing, stop, then do drumming (call and response). I'm going to add the apremprensemma to provide us with the lower frequencies.

Since 1973, Koo Nimo has continued with his rootsy 'up and up' music, as he sometimes calls it, and together with his Band called Adadam Agofomma (roots players) group, his lifelong guitarist friend the late Kofi Twumasi, and his dancers Abena Manu and Nana Yeboah, he has travelled extensively around the world. Around 1980, he met Jacqueline Smith Bonneau who was visiting Ghana. She was the neice of the famous Black American jazz pianist Theonius Monk whom Koo Nimo so much admired. As a result, Koo Nimo was invited to New York in 1982 to take part in a film about Monk. In the late 1980s, Koo Nimo met the Trinidadian calypso musician, Lancelot Layne, who was visiting Ghana and invited Koo to Trinidad, where he met Lord Kitchener and played with steelpan bands. This interaction became part of the 1989 award-winning film 'Crossing Over' that explored the musical and cultural connections between Africa and the Caribbean, such as the brass bands and masqueraders of Ghana, and Carnival and the Orisha religion in Trinidad.

In the late 1980s, I had the pleasure of going to Kumasi with the late Beattie Casely-Hayford to record some of Koo Nimo's instrumental numbers, as background music for a United Nations developmental film called 'The Secret of Wealth'. Some of these recording from my Bokoor Recording Studios mobile unit were later released in 2003 as part of the 'Vintage Palmwine' CD under the Dutch Otrabanda label. In June 2000, I accompanied Koo Nimo, as his second guitarist, on a United States performance/lecture tour of the New England Universities of Yale, Harvard, Wesleyian, Boston and Trinity. A party was thrown for us at Harvard by the historian Emmanuel Akyeampong and many Ghanaian intellectuals turned up, such as the economist Kwesi Botchway and philosopher Anthony Appiah. Besides being Ghana's Segovia-like guitarist, Koo Nimo was, for a while, the President of the Musicians' Union MUSIGA, advisor for the Ghana Broadcasting Corporation, and member of the Ghana National Folklore Board of Trustees (formed in 1991). After retiring from the KNUST Biochemistry Department, Koo Nimo taught in the States for several years at the Universities of Seattle and Michigan. In 1992, he was awarded an Honorary Doctorate by KNUST where he is now part-time teaching at its new Cultural Studies Unit. Koo Nimo has a large collection of books and music on African music at his Adadam Cultural Resource Centre in his house in Kumasi, to which many local and foreign visitors, students and researchers gravitate. Koo Nimo still has time to occasionally play in Accra form time to time. For instance, in 2010, he played at the +233 Jazz Bar and Guitars in the Park. Koo Nimo's adopted son Little Moah now resides in Australia, whereas Koo Nimo's students, George Spratz and William Hanson, are continuing his pioneering work in reviving and deveoping palmwine music and Kyekyeku (Eugene Oppong Ampadu) plays both palmwine music and experiments with fusion music that draws on jazz and Fela Kuti's Afrobeat.

Chapter 29

KOFI GHANABA: HIGHLIFE TO JAZZ TO THE AFRICAN HERITAGE

Ghanaba and his African drum-kit at the Goethe Institute Accra in 1996 (photo Jay Stoller)

I first heard of Kofi Ghanaba (Guy Warren) in 1969 when I was playing in a band with a group of students, including his son Glen Warren, whom I would visit at his dad's house, then in Tesano. I never physically met Ghanaba at the time as he was a rather reclusive person who stayed in his room in which no one was allowed to enter. I finally met Ghanaba face-to-face in early 1973 when I went to his spacious house (by then in Achimota) with E.T. Mensah in connection with the biography I was writing on E.T.'s Tempos band, of which Ghanaba had been a member. Ghanaba, in Buddhist attire, talked to E. T. and me for several hours about his Tempos days and, as we parted, he invited me back for a second discussion which I taped on August 19, 1973.

Ghanaba was born in 1923, a member of the Akwei family of Accra and was educated at the prestigious Achimota College. Early in life he became familiar with both traditional and jazz drumming. The first band he joined was the Accra Rhythmic Orchestra led by E.T.'s elder brother, Yebuah Mensah. This was a fifteen-member group formed in 1936 as an offshoot of the Accra Orchestra and it played a cross-section of the current ballroom music, highlifes and ragtimes. During the Second World War, Ghanaba played at wartime bars catering to American and British servicemen in Accra. In 1947, he was invited to join the recently formed Tempos band. As this was a seven-man group modelled on the swing bands, it was much more to Ghanaba's liking than the earlier colonial dance orchestras. E.T. told me that whenever the Tempos played waltzes, foxtrots and highlifes, Ghanaba would play only half-heartedly, but as soon as it was a hot jazz number he would play full belt. At that time, Ghanaba's eyes were fixed on America and he developed a perfect American accent. In fact, many people thought he was an African American, which, as he explains below, caused him trouble at the Accra Club, a place the Tempos regularly played.

During the intermission, I went over to see a white guy who, like myself, was in publishing. This guy's Canadian friend said, "What's an American nigger doing here?" He thought I was an American and I thought he was one. He pushed me and I nearly saw red, as I had come to dislike the American whites intensely; by then, I had been over there (he had been to the U.S. for a few months during the Second World War) and had found all the propaganda about G.I.'s being friendly a pile of horse shit. I thrashed his arse out. You see, this was the sort of club where Africans were only seen padding about gently, dressed in white tunics, and here I came beating this guy up. It was a sensation. Just about the same time the C.P.P. (Convention Peoples Party) was forming, and I was the editor of a (nationalist) daily paper. So James (James Moxon of the Information Service) talked to me afterwards in my house, and he rushed to the Governor's Castle and told him that the Canadian must be sent away immediately, which he was (it being a delicate time for the British administration).

Ghanaba flew to the UK shortly afterwards, where he joined up with Kenny Graham's Afro-Cubists. Ghanaba returned to Ghana nine months later, bringing back many new ideas for the band.

When I came back from London, I brought bongos and Cuban percussion to Ghana for the first time Also, when I was in London, I went to the Caribbean Club, somewhere near Piccadilly, the haunt of a lot of West Indians. It was all calypso every night and I played these records on a B.B.C. programme I had. When I came back, I brought some of these records and we (the Tempos) learned to play them as I knew straightaway that the musical

Ghanaba and Tempos, circa 1948. Photo African Heritage Library

The band only stayed together about a year after Ghanaba's trip. After a two-week stay in Lagos in 1951, Ghanaba and most of the other members of the Tempos split and left for Liberia. The reason for this was that E. T., who owned the instruments, wanted to create a synthesis of highlife with calypso and Latin-American music, whereas Ghanaba was more interested in fusing jazz with Afro-Cuban drumming. Ghanaba stayed in Liberia for three years working at a radio station, and just before he left he played at President Tubman's inauguration. From there, Ghanaba went to the United States where he went even further with his musical experimentation of combining jazz and African drumming. It was in Chicago that he met his 'muse' which, as he explains, was the realization that 'I would be the African musician who re-introduced African music to America to get Americans to be aware of this cultural heritage of the black people'. It was while he was in America, during the 1950s, that he produced a whole series of revolutionary LPs such as 'Africa Speaks, Africa Answers', 'Theme for African Drums', 'Africa Sounds', and 'Third Phase'. Indeed, what Ghanaba was doing then preceeded the later generations of Afro-fusion artists in West Africa. Ghanaba is really the spiritual father of musicians like Osibisa and Fela Kuti who fused African music with jazz, rock and soul. On returning to Ghana from the States, Ghanaba again switched direction and began to concentrate on his unique style of solo drumming in which he draws heavily on local rhythms and instruments. Because of this, he sometimes chides the young musicians who only have eyes for Western music.

The following is another part of the interview I did with Ghanaba at his Achimota house in August, 1973, in which I talked to him about other aspects of his life, other than the Tempos story. Some parts of the material have been edited and rearranged for the sake of continuity. The first question I asked was whether he had problems playing with Americans musicians and why he thought whites are beginning to play African music.

GHANABA: When I was in the States, I couldn't work with any American bands because they wanted Afro-Cuban sounds and I wanted to play African rhythms. The Black American is playing his version of African music, and then this version is being copied by the youth in the West. The reason why this is happening so fast is because of the rapid communication system we now have.

JC: One of the influences on the formation of highlife itself has been the music of the Black Americans.

GHANABA: I call it bastardisation.

JC: Couldn't you just as well call it an enrichment?

GHANABA: No, bastardisation, because we came before them and the Afro-rhythm are derived from Africa. Afro-Americans were thinking that they would bring the African beat back home to teach it to the people here and it would become popular, like jazz trumpets against an African background. I can't do that. I did that once but now I don't consider this right, I should have done it the other way around.

JC: Could you mention some of the early musical influences on you?

Ghanaba (Guy Warren) with drums late 1990s (photo Yemo Nunu)

GHANABA: I have always been interested in traditional African music and jazz since my young days. We lived in downtown Accra where they had this Gold Coast Bar (the Basshoun Bar) that catered to seamen, prostitutes and pimps. They had a combo there and every night they would play and we would hear them from where we were (living). They played ragtime and I learned to tap-dance. There was this great drummer who died, called Harry Dodoo, a jazz drummer and also a comedian who used to juggle with the sticks and joke around, just like Baby Dodds (a famous African American jazz pioneer). Harry Dodoo was my hero and I used to go to the bar and watch him play and dance. In the house where I lived, there were some Ewe people, and every Saturday light they would hold a traditional drum-session, for they are a very musical tribe. We also used to have masquerade parades in Accra every Christmas and everybody would dance a sort of poor quadrille to the sound of a bass-drum, flute and pati (side-drum). When I was young it was jazz that dominated me. I was naive and thought that was the thing. But it is the African music that is the mother, not the other way around. I had to find this out the hard way.

JC: Why did you change from playing jazz to developing your own jazz fusions?

GHANABA: It was a personal decision I made in my room in Chicago. I remember it very well. I said to myself, 'Guy, you can never play like Gene Kruper, Max Roach or Louis Bellson. They have a different culture, and can never play like you'. I had to make a choice between being an imitation of Buddy Rich or playing something they couldn't play. I could play jazz well, but I possessed something that nobody else had. So I started to play African music with a little bit of jazz thrown in, not jazz with a little African thrown in.

JC: Would you agree that young Ghanaian musicians who are copying black American music today are being turned back to the African culture, as this is where the most avant-garde Afro-American music is moving towards (by this meant the Afro-centric music of James Brown, John Coltrane, Sun Ra and others) .

GHANABA: No, I don't think they can have it both ways, both of the worlds together like that! It's the education system here, it's still the same (i.e. colonial). There's been no revolution in Africa. These (Ghanaian) kids should realize that the last people they should imitate are people imitating them.

JC: But surely, it is a step in the right direction? The next step can only be a conscious turning by young Ghanaian pop musicians towards their own traditional music?

GHANABA: But musicians like my sons (Glen and Guy Warren Jr.) are all the time influenced by Western newspapers, movies and television; and commercialisation (which) affects the whole world. They always force things down and the masses accept it, even if it's rubbish.

JC: It's true that commercial interests usually trivialize music, but as soon as that happens a new layer of musicians turns up with a different sound altogether. Like Afro-beat which may partly be a response to imported 'Afro' ideas from America, but even so it is a blow against the colonial mentality that is still so strong here in Ghana, as you are getting a generation struggle through music.

GHANABA: But this has been going on for a long time. The best that a black American can offer you musically, you dig, but it could never be like African music. So when Afro-Americans, Americans I call them, tell us that we should be proud of our culture, they are actually messing us up; because this (the imported 'Afro' culture) is not our culture, it is theirs.

JC: Western popular music has been greatly influenced by black music in America, and it looks as if it will soon be influenced by music coming directly from these shores; like Afro-beat.

GHANABA: But the powers that be will never allow that to happen. They will always compromise, as it is to their advantage to be flexible. If they ever tell you that you are succeeding (commercially), you are failing… I consider myself anonymous, my music is from the masses and I don't want it to have a commercial appeal. I have been a jazz musician but now I am a folk musician. In other words, I have come home.

Shortly after this interview, Ghanaba put together the first volume of his autobiography or 'Testament'. It is over a thousand pages. Jimmy Moxon gave me a copy to edit and so I helped proof-read in June 1975. It made fascinating reading.

Because of Ghanaba's enormous knowledge on music, gathered from years as a musician and journalist, he set up an archives in the 1980s at his new home in Medie, fifteen miles north of Accra. In this, he has been helped by royalties from his most famous composition 'Happy Feeling' that has a highlife lilt and which became the permanent signature tune for the external service of German Radio. His centre is called the **African Heritage Library** and contains literally numberless boxes containing rare articles, books, photos and tapes. In the early 1990s, I had the opportunity of hearing some of the tapes Ghanaba had made, as he asked me to help him transfer them from reel-to-reel to cassette tape. It was fascinating to sit with him over a number of days listening to his taped reflections on his work with Thelonius Monk, Miles Davis, Max Roach, Billy Strayhorn and other top African-American musicians.

Ghanaba, his grand-daughter, the jazz percussionist Juma Santos/Jim Riley,
and John and Thomas Collins at the African Heritage Library in 2001

Ghanaba has long switched from American jazz or trap drums to a huge array of local drums that he surrounds himself with when playing. He plays either solo or teams up with a number of local percussionists. In the 1980s, this was Nii Amaa and his Akomfrah Afrika Obonu called 'Ghanababii' (Children of Ghanaba) when working with the the 'old man'. Then, there was Nii Noi Nortey's group and, more recently, Ghanaba's own son Glen Warren. On stage in the 1980s and 1990s, Ghanaba was accompanied by the graphic artist Nii Anum Telfer wearing white clay and holding an old-fashioned Dane gun which he would fire for dramatic effect. Ghanaba even had his own personal and long time photographer Yemo Nunu or 'Flick'.

In 1991, Ghanaba was involved in Haile Gerima's feature film 'Sankofa' about an African American model who, while visiting the Cape Coast Castle and Slave Dungeon, is transported into the past. Ghanaba was the mystical oracle in the film and played his huge array of traditional drums on Cape Coast beach. On May 1, 1996, three days before his seventy-third birthday, Ghanaba gave an outstanding solo performance at the closing ceremony of the Highlife Month, jointly organised by the German Goethe Institute and the Bokoor African Popular Music Archives Foundation. In 1998, Ghanaba teamed up with the American/German percussionist Robyn Schulowsky and they performed several shows together in Accra, which resulted in a German documentary film being made on Ghanaba.

In 2001, Ghanaba toured Britain with the 'Yaa Asantewaa – Warrior Queen' musical that also involved the Pan African Orchestra and the UK-based dance company Adzido. It was written by the Ghanaian Margaret Busby and directed by the West Indian Geraldine Connor. Then, in 2002, the UK Retro-Afrik record company released the 'Ghanaba The Divine Drummer Odumankuma' CD consisting of Afro-jazz songs based on West and East African rhythms that he first recorded in London between 1969 and 1970, playing flutes and xylophone as well as percussion. Although the record company had wanted me to get details of that particular recording for the sleeve notes, Ghanaba rather wanted to talk about the Lebanese mystic Khalil Gibran and his book The Prophet. As he told me, that is where his head was at that time and he did not want to dwell on matters of his own past. So I spent an interesting afternoon interviewing Guy about Kahlil Gibran's book, which subsequently became part of the CD's sleeve-notes, for, as Ghanaba told me, 'if you are a fan of mine and you'd like to know more about me, read this book.'

Around 2004, the New York University in Ghana hooked up (via the Nigerian Professor Awam Amkpa) with Ghanaba and helped in refurbishing and equipping his African Heritage Library and digitising his archives – which was formally opened to the general public in 2005.

Sadly, Ghanaba died on 22 December 2008 and the following are some extracts of the orbituary I wrote on him for a funeral brochure produced by his friends – focusing on my own personal reflection on him.

The first time I heard about Ghanaba was in 1969 when I was playing in a school pop band with Sammy 'Slim' Bentil and Bobby Torto, through whom I also got to know Glen Warren. So I would sometimes visit Glen at his dad's house, then in Tesano, bringing with me my electric guitar and its waw-waw pedal and fuzz-box gadgets. At the house there was always a strong small of incense coming from behind a locked door and Glen explained that inside was his father Ghanaba meditating; and that he never wanted to be disturbed. I never did find out what Ghanaba thought of the distortions that Glen and I were pumping out the radio amplifier in the house that we used to get our Jimmy Hendrix type effects. So I only knew of Ghanaba at that time as a mysterious recluse. However, I did see him play his African drum-set at the Soul to Soul concert at Black Star Square in 1971, when he was accompanied by the Damas Choir and the Dahomean Calabash Drum Ensemble.

It was in July 1973, when I was writing the story of E.T. Mensah and the Tempos, that I finally met Ghanaba then staying in Achimota, as he found that the Tesano area had become too noisy. But I even had a problem on this occasion, as the first time E.T. and I went to his Achimota house, Ghanaba told his gateman not to let us in. Ghanaba had not realised that it was his old Tempos colleague E.T. who was coming up the road with a whiteman. So, after profuse telephone apologies to E.T., whom Ghanaba loved dearly, we were invited a second time. On this occasion, I interviewed Ghanaba in connection with his role in the Tempos – and then the following month Ghanaba invited me to come on my own to do a second interview specifically on his own musical career. Even on this occasion he surprised me, as whilst I had brought my cassette tape-machine to record him, he also had his tape-recorder going. He told me this was to double-check me afterwards to make sure that I had got right exactly what he said! In fact, the interview was later published (the first time in my 1985 Music Makers of West Africa book) and he never complained of any inaccuracies.

Then, in 1975, I proof-read and edited Ghanaba's 1000-page autobiography, given me by his publisher and close friend, Jimmy Moxon. However, I didn't meet Ghanaba on this occasion, but after I had returned the typed manuscript to Jimmy with a lot of my comments on it, I received a signed archival document in the post from Ghanaba in September 1975 with the cryptic message 'the mission matter MOST, the personality matter LESS'. At the time I didn't understand this comment. But, later on that year, I went on my motor-bike to visit him with my African American friend, the jazz percussionist Juma Santos (Jim Riley). After Juma did a bit of shouting, Ghanaba rushed out of the house and pulled a pistol from his yellow Bhuddist robe and chased us away from the house, saying we had *disturbed his meditations. After that he wouldn't speak to me for 15 years. I don't think it just was a matter of Juma's shouting and my noisy motor-bike, I think Ghanaba was really annoyed with me for the extensive editing and re-arranging I had done on his book (his 'Testament') which, sadly in the end, was never published.*

By 1986 I had moved into my father's farm-house at South Ofankor (now Bokoor House) and, as it is on way to Medie where Ghanaba had relocated, I attempted to see him again, the first time with an old friend of mine called Kwesi Asare who was a master-drummer and great-nephew of Nana Oparebea, the High Priestess of the Larteh Akonedi Shrine. Kwasi's efforts on my behalf proved unsuccessful and I had to sit outside in the foyer, whilst Kwasi and Ghanaba chatted inside. Other people close to Ghanaba then began to intercede on my behalf, including some artists who accompanied Ghanaba on stage, like Nii Anum Telfer (who carried Ghanaba's Dane guns) and the percussionists Nii Armah and Nii Noi Nortey. Particularly insistent that we get together again was Ghanaba's photographer Yemo 'Flick' Nunu. In fact, 'Flick' had given Ghanaba a copy of an article I had published in the UK West African magazine (15 August 1988) called 'The Power of the Drum' when Ghanaba jammed with the Nigerian drummers Bayo Martins and Remi Kabaka.

So, finally Ghanaba and I buried the hatchet on June 3, 1990 and from that time Ghanaba and I were in regular touch. Sometimes I would go to Medie, then a quiet and secluded place without electricity. On other occasions he would come to Bokoor House where, because of my recording studio and the BAPMAF music archives I had just established, I had equipment to re-copy many of Ghanaba's old reel-reel recording of reminiscences of the great American jazz giants he had known. Then, in February 1996, Ghanaba became involved in a 'Highlife Month' that celebrated Ghana's home-grown music, organised by BAPMAF and the German Goethe Institute in Accra (under its then Director Sabine Hentzch). Ghanaba made a speech and gave an outstanding solo performance at its close.

It was also that year that Ghanaba made several trips to the University of Ghana at Legon when I was the Technical Director of the joint German/Institute of African Studies project to re-document and digitise old records and field recordings done by Professor Nketia, Ephraim Amu, Professor Atta Annan Mensah and others in the 1950s and 1960s. So African Studies had record turntables, and both cassette and digital recorders; so we had the equipment to transfer some of Ghanaba's records onto cassette. Another university trip occurred in 1998 when I arranged for Ghanaba to speak to our School of

Performing Arts students for the Process of Arts course that I was running out of the Music Department where I teach. Ghanaba in his usual quirky way made an announcement that he would only speak in Ga, which backfired somewhat as many of the students didn't speak this particular Ghanaian language. So a translator had to be supplied.

Throughout the 1990s and early 2000s, I made numerous trips to Ghanaba's Africa Heritage Library place, sometimes with my son Thomas who liked to play with "Uncle Guy's" tortoise and also with his grand-daughter (Midie's daughter) Leyla who stayed with him from time to time. We exchanged archival materials and talked about musical history and philosophy. Sometimes on these visits I met his numerous friends, colleagues and fans. Some of those were Eddie Quansah (the black trumpeter); the film-maker Nii Kwartey (who was documenting Ghanaba); Ghanaba's old time friend and promoter Faisal Helwani; Mac Tontoh (Osibisa's trumpeter), Felix Cobson (of the Aklowa African Village just outside London); a relative of Ghanaba called Abooshi Torto (coincidentally she and I had been archaeology students together at Legon), the art-historian Joe Nkrumah, the poet Kofi Awoonor, the politician Kojo Tsikata, the music promoter Panji Anoff and the enthno-musicologist Steve Feld. Two African American jazz musicians I met there were Montego Joe (ex Art Blakey's conga player) and the jazz pianist/ composer Randy Weston who came to Ghana in 1999 for an ACRAG Award.

In February 2005, the BAPMAF music archives that I chair, together with Juma Santos and the US Embassy Public Affairs, organised that year's Black History Month under the title 'African American Heritage Month'. This program culminated in an award ceremony for outstanding Ghanaian artists receiving 'Life Time Achievement Awards' at the DuBois Centre in Accra, with Ghanaba's award being collected on his behalf by his youngest daughter Mawuko. Two years earlier I had put Robin Kelly, an African American jazz researcher, in touch with Ghanaba. This professor of African Studies in New York was doing work on Thelonius Monk whom he knew Ghanaba had played with – and so wanted to get Ghanaba's side of the story of a rhythmic argument that had once taken place between these two jazzmen. The New York University connection later led to Professor Awam Ankpa and the NYU teaching unit being established in Accra, refurbishing, equipping and digitising Ghanaba's African Heritage Library. This was formally opened to the general public on September 28, 2005 and I was asked to present a talk and slide-show on Ghanaba's contribution to both highlife and Afro-fusion music.

On January 18, 2008, Ghanaba handed over his drum-sticks to his son Glen Warren after a performance at the National Theatre in Accra, and he made his very last performance aged eighty-five at the 'African Presence in Jazz' concert organised by the at the Goethe Institute in Accra on September 23rd, 2008. The last time I ever saw Ghanaba was in October 2008 when I paid him a visit with my brother-in-law Ben Ahorlu Ajokpa.

Besides Ghanaba's enormous musical legacy and his African Heritage Library, he left behind four sons and two daughters. His oldest son Guy Warren Jr. is a sculptor, then comes Glen Gillespie 'Ghanaba-ba' Warren who took over Ghanaba's sticks in 2008, followed by Gamal Abdel Nasser Warren and Gamaliel Joseph Warren, a jazz drummer in the US. His daughters are Midie and Gye Nyame Hossana Mawuko.

Chapter 30

GHANA/NIGERIAN DRUM COMMUNION: KOFI GHANABA, BAYO MARTINS AND REMI KABAKA

Ghanaba and two daughters at home with Remi Kabaka (back left standing), Bayo Martins (bearded at back). Standing on right is Edmund Mensah with Nii Anum Telfer on extreme right (photo by Yemo Nunu)

On July 14, 1988, Kofi Ghanaba and the Nigerian drummers Bayo Martins and Remi Kabaka played an extraordinary percussion session together at the DuBois Memorial Centre in Accra, during a three-day 'Focus on Nigeria', when the Nigerian High Commissioner in Ghana presented Nigerian cultural material to the archival documentation project of the Centre.

Remi Kabaka actually began his drumming career in Accra in the early seventies, then went on to play with Hugh Masekela, Fela Kuti and Osibisa and also with the the British rock musicians Paul McCartney, Steve Winwood, Mick Jagger and the (ex Cream rock band) drummer Ginger Baker. In fact, Remi travelled across the Sahara Desert with Ginger in 1971/72, who was on a trip to Nigeria to help set up the sixteen-track ARC (Associated Recording Company) studio in Lagos, the whole journey being filmed for the BBC documentary 'Across the Sahara'.

Fifty-two-year old Bayo Martins worked with the Nigerian dance-band leader Bobby Benson in the 1950s (see photo of him then in Chapter 47) and then formed the Koriko Clan jazz group with saxophonist Chris Ajiloi, trumpeter Zeal Onyia and pianist Wole Bucknor. In 1959, he went for further studios in dance and radio/TV journalism in England where he was influenced by the visiting Jazz Messenger of Art Blakey whom Bayo considered to be 'the most African of American drummers'. As a result, Bayo formed his own African Messengers with the Nigerian saxophonist Peter King and trumpet player Mike Falana. On returning to Nigeria, he helped set up the Nigerian Navy Band and, together with Bobby Benson and Fela Anikulapo-Kuti, was an executive of the Musicians Foundation of Nigeria.

The highlight of this *Nigeria meets Ghana* event was a drum workshop called 'The Powers of Drums in the Society', introduced by a lecture from Bayo Martins. He first talked about the general impact of music on politics, communication, religion, medicine and meditation, summing up by stating that 'a society without music is a society without soul and may be regarded as dead'. He said that drums have both the power to rouse people to frenzy or sedate them. The hostility of Europeans to African drums during the days of slavery and colonialism was a result of this instrument being used to stir up and co-ordinate revolts. He went on to say more about drums music and rhythm.

'What causes the drums to be so revered in Africa and so dreaded by others elsewhere? What is the source of powers the drums are said to possess? How do they influence the mind? Could this influence stem from a numbers of elements rather than just one source? As a drummer myself I can testify to the mysticism of the drums. There is obviously something in the drums which can properly termed "power", and this power has a way of affecting people which is universal. For anywhere the drums are played or displayed, whether made of hollow wood covered in hide or of chrome, people black and white beome excited…Of all the arts, the art of music has in particular been considered divine because it is the exact miniature of the laws working through the whole universe. If we study ourselves, we discover that the beat of the heart, the inhaling and exhaling of the breath are all the workings of rhythms'.

Bayo's talk was followed by musical action, the first being a short musical interlude from Nana Danso Abiam's Pan African Orchestra. This was immediately followed by the three drum maestros from Nigeria and Ghana. Sixty-five year old Ghanaba came on stage coated in white clay, wearing dark glasses and a white cloth. He was accompanied by his two daughters, Midie and Mawuko (likewise covered in clay), Anum Telfer carrying a rifle and the Nigerian talking-drum player, Ayanbode Oluwole. Ghanaba sat down at his amazing array of Ashanti fontomfrom drums, accompanied by Bayo on congas and Remi Kabaka on trap-drums.

These three master drummers then proceeded to weave a complex tapestry of sounds as they explored common features of the 6/8 rhythmic patterns of Nigeria's konkon beat and Ghana's adowa and agbadza beats. It was a perfect sonic combination with Remi's light and crisp jazz-kit, the spacey and mellow tones of Bayo's congas and the deep thunder of Ghanaba's fontomfrom drums. To two of these massive hand-carved drums, Ghanaba had attached foot-pedals; so sometimes, he would play flute or wave the Ghanaian flag around his head while maintaining intricate cross-beats with his feet. It was a brilliant conversation between three master percussionists with each giving the others plenty of room to solo. This amazing Nigerian/Ghanaian drum communion ended abruptly with a pre-arranged finale rifle shot from Telfer who had been standing behind Ghanaba throughout the performance.

For many years Bayo Martins was moving between Nigeria and Germany where he was a university teacher. In fact, it was in Germany that we first met in the mid-1980s at a lecture I gave at the German Unviversity of Mainz organised by Dr. Wolfgang Bender. Really, the way I met Bayo Martins is interesting. At my lecture, I had showed a slide of Bobby Benson's Jam Session Orchestra taken around 1951/2. Unkown to me, Bayo Martins was in the audience and, at the end of my presentation on Ghanaian and Nigerian highlife history, he got up very excitedly and told us that one of the personnel in the Benson band slide I had shown was none other than himself, playing maracas as a very young man (see photo Chapter 47). So after that we became friends and Martins asked me to send him a copy of the photo. He was also running his Music Foundation out of Lagos and I naturally kept in constant contact with him as I was gong similar work in Ghana through the BAPMAF music archives.

Below is an extract of a letter Bayo Martins wrote to me in my capacity as BAPMAF Chair on 8 August 1996:

> *Many thanks for notifying me about the activities of BAPMAF. It is really interesting to observe that, even though separated by four hundred miles of land, we are operating on the same wave length. Fascinating. Your ORGANIGRAM [highlife music tree diagram I designed] tracing the roots of Popular Music in West Africa is in outline interesting, but I have a few questions I would like to raise and discuss with you . This we'll do when I come to Accra. We will talk and explore means of cooperation between our two organisations. I am proud of you man. Take care and best regards, Bayo Martins.*

Sadly we never did meet up again as Martins died in Germany on 12 August 2003.

Chapter 31

WULOMEI AND THE GA "CULTURAL GROUP" EXPLOSION

Agbafoi – one of the many 'Ga cultural groups' of the mid-1970s modelled on Wulomei. Note the giant gome bass-drum on the left

During the early 1970s, there were a number of moves to create more 'rootsy' forms of highlife music. As discussed in Chapter 28, the Kumasi-based guitarist Koo Nimo re-popularised the 1920s 'palm wine' style of Jacob Sam (Kwame Asare). Similarly, C.K. Mann and his Carousel Seven from Cape Coast became all the rage in the early 1970s with their highlife based on the rhythms of the local Fanti 'osode' music. This folk highlife revival also took place in and around Accra where so-called 'Ga cultural groups'[15] sprang up that caught everyone's attention with their Ga folksongs, kolomashies, kpanlogos and highlifes. The most important of these bands, and the first to appear on the scene, was Wulomei (the Ga word for 'traditional priests') founded by the Ga drummer Nii Ashitey in 1972/3. They were soon followed by others such as Blemabii, Dzadzeloi, Agbafoi and Abladei.

On stage the members of Wulomei made an impressive sight, with eleven Ga performers, one Fanti and one Ewe dressed in the white cloth of the Wulomo (priest). The men wore frilly white caps and the three lady singers had their hair plaited like that of traditional priestesses. Nii Ashitey, who composed most of their songs, darted in and out of the musicians directing them with staccato bursts on his long osraman drum slung over his shoulder. The Fanti guitarist sat well to the back of the stage with the rhythm section between him and the vocalists. The percussion instruments included local congas, calabashes, bells and clips. Around the microphones, melody was supplied by three female members singing in western harmony, supported by two male singers on the bamboo antenteben flutes. The bass-line was supplied a giant gome drum that was played by the group's comedian, the beefy Nii Adu Ofoliquaye (Big Boy). As mentioned in Chapter 23, the gome drum used by Wulomei is a Pan African one that was introduced to Accra around from 1900 by Ga artisans returning from the Congo and later by Ga fishermen who visited Fernando Po; in both cases borrowing the idea of the drum from Sierra Leoneans living or working in those countries.

Wulomei not only became popular with Ga's but with most Ghanaians, and its appeal seemed to cross the boundaries between ethnic groups, generations and social strata. At one of their shows in the mid-seventies, I recall being amazed by the variety of the audience, which included elite people in suits and ties, young people in 'Afro-gear', market women carrying babies and sedate elders in traditional cloth. The band's fame was spread by records, especially their LP. 'Walatu Walasa' which they dedicated to the

[15]According to the researcher Gavin Webb in 2011 these groups are now genrally known as Ga' folkloric' groups.

ideals of the early Acheampong government's self-reliance policy. When I asked Nii Ashitey in the mid-1970s what prompted him to form the group, he replied, "To bring something out for the youth to progress and to forget foreign music and do their own thing."

Nii Ashitey started his musical career as a young boy just after the Second World War, when he played the pati side-drum in one of Accra's konkoma groups, the Navy Babies. Later, he became a conga player and joined a number of dance bands starting with E. T. Mensah's Tempos. He then spent some time in Liberia as a member of the Tubman Stars dance band, and returned home to the Police Band and the Brigade Band Number Two, before forming Wulomei. He told me that Wulomei has incorporated material from various local sources, the most important being that of Obiba T.K., a Ga musician who led a guitar band in Accra in the 1940s and 50s (others Nii Ashitey did not mention were the Kpagon Band and the Osu Selected Union). These groups used tambourine-like konkoma drums (also called gome drums), mandolin and guitar and played Akan konkoma highlifes and Ga kolomashies. Another style that Nii Ashitey told me affected Wulomei was the 'something' music popular with Ga fishermen in the fifties, played on guitar with large bass and small lead hand-pianos. Also included in Wulomei's repertoire is oge, a music associated with the Liberian Kru seamen who lived in Accra in the fifties. Wulomei even included a few Dagbani songs from northern Ghana and therefore presented a broad range of Ghanaian folk music to its audience.

Wulomei was given a lot of encouragement by Saka Acquaye the director of the Arts Council. Their first LP 'Walatu Walasa' was released in 1974. It included numbers such as 'Menye', 'Soyama', and the very popular 'Walatu Walasa' and 'Akrowa' which they also released as singles. In March 1975, they signed a three-year contract with Phonogram and the same year released a second LP called 'Wulomei in Drum Conference'. This record consisted of ten numbers: nine Ga songs and an old Liberian song that dates back to the forties. In June and July 1975, Wulomei, accompanied by the Kwaa Mensah Group and the Gonje Group of Salisu Mahama, made a forty-five day tour of America, which began at the Festival of American Folklore held in Washington, D.C.

By the late seventies and eighties, there were dozens of Wulomei type 'Ga cultural groups' or 'Ga folkloric groups', as they are usually referred to, operating in the Greater

Accra Region, such as Blemabii, Dzadzeloi (Night Thing), Abladei, Kyirem, Suku Troupe, Agbafoi, Ashiedu Keteke, Kudoloi, Adzo (Leave It), Dzenbii, Medjeji (Blacks), Lumei (Royals) Degmebii and Odoadebii. There were also two groups formed by ex-Wulomei members. One was the Odumankoma Troupe formed in 1976 by Wulomei's lead lady singer, Naa Amanua. Another was the Bukom Ensemble formed in 1988 by the gome player 'Big Boy' Nii Adu Ofoliquaye, which went on to tour the UK in 2000.

There are still some functioning Ga cultural groups. After Big Boy's death in 2006, the Bukom Ensemble was taken over by his son David Nii Ardy Ofoliquaye and, in 2011, they teamed up with the hiplifer/'contemporary' highlifer Adane Best to release the album 'Yei Pii Ye'. Abladei and Dzadzeloi are still going strong. Other new Ga cultural groups have also entered the scene like Ebaahi Sounds, the Kake Dance Ensemble and the Modin Sane group based at the Fair Gardens Hotel in Accra. Furthemore, Wulomei itself has continued through to a second generation. This is the Sensational Wulomei run by Nii Ashitey's son and daughter, Nii Tei Ashitey and Naa Ashalay, and which is based in Mamprobi, Accra. In 2007, they released an album called 'Wulomei Returns' on Kwesi Owusu's Creative Storm label.

Chapter 32

KWESI ASARE: GHANA'S FOREIGN AMBASSADOR OF RITUAL DRUMMING

Kwesi Asare Asuo Gyebi has unostentatiously been spreading African rhythms abroad for years. To jazz musicians in the late 1950s and 1960s, amongst West Indian and British youth in the late 1970s, and then in the United States where in 1987 he was awarded the title of 'cultural ambassador' by American's oldest black newspaper – the Philadelphia Tribune. Kwesi was born in 1931 in the hill-top town of Larteh-Akuapim. On his Guan maternal side he is the grandson (or more precisely the grand-nephew) of the late Nana Akua Oparabea, President of the Psychic and Traditional Healers Association of Ghana and High Priestess of the Larteh Akonodi Shrine (which even has branches in New York and Washington D.C.)

This important Ghanaian traditional religious centre is today a composite of four spirit cults, each with its own rituals, shrines and music. The oldest of them is the Akonodi spirit shrine founded in the last century by an ancestor of Kwesi's, called Nana Adwo Komfo. Junior to this is the Asuo Gyebi spirit (from which Kwesi gets his name), embodied in a sacred stone discovered in 1900 in a forest by Kwesi's maternal uncle, Yaw Akyea, the master-drummer for the then Akonedi high priestess Nana Okomfo Ansa. The two other spirits of the Larteh Shrine are Asi Ketewa and Adade Kofi, the latter being introduced by Kwesi's grandfather, Kweku Ahia. As each of these four religious cults have their own special dances, songs, drums, and rhythms, Kwesi was brought up in the right environment to be groomed as a master-drummer.

Despite his rich traditional background, Kwesi left Ghana in 1955 to study motor mechanics in the northern British town of Manchester. He soon gravitated back to music and learnt to play alto sax. From then on, he worked in a factory but spent all his spare time playing with a succession of African-American jazz giants who came on tour of Britain. In 1958, he met and jammed with Duke Ellington and the following year began a long relationship with Count Basie. Kwesi and Ellington's guitarist, the late Freddie Green, began working out Afro-rhythms for this large swing group. Green advised Kwesi not to copy Basie's music but rather to use what Basie had taught him. With this good advice, Kwesi stuck to his drums and, in the 1960s, played percussion with a number of African-American musicians; including singer Sarah Vaughan, pianist Thelonius Monk who stayed with Kwesi whenever he played in Manchester, and the multi-instrumentalist Roland Kirk who played with Kwesi at the Club 43. Kwesi explains that he was able to play with these top American musicians because "when I came to England, I studied Western music and could hear that blues, jazz and soul grew out of African music. They go side-by-side, so I can play drums with anybody."

Kwesi Asare with Duke Ellington in Manchester, UK, in the late 1950s

In the late 1970s, and with a growing British interest in Afro-Caribbean music, Kwesi began teaching African drumming to the West Indian community in Manchester. In fact, this is when I first met him, for in 1979/80 two Ghanaian members of my Bokoor Band and I were teaching unemployed West Indian youth African guitar music at the Wolverhampton Centre for Community Relations, and Kwesi often came to help us out. Finally, in 1982, with the help of the North-West Arts Council, Kwesi set up his own band called the Kantamanto Kruti Ayisi Cultural Group (Twi for 'my word is my bond') made up of nine young unemployed West Indian men and women from Manchester's Moss Side. This group began playing all over Britain – at the Royal Festival Hall and Almeida Theatre in London, the Amofini Theatre in Bristol and the International Jazz Festival in Hayfield. At one point, he played in Manchester with the Halle Orchestra and conductor David Fanshaw.

In 1987, Kwesi went to the United States, where he spent six months in Philadelphia. He taught African music at schools, academies and art institutions. He and the African American jazz drummer Edgar Bateman gave a series of workshops entitled 'African Rhythms and American Music' at Coltrane House, dedicated to the sax virtuoso John Coltrane (who died in 1967, aged 40). Coltrane had lived in the house, which became a cultural centre and museum run by his cousin, Mary Alexander. Kwesi also accompanied the poet Elizabeth Suber Bennett (who subsequently became his manager) on talking drums at the Afro-American Historical and Cultural Museum. In spite of his heavy teaching schedule, Kwesi still had time to jam in Philadephia: with trombonist Al Grey at Jewel's Lounge, with Count Basie's Band at the Trocadero Club and several times with the Sun Ra Arkestra at the New York Cafe Club. Indeed, Philadephians liked Kwesi so much and were so inspired by his wise and sensitive teaching approach that he was invited there again.

This modest master-drummer explains the magic of his international success in this way:

> You can't be selfish when you're playing. You have to be sincere. If you have ego problems you have no chance. Don't think about yourself, "Look at me, watch me". That's no good. You have to be honest and put all your heart to it. Don't be afraid of learning. Don't be afraid of asking someone who knows more than you. Don't be shy. If you know you don't know but won't ask, you're being insincere and full of ego. When you're playing, you're gaining sound; then you create more sound and rhythm – but not all at once. So try to hear other things. Listen a lot, listen, listen.

Kwesi Asare and Loius armstrong and wife Lucy, UK 1950

In 1995 Kwesi came back to Ghana to settle in his home town at Larteh, where he established the African Cultural Research Centre. He is now a respected elder or 'Opanyin' and, under the title 'Asare Kwakwe', is the Ankobia or Councillor for the Okuapemhene at Larteh.

OUTSIDE INFLUENCES: 1950s TO PRESENT – AND RESULTING MUSICAL FUSIONS

5

Highlife
TIME 3

This first turns to how jazz, rock and soul influences coming into Ghana, Nigeria, Sierra Leone, Liberia and Cote d'Ivoire since the 1950s have been blended with highlife and other West African popular music styles. It is followed by chapters on the rise of local reggae in West Africa as well as Ghanaian disco-influenced burger highlife, pioneered by George Darko and the Lumba Brothers as well as the more recent rap-influenced hiplife pioneered by Reggie Rockstone.

Chapter 33

LOUIS ARMSTRONG IN GHANA

In 1956 the great African-American jazz trumpeter Louis 'Satchmo' Armstrong visited Ghana, and since E.T. Mensah was the top Ghanaian trumpeter at that time he found himself heavily involved in the visit. The trip was sponsored by the Columbia Broadcasting System which, under the guidance of Ed Murrow, had made a feature film on Africa the previous year entitled 'See It Now' which included shots of Accra and E. T.' s Paramount Club. A film about Armstrong's trip to Europe was already in the pipeline at the CBS studios and Murrow, therefore, decided to lengthen the tour to include Accra and also for Louis to do a jam-session with E. T. at the Paramount. A film of the whole tour, including the four weeks in Europe, three days in Accra and the return to America was later released under the title 'Satchmo the Great'.

Arrangments at the Accra end were in the hands of James Moxon, Head of the Information Service, who arranged a meeting at his bungalow between E.T. Mensah and Gene De Poris, head of the CBS film crew. They had to decide what songs they were going to use in the jam session, and so Moxon pulled out his selection of Armstrong records and began to play them. One song was chosen, sheet music was given to E. T. and the few of his musicians who were present. De Poris asked them to play it and as Armstrong could not play highlife the song 'St. Louis Blues' was chosen for the jam-session. As E.T. explains this was no easy matter.

With Louis on his way, arrangements were made that he would have a jam-session at my club, but we didn't know the type of music that Louis played and he couldn't play our highlife. So when we went to James' house they brought us some of Louis' records. They were wondering whether we could play any thing reasonable together when he came. They wanted us to play a song that we had never heard of at the time. 'St Louis Blues'. Unfortunately, it wasn't the days when Guy and Joe were in, so they weren't very impressed with our playing.

The next day, Wednesday May 23, Louis, his wife Lucille, the blues singer Velma Middleton and the All-Stars arrived. The All-Stars was a five-piece band comprising Edmund Hall on clarinet, Trummy Young on trombone, Billy Kyle on piano and two white musicians, Barret Deems and Jack Lesberg on drums and bass. A large group of local trumpeters, playing an old highlife 'All For You', were on hand to greet the band at the airport. When Louis and the others got off the plane, they pulled out their instruments and joined in. The trumpeters fell in behind them and the whole group of musicians marched across the tarmac to the vehicles that were waiting for them. While the crowd had been waiting for the All-Stars, they had been entertained by the Nigerian comedian Ajax Bukana (see Chapter 7) whom E. T. knew well.

He was originally a member of Bobby Benson's Band as bass player and when he came here he liked the atmosphere and stayed. On any important occasion, you see him dressed up as a clown, getting himself involved by making an unofficial floor-show. He even went to government functions in his peculiar dress. He was very well-known and could go almost anywhere freely. He paraded around that day and when the band arrived he joined us marching along with the trumpets.

When the Ghanaian and American musicians, playing 'All For You', reached their waiting cars, they were driven in a cavalcade from the airport to Accra playing all the time to the crowds lining the streets. The All-Stars then went off to have lunch with Nkrumah and, later in the afternoon, went to the old polo ground to play at a free concert. By the time Louis and his band arrived, they were late and there was an enormous and restless crowd of almost a hundred thousand. Unfortunately, the amplification wasn't up to scratch and some of the speakers had even been knocked over by the vast crowd. So when the band started playing, the crowd surged forward to listen, breaking through the crowd barrier. The Police pushed the mass of people back, employing the normal method of crowd control in Ghana – flicking people's feet with the leather straps of their truncheons. This happened several times and, on each

Louis Armstrong at Accra Airport in 1956 with the Nigerian clown
Ajax Bukana. E.T. Mensah is on extreme left with trumpet and Edmund Hall is on far right

occasion, Louis stopped playing in the mistaken belief that the police were truncheoning his audience in earnest.

The band played for about one and a half hours but the general impression of the music was poor. As E.T. explains:

> *They were playing the sort of jazz that wasn't popular here then; swing was popular but*
> *dixieland was not. The crowd tried to listen to the music but the amplification wasn't so*
> *good and there was such a huge crowd that the music was drowned. The sound wasn't thick,*
> *the trumpet was pitched high so that the music was light and this wasn't popular with the*
> *African audience.*

That evening, the All-Stars came to do the jam at the Paramount with the Tempos. Tickets cost up to £1. 00 and there was such a crowd inside that it caused problems for the film crew. Throughout the evening, the dance floor got smaller and smaller as more tables and chairs were brought in. One little boy was even forced to dance on the roof. The Tempos opened the evening and at about nine o'clock Louis Armstrong arrived. Dan Acquaye recalls that Edmund Hall was particularly impressed by their rendering of 'Stranger in Paradise'. Louis too was impressed as can be seen in this extract from the Daily Graphic (May 25, 1956):

*Armstrong and E.T. Mensah jam together at
the Paramouint Club in 1956 (photo Steve Feld)*

*Mensah and his Tempos were certainly on top form when they played their signature tune,
'Tiger Rag'. This number nearly brought the house down. E. T. himself seems to have been
inspired by the presence of the great Louis; his fingers moved over the valves of his silver
trumpet to produce the best manipulation of this musical instrument by any West African
trumpeter. Louis must have been surprised. He was moved. He was pleased. He went up to
E.T. and shook hands with him.*

The All-Stars then took the stage and started to play the 'St. Louis Blues'. However, it
was in a different key from the one the Tempos had practised at Moxon's house.
Nonetheless, it took E. T. only a few moments to get the right key and shout it out to his
musicians. E.T. was very impressed by Louis' trumpet playing.

*Louis was a great player and when he was playing, he put in all his energy, from his head to
the tip of his toes. We could see everything quivering, sweating all round, saliva coming out
and we could see that a portion of his lip had come out. I observed that if he wanted to play a
note he must force the note to come, come what may. So we could see him pitching high. He*

310

found my range and started above it so that his trumpet sounded like a clarinet. He was pitching high all the time, his lowest note was my top G. We jammed for about half an hour playing the 'St. Louis Blues'. Then they left the stage and listened to us playing highlife. By then, the crowd was huge so there was no chance of dancing. Afterwards we talked to Louis. He liked our highlife as it was something he hadn't heard before. But it was difficult to hear him talk as he was so choked up with his croaky throat.

Dan Acquaye, the Tempos bongo player and vocalist, also has some words to say about Armstrong's performance that night.

Having seen other trumpeters play, I found that Louis Armstrong plays with much feeling and doesn't mind how his face looks. We even saw saliva dripping down his face with his eyeballs about to pop. Because of the smallness of the place, the music was properly contained and the music there was more admirable than it was at the old polo ground.

On Thursday, the All-Stars spent the day visiting schools, lunching at the University Legon and being entertained at Achimota School by a display of cultural music and dancing. For the evening, a charity jazz concert had been arranged at the Opera Cinema. Tickets were three pounds each and Nkrumah was to be there. The concert master-of ceremonies was Beattie Casely-Hayford and the whole event recorded by the Gold Coast Broadcasting Department. E.T. remembers the occasion vividly.

When they started it was bad. The music was thin for us Africans and we wanted more rhythm. For about the first four numbers, when they finished, the audience would just look at them. The people had not known how to give heavy applause at the end of the music as is done abroad, so the musicians were not getting that encouragement. Some of the audience was even going to sleep. It was Trummy Young, the trombonist, who saved the situation. He played reclining on his back using his legs to move the slide and got a huge applause for this. This raised the morale of the public and the musicians and, from then on, the people became interested. The show didn't close till midnight.

The next morning, E.T. went to Moxon's to say goodbye to Louis and his band. While Louis was eating lunch, he told those around that he was on a diet and was taking a special herb for this. E. T. had noticed that Louis was much thinner than his photographs suggested. After lunch, everybody went to the airport to see the musicians off and, as they left, the Rakers Band broke into 'All For You'.

Dr. Nkrumah with Louis Armstrong and his wife Lucille in 1956

An interesting point concerning this particular highlife is mentioned by lain Laing, foreign Editor of the Sunday Times, who was in Accra in 1956 and spoke to Louis. In his article 'Jazz Comes Home to Africa', Laing mentioned that Louis recognised the song as an old Creole melody from his childhood. Laing wondered whether the melody was brought to Ghana some time before or whether it was an old Gold Coast melody taken to America during the days of the slave trade. In fact, 'All For You' is based on the melody of an early calypso called 'Sly Mongoose' first recorded in the 1920s by Lionel Belasco. The first African version of this West Indian song was recorded in 1929 by the West African Instrumental Quintet under the title 'Tinka Tinka'. Then, there is a late 1940s guitar band version of 'All for You' (recorded by the American Arthur Alberts) by Eupheme Cooper who sings a complaint that her man is trying to take her to a location in Monrovia, slit her throat and smash her head with a hammer.

E.T Mensah's version of 'All for You' does not include these strong lyrics.

E.T.'s impressions of Louis were that he had quite an impact on the local music scene of the times. Although jazz had been known in Ghana for some time, it was more of the ragtime and later swing variety. So it was Louis who brought in the dixieland jazz and many Accra trumpeters started using his phrasing;, singers copied Satchmo's gravelly voice and the 'St. Louis Blues' became a standard song for the Tempos and other local dance bands. E.T. also recalled that Louis and the All-Stars were impressed by the standard of music in the Ghana. They also liked the country and Louis expressed a wish to come back. Once, at Achimota market, he had seen a woman who resembled his mother and this led him to believe that his ancestors came from Ghana. One of the All-Stars did, in fact, return to Ghana. This was the clarinettist Edmund Hall who came back to Ghana in 1958 to form a band. As E. T. relates, and like all band leaders in Ghana, Ed had his problems.

> *He came back to Accra and wanted to form a jazz band at the Ambassador Hotel. He got some local musicians together, including one who had been with me for a time, Ray Ellis – a talented pianist. Ed went and bought instruments but he couldn't get the musicians to rehearse in the way he liked and therefore couldn't bring out the sound he wanted. He got fed up and went back to the States. The band was never even out-doored. The conditions are very terrible here for the musicians. In the United States or Britain, if you are a band leader and you want to make a band, all you got to do is make publication and the musicians will come along with their own instruments. When you get an engagement, everybody brings their own instruments; so the task is easier there. But here, Ed could not understand why he should buy the instruments for the musicians to come and play and then pay them; especially when the musicians needed more technical coaching to make them perfect. He couldn't bear it and left.*

Louis Armstrong also came again to Ghana in October 1960 at the beginning of an African tour. On that visit, he picked up Ajax Bukana and took him to perform in Lagos, Kano and Lome. In Ghana itself, Louis and his All Stars played at the Accra Sports Stadium alongside a Ghanaian contingent that included clarinettist/saxophonist Joe Kelly, trumpeter Guy Oke, tenor saxophonist George Lee, guitarist Ralph Quist, double bassist Papa Mantey and drummer Guy Warren (Kofi Ghanaba). Armstrong and his All Stars also played in Kumasi where they made a big impact on the young Koo Nimo. As Koo Nimo told the journalist Kwabena Fosu Mensah in 1986, "America uses its sportsmen and musicians in world politics and, in the heat of the Soviet-American tensions, it was the music of Louis Armstrong that saved the situation."

Chapter 34

POP MUSIC AND ITS IMPACT IN GHANA AND NIGERIA DURING THE 1960s AND 1970s

From about 1960, rock 'n' roll, the twist and pop music generally started coming into vogue with the youth of West Africa. The very first pop bands there were the Avengers of Ghana, the Heartbeats of Sierra Leone and the Blue Knights of Nigeria. Since pop music is sung in English, it predictably first caught on in English-speaking West African nations, and only later spread to the French-speaking areas. As I will deal with the popular music scene in Sierra Leone in Chapter 52, I will examine here the early pop-music scene of Ghana and Nigeria.

Rock 'n' roll dancers Accra. Photo Drum Magazine October 1959

The first pop band in Ghana was the Avengers, formed in 1962 from an army band called the Red Devils. Gabby Nick Valdo (Nketsia – later manager of GANAVA batteries) was the leader and he formed the Avengers after he and some of the members of Red Devils spent some time training in England, where they saw pop groups such as Cliff Richard and the Shadows.

Gabby Nick Valdo (front with guitar) and the Avengers the early 1960s

The Avengers as well as imported records and films of rock music artists subsequently inspired a whole number of student pop bands. One of the earliest was The Avalanches of Adisadel School, formed in 1963 that included Glen Warren on drums (he also played for the school jazz band), Bobby Torto on guitar, Ricky Telfer piano and a Canadian teacher Dave Godfrey on trumpet. This group played side by side with the Avengers band at Accra clubs like the Lido and Metropole. Not to be outdone, Achimota School also set up early pop bands like the Bachelors and the Sharks.

This is what Lash Laryea told me about those times:

We had Cliff Richard and Beatles, and the Avengers were playing sound like the Shadows. They played pure copyright – but well – so everyone got crazy, especially the students. They were actually called the students' band. I was living in a rough neighbourhood of Accra – Opera Square, my family house just by the Glamour Shop and Opera Cinema. That was the first place I saw the first movie by Elvis Presely titled 'Loving You'. I also saw this guy singing with blue eyes and dark hair and girls were screaming. I was a little guy, about six or seven. I also saw Little Richards, Fats Domino and Bill Haley and the Comets. I also used to listen to their records and sing their songs. Chubby Checker also came to Ghana, but that was later.

Then, in 1965, the Adisadel Avalanches (later called the Thunderbirds) organized the first 'Pop Chain' (competition) at Baiden Powell Hall in Accra. Glen Warren was instrumental in this; for, as a small boy, he had sometimes accompanied his father Ghanaba playing at jazz concerts there and so knew the people to contact. According to Glen, the name 'Pop Chain' itself was taken from the title of a British film being shown in Ghana, which featured a string or 'chain' of performance by top UK pop bands like Spencer Davis, and Eric Burdon and the Animals.

By 1966, 'pop chains' competitions were being organized in Accra during the holidays for schoolboy bands like the Road Runners, Blues Syndicate, Circuit Five, Phantoms, Mathew Chapter Five and the Saints – playing the music of Elvis Presley, the Beatles, the Rolling Stones and Spencer Davis. Incidentally, I myself played with one of these schoolboy groups based at Achimota College in 1969, called 'Deep Blues Feeling' (with Sammy 'Slim' Bentil and Johnny Opoku-Acheampong). As I had bought a wah-wah and fuzz-box guitar effects with me from Britain, our group created a sensation playing Jimmy Hendrix songs like 'Foxy Lady'. We won that year's school pop-chain.

As will be discussed in the next chapter, live soul music had already hit Ghana in 1966 when the Heartbeats of Sierra Leone came to the country. The first Ghanaian band to play soul was Stanley Todd's El Pollos, followed by some of King Bruce's B.B. bands. However, imported rock music itself began to change in the late sixties with the 'progressive', 'underground' or 'psychedelic' rock music of Jimi Hendrix, Sly and the Family Stone, and Cream (of Eric Clapton and Ginger Baker) becoming popular in Ghana. One of the first bands to play this new music style in Ghana was the visiting Super Eagles from Gambia (now known as Ifang Bondi and the Afro-Mandigue Sounds), who went on a West African tour in 1968. The first Ghanaian band to play this type of psychedelic or 'progressive' rock music was the Magic Aliens, formed in 1967 by Ricky Telfer with Smart Aperh 'Pozo' Thompson, Lash Laryea, keyboard player Malek Crayem, bassist George Allen and, later, the singer Nadim Tabika. Then came Blue Magic and a B.B. (i.e. Black Beats)[16] band managed by King Bruce called the Barristers.

Pop bands also started appearing in Nigeria in the early sixties, the earliest ones being composed of students and schoolboys; like the Blue Knights and the Cyclops based in Lagos. They were given impetus by the two visits of Millicent 'Millie' Small to Nigeria in 1965 and 1966, and by Chubby Checker's African tour in 1967. By 1968, soul had also made an appearance in the country with a visit by James Brown and with Geraldo Pino's Heartbeats settling in Nigeria.

THE 1970s CHANGE

Around 1970, a great change occurred in the popular music of Ghana and Nigeria as, under the impact of progressive rock and particularly soul music, young musicians began to move away from the straitjacket of 'copyright music', i.e. music imitative of Western pop records. Very important was the birth of Afro-soul and Afro-beat – pioneered by Nigeria's Orlando Julius, Segun Bucknor and Fela Anikulapo-Kuti – and the **Africa '70** that coined the word 'Afro-beat', a blend of Yoruba music with highlife, jazz, Latin music and soul (see Chapter 49). Concurrent with the rise of Afro-beat was the revival and revitalization of West African guitar-band music. In Nigeria, there was the modernized juju music of Sunny Ade, Shina Peters and Segun Adewele, as well as Sonny Okosun's rock version of Victor Uwaifo's Bini highlife music. In Sierra Leone, there was the maringa music of the Afro-Nationals. In Ghana, there was a new surge of interest in folk highlife bands, the most popular being the Ga group Wulomei and the Adadam Agoromman group of the Akan guitarist Koo Nimo.

But let us turn to Ghana and the emergence of progressive rock-music, also known as 'psychedelic' or 'acid rock'. As mentioned, the first Ghanaian bands to play this music were the Magic Aliens, Blue Magic and Barristers. But, by the 1970s, several Ghanaian bands started experimenting with their own 'Afro-pop' styles. The Magic Aliens, first known as the 'Psychedelic Aliens', was the first when it released a recording that was a cross between Jimi Hendrix and African music. It included some songs in a style the group called its 'psycho African beat'. The recording was done at the Nigerian EMI studios in 1968 when the Aliens were based at the Kue Club in Apapa Lagos.

[16] The B.B. Bands were a stable of bands that King Bruce ran.

This is what Lash Laryea told me in November 2009 about this matter:

We were (initially) playing strictly copyright – and from copyright we began to create 'psycho-African beat' sound which began with 'Blofonyo Bi Wo Atale' and 'Extraordinary Women'. This was on an EP (extended play format of 4 songs) we recorded in 1968 at the four-track EMI studio in Lagos at Apapa that was released by Polydor – so there was several songs on it. I composed 'Extraordinary Women', which is like a Jimmy Hendrix kind of song. 'Blofonyo Bi Wo Atale' was more like an Afro-beat. It means 'the white man wearing a shirt…thanks to Prempeh'. That's the Ga proverb the children would use to dance around in the road to play games. We turned it into a song – and Smart and I were the singers. When we came back to Ghana, we did two other singles that we recorded for Polydor at the Phillips studio in Accra. At the time Essiebons was in charge of Phillips. We did songs like 'Homowo' and 'We're Laughing'. They were our creations, pure psychedelic or what we called 'psycho African beat'. Phillips produced the two songs, they became hits and were often played by the Broadcasting Corporation of Ghana.

In Kumasi, there was another band experimenting with African/pop fusion music. This was the the Q-Masters formed by some memberts of the Sierra Leonean Echoes band that had been resident in Ghana since 1967. In 1970, they teamed up with the Sierra Leonean guitarist Papa Maurice Williams and the resulting Q-Masters created what they called the 'Cross-Beat', based on the traditional rhythms of the Poro secret society of Sierra Leone, with Latin and pop influences.

Fela's sound was also catching on and, in 1971, after some members of the El PolIos' second band – the Triffis – went to Nigeria. They returned as the Big Beats and released their own Ga Afro-beat record that was a big hit in Ghana. This was 'Kyenkyenma' which became a catchword in Ghana for anything that is antiquated or not up-to-date. Another Ghanaian band that specialized in Afro-beat was Sawaaba Soundz, which was formed in 1971 and released several singles.

An event which particularly affected Ghanaian pop musicians was the Soul to Soul concert of March 1971. This event will be discussed more fully in the next chapter. Suffice it to say here that its biggest impact on Ghanaians came through Santana, whose fusion of rock and Latin music became a source of inspiration for young Ghanaian musicians. Indeed, 'Santana Man' became a current phrase in the country, synonymous with the terms 'Afro' and 'Psychedelic'.

Yet another stimulus to the Ghanaian pop scene was the London-based Afro-rock band Osibisa, which is mentioned in Chapter 17, was founded around 1970 by Teddy Osei, Mac Tontoh, and Sol Amarfio. Osibisa toured Ghana in 1972. The same year also saw the formation of two more local groups who moved away from 'copyright music' toward their own 'Afro' pop style. One was Cosmic Boom or Boombaya, formed by the Bannerman brothers with Smart Arpeh Pozo from the old Aliens, Kofi Edo and Kofi Adu. The other was Zonglo Biiz, which included the drummer Smart Arpeh Pozo and also the bass player George McBruce who later went on to join Fela Kuti in Lagos. Then, in 1973, Faisal formed Hedzoleh, the first of his Afro-rock bands resident at his Napoleon club in Accra.

The Boombaya Afro-rock group in 1975

Below is a list of some of the Ghanaian pop groups of the mid-seventies (excluding concert guitar-bands and large dance bands), all of which played a wide range of music which included highlifes, Congo music, imported pop music as well as 'Afro-pop' (i.e. Afrobeat and Afro-rock). Because of the prevailing 'Afro' music and fashions, many of these bands used African names:

Alpha-Omega, Ionic Revolt, Bisa Goma, Adam's Apple, Ambollay's Sekondi-based Steneboofs, Bob Pinodo's Winneba-based Sound Coasters, Kukurudu (Earthquake), Gee Dees (formerly the Q-Masters), Tommy Darling's Wantu Wazuri (Swahili for 'Beautiful People'), the Tip-Toe nightclub's Jewels, Sawaaba Sounds and Szaabu Sounds managed by Aunty Naomi, the Sweet Talks managed by Raymond Azziz, Ebo Taylor's Asase-Ase (Underground), the Third Generation and Fourth Dimension army pop bands.

Others were:

- Blemabii, a pop band that turned folk, led by the Headmaster of the Empire School in Odorkor, Mr. Mark Diamond Addy.
- King Bruce's bands: the Black Beats (led by Sammy Odoh), Barbecues, Barristers, Barons, Bonafides, B. Soyaaya and Boulders.
- The bands of Faisal Helwani's 'F' Promotions: Hedzoleh, Basa-Basa and the Bunzus.
- Uppers International based in Bolgatanga, led by Chester Adams and featuring the singers Prince Ali and Christie Azuma. Established by A.A. Ampofo (a.k.a Kofi Charlie) the Upper East Regional Administrative Officer.
- Black Berets, the army Recce Unit's highlife/pop band based at Burma Camp in Accra and led by Bossman. I appeared on TV once in 1974 with them playing harmonica.
- Sweet Beans led by Pat Thomas and run by the Cocoa Marketing Board.
- Pagadeja (from the break-up of EI Pollos). The band later left for England where it became known as Bukutu, based at Harry Appiah's club in Liverpool.
- Apagya Show Band managed by Dick Essilfie-Bondzie and including the musicians Ebo Taylor, Bob Pinodo, Gyedu-Blay Ambollay and Ebo Dadson.
- Marijata, a break-away from the Sweet Talks that played Afro-funk and which included Kofi Electric, Bob Fiscian and Nat Fredua Osamanu.

The most important pop music promotions were those of King Bruce, Faisal Helwani and Raymond Azziz. Faisal Helwani's pioneering role in creating local Afro-pop will be dealt with in Chapter 59. As already mentioned in Chapter 14, King Bruce was running seven youthful pop bands in the 1970s playing 'copyright music' and some original material. 'Ray Publicity' was a music business owned by Raymond Azziz. From 1967, he managed the Black Santiagos and organized a series of 'pop chains' called 'Soul

Brother Competitions'. He also promoted bands from other West African countries, such as the Heartbeats of Sierra Leone, Fela's Africa '70, and Segun Bucknor's Soul Assembly from Nigeria. He later became the manager of Sweet Talks and the singer Joe Mensah.

Before closing this section on the 1970s changes in Ghana's popular music, I should add that there was a definite convergence between two creative movements: the rise of local 'Afro-pop', and the revitalization of the less-westernised music of guitar bands and Ga 'cultural groups'. Hedzoleh played Afro-rock/beat band but also included some folk songs, like the Liberian song 'Rekpete'. Blemabii started as a group playing Osibisa type rock and underground music; then, encouraged by Wulomei's success, ended up playing their own local Ga music. One hit song they had then was 'Maa Fio'. On the other hand, guitar-bands like the African Brothers, Teacher and his Afrikana, and the City Boys began absorbing ideas from pop, soul, and Afro-beat (and later reggae).

Turning now to Nigeria in the seventies where the most important factor was Fela Anikulapo-Kuti's Afro-beat (originally called Afro-soul) and the multitude of bands influenced by him. Fela's influence has been profound. A good example is Sonny Okosun, a musician who joined Victor Uwaifo in 1969 and then in 1972 split away to form his own group which played what he called 'Jungle-rock', a combination of Uwaifo-type rhythms, Afro-beat, and Santana-style Latin-rock guitar. From Kaduna came the Northern Pyramids dance band, which included in its repertoire a Hausa form of Afro-beat; and Sunny Ade who created his 'synchro-system' by fusing his juju-music with Afro-beat.

After the success of Afro-beat, as well as Osibisa's Afro-rock, a large number of young Nigerian pop bands surfaced, each trying to create their own sounds. Typical were the Afro-rock outfits of Berkley Jones' BLO, Ofege that played rock in 6/8 time and Johnny Haastrup's Mono-Mono which ended up in the United States. Another band that left the country was Ofo and the Black Company, which was formed in 1972 and played what it called 'Afrodelic Funk'. It became the resident band for a time at Ginger Johnson's Iroku Club in London. Another experimental group was the Black Ghosts that was led by Twin Seven Seven who was also a well-known painter in the Yoruba 'Oshogbo' art style. The Black Ghosts fused the Ijala drumming of Oyo and Afro-American music. Other Nigerian 'Afro-pop' groups were the Shango Babies, Easy Kabaka, the Gondoliers and Cicada. Then, there was the Baranta Afro-rock band, led

Joni Haastrup leader of Mono Mono, the 1970s Nigerian Afrorock band

by Francis Fuster (ex-Heartbeats) based at the Can-Can club in Lagos where I saw them perform in 1974. The resident band of the Granada Hotel in Lagos at the time, the Granadians, also developed a form of Afro-beat based on the makossa music of the Cameroons, since some of its members had been in a band in that country called Voory's Power. A final example is the Afro-Collection, formed in 1971 by the leading Nigerian pop musicians Tee Mac, Berkley Jones, Laolu Akins, Mike Odumosu, and Joni Haastrup.

Chapter 35

SOUL TO SOUL, FESTAC, PANAFEST AND THE DUBOIS CENTRE

SOUL MUSIC IN WEST AFRICA

Up until the disco music of the 1970s and reggae craze of the 1980s, the biggest wave of black American 'pop' to sweep over Africa was, undoubtedly, soul. In fact, it was Liberia, with its Americo-Liberians, that first got soul through imported records. Liberia, however, didn't produce Africa's first band to play the music of Otis Redding, Aretha Franklin, Ray Charles and also James Brown and Wilson Pickett, who both played in West Africa in the 1970s – and Isaac Hayes who actually settled in Ghana during the 1990s.

Although Liberia was the first West African country to feel the impact of soul records, it was rather Geraldo Pino's (Gerald Pine) Heart-beats of Sierra Leone, a pop band formed in Freetown in 1961/2, which moved on to performing soul in 1964 when it was resident in Monrovia. In 1966, the Heartbeats brought live soul music in Ghana. Then, in 1968, Chris Okotie took them to Lagos where they dominated the Nigerian pop scene for two years. They then split up. Those who stayed in Lagos with percussionist Francis Fuster formed Baranta, whilst Pino went to Kano where he formed the New Heartbeats with the Plastic Jims (formerly called the Triffis) from Ghana. Ghana's first soul group was the EI Pollos led by Stan Todd featuring the soul singer Elvis J. Brown (Bob Pinodo's brother). Others soon followed. King Bruce's old Black Beats dance-band began playing soul in 1969 under the youthful leadership of Sammy Odoh who hired the local soul singer Ray Otis. King Bruce also formed a new B.B. band that specialised in soul called the Barbecues led by Tommy Darling.

In Nigeria, the Heartbeats influenced pop-bands like the Clusters and Hykkers which went overboard for soul. Joni Haastrup became acclaimed as Nigeria's James Brown, whilst Tony Benson, son of the famous old-time highlife band leader Bobby Benson, set up his Strangers band that played soul music at his father's Caban Bamboo nightclub in Lagos. Yet another Nigerian soul fanatic was Segun Bucknor who, in 1968 and after a two-year trip to the States, teamed up with the Nelson Cole brothers to form Segun Bucknor and his Soul Assembly. This group released popular records like 'Lord Give Me Soul'. By 1969, Segun was fusing soul with African music and so changed the name of the group to Segun Bucknor and the Revolution, and released a string of 'Afro-soul' hits like 'Pocket Your Bigmanism' and 'Poor Man No Get Brother' (See Chapter 50). Besides Fela and Segun Bucknor, another important Nigerian Afro-soul pioneer was Orlando Julius who formed his Afro-Sounders in 1967.

Geraldo Pino leader of the 1960s Sierra Leonian Heartbeats soul band

So, through the influence of soul and funk music and their associated 'Afro' fashions, creative young African musicians were turned back to their own indigenous resources, for African musicians took James Brown messages of 'doing your own thing' and 'black and proud' to heart. Nigeria's highlife star Victor Uwaifo began to develop his soulish 'mutaba' beat. The Congolese guitarist Dr. Nico used soul elements in his 'Kirri-Kirri' beat, as well as releasing the archetypal African soul song 'Suki Shy Man' which even became a hit in Ghana in 1969. And, in Ghana, in the early seventies bands like Hedzoleh, the Big Beats and Sawaaba Sounds were developing their own brands of Afro-beat. Guitar bands also played soul music. For instance, Nana Ampadu's African Brothers created their soul and Afro-beat inspired 'locomotive' and 'Afro-hili' beats.

THE 'SOUL TO SOUL' CONCERT

As mentioned in the previous chapter, another stimulus to the creative music scene of the 1970s was the 'Soul to Soul' concert held in Accra in 1971. At this massive two-day event, top African-American bands played by side with Ghanaian groups and tens of thousands flocked to Accra's Black Star Square. Even the African American politician Jesse Jackson attended the event. This unique happening was organised by the US Cinerama Company (Ed and Tom Mosk) and the Ghana Arts Council (Saka Acquaye then being its Director). However, the original idea (although not the name) of such a concert was muted as early as 1967 by the African American writer Maya Angelou, when she was living in Ghana.

At Soul to Soul, there were the American artists Roberta Flack, the Voices of East Harlem, the hot-gospel songs of the Staple Singers and the soul singers Ike and Tina Turner – and Wilson Pickett who so excited one policemen on duty for the show that he jumped up on stage and started dancing with his hero. Ghanaian acts that played at this marathon event were the palmwine guitarist Kwaa Mensah, Charlotte Dada backed by the Barbecues and the Anansekromian Soundz, the resident folkloric group of the Ghana Arts Council. The Psychedelic or Magic Aliens also played some of their 'psycho African beat' songs, like 'Blofonyo Bi Wo Atale' and 'Extraordinary Women'.

Other new creations were also aired at the Soul to Soul concert. Ghana's Kofi Ghanaba (Guy Warren) played way-out drum solos backed by the Damas Choir. The African American jazz group of Les McCann and Eddie Harris teamed up with Amoah Azangeo. He was the master of the Frafra calabash rattle of northern Ghana who was based at the Arts Council in Accra. Unlike the maracas which are simply shaken, the Frafra instrument is thrown around the body in a sort of juggling act, providing the kinetic framework for complex rhythmic sound. The high energy scintillations created by the combination of Frafra and jazz music galvanised the audience. Incidentally, it was after this international exposure at Soul to Soul that Amoah joined up with the Afro-rock band Basa-Basa. Santana's performance during this marathon show made a particularly deep and long-lasting impression on the Ghanaian music scene, as their blending of Afro-Latin percussion and rock inspired a generation of young Ghanaian musicians who went on to do the same thing with African music and rock. The Soul to Soul show was released on film and record in 1971 by the Nigram Corporation and Aura Productions, and then re-released as a DVD in 2004 by the Reelin' In The Years Productions (a part of Warner Brother). The significance of this concert is emphasised by the fact that a retrospective film about the making of this event called the 'The Story of Soul to Soul' and made by Kwesi Owusu of Creative Storm was broadcast in 2004 on BBC Channel Four.

NIGERIA'S FESTAC '77

The biggest 'soul to soul' experience of the 1970s was undoubtedly Nigeria's FESTAC, the Second World Black and African Festival of Arts and Culture held in Lagos and Kaduna in 1977. FESTAC brought together the traditional and contemporary arts of the eight hundred million blacks living throughout the world. This spectacular festival was attended by black delegations from sixty-two countries. Events included traditional durbars, regattas and performing arts from the host country Nigeria, and a colloquium on black civilisation attended by seven hundred scholars. There were also fifty plays, a hundred-and-fifty music and dance shows, eighty films, two hundred poetry and literature sessions, and forty art exhibitions.

It would be impossible to list all the music and dance events, but here are a few. From other African countries came Miriam Makeba, Osibisa, Bembeya Jazz, Les Amazones, the Golden Sounds, Louis Moholo, and Dudu Pukuwana; from the Caribbean the Mighty Sparrow and the Cuban National Dance Troupe; from Latin America, Omo Alakuta and her Yoruba Brazilian priestesses and Gilberto Gil's Afro-Latin music (incidentally Gil later became Brazil's Minister of Culture) and from North America came Stevie Wonder, Sun Ra and Donald Byrd; from Australia and New Guinea aborigine dancers.

PANAFEST (THE PAN-AFRICAN HISTORICAL THEATRE FESTIVAL)

Yet another African festival that, like Soul to Soul and FESTAC, has brought African and black diasporic artists together is the Ghanaian PANAFEST that began in December 1992. On its initial International Advisory Board were the American soul singers Stevie Wonder, Isaac Hayes, Dionne Warwick and Roberta Flack. The event takes place every two years at the old European fort and slave dungeon of Cape Coast Castle. The event includes traditional durbars of chiefs, colloquiums on Pan-Africanism, theatre workshops and performances. PANAFEST is designed as a cultural forum for Africans and people of African descent, as well as friends of the continent. Through the medium of the performing arts, PANAFEST is helping portray the history of Africa, affirm the common heritage of Black and African peoples and define their contribution towards the development of the African continent and world civilisation.

The theme of the first PANAFEST '92 (12-19 December) was 'The Re-Emergence of African Civilisation' and papers were read by Marcus Garvey Junior, Mana Farrakhan and Akbar Mohammed (Nation of Islam), Isaac Hayes, Elain Thomas (a Jamaican poetess), Efua Sutherland (the original inspirer of the PANAFEST concept), Gary Byrd (a New York broadcaster), Dr. Mohammed Ben Abdullah (the National Commission on Culture's Secretary at the time) and Lord Anthony Gifford (a prominent British human rights lawyer). There were also numerous musical dance and dramatic performances at both Cape Coast (even inside the Castle) and Accra. From Jamaica came Greg Isaacs, the Child Drummers of the Content Model School, and L' Anla Antoinette Stines and L' Acadco. From the United States there was Isaac Hayes, the Muntu Dance Theatre of Chicago and the rap group Public Enemy. From Britain came the Adzidza Pan-African Dance Ensemble. Then there were the ZITIC National Theatre Group of Togo, the Batsranai Theatre Group of Zimbabwe, the Jalibah Kuyateh Kora Group from Gambia and the University of Benin Arts and Culture Group. Ghana, of course, was well-represented with traditional performances by the Ghana Dance Ensemble, Abibigromma, the Pan African Orchestra, The School of Performing Arts Ensemble of Legon and Nii Tetteh Addy's Obonu Drummers. Ghanaian popular music acts included the local reggae stars K.K. (Kwabena Kwakye). Kabobo and Kojo Antwi, the Wulomei 'Ga cultural group' and the highlife of Nana Ampadu, Jewel Ackah, Amakye Dede, Pozo Hayes, the Marriots Band, Joe Mensah and alto saxist Asabea Cropper in her usual kente attire. With various ups and downs, PANAFEST has continued and, over the years, many other Black Diasporians have visited Ghana to perform at it. These include Rita and Ziggi Marley, Jermain Jackson, Akilah, the Andrew Cyrille Jazz Quartet, the Jamaican reggae poet Mutabaruka, the Saamaka Maroon Society of Surinam and the Caribbean Dance Company of the US Virgin Islands.

THE W.E.B. DUBOIS MEMORIAL CENTRE, ACCRA

Although not strictly in the popular music area, mention must be made of the Dubois Memorial Centre for three reasons. Firstly, in the context of 'Soul to Soul', William Edward Burghart DuBois was an archetypal African American figure who, not only returned to his African roots at the invitation of President Nkrumah, but died in Africa. In fact, it is his house that was turned into the Pan-African Dubois Centre. Secondly, amongst its archives, the Centre has a collection of works of black and African popular music. Thirdly, the Centre hosts numerous musical performances.

DuBois was born in 1868 and was the first African American to receive a degree from Harvard University. In 1905 he set up the Niagra Movement, a precursor of the National Association for the Advancement of Coloured People which figured so prominently in the civil rights movement of the 1960s. In 1919, DuBois was the leading light behind the First Pan-African Congress in Paris. In 1945, he chaired the key Sixth Pan-African Congress in Manchester, England, which budding African leaders like Kwame Nkrumah, Jomo Kenyatta and Nnamdi Azikiwe attended. As a result of his political activities, DuBois was accused by the US government of being an 'unregistered foreign agent' during the McCarthy anti-Communist witch-hunts of the 1950s. Fortunately, in 1961, Nkrumah invited DuBois to come to Ghana and head the Encyclopaedia Africana project in Accra, one of his life-long ambitions. Two years later, President Nkrumah conferred Ghanaian citizenship on him. On his death in Accra in 1963, DuBois was given a state funeral and buried at Christiansburg Castle. In 1985, he was given a second state funeral when his body and the ashes of his wife, Shirley, were re-interred at his house in Accra.

The Memorial Centre itself was formally opened on June 1985 by Flt-Lt. J.J. Rawlings. Its first major project was to see to the construction of a tomb for DuBois. The re-interment ceremony turned out to be a huge event. Thousands of people lined the route from the Castle to Circular Road while a special detachment of the Ghana Armed Forces carried the remains of DuBois and his wife on a gun carriage. Among the crowd were the African American writer Maya Angelou, Betty Shabazz, the widow of the black nationalist Malcolm X, and the scholars Professor Gerald Home and Professor Chukwuka Okonjo. Ghanaian personalities included members of the government, the Wulomo (Ga priest) of the Osu Traditional Area in which the DuBois's house is situated, the State Linguist Okyeame Kwasi Akuffo and the drummer Kofi Ghanaba. The Ghana Dance Ensemble gave a special performance and Kobena Eyi Acquah, Kofi Anyidoho and Kwesi Brew gave poetry recitals.

The Centre has a gallery of DuBois memorabilia and his personal library, as well as lecture rooms and 130,000 micro-filmed documents donated by Professor William Strickland, Director of the DuBois Papers Collection at the University of Massachusetts. The Centre has hosted a string of interesting events. Some of the speakers include the Black Muslim Louis Farrakhan and the Barbadian poet and historian Edward Kamau Brathwaite. In 1987, Chief M. O. Abiola of Nigeria came to the Centre and donated $25,000 to the DuBois Pan-African Book Award. In 1988 the three-day 'Focus on Nigeria' event took place at which Ghanaba, Bayo Martins and Remi Kabaka played (see Chapter 30). The Centre also held a festival marking the centenary of the birth of the West Indian black nationalist Marcus Garvey. It was Garvey's Universal Negro Improvement Society that gave Ghana the red, gold and green colours of its flag, as well as the name of its state shipping company, the Black Star Line.

*Kofi Ghanaba on left leading Betty Shabazz (wife of Malcolm X)
at the Dubois Memorial Centre in 1986*

Chapter 36

REGGAE AND AFRO-REGGAE

THE ORIGIN OF REGGAE AND ITS INITIAL INTERNATIONALISATION

Western 'progress' with its environmental pollution, arms race and unequal division of the world resources has resulted in many African and African American artists questioning technological society and re-evaluating cultural traditions. An example of this was the immense success of the African American Alex Haley's book 'Roots', which traces his slave ancestors all the way back to Africa. Another was the Afro-centric message of soul music and the militant Pan Africanism of Fela Kuti. Yet another upsurge of the 'back to Africa' theme has come from Caribbean reggae music, preaching the doom and downfall of 'Babylon', or Western civilization and imperialism.

Reggae is, in fact, the most recent of a number of Jamaican dance-styles following the calypso-like 'mento' of the 1950s. The first was ska, a fast dance-music that combined mento with black American rhythm and blues, but with the guitar beat 'skanked' or reversed. The biggest commercial success of this music was Millicent Small's 'My Boy Lollipop' released in the early 1960s, which led to 'Millie' making two tours of Africa in the late sixties. This record was, incidentally, the first commercial success of Chris

Blackwell's Island Record, through which Bob Marley shot to fame. Ska was followed in the late 1960s by a slowing down of the beat to 'rock steady' played by the Heptones and Ken Boothe. Around 1970, the bass became more dominant, and the tempo was sped up a little into 'reggae' by Desmond Dekker, Jimmy Cliff, Toots and the Maytals, the Heptones, Peter Tosh and Bob Marley.

Linked with the waxing of reggae music was the surfacing of the Jamaican millenarian cult, Rastafarianism, which protests discrimination, forecasts the collapse of the Western world and urges its followers to return to a simpler and more natural way of life. This church is based on biblical beliefs laced with those of the black nationalist Marcus Garvey who, in the 1920s, predicted that a 'King of Kings' would be crowned in Africa, which would signal the downfall of the West and the repatriation of blacks to Africa. This seemed to come true in 1930 when Haile Selassie was made the Ethiopian Emperor, given the title 'King of Kings' and 'Lion of Judah', and later defeated the Italian colonialists. The word 'Rastafarian', in fact, comes from the royal title of Haile Selassie 'Ras Tafari'. It was also widely believed in Jamaica that Selassie was the leader of a secret society called the 'Nyabingi' whose members had long matted 'rasta' hair, used 'ganja' as a religious sacrament and were dedicated to overthrowing white and black oppressors. The dreadlocks of the Rastas were copied from these legendary 'nyamen', as the West Indians call them, reinforced with the biblical story of Samson and Delilah. The Rastas also created 'nyabingi' drumming based on the 'akete' and 'buru' drum rhythms derived from the descendents of Akan slaves and the Congo-derived Jamaican Kumina spiritual-healing cult.

In the early 1950s, this religious cult was led by Leonard 'Gong' Howells, but the British colonial authorities, hating the cultivation of marijuana by the Rastafarians, destroyed their original settlement in the village of Pinnacle. As a result, Rastafarians scattered all over Jamaica spreading their beliefs. This included their spiritual music played with hand-drums and rumba boxes which were used to create a state of possession or 'trumping', through dancing, chanting and rhythmic deep-breathing. This religious and nyabingi music of the Rastas found its way into the ghettoes of Jamaican towns like Kingston where it deeply influenced urban popular music. By the early 1970s, it was turning reggae into the apocalyptic 'roots-reggae' of Bob Marley and the Wailers. Indeed, Bob Marley helped introduce neo-African 'nyabingi' drum patterns to reggae. Despite all opposition, reggae music and the Rastafarian faith not only flourished in their birthplace, but throughout the world. And even in Europe, the very heart of

Babylon where the first Industrial Revolution took place and the African slave trade initiated. Britain became a particularly important focus for reggae and Caribbean music generally, as many West Indians were invited to settle there in the 1950s with the hope of a bright future. But many of these immigrants saw their children condemned to unemployed life in city ghettos like Saint Paul's in Bristol, Notting Hill and Brixton in London and Toxteth in Liverpool, the very places where there were major black riots during Margaret Thatcher's rule. Even the Notting Hill Caribbean Carnival in London, that now attracts a million tourists a year, began with violent clashes between youths and the police. This disillusionment with British life-style and establishment was expressed by the Brixton-based dub-reggae poet Linton Kwesi Johnson who was born in Jamaica but came to England as a youth in 1963. In his poetry, he drew on both the Jamaican toasting and African griot style of combining poetry music and dance with social commentary. His first album released in 1978 was 'Dread Beat an' Blood' that contained the song 'Dread Inna Inglan'.

On the more positive side, West Indian immigration into Britain led first to an interest in Afro-Caribbean and then African music and culture, provided by institutes such as Aklowa House run by the Ghanaian Felix Cobbson, the Iroqo club of the late Ginger Johnson of Nigeria, and the Africa Centre run by the African Union (formerly the Organisation of African Unity). As a result, many bands and dance groups playing Afro-Caribbean and African music were formed by West Indians and Africans. An early one was Steel and Skin set up in the mid-1970s by Jamaican-born Peter Blackman which included a number of Ghanaians. Then, there was Lanzel (Unity) formed in 1978 by the Ghanaian master-drummer Ben Badoo with some unemployed West Indian youths who were members of the Harambee self-help organisation. Others mixed African/Caribbean bands were Ekome, Mystic and the Israelites, Kutamba, Black Velvet, Matta Fancanta, Mass Movers, the Ujaama Players, Uzuri Binti, the Cardiff Afro Caribbean Dance Troupe and Adzidza. White youth also became interested and Afro-Caribbean and African music drumming and dancing began to be taught in British schools. Another Caribbean musical impact was that, during the 1980s, mixed black and white 'Two Tone' bands appeared, such as the Beats, Selector, UB40 and the Specials. These combined the upbeat of ska and reggae with the downbeat of rock music, thus creating a cross-rhythmic dance style that helped pave the way in Britain for the polyrhyhmic music of African itself.

THE AFRICAN CONNECTION

Besides Africans teaming up with West Indians in Britain, many West Indian reggae artists have visited Africa since the 1980s. These include Jimmy Cliff, Misty and Roots, Aswad, Steel Pulse, Musical Youth, Greg Isaacs and Yellow Man – as well as Bob, Rita and Ziggi Marley. These artists, together with imported reggae records, sound systems, films and videos have led to the emergence of African versions of reggae which are, in turn, feeding back into the international reggae scene. Some of the most internationally well-known African reggae stars since the 1970s have been Nigeria's Sonny Okosun, Ras Kimono and Majek Fashek and Lucky Dube of South Africa; Alpha Blondy of the Cote d'Ivoire and Ghana's Kojo Antwi and Rocky Dawuni. We will turn to Ivorian and Ghanaian artists later, but here let me first say something about Nigeria.

Jimmy Cliff toured Nigeria in 1974. Around that time Nigeria's famous highlife exponent Victor Uwaifo and his Melody Maestros started experimenting with Jamaican music in such songs as 'When the Sun Shines' and 'Five Day a Week Love'. Bongos Ikwue was also playing reggae at the time. In 1977, ex-Melody Maestros member, Sonny Okosun, released a string of militant reggae songs starting with 'Papa's Land' and 'Fire in Soweto' (see Chapter 51). One of the most successful blends of reggae and African music in the late 1970s was 'Sweet Mother' by the eastern Nigerian Rokafil Jazz of Prince Niko Mbrarga that combined pidgin English highlifes and Cameroonian music with a reggae type bass-line. Around 1980, the Nigerian band Cloud Seven released a twelve-inch Afro-reggae record (a format popular in discos) on the Otis Brothers label. And the London-based Nigerian Gaspar Lawal's 'Ajomase' album of 1983 also contained reggae tracks like 'Kita Kita'. Victor Essiet and Peggy Umanah of the Mandators had two hit reggae albums in Nigeria called 'Crisis' (1987) and 'Rat Race' (1988), whilst Nigeria's top reggae woman, Evi Edna Ogholi-Ogosi, released three albums from 1987 ('My Kind of Music', 'On the Move', and 'Happy Birthday'). Then there is her contemporary, Majek Fashek, who released 'Prisoner of Conscience' and who was influenced by Bob Marley and also Steel Pulse who visited Nigeria in the early 1980s. Some of the songs on Fashek's album (like 'Police Brutality') and the fact that he wore hand-cuffs on the album cover led to him being detained by the Nigeria police for a while. Other top Nigerian reggae artists are Blakky, Orits Williki as well as Ras Kimono, who made his debut album 'Under Pressure' in 1988, followed in 2004 by 'What Gwan'.

ALPHA BLONDY OF THE COTE D'IVOIRE

Alpha Blondy is the biggest Ivorian reggae star and, as will be discussed further on, his use of local language lyrics made a major impact in the 1980s on Ghanaian reggae musicians. Alpha Blondy, which means 'first bandit', was born in 1953 in the town of Dimbokro as Seydou Kone. As a schoolboy in Abidjan, he played for his school's Atomic Vibrations Afro-rock band, which was influenced by the music of Jimmy Hendrix, Pink Floyd, Wilson Pickett and Otis Redding. He went to Liberia and then on to New York, where he studied at Columbia University to become an English teacher. He then stayed in Jamaica and returned home in 1980. While abroad, he had become affected by the music of Bob Marley, embraced Rastafarianism and wanted to combine Rasta ideas derived from the Bible with those of Islam. Because of his strong new beliefs and his decision to become a musician rather than a teacher, his parents put him under psychiatric care for two years after his return. But then, in 1982, he made his first hit single 'Brigadier Sabari/Operation Coupe de Poine' about the then current police clean-up of Abidjan's gangsters, and then there was no question about his future in music. This was followed by a string of reggae albums sung in English, French, and Dioula (a Mandingo language) like 'Jah Glory', 'Cocody Rock', 'Apartheid Is Nazism', 'Jerusalem' (recorded with the Wailers) and later 'Revolution' which features the Cameroonian saxist Manu Dibango and the top Ivorian female vocalist, Aicha Kone.

In the late 1980s, Blondy's thirteen-piece Solar System band, which includes musicians from the Cote d'Ivoire, Ghana, Togo, and the Cameroons, toured Ghana and appeared onstage in in the red, green and gold colours of the Ghanaian flag (as well as that of Marcus Garvey and Rastafarians). As a result of seeing an African reggae star singing in an African language, many Ghanaian reggae artists subsequently started to sing in local Ghanaian languages as well as English.

In 1987, the American record company Shanachie released two of Alpha Bloody's albums and he went on a forty-city tour in the United States where he and Ziggy Marley were seen as the true heirs of Bob Marley. In the same year, Alpha Blondy received the Senghor Award for the best male singer in Francophone Africa. In 1991, he released his sixth album 'SOS Tribal War' about the Liberian Civil War. This was followed in the late 1990s with 'Guerre Civile' that criticized the policies of President Bédié and was repeatedly played on the radio the day of General Guei's military coup in 1999.

The Ivorian reggae star Alpha Blondy

Other top Ivorian reggae musicians are Jah Tiken Fakoly, and Tangara Speed Ghada and Zaga Zigi who started out with Alpha Blondy's band.

REGGAE IN GHANA

The early reggae records of the Maytals, Desmond Dekker and Jimmy Cliff became popular in Ghana in the early seventies. Almost instantly, local highlifes and reggae rhythms were fused together by guitar bands like African Brothers, City Boys and Teacher Boateng and his Afrikana; later followed by the Kumapim Royals, Amakye Dede, K.K. Kabobo and Nana Tuffuor's Sikadwa Band. Reggae became even more popular in Ghana after 1977 when Bob Nestus Marely released his 'Exodus' album on Chris Blackwell's Island Record label. This was also the year that the first reggae sound-system was brought to Ghana by the Jamaican Raas Wolde Mikael who set up

335

base in Tema and Accra. Reggae became so pervasive that Ghanaian bands were set up in the late 1970s that exclusively played reggae, mainly imitative cover versions of this Jamaican music. These were the Classic Handels and Classic Vibes (with Kojo Antwi, Obibio and Henry Ayi Soloman) which left Ghana for Europe in 1983, and Roots Anabo, set up in Germany in the late 1970s by Sammy Mawuli Nukpese. Roots Anabo included the percussionist Ekow Savage Alabi and also Ekow Micah who, in the late 1990s, coined the name 'Sunlife' for the Ghanaian variety of reggae. In 1993, he had a hit in this style with his song 'Hemaa' that talks on the need of Africans to shirk the slave mentality. This song was later remixed by the artist Samini who began his career as a hiplife artist. Besides Roots Anabo, another Germany-based Ghanaian roots-reggae band that Ekow Savage Alabi played with from 1989 was Vitamin X, formed in Hannover in 1981. Its lineup included the drummer Gazo Jones, bassist Emmanuel, guitarist B.B.Cornell and the two keyboardists Sledge and Sello Sihlabeni.

Then, in the early 1980s, there were visits to Ghana by the Jamaican reggae artists Misty and Roots, Musical Youth and Yellow Man. Moreover, the 'Hi Power' reggae sound-system was brought to Ghana by the British West Indian 'Jah Power' that featured the Ghanaian MCs Preacher Levi, General Marcus and Wahesh Simeon. As a result, more local reggae artists appeared on the scene like Felix Bell, Kojo Ashakanor, the SO2 Squad (later called Sons of Zion), Kindred, Grassroots, Nazarite Vow (with Ras Korby and General Stano), Ras Kente's Root of David and Black Empire. Vitamin X also came to perform in Ghana in the late 1980s.

It was the 1980s success of the Alpha Blondy Mandinge language reggaes that encouraged Ghanaian reggaes artists to sing in their own local languages as well as English, and sometimes use local instruments. From the mid-1980s, artists playing in this more local style appeared. One was Salaam's Cultural Imani Band that combined reggae and highlife, used traditional percussion and sung in the Ga language. Then came Kojo Antwi (ex-Classic Vibes) who sings reggae songs in Twi, followed by Fred Dred's Kente group that was managed by Bob Berrings, the Duch owner of the Zaya Soundz sound-system. During the 1990s came Sly Dennis's Exodus group from the University at Kumasi, Alaine Courage Man, Ras Tonto, Carlous Man, United Spirit run by the German keyboards player, the late Chris Luhn. Then, there is Shasha Marley (Julius Amua-Sekyi) who often used to dress onstage as a monk. He released his debut album 'Tell Freedom' in 1999 and has gone on from success to success. In 2010, he won the Best African Reggae Artiste trophy from the KORA Music Awards held in in

Ouagadougu, Burkina Fasso, for his song 'Mataa Family' ('Lost and Found' album). More recent examples of Afro-reggae artists, influenced by both roots reggae and the newer dance hall reggae, are Black Prophet, Shariff Ghale, Samini, Fiifi Selah, Wutah, Sammi B, Na U and Sonni Balli. Another is Blakk Rasta, a radio DJ who has released seven albums since his 2000 'Rasta Shine'.

Since the 1990s the Ghanaian reggae scene has also been enriched by visiting reggae bands. South Africa's Lucky Dube came, as did Nigeria's Ras Kimono. Another Nigerian visitor was the lady reggae star Evi Edna Ogholi-Ogosi, whose nine-piece band includes six Ghanaians, originally belonging to the Ghanaian reggae group, Big Eye. Jamaican reggae artists have continued to visit Ghana, like Gregg Isaacs, Mutabaruka, Ziggi Marley and Shaba Ranks. Some of these have even settled in Ghana. One is Zion's Children and another is Rita Marley who built a recording studio in Aburi equipped with the old Abbey Road Studio that recorded the Beatles way back in the 1970s. Then, in 2010, the 62 year-old Jimmy Cliff made a stop-over in Ghana on his way to the Sierra Leone ECOWAS Peace Pageant. Although this man, so famous for his 'The Harder They Come' album and film did not play, he spoke about the detrimental influence of foreign cultures on Africa. That same year, the 32-year old Jamaican dance hall reggae exponent and pan-Africanist Sizzla Kolanji (Miguel Orlando Collins) played in Accra and Kumasi in a program organised by Lalibela Music and Adunaba Promotions.

To conclude, let me say something about two of Ghana's most well known reggae men, Kwadwo (or Kojo) Antwi and Rocky Dawuni.

KOJO JULIUS ANTWI is popular for his romantic Twi songs in which he fuses highlife motifs with the slow and sentimental romantic 'lovers rock' form of reggae popularised by the late Gregg Isaacs. Kojo began his career as the singer in two early Ghanaian reggae bands of the 1970s: the Classic Handels and then the Classic Vibes. It was with the six-piece Classic Vibes band that he first left Ghanaian shores. In 1983, the group went to Denmark after having made a successful demo-recording in my Bokoor Studio in 1982, produced by Mike Bonsu. The Classic Vibes broke up after a few years and its members, like bassist Nana Osibio and percussionist Ayi Soloman, remained in Europe. Kojo Antwi himself went solo in 1985 and settled in Switzerland. Since then, he has released a string of successful records and CDs. In fact, he married a Swiss lady who often sings choruses on his records. Kojo's first albums were 'All I

Kojo Antwi with guitar. Photo Mirror (Jan 19 1991)

Need Is You' and 'Saman' released in1986 and 1987, respectively. From the 1990s, Kojo produced many solo albums, such as 'Akwanoma Anokye', 'Don't Stop the Music', 'Akuaba'and later 'Mister Music Man', 'To Mother Africa', 'Densu', 'Groovy' and 'Superman.' Antwi's latest album 'Mwaah', released in 2009, features singers Freddie Meiway, Nana Yaa and Beverly Tawiah. Music styles that appear on the fourteen track album draw on Antwi's usual mid-tempo reggae-highlife with dance hall, Ivorian zoblazo, kpanlogo and R&B. It also has a remix of the old highlife song 'Mesan aba' by Yamoah's guitar Band. Every Christmas year, Antwi returns to Ghana to do a live performance for his numerous Ghanaian fans at top venues like the

338

National Theatre. In June 2010, Antwi received the US Black Entertainment Television (BET) Awards for Best International Act. This event was hosted by Queen Latifa and was the first time since the formation of BET in 2001 that BET has honoured African artists[17].

ROCKY DAWUNI was born 1969 in Tema but his family is from Bonbonayili near Yendi in Ghana's Nothern Region. He was raised and went to school in Tamale, Koforidua and often visited the Michel Army Camp in Accra where his father was an army sergeant. The young Rocky was, therefore, influenced by the Hot Barrels army band in the barracks. He went to the University of Ghana Legon to study Philosophy and Psychology and, whilst there, formed his first reggae group in 1991 called Local Crisis. Rocky then left for the USA and, in 1996, released his first album 'Movement', followed two years later by 'Crusade' recorded in Ghana and celebrating Ghana's 40th anniversary. It was released on the Aquarian Records Company run by his wife Carey Sullivan and by Rocky's older brother Bob Dawuni. 'Crusade' was first performed at a special concert in Abidjan that also featured Steel Pulse, Rita Marley and Sister Carol. In 2000, Rocky made his first of many US tours. In 2001, Rocky released his third album 'Awakening' at the Rocky Dawuni Reggae Sunsplash in Accra to a crowd of 20,000. He also established 'Africa Live', a non-profit NGO that promotes live music in Ghana and helps provide music education in Ghanaian schools. In his fourth 'Book of Change's album, he began to fuse reggae with Fela-type Afro-beat into what he calls his 'Afro-Roots' music. As he explained to the journalist Nii Laryea Korley[18], "Afrobeat forms part of the kind of music I express – dimensions which you cannot find in Bob Marley or any other known reggae artist's music." His fifth album – 'Hymns for the Rebel Soul' – was released in 2009, followed in 2015 'Branches of the Same Tree'. He continues to play in Ghana every Independence Day. For instance, in 2011, he played at the Tamale Sport Stadium alongside DJ Blakk Rasta, the northern reggae man Sheriff Ghale and the northern hiplifers KKC, George Cliff and Lil Malik. The program was organised by Dawuni's Live Africa NGO and its theme was the eradication of the guinea-worm disease.

[17]The others were the Nigerian rapper M.I., the P-Square singing duo and and South African rapper HHP.
[18]Graphic Showbiz 11-17 March 2010, p.7

A poster for a Rocky Dawuni Sunsplash festival

Some newer additions to the Ghanaian reggae scene are the roots reggae artists Black Prophet, the northern Ghanaian artist Sheriff Ghale and Blakk Rasta whose 'kuchoko' reggae style employs local xylophones and drums. Those influenced by the newer Jamaican dance-hall style include Samini, Wutah, DJ Blakk, Grace 'Kaaki 'Ocansey, MzVee, Stonebwoy and Shatta Wale who are discussed in this book's Prologue.

Stevie Wonder and Rocky Dawuni in 2004. Photo www rockydawuni.

Chapter 37

LIVE MUSIC COLLAPSES, DISCO 'BURGER HIGHLIFE' RISES

As mentioned in the introductory chapter, there was a high point in the Ghanaian popular music scene around the early 1970s when the country boasted of four recording studios and two record pressing plants. Then, there were literally hundreds of highlife guitar and dance bands, concert parties, Afro-fusion bands and student pop groups – as well as numerous night-clubs catering for them (60 in Accra alone). The recession began from the mid-1970s with the economic 'kalabule' mis-management of the latter part of the Acheampong/Akuffo military regimes. Record companies (Ambassador and Polygram) folded up due to a lack of vinyl, whilst many artists began to leave in a "musical 'brain drain" to Nigeria and overseas to Europe, Nigeria, Australia and North America. Indeed, by 1979, the Musicians Union of Ghana (MUSIGA) estimated that one quarter of its membership had left Ghana. Then came the two coup d'etats of Flight Lieutenant J. J. Rawlings in 1979 and 1981, followed by over two years of night curfew, a massive 160% import duty on musical instruments and the demotion of music in the education system. Because highlife bands and concert parties could not obtain imported equipment, there was a drastic reduction in the number of popular music groups, and most school pupils were no longer taught to play band instruments. In short, live music was given a series of body blows.

Technological factors also contributed to the decline of live music bands. First, there was the rise of discotheques during the 1970s whose 'disco-music' is basically black American soul and funk music with a drum-machine beat. Some of the discos in Accra in the early 1970s were the Gondola, the Cave de Roi, Club Keteke, Blow Up, Club Edward, Pussy Cat, Moon Club, Club Tabela, Windmill, Flamingo Club, Climax and Pagoda (renamed the Napoleon Club in 1973). By the late 1970s, even more discos were opening in Accra, like the Moustache, High Society Lodge, Club Faleisa and Club Eleganza. Another was Funky Town Disco set up in Dzorwulu by Sidiku Buari in 1978 after he returned home from the United States where he had released some disco records.

Sidiku's career actually began with sports when, in 1963, he won the silver medal running for Ghana at the All African Games in Dakar. As a result, he obtained a sports scholarship to study at the Bronx Community College. Whilst there, he became the school's baseball team captain and taught the players African 'macho' war songs. His strong voice caught the attention of Irving Mechanic (Chubby Checker's manager) who, in 1974, got Sidiku to record his first album "Buari: Karam Bani'm", followed in 1977 by his 'Disco Soccer' which was a huge hit in Ghana. Besides Sidiku's Funky Town and all the other numerous indoor disco's clubs, mobile discos or 'spinners' become popular in late 1970s. These gradually took over the open-air dance spots during the 1980s. Unlike highlife and concert bands, the spinners were cheaper to run as they used less equipment and only needed three operators: a D.J., a technician and gateman. Then, during the 1980s, cheap-to-produce local video productions began in Ghana which, like the 'spinners', also went mobile. So, in the 1990s, mobile videos gradually eclipsed live concert parties in the rural areas.

As a result of all the above problems in running large live bands and the arrival of new electronic equipment, the Ghanaian youth of the early 1980s turned to a 'techno' alternative that did not involve large numbers of instrumentalists and instruments. This was a form of highlife that became known as 'burger highlife'. It borrowed the drum-machines and synthesisers of disco–music and so cut down the number of musicians needed in a band, particularly percussionists and horns-men. Furthermore, disco-music is mainly played on records rather than through live performance, so it was the perfect musical vehicle for young Ghanaian of the 1980s, few of whom could either play or had access to musical instruments. In short, this 'disco form of highlife' was easier to play and cheaper to perform, record and produce. It was given the name 'burger highlife' as it was created in the German town of Hamburg[19] by some of the many musicians who had fled Ghana in the 1970s for economic reasons. Many Ghanaians were attracted to Germany then, as its immigration laws at the time were quite relaxed as compared to Margaret Thatcher's Britain. Ghanaian musicians who settled in Germany include Allan Cosmos Adu, Charles Amoah, Andy Vans, Seth Dako, Nii Edmund Aryittey, McGod, Rex Gyamfi, the Lumba Brothers (Nana Acheampong and Charles Kwadwo Fosu), Ekow Savage Alabi and Amakye Dede. Hamburg was the favourite place for many of these musicians as it was a port town and so already had a small established Ghanaian community. As disco-music was then all the rage with German youth, Ghanaian musicians blended it with highlife music and Ghanaian lyrics. It was the guitarist George Darko who formed the Bus Stop Band with a group of session musicians that consisted of the singers Albert Jonesa and Lee Dodou[20], key-board/synthesizer player Bob Fiscian, bassist B.B. Dowuona and the German hornsman Steve Szabo (or Zzabo). This group released the first burger highlife hit in 1983 called 'Akoo Te Brofo' on their 'Friends' album, followed by the 'Highlife Time' album in 1984. Being influenced by the music of George Benson, George Darko also added a touch of jazz guitar. In 1984 Lee Dodou left the group and Darko then formed 'Kantata' which in 1986 released successful burger highlife albums

Bus Stop Band with George Darko (check shirt) and Bob Fiscian (back right)

[19] According to the University of Ghana research student Eric Sunu (2011) and George Darko himself, the word comes rather from the German word for town 'burgh', and therefore a burger is a (German) townsman.
[20] Eric Sunu (2011) says he replaced the group's first singer Nkansah. Sunu also mentions that the group included a bass guitarised called Sylvestor Kwame.

like 'Asiko' and 'Moni Palava'. This group included Ekow Savage Alabi who played percussion.

Ghanaians in other European countries followed the burger highlife trend, such as Sloopy Mike Gyamfi, Charles Tetteh, Chikinchi and Captain Moro in Holland.

Then, in the UK, was the late John Kay who wrote the signature tune for the Ghanaian comedy series 'Taxi Driver'. Another was Ben Brako who began his musical career in Cape Coast with the Flames group of his St. Augustine's College and then, in the early 1970s, the Agromba Gudureba group at the University of Ghana where he was studying. He then went to the UK for further studies and began releasing albums that were hits in Ghana in the late 1980s, like 'Baya' and 'Everybody'. Much later, around 2010, Ben Brako set up his Highlifer Institute (not to be confused with the much older BAPMAF Highlife Institute).

Another burger highlife musician was Khodjo Aquai who settled in the US, studied at Juliard Music of School and experimented with a disco blend of highlife fused with Caribbean music. During the 1980s, he released hits in Ghana like 'Anadwo Fa' and 'Mese Saa Nso Mentse Sa'. He sadly died in Ghana in 2007 after returning and setting up a recording studio in Accra. Khodjo Aquai's close friend and colleague in the recording busines is Charles Amoah who, as mentioned, was one of the pioneers of burger highlife. He had originally played in Ghana with highlife groups like Konadu's, the Parrots, Happy Boys and Precious Jewels before re-locating to Germany in the late 1970s where he began releasing burger highlife hits in the mid 1980s like 'Sweet Vibration', 'Fre Me', 'Me Ne Wo Begoro' and ' Eye Odo Asem.'

During the 1980s, this disco style 'burger' music subsequently became popular in Ghana, first through records and then, towards the end of the 1980s, when the Ghanaian economy started to pick-up, through 'burger' Ghanaian musicians returning home. Burger highlife became much favoured by the Ghanaian youth of the 1980s who began to treat the older brands of highlife that used live percussion and horns as 'colo' or old-fashioned. Furthermore, whereas some of the early burger highlife bands like the Germany-based Bus Stop and Cantata performed live show, the trend in Ghana was towards singers miming to backing tracks. Taking into account the poor state of the Ghanaian economy and music scene at the time, the small burger highlife bands and mimed shows provided a solution, as they were more economical to operate than big highlife bands.

As George Darko is such an important burger highlife artist, it is worth looking at his musical career in some detail. He was born in 1951 at Akropong and learnt guitar at the Presbyterian School at Akropong from his Canadian biology teacher Mr. Dobson. Darko's father (a Paramount Chief) wanted him to become a lawyer, so he had to leave home and stay with his uncle Nana Boafo. George then joined Gabby Nick Valdo's Avengers rock 'n' roll band in 1969 and then moved on to the Soul Believers, the Blue Monks and the Fourth Dimension army band, with whom he stayed for six years entertaining troops in the Middle-East. On returning to Ghana, he formed his first band called the Golden Stool Band, which left for Germany in the late 1970s. In Hamburg, he went solo where he was also influenced by the jazz guitar playing of George Benson. In 1979, he formed the short-lived Golden Stool band and then, in 1982/3, the Bus Stop Band. George Darko finally returned to his home-town of Akropong in 1988 and was made a chief there in 1991 with the stool (throne) name of Nana Yaw Ampem Darko.

The most popular of the burger highlife artists today is Daddy Lumba (Charles Kojo Fosu) who broke away from the Lumba Brothers and had an enormous hit in 1998 with his contentious song 'Aben Wo Ha' (it is already cooked [here]), which was banned by some radio stations due to its lyrics thinly disguising the idea of a sexually-aroused woman. Other popular burger artists today are 'Lover Boy' Nana Acheampong and Nana Aboagye Da Costa, who had a big hit on the Megastar label in 2000 with 'Odo Menkoaa'. Indeed, most of the lyrics of burger highlife are about 'odo' or romantic love[21]. This is quite different from the lyrics of old-time highlifes in which romantic love was a minor theme, with the majority of lyrics covering a range of topics that covered topical social issues, family problems, moral advice, money 'palavas' and philosophical and proverbial comments on life and death. Burger highlife bands mainly generate their incomes from recordings rather than live shows and so, today, this form of highlife is mainly played at indoor discos, open-air 'spinning' events and also on FM radio and music video clips. Because of their focus on working in audio and television recording studios, when some burger highlife bands do perform on stage or in front of a TV studio audience, they prefer to mime or lip-synch to their pre-recorded tracks rather than play live.

Demontrating the staying power of burger highlife, Eleonore Sylla and the Goethe Institute in Accra organised two shows in Accra and Kumasi for this 'Made in

---

[21]Eric Sunu (2011) says that lyrics on the problem of migrating away from one's family and and moving to a foreign land was also a topic of some Germany-based burger groups, like Kantata.

Germany' music. For these, the artists were asked to perform live. The first in 2007 was linked to the celebrations marking Ghana's fiftieth independence anniversary and it included performances Nana Acheampong, Daddy Lumba, George Darko, Lee Dodou, Bob Fiscian, McGod, Albert Jones and Nana Aboagye da Costa. These performances, as well as interviews with musicians, producers and musicologists, were packaged together as the film 'Who is Highlife', made by Dieter Matzka and Wilma Kiener, with local assistance from Alpha Suberu.

Another 'Made in Germany' burger highlife concert was held in 2008 and then, again, in 2011. The third Goethe Institute-organised burger festival took place at the National Theatre and the Alliance Francaise premises. These shows naturally featured Bob Fiscian, George Darko and Lee Duodu of the old Bus Stop band. McGod did his 'Highlife Agogo' and also his popular 1980s 'Wo Ye Bue, Wo Ye Kenken' that praises hardworking people, whilst Charles Amoah danced and sang his 'Eye Odo Asem' and 'So Medo Hwe.' Pat Thomas, who was also based in Germany at one point in his career, did his old highlife hits 'Sika Ye Mogya' and 'Bisa'. Ben Brako, was the only burger artist at these shows who had not been based in Germany, but rather the UK – and he played tracks from his his 'Baya' album. All the artists were backed by the excellent New System Band that includes the bass player Emmanuel 'Shabo' Koomson and guitarist Akah Blay was managed by Zapp Mallet.

Chapter 38

GHANAIAN RAP AND 'HIPLIFE' (HIPHOP- HIGHLIFE)

G hanaian vernacular rap (or 'hiplife') has it origins in American hip-hop that became popular in Ghana in the early 1990s when teenagers listened and danced to rap at Accra clubs like the Matador, Red Onion, Balm Tavern, Ringway Hotel, Pizzazz, Miracle Miraj, Stallone Catabaron, the Orion and Globe cinemas and at parties at La Beach. Their local heroes and MCs who rapped in English over a beat-box were Burgey, Joe B., Bubee, Areka, Ricky and Ayoko, Bernard Teming, Stanley, Ded Buddy, Jellycone, Sammy B, Chief and the Tribe, Taboo Tribe, Kwame Fakye 'Swiftman', Little Shaba, Eddy Blay Junior, General Marcus, Best MC, KKD and Cy Lover.

Some rappers then began using the local Ghanaian languages. And one of the earliest to do this was Mahoney P, based in Holland, who in 1994 released the 'In Gang Amsterdam' album that contained the rap song 'Ebe Ye Yie'. More important was Reggie Rockstone who released 'Tsoo Boi' in 1995 and (with his then current manager Panji Anoff) coined the name 'hiplife' by fusing the words hip hop and highlife. Rockstone is considered to be the 'god-father' or as he is called now the 'grand papa' of local Ghanaian rap. Rockstone was born in England in 1963 and so spent most of his childhood between London and Accra. At eighteen, Rockstone moved to New York as his father, the fashion designer Ricky Osei, married an African American. Rockstone, therefore, spent fifteen years in Brooklyn and Queens and so witnessed the emergence of the hip hop of Grandmaster Flash and Lou Rodney C. It was in New York that Rockstone began rapping and then he continued in London, working with the Sierra Leonean Freddie Funkstone in their PLZ group. In 1992, Rockstone attended PANAFEST and decided to move back to Ghana, where he set up Kassa Records with DJ Rab, a rapper from Queens.

Reggie Rocktone Poster BDN Productions

Other early hiplifers were Nananom (made up of Sidney Ofori, who is cousin to Rockstone; Omanhene Pozo and Jyoti Chandler aka Ohemaa), who released their first album 'Nana Kasa' in 1997; Lord Kenya, Akatakyie, Lifeline Family, Buk Bak, the DC All Stars, Nana Kwame and the Native Funk Lords who sang in pidgin English. Then there was Nana King who was raised in the US, playing with the Los Angeles rap group 2-Pack before returning home to Ghana and releasing his first hit 'Ama Serwah'; followed in 2000 by 'Champion' that uses music loops from Fela-Kuti's Afro-beat song 'Lady'. As his Twi is not so good he rapped in English. Some hiplifers concentrated more on the West Indian dance hall ragga style of rapping or 'toasting', like Mad Fish, Batman (later called Samini) , Yoggy Doggy, Bandana (now called Shatta Wale) ,

Abortion, Sonni Borley, Bacteria, Aberewa Nana (Dorcas Opoku Darkwah), Slim Busterr (Ebenezer Asare) and the late Terry Bonchaka. A striking feature of hiplife is its lack of women rappers. An early exception was Jyoti Chandler (Joe T) who was a member of Nananom with Omanhene Pozo and Sidney, but she then married a pastor and moved into gospel music. There are only a few female rap artists: Aberewa Nana, who went into dance-hall; Tiffany Hayden .and Mzbel (Nana Ekua Amoah) who released her debut album 'Awosome' in 2004. In 2005, the gospel singer Jeal Wiafe began released rap versions of local gospel music she calls 'hip-gospel'. Then there is the Triple M trio of Mildred Hansen, Mercy Quarshie and Monica Tawiah, who started of as a gospel group – until 2003 when they released the first hiplife ablum 'Koti'. Mildred Hansen or 'Shegee' is Jerry Hansen's daughter and she has also produced solo albums, like her 2008 'My Time: Shegee Styla'. As mentioned in the Prologue a newer lady rapper is Eno (Ruth Nana Serwaa Nyame) who is from Kumasi and performs in English and Twi. In 2012, she collaborated with Afriyie for the 'My Love' single and in 2014 with Abrewa Nana for 'Megye Wo Boy' (I'll Take Your Boy). Eno's debut album 'Yaa Asantewa' was released in 2016.

Many of the older Ghanaian generation complained that hiplife lyrics are too hurried ('kasa hare') to be deciphered, that they contain lyrics that are sexually explicit and misogynist, or are of the violent African American 'gangsta-rap' variety. Local examples of such 'gangsta rap' are hiplifers who denigrate each other in song. For instance, the musical duals or 'dissing' (disrespecting) between Ex Doe (his song 'Maba') and Chicago's rude reply ('Wo Beko'). These musical battles caused controversy in Ghana for introducing what the newspapers call 'protest gangsterism'. A later example in 2010 was Okomfour Kwadee's 2010 song 'Hmmm' in which he tells Obrafour (Michael Kwabena Okyere Darko) to revive his dead musical career after Obrafour called Kwadee a mad person in one of his raps. But these musical duels are more for publicity and of less serious nature than the aggressive American 'gangsta-rap' street-music linked to the violence, drugs and oppression in U.S. black city ghettoes.

Public concern for sexually suggestive lyrics rap lyrics often appear in newspaper reports condemning songs like Batman's 'Linda', Kaakyire Kwame Appiahs's 'Nketewa Do' (Small Love), Lord Kenya's Bokoboko (Slowly), Max Kofi's 'Akwaada Ketewa Bi' (Youngster) and Michael Dawamena and Cool Joe's 'Te Bi Di' (Pluck and Eat). An example of misogyny was Sidney's 'Abuskeleke' which makes fun of the recent female fashion of baring the waist mid-riffs. Another was Nana Nsiah Piese's rap on the topic of women being sexually attracted to a policeman's 'Abaa' or baton. And then there was Tic Tac's 'Philomena' which criticizes the imported female fashion of allowing body hair to grow. As the song refers to genital rashes, it is sometimes also rudely danced with the dancer scratching his or her pubic area. Tic Tac, however, says it is a song about personal hygiene. Another example is Atumpam's 2011 song 'Akwalatin' (a child's thing) about how he is teaching a small girl the 'tin'. When the public accused him of indecent lyrics, he tried to wriggle out of it by saying that it was a children's folk song. This was a convenient reaction, as the hilplife artist Fita also claimed authorship of this song – and if it is a folksong then it is in the public domain.

Not only did local newspapers accuse hiplife of being 'lewd' but, in 2002, the Director of the International Federation of the Women Lawyers (FIDA) stated that some hiplife lyrics 'debase femininity and the bodies of women…(and) constitutes violence against women on the airwaves'. As a result, FIDA threatened high court actions against some radio stations and disc jockeys. Furthermore, both FIDA and the Musicians Union of Ghana (MUSIGA) asked the Ministry of Information and the Ghana Media Commission to closely monitor the local FM stations for indecent lyrics. At a seminar in Kumasi in April 2005, the Centre for Moral Education suggested that National Communication Authority of Ghana should ban hiplife and profane songs. But, as the journalist William Asiedu commented, hiplife songs that are banned or "come under fire for spawning immorality amongst the youth make good sales throughout the country and become instant hits and chart busters". Not only does this criticism of hiplife by the older generation make it more commercially popular, as Asiedu rightly says, but it is precisely what the hiplife musicians and fans like, for these controversial lyrics puts a distance between them, the older generation and their music.

Hiplife, with its outspoken lyrics, electronic instrumentation, solo artists and video-clip format became an identity symbol for the present generation of Ghanaian city youth moving away from the live bands and performance venues of the older generation. The use of electronic drum beats, vo-coders, auto-tuners and other hi-tech gadgets also adds an artificial flavour that clearly distinguished the hiplife sound from older forms of live popular dance-music. This artificiality is not a result of some sort of failed imitation of western electronic techno-pop, but is rather the sought-out flavour of the hiplife generation that also helps distance this new music from that of the older Ghanaian. In short, hiplife became an anti-establishment musical icon for the youth.

Besides its profane lyrics and artificiality, a more serious objection to hiplife from the older generation was that hiplife was not initially ever performed live. There were a few early exceptions, of course; such as VIP, the university music graduate Obour and Sidney (Ofori), whose manager Goodies got him playing live with the Dzidudu Afro-rock band as early as 2002. But, generally, the first wave of hiplife musicians (like the burger highlife artists) rather mimed or 'lip synched' to pre-recorded computerised backing-tracks, even when appearing on stage in front of live audiences. However, it is not fair to blame the youth for, as already mentioned in earlier chapters, during the late seventies and eighties, Ghana's live popular music scene collapsed and there was musical 'brain drain' of talented artists. So without the hiplife option of rapping over easy-to-produce electronic music, the Ghanaian youth of the 1990's would not even have had their own musical medium. Where were all the live bands of yester-year who could act as role models and teachers for them? Furthermore, the music lessons were downgraded in Ghanaian schools in the late 1980s so who was going to teach the youth harmony and stage-craft? But every generation has to find a musical medium and the Ghanaian youth of the 1990s did the only logical thing – they borrowed ready-made musical backing-tracks from American hip hop that only needed few musical studio-technicians to lay down; then overlaid this with a poetic rap session rather than the melodies and harmonies of highlife. So hiplife provided a voice for the youth even if the older generation does not like it.

Earlier, it was mentioned that some hiplife lyrics were condemned as profane by the press and older generation. However, many hiplife lyrics also made social commentaries and dwell on positive topics. Some even warn against promiscuity. For example, 'Wobedesen' by Queens Block (their 2005 'Freedom Song') tells men they should respect women; Mighazi and Sabato's 'Sugar Daddy' warns young girls to beware of elderly men who lure them into sex, whilst raps on the AIDS epidemic was the topic of Timber's 2002 'Kasa Kron' release. Other songs comment on current events and the concerns of the youth. Like Reggae Rockstone's 'Do the Do' on the problem of obtaining a foreign visa; Buk Bak's 'Tankasse' (on their 2004 Goldcoast CD) supports town council campaigns to clean up urban filth, Don King's 2003 song 'Kotofa' endorses the government's campaign against indiscipline. And, Obrafour's very popular song against indiscipline, 'Nya Ntetee Pa,' released during the campaign by former Vice President Aliu Mahama. There are also a few political hiplife songs, such as the Native Funk Lords 'Vote For Me Make I Chop President' made during the 2000 elections, 'Freedom of Speech' released in 2004 by A Plus, and Sidney's humorous 2003 song 'Scent No' on personal hygiene, which mentions that even 'honourables" (i.e. parliamentarians) have smelly socks. A very controversial song by the Nkasei duo (Kwame Godlove Yeboah Prah and Isaac Mensah) was their 2005 'Yefri Tuabodom' which the people of the farming town of Tuobodom believed ridiculed them as being too 'bush.'

Whereas hiplife lyrics were quickly indigenised by local rappers (like Rockstone in 1995) who moved from English to local language raps, the musical and rhythmic backings of hiplife remained as mainly imported American hiphop. But this has gradually begun to change as some hiplifers began turning to old-time highlife. Sometimes, these hiplifers rap over short samples of highlife songs. An early example was Reggie Rockstone's 2002 'Keep Your Eyes on the Road' that drew on Alhaji K. Frempong's 'Kyenkyen Bi Adi M'awu'. Then came Lord Kenya's 'Baby Nayaku' that sampled Smart Nkansah's Sunsum Band, whilst Kontihene 'Medofo Paa Beko' uses a chorus from the old hit 'M'Adanfo Pa Beka' by Ani Johnson's Parrots. Other short samples of highlifes include Akyeame's 'Ano Bebre' that draws on an old Uhuru dance band tune, and Akasonoma's 'Osobrokyire' and Omanhene Pozo's 'Comfort' that both use samples from the highlife singer Paa Bobo. Tic Tac uses samples of two of Pat Thomas's songs ('Menka Bio' and 'Santrofe Anoma') on his 'Masem' album, which landed him in trouble in 2005 when he had to pay Pat 25 million cedis (about $2,500) for the use of this material without his permission. In other cases, the hiplife artist raps over a whole highlife recording, like the hiplife-highlife singer Adane Best and his 2004 rap remix version of 'Maa Fio' that was originally made by the Blemabii 'Ga cultural group' of mid-70s[22], or Omanhene's remake of 'Joromi' by the Nigerian highlife star Victor Uwaifo. Hiplifers also sometimes team up with the original highlife artists who composed the tune, so combining the two music styles. Obour did this with A.B. Crentsil, Ex Doe did this with Paa Bobo, whilst Omanhene Pozo's 'Ayede Volume One' album contains the song 'Medofo Adaada Me' that he remade with the lady highlife singer Ewurama Badu. Another is the hiplifer Omanhene Pozo who did a remake of 'Kyenkyen Bi Adi M'awu' and 'Yellow Sisi' with their composers Alhaji K. Frempong and Kofi Sammy, respectively.

[22]This group was managed by the Empire School headmaster Mark Diamond Addy.

Highlife and hiplife collaboration. Obour and AB Crentsil

There are also some hiplifers who began doing cross-overs between the two genres, combining highlife singing with rapping. An example is Daasebre Kojo Gyamenah who sings in his 2001 'Kokooko' release, with Lord Kenya doing the hiplife rap section. Other early examples were the late Terry 'Bonchaka' Adjetey, Nana Quame, Nana Fynn (Acquah-Harrison) and Slim Busterr. More examples are Papa Shee, Samini, Ofori Amponsah, Kwabena Kwabena, K.K. Fosu, VIP, Obrafour, Castro, Kwaw Kese and Okyeame Kwame (Kwame Nsiah Apau of old Akyeame group). In fact, and as will be mentioned again later, some of this new generation have actually begun to call their new brand of hiplife 'contemporary highlife.'

Although hiplife was initially sung mainly in the Akan, other artists began to sing in other Ghanaian languages. Hausa is sometimes used by VIP, Jaz Dee and D-Flex, whilst Tinny, Bepo, Buk Bak and Adane Best rap in Ga. The previously-mentioned Chicago and Ex Doe sometimes rap in Ewe as do a newer crop of hiplifers like Ayigbe Edem, E.L. and Agbeko.

Traditional rhythms and instruments are also being used more and more by hiplifers such as Adane Best, Omanhene Pozo, Akatakyie, Obour and Okomfour Kwadee. Some specific instances are the use of Ga kpanlogo rhythms by Castro, Buk Bak and Lord Kenya, and the use of Akan rhythms by Bones Nkasei (his 2005 'Ekomamu' album). A few groups have employed some traditional instruments, like the Native Funk Lords, Terry Bonchaka and, Okomfo Kwade (his 'Boys Boys' CD) that used the northern Ghanaian Frafra koloigo or koliko lute. The recording enginer of Daniel Adjeio's Hush Hush Studio, Jeff Quaye (J. Que), is actually concentrating on the use of traditional rhythms, highlife rhythms and live percussion for his ragga-influenced hiplife artists Batman-Samini and Wutah. He calls this more indigenous hiplife style 'jama' (or dzama) which is the Ga word for animated dancing. Going the other way around in 2003, the neo-traditional Hewale group produced their 'Bakuye' album which combined traditional instruments with raps in Ga and Twi. More recently, the hiplifer/contemporary highlifer Adane Best was collaborating with the Ga cultural/folkloric group Bukom Ensemble and, in 2011, they released their joint album 'Yei Pii Ye'.

I must mention that hiplife generates considerable incomes for the artists and those involved in its recording, production and marketing. Besides Hush Hush studio, others that have recorded hiplife include the Combined House of Music, Lisarf, Goodies Records, Megastar and Big Ben that are based in Accra and Quantum Leap Studio in Kumasi. Others are Kays Frequency, TLC Studio, Pani Anoff's Pidgen Music Studios, the Hitz Factory, Charles Amoah's Studio, Slim Busterr's Studio in Darkuman and Best Brain Studio. The top engineers for this music are Max 'Babyface' Morris Twumasi, Zapp Mallett, Saage, Appietus, Nana Quame, Hammer, Panji Anoff and Roland 'Roro' Ackah. Important radio disc jockeys for hiplife are Bola Ray, Sammy B and Cox Tamakloe of Joy FM and Ashley of Peace FM. There are also numerous companies that produce and promote hiplife. These include Frimprince, Soul Records, Agiecoat, Precise Music, Slip Music, Kampsite Records, Creative Storm Records, and Kaakyire Music. Others are Metron Music, Mepo Music, Mount Kenya Records, Abib Records, K. A. B. Records, ITC Productions, Ken Kwame Boakye Productions, True

Dream Label, In House Music, Family Tree Enterprises, Lexyfri, U Name It, PSI, O.M. Music, Prince Dave Records, Brain Cee Music, Executive Enterprises, Nana Quame's NG Promotions, Mercury Music, Vyvetown, S.B. Productions, Noise, Ashanti International, Bibini, Records, the Kon-Te (mastering) Studio and Richie Mensah's Lynx Entertainment.

Business companies and brands have also become involved in the promotion of hiplife shows and competitions, such as Club Beer, Star Beer, Nescafe, Coca Cola, Air Afrique, TV3, the Media Whizz Kids and Universal Entertainment. The connection between hiplife and commercial companies is also evidenced by the use of hiplife artists to advertise their products on television and billboards. Reggae Rockstone has advertised for Guinness, TicTac for Ashfoam beds and Castro (Theophilus Tagoe) for the Fanta drink. Some hiplifers also produce commercial music videos. For instance, in 2005, Lucky Sounds released the 'Breakthough' DCD/VCD that includes performances and interviews by Reggie Rockstone. Other hiplife artists who have moved into this media format include Slim Busterr, Mad Fish, FBS, Kwadee and also Mighazi and Sabato. In 2003, the VIP trio[23] won the best hiplife Ghana Music Awards video. In 2005 Okomfour Kwadee won this award, whilst Reggie Rockstone won best music video award at the South African Kora Awards in 2004.

On the matter of video, it should be noted that in the late 2000s, two documentary films were made on hiplife. Firstly in 2007 came Jesse Shipleys 'Living the Hiplife' (Coltan Media) that looked at the origin and development of hiplife and featured Reggie Rocksone and the Mobile Boys. Then, in 2009, came Mantse Aryeequaye's 'Rhythm Rising' that is about the political history of hiplife and includes interviews with artists like Kwaw Kese, Kwaku Tutu and Obrafour. Furthermore, in 2010, the Pidgin English feature film 'Cos of Money' was released that stars the London-based rapper Mensah and the half Ghanaian/Romanian Wanluv the Kubolor (Emmanuel Owusu Bonsu) who became famous for his song 'Konkonsa' and moves between hiplife, highlife and even gypsy music. This film, shot in Accra and Cape Coast, features hiplife, Afropop and Afrobeat music; it was produced by Panji Anoff and directed by King Luu.

I should also add that there have been fruitful interactions and contacts between Ghanaian hiplifers and Nigerian or Naija hip hop and Afro-pop artists. For instance,

---

[23]VIP or Vision in Progress is from Nima in Accra and consists of Promzy (Emmanuel Promzy Ababio) Prodigal (Joseph Nana Ofori) and Lazzy (Abdul Hamid Ibrahim).

Tony Tetuila (Anthony Olanrewaju Awotoye Awosanya) who had been a member of the pioneering Nigerian hip hop group the Remedies collaborated with Ghana's Tic Tac in the mid 2000s remix of the Fela Kuti song 'Fefe Ne Fe'. Then, there have been performances in Ghana of Nigerian groups. One is Peter and Paul Okoye's P-Square that was formed in Anambra State in 2001 and whose third and fourth albums in 2007 and 2009, called 'Game Over' and 'Danger', both sold a million of copies worldwide. Another is M.I. or Mr. Incredible (Jude Lemfani Abaga) who shot to fame after his 2008 release 'Let's Talk About It'. Yet another Nigerian who has played in Ghanaian clubs is Tuface or 2face Idibia (Innocent Ujah Idibia) who comes from Jos. Today, he is a solo artist but he began his career together with Blackface and Faze in the the Naija rap group called the Plantashun Boiz that, in 2004, released the hit 'African Queen' which also became a big seller in Ghana.

Since 2004/2005, there has developed a distinct split in the Ghanaian hiplife scene. There are the younger hiplifers who sing in highlife or ragga-dancehall style or incorporate local 'jama' rhythms and occasionally use some live instruments. These include Batman-Samini, Kokoveli, X-Doe, Castro, Wutah, Praye, Tic Tac, Mad Fish (Raymond Frimpong), Yoggi Doggi and Wanluv the Kubolor. There is also the other group associated with hiplife but who focus on singing and call their music 'contemporary highlife'. This includes Ofori Amponsah, K.K. Fosu, Lucky Mensah, Oheneba Kissi, Nana Fynn and Nana Quame. Also there is Kwabena Kwabena and Daasebre Gyamenah who both won the MTN highlife awards in 2011. Another is Adane Best whose songs 'Maa Fio'[24] and 'Adesa' won the Ghana Music Awards highlife song of the year in 2003 and 2008, respectively. These acts are also increasingly performing live shows at concerts, or on television programs such as Music Music and Mentor House. As discussed in the book's Coda and Prologue, the 'contemporary highlife' form of hiplife has now become a separate music genre in its own right, popularised by the likes of Kofi Kinaata and Bisa K'dei.

Besides the highlife and 'jama' forms of hiplife, there are more American-influenced genres. One is 'crunk' music that combines hiphop with drum-and-bass and is, therefore, focused more on party dance rhythms than on rapping. A Ghanaian exponent of this is Richie. Then there is 'underground' or 'GH rap' that sticks more to the American hiphop mode and so is often sung in English (Pidgin), utilising improvised 'freestyling'. Artists include 50 Cedis, Ali M, Osrane, Agbeko, Hot Core,

[24]A remix of the mid-70s hit song by Blemabii

Hammer, the 'rap doctor' Okyeame Kwame, Blitz, Bollie Babeface (now part of the duo Reggie 'n' Bollie of X-Factor fame), K'gee, P.M. Motia, Bra Kevin, and Lil' Shaker. The GH rappers often dwell on socially-conscious lyrics and consider the lyrics of jama and crunk-influenced hiplife to be too light-hearted. An important engineer and beat man for the underground medium is Hammer (Edward Nana Poku Osei) through whose hands many top hiplife artists passed from 1998 – like Kwaw Kese, Ayigbe Edem, Obrafour, Tinny and the fast-rapping Sarkodie. Some of the current GH rappers are Asem, 50 Cedis, Okyeame Kwame, Ali M, Hot Core, Sarkodie (Michael Bonsu), Scientific, Tinniequaye and B. Black.

However, it would be true to say the 'jama' and highlife ('contemporary highlife') styles dominate the youthful hiplife scene at present, with an increasing trend towards live performance, the use of indigenous musical and rhythmic resources and singing in an R&B-influenced 'Afropop' mode. One specific example of this trend towards local instruments and live rather than mimed shows was the 2009 'Cultural Caravan' project. This was a series of countrywide hiplife shows organised by the French Embassy's Alliance Francaise and Panji Anoff's Pidgen Studio. This touring road-show included a live dance band, Stephen Yaw Kontor's traditional drummers, the koliko/kologo lute player King Ayisoba and live performances by the hiplifers Reggie Rockstone, Kwaw Kese and Wanluv the Kubolor. More will be said about recent developments in Hiplife, including its link to Afro/Twi-pop and the azonto dance craze, in the concluding the Coda of the book.

HIGHLIFE, FOLKLORIC GROUPS AND AFRO-FUSION FROM THE1990s

6

Highlife
TIME 3

This firstly looks at the old-time highlife musicians who have survived the 1970s to 80s' collapse of the Ghanaian popular music industry and who are still active. It then turns to the younger generation of highlife musicians who have appeared during the1990s, such as Amandzeba, Rex Omar, Bessa Simons, Ackah Blay and others. This Section also deals with various forms of current crossovers between traditional folkloric music and highlife and other popular musical idioms. It also has a chapter on the local Ghanaian jazz scene and the new wave of Ghanaian Afro-fusion music (Afro-rock, Afro-beat and Afro-jazz) that has emerged since the 1990s.

Chapter 39

A NEW GENERATION OF POST 1990s HIGHLIFE MUSICIANS

Before discussing current highlife musicians and bands, it should be mentioned that many old time old-time highlife artists survived the 1970s/80s down-turn in live music and were still performing into the 2000s, such as Jewel Ackah, Pat Thomas, Paapa Yankson, C.K. Mann, Eric Agyeman, A.B. Crenstsil, Osei Kofi, J.A. Ampofo, Nana Tuffour, Kofi Sammy, F. Kenya, Nana Tabiri, Gyedu-Blay Ambolley and Amakye Dede. Some of these highlife 'survivors' are discussed in the next chapter.

But, first, I will say something about two outstanding highlife musicians who were still operating until they died between 2005 and 2006. Firstly, there is Akwasi Ampofo Adjei, leader of the Kumapim Royals, one of the last concert parties to regularly tour Ghana. Mr. A.A.A. began life as a school teacher in the Brong Ahafo Region and moved to Kumasi where, in 1972, he was given instruments to form the Kumapim Royals by Mr. A.K Brobbey, who released their songs like 'Ehye Wobo', 'Gye Dabi' and 'Saa Na Onipa Teɛ'. The Kumapim Royals also toured Europe and won the ECRAG Guitar Band Award for three consecutive years. He died in 2006. Ghana also lost another outstanding musician in 2005, this being 'Alhaji' K. Frempong who ran the Cubanos Fiesta guitar band and concert party from the 1970s. Frempong released six albums, the most famous songs being his minor highlifes 'Kyenkyen Bi Adi M'Awu',

'Aboagyewaa' and 'Hwehwe Mu Na Yi Wo Mpena'. He recorded these in 1977/8 working with Isaac Yeboah's Vis-à-Vis band (guitarist Sammy Cropper and drummer Kung-Fu Kwaku) with George Amissah and Arthur Kennedy on horns. These songs have inspired many current musicians including the hiplifers Reggie Rockston and Omanhene Pozo – and have been also picked up by World Music fans.

After the collapse of the highlife scene in the late 1970s and 80s, and the appearance of the 'spinners' and 'techno-pop' styles like burger highlife and early local rap, the first signs of a renewed interest in old-time live highlife music emerged in the early 1990s. At that time, there was a popular outcry against the mimed ('lip-synched') music videos on prime-time television, and so live music programs like 'Music For Your Dancing Feet' were established, featuring the few operating highlife big bands such as the Western Diamonds, Golden Nuggets, Ghana Broadcasting Band and Marriots International. In fact, the Marriots was first formed in 1981 and included the bass guitarit Gilbert Armah 'Marshall', singer Princess Cynthia, singer Armah Pino and keyboards player Kwadwo Akwaboah (son of the guitar band leader of that name). Then it transmuted into the Ozimzim band in 1994 until the Marriots reformed in 1997.

It was from the mid-1990s that the privatisation of the airwaves began and many of the multiplying FM radio stations started broadcasting programs that specialised in 'classic' highlifes (the first being Paa K. Holbrook-Smith's program on Groove FM). Palm-wine highlife cassettes and CDs then began to be released – of The Kumasi Trio, Koo Nimo, Kwaa Mensah, T.O. Jazz and Kwabena Nyama. Then, a whole new generation of highlife dance bands were formed like, Ankobra, the Megastar Band, Desmond Ababio's Alpha Waves, Komla Amoaku's Visions, Wellington's Band, the Octopus Band, the Zoom Band, Avalon's Gold Coasters, Malek Crayem's Qu'est-ce Que C'est, the recently re-constituted Ramblers and Tex Korley's Y2K Band.

Korley (born 1935) is a sax player and has played with numerous bands in the past, such as the Hot Spears, Springbok, Golden Eagles, Ambassadors, Golden Pods, Great Pilsners and Sweet Talks. He operated his Y2K highlife band at the Chez Afrique in East Legon, Accra. Furthermore, two university music departments have set up highlife bands. The first, formally launched at Legon in 2002, is directed by the highlife veteran, Ebo Taylor. This was followed in 2005 by the highlife band of the University of Winneba directed by Bob Pinodo, creater of the 'Sonobete' beat (a traditional Efutu rhythm), who began his career in the sixties and seventies with the Magic Aliens, Blue Monks, Skippers, Apagya Show Band and Szaabu Sounds.

A new generation of younger highlife artists also surfaced. One group are the 'contemporary highlife' singers, mentioned in the previous chapter that, although associated with hiplife, specialise in song rather than raps. These include Nana Quame, Daasebre, the Praye Trio, Slim Busterr and K.K. Fosu. Another is Ofori Amponsah, who began his musical career singing on Daddy Lumba's burger highlife 'Woho Kyere' album. In 2001, Ofori went solo and, in 2006, established his 4Reez Westside Music Acadamy to teach young people studio and engineering techniques. In recent years, this 'contemporary highlife' trend has been continued by Bisa K'dei, Kofi Kinaata and others mentioned in this book's Prologue.

Another group of current highlife musicians have been influenced by the interest in old-time 'classic' highlife by international 'World Music' fans. World Music surfaced in the mid-1980s when there was an increasing global recognition of African stars like Sunny Ade, Fela Kuti, Papa Wemba, Youssou N'Dour, Salif Keita and Angelique Kidjo. At the same time, western rock superstars like Peter Gabriel, Stuart Copland and Paul Simon began to incorporate African elements into their music. For instance, in the late 1980s, Paul Simon's released the 'Rhythm of the Saints' album that included the 'Spirit Voices' that drew on the Yaa Amponsah highlife melody.

It is both the global interest and Ghanaian renewed interest in highlife that has helped foster a new generation of highlife artists in Ghana and abroad. Some other foreign-based Ghanaian highlife artists are Nana Tsiboe whose London-based Supa Hi-Life Band specialises in acoustic highlife, and Dr. Kwasi Ampene who runs a highlife big band in the American state of Colorado. In Ghana, there is Oheneba Kissi, K.K. Kabobo, Smilin Osei and Felix Owusu. Felix passed through the Osabarima and Sappers army bands, then in the late 1970s teamed up with Bessa Simon in the U.K. In 1995, he helped the Western Diamonds with their 'Passengers' album. Felix released his material on the Megastar label before settling in the United States for ten years. He came back with his ninth album 'Sika Ye' and performed at the Music of Ghanaian Origin (MOGO) Awards in 2010[25]. Smilin' Osei worked in Nigeria for some years and also released a contemporary highlife album in 2001 called 'Alarm Blo', produced by Dakar Sounds.

[25]This Annual festival was launched in 2005 and is organised by Citi FM and MTN.

Another contemporary highlife artist is Kwabena Kwakye or K.K. Kabobo who formed his first band, the Explosive Jets, in 1978 when he was just twenty-eight years. In 1981, he release first album 'Nyatse Nyatse' and, since then, has released eight more, including his popular 1992 'Onyame Ehuwo'. This drummer and singer obtained his musical training with the Kumapim Royals and F Micah's guitar bands. He has backed artistes like Nana Ampadu, Akosua Agyapong, Kofi Sammy and Dr. Paa Bobo, and played with bands like the Black Berets and Sweet Beans. He has developed a music style that combines highlife and ragga. Kabobo was at one point the Musicians Union of Ghana (MUSIGA) Welfare Officer and is also a church apostle.

Two other musicians who need to be mentioned are the 'contemporary highlife' artists Adane Best and Alex 'Lucky' Mensah who both started operating in the early-mid 1990s. Adane Best both sings and raps and released his first album 'Ayitey' in 1992. He then went on to release a string of albums like 'Se Wu Bre', 'W'anu Pe Asem', 'Rabbi', 'Soja Go Soja Come', 'Ayekoo' and 'Mamamia'. His 'Maafio' and 'Adesa' releases won him the 2003 and 2008 Ghana Music Awards (GMA) Best Highlife Album Award, respectively. Lucky Mensah released his first albums 'Nsawa Bo' and 'Wope a Hwe' in 1993 and 1995, in that order. Then he had a huge hit in 2001 with 'Agooji Baby' which he followed up with 'Brofre Nie' and 'Aduu Sumo Akwadu'. His title track song 'Aduu Sumo Akwadu' won the GMA Best Highlife Song in 2005 and, after this success, he released the the highlife album 'Old School.'

Other highlife artists who have risen to fame since the 1990s are discussed in more detail below.

NAKOREX (NAT 'AMANDZEBA' BREW, AKOSUA AGYEPONG AND REX OMAR)

A very popular band of the 1990s, set up by three young musicians who wanted to create a contemporary brand of highlife, was NAKOREX, the acronym for Nat 'Amandzeba' Brew, Akosua Agyepong and Rex Omar (Owusu Marfo). Amandzaba got his musical training with Sammy Odo's Blackbeats and the Osabarima Band of the Atlantic Hotel Takoradi. Akosua Agyepong was a singer for Nana Ampadu's African Brothers and in 1990 – at twenty-six years old – released her first album 'Frema', followed by 'Esiwa' and then joined NAKOREX. Rex Omar who was born in Kumasi and played for the Nigerian Universe Band in the late 1980s. NAKOREX was formed in 1990 (actually December 1989) under Smart Binete's SECAPS management and had popular hits like 'Amu Money' and 'Kpanlogo Yede'. The three NAKOREX members then went solo. Amandzaba has had a number of successful releases based on indigenous Ga rhythms, like his 'Kpanlogo Fever' and in 2000 the 'Demara' CD that utilizes local Ga 'La Kpa' rhythms. He toured West Africa in 2003; in 2005, he released 'Lilo Juju' that uses traditional Ghanaian and Nigerian rhythms.

L-R Amanzeba, Smart Arpah and author. Mid-2000s

When Rex went solo, he had a big hit with his risque highlife song 'Abiba Wadonkoto Ye Me Fe' (Abiba's Beautiful Movements Sweet Me) that appears on his 1998 album 'Dangerous' which sold 300,000 copies. In 2002, Rex Omar formed his Nu Ashanty Band that released the albums like 'African Roots 2' and 'Ajala', followed by a twenty-month African tour organised by the French AFAA Agency. In 2004, Rex collected the South African Kora Award for this album. Then, in 2005, he played in France and South Africa and released another album called 'Who Am I'. He also runs the 'Do It Yourself – Africa' NGO with his manager Ebo Hawkson. Over the years, Akosua Agyepong has made five albums besides the two she did with NAKOREX. These include 'Frema' and 'Asiwa' that included the hit songs 'Born Again, 'Mi Ye Obaa' and 'Kokooko.' After her divorce from Nat Brew, Agyepong married a Reverend and, in

2008, released the gospel album 'I Belong to You'. In 2010, she launched her eighth album 'My Time' to celebrate 20 years in the music profession.

THE CULTURAL IMANI GROUP

Singer/guitarist Ellis 'Salaam' Lamptey was born in Accra in 1955, obtained his first musical training in the Ga cultural groups Cultural Voodoo and then Sammy Brown's Agbafoi that combined traditional Ga instruments with West African finger-picking guitar. Salaam then moved on to play with E.T. Mensah's famous Tempos highlife dance-band and later the Barristers and El Beats. In 1980, he formed his Cultural Imani acoustic group that consisted of guitar, gome bass drum and percussion, and played an acoustic combination of highlife and reggae. In August 1981, the band recorded at Bokoor Studio. Some of the songs (like 'Mama Shile Oga' and 'Momo Baba') were released on the 'Guitar and Gun' compilation highlife album by Cherry Red Records of the UK and then re-released on CD in 2003 by Sterns African Records of London. Besides the influence of highlife and traditional music, Salaam has also been influenced by Bob Marley's singing style –he sports dreadlocks and some of his songs are in local reggae vein. In the 1990s, Salaam teamed up with his manager Kobena Andah and expanded the Cultural Imani band to include bass guitar and horns. In 1992, this group recorded the cassette album 'Djemba' (the Ga word for character) at the Accra studio of Nana Danso (Director of the Pan African Orchestra), financed by the German Development Service. Salaam's group then moved on to a second release entitled 'Weku Sie' (Family House).

TAKASHI

This is a highlife and fusion group put together by guitarist Cliff Asante and vocalist/percussionist Kojo Esseh. This ten-piece band combines the western guitar and trumpet with the traditional antenteban bamboo flute and wooden gyil xylophone, with African percussion from the Ga 'kpanlogo', Akan 'fontomfrom' and Malian 'djembe' traditions. The group also uses tuned cow-bells and its bass-line is provided by the giant gome frame drum popular amongst the Ga people of Accra. Its horn player is the veteran highlife saxist George Emissah, ex-leader of the old Uhuru band. The aim of Takashi is to provide creative and progressive African based music to local and international fans. Takashi is also an NGO that doubles as an African research centre and music consultancy. This interesting group was for many years the resident band at the La Palm Hotel in Accra.

THE LOCAL DIMENSION ACOUSTIC HIGHLIFE BAND

This band was started in 1997 by Aaron Bebe Sukura (seprewa harp-lute, xylophone and mbira thumb-piano), myself (guitar and harmonica) and some other students and staff of the Music and Dance Departments of the University of Ghana at Legon. This acoustic group combines plays a range of West African popular music styles, such as highlife, palmwine music, Afro-beat and songs in the traditional adowa, agbadza, kpanlogo and northern Ghanaian Dagari 'sahelian' styles. Percussion was initially supplied by Mary Agama (also vocals), Francis Akotuah, Isaac Tagoe and Isaac Accrong. Frank Ata-Baah was on giant premprensua hand-piano but this instrument was later replaced by the gome drum played by Bernard 'Solar' Quarshie and later Nii Okai. The band's drummers included Emmanuel Kwashi and Aryitey. For several years, Local Dimension also included the late T.O. Jazz (of Ampoumah's guitar band) whose long-time singer Peter Kojo Menu is still with the group. Local Dimension also occasionally played with the late S. K. Oppong. This university-based band has performed many times in Accra and and has appeared on local Ghanaian TV several times. In 2002 (together with Kwabena Nyama's band), it toured Germany, Switzerland and France and played at clubs like the Birds Eye in Basel, Moods in Zurich and the Satellite Café and Baiser Salee Club in Paris. In 2003, Local Dimension released its N'Yong CD (recorded at Pidgen Studios Accra by Panji Anoff) on the French Disques Arion label. In 2004, the band played at Hannover University and, in 2006, it toured Belgium and Holland, playing the Zuiderpershuis (Antwerp), Korzo (The Hague), Rasa (Utrecht) and the Tropical Museum (Amsterdam). In 2011, the group consisted of Aaron Bebe and myself with Nii Okai and Moses Akutu on percussion, singer/percussionist Peter Kojo Menu, and the guitarist Kofi Labayili Kudonu and bassist Koffie 'Fish' Mark Millas, both ex-students of the University of Ghana Music Department. Later the personnel changed and I dropped out, but Aaron Bebe Sukura still continues to operate the group.

AFRO MOSES AND THE NGOGO HIGHLIFE BAND

This World Music band is made up of Ghanaians and Danes. Ernest Safo or 'Afro Moses' began his music career in the 1980s with Kris Bediako's Afro-rock band Third Eye (based at Temple House in Jamestown Accra) and then moved to the Talkatives. In 1986, he settled in Denmark where he hooked up with the Danish Ngogo Highlife Orchestra established in Aarhus in the 1980s. This was a time of an efflorescence of mixed Danish Afro-pop bands such as Kutatshi, Zebra and Dr. Livingstone, and the Presumers. He then went on to form his own Moses O' Jah band which combines western instruments with kora, atenteben and xylophones. Their 'Makola' album won

Local Dimension at the 2000 ACRAG Awards Night at the National Theatre. Aaron Bebe Sukura is on left. Guitarist T.O Jazz and singer Kojo Menu are on the right

the best song award of the Scandinavian Music Charts in 1998. Afro Moses is currently based in Australia but often comes to Ghana. For instance, in 2010, he played at the New Music Ghana festival organised by the Institute of Music and Devlopment, an NGO run by Korkorkor Amarteifio and Professor Komla Amoaku. In Sydney, Australia, Afro Moses runs his twelve peice Afro-Reggae Spirit Band and, in 2010, was awarded the best Afrobeat/African Music Act of the Australia (AAMMA) Award.

OBIBA SLY COLLINS

Obiba ('someone's son') was born in Bekwai Ashanti in 1961 and played with Konadu's guitar band in 1977/8. He went on to join Kofi Sammy's Okukseku guitar band in 1979, then resident in eastern Nigeria. In Lagos, Obiba played percussion and bass with Fela Kuti between 1980 and 1984, and then joined a number of artists and bands in Nigeria: the Blue Diamonds run by the Ghanaian Techi Menson, Alex Zitte (a 'lovers rock' band run by a Ghanaian), reggae star Ras Kinomo, Danny Wilson, Tera Cota, and the South African singer Yvonne Chaka Chaka. Obiba also ran three bands himself in Nigeria, namely Kazz, the Preachers and Goldfinger. He returned to Ghana in 1998 and went under the management of the Nigerian Fransesca Nielson of Universal Entertainment in Dworulu, Accra. In 2001, Obiba released his 'Odo Fantastic' CD at the Alliance Francaise in Accra.

BESSA SIMONS

This highlife keyboards player first got a taste for music with the band of his Aggrey Memorial Secondary School in Cape Coast, and then he studied at the Winneba National Academy of Music. During his youth, he played with many bands, including the Dutch Benglos, Third Eye, Tommy Darling's Wantu Wazuri as well as Pepper, Onion, Ginger & Salt. He also ran his own band for a while called the Pelicans. Bessa then went to the UK to study engineering and stayed for about twenty years. During this time, he played and recorded with many bands and artists such as Francis Fuster, Alfred Kari Bannerman, Paulina Oduro and also joined Osibisa on their 1999 home tour of Ghana. He recorded on albums with C.K. Mann, Ebo Taylor, Gyedu Blay Ambolley, the Tagoe Sisters, Pat Thomas, Paapa Yankson and Felix Owusu whenever they travelled out of Ghana. Bassa formed his own Bessa Band in the 1986 that played alongside big acts like Hugh Masekela and Manu Dibango, and toured Ghana in 1994. The Bessa Band began recording at Dave Yowell Sultan Studio in London from the early 1990s, producing a string of contemporary highlife albums that became hits in Ghana, like 'Sii Nana', 'Accra Station/Junction', the 'Akwaaba' live album and the 'Best of Bessa'. Bessa Simon returned home to Ghana in 2001 and set up his DiBess recording Studio in Accra.

KWAME YEBOAH

This guitarist and keyboards player was born in 1978 and comes from from Wasa Akropong in the Western Region. He comes from a rich musical background. He is the son of Abinfour Nana (Anthony Kwabena) Yeboah of K.K.'s No 2 band and nephew of the ace guitarist, the late Paa Gyimaa who played for Eddie Donkor, Jewel Ackah, F. Kenya and Sloopy Mike Gyanfi's Adinkra. Kwame Yeboah began his musical career with the EX93 group, the Tagoe Sisters and the Amazing Six jazz-oriented group that became the Megastar Band. He has played regularly with Kojo Antwi since 1996, when he was introduced to this local reggae maestro by the keyboardist Kwabena Akwaboah. Kwame Yeboah moved to London in 1999 and played with Miss Dynamite, the late Amy Winehouse and the R&B and pop musician Craig David, whose group also included drummer Frank Tonto, son of Mac Tontoh. Yeboah also produced Osibisa's 2010 album 'Osee Yiee'. In 2010, Kwame Yeboah was awarded the Best Instrumentalist of the Year at the 11th Ghana Music Awards. He currently moves between London and Ghana. In Ghana, Yeboah manages the Mixstation Studio in Accra and since 2011 runs his O.B.Y. (Ohia Beye Ya) Band.

Kwame Yeboah. Picture kwameyeboah.com

WIND AFRIQUE

The Wind Afrique band is a fourteen peice big-band that plays highlife and Afro-fusion music. It was formed in 2005 by trumpeter Joseph Darko, singer Anthony Simpson, drummer Evans Kumah and keyboards player Daniel Yeboah. This band has been influenced by Osibisa and so, like this pioneering Afro-rock group, it utilises plenty of African percussion. It is also influenced by the World music Angelique Kidjo, Youssou N'dour and Salif Keita. The group has won various awards, including the Best Afro Band of 2007, the Best Young Achievers band of 2008 and, in 2009, it was selected by the New Music Ghana Project to represent Ghana in the Music Cross Roads Festival. Consequently, the organisers of this project, the Institute of Music and Development, flew them for the event to Johanessburg in South Africa and Livingstone in Zambia. In 2010, the group played alongside Afro Moses and the Royal Echoes of Ho for the New Music Ghana Festival. The group also arranges workshops to teach young Ghana musicians music and stage-craft. Their maiden album is called 'Aaya'.

ACKAH BLAY

The ace highlife guitarist Ackah or Aka Blay is from Nzima in Ghana's Western Region and is the nephew of the guitar band leader F. Kenya. Ackah Blay began his music career playing with the Western Diamonds for a decade and, over the years, has been a session-musician and bandsman for many artists, such as Kojo Antwi, Rex Omar, Amandzeba, Ofori Amponsah, Daddy Lumba and the Zimbabwean chimurenga musician Oliver Mutukudzi (Mtukudzi). Around 2007, Ackah Blay set up his own band called the Abiza Band made up of bassist Emmanuel 'Shabo' Koomson, keyboardist Robert Johnson, percussionist Eric Owusu and drummer Francis Osei. This group released its debut album 'Life in the Pot' in 2007, followed by 'Flipside of Life' in 2010. It was also in 2010 that the band toured Denmark. The Abiza bands also features star artists like Paulina Oduro and Atongo Zimba. Ackah Blay himself also sometimes features with other bands, for instance Zapp Mallet's System Band and the Ogya Afro-fusion set up in 2011 by the flotist Dela Botri.

Chapter 40

BIOGRAPHIES ON SOME STILL-OPERATING OLD-TIME HIGLIFE SURVIVORS

KWABENA NYAMA

The late Kwabena Nyama was a guitar band musician from Kumasi was still going strong in the early 2000s when he was in his eighties. With Kofi Poku on premprensua and Agyemang Duah tapping out a rhythm on a beer bottle, they released some of Kwabena's old palmwine highlifes hits in 2000 on the 'Sunday Monday' album (on the French Arion Disques label). In 2002, this band, together with the Local Dimension highlife, toured Germany, Switzerland and France and Kwabena was so frail that he had to use a wheelchair and be carried onto stage. So I had the pleasure of playing beside this veteran. The following year Kwabena again played in France in a tour organised by his European manager Thomas Dorn.

THE MUSICAL COUSINS ART BENNIN AND REDCAP JAMES

The guitarist Art Bennin was born in 1926 in Elmina and comes from a musical family. In 1953, he joined the old Nanshamak Dance Orchestra of Sekondi (run by the pianist Entsua Mensah). Then, in 1956, he joined the Alkot Dandies dance band in Accra, moving the following year to the Skylarks of Takoradi. In the early sixties, Art spent some time in Lagos where he played with the Steve Rhodes Jazz Band. Art returned to Ghana and played with the Dominant Seventh Jazz Band of the Ambassador Hotel in

Accra between 1963 and 1965. In 1965, he joined the Beach Melodians based at the Busua Pleasure Beach, owned by E. K. Dadson of Ocean Fisheries (an ex C.P.P. Minister and one-time concert party performer). From 1967 to 1984, Art was a member of the Ghana Broadcasting Band. After retiring from there, he played with the Wassa International Band and did studio work with various artists, such as Morwan Kalmoni. From 2002 to 2004, Art helped Professor John Collins put together the non-commercial educational highlife score-book 'Classic Highlife Tunes' for university students, assisted financially by the Public Affairs Section of the American Embassy. Art Benin's cousin, James Ato Scott Bennin (Bannin) or 'Redcap', learnt keyboards at Mfantsipim School in Cape Coast in the 1960s. In 1974, he was briefly with the GBC Orchestra and from 1976 to 1981 was Director of Music for the Ghana Prisons Service. In 1981, he moved to neighbouring Cote D'Ivoire where he became Director of the Ivorian RTI (Radio and TV) Dance Orchestra. In 1985, he released his maiden album on the London Afroboom record label called 'Redcap James Plays Broadway and Uhuru'. In this, he was assisted by guitarist Smart Nkansah, drummer Thomas Frempong and Hermann Asafo-Adjei on bass-guitar.

DAN TACKIE

Dan was born in 1937 in Accra and was exposed to music early as his grandfather was organist of the Freeman Anglican Church. Dan attended the Adabraka Methodist School from 1944 to 1951 where he learnt to play flute in the school's mass band that played at Empire Day Parades. Around 1954, he was called in as saxophone player for E.T. Mensah's second band, the Star Rockets, led by guitarist Scorpion Mensah. This band, that also included Dan Acquaye, Herbert Thompson and drummer Tom Tom Addo, had been formed by E.T. to take over from the Tempos whenever it was on its frequent Nigerian tours. In 1957, Dan's brother-in-law was running the Weekend-in-Havanna club in James Town and so invited Dan to form the Havanna Dance Band with Ebo Taylor and some members of the Star Rockets[26]. The Havanna Band travelled to the Ivory Coast and Liberia and, on returning home in 1957, Dan helped re-organise the Spingboks Band for two years. Subsequently he invited to join two governmental bands: the Farmer's Dance Band and then the City Council Band led by Joe Kelly. It was when Dan was with the Farmer's Band that he was injured in a bomb explosion, which happened when they were playing their last number before an important football match at the Accra Sport Stadium. President Nkrumah was attending this match and the bomb, thrown by a certain Teiko Tagoe, was meant for

[26]E.T. Mensah's third band was the Paramount Stars led by Amoo Dodoo.

him. Amidst the pandemonium, Dan had to be rushed to the 37 Military Hospital and still today bears the scar on his right ankle. From 1966, Dan led the Caprice Band of Nana Osei Poku's Caprice Hotel in North Accra. In recent years, Dan Tackie has had a comeback playing saxophone for Alpha Waves, the resident dance band at Bywels Club in Osu. Alpha Waves was set up in the 1990s by ex-member of King Bruce's Black Beats, the keyboard player Desmond Ababio and released the CD 'Roko Party' in 2003.

Veteran highlife sax player Dan Tackie in 2001, who plays with Desmond Ababio's Alpha Waves

NAT BUCKLE

Nat Buckle was born in James Town Accra in 1936; his professional musical career goes back to 1959 when he joined the Rakers dance band, and then Spike Anyankor's

374

Rhythm Aces, considered by many to be the best highlife dance band of the period. It was at this time that Buckle wrote the popular highlife song 'Abele' which E.T Mensah's Tempos later popularised through a record. When the Rhythm Aces broke up, Buckle moved to Kumasi to join Eddie Quansah's Stargazers where he met Glenn Cofie, Sol Amarfio, Teddy Osei and Pete Vanderpuie. Buckle then left for Nigeria and joined the Jobafro Aces with whom he sang jazz and blues, as well as highlifes. Whilst there, he also sang with the Nigerian pianists Fela Sowande, Sammy Akpabot, Sid Morris, Art Aladay, Keri Miko and also with the top highlife bands of Zeal Onyia and Eddie Okonta. Buckle came back to Ghana in 1976 to join the Ghana Broadcasting Corporation dance band and then travelled to the United States to work with the Nigerian Josamic International band. He returned again to Ghana in 1988 and worked as singer for the late Ray Ellis Quartet at the Novotel Hotel. In 1999, he met Faisal Helwani at Ray Ellis's memorial service and Faisal's Bibini Company released some of Nat Buckle's old hits, including 'Abele'.

ORLANDO JULIUS

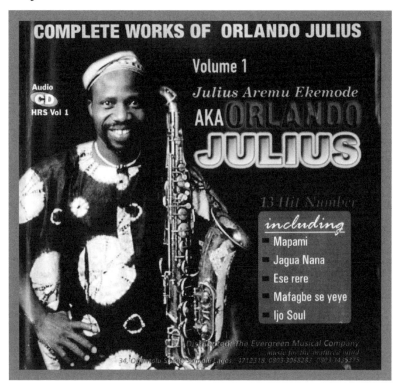

The Nigerian highlife musician and Afrobeat pioneer Orlando Julius

This famous Nigerian highlife saxophonist from Osun State was resident in Ghana during the late 2000s. Orlando Julius Aremu Olusanya began his musical career in 1958 with the Modupe Dance Band and Flamingo Dandies and then, in 1959, joined Eddie Okonta's Top Aces highlife dance band in Ibadan. It was during that time that he played with Louis Armstrong on this American jazz trumpeter's second African trip in 1960. For a while, Orlando was with I.K. Dairo's juju music band and then, in 1963, he formed his own Modern Aces highlife dance band in Ibadan and made his first hit record entitled 'Jaguar Nana' (released on the Phillips label). His music at the time was a fusion of highlife and jazz. Later in 1966, when soul music became popular in Nigeria, he released his album 'Super Afro-Soul'. As a result of this soul influence, Orlando changed the name of his band, in 1967, to the Afro-Sounders. Like fellow Nigerians Fela Anikulapo-Kuti and Segun Bucknor, Orlando began to pioneer what later became called 'Afro-beat'. In 1974, Orlando went to live in the United States for a while and joined the Ghanaian musicians Stanley and Frankie Todd, Glen Warren and Okyerema Asante in their Umoja, formed after the break up of Hedzoleh. With the Umoja band and Hugh Masekela, Orlando recorded on the classic Afro-rock highlife album of 1975 called 'The Boy's Doing It'. He recorded under the name O.J. Ekomode and the 'Ashiko' song on the album was actually composed by him. Whilst in the States, he also worked alongside Hugh Masekela's Ojah band, the Crusaders, Isaac Hayes, Gil Scot Heron and Gladys Knight. Then, between 1977 and 1998, Orlando ran his own Ashiko band there. He then returned to Nigeria to set up a recording studio in Lagos and formed the Nigerian All Stars band. Around 2003, Orlando and his African American wife and singer Layoya Aduke settled in Ghana. They later moved back to Nigeria.

JEWEL ACKAH

'Jewel' Francis Kofi Ackah hails from Nzema in Ghana's Western region. He began his career with C.K Mann's group in 1967 and then moved on to a succession of bands: Ebo Taylor and the Railway Band, the El Dorados (of the Aboso Glass Factory) and the Lantics, the resident band of the Atlantic Hotel, Takoradi. In 1973 he joined A.B. Crentsil's Sweet Talks in Tema (leading them at one point) and then in 1985/6 the Talkatives. In 1974, Jewel recorded his first album 'Gyaki Me' that he sang in Nzima and which won him several awards. The same year he and Pat Thomas recorded the song 'False Lover'. Jewel formed his own Butterfly Six in 1988 (with Marshall on bass) and signed up with the local Megastar label in 1995. Later, Jewel began releasing gospel albums such as 'Me Su Fre Wo' in 1994 and 'Ahwere How' in 1995. He was an active member of the Musicians Union of Ghana. Over the years, he released twenty seven albums and up to a few years ago still occasionally played – for instance at the Highlife Parties that took place at the Alisa Hotel. His son, Kofi Ackah, continues in his father's footstep and now resides in Canada. I recall the son and father playing together in Toronto in 1988, with the then very young Kofi playing drums and singing highlifes in a beautiful clear voice. Jewel Ackah passed away in April 2018.

Jewel Ackah, Legon University 2007 show. Photo Titus

KOFI SAMMY AND OKUKUSEKU

Abirekyireba Kofi Sammy (or Kofi Anese) of the famous Okukuseku guitar band is an Ewe highlife singer who was born in Amedzofe in Ghana's Volta Region in 1942. However, he was raised in the Akan town of New Juaben near Kororidua, the capital of Ghana's Eastern Region. And it was in New Juabem that I first met Kofi Sammy in 1973 when I was teaching chemistry at a secondary school in Koforidua and he was on a break from a local tour. He started his musical career at the age of fifteen with the Albella Band in Kumasi. He also played with Boakye's guitar band between 1959 and 1961, E.K.'s band in 1961, the Jaguar Joker's 1961 to 1962, K. Gyasi's band 1962 to 1964, Ahamano's 1965 to 1967 and again K. Gyasi's band from 1967 to 1969. Kofi Sammy finally teamed up with the singer comic actor Waterproof (John Grahl) to set up the Okukuseku Number Two band and concert party in 1969 in Accra; Waterproof was previously a singer and comic 'Bob' actor for E.K.'s Nyame's group.

377

Okukuseku released its first record, the single 'Osona Ba' in 1969, recorded at Ghana Films Studio in Accra. Then, at the invitation of a Kumasi record producer Mr. A. K. Badu, who supplied the band with instruments, the Okukuseku band moved north to Kumasi. They began recording for Mr. Badu's Ambassador Records in Kumasi. Between 1970 and 1975, Okukuseku released 'Agyanka Due', 'Bosoe Special' and over thirty other singles, as well as several albums for the Ambassador label. Kofi Sammy's Okukuseku began touring Nigeria in 1977 and stayed in Onitsha for over a year where they recorded 'Yellow Sisi' sung in Pidgin English, which sold like hot cakes in Nigeria and Ghana. They also released 'Menso Odo' on Sounds Linacco label of Nigeria in 1978. Okukuseku toured Nigeria several times and finally decided to stay in Nigeria on a more permanent basis from 1979 because of the economic depression at home. They were first based in Lagos, where they released the albums 'Okponku Special' and 'Original Kekako', and then, in 1980, released 'Yebre Ama Owuo' for the Roger All Stars company in Onitsha. Okukuseku's highlifes sung in Akan, Igbo and Pidgin English were so successful in both Ghana and Nigeria that Kofi Sammy and his band relocated to Onitsha where, between 1981 and 1984, they released half a dozen albums on the Rogers All Star label, such as 'Suffer Suffer', 'Take Time', 'Black Beauty' and 'Odo Ye De'.

After the Nigerian oil boom ended, Okukuseku returned to Ghana in 1985 and Kofi Sammy settled back in his home town of New Juaben. In the late 1980s and early 1990s, he was an active member of the Musicians Union of Ghana, MUSIGA. Waterproof became involved with the 'Keysoap' concert party shows at the National Theatre in Accra and was an occasional host for FM Groove Radio in 1989. He also recorded a 'dialogue' cassette for the local Quantus Productions at my Bokoor Studio in Accra, a format that combines music and humorous dramatic sketches. In the early 2000s, Kofi Sammy became involved with Faisal Helwani's Bibini Record Company. He also started to release local gospel records and formed the Okukuseku Practical Angels Band International. In all, Kofi Sammy has released about a hundred and twenty single records and sixty albums, many of which he has recently re-released on cassette. In 2017, Abirekyireba Kofi Sammy was given a Lifetime Achievement Award in Koforidua by the Hi5 Productions, Presenters Association of the Eastern Region (PATER) and the Musicians Union of Ghana (MUSIGA).

THE FANTI GUITARIST C.K. MANN

The guitarist and singer C. K. Mann (Charles Kofi Amankwaa Mann) was born in the late 1936 in Cape Coast/Elmina and spent his childhood in the twin city of Sekondi-

Takoradi, learning guitar at the Zenith Hotel. C.K. began his music career in the mid-fifties with Kakaiku's guitar band (see photo in Chapter 11) and then formed the Ocean Strings which he led until 1966. Then, C.K. and singer Kofi Paapa Yankson formed the Carousel Seven that became the resident band at the Princess Cinema in Takoradi-Sekondi owned by Annis Mubarak. This band blended highlife with traditional Fanti Osoode recreational music. In 1969, the band had its first hit song 'Edina Benya' – and others followed like 'Araba Lucy', 'Me Dowo' and 'Mawere Kyekyer'. In 1971, the Carousel Seven released the album 'Party Time with Ceekay' on the Esseibons label that also featured the young singer Pat Thomas. The album included the song 'Nimpa Rebree' that was a huge hit with the public. This was followed by 'Funky Highlife', one of the first Ghanaian albums to fuse highlife with western funk music. In 1976, C.K. released his first gospel music album 'Enigye Wo Sor Ho' in which he was accompanied by the Melodic Trio singers. In 1979, C.K. and Paapa Yankson teamed up with Ebo Taylor to produce the Essiebons album 'C.K Mann and the Masters' which featured prominent musicians like Bessa Simon (keyboards.), Osei Tutu (trumpet) and Okyerema Asante (congas). In the late 1980s, C.K. travelled abroad and released 'Timeless Highlife' in Canada. After returning, he was briefly with the Western Diamonds and was also guest vocalist on the mid-1990s 'Con Ghana Cuban' album that fused highlife and salsa music. One of his top hits of the time was his 1995 'Adwoa Yankey' that consoles a women of that name who has lost a family member. This song became an even bigger hit when it was banned from radio as, for some unknown reason, it became associated with a criticism of local cloth. Some of his hits have, in the late 2000s, been released by the world music Tropical Vibe Company, whilst his Ghanaian producer Dick Essilfie-Bondzie (Essibons label) is planning to bring out a backfile of his old hits on an eight-CD pack. In his home town of Takordi, this veteran artist runs his C.K. Mann Charity foundation for sixty under-privileged school children. In 2006, he was awarded the Grand Medal of Ghana by President John Agyekum Kufuor. Then, in 2010, C.K was given the MOGO lifetime Achievment Award for epitomising 'the best of original Highlife, authentitic Ghanaian music, Music of Ghanaian Origin'. In his later years, C.K. Mann was on retirement in his home town of Takoradi. He passed away in March 2018.

THE HIGHLIFE SINGER PAAPA YANKSON

C.K. Mann's longtime singing colleague is Paapa Yankson (Benjamin Paapa Kofi Yankson) who was born in 1944 at Winneba into a musical family, as his mother was in a church band and his father a trumpeter in the local Apam Brass Band. The first band Paapa Yankson joined was the Big Sound Band of the United African Company

(UAC). In 1966, he teamed up with C.K. Mann and his Carousel Seven and then, in 1975, Yankson did a Diploma at the National Academy of Music at his home town of Winneba. During the 1980s, he was music organizer for the Garrisons Education Unit at Burma Camp in Accra. Then, in 1991, the businessman and hotel owner, Mr. Ebo Coker, invited Paapa Yankson to Takoradi to help form the Western Diamonds Band. After C.K. left the group, Paapa Yankson became the leader of this band which released albums like 'Diamonds are Forever' (Sterns, UK label). After two years with the Western Diamonds, the then Chief Executive Officer of the Ashanti Goldfields, Sam Jonah, asked Yankson to help form this company's band, the Golden Nuggets, based in Obuasi and later Accra. In 1995, Paapa Yankson decided to go solo and went on many foreign tours. He released gospel albums like 'I Need Thee' and 'Rejoice' and in 1997 had a huge hit with his composition 'Yaaba'. In all, Paapa Yankson released around fifteen albums; some of the top ones are 'Wiase Mu Nsem', 'Show Your Love', 'Wo Yere Anaa Wo Maame', 'Okukuseku' and 'Tsena Mentsen'. Occassionally, Yankson and C.K Mann continued to team up and one example was in 2006 when they performed at the Highlife Extravaganza organised by the Ghana Music Foundation at the house of the Country Director of the World Bank, Mats Karlsson.

The same year, and together with C.K. Mann, Yankson was awarded the Grand Medal of Ghana by President Kufuor during National Honours and Awards Ceremony. During his career, Paapa Yankson recorded fifteen albums and performed in many countries across the world, including United States, Canada, Belgium, United Kingdom, Germany and Holland. Sadly, Paapa Yankson died in 2017.

THE CITY BOYS

This is a guitar highlife band and concert party formed in 1970 by Jackson Alfred Adofo (born 1951), together with Elvis Yeboah and P.P. Lamptey. Ampofo started off life as a lotto receiver in Accra. But, luckily, he is the nephew of Nana Ampadu of the African Brothers who encouraged him to go into the music field. Adofo is popularly known as the 'Black Chinese' and his City Boys has released numerous record singles and albums over the years. The City Boys concert party has also 'trekked' or toured to practically every village and small town in Ghana, and its highlife music section has also made several tours abroad. The City Boys was experimenting with Afro-reggae way back in the 70s, long before Alpha Blondy and Lucky Dube were on the scene. The City Boys band is currently one of the few operating concert parties and some of its later releases have been in the gospel vein, like its 1996 hit 'Osoro Aye Kom'. Adofo

Paapa Yankson. Mirror 31 July 2004

and his band still play and, over the years, he has released over 300 songs as singles or on record albums.

A.B. CRENTSIL

Singer and rhythm guitarist Abraham Benjamin Crentsil (born 1950) began his musical career with the El Dorados of the State Aboso Glass Factory and the Lantics in Takoradi. Then, in 1973, he joined the Sweet Talks that included Eric Agyeman, Smart Kwaku Nkansah and Pope Flynn. This group was the resident band of the Talk of the Town Nightclub in Tema owned by owned by Jonathan Abrahams, the brother of the highlife singer Joe Mensah.

Crentsil's Sweet Talks (later re-named Super Sweet Talks) released albums such as 'Adam and Eve', 'Mbesiafo Nto Nsa', 'Kusum Beat', 'Spiritual Ghana' and also 'Hollywood Highlife Party' recorded in the United States. In 1979, the group broke up.

Whilst its lead guitarist Smart Nkansah moved on to form the Black Hustlers and then Sunsum, Crentsil set up the Super Brains, which released (featuring guitarist Smart Nkansah) the song 'Atia' which warns of the danger of drinking too much local gin. Crentsil then formed Ahenfo (Kings) in 1982 which released 'Tantie Alaba' and the controversial and erotic song 'Moses'. During the 1980s, Crentsil mainly recorded in Canada and his band toured abroad extensively. His top 1980s releases include 'Kafo Mpo Dzidzi', 'Abrokyiri Abrabo', 'Party Time with The Stars' and 'Toronto by Night'. More recent recordings are 'Highlife in Canada' and a 1991 re-release by World Circuit Records of his 'Hollywood Highlife Party'. Since the 1990s, many of his hits have also been released on CD by the UK-based companies World Circuit Records and Sterns. In the mid 2000s, he teamed up with the highlife artist Obour to produce a collaborative highlife-hiplife album. Crentsil still makes occasional appearances, for instance at the Highlife Festivals and Parties organised peridocially in Accra by Mark Okraku-Mantey of Slip Music.

ERIC AGYEMAN

This great highlife guitarist was born in Kumasi, joined Afro Boateng's Midnight Movers in 1963 and then Dr. Gyasi's Noble Kings in 1972; which two years later released the classic 'Sikyi Highlife' with bassist Ralph Karikari, the drummer Thomas Frimpong and the trumpeter Tommy King who had previously been with P.P. Dynamite's Henrikos Dance Band and the Complex Sounds of the Tema Food Complex. From Dr. Gyasi's band, Eric, Frimpong and King then moved on to help A.B. Crentsil form the Sweet Talks. Then Agyeman went solo and formed the Super Sweet Talks with A.B. Crentsil, Frimpong, King and singer Agyaaku, released 'Safari Highlife' and 'Living in the Cold'. In 1982, Agyeman formed the Kokroko (Mighty) band and, in the 1990s, the Highlife All Stars; which did a live recording in 1996 at Amsterdam's Milky Way that was released on the Ghana Gold label.

NANA TUFFOUR

James Kwako Tuffour (also called Nine-Nine-Two-Four or 9-9-2-4 by his fans) was born in 1954 in Adwuman near Kumasi. He studied at St. Peter's Cathedral School and Asanteman Secondary School in Kumasi between 1960 and 1975. He played piano whilst a student and then joined Konadu's guitar band in 1976 as keyboard player and singer. He later moved on to other bands like Kofi Ani Johnson's Parrots, Santiano Damfo Domino's band, Tommy Darling's Wantu Wazuri and the Waza Afriko Band. In 1980, Tuffour released his first composition 'Highlife Romance' and later had a big hit with his 2003 song 'Abeiku'. In 1979, he spent some time in Lagos where he played keyboards for the Nigerian juju-music star Sunny Ade (whose band had also previously featured another Ghanaian guitarist Osei Bonsu Senior). On returning to Ghana, Nana built a house in Kumasi and formed his Sika Dua band with which he toured the States in the 1990s. In all, he has released seventeen albums and his band still plays occasionally. In 2011, he contested elections for the position of President of the Musicians Union of Ghana (MUSIGA).

WOFA ROCKSON

Singer, composer and guitarist Wofa (Uncle) Rockson Opoku Amponsah was born in 1947 near Kumasi. His mother, Abenaa Foriwaa, was a famous traditional nnwonkoro (Akan female music genre) singer and his brother is the well-known highlife folk guitarist Koo Nimo. Rockson began his musical career in the late-sixties with the Afro-Peace guitar band in Brong Ahafo. In 1971, he moved on, first to Ani Johnson's Parrots guitar band and then the Arakan's Dance Band. In 1975, he joined the army and became a corporal and leader of the Army Magazine Two Dance Band of the Second Battalion of Infantry at Takoradi. He recorded at Bokoor Studio in 1984 after leaving the army. These songs appeared on the 'Guitar and Gun' album and on 'Business Women' released in the mid-eighties by Hot Blow Productions. He later tried his hand at farming; he is currently a musical pastor in Accra and helps run a gospel band.

EDDIE ANSAH FROM THE VOLTA REGION

'Togbe' Eddie Ansah hails from Ghana's south-eastern Volta Region and so his highlifes are in Ewe. Eddie learnt to play the guitar from the American Peace Corp volunteer Andy Brunner and local guitarist Mr. Aoli. In 1970, he joined the Liberty Dance Band of Odumase and, the following year, the Police Band. From 1974 to 1978, he was with the army Barrels Band of the First Infantry Battalion at Michel Camp and, after this, he ran his own 'E' Band at Reno's Hotel in Tema. He recorded at my Bokoor Studio in 1985 with the Saka Saka musicians as session-men. These songs were released in Holland on the Wawa label. One of the songs with a 6/8 agbadza lilt called 'Mewu Mo DziI' was later released in 2002 on the world music 'Electric Highlife' CD (Naxos label). In 1989, Eddie moved back to the Volta Region where he became an executive member of the Volta branch of the Ghana Musicians Union (MUSIGA) and Director of the Canons Band of the Mortar Brigade in Ho. Eddie was also the inspiration behind a series of mobile Bokoor recordings I did in the Volta Region, based in the town of Tsito. In 2006, Eddie became involved with the businessman Devine Dzegbia to launch a live music band and rehearsal space at the Woezar Hotel in Ho, in order to counteract the tendency towards computerised music and mimed performance.

ANTHONY AND THE BEACH SCORPIONS

Anthony Scorpion Entsie is a Fanti guitarist from Mankesim who began his music career in 1971 with Nana Ampadu's African Brothers. In 1973, he formed his own Beach Scorpions guitar band which had an instant hit with its record 'Momma Yengye Yeni' (Let's Celebrate). In 1977, he went to eastern Nigeria for seven years and released highlife songs there on the Roger All Stars label and Ben Okworko's Grover Records. One of his Roger All Stars records was the 1981 'Original Beach Scorpions'. After returning to Ghana, he teamed up with the American percussionist Joyce Gilbert from San Francisco who plays Afro-Cuban drums and had come to Ghana in 1973 when she joined the Saints Band and, briefly, Boombaya. Together with Joyce Gilbert, Anthony reformed the Beach Scorpions as an acoustic guitar band in the mid-1980s which recorded at my Bokoor Studio in Accra in 1989. Two of their songs 'Jealousy' and 'Friends Today Enemies Tomorrow' were later released in 2002 on the Naxos world music label. This 1989 recording featured the clarinettist Jimmy Beckley and mandolin player Papa 'T' (Tornado) Teiko. Beckley was at the time running his Jimmy's Jazz Combo and Jazz Club in Accra whilst Teiko had settled in the seaside town of Kokrobite. Teiko himself had been a horse jockey in Accra as a young man before playing in the 1970s with the Ekome Faloi Cultural group and Ricky Tee. Sadly, Papa 'T' died in 2017.

MASTER DRUMMER OKYEREMA ASANTE

Okyerema was born in 1949 in Koforidua and his uncle was the master drummer of the King's Palace at New Juaben. As a youth, Okyerema was a member of Nkrumah's Young Pioneers band and then moved on to join the Togolese group L'Orchestre Los Huefanron and the Ghanaian Zonglo Biiz. He then joined Hedzoleh, travelled to the States with them in 1974 and settled there – as is more fully discussed in Chapter 59. Then, in 1987, Okyerema Asante performed on Paul Simon's South African 1987 'Graceland' tour. Much later, in 1998, Okyerema was involved in a big-band highlife release called 'Crabs in a Bucket' whose songs were composed by himself and the American vibes player Nick Robertson. The arranger was Stan Plange and the CD was released in the United States on the Asante/Oyigbo label.

I first came across this versatile musician at the Napoleon Club in 1974 when Okyerema was playing with Hedzoleh Sounds or Soundz. This Afro-rock band led by guitarist Stanley Todd was formed by the Napoleon Club owner Faisal Helwani. In 1973, it recorded the album 'Introducing Hedzoleh' with South African trumpeter Hugh Masekela (see Chapter 59 and picture of Okyerema with this group). Hedzoleh then went on US tour with Masekela but the group subsequently broke up and Okyerema stayed on in the States. As a result in 1980, he became involved in Mick Fleetwood's filmed musical safari to Ghana 'The Visitor' when this famous British drummer of the American Fleetwood Mac rock group came to Accra with twelve tons of equipment and a 16-track studio. Two years later, Okyerema came to my Bokoor Studio with producer Malcolm Ben to play percussion and xylophone for the Yaanom Band (see Chapter 61). After this, Okyerema went back to the States where he played with top artists and bands such as Laurie Smith, the Crusaders, Herbie Hancock, Roy Ayers, Third World and Paul Simon. Okyerema is currently based between the States and Ghana.

PAT THOMAS – THE 'GOLDEN VOICE' OF GHANA

This singer-composer was born in Kumasi in 1950 and was introduced to highlife by his uncle, the famous guitarist Kwabena Onyina who ran a guitar band and concert party. In the late 1960s, Pat worked with Ebo Taylor and the Broadway big-band. Then in 1972, he and Ebo were invited to form the Blue Monks by two of Ghana's leading radio disc jockeys, Mike Eghan and Carl Bannerman. Pat then moved to Cote D'Ivoire for a while and then back to Ghana where he led the Ghana Cocoa Marketing Board's Sweet Beans band with singer Lola Everett (whom he was briefly married to). Until it broke up in 1978, the Sweet Beans played regularly at the Tip Toe Gardens in Accra and for Cocoa Day celebrations. Some of his hit tunes then were 'False Lover' released in 1974, 'Odo San Bra', 'Mmesiafo Yi' and 'Eye Wo Asemben'. Pat also recorded in 1976 with the Marijata band composed of the Sweet Beans musicians Kofi 'Electric' Addison, Bob Fiscian and Nat Fredua Osmanu. Due to the collapse of the music industry in the late 1970s, Pat settled in Germany in 1977 where he released 'Yesu San Bra' and a disco highlife called 'Pat Thomas 1980'. He then spent a year in Abidjan where he released 'Asante Kotoka' and 'Pat Thomas and Marijata'.

In 1986, he settled in Canada and, that year, he released his album 'Highlife Greats Mbrepa' for JAP Records. This was recorded by F.K. Kwakye at the Office Togolaise du disque in Lome. The line-up on that album was bass, rhythm and lead guitarists

Marshall, Frank Donkor and Aweke Yaw Glyman, respectively; drummer Asie Dee, congoist Seth Otinkorang, keyboardist Abee Mensah and the hornsmen Mike Nielson Sam Torto and Laryea. Its title track was 'Mbrepa Beba' (Good Times will Come). Other popular songs followed like 'Sika Ye Mogya' (Money is Blood, released 1991), 'Me Gyedi So' and 'Gye Nyame Di'. Pat returned home in 1997 and signed up with the Megastar Company that produced his 'Sika Nantie' release. Pat is still active in the local music scene and, for instance, appeared in the 2007/8 celebrations of the 'Made in Germany' burger highlife festival organised by the Director of the Goethe institute in Accra, Eleonore Sylla. Pat Thomas's daughter with his one-time wife and singing partner, Lola Everett, is the up-and-coming singer Nana Yaa. Pat Thomas currently tours with his Kwashibu Area Band which includes Kwame Yeboah.

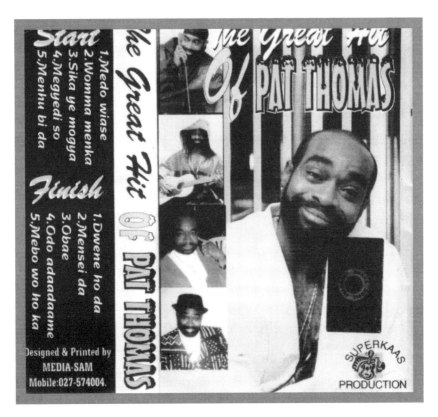

Pat Thomas from the Great Hits cassette cover

AMAKYE DEDE, HIS APOLLO HIGH KINGS AND HIS ABRANTIE SPOT

Dan Amakye Dede, or 'Iron Boy' as he is often called, was born in Agogo in the Asante Region in 1958 and began his music career in 1973 as a back-up singer with the Kumapim Royals led by the late Akwasi Ampofo Agyei (A.A.A.). Amakye Dede composed several big record hits for this guitar band/concert party, like 'Abebi Bewua Eso', 'Wanware Me A', 'Odo Mani Agyina' and 'Ohoho   Batani'. He then formed his own Apollo High Kings, in 1981, after returning from one of his stays in Nigeria. He moved between Ghana and Nigeria for some years from 1979 and had a number of popular hits there sung in Yoruba, Pidgin English and Akan, such as 'Kechi', 'Jealousy Go Shame', 'Beautiful Women', 'Sansa Akroma', 'To Be A Man Naa Waa', 'Ifa Anyi Chuku' and 'Taxi Driver'. For a while, his Apollo High Kings actually operated in Nigeria as the resident band of the FESTAC Hotel. In 1983, he released 'Ifa Anyi Chuku' but that year, and with so many other Ghanaians, he had to return home during the Nigerian Aliens Order. Consequently, he released a song called 'Ye Ko Ye Yaba' or just 'Yaba' about his time in Nigeria and having to return home. Then, in 1986, he had his first notable Ghanaian hit 'Kose Kose' released by A.K. Brobbey and, three years later, made his first American tour where he recorded and released 'Dabi Dabi'. By 1991, Amekye Dede's Apollo High Kings had released eight albums, some of these being recorded in Germany, a country he also began to tour. Although his songs are typical guitar band highlifes complete with proverbial type lyrics, he often gets his drummers to use reggae type beats. By the late 1990s, he had released fifteen albums, including many in reggae-highlife style.

By 1995, with money coming in from his records and German tours, Amakeye Dede was able to set up his Abrantie (i.e. Gentleman) Spot in Lapaz, Accra, the only live music venue to be owned by a Ghanaian highlife musician. Amakye changed the name of his band to the High Kings and also signed up on the local Megastar Label. Today, he is still going strong, operating and playing at his Abrantie Spot, with well over twenty albums to his credit.

Some of his big hits over the years have been 'Handkerchief', 'Seniwa', 'Brebrebe Yi', 'Mensuro', 'Mabre', 'Broken Promises', 'Nsuo Amuna', 'Sokoo Na Mmaa Pe', 'Mefre Wo', 'Okyena Sesei', 'Odo Nfonii', 'Nka Akyi', 'Iron Boy' and 'M'ani Agyina'. For his untiring work Amakye Dede has won the prestigious Ghanaian ECRAG awards on five occasions and, on one of these (in 1994), I had the pleasure of handing out the award that was in the form of a small royal stool or throne. Other awards he obtained that are mentioned by the Ghanaian journalist Nanabanyin Dadson[27] were the 1988 Leisure Guitar band of Year, the 1990 Leisure Contemporay Music Awards, the 1991 Album of the year (for 'Dabi Dabi'), the 1996 South African Kora Music Award and the 1997 Konkoma Music Award.

In 2000 and 2002, he released the 'Broken Promises' and 'Krokro Me' albums, after which there was a gap in his recording for a number of years. However during this time, he continued to play at his club and at important functions. For instance, in 2010, he played at the MOGO Award Night, the Night with Wole Soyinka, the GBC Gala Night, the Ghana Journalists Association Awards and in December of that year at a solo concert at the International Conference Centre in Accra. At these show, his 12-peice High Kings included the veteran trumpeter Osei and the German violinist 'Kwame' Thomas Woermle. It was also in 2010 year that he released his album 'Akonaba'. Then, in 2011, portions of the two-and-a-half hour of the Dember solo concert was released by Stebo Records as a video entiled the 'Amakye Dede Best Concert Video.'

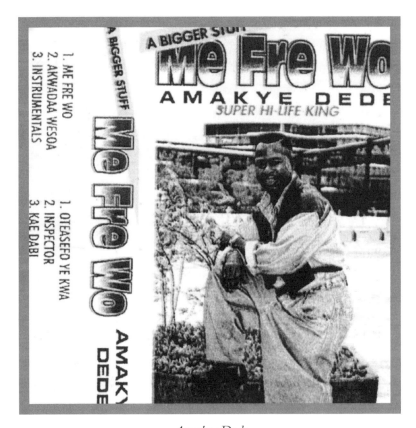

Amakye Dede

[27]See Dadson's article on Amakye Dede in the Ghanaian Graphic of 18 December, 2010.

ABEBE AND THE BANTUS

Abebe Jonathan Kakraba was born in 1949 at Anfoega in the northern part of Ghana's Volta Region. As a youth, he was a vocalist in the town's borborbor drum-dance group. Then, in 1960, his father moved to Vakpo in the southern Volta Region where the schoolboy Abebe joined the local agbadza drum-dance group as as a percussionist playing kagan (stick drum), gangogwe (bell) and axatse (maracas). In 1970/1971, Abebe became the singer for the G.D.'s (or Gee Dees) dance band that was the resident band of the Silver Cup Club in Accra. This was a band composed of Sierra Leonian and Ghanaian musicians. The Sierra Leonians were the leader and guitarist Papa Maurice, percussionist Samuel Oju King and bass guitarist Bola. From Ghana came the group's lead singer, the late Prince Ali of northern Ghana, with other Ghanaian artists who passed through being the keyboardsman Ernest Honney and the drummers Kofi Electric and then Judas.

In 1973, Abebe started his Bantus band and it became based at the Tabela night-club in Accra (near the Caprice Hotel) run by the Lebanese proprieter Mr. Hadad. Coincidentally, the Bantus and my own Bokoor Band shared the same stage on several occasions at this club around 1977. In fact, we lost one of our python snakes we used in our Bokoor floor-show in the club's bamboo decorations. Abebe could not then sustain his Bantus group and so briefly joined the Funky Millionaires dance band; then, in 1978, he joined the Tata Brewery's Great Pilsners band led by Jimmy Kwapps. The same year, Abebe recorded his first album called 'Mawuana' (God will do it) that used borborbor rhythms. Abebe then travelled to the Republic of Benein to join Ignace de Souza's Black Santiagos Band based in Cotonou.

Six months after returning to Accra from Benin, the Ewe producer John Tamson of Johnny World Music became so interested in Ababe's Ewe compositions that he produced three more borborbor-type albums that were distributed in the Ewe territory of eastern Ghana and Togo. In fact, Abebe and his Bantus went on to record sixteen borborbor-type albums. In 1991, the Bantus embarked on a West African tour and released 'Gbekagbe Soka Borborbor', an album that combined borborbor, soca, reggae and funk. Artists on this album included Sammy Lartey Junior on tenor sax, Ani Laryea and Edmund Mensah on trumpets, Laryea Torto on trombone, Sam Incoom on guitar, Kojo Dadson on bass, Daniel Safo on keyboards with K.K. Kabobo doing the drum programming. This album was produced by BGI productions and was financed by Kojo Dadson of the Black Generation Band. Around this time, Abebe also made albums that explored the traditional Ewe 6/8 agbadza drum style. Up to 2007, he made nine such records utilising this southern Ewe music as well as highlifes, borborbor and reggae. I should add that two of his 1990s recordings were made at my own Bokoor Studio, which in 2010 I digitally re-mastered for his CD current releases.

Chapter 41

THE RISE OF FOLKLORIC CROSS-OVERS AND NEO-TRADITIONAL ARTISTS

Since the liberalisation of the Ghanaian economy in the late 1980s, there has been a boom in the tourist industry with many of the foreigners and world music fans who are interested in Ghanaian live bands, cultural displays and folkloric groups. As a result, many private clubs and beach resorts have sprung up that cater for these foreign visitors, like Big Milly's, Chesters, Akoma Village, Next Door, Bywels and Osekan. Also patronised by foreign visitors are international venues like the Alliance Francaise and Dubois Memorial Centre, and government-sponsored international festivals such as PANAFEST and Emancipation Day.

Also very important are the now numerous private cultural centres that teach traditional music and dance to foreign visitors, the earliest being the African Academy of Music and Arts (AMAA) set up at Kokorobite in 1988 by the master drummer Mustapha Tettey Addy who leads the Royal Obonu Drummers. Others are Kasapaa at Ninyano, the Odehe Dance Company centre in Nungua and the late Godwin Agbele's Dagbe Institute at Kopeyia in Volta Region now run by his sons. There is also the cultural centre guesthouse associated with the Kukye-Kukye Bamboo Orchestra at Masomogor village near the Kakum Nature Reserve. More recently is the Dagara Music and Arts Centre that was set up at Medie by Bernard Woma, previously with the

National Dance Ensemble. There are also private neo-traditional folkloric groups that double up as both performance ensembles and teaching outfits for foreigners. For instance, Hewale Sounds, Nana Danso Abiam's Pan African Orchestra (PAO), Stephen Yaw Kontoh's Bomsaka Cultural Group, the Suade group in Nungua, Nii Tettey Tetteh's Kusun Ensemble and Richard Danquah's Kusum Gboo drum and dance ensemble. To everybody's shock, Richard died in October 2006, at just 36 years old, but the group still continues.

Many of these cultural/folkloric groups and artists who perform at hotels, beach resorts and festivals also sometimes record for the local and international 'World Music' market; like the afore-mentioned Hewale Sounds, PAO, Kusum Gboo and Royal Obonu Drummers. Then, there have been recent local cassette releases of Akan Nwonkoro music by groups like Onyame Krabae, whilst Osei Korankye has been reviving, teaching and recording the Akan seprewa harp-lute. Examples of current Ga 'cultural' groups that are releasing music are the Sensational Wulomei, Ebaahi Soundz, Modin Sane and the Kusun Ensemble. From north-eastern Ghana comes the African Showboys; and also tha late Captain Yaba, King Ayisoba and Atongo Zimba whose CDs combine the Frafra koliko/kologo lute with western instruments. Atongo got his training as the young guide for the blind musical street-beggar Onipa Nua (Brother Man), a Frafra hand-piano player who shot to fame in the 1980s when Faisal Helwani began recording him and took him to Paris to appear on prime-time TV. From northern-western Ghana came the late Kakraba Lobi, an internationally-recognised teacher of the Dagari pentatonic xylophone who also makes recordings. There has also been a resurgence in sales of the 'palmwine' highlife recordings of the Akan acoustic folk guitarists Koo Nimo, Kwabena Nyama and the late T.O Jazz.

But before turning to more detailed biographies on some of these folkloric and neo-traditional artists I will first present the stories of some pioneering Ghanaian symphonic art-musicians and stage choreographers who, many years ago during the Nkrumah era, began combining traditional and contemporary performance as part of a search for a national and Pan African identity.

Richard Danquah (in white cloth) and his Kusum Gboo

SOME EARLY GHANAIAN PIONEERS OF CULTURAL CROSS-OVER BLENDING

EPHRAIM AMU: FATHER OF GHANAIAN ART MUSIC

Ephraim Amu was born in Peki in the Volta Region in 1899 and composed an enormous number of hymns, choral compositions and patriotic songs in Ewe and Akan from the 1920s, including 'Yen Ara Asasi Ni' (This Land is Ours) that has become Ghana's second national anthem. In 1927, he joined the staff of the Akropong Presbyerian Training College and his endeavour to Africanise the Church, by wearing traditional cloth on the pulpit, led to his dismissal from the College in 1932. This actually opened the way to a long academic career. He taught as music teacher at Achimota College where he introduced the idea of so-called 'tribal nights' when the students had to get out of their school uniforms and wear their ethnic clothes and play ethnic music and dance. In the 1950s, Amu went on to teach at the university music

393

departments at Kumasi, Winneba and, finally, Legon. From 1962, Amu became a Research Fellow at the Institute of African Studies at Legon and made many field trips recording music on reel-to-reel tape. He therefore (with Professor Nketia, Atta Annan Mensah and others) contributed to the important collection of six hundred hours of recordings of Ghanaian ethnic and popular music, folk-tales and dramas now lodged with the Institute of African Studies at Legon. From 1965, Dr. Amu became the Head of the School of Performing Arts at Legon until he retired in 1971. He died in 1995 but his daughter, Misonu, continues his university work as she is based at the Institute of African Studies. Amu is remembered not only as a nationalist composer but also as the developer of the traditional Akan atenteben bamboo flute. His remarkable legacy is reflected by the fact that Amu was given a State Burial and his picture is the first of a contemporary musician to appear on a Ghanaian currency note.

J.H. KWABENA NKETIA: THE GURU OF AFRICAN ETHNO-MUSICOLOGY

Another Ghanaian art-musician is Professor Nketia who was born in Mampong Ashanti in 1921. He attended the Presbyterian Training College at Akropong between 1937 and 1941, and then spent three years in London at the School for Oriental and African Studies and Trinity College of Music. He then did further studies in the U.S. at the Juliard School of Music, Columbia College and North-western University. He joined the staff of the University of Ghana in 1952 and made extensive field trips to collect traditional music on a portable recording machine. He was also a member of the African Music Society that encouraged the music of local highlife guitar bands such as Onyina, Yamoah and E.K Nyame. He has over two hundred publications to his credit, including the book 'Music of Africa' that has become a pioneering ethno-musicological work. He is a 'creative ethnomusicologist' who draws inpiration from ethnic music and has composed eighty pieces of Ghanaian art-music for piano, flute piano and atenteben bamboo flute. In 1966, he became Director of the Institute of African Studies at Legon until he was awarded an Emeritus Professorship from UCLA where he taught from 1969 to 1982. He then became Andre Mellon Professor Emeritus at the University of Pittsburgh where he taught from 1981 to 1991. In the mid-1990s, he returned home to Ghana to establish the International Centre for African Music and Dance (ICAMD) that is located in the School of Performing Arts at Legon. Over the years I have often interacted with Professor Nketia; infact, we went together, in 1998, to the Afromusique/Africania Colloquium at Grand Bassam in the Cote d'Ivoire, and in 2011 we both gave keynote speeches at the symposium on

'Enhancing Contemporary Ghanaian Music' organised by MUSIGA, the ICAMD and the Dutch Royal Music Conservatory, held at MUSIGA House. More recently, in 2016, Professor Nketia and I were on the panel of 'Your Story - Don't Lose It' organized by the Institute of African Studies to mark UNESCO's 'World Day for Audiovisual Heritage'. So well into his nineties, Professor Nketia is still going strong.

Prof JHK Nketia and Anis Haffer 2009. www.myjoyonline.com

PROFESSOR A. M. OPOKU AND HIS DISCIPLE FRANCIS NII YARTEY

The late Professor Albert Mawere Opoku (1915-2001) was a pioneer in choreographing Ghanaian dances and putting them on the professional stage. He was born near Kumasi. Between 1921 and 1930, he went to Achimota College to obtain an Art Theatre Diploma, which he further pursued at the Camberwell School of Art in Britain. On his return to Ghana he taught in a Kumasi school from 1935 to 1937, and then moved on as an Art Tutor at Achimota from 1937 to 1944. In 1944, Professor Opoku and his musicologist colleague Professor J.H K. Nketia went to the UK on Commonwealth Scholarships. Both returned to Ghana in 1952, Nketia going to the

University at Legon and Opoku to the university at Kumasi, now called the Kwame Nkrumah University of Science and Technology (KNUST). In Kumasi, Professor Opoku became involved with the Asanteman Cultural Centre that taught the local public to learn Akan dances like the adowa and fontomfrom. In 1957, both Opoku and Nketia, as well as the sculptor Dr. Seth Cudjoe and the composer Phillip Gbeho, were put on a committee by Kwame Nkrumah to organise the performance side of the Independence Day celebrations.

Opoku was a lecturer at KNUST until 1962 when he became a Senior Research Fellow at the Institute of African Studies at Legon and then Artistic Director of the newly-formed Ghana Dance Ensemble. For its intensive training in traditional performance, Opoku brought onto the university campus talented local drummers/dancers from the provinces to teach the students. These included Seth Kobla Ladzekpo and Michael Kojo Ganyoh (Kojoga) to teach Ewe drum-dances, Mustapha Tettey Addy for Ga Adangme styles, Osei Bonsu and Kwesi Badu for Ashanti drum-dances, and Iddrisu Alhassan for the Dagbani variety. The Ghana Dance Ensemble made trips numerous to Africa, Europe, the Soviet Union, Eastern Europe, north America, Latin America and the Caribbean. After his Opoku's retirement in 1976, his talented student Nii Yartey became Artistic Director of the Ghana Dance Ensemble, later renamed National Dance Company.

Nii Yartey himself was was born in the Bubuashie traditional quarter of Accra into a royal family and was influenced by the local songs, poems and dances of his grandmother. During the 1960s, he also played and danced with local kpanlogo drum-dance groups of the Ga youth of Accra. Between 1966 and 1971, he took a dance diploma course at the University of Ghana at Legon where he was mainly taught by Professor Opoku, as well as some foreign dance teachers like Deborah Bertanoff, Odette Blum, Drid Williams and Peggy Harper. In 1972, Nii went to the USA to do an M.A. degree in dance at the University of Illinois. He returned to Ghana and, in 1976, became Director of the university-based Ghana Dance Ensemble. Then, in 1992, Nii became Director of the resident National Dance Company of Ghana group of the newly-built National Theatre in Accra, taking the ensemble on many national and international tours. He became Director of the Noyam (Moving On) Dance-Theatre Company established in 1998 to help develop contemporary African dance. He also became a university professor but sadly died whilst on tour of India with Noyam in 2015.

BIOGRAPHIES OF SOME CURRENT FOLKLORIC/NEO-TRADITIONAL ARTISTS, PLUS TRADITIONAL MASTER MUSICIANS WITH INTERNATIONAL CONNECTIONS

KAKRABA LOBI: AMBASSADOR OF THE NORTHERN XYLOPHONE

The late Kakraba Lobi was born in Kalba Suru in the Lobi/Brifo and Dagara area of Upper West Region of Ghana (and northern Cote D'Ivoire and southern Burkina Faso). Kakraba was taught the pentatonic wooden 'gyil' xylophone by his father, an instrument that is played at weddings, funerals and festivals. They are played alone, in pairs, or in ensembles with singers and drummers. In the 1950s, the young Kakraba went to Accra where he did some broadcasts for Radio Ghana. In 1957, he met Professor Nketia who offered him a teaching post at the Institute of African Studies where Kakraba was a full time teacher until 1987. Over the years, Kakraba has given guest lectures in Germany, Scandinavia, the U.S. and Africa, and has hundreds of gyil disciples in Japan. In 2000, Kakraba released the 'Song of Legaa' CD, followed in 2004 by the 'Song of Niira'. In both, he was accompanied by Valery Naranjo and Barry Olsen, and the CDs were released on the Kalaeidoscope Sound label in the United States. Kakraba's son, S.K. has also become an excellent gyil player.

MUSTAPHA TETTEY ADDY: INTERNATIONAL GA MASTER DRUMMER

Mustapha was born in the Ga village of Avenor near Accra in 1942. He and his brothers Yacob, Emmanuel and Obo learnt traditional music from their father who was a traditional Wonche or Akon priest. In the early 1960s, Mustapha and his brothers created the Obuadi group that helped pioneer the kpanlogo dance of the 1960s (see photo in Chapter 26). He and his brothers were also instrumental in creating the neo-traditional 'fume-fume' music by re-working older Ga, Adangbe and Ewe drum-dance styles. Around 1960, Mustapha began working as a master drummer at the School of Performing Arts of the University of Ghana. In the late 1960s, he began to make international tours; between 1972 and 1981, he released seven record albums on the British Tangent, French Arion and German Insel Hombroich labels. In 1982, Mustapha moved back to Ghana where he set up his Royal Obonu Drummers and, in 1988, founded the Academy of Music and Arts (AAMA) in the beach village of Kokrobite near Accra This hotel-cum-cultural centre became the first major private center that taught traditional music and dance to international visitors. Between 1990 and 1999, he released six albums (like the 'Royal Drums of Ghana') on the German

Mustapha Tettey Addy (middle at back) and his Royal Obunu Drummers.
Kakraba Lobi is playing the 'gyil'l xylophone

Weltwunder label. In 1992 and 1993, the Royal Obonu Drummers played at the international WOMAD (World Music and Dance) festival. Through his records, international tours and AAMA drum centre, Mustapha has became a major player in spreading Ghanaian drum culture internationally. His brothers have settled in the United States where where the late Obo was running his Kukurudu and Okropong ensembles, and Yacob was teaching traditional drumming. Mustapha had a mild stroke a few years ago and so has now retired to his house in Kokrobite.

JOHNSON KEMEH: UNIVERSITY MASTER DRUM TEACHER
Johnson hails from Ghana's Volta Region and has been teaching drumming at the University of Ghana since the 1970s. He is currently the longest standing member of the University Music Department and hundreds of Ghanaian and foreign students have passed though his practical course. He formed the Brotherhood Foundation Cultural Group of Alajo (an Accra suburb) in 1976. With this drum-drama and dance

group, he has also trained many artists, including members of the Dance Company of the National Theatre and the Dance Ensemble at Legon. The group has played at Kiddifest and Black History Month in Ghana and toured Holland in 1997.

THE AFRIKA OBONU MUSIC THERAPY DRUM ENSEMBLE

This group is led by the Ga percussionist Nii Amaa Akomfrah who was born in 1945 in Accra. At seven years, Nii began to learn talking drums (obonu drums) and formed the Afrika Obonu Drum Ensemble in 1980. The group worked with the Afro-jazz percussionist Kofi Ghanaba (Guy Warren) in the mid-1980s under the name 'Ghanababii' (Children of Ghanaba). In 1986, Kojo Arkorful joined Afrika Obonu as band coordinator, and both Nii Amaa and Kojo began serious research into African musical therapy and the medicinal use of music and plants. In 1999, they worked with South African musician/music therapist Sharon Katz. Afrika Obonu provided music therapy drumming and dancing at many Ghanaian psychiatric wards, borstals, hospitals, occupational therapy departments, orphanages and children's homes. Sadly, Nii Amaa passed away in early 2011.

OSEI KWAME KORANKYE REVIVES THE SEPREWA HARP-LUTE

Osie Korankye was born in 1967 in Sefwi of the Western Region. He lost his father when very young and joined his grandfather who taught him at eight years old to play the local Akan seprewa (or seperewa) harp lute. Osie could not complete school so went into farming and joined the local village group as seprewa player which he says means 'small touched and speaking instrument'.

The Akan lute seprewa harp-lute was first introduced into Ghana in 1740 when the Ashantis defeated the Gyaman State in what is now northern Cote d'Ivoire. This court instrument was taken as war-booty from the Gyaman capital Bonduku (Bondoukou or Buntuku) to Kumasi and became a favourite 'sankwa sika' instrument of the Asante King. It was initially King's instrument but later was taken up by sub-chiefs and then became 'democratised', spreading into even the smallest villages, where it became associated with funeral appellations, palmwine drinking and musical philosophising. But, gradually, this six-stringed instrument had died out and so, in 1990, Professor Nketia and Koo Nimo arranged for it to be taught at the University of Ghana by Osei Korankye who, as mentioned, had been playing it from 1979. Osei has developed this instrument into a ten-string one and has even added modern tuning pegs. He has travelled all over the world with it and has recorded both with Koo Nimo and the London-based highlife guitarist Alfred Kari Bannerman. In 2009, Osei Korankye's song 'Emmaa Mmo' won the music competition of the 'Pathways of Womens Empowerment in Popular Culture Project' organised by Professor Akosua Adomako and the CEGENSA (gender advocacy) section of the University of Ghana, then part of the Institute of African Studies. Osei is still teaching as the seprewa instructor at the University of Ghana's Music Department.

THE AFRICAN AMERICAN/GHANAIAN ETSI KUSUM AGOROMBA CULTURAL GROUP

This is a thirty-piece cultural group based in Cape Coast set up in the mid 2000s, made up of children who play drums, shekeres, claves and bamboo sticks. Its Director is the African American Zakia N. Alston and the Ghanaians Ebo Otoo and the late Professor Joe Nkrumah. The group was established in 2001 and performed at PANAFEST 2003, the National HIV/AIDS Day, the Cape Coast Black History Street Theatre Project and the Assin Manso Emancipation Day sponsored by the Ghana Heritage Conservatory. It also featured at the US Embassy's African American History/Heritage Month in 2005.

NANA DANSO ABIAM AND THE PAN AFRICAN ORCHESTRA (PAO)

Danso Abiam was trained at a French music conservatory, taught at the University of Ghana from 1979 to 1984 and, then, became Director of Ghana's National Symphony Orchestra. Whilst at the University, he devised a chromatic fingering system for the local atenteben bamboo flute. His forty-eight strong PAO was established in 1988 to develop an Afrocentric system of making symphonic music. Consequently, the Orchestra uses solely African instruments, but organised into symphonic-like sections and led by a conductor (i.e. Nana Danso). So it is presented in an art, rather than a dance music context. The repertoire includes Nana's own compositions as well as his arrangement of traditional songs, highlifes, Osibisa's Afro-rock and Fela-Kuti's Afro-beats. After performing at the 1994 WOMAD festival in Britain, the Orchestra recorded at Peter Gabriel's Real World Studio in the West of England. In 1996, the resulting 'Opus One' CD went to the top of the International New World Music Charts for six weeks. In 2001, and in collaboration with the UK based dance company Adzido, the PAO toured the UK with the musical play 'Yaa Asantewa – Warrior Queen', written by Ghanaian Margaret Busby and directed by West Indian Geraldine Connor. In 2003, the PAO collaborated with the Nigerian Kora player Tunde Jegede. Nana's last project was to establish a Ghana International Conservatory of African Music. Nana was also working with the orchestra of Bishop

Otabil's International Central Gospel Church, but was killed in car crash in November 2014. The Pan African Orchestra is being continued by Nana's son, Yaw Kwakye.

THE NEO-TRADITIONAL HEWALE SOUNDS

Hewale Sounds is a twelve-person ensemble that, in 1996, became based at Professor Nketia's International Centre for African Music and Dance (ICAMD) at the School of Performing Arts, University of Ghana, Legon. Its leader, Dela Botri, was born in Accra in 1956 and joined his first group in 1978/79, called the Okotobrigya Cultural Troupe. In 1980, he joined the Nyame Mei Cultural Troupe and subsequently, in 1990, the Pan African Orchestra where he was taught advanced techniques on the bamboo antetebem flute by Nana Dansa Abiam. In 1995, Dela began to put Hewlale Sounds together – that was outdoored in 1996. Being a neo-traditional group, Hewale's instruments come from various ethnic regions and includes antenteben bamboo flutes, the Akan seprewa harp-lute, the goje one-stringed Dagbani fiddle, two northern xylophones and the giant Ga gome frame-drum. It also includes two lady singers/dancers. The repertoire of Hewale Sounds consists of Ghanaian and other African traditional music, their own compositions and some contemporary music; including their own renditions of highlife, Afrobeat, Afrorock and American jazz songs. The group has played extensively around Ghana and has made international tours of the United States, Europe, West African and South Africa. In 2004, they played alongside Stevie Wonder at the International Conference Centre in Accra. The group is now based at the Dubois Centre in Accra and organizes workshops for music students from home and abroad.

AARON BEBE FROM THE UPPER WEST REGION OF GHANA

Aaron Bebe Sukura was born in 1970 in the village of Tanchara in Ghana's Upper West Region and has been playing the local gyil (wooden xylophone) since boyhood. In 1992, he moved to Accra where he began teaching at the Music Department of the University of Ghana at Legon. Aaron is also an accomplished player of the mbira (Zimbabwean hand-piano) and traditional Akan seprewa harp-lute. Besides teaching at the university, Aaron has played with the Novisi dance group, the Ghana Dance Ensemble, the Pan African Orchestra, the Abibigromma Theatre Company of the University and Hewale Sounds. Aaron is co-leader (with myself) of the Local Dimension highlife band started in 1997 by some students and staff of the University of Ghana Music and Dance Departments (see his picture with this band in Chapter 39).

Hewale Sounds. Dela Botri is standing second on left and
Aaron Bebe Sukura is on extreme left

NII TETTEY TETTEH AND THE KUSUN ENSEMBLE

This Accra-based master-drummer and atenteben flute player obtained his musical training in his family house in James Town and then was a member of Nana Danso's Pan African Orchestra. In the 1980s and 1990s, he was running a band called the Allen Family. Then, around 2000, he formed the Kusun Ensemble which in 2003 released 'Nokoko' (something-something) recorded/distributed by the Pidgen Music Company of music promoter Panji Anoff. In it, Nii Tettey combines his traditional percussion group with trap-drums, guitars and trumpet. The Kusun Ensemble also runs the Kusun Study Centre in Accra which teaches drumming and dancing to both local and international students from Australia, the U.K. and South Africa.

THE NORTHERN LUTISTS: ATONGO ZIMBA, CAPTAIN YABA AND KING AYISOBA

Both Atongo Zimba and Captain Yaba (Azongo Nyaaba) were born in the northern Ghanaian town of Bolgatanga in the late 1960s, sing in the Frafra language and play the two-stringed or 'koliko/kologo' lute. Atongo, in his youth, was a traditional minstrel in Accra and worked with the blind street musician Onipa Nua. He then moved on to Fela's Afrika Shrine doing opening acts. He has also opened shows for Osibisa, Manu Dibango, Hugh Masekela and Angelique Kidjo. His first recording, in 1994, was with drummer Gabriel Schildnecht and guitarist Ljubo Majstorovic. In the early 2000s, he performed the griot role in the London National Theatre play 'Elmina's Kitchen' by Kwame Kwei-Arma. In 2004, he released an album called called 'Savannah Breeze' on the Dutch Hippo Records label and is currently a popular artist on the World Music circuit.

Captain Yaba was brought to Accra with a cultural group in the mid-1980s by Osibisa's Mac Tonto, and subsequently teamed up with xylophonist Joseph Kobam and with Jimmy Beckley's Jazz Combo. Captain Yaba made his first recording in 1989 with the producer Faisal Helwani; followed by another recorded at the ARC Studios in Tema, produced by the Sierra Leonian Francis Fuster and his Ninkribi Afro-rock band. In the mid-1990s, Captain Yaba toured Europe with Ninkribi but, after returning to Ghana, fell sick and died in 2001.

The newest northern lute player on the commercial Ghanaian music scene is King Ayisoba (Albert Apozori) who performs traditional music, Afro-beat and collaborates with hiplifers. He is managed by Panji Anoff's company Pidgen Music.

THE GHANA-NIGERIAN DZEMBII GROUP

An important neo-traditional group is Dzembii set up in Accra in 2000 by 'JB' Daniel Koranteng Crentsil. Daniel, who is half Ga and half Fanti, was born in 1948 in the Accra Police Depot. In the 1960s, he was a drummer in the 'Play and Laugh' kpanlogo group and the soul dancer for the Bugulu Dance Group of Accra Newtown. That's where he got his nickname 'JB' (i.e. James Brown). Dancing took him to Nigeria where he joined Fela-Kuti's Africa 70 band and became one of its conga players between 1971 and 1975. After leaving Fela, he joined the Juju Rock Stars and Sonny Okosun's reggae band. Then, in 1977, JB taught drumming at the Lagos University Centre for Cultural Centre Performing Arts until he retired in the late 1990.

On returning home, he set up his Dzembii group in Accra that can play Nigerian as well as Ghanaian traditional music. In fact, some of his performers are Nigerians and they subsequently broke away from Dzembii to form the Sogo cultural. Besides being a performance group, Dzembii also teaches drum-dances to Ghanaian and foreign students.

THE GONJE CONTEMPORARY FOLK INSTRUMENTAL GROUP

This is a fairly recent addition to the growing list of neo-traditional or folkloric bands. This band, which plays local folk songs and their own compositions, was formed in 2005 by Boateng Kudua Aheampong with Akuetta Nunoo, Athony Awingura, Odai Laryea, Kwabena Darko, Nii Dodoo, Baosiga Abalem and Yaahemma. It is a folk instrumental group that uses local instruments from the various ethnic groups in Ghana such as the Ga gome drum, the Fra-Fra koliko, the Dagari pentatonic xylophone, the Akan-derived atenteben flute and various types of northern and southern Ghanaian drums. They released their first album in 2005 titled 'Bolgatanga' and I saw them for the first time at an event held in Accra in April 2006 to say farewell to Mali's Ali Farka Toure who had just died.

THE AYEKOO DRUMMERS

The seven-member Ayekoo Drummers were formed in 2006 by musicians who had belonged to the Indigen Afrika childrens group of National Theatre in Accra that was managed by Professor Komla Amoaku and Korkor Amarteifio. This youth group lost its patronage at the theatre when this national venue was reorganised in 2005. Mr. Walter Espoito of Switzerland who works for Akosomba Textiles stepped in to help the group. It was renamed as Ayekoo and it began making trips to Euorpe to perform and teach music.

Chapter 42

CURRENT AFRO-ROCK, AFRO BEAT AND AFRO-JAZZ

NEW WAVE OF AFRO-FUSIONS BANDS IN GHANA

As mentioned in an earlier chapter, Afro-rock was created around 1970 by the London-based Ghanaian band Osibisa whose music became popular in Europe in the 1970s. Together with Fela Kuti's Afro-beat, Osibisa's Afro-rock also influenced many West African bands, such as the Liberian group Kapingdbi (run by Ebenezer Kojo Smith), Nigeria's BLO, Mono Mono and Ofege, and Ghana's Psychedelic Aliens, Boombaya, Zonglo Biiz, Wantu Wazuri, Pagadeja, Sawaaba Sounds and A Band Named Bediako. Also important were the resident Afro-pop bands at Faisal Helwani's Napoleon Club in Accra in the 1970s –Hedzoleh, Basa-Basa, Bunzus and Edikanfo (see Chapter 59).

However, none of these 1970s Ghanaian Afro-fusion bands (except the London based Osibisa) survived the late 1970s to late 1980s military government interegnum when Ghanaian popular music industry collapsed. Indeed, many Afro-rock musicians left the country, some permanently. Alfred Kari Bannerman, Kofi Adu and most of the Boombaya musicians stayed in the UK after doing a tour there. Members of Pagadeja packed up and also left for Britain. The British-born rock guitarist Kris Bediako returned to the UK in the early 1980s after valiantly attempting to run his band in Accra. Tommy Darling of Wantu Wazuri, on the other hand, settled in the US. Lash Laryea of the Magic Aliens and Jagger Botchway of Hedzoleh also went to the States, although these two did come back briefly in the early 1980s; when, as the group 'Amartey Hedzoleh', they did some recordings at my Bokoor Studio. Two other Afro-rock bands that recorded in my studio around this time were Saka Saka led by Jerry James Lartey (ex-Basa Basa) and Smart Arpeh Pozo's Nokoko band. Smart had been in Britain with Boombaya and came back to Ghana in the late 1970s and early 80s to make a go of it; but, in the end, he went back to the UK and did not return until the 1990s. None of these early '80s groups could do gigs due to the instability of the country and the night curfew.

However, from the early 1990s and after the liberalisation of the Ghanaian economy, 'Afro-pop' fusion bands began to re-appear in Ghana, formed by a newer generation of musicians or by musicians returning from abroad. In the 1990s, the Bawasaba Afro-rock band was put together by the drummer Smart Arpeh Pozo on returning from Britain, followed in the late 1990s by Dabatram run by the university lecturer Kodzo Gavua after completing his studies in Canada. Another was Dzidudu formed by the guitarist Nana Kwesi Danquah who had settled in Sweden for a while. Also, in the 1990s, the Ninkribi band led by the Sierra Leonian percussionist Francis Fuster became partly based in Ghana. Like the earlier Osibisa and the Afro-rock bands of the 1970s, many of these new generation Afro-fusion groups continued utilising traditional instruments. For instance, in the mid-1990s, Ninkribi teamed up with the northern Ghanaian (koliko/kologo) lute player Captain Yaba to release 'Yaba Funk'. Likewise, Dzidudu worked with the local percussionists of Group Afrika, whilst Dabatram uses guitars with Ewe drums. In the 2000s, Lash Laryea (a.k.a. Amartey Hedzoleh) came back to Ghana and has combined electronic instruments with traditional xylophones, flutes and drums. A more recent Afro-fusion band is the Ogya Band set up in 2011 by flotist Dela Botri, guitarist Ackah Blay, bassist Baba Umar Ahmed, drummer James Begyina and keyboards player Opoku Ayim.

It should be noted that the current wave of Afro-rock music is not particularly liked by the hiplife generation of urban youth of Ghana, who see it, like highlife, as being too old-fashioned. This music is rather appreciated by foreign visitors, musicians and 'world music' fans, as well as older Ghanaian returning home after long stays abroad. It is precisely this class of Ghanaian who also patronises local jazz, the topic to which we now turn.

THE LOCAL GHANAIAN JAZZ SCENE

Before examining the growth of local jazz in Ghana since the late 1980s it should first be mentioned that from as early as the 1950s, a number of important jazz musicians have visited Ghana, beginning with the Louis Armstrong's trips in 1956 and 1960 (see Chapter 33). These were followed in the 1970s by artists such as Max Roach, Randy Weston, Pattie Bown, Eddie Harris and Les McCann. Even more important is the role of Kofi Ghanaba who, as mentioned in a Chapter 29, went to the US in the 1950s where he worked with African American jazz musicians like Thelonius Monk, Miles Davis, Max Roach and Billy Strayhorn and released several pioneering Afro-jazz albums. After returning to Ghana in the 1960s, Ghanaba established his African Heritage Library and became an inspiration to a young generation of local jazz and Afro-jazz enthusiasts.

During the late seventies to mid-eighties, little happened in the local Jazz scene due to the various problems the country was then suffering from (Ghanaba became almost a recluse at the time). However, when the Ghanaian economy and the tourist industry began to pick from the end of the eighties, this stimulated the local jazz scene in two ways. First of all, foreign and particularly African American jazz musicians started coming to the country. Randy Weston and Max Roach re-visited the country. Other African American jazz-men who came were James 'Plunky' Branch, Andrew Cyrille and his Quartet, Donald Byrd, George Cables, Nathan Davis, Idris Muhammad, Milton Mustapha, Clark Terry and Joe Williams. Contributions to the Ghana jazz scene also came from the South African trumpeter Hugh Masekela, the white American vibes player Nick Roberts, the Cameroonian sax player Manu Dibango, the Liberian vocalist Miatta Fahnbulleh and, in 2005, the Black British sax player Courtney Pine.

Even more important was that, with the late 1980s liberalisation of the economy, many Ghanaians who had left home for economic reasons began to come back. Some of these 'been tos' (i.e. those who have been abroad) have been exposed to jazz abroad and are also relatively well-to-do. So, a number of exclusive jazz clubs sprang up in Accra and elsewhere to cater for them. The first in the early 1990s was Jimmy's Jazz Club run by clarinettist and sax player Jimmy Beckley. Others that later sprang up were Diane's Café, Village Inn, Baseline (later called the Jazz Optimism Club), Bywels, Hoops Nightclub, the Jazz Tone Club (established by African American jazz vocalist

Toni Maneison), the Odo Rise Jazz Club, and jazz clubs in hotels like the Golden Tulip and La Palm Beach. Another jazz spot is the Mojo Lounge (part of the Next Door Club), opened in May 2006, which featured the Dzidudu band. These jazz clubs are mainly patronised by middle-class Ghanaians and foreign visitors and residents.

As a result, small jazz groups multiplied, such as Jimmy's Jazz Combo, Unconditional Love, the D Minor Band, the Asanaba Jazz Combo, Young's Karmah Jazz Band, Charles Dewey's Wala Band, Big Wellington's Band, the Jazz Music Makers and Ray Allen's Jazz-life. One interesting Afro-jazz group was Febeja, the resident band of the Baseline Club in the late 1990s, with keyboard player Soroko, guitarist Cliff Eck, the Togolese bassist Gautier and trap-drummer Frank Sisi-Oyo (who was Fela-Kuti's drummer from 1982 to 1997).

Individual Afro-jazz artists include the trumpeters Osei Tutu, Long John and Mac Tontoh, singers (and sisters) Rama and Bibie Brew, Amanda and Cameroonian horn player Fru 'Fats' Tanga. Kofi Ghanaba, the 'old-man' of Ghanaian Afro-jazz, was still active up until his death; for instance, in 1998, he collaborated and made a film with the German free jazz percussionist Robyn Schulkowsky. The jazz scene received a boost when +233 (the old Jazz Optimism) Club was opened off Ring Road Central in Accra. The joint features the Sound Factory jazz group consisting of trombonist Eli Amewode, bassist Phillip Acquah, guitarist Cliff Eck and singer Sandra Housonon. Also, the verteran saxophonist Ray (Ekow Otoo) Allen put a small Afro-jazz quartet together with Victor Dey on piano, Daniel Black on drums and Phillip Acquah on bass. It was 'outdoored' in 2010 at the Italian Cultural Week Celebrations show held at the Citiz en Kofi Entertainment Centre in Osu, Accra.

In 2004 and 2005, Jazz Festivals were staged at the W.E.B. Dubois Centre in Accra, connected with European Week celebrations. Both were organised by Jimmy Beckley. Besides local bands, they included bands from Germany (Cafe de Sport), Nigeria (Orlando Julius), Liberia (Miatta Fahnbulleh) and Niger/Mali (Eddie Abdelrahmani). Moreover, in 2004, the Jazz Society of Ghana was formed by Sam Mensah and others which, in May 2005, hosted a tour of Ghana by the sixteen-piece University of Maryland Eastern Shores Jazz Ensemble. In 2006, the society invited the Amerucan blues singer and harmonica player Kellie Rucker. The most recent jazz spot in Accra is the +233 Club that opened around 2010, is located on the premises of the old Bassline/Jazz Optimist Club and whose resident jazz group is the Sound Factory that includes trombonist Eli Amewode, bassist Phillip Acquah, singer Sandra Housonon and guitarist Cliff Eck. In 2011, this club featured the American cool jazz soprano saxophonist Marion Meadow and his native Vibe Band. As mentioned in the Prologue, other later visiting jazzists were the vibes player Kenny Drew Junior (son of the famous jazz pianist of that name), the jazz guitarist Earl Klugh who played in Accra in 2015 alongside Big Wellingtons local jazz group, and the drummer Royal Hartigan who has recently brought his 'Blood Drum Spirit Ensemble' to Ghana on several occasions. Again, as mentioned in the Prologue, there are a number of important ongoing jazz festivals such as the Afrojazz Festival that began in 2013, organised by Paa K. Holbrook-Smith and Kofi Amoakohene of Scratch Studio; and the 'Stanbic Jazz Festivals' hosted since 2014 by Stanbic Bank, which in 2017 featured the American jazz saxophonist Gerald Albright and Cameroonian-born bassist Richard Bona. Then, in April 2018, the Alliance Francaise organised its fifth 'Live in Accra' Jazz Festival.

BIOGRAPHIES OF SOME AFRO-FUSION AND AFRO-JAZZ ARTISTS AND BANDS

BAWASABA

This Afro-fusion band was formed in the early 1990s by the trap-drummer Smart 'Afrakabi' Apeh Pozo Thompson who had his musical training with Ricky Telfer's Magic/Psychedelic Aliens and then Zongli Biiz (that included percussionist Okyerema Asante and bassist George Mc Bruce). He then joined Boombaya (originally called Cosmic Boom) that was the resident band at Wato's Club in Accra in the early 1970s. Smart went to the UK with this band on a trip organised by the Ghana University lecturers John Burney and Phillip Dean, and then he returned for a brief period to form Nokoko. This group actually recorded at my Bokoor Studio in 1982, but the situation in the country at the time was very difficult; so Smart left Ghana for the UK. He finally setteld back home in the late 1990s and formed his eight-member Bawasaba Afro-rock group in 2002 that is based at the restaurant belonging to him and his wife – Odo Rice Jazz Club in Kokomlemle. Bawasaba band, which specialises in Afro-jazz, includes guitarist Mallam Isaaka, Seth Amamoo on keyboards, Emmanuel Ashiagbor on bass guitar, Kofi Karikari on sax and Sir Isaac on trumpet.

THE AFRO-ROCK OF AMARTEY HEDZOLEH

Nii Amartey 'Lash' Laryea II is a singer and multi-instrumentalist from Accra who plays guitar, the one-stringed 'goje' fiddle of the Dagbon traditional area of northern Ghana, the 'wui' flute of Ghana's Upper East Region, the 'gyil' xylophone of the Upper West Region, as well as the West African 'donno' or 'dondo' pressure-drum and the Zimbabwean 'mbira' hand piano. I first met him when he and the bass player Jagger came to record at my Accra-based Bokoor Studio in 1982, 1985 and 1986. By this time, Amartey was calling his group 'Amartey Hedzoleh' and one of the Afro-rock songs I recorded in 1986, 'Dza Hunu Tso' appears on the 'Ghana Funk' album released by Hippo Records of Amsterdam in 2010.

At boarding school, Amartey learnt bass guitar from George Allen of the school pop-band. George later brought Amartey into the Magic (or Psychedelic) Aliens pop band for which George was the bass player. This Accra-band was led by Ricky Telfer and included the drummer Smart Apeh 'Pozo' Thompson, keyboard player Malek Crayem and Jagger Botchway on guitar. It released an 'Afro-pop' EP in the late 1960s that combined African rhythms with soul music and progressive rock.

The Magic Aliens also performed at the marathon Soul to Soul show held at Black Star (Independence) Square in Accra in 1971. The famous Ghanaian playwright Saka Acquaye was the then Director of the Ghana Arts Council that helped organize this show. In 1973, he provided some instruments to help Amartey form Hedzoleh Sounds ('peace' or 'freedom' in Ga) which included Jagger Botchway, Nat Hammond Leepuma on the local bamboo antenteben flute and ace congaist Nii Urpah 'Kanido' Fletcher of the Ramblers dance-band. Amartey then went on to get help from Faisal Helwani, the Ghanaian-Lebanese music promoter and owner of the Napoleon Club in Osu, Accra (see Chapter 59). Unfortunately, there was a misunderstanding with Faisal, and Amartey quit the band. Amartey travelled to the UK where he joined the Obuade drumming group, consisting of Mustapha Tettey Addy and others from the Addy family, and a group of dancers. After touring with Obuade, Amartey went to the US where he joined up with some members of the, by then, defunct Hedzoleh Sounds who had stayed on in the States after Faisal had sent them there on tour in 1974 with Hugh Masekela.

In the 1980s, Amartey did the sound-track for King Ampah's feature film 'The Road to Kukurantumi' with Amartey making a brief cameo appearance onstage at the Apollo Theatre in Accra. During the 1990s, Amartey spent a lot of time in the US as a solo artist and made appearances such as at President Clinton's inauguration show 'Americas Reunion on the Mall', the Smithsonian Institution's Festival of American Folklife, the Washington Folk Festival and the Takoma Park Festival. Amartey returned to Ghana in 2003 and still makes occasional appearances in Accra as a solo artist; for instance, at the British Council, at the Alliance Francaise (in 2009) and, in 2011, for Dick Essilfie-Bondzie's 80th birthday bash.

NII NOI NORTEY: AFRO-JAZZ FUSIONS

Afro-jazzist Nii Noi Nortey (on sax) and Mau Mau Musiki

Nii Noi was born in Accra in 1953. In the 1980s, he spent some time in the UK where he played saxophone with the Dade Krama group and the reggae band Misty and Roots. In 1988, he returned to Ghana and in the 1990s ran his Mau Mau Musiki band consisting of traditional African flutes hand-pianos flutes, percussion, wooden xylophones, blown conch-shell and the double-reed North African shawm. The group worked with Ghanaba and, in 1992, with the Pharoah Saunders Quintet at the Togolese Taxi Jazz Festival. Nii Noi's group is now known as Muziki w'Afrika and it plays a combination of traditional African music and free-jazz. Nii Noi is also the Director of the Anyah Arts Library in Accra that has a wide collection of music, books and art-pieces. His jazz inspiration comes from the late John Coltrane. Nii Noi has several Afro-jazz compositions based on the music of this famous African American saxophonist, who himself was inspired in the 1960s by African music. In 2007, Nii Noi's band, with percussionist NiiOtoo Annan and American musician and musicologist Steve Feld, released the CD 'Another Blue Train' dedicated to the 50th anniversary of both Ghanaian independence and the release of John Coltrane's classic 1957 album 'Blue Train.' Around 2010, Nii Noi he set up his latest outfit – the African Sound Project – with Ralph Karkari on guitar and Aminu and Naziru Kalangu on percussion. Nii Noi himself plays an Africanised form of the saxophone he calls an 'Afrifone'.

DABATRAM

Dabatram was an Afro-rock band run by the guitar-playing archaeologist Dr. Kodzo Gavua. It toured Ghana extensively in the 1990s and I once met him in the Ewe town of Tsito in 1995 (where I was doing some mobile recordings) playing to a thousand school-kids of Awudome Secondary School. Kodzo himself is an Ewe and was determined to expose the youth of the Volta Region to his brand of live music. Dabatram released two CDs that consist of highlifes, Afrobeats and Afro-rock songs in 4/4 time and in the 6/8 time of the Akan adowa and Ewe agbadza drum-dances. Violin and one-stringed gonje fiddle licks were added by German Thomas Woermle who is a long-time member of Ghana's National Symphony Orchestra. Dabatram's lyrics are in English, Ewe and Akan and dwell on issues of gender, Pan-Africanism and social commentary. He released a third CD in 2005 called 'Borborbor Mapouka'. Dr. Gavua is a member and one-time head of University of Ghana's Archeaology Department, specialising in ethno-archaeology. As many years ago I also did my B.A. degree in archaeology at that same Department, myself and Kodzo sometimes joke that we represent the tiny contingent of musical archaeologists in Ghana.

JIMMY BECKLEY: THE AFRO JAZZ COMBO

Saxophone player Jimmy Beckley began his musical career in the 1970s as a clarinettist in bands with his guitarist brother Robert. In fact, it is though Robert that I first met Jimmy in 1971 as a tall and gangly twelve year old boy, as Robert and myself were running an early version of Bokoor Band, then the second band to the Uhuru Dance Band. In the late 1970s, Jimmy often came to my flat at Temple House in James Town with Robert for jam sessions. Between 1983 and 1987, Jimmy ran his Jazz Club in Tesano, out of which came his Jazz and Highlife Combo. In 1989, the Combo released the 'Twilight of the Volta' album. Many top artists have played and jammed with

Jimmy's Combo, including the local jazz singers Rama Brew and Avalon, the traditional artists Captain Yaba and Atongo Simba, the highlife musicians Nat Buckle and Anthony Scorpion and the famous Cameroonian sax player Manu Dibango. Jimmy's Combo regularly played at the Labadi Beach Hotel and the Friday night jazz sessions at the Golden Tulip Hotel. He and his wife Dawn spent several years in the UK, but Jimmy is currently back in Ghana running his jazz group.

THE SANE KO YE AFRO-JAZZ ENSEMBLE

This fifteen-piece group was formed 2002 by master drummer Asabre Quaye (born 1971) and operates out of the Fair Gardens Hotel in Accra. As a youngster, Asabre was with the Egbaahi Gbiko children's Ga cultural group. His drumming talent was spotted by Faisal Helwani in 1980, who included Asabre in the Ebaahi group that worked with Mick Fleetwood, who was in Ghana that year making his 'The Visitor' film. After playing with Onipa Nua, the Pan African Orchestra and George Darko, Asebre left for London and arranged two tours for his cultural Saneko cultural group. The members of his current Sane Ko Ye Afro-jazz goup has moved from traditional to Afro-fusion music and includes members of the GBC and Marriots dance-bands, Kwesi Dankwah's Afro-rock Dzidudu outfit, with the bass player coming from the original Wulomei. Asabre spends some time in UK teaching drumming at schools organised by his partner Thomas Dadson who is the son of E.K. Dadson, one-time concert party performer and Minister in Nkrumah's CPP government. The bands patron is the chief of Shiashie, Nii Tetteh Opremeh II.

The Saneko Ye Afro-fusion group. Asabre Quaye on drums (photo Yemo Nunu)

MAC TONTOH AND THE OSIBISA KETE WARRIORS

The late Mac Tontoh of the pioneering Osibisaba Afro-rock band returned to Ghana in the 1990s and became an Executive of the Musicians Union of Ghana as well as a member of the National Commission on Culture. Mac built a recording and rehearsal studio in his house in Accra. He also set up his Osibisa Kete Warriors that comprised Mac on trumpet/flugel-horn with a huge battery of local percussion, which played everything from traditional music to Afro-fusion. His band played at a variety of venues, at jazz clubs, the National Theatre and at the more local setting of wake-keepings. According to Mac, his group combined the rhythms of the Ashantis with modern jazz. His Kete Warriors made several international tours and featured at the 2000 Edinburgh Festival.

ALFRED YOUNG

This guitarist comes from Peki-Kpalime in the Volta Region. He was influenced by rock guitarist Jimi Hendrix and jazz guitarists Wes Montgomery, Charlie Christian, Kenny Burrel and George Benson, as well as the homegrown highlife musicians Koo Nimo, Onyina and Kakaiku. He has been a professional guitarist since 1977, beginning in Kofi Ani Johnson's Parrots guitar band. He later joined the Talkatives in Tema, before moving to Abidjan for twenty years where he played with Alpha Blondie and the Asabea Cropper group that included her brother Eugene Cropper and Pope Fynn. Young then lived in South Africa for a while. When he returned to Ghana, he formed the Karmah jazz Band. Around 2010, he and his band played at the second 'Jazz and World Music Festival' held at the Alliance Francaise. From 2011, and with a smaller quartet, Young was playing regularly at the +233 Jazz Bar on Friday nights and for several years after that he worked with Aaron Bebe Sukura's Local Dimension band.

THE GOSPEL EXPLOSION – WOMEN ON STAGE

7

Highlife TIME 3

This looks at the main ways the initial hostility to women operating in the Ghanaian commercial popular has been overcome since the 1950s. Very important in this feminisation of popular music is the role of highlife gospel bands of the local separatist churches, which are providing a major avenue for women into Ghana's commercial music profession. Included are interviews with the concert party actress Vida Oparabea, singer Bibie Brew and leader of the Christo Asafo Mission, Prophet Safo.

Chapter 43

GHANAIAN GOSPEL MUSIC

The biggest development in the area of popular dance music in Ghana since the 1970s has been the efflorescence of local 'gospel-highlife' for both worship and outreach purposes by the hundreds of African separatist churches. Local gospel is now so prevalent that it is estimated that between 60 and 70% of all Ghana's local CD and cassette production are of this danceable religious music. But, before looking at the history of gospel, it should be noted that in Ghana there has been a long relationship between sacred church music and secular commercial local popular music. In fact, early forms of highlife music were influenced by missions, particularly the protestant ones that were set up in mid 19th century in southern Ghana, spreading western music through their churches, schools and trading posts. They taught Ghanaians to sing hymns, anthems and school songs; taught them to play harmoniums, pianos and brass instruments and introduced musical practices such as the diatonic scale, I-IV-V harmonic progressions, part singing, four-bar phrasing and the sol-fa notation.

The origins of the current gospel music boom goes back to the 19th century creation of vernacular language hymns, and the early 20th century use of dance by the Ghanaian separatist churches. Both the use of local languages and dance was initially strongly opposed by the white missionaries. The first evidence of hymns in local Ghanaian languages were the 'Ebindidwom" (Indigenous music) of the Cape Coast area of Ghana, created by local catechists as early as the mid-19th century due to the shortage of European missionaries, who quickly died of malaria in Ghana, then known as 'the white-man's grave'.

However, a more important wave of vernacular hymnody began from the 1880s which resulted from a switch in the British colonial system of administration. Before the 1880s, the British had fostered the growth of a local christianised African coastal elite made up of merchants, clerks and lawyers who had acted as middlemen on the matter of inland trade. However, after the 1880s, the British moved to a policy known as 'indirect rule' through traditional chiefs and thus began to see the local educated elite and merchants as a threat. So they enacted various pieces of racist legislation to prevent these elites from holding any institutional power. This change of policy was a result of two factors. Firstly there was availability of the anti-malarial drug quinine which, at first, had been derived in small quantities from the bark of a South American tree; but which, by the 1880s, was being grown in large plantations in Ceylon and industrially manufactured in Germany. As a result, British traders and colonial officers could move inland, even into the most strongly malarial areas and therefore no longer needed the services of the Ghanaian coastal middle-men who, being African, had a natural partial defence against malaria (i.e. the sickle cell factor). The second reason for the shift in British colonial rule was the Berlin Conference of 1884/1885 in which the European powers divided up Africa. It was after this 'Scramble for Africa' that Britain decided to rapidly expand its rule through local inland chiefs and emirs rather than though the coastal elites who, as a result, became marginalized from institutional power.

Not surprisingly, members of these African elites became disillusioned with the British and their new policy of 'indirect rule' through traditional chiefs. As a result, some of them, like J.E. Casely-Hayford of Ghana and Herbert Macauley of Nigeria, began to establish the early West African nationalist movement. Other educated Africans began to set up separatist churches such as the Native Baptist Church and United African Native Church, which pioneered the use of vernacular hymns. By the 1920s, important composers of this local choral genre were Reverend Allotey Papoe and Dr. Ephraim Amu of Ghana as well as Thomas King Ekundayo Phillips and Reverend J.J. Ransome-Kuti of Nigeria (Fela Kuti's grand-father). The South African equivalent was Enoch Sontonga who in the 1890s wrote the famous African nationalist hymn 'Sikelele I'Afrika' (God Bless Africa).

During the 1920s and 1930s, a second wave of separatist churches appeared which, rather than drawing on local elite congregations, appealed to the new rural migrants and poor of the rapidly-growing towns and cities. Unlike western Christian churches, these more proletarian 'spiritual' or apostolic churches followed the traditional African practice of spiritual healing, exorcism, divination (i.e. prophecy), possession (i.e. by the Holy Ghost) and the worship of God on one's feet through dance. Early examples of such Africanised Christian churches that allowed religious dancing were the African Faith Tabernacle, the Musama Disco Christo Church, the Apostolic Revelation Church in Ghana; and in Nigeria, Aladura Church and the Cherubim and Seraphim Church. Another was the Church of the Twelve Apostles set up in Ghana during the 1920s by followers of the Cote d'Ivoire-based Liberian prophet William Wade Harris, after he had been imprisoned in 1914 by the French authorities who believed that his African version of Christianity was anti-colonial.

African Separatist Christian Church with singing and dancing congregations

Besides dancing, these break-away churches also allowed the use of local percussion instruments. For instance, the Church of the Twelve Apostles not only clapped and swayed but also danced to the rhythms of gourd rattles, whilst the Musama Disco Christo Church employed traditional Fanti 'asafo' (warrior) drums. By the 1940s, the

419

'praises' and 'choruses' of these spiritual churches were being influenced by highlife songs, as were their acapella 'singing bands' (like the See There group in Kumasi) that began to record in the late 1930s. By the 1950s, some of these churches even began to employ highlife band instruments. The Mark Hayford Baptist Mission, the Zion Church, the Nigrition Church and Apostolic Revelation Society Church all played religious versions of danceable brass-band highlife, whilst church-based singing bands like the Yaw Ofori Singing Band of Kwahu employed the guitars, bongos and double bass of contemporary highlife guitar bands. Partly helped by their Africanised format, the spiritual churches began to proliferate; so that by 1955 there were seventeen denominations in Accra alone.

Whilst during the 1940s and 1950s the spiritual churches were beginning to use local popular dance music, a few highlife guitar band of those times also began to compose highlife songs with Christian messages. For instance, between 1950 and 1955, E.K. Nyame released 'Mo Nnyi Nyankopon Aye' (Let's Praise God) and 'Jesus Christo' on the local Teymani label, whilst Gyak's guitar Band released 'Pepeepe' (Equal before God) in 1954 via the Swiss Union Trading Company.

By the early 1970s, the first anticipatory ripples of the current wave of gospel music surfaced, partly infuenced by Amercian 'hot' gospel music introduced by records. This danceable Black American music was pioneered in the 1930s by Thomas Dorsey, Mahalia Jackson, Speer Family and Soul Stirrers; followed in the late 1940s and 1950s by the Sensational Nightingales, James Cleveland, the Davis Sisters and Jim Reeves- and then the 1960s gospel-soul artists like the Staple Singers, Al Green, Aretha Franklin, Dinah Washington and Sam Cooke. One of the first Ghanaian gospel bands was Emmanuel Lartey's Joyful Way Singers of Cape Coast, formed in 1972. According to George Brenyah[28], the Joyful Way Singers group was formed in 1972[29] by students from Mfantsipim School, Adisadel and Wesley Girls one year after the African American Evangelist Danny Santa Lucia came to their schools with a team of tambourines players and guitarists who sang 'negro spirituals' and gospel songs.

It was also in 1972 that the secular highlife composer Love Nortey (co-leader of the Happy Stars concert party) began releasing gospel-highlifes such as 'Mesi Me Dan Wo

[28]A University of Ghana student who wrote a paper on local gospel for my Process of Art course in 2010 in which he interviewed one of Joyful Way's early members, Gordon Egyir-Croffet.
[29]Actually, two groups – 'Noise of Joy' and 'Evangels' - came together to form Joyful Singers in 1972, having existed at least a year before as separate groups. The members were drawn from Mfantsipim and Wesley Girls for 'Noise of Joy', and Adisadel and Wesley Girls for 'Evangels'.

Obotan So' (I Will Build my House on a Rock). 1972 was also the year that the guitar band musician Kofi Abraham in Kumasi formed his Sekyedumasi Gospel Band that released 'Hwehwe Na Wo Be Hu' (Look and You Shall Find) on the Ambassador Records label, followed by other gospel-highlife hits such as 'Spiritual Osode', 'Amen' and 'Sweet Jesus'. In the mid-1970s, Ani Johnson's Parrots guitar band released its first gospel song 'Iesu Wo Nkyen Na Metene' whilst the highlife singer and guitarist C.K. Mann released 'Enigye Wo Soro Ho'.

However, the current gospel 'explosion' of the spiritual charsimatic and later pentacostal churches really began in the late 1970s, when it became obvious that use of popular dance music for church 'praises' and 'choruses' drew large congregations. A critical trigger for this 'explosion' was a series of economic and political changes that began in Ghana from the late 1970s.

The first factor was the economic decline of Ghana during the 'kalabule' (corruption) military regime of Acheampong-Akufo, when the music industry collapsed and many musicians left Ghana. For the many artists who remained behind in Ghana, the local dancing churches provided one of the few venues for their music. After 1979, the economic problems facing the Ghanaian commercial pop artist got no better due to revolutionary upheavals, night curfews and a massive import duty on band instruments which are the 'tools of trade' for musicians. On the other hand, the churches, being charitable bodies, did not have to pay import duties, or for that matter a pre-paid entertainment tax on gate fees. So, even more popular music performers went under the wings of the churches, who provided instruments and, in many cases, a small salary.

Some of the highlife artists who moved into gospel-highlife to varying degrees in the 1980s were A.B Crentsil, C.K Mann, Paapa Yankson, Kofi Sammy, Carlos Sakyi, Nana Ampadu, Jewel Ackah, T.O. Jazz, A.K. Yeboah, Ani Johnson, J.A. Adofo, Daddy Lumba, Francis Kenya, Safohene Djene and K. K. Kabobo. I also saw this actually happen in my own Bokoor Studio as, in 1981, most of the highlife artists coming to record were from the secular side, with gospel bands being in the minority. By the late 1980s, the situation had completely reversed, with most of the bands being church-based ones, recording the same danceable highlife and played by the very same musicians, but of course with the lyrics being of a religious nature.

By the 1980s, local gospel music was in full swing. In 1983, Kofi Abraham formed his Nyame Bekyere (God will Provide) Band whose first release was 'Psalm 23'. Then, in 1987, he set up the Kofi Abraham Gospel Band which went on to release twenty-five commercial cassettes and albums. Other big names of the 1980s were Mary Ghansah, the Tagoe Sisters, Samuel Grippman and his Ministries Gospel Group, Ola Williams, Stella Dugan, Leslie Tex Buabasah and the Saints, Reverend Yaw Agyeman-Benjamin (YABS), Daughters of Glorious Jesus, Jesse Jones and the various gospel bands set up by Prophet Safo (see chapter 45). By 1990, gospel music had become so popular that the Rawlings' PNDC government of the time instructed the state Ghana Broadcasting Corporation to reduce the amount of gospel music radio air-play time by half – down from sixty to thirty percent.

Despite these government sanctions, gospel music continued to boom. So much so that, during the 1990s, a whole host of new local gospel artists and stars came onto the scene, such as Diana Akiwumi, Stella Dugan, Mary Ghansah, Soul Winners, Reverend Michael Osei Bonsu, Reverend Charlie Sam, Suzzy & Matt, Reverend George Owusu-Mensah, Cindy Thompson, Carlos Sakyi, Naana Frimpong, Javes Jonathan Addo, Helena Rhabbles, Yaw Sarpong, Francis Adjei, Joe Beecham, Hannah Marfo, Juliet Antwi and Amy Newman. Then came Alabaster Box, Elder Collins Amponsah, Akwasi Boateng and Jane & Bernice. More recent are No Tribe, Miracle Wave Band, Ohemma Mercy, Ernest Opoku, Nii Okai and Celestine Donkor. As can be seen, women singers played a prominent role in gospel and, as will be discussed in the next chapter, it would be true to say that they have came to dominate this music genre.

I should mention that yet another reason for the upsurge of gospel highlife is that the message of the local separatist churches was 'this worldly' rather than the 'other-worldly' one of the orthodox European churches which preach that one can only attain heavenly happiness after ones dies. It was this 'prosperity message' (in this life) of the spiritual, charismatic and Pentecostal churches that led them to develop a quasi-commercial business orientation (including musical enterprises). With their Christian businessmen's breakfasts and fellowships, these churches filled an entrepreneurship vacuum in the early revolutionary and anti-private-business early to mid-eighties' period of the PNDC government.

Cinemas like the Orion and Palladium as well as open air dance-spots like the Apollo Theatre have been taken over by huge all-night church crusades and filled with the gospel music.

Some churches have even set up their own recording studios. One of the earliest was the Jesus Above All Studio set up in East Legon Accra in the late 1980s. Others that followed include the Gentiles Revival Ministry and Christian Music Studios in Accra; and the Holy Spirit Digital and Jehova Nissi Studios in Kumasi. Many other leading general music studios in Ghana are also involved with gospel recordings. Here, I will name a few of these studios (and their engineers). In Accra there is Quantum Studio (engineer Morris), Vision Audio Laboratory (T.V.O. Lamptey), TLL Studio (Zapp Mallet), Brain Studio (Roland Best), Albert Oparrah Mensah's Digital Studio, PSI Studio, Nacy Studio and Despite Studio. In Tema, there is Master Mix (Sammy Helwani), Crystal Bay (Steve) and ARC (Boamah) and, in Kumasi, Nana Yaw Owoahene's Audio Logic Studio and Garth Studio.

Since the 1990s, many of the local churches and their musicians have also gone into cassette/CD production and distribution. Some examples of these companies are JaBenz (Jane and Bernice), Daughters (of Glorious Jesus) Productions, Esther Smith Productions, Joyful Way Incorporated, Uncle Fifi's Productions, Reverend Michael Osei Bonsu's KMP Company, His Majesty Gospel Music Shops in Accra and Kumasi, the Church of Pentecost Productions, Christian Music Shop, Spirit Records, Holy Ghost International, SDA Missionary, Reverend Ben Danquah Productions, Diana Akiwumi Productions, Reverend Francis Boahene Productions and the JBA Missionary.

Local churches have also initiated national gospel award competitions and taken over commercial cinemas and open air dance-spots – like the Orion, Palladium and Apollo Theatre – for huge all-night church crusades filled with gospel music. Morevoer, since the late 1990s, some churches and gospel artists have moved into film and video TV clip production, like the Tagoe Sisters 'Anka Matete', Edward Akwasi Boateng 'Ntie Atesem Hunu' and Lord 'Cosky' Amofa's 'Atenbuo' that is about a preacher trying to dissuade a man from taking alcohol, cigarettes and cocaine.

Gospel has become so prevalent that unions for gospel artists have been established in the 1990s such as the Presbyterian Singing Band Union, the Gospel Pioneers Association and the gospel branch of the Ghana Musicians Union (MUSIGA). Indeed, a past president of MUSIGA was the gospel singer Diana Hopeson (previously called Akiwumi). Furthermore, in just the last few years, a new FM radio station Radio or Channel R (i.e. Religion) was set up in Accra that exclusively played gospel music.

In short, the local Ghanaian churches and their new gospel highlife have become training grounds for dance-band instrumentalists, a haven for old-time highlife artists, a ritual space for cathartic dance sessions, an arena for moral sermons, a sector for the music business and a major avenue for professional female singers.

Chapter 44

WOMEN ENTER GHANAIAN POP MUSIC: VIDA OPARABEA AND BIBIE BREW

Up until the 1950s, there were very few women operating in the Ghanaian popular music and concert party scenes. These were not thought to be 'decent' professions for women to enter, as they involved exposing themselves to the public gaze on-stage. Moreover, highlife bands and concert bands were associated with palm-wine bars, drunkenness, loose living and an itinerant life-style. The few exceptions in the late 1920s and 1930s were the singers Akosua Bonsu and Aku Tawia who respectively accompanied George Aingo's Fanti guitar/accordion songs and Squire Addo piano songs, released by the British Zonophone Recording Company. Then there was Lady Wilmot, the actress who was with the Axim Trio before it began the practice of undertaking long tours of Ghana, and so had to begin employing female impersonators who could put up with the rough life on the road.

However, in the mid-1950s, some of the dance bands began employing women singers, like Julie Okine and Agnes Ayitey who worked with the Tempos. Then, in the 1960s and early 1970s, many female highlife and pop musicians entered the scene, such as Lola Everett, Charlotte Dada, alto-saxist Eugenia Asabea Cropper, Christie Azuma (with the Upper Internationals), the concert party leader/guitarist Vida Rose and Joanna Okang who sang with the Uhuru band (see her photo in Chapter 58). In

Julie Okine at the Coconut Grove Accra. (Photo Drum Magazine July 1961)

addition, there were the more traditionally-oriented pop musicians such as the Ewe singer Efua Dorkenoo and Naa Amanua who was with the Wulomei and Suku Ga cultural groups, before forming her own Odumankoma Troupe. At the same time, a host of top concert party actresses also began to appear on the local entertainment scene, such as Margaret Quainoo, Adelaide Buabeng and Esi Kom, who will be referred to again later. It was also in the 1970s that a wave of important guitar band highlife singers came onto the scene like, like Mum Bea, Janet Osei, Awura Ama and Nana Adjele.

They were followed in the 1980s and 1990s by Abena Nyanteh, Akosua Amoam, Akosua Agyepong, Yaa Oforiwa, Nana Yaa, Philo Selassie, Lady Lartey, Lady Burger and ace Liberian drummer Esther Muna Binta who played with the GBC band.

Another was Lady Talata Heidi from northern Ghana, who began singing professionally in 1975 at fifteen years old with the Skyhawks/Sweet Melodians, and then in 1977 with the Black Anchor of the Black Star Line state corporation, Tommy Darling's band and the Sweet Beans, before moving on to release her own albums.

More recent is the trumpeter Joana Denaka (played with Amakye Dede, Paapa Yankson, C.K. Mann and Ebo Taylor) and the vocalists Ivy Stone (who owns her own recording studio in Kokrobite), Princess Cynthia (ex-Marriots band and now a solo artist) and Afua Ampofowa who has worked with Nana Tuffour, Daddy Lumba, Sloopy Mike Gyamfi, Kwame Appiah and Oheneba Kissi. Then, there is Nana Yaa, the daughter of Pat Thomas and Lola Everett, who made her first public appearance in the mid-1990s during a youth show at the Efua Sutherland Children's Park to raise funds for SOS Ghana Children's Home. Another is Paulina Oduro, a Fanti raised in Ghana, Japan and in the UK, who has worked as a singer with Alfred Kari Bannerman and numerous reggae and soca artists like Casanova, Mighty Sparrow and Lord Kitchener. In the mid-1990s, Oduro recorded with the Western Diamonds and, in 1999, released her first album 'Women Power' in which she was supported by Bessa Simons, Kwame Yeboah and Kari Bannerman. In May 2011, she teamed up with Ackah Blay and his Abiza Band for the celebration of Mother's Day at the Citizen Kofi Entertainment Spot in Accra.

Another important lady singer is Della Hayes who obtained her training with Sunsum and the GBC Band before forming an all-female band in 2009 called Dzesi (or Women of Colour) that was for a time based at the MUSIGA headquarters in Accra and currently regularly plays at the +233 Jazz Club. There are also a few lady hiplifers like Aberewa Nana, Triple M and Mzbel and others mentioned in Chapter 38 as well as a growing number of artists who do Afro-pop versions of contemporary R&B and soul. These include Efya (Jane Awindor), Sala Yacubu, Eazzy (Mildred Ashong), Irene Logan, Raquel Ammah, Ruby Nunoo, and the Liberian-born Jane Logan. Then, there is Yasmin Helwani, the daughter of music promoter Faisal Helwani, and Becca (Rebecca Akosua Acheampong) who obtained her musical training in the church choir to which her mother and father belonged.

Mention must also be made of some of the recent crop of artistess who began their careers as studio backing singers. One is Yvonne Ohene Djan who has worked with numerous artists including Daddy Lumba, Ofori Amponsah, George Darko, Tic Tac,

Sidney, Lord Kenya, Reggie Rockstone, Kwabena Kwabana and Obour. Then there is Anomaa Okore who, since 2008, has worked with Lucky Mensah, Rex Omar, Samini, Castro, Kofi B and Amandzeba. Then, there is Afua Ampofowaa who began her singing career with the Kristo Asafo Band at eleven years old and then worked as a backing singer with Daddy Lumba, Sloopy Mike Gyamfi and Nana Tuffour before releasing a number of albums from 1995 in a modern highlife mode. Some others are Elivava (Tina Mensah Gbevi) who released her first album 'Elivava' (God is truly alive) in 2008 and Beverly Tawiah who appeared on Kojo Antwi's 2009 album 'Mwaah'.

A number of women now perform in the contemporary R&B and neo-soul influenced 'Afro-pop' style that has recently emerged in Ghana. This style is dealt with in both the book's Coda and Prologue – and some of the women artists discussed are as follows: Rebecca 'Becca' Akosua Acheampong, Jane 'Efya' Awindor, Irene Logan, Sala Yacubu, Lady Jaywah, Mildred 'Eazzy' Ashong, Bertha 'Yaa Yaa' Kankam, Antoinette 'Tiffany' Owusu, Joy Jasmine Onyinyechukwu 'Adomaa' Serwaa Adjeman, Raquel Naa Ayorkor Ammaha, MzVee, Ebony, Kaakie, Adina Thembi Ndamse and Noella Wiyaala. Many of this new crop of Afro-pop divas obtained their music training in church choirs and gospel bands. Infact, women singers dominate the local Ghanaian gospel scene that surfaced in the 1970s and 80s. This religious form of dance music and some of its outstanding singers are dealt with later in the chapter.

REASONS FOR THE ENTRANCE OF WOMEN INTO GHANA POP SINCE THE 1950S

The growing prominence of Ghanaian women pop artists over the last fifty years or so can be put down to five major reasons: the effect of Nkrumah's government policies, the impact of foreign women super-stars, the television medium, the utilisation of traditional music by commercial Ghanaian 'folkloric' or 'cultural' groups, and the boom in local gospel dance-music. Let us take each of these in turn

ONE: NKRUMAH'S GOVERNMENTAL POLICIES BOOSTS WOMEN ONSTAGE

In the early 1960s when President Nkrumah set up concert parties that were associated with the Workers' Brigade and Farmer's Councils, he encouraged the employment of actresses, most important being Margaret Quainoo (stage name Araba Stamp), Comfort Akua Dompo and Adelaide Buabeng. Female roles had previously been performed by 'lady impersonators', with the exception of the previously-mentioned Lady Wilmot, and later Perpetual Hammond of the Bob Vans Ghana Trio. When Nkrumah's state-supported concert parties were dissolved, many of the actresses then joined Efua Sutherland's group, Kusum Agoromba, that itself had emerged out of the Nkrumah-supported Ghana Drama Studio.

TWO: FOREIGN FEMALE POP STARS ENCOURAGE GHANAIAN FEMALE ARTISTS

This liberating influence began in 1940s and 1950s with the records of American (particularly black) women who sang with swing type jazz bands; like Ella Fitzgerald, Sarah Vaughan and also Velma Middleton who came to Ghana in 1956 with Louis Armstrong. E.T. Mensah's Tempos was influenced by imported swing music and so, in the mid-1950s, they began to include lady singers on stage, like Julie Okine and Agnes Ayitey. Later came the music of foreign women who sang pop-music and soul. Particularly important were Millicent Small (who toured Ghana in the 1960s), Tina Turner, Roberta Flack and the Staple Singers who visited Ghana in 1971. Also significant was the South African singer Miriam Makeba (herself affected by the Andrew Sisters and Ella Fitzgerald) who made several tours of Ghana during the seventies. More recent are visits by Dionna Warwick, Jermain Jackson, Nina Simone and Rita Marley.

THREE: TELEVISION PROVIDES AN AVENUE FOR CONCERT PARTY ACTRESSES

Television concert parties started soon after this media was created by Nkrumah in Ghana in the mid-sixties. And both for the sake of TV realism and because they did not involve the on-the-road hazards of touring concert parties, TV groups included many women. From the early seventies, long-lasting concert party television series began with Jatakrom, Osofo Dadzie and later Obra, the Adabraka Drama Group and more recently Cantata. Some of the most well-known TV concert actresses/singers who have passed through these groups are Esi Kom, Beatrice Kissi, Joyce Agyeman, Florence Mensah, Mary Adjei, Cecilia Adjei and Grace Omaboe or 'Maame Dokono', the leader of the Obra concert group. Many are now TV personalities (Grace Omaboe is Ghana's equivalent of Oprah Winfrey) or are involved in the local video productions that have become popular since the late 1980s.

E.T. Mensah and his Tempos with Agnes Ayitey in the mid-1950s

FOUR: THE TRADITIONAL 'FOLKLORIC' FACTOR

Also helping women artists is that some highlife musicians have been going back to their roots and taking traditional performance out of the local communal context and 'folklorising' them by them putting them onstage and/or into recording studios. As traditional Ghanaian music has always involved women, these folkloric or 'cultural' highlife artists also employ women. For example, when the Ga highlife musician Nii Ashitey formed Wulomei (traditional priests) in the early seventies that utilises Western guitars and indigenous percussion, he also included women singers and percussionists, like Naa Amanua; for the traditional Ga priesthood always included women. Likewise, when Koo Nimo's appears onstage with his odonson style group that combines palmwine guitar with local percussion, he employs lady singers, as is common in traditional Akan music-making.

FIVE: THE GOSPEL AVENUE FOR FEMALE SINGERS & RECORDING ARTISTS

The fifth factor empowering professional female artists in recent years is linked to the gospel dance music of the multiplying African separatist Christian churches. As mentioned in the previous chapter, gospel music has become so popular that, today, it comprises about sixty percent of the commercial output of CDs in Ghana. And, as

430

over half the gospel singers are women, one could truly say that women are now the dominant voice in Ghanaian popular music. A far cry from the situation of sixty years ago. This has happened because highlife bands have moved into the churches and so parents can no longer forbid their daughters from singing this type of dance-music, as it is now classed as religious music. As a result, today a new generation of trained women singers, such as the Afro-pop ones mentioned above, are making an impact on Ghanaian popular music similar to that African American gospel-trained singers like Aretha Franklin, Dina Washington and Tina Turner made on the United States pop scene in the 1960s and 1970s.

Although it is impossible to list all the Ghanaian lady gospel artistes over the last twenty years, the following are some of the top names: Mary Ghansah, Daughters of Glorious Jesus, Tagoe Sisters, Stella Dugan, Mary Ghansah, Josephine Dzodzegbe, Mavis Sackey, Evelyn Boakye, Esther Nyamekye, Suzzy and Matt, Diana Akiwumi, Cindy Thompson, Helena Rhabbles, Juliet Antwi, Esther Quartey, Juliana Acheampong, Marian Anquandah, Amy Newman, Akua Serwaa Rita, Getty Oduro, Bertha Oboagye, Naana Frimpong, Mary Agyepong, Sandra Oduro, Jane and Bernice, Ama Boahemma, Esther Smith, Esther Amoako, Hannah Marfo, Lady Prempeh, Diana Asamoah, Agnes Opoku-Agyeman, Margaret Mensah, Abena Amponsah, Abena Amankwa, Florence Obinim, Grace Ashy, Phillipa Baafi, Christiana Love, Sister Vivian, Jude Lomotey, Celestine Donkor and Diana Bimpong.

To close this chapter on how women have entered the popular music field, I will let four women speak. Firstly I will briefly turn to the previously mentioned 1950s highlife singer Julie Okine and, then, the choral musician Dinah Reindorf.

Below are the lyrics of Julie Okine's song 'Nothing But A Man's Slave' that was released by the E.T. Mensah's Tempos dance band (Decca WA 808) in 1957/8.

VERSE

I went down town one Saturday night just for a bottle of beer,
I met a lovely Cape Coast boy looking so nice and sweet,
He stepped into a taxi-cab heading straight for me,
We went to a busy nightclub and he asked for table for two,
We went into a private saloon and he asked for gin-and-lime,
I searched into my breast pocket nothing was left for me.

Nungua Minstrel Choir in 1984 (this church band recorded at Bokoor Studio)

CHORUS

He want to know my name, he wishes to know my game
If I died of a man's love, I'm nothing but a man's slave.

Secondly, here are some reflections on women in music by Dinah Reindorf, one-time Head of the Ghana National Symphony Orchestra, and Director of the thirty-two strong Dwenesie Choir that she formed in the mid-1970s. This group has released records, appeared on television and represented Ghana at festivals like Nigeria's FESTAC 1977.

People here tend to look upon music as something of a man's world; and I remember being asked at FESTAC '77 after a performance how I felt about being in a man's world, during a television interview. I found the question rather amusing because I cannot find any good reason why women cannot progress in music or any other field of work. I believe there should be no labels. I even have a lady in my choir who is a welder in the Fire Service. We have two hands, two feet and a mind we can apply. In music, the main thing is to have a feel for it and to be able to express yourself through it. Women, especially in Africa, find it

432

easier to express themselves. So I think the idea of keeping them in the background is out of this time. There is so much women can do – and with such grace. They bring enhancement and balance to most things.

Finally, and in more detail, I will let the concert party singer/actress Vida Oparabea Hynes and the pop diva Bibie Brew speak about how they got into the music profession and the various problems they encountered[30].

THE STORY OF VIDA OPARABEA HYNES

VIDA: I used to see concert parties when I was a child in Adeiso [Central Region] as two or three of them used to come a week as Adeiso is on a main route. I used to do odd jobs for them as I was a tomboy. Then, when I was about eleven (1961), I do remember watching Akompis concert party and when I saw all these women on stage (actually men in drag), I thought *great then I've got a job*. So I asked the leader and he asked me how old I was; I lied and told him thirteen. He told me to wait until I had grown up a bit and he'd marry me instead. That was a joke he made, but it gave me the inspiration to keep on trying.

And the very first time I joined a concert was when I really was thirteen and I went with my cousin Amma, who was four years older than me. She was playing in a band called Okutieku (Oku listens to Oku) run by a Fanti from Agona Swedru who played guitar, sang songs and did magic tricks – he was a 'Professor.' Amma, whose boyfriend was in the group, dressed as a female or played the parts of an Agyanka Ba (orphan child). Amma had also run away from home to join the concert and she had had a baby with a bandsman which had made her parents disown her. I went with her on trek (tour) for three months and I played sticks (claves) in the band, as well as running errands and doing laundry so that the group would let me act on stage later on.

After the three months, I came back to Adeiso as the concert party was on break. My mum was panicking and the whole town was thinking that I had been killed. I hadn't told my family, as I knew they wouldn't understand. After the break, the band went on the road again and was coming through Adeiso to perform at another town fifty kilometres north. So Amma and I both got ready to be picked up and were waiting at the central mango tree when I saw some police, but it didn't occur to me that they were after me. Then, when we saw the concert bus coming and ran towards it, the next thing

I inteviewed Vida in the early 1990s and Bibie in 2009.

433

I know is that four policemen caught me and put me in jail overnight as a runaway child, so that I wouldn't get chance to join the concert at the town where they were playing. The police told me that my sister's husband had put them up to it, to capture me and stop me joining the band. So next day I refused to go to the farm with my mum. I knew where the band would be as I had their itinerary. I packed up my things next morning and told my mum that I was going to market to buy things; but I went off and joined the band. I acted twice with them on that tour, once as an Agyanka Ba and once as a prostitute.

JC: What was the attitude of the band members to having women on trek with them?

VIDA: At first the band manager didn't like the idea as he thought it a bad omen or bad luck for women to move around with males, even as wives or girlfriends. Especially when a female has menstruation and touches band instruments, as the band may not then succeed. The leader thought menstruation affects the spirit or energy of the group. A lot of men in Ghana think that if a female is having menstruation, she should not cook dinner for her husband or should not sleep with him. Menstruating women should just lay low. My friend Amma was accepted because she was doing a very good job bringing a lot of crowd, and a lot of women came in to see a female doing something, besides watching men impersonate women. When I came in, I was accepted as I helped cook.

JC: As a woman did you ever had trouble with the audience?

VIDA: The townspeople used to call us 'ashawo' or prostitutes and I remember once beating one of them up. It was a woman and she said to me 'You small kid, you should be at home helping your mother or going to school.' This was before the show and I was outside the theatre collecting tickets whilst someone else with me was stamping hands. So I said 'Look it doesn't mean if you play band, all the band members sleep with you, unless you want them to; and that's your choice. So none of them are my boyfriends and anyway I'm too young to have one. I'm just trying to learn the concert ropes'. The woman said she didn't believe me and said I was a little prostitute. One of the men who was with her said 'We men are waiting for you to grow up so we can marry you and all you can do is follow a bunch of musicians around'.

Then the woman said that if she was my sister she would beat me. I said 'O.K. go ahead and pretend I'm your sister and come and beat me.' So I called her 'kwasia' (foolish) and provoked her and she slapped me. I got hold of her and twisted her neck and I nearly snapped it. I also scratched the women's face like Ga people do. When the police came in and asked who threw the first punch, everybody said it was her. So I was released and the police told my boss to tell me not to punch the audience.

JC: Didn't your family every try again to stop you working with concert groups?

VIDA: Once when I came back on trek with Okutieku's band and we were on a three-month break, my mum took me and three of my girlfriends, who she thought were a bad influence on me, to the chief's house in Adeiso. Two were prostitutes and the other my cousin Amma. My mum blamed them, as they are older than me and should know better and not give me that encouragement to join a concert party. The reason they encouraged me was that I was a good dancer. You see, from when I was four until I was nine years old, my uncle, who was a salesman, took me to Nigeria and Kano, and you should see me do a Nigerian dance, you'd just fall in love with me. I was into all kinds of dances, although nobody taught me, as I was exposed to the Tigari and Koku cults on my father's side and the Blekete and Yewe cults on my mother's side. Every time I hear music my body tells me how to move and what to do.

So my three friends and I were taken to the chief's house at three in the morning and my mum gave him a bottle of schnapps to have him talk to us. The chief gave us a long lecture and we didn't leave until seven in the morning. The lecture was on what a woman should do and be, and what her chores are. A woman should get married and have and raise a child. A young woman should be at home helping her mother and should be going to farm. A woman should have her own job, like trading and marketing. A woman has no place where a man is and should understand that she is the last person who counts when it comes to men.

These were heavy, heavy talks. I was yawning and the four of us girls were making little laughs. But the chief didn't notice, otherwise he would have charged us for that. In the end, he said 'I have a job for you' as he had a huge sugar-cane farm three miles from Adeiso. He said "You guys look after this farm and I'll give you about two acres of it'. We looked at each other and we knew we could use the money, so we said "Sure we'll take it". So we took over the sugar-cane farm and did a lot of weeding, cut the sugar-

435

cane and hired people to come in and carry the cane to the market where we sold it. We paid the chief fifty percent and kept fifty of the money. That was the deal.

So when three months passed, I told the chief that I was going to Accra to go to school and he said that was a good idea. But, actually, I joined another concert party in Labadi (Accra) for a while. Later, I remained in Accra and bought myself a kiosk in Makola Market and used to travel to Togo, Benin and Nigeria to buy perfumes, cosmetics and things to fill up my kiosk.[31]

THE INTERNATIONAL SINGING DIVA BIBIE BREW

Bibie Brew was born in Accra in 1957 and comes from a musical family, as her uncle was King Bruce of the Black Beats band and her father the famous ex-Tempos and Rhythm Aces saxist Spike Anyankor. However, she and her sisters were raised by her grand-parents Mr. and Mrs. Kwesi Brew who they came to call 'mum' and 'dad'. As Bibie's grandfather Kwesi Brew was an international lawyer, diplomat and poet, he and his family travelled a lot. As Bibie explained to me, it was on these trips abroad she first realised she had a musical talent.

> *The first time I realised I could sing was in Mexico. I was seven years old and was watching a pop show on television where they were doing the jerk and popcorn, and the Beatles were doing 'She Loves me Yeah Yeah.' Then, when I was eleven, we moved to Senegal and my (grand) parents were completely gaga for good music; people would come over and bring records of Stan Getz, Nat King Cole and Motown. I was naturally singing these songs. When we were holding receptions, I would be good for the whole week so that I could beg my mum for me to plan a mini show with my friends. Initially my mum said 'no way.' So I said, "Let us do a rehearsal for you" and she let us do our first show.*

Back in Ghana, 1971 Bibie was musically 'outdoored' when she took part in a talent scout show at the Workers College Institute of Language, organised by her 'Uncle Beattie' – Beattie Casely-Hayford, the Director of GBC. This led to her doing her first television program, singing the Nat King Cole song 'Answer Me' at the Arts Centre in Accra and supported by her sisters Rama and Ginger – as she describes:

---

[31]Vida later married and settled in Canada where she ran the mixed Ghanaian Afro-Caribbean 'Afro-Canada Dance Troupe' in Toronto. Twenty-years ago, and with her husband Julian, she returned home to Adeiso.

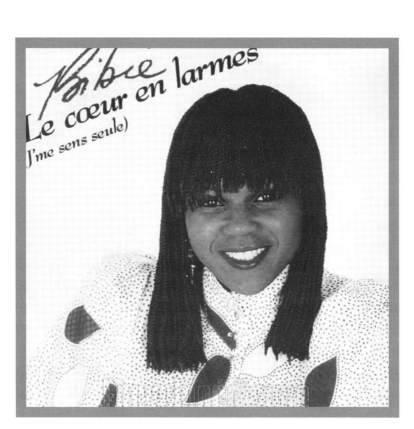

Bibie Brew album cover

We had to hide it from my (grand) parents because, at that time of the night, we were not supposed to be out. And this driver would pick us up from school and we had to find a plot tell our parents. So our Aunty Nora had to plan the whole thing and work on the costumes with me and my sisters.

She then started to sing with one of her uncle King Bruce's bands, the Barbecues and also played with Charlotte Dada at concerts at the Orion Cinema. As she explains, in 1972, she went to Lome.

I went to sing 'Let it Be' by the Beatles at the Congress Hall and stood in front of President Eyedema. And also in front of Miriam Makeba, who told me that 'you have a beautiful voice and that you must continue as Africa needs to hear from you.' She encouraged me so much that day and I was only fifteen years old.

After a period of schooling in Beirut, Bibie continued her musical career in Ghana by joining the Afro-rock band Boombaya in 1973 that played at WATO's club in downtown Accra.

The leader was Alfred ['Kari'] Bannerman with Kofi Edu from Cape Coast on keyboards and Kofi Adu from Kumasi on drums. Then there was Ben Jerry Telfer who played rhythm guitar and flute, George [Mensah] the bass guitarist and MB [Mogens Bollerup] a Swedish guy who blew saxophone. We were very in tune with what was happening abroad and it affected our musical influences here. You know, we had people like Ginger Baker and Fela coming in and out of Ghana. Boombaya was influenced by Carlos Santana and Jimi Hendrix, but Alfred Bannerman wanted to go further by experimenting on the guitar to make his own Afro-fuse, that was a mixture of R&B and soul with African indigenous sounds and a lot of percussion.

In 1974, John Burney and Phillip Dean, the British university lecturers who were promoting Boombaya and running a charter flight company, decided to take the group to England to tour, where they recorded the album 'The Cry of the Pygmy' at EMI studios in London. As Bibie told to me:

The hard part of that was to convince my [grand] parents to let me go, as I had just taken my exams and was waiting for the results. So I went to my father's library downstairs and said to him that I had decided that I wanted to make music my life and intended to become a success. After I made my big speech, he said "OK fine, in that case I have two things to say to you too. Don't take the broad and wide road; take the straight and narrow one, and if you get to a crossroads stop and think it over. Secondly, if it all goes wrong, you can always come back home". So my [grand] mother and father talked it over and they agreed – my dad even drove me all the way to the plane. I was just seventeen and that was a big trust from my parents to go with all these boys. But I think they had sussed them out as educated young lads who had been to university and good Ghanaian school like Mfantsipim and Saint Augustine's in Cape Coast. They weren't just walk-abouts hanging around.

Boombaya played at universities like Birmingham, Manchester and Hamburg, the Windsor Festival and at Ronnie Scott's jazz club. However, the band soon broke up and Bibie returned to Ghana. Then, in 1979, Bibie went to Lagos where she met Fela, Sonny Okosun and Manu Dibango, and ended playing with the Gondola dance band for three months. In 1980, she went to Lome to record the album 'Va Ho Nam' with Wellborne Ativo, Togo's top guitarist. This was recorded at the Studio De la Nouvelle Marche where she also met the Senegalese singer Youssou N'Dour, Mory Kante, Mamadou Doumbia – as well as her old Boombaya keyboardist Kofi Edu, with whom she had had a daughter in London. Kofi Edu suggested she go to Abidjan where he was currently playing.

However, Bibie returned to Ghana and, in 1981, began working with the musical lead and bass guitarist brothers Pinnock and Ralph Casely-Hayford in their Overdrive Band, promoted by the Armenian-Ghanaian owner of the Takoradi Flour Mills, Serge Bakalian. However, with the 1981 Rawling military coup and curfew, things got difficult for musicians in Ghana and so, in 1982, Bibie took up Kofi Edu's invite and joined him in Cote D'Ivoire.

Kofi Edu was with Les Stars Shine band and Bibie sang with them for two and a half years. This band was based at La Canne Sucre Club in Abidjan and its musicians mainly came from Ghana, with some others from Liberia (Robert Tecumsay), Guinea-Bissau, Senegal and the Caribbean island of Martinique. Whilst singing with this band, Bibie met the Malian singer/flotist Boncana Maiga, who had had his debut album produced by Guy Gluck, the Commercial Director of WEA (Warner Electra Atlantic) Records, which had a West African branch in Cote D'Ivoire. Guy Gluck subsequently became Bibie's manager and, through him, she went to France where she released her 'Tout Doucement' album song that became a French smash hit in 1985. It was number two in the French charts for months and got her a Sony Gold Disque. This was followed by five other hit albums between 1987 and 1992. Bibie became a hot item in France.

In the early 2000s, Bibie returned to Ghana where she set up her New Morning band that plays R&B, highlife, blues and jazz ballads in contemporary African style. This small group includes drummer Ekow Quaye, bassist Obed Ocansey, keyboardist Master Richards and percussionist Moses Akutu. Bibie also opened her New Morning Star Club in Tesano, Accra which features, cultural events, poetry readings and live shows by other bands as well as hers.

Bibie Brew

Chapter 45

THE MUSICAL PROPHET SAFO AND HIS KRISTO ASAFO MISSION

Prophet Safo of Kristo Asafo Mission in 1983 (photoTon vander Lee)

One of the backbones of gospel highlife in Ghana has been the Kristo Asafo (Christian Community) Mission led by Prophet Kwadwo Safo. It is one of the fastest-growing churches in the country and, within ten years of its founding in 1971, it had some 20,000 members. It has also supported seven gospel bands and, through its numerous farms and charities, has played an important role in feeding the nation.

Prophet Safo told me in 1985 how he came to found his church, aged just twenty five. It began with a dream.

> *I was first a welder at Tema working at VALCO (the Volta Aluminium Company). Then, through a vision 1967, I had that call to become a pastor. I had a dream that night calling me to do the work of God, so I resigned the job and left everything behind before starting to preach the Gospel. So, now, every time I have a dream, I act upon that dream. Like when I had a dream about music; I woke up in the morning, started to buy instruments and straight away began to teach my people, as I was able to control all the instruments and amplifiers by the dream. I even began to compose and arrange in my dreams, as the music used to just come into my head. That's why I formed my group, the Voices of Wilderness. I've composed over three hundred songs.*

As Prophet Safo explains, his church went on to sponsor even more gospel bands.

> *You see, up to the time of my music dream, we had no bands at all in the church; we only used to clap our hands and sing hymns in Twi. Now there's my group, the three on your record [Guitar and the Gun – see below], plus the Faith Spiritual Band, the Christ Re-formed Band and the Good News Gospel Band.*

Prophet Safo went on to state the teaching of his church to me.

> *If you have something, and you know your brother doesn't, or is handicapped and you don't help him, it means your church is nothing. To help your neighbour – that means you are worshipping God. That's our main principle. Also we like to eat our traditional foods, like cocoyam, plantain, oranges and pineapples and nothing intoxicating. Spiritual healing is one of my main principles. I can cure people of bad spirit by prayer and telling them to go and sleep. So afterwards they're healed.*

Prophet Safo shared his thoughts on the European and African versions of Christianity:

African Christianity is different from the European one, as Christianity started in Africa. The Europeans wrote books about Jesus Christ but they didn't ever see Him, as He didn't come from Europe. Even He spent time in Africa, in Egypt. So Africans can know Him and worship Him properly. The Europeans only translated the Bible from Greek into Roman [Latin] and then into English. They didn't write it as it was originally in Hebrew, so they can never know the Bible more than us, or follow His laws properly. They knew Him not. And when the missionaries came to Africa holding the Bible, they were holding this European copy.

When I asked why his church sings only Akan, Ga and Ewe highlife hymns, Kwadwo Safo said:

Even the songs that Jesus and the disciples sang weren't European ones. If you look at Matthew 26-30, you will read that Jesus told the disciples at the Last Supper that they should all sing a hymn with him. Europeans would consider that a pagan song. So there's nothing wrong in us using our highlifes.

In the above conversation, Prophet Safo mentions his three bands that appear on the Guitar and Gun albums. These were two highlife compilation albums I recorded in my Bokoor Studio in the early 1980s and released on the British Cherry Red/Africa-gram Label (re-released as a CD by Sterns in 2004). The three Kristo Asafo bands on the albums are the Genesis Gospel Singers, Kuntum Thirteen and the Supreme Christian Singers (also known as Calvary Bells). The most popular of the songs was the recording I did of the Genesis Gospel singers entitled 'Momma Mo Akoma Ntutu' (Let Your Heart Be Cool) whose lyrics are basically part of the Gospel According to Saint John. They are sung in Akan by the late Nathanial Akwesi Abeka (leader of the group), Yao Boye, Frank Edwin, Justice Asare, Dora Owusu and Rebecca Danso. They were accompanied by Slim Manu on bass guitar, Samuel Paa Gyima and Agyeman Opoku on rhythm and lead guitars, Sloopy Mike Gyamfi on keyboards, Captain Moro on drums and Kofi Ackah (Jewel Ackah's son) on congas.

Kwesi Abeka took me to the church's New Year celebration in Adabraka 1984 at which the church donated food and a mountain of Fanti kenkey from its many farms to needy charities. As I had coincidentally recorded several bands of the Kristo Asafo Mission, I was treated as one of the guests of honour and was brought forward to wave the record albums about for the huge crowd.

The Christo Asafo band the Genesis Gospel Singers in 1983

Never one to remain still, Prophet Safo went on to build orphanages where music is taught, establish experimental engineering workshops and move on from gospel music to gospel plays and movies. In the 1990s, the Kristo Asafo Mission concert party was set up that stages light-hearted religious and moralistic dramas and through which comedians like Nkomode, Agya Koo and Akrobeto have passed. Then, in 2002, this church released their melodramatic film 'No Easy Target' that stars 'Solo' Soloman Sampah and was directed by Veronica Quarshie.

Prophet Safo continues with his philanthropic and scientific work. In 2004, he was awarded the Platinum Service to Humanity award, he received the order of the Volta in 2007 and, in 2010, he and the Christo Asafo Mission held their 29th Technology Exhibtion in Accra.

NIGERIAN HIGHLIFE,
JUJU MUSIC, FELA'S
AFROBEAT & OTHER
NIGERIAN POPULAR
MUSIC STYLES

8

Highlife
TIME 3

This examines the palmwine ('native' blues) music, juju, apala, highlife and Fela Kuti-type Afro-beat of Nigeria, as well as the makossa guitar music of neighbouring Cameroon. It also supplies interviews with and biographies of some of Nigeria's leading musical stars such as Victor Uwaifo, Fela Kuti, Sonny Okosun, Segun Bucknor and Nickolas Mbarga.

Chapter 46

YORUBA JUJU-MUSIC, APALA AND FUJI

SOUTH-WESTERN NIGERIAN JUJU MUSIC

Nigerian juju band the Rainbow Quintet 1958

447

Juju music is the Nigerian cousin of highlife. It grew up in the 1930s as a synthesis of many traditions: traditional Yoruba praise music, the 'native blues' of Irewolede Denge and Alabi Labilu, local 'agidigbo' hand-piano and Nigerian palmwine music of the Jolly Orchestra led by the Liberian Kru penny-whistle player Sunday Giant. Palmwine music itself was influenced by the 'krusbass' finger-picking guitar style of the Kru sailors who were located in Nigerian port towns. Also important for emerging juju music was the influence of the Brazilian samba and carnival music, introduced to Lagos by freed slaves from Brazil in the late 19th century. Another input for early juju music was gombe music and ashiko, whose origins can be traced to 19th century Sierra Leone where freed slaves were settled in the town of Freetown and from where many of Nigerian descent later returned to Lagos as the 'Saro' people. Finally, there was an infusion of konkoma or konkomba highlife into the Nigerian musical melting-pot, coming in from Ghana in the 1930s and 1940s. This, as mentioned in Chapter 24, was a poor-man's version of Fanti brass band 'adaha' music.

There are two thoughts on the origin of the word 'juju', neither of which which has anything to do with the derogatory word for African traditional religion 'ju-ju', which comes from the French words 'jouer-jouer' or 'play-play' that demotes African religions to childish beliefs. One origin of the musical term 'juju' is that it is an onamatopoeic word that comes from the low-high tones of the wooden tambourine used in early juju bands. However, another explanation offered by Benson Idonije is that the word comes from the act of throwing the 'juju' tambourine up in the air and catching it on time as it comes down, as the Yoruba word 'ju' means to toss and therefore the double up-and-down motion becomes the word 'juju'. Whatever the meaning of the term, it surfaced in Lagos as a distinct genre around 1932 when the mandolin player Tunde King coined the word 'juju'. Other early juju music pioneers were the banjoists Ojoge Daniels, Tunde Banjo and the guitarists J.O. 'Speedy' Araba and Ojo Babajide. It was the the guitarists Ayinde Bakare and Akanbi Ege Wright who were the first juju musicians to use amplified guitars and start adding traditional Yoruba gangan pressure drums to their ensembles.

In the 1950s, the most popular exponents of this Yoruba guitar-band music was the Blue Spots whose leader, I.K. Dairo, used amplified instruments and assorted local and Afro-Cuban perfcussion and made literally hundreds of records. He was even awarded the British MBE for his musical success, and continued composing up until his death in 1996. Dairo paved the way for many other juju bands like those of Prince

I. K. Dairo's juju-music band in 1961 (photo Andy Frankel)

Adekunle, Lady Balogun and Moses Olaiya who also ran a travelling theatrical group. However, up until the mid-1960s, juju music was a 'poor relation' to Nigeria's dance band highlife, as it was music played in palm-wine bars and for streets functions. The top-notch nightclubs were in the grip of a dance band highlife fever, sung in Yoruba, Igbo and Pidgin English.

Everything changed with the 1967-1970 Nigerian Civil War (or 'Biafran' war) when in western Nigeria highlife declined and juju music became more popular. Many of the top highlife bands in Lagos had been run by easterners and therefore broke up, as their members, who belonged to the breakaway Biafran Igbo ethnic group, had to leave. The only dance-bands were left in the Lagos area were those of Bobby Benson, Victor Olaiya and Roy Chicago who were Yoruba, and Chicago's band collapsed when his musicians were drafted into army bands. From this point on juju music had the field to itself in Lagos and western Nigeria. Whereas highlife continues to be popular in the east of the country, it never recovered in the south-western Nigeria where juju (and more recently fuji) has held sway.

During the seventies and eighties many juju exponents appeared. There was Ebenezer Obey who slowed the music of I.K. Dairo to a relaxed tempo. Also playing in this style were Sir Skiddo and his Mountain Millionaires, a twelve-man band based at Abeokuta, and Oladunni Oduguwa or 'Mummy Juju' and her Decency and Unity Orchestra. Then came Sunny Ade, who retained the slow juju tempo but added some ultra modern effects and infused pop and Afro-beat to create his 'synchro system' sound. This crossed over the international market in the early 1980s and became one of the first 'World Music' successes. Also influenced by pop is the high-speed 'Afro juju' of Sir Shina Peters, the 'sedico system' of Thony Alex and the 'adawa system' of Prince Dele Abiodun's Top Hitters, Another was the 'Yo-pop' (Yoruba pop) of Segun Adewele who had worked with Shina Peters in the 1970s and in the mid-1980s was managed by Sterns Records In London who organised European tours for his band and released albums of his like 'Ojo Je' on the World Music market. Juju bands particularly affected by Fela's Afro-beat include Prince Adekunle's Western State Brothers, Pick Peters and Bob Aladeniyi, originally second in command of Sunny Ade's African Beats. Aladeniyi then split away in 1975 to form his Jungle Rock Stars which actually recruited two of Fela Kuti's musicians, Edo and Tutu Shorunma. As the juju field has been dominated by Ebenezer Obey and the younger Sunny Ade, I will say something on them in more detail.

EBENEZER OBEY

In November 1974, I visited Ebenezer at his home off Palm Avenue in the Mushin area of Lagos. He told me that the first bands he joined in the 1950s, were the Royal Mambo Orchestra and the Guinea Mambo Orchestra. He moved on to Fatai Rolling Dollars Band and the Federal Rhythm Brothers, before forming his own the International Brothers band in 1964, after obtaining a recording contract by Decca West Africa (Afrodisia). The International Brothers first release was the single 'Ewa Wowum Ojumi Ri' (People Come and See What I See), after which they released a series of albums for Decca. In 1970, he changed the name of the band to Chief Commander Ebenezer Obey and the Inter-Reformers Band and continued to release on the Afrodisia label. One very popular song was dedicated to the 'Late General Murtala Muhammed and another expounded the government policy of 'Operation Feed the Nation'. Many have a strong moral behind them. By the mid-1970s the Inter-Reformers was an eighteen-piece band based at Obey's Miliki Spot nightclub in Lagos. The group's instruments included electric guitars, wooden tambourines, the squeeze or talking-drum, the shekeres (maracas), agogo (clips), and a type of 'goumbeh' drum.

Not only did the musicians weave a web of complex percussive rhythms, but they also embroidered and crossed the main melody with snatches of other tunes.

The 1950s juju music which I.K. Dairo used to play was similar in tempo to the fast and bubbly highlife music. Obey's style on the other hand is much slower and spacey. Indeed, it is so relaxed and the live shows are so long that the bandsmen often sit down behind their amplifiers when playing in public. Obey's band is typical of many of the hundreds of juju bands. In all of them the bass-guitar is used like a bass-drum, traditional percussion is employed and horns are absent. Like many other bands, much of the music of the Inter-Reformers is praise music: praising God, or praising big men and patrons. Sometimes huge sums of naira currency notes have been showered or 'sprayed' over Ebenezer and his bandsmen by flattered patrons. In the eighties pop music began to make Ebenezer Obey change his tune a bit, when he came out with a juju/rock fusion. This even became popular with European 'World Music' fans and his records were released in London by Rough Trade. He also did some recordings for Virgin Records (with Ghana's Joe Mensah as producer) and toured the United States with his band. In recent years Obey's juju music lyrics have moved towards Christian themes and he became known as Evangelist Ebenezer Obey-Fabiyi.

SUNNY ADE

Obey's younger rival, Sunny Ade, whose African Beats not only uses the guitars and traditional percussion of orthodox juju, but also the vibraphone, synthesiser and steel guitar played by Denola Adepoju. Sunny, whose real name is Sunday Adeniyi, was born in the Ondo State in 1946. He picked up his musical inclinations from his father who was an organist, and his mother who was in the church choir. He completed his secondary education at Oshogbo and became leader of the school band there. Then he worked for a time as samba (frame-drum) player with one of the popular travelling comic theatres; that of Moses Olaiya (Baba Sala) based at Ibadan. He then moved to Lagos and joined Victor Olaiya's highlife band at the Papingo Club. In 1966, he formed his own Green Spots band based at the Kue Club in Lagos. The band's first success came in 1967 with their football song, 'Challenge Cup' and since then Sunny has released scores of albums. He records and releases everything on his own label, Sunny Alade Records, as he does not trust the big companies. Sunny's is deeply spiritual and has been a devout Christian since the age of seven. He neither smokes nor drinks and believes that everyone has a special destiny, which in his case is juju music. He calls his Ariya (Enjoyment) Club a 'church from where my message will reach the masses'. His music, like all juju music, has a strong religious and moral bias and there is a definite overlap of juju music and the Yoruba hymn music of the aladura or 'praying' churches, which is often played by electronic guitar-bands. Many of Sunny's lyrics are pessimistic predictions of doom, but again this is in the tradition of the revivalist African churches. Sunny denies that his songs are anti-establishment, they are simply about the happenings in society, including its ills.

At the height of his popularity Sunny regularly sold two hundred thousand copies of his albums in Nigeria, and in 1983 he became an international star when Island Records (who produced the late Bob Marley) signed him, released 'synchro system' and organised American and European tours for the African Beats. Here is a comment by a journalist for the London Guardian newspaper at that time that clearly reflects the western fascination with this musician and his music

> *Sunny Ade proved why they call him the 'Chairman''. He functions less as a star performer than as a conductor orchestrating a series of musical dialogues. The show offered a marked contrast with western song structure and our notions of musical climax. Although the set was divided into songs of varying mood and tempo, one had the impression it was all part of the same fabric. Each number ended abruptly, in mid-sentence as it were, yet without any feeling of discontinuity. They could have all started at any point and played forever. Their skills and joyful dedication had the effect of making the panorama of English rock music look jaded and trite.*

In the 1980s 'King' Sunny Ade became a founder member of the Nigeria anti-music piracy organisation, the Performing Artists Association of Nigeria (PMAN) and in 1994 established the King Sunny Ade Foundation in Lagos. He also continued with his musical career and in 1998 was nominated an American Grammy Award for his 'Odu' album, in 2008 won a world Reggae and World Music Award in New York and the following year won the US Public Radio 'Afropop' program Hall of Fame Award.

APALA, SAKARA AND FUJI

Ironically, as juju music went international in the 1980s, at home in Nigeria it began to decline in popularity and a new home-grown form of Yoruba popular music began to replace it known as Fuji. This music represents a quite different current of commercial music in south-western Nigerian popular music as it evolved out of Muslim Yoruba music-styles like waka, were, sakara and apala. Were music is an old Muslim tradition of men's Ramadan celebratory music and its female counter-part is 'waka' whose most popular exponent has been Queen Salawa Abeni. Sakara music is another Muslim influenced style that emerged in the early 20th century and uses only traditional Nigerian instruments such as the pressure talking-drum, the one-stringed goje violin, calabash drums and the 'sakara' or 'sahlar' drum, a small tambourine made of clay or bamboo. This music arose as a Muslim Ramadam Festival music in the northern Nigerian town of Nupe, and then spread southwards amongst the Yoruba. Apala is another Yoruba-Islamic popular music that emerged in the mid-1940s as a mixture of traditional Yoruba music and sakara. Therefore it uses the same instruments as sakara, but with the addition of the 'agidigbo' hand-piano.

At first apala was called 'area' in Lagos and 'oshugbo' in Ibadan, with the name 'apala' being coined in 1947 by the late Haruna Ishola. Up until his death in 1983 his Apala Band released scores of singles and twenty-six albums on the Decca label. Ishola also helped consolidate the apala scene when he opened a twenty-four-track recording studio in 1979 at his home town of Ijebu-Igbo near Ibadan. Other apala musicians include Ayinla Omowura, Kasumu Adio, Sefiu Ayan, Adaran Kareem and Adisa Ariyameta. One juju musician liked the indigenous apala sound so much that in the seventies he specialised in fusing juju with apala. This was Idowu Animashaun, a man of huge proportions who had formed his Lisabi Brothers in 1966.

A newer craze in the western Nigerian scene since the 1970s has been 'fuji' music that is influenced by both Muslim sakara and 'were' music, as well as the more commercialised Yoruba apala style. The name 'fuji' itself was coined by Ayinde Barrister after either the Japanese Fuji (Beautiful) Mountain or the Japanese brand name. Ayinde Barrister himself initially played the agidigbo hand-piano for a Muslim Yoruba "were" band, then joined an army dance-band and formed his thirty-five strong Supreme Fuji Commanders in 1970 with the encouragement of Ebenezer Obey. His main rival is Ayinla Kollington who also started off as a "were" musician, then he joined the army Olumo Dance Band as sax player before forming his fuji band in 1978. Both Barrister and Kollington have released scores of records and have added keyboards and guitars to the agidigbo and sakara instruments, as well as the bata drums of the Yoruba Shango thunder-god cult. Other important fuji pioneers are Wasui Barrister, Wahabi Ejire and Wasia 'Marshall' Anifowoshe (an ex-Barristor member) and the Ibadan based Dauda 'Epo Akara' Akanmu, followed later by Adewale Ayuba and Abass Akande Obesere. The Nigerian writer Paul Ademowo (1993) lists sixty fuji groups in western Nigeria and says these and others have developed hundreds distinct styles of fuji: such

The Nigerian Idowu Animashaun who fused juju music and apala

as raggae, synchro, Afro, merengue, waka, miliki, apala, Jackson, Oklahoma and gospel-fuji, etc.

Chapter 47

NIGERIAN HIGHLIFE AND THE MAKOSSA OF THE CAMEROONS

HIGHLIFE IN NIGERIA

Nigeria is now a major centre for highlife. However, the music was introduced to the country from Ghana in a variety of ways. At first through the diffusion of konkoma highlife and 1937 Nigerian tour of the Cape Coast Sugar Babies Orchestra. Later came the 1950s records E.K. Nyame's and Onyina's guitar bands and most importantly the early fifties tours of the Ghanaian Tempos band. The jazzy style of highlife of this dance band led by E.T. Mensah was copied by numerous Nigerian band leaders who had previously mainly been playing the imported swing, calypso and rumbas; such as Victor Olaiya, Bobby Benson, Rex Lawson and E.C. Arinze.

Highlife dominated southern Nigeria in the 1950s and 60s. But as mentioned in the previous chapter, everything changed because of the 1967-70 Nigerian Civil War. Many of the large dance-bands in Lagos that were led by Nigerians from the east, collapsed: like those of Charles Iwegbue, Enyang Henshaw and Zeal Onyia. E. C. Arinze who had operated his band in Lagos from 1952-65 quit the city during the war and later ran his band in Enugu. Rex Lawson Mayors dance band relocated to the east as the Riversmen until his death in a car accident in 1971. Some of the 1960s bands already located in eastern Nigeria did manage to survive, although there was a

Bobby Benson (centre with sax) and his band in the early 1950's. At the back and second from left is Ajax Bukana with maracas on on the right of the trap drummer is the young Bayo Martins.

tendency to move away from the large dance-band to the smaller guitar band format. Examples of these were the bands of Stephen Amechi, Paulson Kalu from Aba and Celestine Ukwu who in 1962 joined Michael Eleagha's Paradise Rhythm Orchestra based in Enugu, and then in 1966 started his own Music Royals group in Onitsha.

With the collapse of the big highlife dance bands during the Nigerian Civil War the field was left open for the smaller guitar-bands, which surfaced as a dominant factor in the 1970s throughout southern Nigeria. In the south-western Yoruba part of Nigeria this guitar-band music was that of juju music, discussed in the previous chapter. In the mid-west it was Bini (i.e Benin) highlife based on local 'native blues' and played by artists such as Victor Uwaifo who set up his Melody Maestros in 1965, and through whom many Bini highlife artists passed, like Collings Oke Dandy Oboy and Sonny Okosun (see next chapter).

Palm-wine music and 'native blues' guitar bands became popular in the eastern part of Nigeria well before the Second World War. However, in the 1950s the Ghanaian dance

456

band and guitar band highlife was also a formative influence. As a result, eastern guitar groups sprang up in Nigerian that combined highlife and local native blues like those of Okonkwo Adigwe, Israel Njemanze (Three Night Wizards from Asaba), Stephen and Aderi Olariechi from Owerri. Another was Stephen Amechi's Rhythm Skies Band formed in the late 1950s and which included the young Steven Osita Osadabe. Osadabe was born in 1936, and whilst playing with Amechi's band became a side-man singer for various highlife dance band run by the eastern Nigerians E.C. Arinze, Eddy Okonta, Charles Iwegbue and Zeal Onyia. Osadabe went on to form his own Central Dance Band in Lagos and then the Soundmakers in 1964, which shifted more to a guitar band format after he relocated to eastern Nigeria during the Nigerian Civil War. The Soundmakers became a leading guitar band in Igbo-land and released seventy albums.

After the Nigerian Civil War the Nigerian highlife tradition was mainly kept alive in the east by the guitar-bands. For example after Rex Lawson's death in 1971 his Riversmen formed the Professional Seagulls which was one of the top guitar-band for many years. Another was the Peacocks, formed in Owerri in 1972 by Raphael Amanabae who had been a member of the Riversmen. Incidentally, Amarabem was in Ghana between 1949 and 1962 and as as a member of the Abaraka highlife guitar band learnt guitar from its leader Robert Osuji. Another Nigerian guitar band artist of the 1970s was Celestine Ukwu who had changed the name of this band from the Music Royals to the Philosophers National. At the same time Paulson Kalu was running his popular 'Africana' Igbo guitar highlife. Then there were Sunny Neji, the female singer Onyeka Onwenu and also the Ikengas and Oriental Brothers that pioneered 'Ikwokilikwo' or 'Ikwokirikwo' guitar band music. This a fast-paced form of highlife combined elements from the Igbo blues and imported Congo Jazz. The Ikengas or Nkengas Super Stars was formed by Vincent Okoroego in 1973 who had previously played with Steven Osita Osadebe's Soundmakers. The Oriental Brothers was formed in Owerri in 1974 by three brothers; Dan Satch Opara, 'Sir Warrior' (Christogonus Ezebuiro Obinna) and Godwin Kabaka Opara. Feuds between the three of them ultimately led to a split in 1977, resulting in each of them forming his band. These were Kabaka International and two wings of the Oriental Brothers band that were both marketed by the same company, Decca West Africa.

More recent addition to the eastern Nigeria highlife scene is Oliver de Coque from Anambra State. He learnt guitar from a Congolese musician and played with several juju bands in Lagos before moving eastwards and setting up his Super Ogene Band that released eighty albums between 1976 and his death in 2009. His 'ogene' highlife combines Congolese soukous, Cameroonian makossa and traditional Igbo music: In fact, the name 'ogene' derives from the name of the Igbo bell and social dance. Also important was Nicholas Mbarga from Anambra state who developed his own distinct 'panko' style of highlife in the 1970s that blends in Cameroonian and Congolese music. I will say something more about this important artist, but first let me say something about some of the Ghanaian guitar band artists who were attracted to Nigeria at this time.

GHANAIAN HIGHLIFE GUITAR BANDS IN EASTERN NIGERIA

As eastern Nigeria became an important 'highlife zone' during the 1960s and 70s the Igbo version of this music made an impact on Ghana through records and particulary through the numerous Ghanaian guitar bands that relocated to Nigeria during the late 1970s and early 1980s. These were the harsh economic days of Ghana during a series of the military regimes, which forced some highife band to travel to Europe, the US and various African countries like the Cote d'Ivoire and Nigeria. Those that went to Nigeria played for the tens of thousands of Ghanaians economic migrants in that country, and these Ghanaian bands also included highlifes in Pidgin English to make them attractive to Nigerian audiences.

One such Ghanaian group was Alex Konadu's band that often toured Nigeria from the late 1970s – and a break-away from it, called the Canadoes, settled in Nigeria between 1980-5. The Canadoes led by Robert Danso recorded albums liked 'Oga Sorry', 'Fine Women' and 'Never Lose Hope' at the 24 track studio of the Roger All Stars record company set up by the Igbo music entrepreneur Chief R. E. Okonkwo in 1977.

Anthony Entsie's Beach Scorpion spent seven years in Nigeria from 1977 and also released songs for the Roger All Stars, like his 1981 'Original Beach Scorpions'. Another Ghanaian guitar band that recorded for the Roger All Stars was Nana Agyeman Opambuo. His Opambuos guitar bands released several albums between 1982-4 including 'My Darling' and 'Kiss Me and Smile'. Likewise, the Golden Boys Band of Ghana produced their 'I Don Tire' in 1984 for the Roger All Stars label. Then there was T.O. Jazz who, together with three of his bandsmen, settled in Nigeria for almost two years as the resident band of Stephen Osita Osadebe's Hotel. In 1980, T.O. Jazz released the Nigerian 'top ten' album 'Ojukwu Welcome' that marked the the return from exile of Lt. Col. Odumegwu-Ojukwu, the leader of the attempted break-away state of Biafra,

Some other Ghanaian guitar bands that resided in Nigeria were the Kuul Strangers who released their 'Paddle Your Own Canoe' for the Smart label in 1981, the Dytomite Starlite Band of Ghana that recorded in the early 1980s on the Tabansi Records, the Super Seven that released the album 'Travel and See' and Eddie Maxwell's Odoyewu International Band that released 'Monkey Chop' in 1982 for CY Records. Amakye Dede's Apollo High Kings also relocated to Nigeria from 1979 to 1983 where they released several albums, like 'Jealousy Go Shame', 'To Be A Man Nawaa' and 'Ifa Anyi Chuku'. Two others were Paa Bobo and his Three Axes that produced their 'Osaobrokye' album in Nigeria in 1982 (Janco label) and Kofi Sammy's Okukuseku band. Okukuseku first toured Nigeria in 1977 and then resided in Onitsha from 1981-4 when they they recorded albums such as 'Suffer Suffer' and 'Take Time' for the Roger All Star Company.

As can be seen from the above, all the Ghanaian artists had returned home by the mid 1980s. The reason for this was that it was in 1983 that the Nigerian Govenrment enacted its Aliens Order Act which led to the deportation of tens of thousands of Ghanaians and other Africans who did not have the required work permits. Nevertheless the Ghanaian bands brought back with them the Igbo variety of highlife which influenced the local music scene. For instance Okukuseku's 'Yellow Sisi' sold like hot cakes in Ghana. Furthermore, Ghana itself had been primed for the Igbo style of Pidgin English guitar band music through the massive late seventies hits or Nicolas Mbarga and his Rokafil Jazz – to which we now turn.

PRINCE NICO AND THE ROKAFIL JAZZ
Nicolas Mbarga's Rokafil Jazz had a huge smash hits in Africa and the Caribbean after their 'Sweet Mother' album was released in 1976. That year everyone in West Africa began playing 'Sweet Mother', and African prints, nightclubs, chop-bars and local transport vehicles began bearing this name. The reason for this is that in the 'panko' style Rokafil Jazz combined all the best from several African countries: the Igbo highlife style of eastern Nigeria, the fast makossa music of the Cameroons, and a touch of the soukous guitar-style from the two Congos. In fact, the leader of the band, Nicholas Mbarga or 'Prince Niko', was half-Nigerian and half-Cameroonian and during Nigeria's Civil War his family temporarily settled in neighbouring Cameroon.

459

As a result, the first band he played guitar for was the Cameroonian band the Melody Orchestra – and on returning home Prince Nico formed his Rokafil Jazz in 1972. This released several records but the popularity of his 1976 'Sweet Mother' was enhanced by the lyrics being in Pidgin English and so could easily understood from country to country, and by Prince Niko using a bass-line that had a reggae lilt. Rokafil Jazz quickly followed their first highlife hit with fourteen more highlife albums in their fast, bouncy 'panko' style, like 'Dear Father' and 'Free Education in Nigeria'. 'Music Line' is another example, which is literally the story of Nicholas and his band. The song starts with a father warning his son against going into the music business, as he will never be able to save enough money to get married and settle down. But it ends happily with the son becoming so successful through music that he can afford several wives and a big car.

In the late 1979 Nicholas was interviewed at the BBC's External Broadcasting Centre at Bush House. I was on the same programme and was astonished to see his diminutive figure breeze in flanked by a group of beefy minders. Unlike his boisterous and noisy companions Nicholas turned out to be a quiet and shy person. I noticed that physically he had a lot in common with Nana Ampadu, leader of Ghana's African Brothers band. Both were wiry, slightly built men with sensitive and finely chiselled features. Both are wizard musicians and there is even a resemblance in the highlife music they play. Although quiet off-stage, Nicholas is completely different in the limelight where he looks larger than real life, as in those days he used to he wears stacks, or 'guarantee shoes' as they are called in Ghana, that added inches to his height. He invited me to his show in London and by the end of the program he had the audience in the palm of his hand. They were dancing in the aisles and in front of the stage and would have gone on all night if the caretaker had not come and closed the place. The following day Prince Niko flew off to Paris to do a promotional tour. Prince Niko went onto become so successful that he set up his own hotel and club in his hometown Onitsha, where he also ran a multi-track studio. He died in a motorbike accident in the late 1990's. As both Nicholas Mbarg's 'panko' and Oilver de Coques 'ogene' style of highlife were influenced by the makossa music I will say more about this popular music of the Cameroons

THE MAKOSSA OF THE CAMEROONS
Just as Ghana and Nigeria have highlife, the Cameroonians dance to makossa music: the latest of a series of guitar-band styles played in palm-wine dives and bar-rooms. Makossa is a southern Cameroonian popular dance music that emerged in the 1940s as

a blend of local styles with the maringa of the neighbouring Congos and an early West African guitar/accordian music known as ashiko (or asiko) brought by English-speaking West African seamen. The most popular ashiko groups in the Cameroons in those days were those of Jean Aladin Bikoko and Uncle Jospeh Medjo. Makossa followed in the wake of maringa and ashiko and the top makossa artists of the 1950s and 60s were Eboa Lotin, Misse Ngoh, Mama Obandja and Ebanda Manfred. Their guitar band music even affected the local dance-bands of the period, such as the Black and White Jazz Orchestra and Los Negros.

Manu Dibango of the Cameroons

However, the word 'makossa' didn't surface in the international music scene until Manu Dibango released his 1972 'Soul Makossa' hit in the United States that fused disco-music with jazz and African rhythms. Sax player Manu Dibango was born in

1933 and played with Kalle's African Jazz in the D.R. Congo from 1961 to 1965. He then went to Paris and in 1975 moved to the Cote d'Ivoire where he became director of the RTI Radio Orchestra. He also worked with the late Bella Bellow of Togo and Francois Lougah of Cote d'Ivoire – and in recent years has made several trips to Ghana to perform. Younger makossa artists include Moni Bile, Tity Edima and Sam Fan Thomas (of 1984 'African Typic Collection' fame) who are popular in both the Cameroons and Paris. There is also Lapiro de Mbanga who is known for his anti-establishment lyrics. In Paris, during the 1980s and 1990s, some Cameroonian artists, like the guitarist Toto Guillaume and Alhadji Toure, began fusing makossa with the Caribbean zouk music of the French Antilles. This fusion followed in the wake of another Cameroonian band, Voory's Power, which in the seventies worked with the Granadian dance-band in Lagos and combined makossa with Afro-beat. Another makossa artist is the guitarist Vincent Nguni who spent some time in Ghana in the 1980s (he visited my Bokoor Studio) and then worked with Paul Simon in the States on his late 1980s 'Rhythm of the Saints' album.

A faster style of urban music than makossa that has recently surfaced in the Cameroon is 'Bikutsi', associated with the Beti people of the capital city Yaounde. This was originally an up-tempo bar-room music with rude and controversial lyrics sang in the 1950s by artists like Anne-Marie Nzie to the accompaniment of local xylophones. From the 1960s the music went electric with dance bands like Los Camaroes and Confiance Jazz. In 1987 Bikutsi went international when the group of young musicians in colourful body-paint and called Les Tetes Brulees (Burnt Heads) began releasing records on the World Music market. Others are Govinal, Zelel and the lady singers Sally Nyolo (ex-Zap Mama band) and K-Tino.

Mention must also be made of the late Francis Bebey (born in Douala in 1929), the famous Cameroonian poet, guitarist, recording artist, novelist and a musicologist who wrote an important book on traditional music in 1968 called 'African Music: A People's Art'. In the fifties he studied at the Sorbonne University. In the sixties he played with Manu Dibango in France and spent time in Ghana as a journalist during the Nkrumah period. He then travelled to the US to study broadcasting. In all he released twenty-four record albums that combined traditional and popular African music, including makossa, with jazz and the classical guitar style of Segovia. He died in 1991, but his musical legacy is continued by his son, Patrick, who runs a jazz music trio in Paris.

Chapter 48

THE 'BINI' HIGHLIFE OF 'SIR' VICTOR UWAIFO

Victor Uwaifo was born into a musical family in 1941 in Benin City, the ancient capital of the Benin Empire. He has released over one hundred singles and a dozen albums since he formed his Melody Maestros in 1965. His highlife music is based on the Bini local folk music from the Edo (formerly Bendel) State of Nigeria. He rose to fame in 1966 when his band released three smash hits on the Phonogram label. These singles were 'Sirri-Sirri', 'Joromi' and 'Guitar Boy'. 'Joromi', based on the story of a legendary hero of Benin City, was so popular that it earned Uwaifo Africa's first Gold Disc Award in 1969. Joromi also became the name for one of the brightly embroidered African cloth designs. In fact, Victor became so famous in Nigeria that that the students of Nsukka University knighted him 'Sir' Victor Uwaifo. The Melody Maestros made many international tours: they represented Nigeria at the Black Arts Festival held in Dakar in 1966, played at the Algerian Arts Expo in 1969 and the 1970 World Expo in Japan. They also toured in the United States, Europe and Russia. Many of the top Bini highlife musicians played with Victor's Melody Maestros. Like Collings Oke and the Odoligue Nobles, as well as Dandy Oboy and Mudogo Osegie who left Uwaifo in 1971 to form the Musketeers that played what they called 'bushpower'. Another leading Bini musician who was with the Melody Maestros is Sonny Okosun and his 'ozzidi' music that are discussed in Chapter 51.

I first met first met Victor in Accra in 1975 when he was making a trip to the home-town of his Ghanaian lawyer wife, Adelaide. I was introduced to him through John Chernoff, an American musicologist who had become involved in the production of Victor's album on the Black Bell Label called 'Laugh and Cry'. Immediately after our meeting I did a recording session with Victor, playing harmonica on the song 'West African Safari' for the Laugh and Cry album. I also arranged for Victor to play at the Napoleon Club in Accra where I was guitarist with the resident Bunzus band. We then discussed the idea of me writing his biography, and he invited me to stay with him at his home in Benin City during the Christmas/New Year holiday to work on the project and travel with his Melody Maestros band.

I travelled by road in December 1975, staying for a few days in Lagos at Fela's Afrika Shrine and then taking a Peugeot car to Benin City in the mid-western Edo State. I was lodged at Victor's Joromi Hotel on the outskirts of town with some of his bandsmen: like the bassist Sulley, Richard, the manager Patrick and the Ghanaian guitarist Osei Bonsu Senior. The Joromi Hotel was built in 1971 and was full of sculptures and art-works by Victor who had done a B.A. Degree in Graphic Arts. But the hotel was undergoing repairs and so the first time I saw Victor play was at his newly opened Club 400 discotheque in the centre of Benin City.

Victor Uwaifo and John Collins at a recording session in 1975

His shows started with the ten-man group warming up with some pop numbers, sung that Christmas by Ghanaian soul-music vocalist Picket (now known as McGod). Then in would come Victor wearing spectacular clothes he designed himself, and playing his 'akwete' and 'ekassa' music that blended of highlife with local Bini (i.e. Benin) styles. He would dance, sing and play instruments such as traditional xylophone, western flute and electric organ, which he sometimes played with his chin. But his main instrument was the guitar and he left everyone spellbound with his amazing solos. Sometimes he would use a double 'Siamese guitar' that he would spin around a pivot on his belt. Victor was accompanied by two midgets playing wooden claves and maracas, who moved backward and forward across the stage darting in between Victor's legs. One of them, King Pago, had been with the famous Lagos-based Bobby Benson's Dance Band during the 1950's. A support band that also played at his club that Christmas was Ignace de Souza's Black Santiagos from Cotonu in the neighbouring Republic of Benin: so it was literally Benin meets Benin.

The 'guitar boy' Victor Uwaifo in the mid-1970's with his Siamese guitar

I discovered the Victor did not smoke or drink and was a strict disciplinarian with his bandsmen. He was also a restless person always on the move and looking for things to do. Having been a semi-professional athlete and wrestler he was physically very strong and so even after a night's show he would sometimes take me in his sports-car to cruise around town and check the other night-spots. On Sunday mornings he took me to Camp David, a drinking spot located in a palm-tree plantation that was the haunt of many of the town's 'bigmen'. Here fresh palm-wine was tapped from living trees and Nigerian and Ghanaian highlife was played from portable radios hanging from branches. During this trip I toured eastern Nigeria in a minibus with Victor and his group, first crossing the Niger River Bridge, partially wrecked during the 1967-70 Nigerian (Biafran) Civil War. The band played in and around Enugu, Onitsha and Aba and we saw many destroyed tanks and aircraft from the civil-war era. However, south-eastern Nigeria is musically in the 'highlife zone', so the ambience of the shows reminded me of what I was experiencing from my own band tours in Ghana. Here are some extracts of the interviews I made with Victor on that 1975 trip, and I first asked him how he became so interested in the guitar and how his parents reacted

I used to go around to the palm-wine guitarists downtown. The most famous of these guitarists in Benin was We-We, who had been a soldier during the Second World War. So I made a crude guitar myself, with high-tension wires for strings and bicycle spokes for frets. I begged one of the guitarists to teach me how to tune the guitar and he said he wouldn't, unless I bought him a jug of palm-wine. I found my home-made guitar very inferior, so I decided to buy one for myself. But it was difficult as I didn't know how to put it to my father. He would never agree. But I earned my one guinea and bought a second-hand guitar. The first time my father saw me playing it he seized it and threatened to destroy it. But my mother saved it.

Victor left Benin City and went to secondary school at Saint Gregory's in Lagos and in his spare-time he joined Victor Olaiya's highlife dance-band. In 1962, Victor won a scholarship to the Yaba College of Technology where he spent his time on his three main interests: studying in the morning, wrestling and athletics in the afternoon and playing with E.C. Arinze's highlife band at the Kakadu Club in the evenings. In 1964 he joined the Nigerian Television Service as a graphic artist and began putting his own band together. The first sound Victor created was the 'akwete' beat and his first three hit singles were based on that rhythm. As he explains, it was his knowledge of art that helped him create this, by using colours to represent musical notes.

It was at art school that I discovered colours in sound, and sound in colours. I was able to transpose them so that "do", the strongest note was black, "ray" was red, "me" was blue, "fa" was green. "so" a neutral colour and sound was white, "la" was yellow, and "ti" violet. But the whole change came when I transposed the colours of akwete cloth, hand-woven cloth made in eastern Nigeria. It is a very beautiful cloth and you will see that different colours recur, creating a moving rhythm of colour. When I interpreted this, it gave the akwete sound.

By the late 1960s he was fusing this akwete beat with pop influences like rock music, soul and later reggae.

I developed the 'shadow' which was a link between the akwete and the twist. The shadow lasted a year and I made an LP of it, but then soul came, and I started losing. So I had to bridge the gap. I had to create a rhythm similar to soul as well as my original sound. This was 'mutaba'.

Some critics condemned Victor for this modernising influences, but Victor had an answer.

They fail to see that the foundation of my music is very cultural, as demonstrated in the beat and the lyrics. The fact that I use modern instruments to produce my sound has not altered the basic character of the music, otherwise we might as well argue that a historian writing ancient history with modern tools, like a Parker pen and paper, is a farce. The tools he uses to write history will not alter the facts and dates of the book. We have experimentation and evolution of ancient African cultures and my music is no exception to this.

As Victor explains he has also based much of his music on the folk rhythms of Benin, like 'ekassa' and 'sasakossa'.

Ekassa was a royal dance performed during the coronation of a new king. Some people thought it an abomination to hear 'ekassa' while the king was still alive, but I didn't mind them, as the first tune was a brilliant hit and others followed. Here is how I got the rhythm for sasakossa. There was a time when the Benin Kingdom was overpowered. It was when the king of England sent explorers to Africa to trade with the king of Benin. But the king had an important festival and said he would not grant the British an audience. But they were determined to come and were intercepted and killed. A few managed to escape to England

467

where they were reinforced and came back for revenge. It was then that Benin was almost completely destroyed and the oba (king) went into hiding. The king had an orderly called Sasakossa who used to sing in a popular way to warn him when there was danger and it was not safe to come out of hiding.

During the late 1970's when he was developing his 'sasakossa' beat Victor set up a recording studio in Benin City. Then in the 1980s and again in his home-town he established a Music Academy, an Art Gallery and Nigeria's first private television studio with which he produced TV programs and made many commercial videos of his own and other music groups. In the 1990s he took an M.A. degree in Art, wrote and published a book of poems and essays called 'The Philosophy of Life' published in 1995 by his own book company, Joromi Publications. And to top this he then became Commissioner (i.e. Minister) of Arts and Culture for the government of the Edo State.

Over the years I have kept in touch with Victor and the following is a letter he wrote to me on 3rd November, 2000.

My Dear John, I want to thank you for your letter and was very delighted to read about you in some of the journals. I guess you must be doing well both academically and practically, especially, with your guitar band. I remember that you used to play the harmonica (mouth organ) but I didn't know when you started playing the guitar and it didn't ever occur to me also that you were left-handed. Maybe you're ambidextrous. On my own side, I have made some significant inroads into the intellectual ivory tower. When I had cause to go back to the University to study sculpture, I made First-Class honours and immediately enrolled for my Masters degree which I also completed in record time. My Art Gallery and my Recording Studio were run side-by-side along with my band the Titibitis that embarked on many international trips. John. I am sending you some of my past and recent catalogues of information about myself. I hope you'll like them. By the way, you should know Joe Mensah the President of the Ghana Association of Musicians, a highlife maestro who in the sixties recorded a chart buster with a popular hit tune entitled 'Bosue' which swept across West Africa. If you can get in touch with him, please tell him that I've not heard from him since the last time we spoke on the line last year. I hope he's well, up-and-doing and please extend my regards to him. Let me use this opportunity to invite you to visit me in Nigeria at your convenience, I would love to see you and hear you play. I would also love to arrange a musical concert for you or feature you alongside other bands. The Arts Theatre in Benin City named after His Majesty Oba Akenzua II is under my Ministry. I remember John Chernoff who used to accompany you to my place whenever I was in Ghana. I wonder where he is now. If you ever come across him, please give him my regards. I'm looking forward to hearing from you and I wish you the best. Dr Victor Efosa Uwaifo (MON, JP) Hon. Commissioner for Arts, Culture & Tourism, Ezoti Street, Benin City, Edo State, Nigeria.

I contacted Victor in 2003 when I helped him liase between the media man and sports commentor Moses Foh-Amoaning and the organisers of PANAFEST (Ghana's biannual Pan African Festival). As a result Victor Uwaifo visited Ghana and teamed up at with local highlife musicians to play some of his old hit tunes at Cape Coast for that year's event.

My most recent correspondence with Victor was in 2011 when I was put in touch with him through the Nigerian media man Taiwo Obe of Taijo Wonukabe Limited who was involved in Victor's 70th birthday festivities. By this time Victor had opened his Legacy Museum and Revelation Tourist Palazzo and and he sent me many packages of information on this and his current activities. As a result we decided that I should write his biography – continuing the work that I had started way back in 1975. The tentative title of the book will by 'Victor Uwaifo: Highlife Pioneer, Legend' and it will be published in Nigeria.

One interesting point I learnt from Victor in this correspondence concerns Ghana and his 1966 hit song 'Guitar Boy'. He informed me that this song became the name for the failed April 17th 1967 'Operation Guitar Boy' counter-coup against the Ghanaian National Liberiation Council government by a group of junior officers – which resulted in the assassination of General Kotoka. According to Victor, the reason the coup plotters used his song was that 'just like the staccato sound you hear in my Guitar Boy song they said that was the way their gunfire was sounding when the shooting started'. But of course the song itself had nothing to do with any coup. Nevertheless, the song was banned from Ghanaian radio by the NLC Government for a while.

Chapter 49

FELA ANIKULAPO-KUTI NIGERIA'S CONTROVERSIAL AFROBEAT KING

Fela and his Africa 70 band at the Afrika Shrine in 1971

The late Fela Anikulapo-Kuti was the main creator of Afrobeat or Afro-beat, a fusion of jazz, soul, Latin music, highlife and traditional Yoruba music. His blunt anti-establishment protest lyrics made him the Bob Dylan, Mick Jagger and Bob Marley of Africa rolled into one person. In Lagos everywhere he went, people stopped what they are doing, shouted his name and gave him the Black Power salute. Once, at the Surulere football stadium in Lagos, he received an overwhelming ovation greater even than the Head of State. Fela even had a larger retinue, with scores of musicians, chorus girls, dancers and bodyguards accompanying him. In 1974, at the same stadium, another demonstration of his popularity occurred during a Jimmy Cliff show. Towards the end of this Jamaican reggae star's performance, Fela was spotted by the crowd, a huge roar went up and the crowd carried him on their shoulders and circled the stage in the middle of the football field. After that, Jimmy Cliff decided that there was no point in going on.

Before it was burned down by the army in 1977, Fela's first home-base was in the ghetto area of Lagos known as Mushin, just across the road from his club, the Africa Shrine in the old Empire Club. He called his house the 'Kalakuta Republic', which in Swahili means 'Rascal's Republic' As he explained to me in 1975 the got the name from the wall of a Lagos prison cell:

> *It was when I was in a police cell at the CID headquarters in Lagos, called Alagbon Close. The prisoners called the cell I was in 'The Kalakuta Republic'. So if rascality is going to get us what we want we will use that name, because we are dealing with corrupt people so we have to deal rascally with them.*

In every way, the Kalakuta was a republic. It had its own rules, court, prison, clinic and barbed-wire security system. Fela lived inside with his musicians, dancers, twenty-seven wives, his brother, mother and three children, not to mention a donkey, a baboon and an Alsatian dog. Fela ruled the place like a traditional chief. Attendants waited on him and he fined and punished wrongdoers at his own court

I first saw Fela in 1972 when I was a student at the University of Ghana when he came to play (at that time he was on keyboards) at the Legon campus above the Central Cafeteria. But I met him personally in November 1974 when I was on a recording trip to Lagos with two of Faisal Helwani's bands (Basa Basa and Bunzus), and we played at Fela's Shrine and Fela assisted Faisal with our recordings. At that time Fela would often hold court and entertain in the Kalakuta Republic's 'session-room' whilst sitting on an adjacent toilet without a door. By 1975, when I went there the second time, he had put a thin curtain between the toilet and the session-room so that you could only see his legs and knees. As a result of his growing international popularity he had been advised that some sort of partition was necessary because of the increasing number of foreign visitors who might be shocked. I was surprised myself, but later on discovered that King Louis XIV the 'Sun King' of France, also sometimes held court for their privileged intimates while sitting on a special throne that doubled as a toilet.

The shows at the Africa Shrine I saw in the seventies always started with Fela as 'chief priest' pouring a libation at a small shrine dedicated to Kwame Nkrumah and other Pan-African leaders. A shrouded figure then leapt on stage and the show began with the Africa 70 band doing a long warm-up, before Fela appeared holding his sax. While playing, Fela was always flanked by two musicians playing claves and maracas. The rest of the band was stretched out behind him and included trumpeters, sax players, guitarists, conga-drummers and the trap-drummer Tony Allen, who incidentally is half Ewe. Six chorus girls performed sexy dances on raised platforms. Fela had a foot switch attached to these platforms so that if one of the dancers tired, he switched off her particular platform light and a fresh dancer took her place.

The compositions I heard at the Afrika Shrine in the mid-seventies were 'Lady' and 'Gentleman', about the way some Nigerians copy Europeans. Another song was 'Yellow Fever' that condemns Nigerian women for using bleaching creams. 'Confusion' was about the problems of modern urban life and 'No Bread' was a political song. In between songs Fela speaks or 'yabbis' to his audience about black consciousness, the colonial heritage, government corruption, and of course the need to legalise NNG, or Natural Nigerian Grass, for he hated anyone to call it Indian hemp. He was charged many times for possession of this leaf and once, when the police thought he had swallowed the evidence, they examined his stool under a microscope, but could find no trace of the weed. Fela captured the incident in his song 'Expensive Shit'. In fact, Fela was always turning his problems and palavers into music. For instance, in 1975 when one of his girls had been misbehaving, she had been put inside a little prison in the backyard of Kalakuta called the 'Kala Kosu'; a symbolic prison I might add, as the door was only tied with string. The young women made such a racket that she was finally let out into a circle of Kalakuta people, whom she shouted at and they shouted back, and they soon they had a call-and–response song going.

472

A more serious incident is described in Fela's song 'Kalakuta Show', about an attack on his house in 1974 by sixty riot police. They were looking for a young girl who had been playing truant from home and who was believed to have become one of Fela's dancers. By coincidence I was at the Akrika Shrine (the Empire Hotel) at the time, staying, as mentioned earlier, with a group of Ghanaian musicians on a recording trip. None of us had been in Lagos before and so our manager, Faisal Hewani, had warned us about the place the first night we arrived. The very next morning we woke to the smell of tear gas, as we were across the road from the Kalakuta. We could see the whole thing, including the stiff resistance put up by Fela's people who were throwing stones from the roof of the Kalakuta down onto the police. There was a show that night, so Fela's stand-in, his lawyer Tunji Braithwaite, known as 'Feelings Lawyer', took over the singing. By the next day an injured Fela was back on stage joking about the bandages on his head that he said made him look like the pope. The day after that he had even more trouble after a court case involving Indian hemp. But he won the case and a crowd of thousands followed him back from the court to Mushin, creating yet another 'go slow' (traffic jam) in overcrowded Lagos.

Because of his continual dicing with danger and because he didn't like the colonial name Ransome, Fela changed his surname from Ransome-Kuti to Anikulapo-Kuti, which means a person who carries death in his pocket. I travelled up and down with him to Abeokuta so I know that as he loved racing against Mercedes Benz cars. Fela would never give way, even with a truck coming the other way and in this test of wills, the other driver always gave way. This exhilarated all of Fela's people and put them into a good mood.

Fela's most serious confrontation with the establishment was just after the Nigerian Black Arts Festival, FESTAC of 1977. Fela had been needling the authorities for some time before this as he and his Young African Pioneers (YAP) organisation had distributed a half-million pamphlets criticising the recently introduced law of on-the-spot whippings for motor offences. They did not think it a good idea for the visitors to FESTAC to see these whippings as it was too reminiscent of what was happening in apartheid South Africa. YAP then released another half-million pamphlets condemning the organisers of FESTAC itself for corruption. On top of this Fela had just released his 'Zombie' album that lampooned the robotic military mentality. Indeed 'zombie' became a term of abuse for the military governments throughout Africa. The final straw for the Nigerian authorities came when a couple of Fela's people set fire to a motorbike belonging to a soldier from a nearby barracks. Fela refused to give up the culprits to face court charges and played Zombie at the soldiers whenever they came. Using the excuse that Fela was declaring his Kaluta to be an independent 'republic', which is against Nigerian law, the soldiers hit back by raiding the Kalakuta. They beat up everyone there, including Fela's mother, and set fire and completely gutted the premises. It should be added that an additional reason for the military government's hatred of Fela at that time was that he was planning to stand for President of Nigeria and was actually working on a biographical film called the 'Black President' at the time of the attack.

FELA'S BACKGROUND STORY

Both Fela's parents were famous. His father was a leading Yoruba educationalist and his mother, Funmilayo Ransome-Kuti, was a leading political figure in Nigeria. Fela's grandfather was the well-known Reverend J.J. Ransome-Kuti who composed Yoruba Christian hymns for the piano in the 1920s. When I interviewed Fela at the Kalakuta Republic in December 1975, he told me about his grandfather:

> *He was a preacher and was responsible for bringing Christianity to the Yoruba country here, which I think is very bad, so I have to undo what he has done. His mistakes are colonial and we are now trying to get the colonial thing out.*

Fela was brought up in Abeokuta and began his musical career as a highlife musician with Victor Olaiya's Cool Cats band in Lagos. He formed his own highlife group in England called the Highlife Rakers when he was studying music at Trinity College, London. Whilst there, he was influenced by the jazz of Miles Davis, John Coltrane and Thad Jones. When he returned to Nigeria in 1963 he formed his Koola Lobitos, which combined highlife and jazz. During the 1960s his band was based at the Afro-Spot (Kakadu Club) in Yaba and competed with other highlife bands of the time; like Rex Lawson's, Roy Chicago's and Eddie Okonta's. The Koola Lobitos got a big boost when they backed Millicent Small and Chubby Checker in their tours of Nigeria in the mid-1960s. Yet Fela's music did not catch on in a big way in Nigeria. But he was popular in Ghana where Fela made many tours in the late sixties organised by Raymond Azziz and Faisal Helwani. He was much impressed by the Uhuru big-band sound and whenever he was in Accra he stayed with this highlife band's leader Stan Plange. Stan explains what happened the first time Fela came:-

In 1966 or 1967 Zeal Onyia wanted to bring Fela and his Koola Lobitos group to Ghana. Zeal brought him to Uhuru House (in Asylum Down, Accra) and told me to take care of Fela. So we went around to book clubs, but Fela wasn't known in Ghana then at all and didn't have any recordings. Anyway Fela came back with his band which was playing highlife but in a very jazz mood. We got the Koola Lobitos to play at the Ringway Hotel, Accra, when Ignace de Souza's Black Santiagos was the resident band. The Uhurus also played there, as did other bands like the Ramblers and Geraldo Pino's Heartbeats. Fela's boys were staying at Ringway Hotel and he was staying with me at Uhuru House. But he had been wasting all his gate-money on their accommodation, so I suggested to Fela why don't you bring your boys to stay with mine, because Uhuru was a big band and Fela's was just a small combo. It was after that trip that Faisal Helwani began bringing Fela to Ghana. Fela so loved Ghana that the least time he stays in Nigeria, he rushed back down to Ghana for a holiday, and then would stay with me. I could guess that he used to come five or six times a year.

In 1969 Fela went to the United States and came into contact with black militants. As Fela explained to me, this completely revolutionised his approach to music.

At the beginning, my musical appreciation was very limited, but later I got opened to many black artists. And I saw that in Africa we were not open, as at that time they only let us hear what they wanted us to hear. When you played the radio it was controlled by the government and the white man played us what he wants. So we didn't know anything about black music. In England, I was exposed to all these things, but in Africa they cut us off. It was after I was exposed that I started using jazz as a stepping-stone to African music. Later, when I got to America, I was exposed to African history which I was not even exposed to here. It was then that I really began to see that I had not played African music. I had been using jazz to play African music, when really I should be using African music to play jazz. So it was America that brought me back to myself[32].

When he came back from the States, Fela changed the name of his band to the Africa 70 and concentrated solely on the soul influenced music he had begun experimenting with even before leaving for the U.S. In 1968 he coined his new sound 'Afro-beat' which, according Carlos Moore in his 1982 book 'Fela: This Bitch of a Life', he did whilst listening to the music of James Brown's in Accra with the Ghanaian/Nigerian

[32]There are many resemblances between Fela and the Ghanaian Afro-jazz drummer Ghanaba: elite family background, Nkrumahist and Pan-African politics, rebelliousness, dislike of their fathers and idealisation of their mothers, background in highlife and jazz, and becoming Africanised in the USA. I expand on this on pages 147-8 of my **'Fela: Kalakuta Notes'** book published by Welseyan University Press in 2015.

music producer Raymond Aziz. The American trip also got Fela to radicalise his lyrics in support of the down-trodden Nigerian masses, or 'suffer-heads' as he called them. His first two Afro-beat singles were 'Jeun Koku' (Chop and Quench) a proverbial song against inequality and 'Mister, Who Are You' that complained against 'bigmanism' which were instant hits in Africa in 1970. In 1971 the band went to London and recorded their first album at the famous Abbey Road studio called 'Fela Live with Ginger Baker'. On this album one of Fela's conga players was the Ghanaian dancer and percussionist Daniel 'J.B.' Koranteng.

Over the years Fela went on to release about one hundred record albums. During the seventies the Africa Shrine became a focus for musicians from Africa and abroad. Ginger Baker, the drummer with Cream, visited and played at the Shrine. Sandra Isodore, an Afro-American vocalist whom Fela had fallen in love with from Los Angeles recorded 'Upside Down' with Fela and the Africa 70. Paul McCartney and Wings also hung around the Shrine for a time and got into trouble for pinching some of Fela's musicians for a recording session without permission.

John Collins as a colonial officer with Fela Kuti as a schoolboy (left) and J.K. Braimah at Abeokuta School in 1977 for the shooting of the Black President film.

476

THE BLACK PRESIDENT FILM

By 1977 Fela thought it time to make a film of his life. He teamed up with the Ghanaian-Lebanese producer Faisal Helwani, the Ghanaian poet and film director Alex Oduro, and the Ghana Film crew. The film was called 'The Black President' and was shot in Accra, Lagos and Abeokuta. I played the part of a colonial education officer called Inspector Reynolds. I was meant to have spent four or five days in Abeokuta filming my part. But things went wrong as the Ministry of Education prevented the shooting of the part of the film at Abeokuta School where Fela's father, played by Feelings Lawyer, attacks me playing the role of a colonial school-inspector called Mr. Reynolds (coincidentally my maternal grandfather was called Reynolds). During this scene Fela's father chases Inspector Reynolds out of the room who, in his flight, knocks down Fela playing himself as a schoolboy. The Ministry thought this whole scene might embarrass the British government and so we had to shoot this sensitive part back in the Lagos office of Fela's younger brother, Dr. Beko Ransome-Kuti, and edit it into the shots at Abeokuta School. Incidentally, I had to repeat the shot of me knocking down Fela twice, as the first time it was not realistic enough for him. The second time I really sent Fela flying and much later the writer Carlos Moore[33] told me that Fela complained that I really winded him. Nevertheless it was the realism he wanted on the film and he never said anything to me about it. In fact, during one of his pre-show 'yabbis' early 1977 Fela mentioned the incident of how a white man had come down all the way from Accra to help in the film – and the Nigerian authorities had tried to put obstacles in the way.

Fela had enormous respect for his mother, Funmilayo Ransome-Kuti, a leading nationalist and feminist in Nigeria. One day on my 1977 trip and when I was teaching Fela's children (Femi, Remi and Sola) some science at her family house in Abeokuta, Fela burst into the room and told me to stop, accusing me of teaching his children colonial mentality. His mother blasted him for this and told Fela she wanted her grandchildren educated even if he didn't, and told him to leave the room, which he did. Even though Fela had invited me and paid for me to do the film, for some reason (probably his dramatic imagination) he sometimes confused me with the part I was acting, and actually seemed to think I was the colonial Inspector Reynolds. However, Mrs. Funmilayo Ransome-Kuti looked kindly on my acting and teaching efforts, and when I left Abeokuta she gave me a huge bag of soaps and other commodities that she knew were in desperately short supply in Ghana at that time.

---

[33]Who wrote the biography 'Fela: This Bitch of a Life' in 1982.

Unfortunately, after the filming was completed, the soundtrack was destroyed when the Kalakuta was burned by the army, an awful event that myself, Victor Azziz and the Ghana Film crew narrowly escaped, having left for Ghana a few weeks before. An attempt was made later in Ghana to re-dub the sound, but it was largely unsuccessful as most of the film had been ad-libbed and no one could remember their exact lines. I was able to do mine as it was scripted. At the Ghana Film dubbing studio I again met Mrs. Ransome-Kuti. She looked frail and was quite unable to recognise me, for during the attack on the Kalakuta she had been thrown out of a window on its second storey by a soldier. Shortly after leaving Ghana for Nigeria she died. Fela expressed his outrage about this in his song 'Coffin for Head of State' directed at President Obasanjo.

After that attack Fela moved both his Kalakuta Republic and Africa Shrine from Mushin to Ikeja and continued pumping out his music, with his son Femi playing sax. The Africa 70 made several international tours, particularly of Europe. On one of these tours I saw Fela play in the summer of 1981, at the Amsterdam Woods. On that trip he brought with him several hundred copies of his latest album ITT (International Thief Thief), the lyrics of which condemn the American multi-national company of that name.

At the press conference after the show the questions were, however, all about Fela's attitude toward women. A few years earlier, Fela had made the controversial decision to marry twenty seven wives. But he had not actually married them for sexual reasons; he had simply been trying to deal with the Ghanaian immigration authorities. He had gone with his band and numerous dancers and girl-friends to Ghana during the military government of Colonel Acheampong, which was not happy with the song 'Zombie', or Fela's radical speeches to Ghanaian students organised in Accra and Tema by the African Youth Command. So the airport customs officials used the excuse that he was accompanied by too many unnecessary women and deported the band back to Nigeria. Back in Nigeria, Fela promptly married the ladies in the traditional way, as he knew that Ghana, like Nigeria, allowed 'customary marriages'. So he, his band and all his twenty seven wives were able to return to Ghana with no problem from the immigration officials. So Fela did not marry these women for romantic or sexual reasons, but rather as a ploy to confuse the Ghanaian immigration authorities Nevertheless, he became notorious for having so many wifes and around 1980 at a press conference in Amsterdam many of the Dutch reporters did not know

478

the resosn for this group marriage and so demanded to know how he could claim to be a progressive and yet dominate a large harem of wives. One Dutch woman accused him of having no respect for women. Fela replied that women had their own specific duties to perform and that he would never enter a woman's kitchen, as it is her domain. He went on to say that in Africa, categories like male and female, old and new, day and night are never mixed-up as 'nature is clear with no confusions'. He added that unisex and uniformity may be fine for Europe but would never work in Africa.

I visited Fela, J .K. Braimah and the band (by then called the Egypt 80) at their Amsterdam hotel on that 1981 trip and met a very vexed Fela. He had just discovered that his British tour had been cancelled due to visa problems and put it down to the work of the American CIA and ITT. He talked about the psychological warfare these organisations used against so-called 'Third World' countries in terms of language. He could not see why the terms 'third', 'undeveloped', or even worse 'non-aligned' should be used. Non-aligned, for instance, means not straight, crooked or bent, all of which imply inferiority. His annoyance with all these derogatory terms found expression in his 1982 album called 'Original Sufferhead'.

After his mother's death Fela became interested in the occult, and in order to communicate with her spiritually he was helped by the Ghanaian concert party magician Professor Hindu (Kwaku Addae) who became Fela's religious guru in 1981. In 1984, Fela was arrested in Lagos for contravening the Nigerian currency laws and was sentenced to five years in prison, but served only nineteen months due to pressure from Amnesty International. During this time his son Femi managed his forty-strong Egypt 80 band. Due to his imprisonment Fela became even more internationally famous and in 1986 released 'Army Arrangement' on the U.S. Celluloid Records label. This was followed in 1988 'Beasts of No Nation' criticising the multi-national companies.

In 1994 Fela made his last brief trip to Ghana when he was invited by hotel manager and music promoter Smart Binete (himself a Nigerian). Then in early 1997 Fela was again arrested on hemp charges by the National Drug Law Enforcement Agency of Nigeria and was subsequently paraded in manacles before press and television reporters. He was released five days later and filed a court case against the NDLEA for illegal detention and displaying him in chains. In July 1997 Fela fell sick and was nursed at the Kalakuta house by his elder sister, Oludolupo Ransome-Kuti, a retired nurse.

Fela died on Saturday the 2nd August in Lagos and his death was officially announced by his elder brother, Professor Olikoye Ramsome-Kuti, who not only stated that Fela had died of AIDS, but warned the journalists and crowd present that ten percent of them were probably HIV positive. Tens of thousands of Nigerians filed past Fela's glass coffin at his funeral in Lagos on the 12th of August in the biggest funeral the country had ever seen, bigger than for any Head of State.

In Ghana, the country that Fela had loved and visited so much, there were two wake-keepings. On Monday the 11th of August the Musicians Union of Ghana (MUSIGA) held a vigil at the Centre for National Culture (the old Arts Council) in Accra, with music supplied by the African Brothers, Joe Mensah, Jewel Ackah, Paapa Yankson, A.B. Crentsil and Ebo Taylor. At the same venue on Sunday the 17th of August a wake was held for Fela by the Copyright Protection Committee, organised by Faisal Helwani and Stan Plange who had just returned from Fela's funeral in Lagos with Fela's son, Femi. That night Femi played some of his dad's numbers like 'Palava' and 'No Agreement' backed by the Ghana Broadcasting Band under its then leader Stan Plange. Some of the others who played that night were the Kumapim Royals, Kofi Sammy's Okukuseku, Professor Abraham and the master drummers Okyerema Asante and Tetty Addy. A funeral speech in honour of Fela was given by Nana Kofi Omane, the Chief of Akyem Nkwantanan, who had helped organise the student African Youth Command lectures for Fela in the 1970's.

Although Fela is dead, his Afrobeat music lives on in Nigeria and Africa. Femi runs the Positive Force band and his younger brother Sehun continues the Afrika 80 band at the new Shrine with Fela's long-time members, trumpeter Tunde Williams and, up until his death, the baritone saxist Lekan 'Baba Ani' Animashaun. Then there are the Afrobeat-influenced artists Kola Ogunkola, Dede Mabiaku, Bodun Ajayi, Kayode Olajide, Olaitan Adeniji, Funso Ogundipe, Biodun Adebiyi, Funsho Ogundipe (Ayetoro) and the masked performer Lagbaja, who in the late 1990s opened his 'Motherlan' amphitheatre in Lagos. Other well-known Nigerian Afro-beat band outside of Nigeria are those of Ken Okulolo (Kotoja band), guitarist Soji Odukogbe and Tony Allen now based in France. In the neighbouring Republic of Benin, the Gangbe Brass Band released an Afrobeat tribute in 2000 called 'Remember Fela' and South Africa's Hugh Masekela released a version of 'Lady'. In Ghana, the late Nana Danso scored several versions of Fela's music with his Pan African Orchestra and the hiplifer Nana King 2000 hit 'Champion' was based on and Afro-beat loop.

In 2008 a New York off-Broadway musical on Fela was staged, written by Jim Lewis and Bilt Jones and featuring Aaron Johnson and the Antibalas band. This was so successful that, in 2010, it became a full Broadway production financed by Stephen Hendel, Jay-Z and Will and Jada Pinkett Smith. Sahr Ngaujah played the part of Fela and Lillias White (later, Patti LaBelle) the role of Fela's mother, Funmilayo Anikulapo-Kuti. The Broadway show moved to London in late 2010 and, in 2017, was taken to Lagos.

For more detailed information on this amazing musician who released around 200 songs, see my book 'Fela: Kalakuta Notes' published in 2009 by the Royal Tropical Institute in Amsterdam, with an expanded version published in the United States in 2015 by Wesleyan University Press. Although several books have been written on Fela my book includes my personal recollections of working with him and also it puts a particular emphasis on the Ghana side of Fela and his music – as it includes interviews with Ghanaians who worked with or were close to Fela. These include Stan Plange, Joe Mensah, Faisal Helwani, Mac Tontoh, Daniel 'J.B.' Koranteng, Obiba Sly Collins, Frank Siisi-Yoyo as well as Professor Willie Anku of the University of Ghana and Nana Danso Abiam of the Pan African Orchestra who analysed some of Fela's music in the book.

Chapter 50

SEGUN BUCKNOR AND THE 1960s-1970s NIGERIAN POP SCENE

Segun (born 1946) was an active member of the Nigerian pop scene of the sixties and together with Orlando Julius and Fela Kuti helped create Afro-beat, also known as 'Afro-soul' in its early days. I visited Segun at his house in December 1975 when I was in Lagos staying at the Empire Hotel/Afrika Shrine with the Basa Basa musicians who were doing some recordings. Segun was then a journalist and he told me that he became interested in music as a schoolboy, from being in the choir of his King's College secondary school and from playing and recording with Roy Chicago's highlife dance band.

Then in 1964 and together with Sunni Smart-Cole and the Nelson Cole-Brothers, Segun formed a school pop band called the Hot Four. In 1965 he did studies in the U.S. where he fell in love with the soul music of Ray Charles, and on returning home in 1968 he found that Gerlado Pino's Heartbeats and Tony Benson's group were already playing soul. Segun quickly got his Hot Four school-friends together and they formed the Soul Assembly which immediately recorded two numbers, 'Lord Give Me Soul' and 'I'll Love You No Matter How', and then visited Ghana.

In 1969 this group disbanded and then reformed under the name Segun Bucknor and the Assembly, which he later changed to Segun Bucknor and the Revolution. The

Assembly (or Revolution) did not concentrate exclusively on soul but also developed its own style of Afro-soul. Segun based his group at the Crystal Gardens in Lagos, shaved all his hair from his head and brought in three women dancers. The band recorded many numbers which combined highlife, soul and jazz like 'Poorman Got No Brother', 'Sorrow Pass Sorrow', 'Son of January 15th' (a commentary on post-colonial Nigerian history), 'Who Say I Tire' (a satire on Nigerian society), and 'Pocket Your Bigmanism' (a song against the Nigerian nouveau riche).

The following is a portion of the interview I did with him at his house in Yaba, Lagos in 1974 and the first questions I asked him was to tell me about the first pop bands in Lagos.

BUCKNOR: They were school bands, and the first one was the Blue Knights. Then the first serious rock 'n' roll band we saw was called the Cyclops; they were just out of school and were formed in 1964. The beginnings of pop and rock 'n' roll was at the United States Information Service as they had an amplifier and P.A. System. We used to go there on weekends but there were no permanent groups, as we would just team up and give ourselves a name. Soul groups like the Hykkers International and Tony Benson's Strangers came later, around 1968.

JC: What were the main influences on Nigerian pop music?

BUCKNOR: There were imported pop magazines like Mirabelle and Fab. Then we were listening to the records of James Brown, Wilson Pickett, Otis Redding and Rufus Thomas. Around 1967, Chubby Checker and Millicent Small came as there was a growing interest in pop.

JC: Tell me more about the actual pop bands in Lagos.

BUCKNOR: Around 1964 to 1968 you had people who, even if they were not schooled in music, had the innate talent. They could listen to a record, pick it, play it, and sometimes do it better with their own innovations. The Hykkers guitarist was very good, and so was Berkeley of BLO. Then around 1970 to 1971 there came an urge, not just to play what you hear on records, but for compositions. I will say modestly that this trend has been around since 1969 when I started my own band and we were doing our own songs. Then you had band-boys coming up with their own beautiful

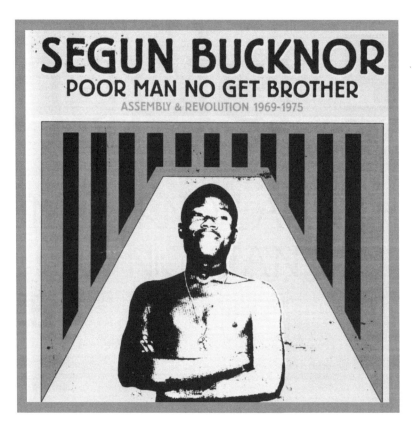

The Nigerian Afrobeat pioneer Segun Bucknor

compositions: the Hykkers, Ofo, Johnny Haastrup of Mono-Mono and Sonny Okosun. For you to thrive here in Nigeria you have to be very prolific and good at your compositions, even though you have to play a few pop numbers for the nightclub clientele. I've heard it is a bit different in Ghana. There, all the nightclub audiences want to hear is copies of the records they've heard on the radio. However, although there has been a great proliferation of pop bands, in the last two or three years there has been a decline, and they have faded due to the steady increase in support of juju music. I don't think Wings and Hykkers exist anymore. Johnny Haastrup's group is between life and death, I have stopped active involvement, and Ofo and the Black Company are overseas. Another thing that created a decline in pop music has been the rise of the army. Initially, they supported groups, as almost every brigade wanted to have a group or band attached to it. They brought instruments and recruited boys; so they started poaching which affected the civilian bands.

JC: You say the main competition to pop music is from juju music. Tell me about this music.

BUCKNOR: It's been going for years and has always been a variant of highlife, especially the guitar-band type like E.K. Nyame of Ghana. At first juju music didn't enjoy much popularity because of our rush to look modern. People here were enjoying going to the highlife bands with all their expensive instruments, so that juju bands were relegated to the background. In the fifties and up to 1966-1967, highlife was the main thing, and most of our highlife musicians came from the east. But with the (Nigerian Civil) war most of the easterners went to Biafra and highlife bands were grounded in Lagos. Some musicians who left were E.K. Arinze, Charles Iwegbue, Zeal Onyia and Rex Lawson who was then currently the highlife superstar. So, there was a dearth of musical entertainers in Lagos and since people must have their fun they turned around to juju bands. There was a vacuum, since places like the Lido, Empire Hotel and Kakadu all lost their resident highlife bands. Only Victor Olaiya and Roy Chicago stayed because they were from western Nigeria. The result is that today ears have been tuned to the easy style of juju, and highlife is considered to be too rigid and formalised. But, as you know music can never remain static and juju music, now, has a lot of imported influences from pop, Afro-beat and so on. For instance, in Obey's last album one of his numbers is an old (Ghanaian) konkoma number called 'Calabar'.

JC: Tell me more about the early music scene in Lagos.

BUCKNOR: You have to take it on two levels. One was the European influence from the turn of the century, with people forming English-style orchestras like the Lagos City Orchestra. Many of the members today are judges and company directors. Also coming in was the influx of Brazilians and we had a Brazilian Yoruba section of Lagos, like the Gomez family. As a result we had a diffusion of Latin American dance music. On the other hand by the early thirties you had informal dance-steps like konkoma (nb: originally from Ghana). This was not like the dance bands but was what you would now call highlife, but without the guitar. This dance-step was later called agidigbo, as it took the name from the Nigerian instrument which is a box with five strings (i.e. a hand-piano). These groups also used conga-like drums, bongos and local drums. Later they started adding guitars. This highlife music was called different names in different parts; in Western State it was called ashiko and in the Mid-West it was called konkoma: later it was all called juju music. So the low-class konkoma and the E.T. Mensah type of highlife existed side by side. E. T. Mensah's music was liked by people who took the English way and were the first middle-class Ghanaians and Nigerians. There was a kind of snobbery in that the man who was in the dance bands felt himself nearer the white man, as he would put on hat, tie, and jacket and would be called to balls and formal occasions. On the other hand, konkoma highlife was informal. During weekend labourer or carpenters would form a group to play at naming ceremonies for some few drinks, and a couple of pounds. While the dance bands tried to be more polished, konkoma was swinging in its own way and has come out in the world as juju music.

JC: What were too trying to do with your Revolution band and what are your future plans?

BUCKNOR: After the Assembly, I changed the name to Revolution because I was experimenting with pop music but using the real basic African beat, the African jungle beat. We sounded like a current group called Ofege which uses a similar basic West African beat 6/8 beat called 'kon-kon'. It's like what Santana did with Latin music and pop. Before Santana there were Latin-American groups that were making it, but not that big. But since Santana came out with a rock-Latin beat, older Latin-American musicians are coming up, like Mongo Santamaria who is a bongos player and is now enjoying some success. You know Latin-America's and our music is virtually the same. It's all in 6/8 time, but when you play Latin-American music you have to double the tempo. However, at the moment I don't operate a band. What is happening now is that I'm not playing publicly, although I am still playing for my own enjoyment. Like you, I write for newspapers and magazines.

Chapter **51**

THE OZZIDI, AFRO-REGGAE AND AFRO-DISCO OF SONNY OKOSUN

Sonny Okosun during his 'Ozzidi' period

Over the years Sonny Okosun has pounded out a series of distinctive styles that blend the local roots music of the mid-western Nigerian Edo State with western rock, disco and reggae. For three years he was a member of Victor Uwaifo's Melody Makers (see Chapter 48). Then in 1972 he formed his own Ozzidi band that played the 'ozzidi' beat which combined Bini highlife music, Afrobeat and Santana-style guitar: the name 'Ozzidi' coming from the Ijaw god of dancing and singing. In 1977 Sonny moved on to composing Afro-reggae hits followed by his own special type of disco music. His music was heard all over Africa, the Caribbean and the black communities of Europe and the States. During the late 1970s and 80s Sonny worked at the London-based EMI where the final touches to his releases were done, but the basic tracks were laid down at the EMI studio in Lagos. His engineer there was the dedicated and tireless Emmanuel Odemusi, one of the best sound engineers of West Africa whom I had the pleasure of working with in 1974 when I recorded with the Bunzus band of Ghana.

But let's start in the eastern Nigerian town of Enugu, where Sonny was brought up and where both his mother and grandmother were expert singers, dancers and traditional story-tellers. As Sonny told me when I met him in 1981, his first intention was to become a Hollywood actor and then as a teenager he became a pop fanatic.

> I was inspired by Elvis Presley and watched his film 'Loving You', and also Cliff Richard's 'Expresso Bongo'. I wanted to be a great man like them when I saw how many fans they had. Sometimes I used to sleep at the Rio Cinema in Enugu after watching all the films.

When Sonny left school, it was towards acting that he first turned.

> When I grew up, I joined a drama group called the Eastern Nigerian Theatre led by John Okwerri, who started the Mbari Centre in the East. The Mbari Centre was an organisation originally started by a white man to force us to know our roots. It had offices at Ibadan and Enugu and Nigerian writers like Wole Soyinka and J.P. Clarke were seriously involved.

At the Centre, actors, playwrights and musicians could meet. It was there that Sonny first took an interest in the guitar. His first guitar was actually bought for him by Miriam Okagbue, later head of the Imo State Broadcasting and Television station. In 1966 he formed his first group called the Postmen which he told me was the 'the first pop group in the eastern region and we played the music of Elvis, Cliff and the Beatles.'

When the Nigerian civil war broke out Sonny moved to Lagos where he started to work as a graphic designer for television in order to 'get as close to acting and music as possible'. In 1969, he teamed up, as second guitarist, with the 'Sir' Victor Uwaifo's Melody Maestros. Sonny toured Europe and Japan with them and learned a great deal during the three years he was a member of this band. By 1972, Sonny decided it was time to form his own group which he first called Paperback Limited, but shortly afterwards and as he explains, he changed the name to Ozzidi.

> *I originally wanted to be a playwright and tell the world about Shango, Chaka Zulu and the deep history of Africa. That's why I named my band Ozzidi. I studied Victor Uwaifo's style of composition, so when I left, I thought if I am to be recognised I must have my own rhythm. So I combined the African rhythm with the Beatles' style of playing, as I wanted a rhythm that anyone in the world could listen to. I am very proud that they can appreciate my records in America, Britain and even South Africa.*

Sonny's first recording success with his ozzidi music was the single 'Help" which sold over one hundred thousand copies in Nigeria. This was followed by three ablums – 'Ozzidi', 'Living Music' and 'Ozzidi for Sale', each of which sold one hundred thousand copies in Nigeria and were heard up and down the West African coast. Sonny made many tours with his band and dancers. Then in 1977 Sonny changed to a reggae sound, which happened by chance.

> *It was almost an accident, as I was recording six tracks for EMI and needed a seventh to fill the record up. That was my reggae song 'Help' which ended up being the biggest hit. It is a simple traditional Bini song but written in English. I got the rhythm from Ogunde the playwright. I do believe the reggae rhythm came from our side, for when I met Jimmy Cliff in New York, before he came to Nigeria [in 1974], he actually said he was playing highlife. And, in fact, if you listen deeply to reggae it has a highlife formation. The only difference is the modified beat.*

It was Afro-reggae that really made Sonny a superstar and his first album of this was 'Papa's Land' which sold 150,000 copies in Nigeria. The EMI record company was so pleased that in 1977 they sent Sonny to their Abbey Road studio in London, made

Sonny Okosun

famous by a band that Sonny idolises: the Beatles. At this London studio he recorded the two best selling albums 'Fire in Soweto' and 'Holy Wars'. Never one to stand still for a moment, Sonny then went over to a third sound, a disco version of his earlier Ozzidi music. I asked him in 1981 what made him decide to do this.

American disco music has taken over Africa. During the days of Victor Olaiya, the Uhuru and Ramblers dance-bands there was jazz music from America. Then there was pop music. It never gave us musicians a chance to move out. And you know with Africans, anything that comes from England is a gas. Then during the time of Victor Uwaifo and Fela there was this soul music. I always remember that one day Victor Uwaifo printed some handbills saying that no one should listen to soul music. But I think that soul music is like our aladura [praying] songs, it's a spiritual music. But they came down and took the business from us. Now these days we have funk, but I'm not lying low and I won't let it take gari [a type of food] from my hands. So I have decided to create my own type of African disco music. Believe me sincerely, it is catching on like wildfire. This music we hope to export to America and England.

His first disco song was the track 'No More Wars' which appears on his 'Third World' album and is sung in Yoruba. This was followed by 'The Gospel According to Ozzidi' sung in both Yoruba and English. When I saw Sonny in 1981 in London he was putting the finishing touches to a follow-up to these disco hits. Many of Sonny's songs, especially the later one, have a strong theme of African liberation and peace. In fact, his songs of peace were in such demand that in 1980 he was the first Nigerian musician to play in newly independent Zimbabwe. I asked him what he thought the role of a musician in society should be.

It is a God-given talent, just like a great football player, a boxer like Mohammed Ali, or Bruce Lee. So a musician owes a lot to society, as he sees more. Whatever we see, we store it in our memories and it explodes in the studio or on stage. We are talking to the world. You see, a musician is a lecturer and he can't do anything he likes. He has to wear a good dress or trousers. A musician has to correct society, as he has followers and fans. I sing protest songs and songs of truth, like 'We Don't Want to Fight Wars No More' which was played on radio and television in Nigeria when the Nigeria and Cameroon conflict burst. I don't sing Tom Jones type songs about love.

Sonny's social awareness is not only expressed in the lyrics of his songs, as he was also actively involved in helping set up a Musician's Industrial Board to defend artists' rights and replace the fragmented Musician's Union of Nigeria. As he explained to me in 1981 he wanted Nigeria to catch up with the Cote d'Ivoire.

When I was in Abidjan I was handled by the Ivory Coast Musicians' Union, a very strong union as you get all your royalties and mechanical rights. It's one of the best music unions in Africa. About 1978, I discussed with my manager about setting up a Musicians' Industrial Board and we went about getting some guys together, like Sunny Ade, Ebenezer Obey, Victor Uwaifo and musicians from the east. In the near future the government will recognise us. We want the board to be represented by a single Minister of Culture. When the Industrial Board is recognised it will be stronger than the old musicians' unions.

In his later years, Sonny became a born-again Christian and played and released danceable gospel songs. He visited Ghana in this capacity in 1996. After a protracted illness, he died in the U.S. in 2008.

THE POPULAR MUSIC OF SIERRA LEONE, LIBERIA AND FRANCOPHONE WEST AFRICA

9

Highlife
TIME 3

This provides an overview of maringa and other popular music styles of Sierra Leone. Following this are some details of the early Liberian guitar styles that made a formative impact on highlife – and a number of short profiles of some of the top recording artists of Liberia during the mid-1980s. The last chapter in this section looks at Francophone West Africa and particularly the popular music scene of Ghana's close neighbours: Cote d'Ivoire, Togo and Benin.

Chapter 52

MARINGA AND THE POPULAR MUSIC OF SIERRA LEONE

The Accra-based (partly Sierra Leonian) Gee Dee's, early 1970s.
Samuel Olu King is standing middle with Prince Ali on far right. Maurice is crouching on the right

Sierra Leone was founded in 1780s by the British for freed black slaves who were settled in Freetown and who created their own language called Krio (or Creole). Being a port, Freetown's music was also influenced by seamen from America, Caribbean and other parts of West Africa.

According to the Freetown percussionist, Samuel Olu King (who I met in Accra in the mid-1970s), there were three forms of Krio music in existence before the Second World War. These were goombay, palmwine music and maringa. Goombay or gumbay frame-drum music was, as mentioned in Chapter 23, introduced by the Krios who were descended from Jamaican freed slaves or 'maroons's. Palmwine music was Sierra Leone's equivalent to Ghanaian osibisaaba, Nigerian 'native' blues and the guitar songs of Liberian Kru's who had a large quarter or 'Kru-town' near the Freetown docks. Palmwine music (according to Oju sometimes called 'ragtime') was a low-class guitar music played around the bars in Freetown by artists like 'Useless Man' Foster and the seaman Eku who were accompanied by percussionists tapping on cigarette tins and bottles.

Maringa came later and was played using a a variety of instruments that included a large 'congama' hand piano with four hacksaw blade keys, guitars, concertinas hand-drums goombay drums, cigarette tins and bottles, musical saws and a small metal trumpet that produced only one note. It was sung in the Krio language or an indigenous ethnic language and was danced to in 4/4 time. Interestingly, maringa is the same name as the earliest popular guitar music of Central Africa and the Spanish island colony Fernando Po discussed in Chapter 55[34]. As Sierra Leonians settled in this West African island in the late 19th century they may have introduced the maringa to Freetown from the early 1900s. Whatever its exact origins, maringa seems to have surfaced in Freetown in the late 1930s as a development of local palm-wine music influenced by local goombay and West Indian calypso music.

Below are a few examples of the Krio lyrics of some of the songs of these early palm-wine and maringa groups.

[34]The Fernando Po connection is according to the Spanish researcher Isabela de Aranzadi (2010 and personal communication 5th August 2011). She says maringa was present there as early as 1910.

KING JIMMY

King Jimmy around the water side, Bonga fish (herring) you get them every day,
So if you want to cook your bonga fish, You can take a walk to the water side,
Give me occra bongo soup, Boborombo na so we de (that's how we are)
Get your fish from down K. baby, Fufu ne de fiti yie occra soup

A LAZY WOMAN

I cook fufu it turn to starch,
I cook agidi (unsweetened blancmange) it turn to pap,
You just sit down like Cinderella, Ee mon ami, ee mon ami.

TRUNGAYAISE ('RUFFIAN')

Me Papa say make I no come out, Me Mama say make I dey na house,
But me Paddy come we go Lumley beach, Moto-car go broke my waist.
Trungayaise no good-o, Trungayaise no good-o
I follow me Paddy we go Lumley beach, Moto-car go broke my waist.

SWEETIE PALM WINE

I catch a bus to Lumley, I meet a nice conductor,
Five shillings he charged me, because of my education,
The boys and girls were laughing, they say I am a drunkard,
Thank God I am freeborn, and Freetown is my colony,
Anywhere I go sweetie palm wine de wait for me.

E.T. Mensah and the Tempos visited Sierra Leone in 1958, and below is E.T.'s description of the music scene there at that time.

> *There were no dance bands in Sierra Leone and at the clubs they danced to gramophone records. Highlife was there but not under that name. We didn't see any guitar-bands, although we did meet one boy who was popular for his guitar playing. We did hear some local highlife records sung in Pidgin English, with the vocalist backed by one guitar. We picked up some of these songs from the town and two of them we later recorded. One was about a river and we called it 'Volta', and the other was 'Fire de Come'.*

The song about a river that E.T. Mensah mentions is a local one called 'River Rockel', and it has the refrain that goes 'River Rockel, me no savvy swim, water de carry me go.'

E.T. changed the word to 'River Volta' and according to Godwin Yirenki it was later again changed into the Ghanaian 'abongo' marching song 'River Congo' by Ghanaian soldiers who were with the U.N. Peace Force during the 1960s Congolese Civil War.

E.T. mentions that, in 1958, he heard a local music that was similar to highlife music. In fact, this was the previously mentioned 'maringa music', a development of local palm-wine music that evolved in the late 1930s and was influenced by Caribbean meringue and West Indian calypso music. Some of the early Krio maringa musicians of the 1940s and 50s were Ali Ganda, Famous Scrubbs, Chris During and Tejan-Se, with the most popular being Ebenezer Calender whose father had been a ship's barber from Barbados. It was Calender who released 'River Rockel' and many other popular hits of the 1950-60s; like 'Double Decker Bus', 'Jollof Rice' and the love song 'Fire de Come' that was a big hit in Ghana and I recall hearing it played on records when I was a child in Ghana in the early fifties. In 1956 Calender formed his Rokel River Boys and below are Samuel Oju King's comments on this important musician.

Calender originally played goombay and later formed his band which was a brass band with one goombay drum, two frame drums, guitars, flutes, recorders, trumpets and a sousaphone that you wrap around your body. By the time I quit Sierra Leone in 1967, he was a fairly old man and had stopped music and was made a producer on Radio Sierra Leone.

Ebenezer Calendar and his Sierra Leonean maringa group 1947.
(Photo Professor Wolfgang Bender)

496

Other popular maringa groups of this period were those of the street musicans Peter Na Leopard and W.P. or Waking Profit (because they made money from wake-keepings) These bands had no brass instruments, but featured the musical saw, guitar, drums and triangle. Like Calender's group, they played at weddings, funerals and picnics, and were considered to be more respectable than the palmwine groups. Below is an old maringa song that Peter Na Leopard used to sing. It is in praise of a bride's mother and Oju King says that his grand-mother used to sing it:

YAWHO ('BRIDE'S) MAMMY

Yawho mammy hebe (heavy) so,	(chorus)
Who that you give 'em to,	(Peter)
I give 'em to that little boy tonight,	(chorus)
Where de bottle,	(Peter)
Bottle de na room.	(chorus)

In addition to maringa, a newer form of goombay drum music appeared on the Freetown streets in the 1950 and 1960s known as 'milo' or mailo jazz'. The name of a cheap local gin. This was created by 'Dr. Oloh' (Olufemi Cole) who used goombay drums, agogo bells, shakers, a wooden 'kuma' box-drum, harmonica, trumpet and local ethnic Mende, Temne and Limba drums.

By 1960, Sierra Leone dance bands were being influenced by Ghanaian highlife and western rock music, as explained below by Olu King.

> Highlife was very popular, and we had a couple of groups that played this music. One was the Ticklers, which had saxes, trumpets, guitars and was rather like the (Ghanaian) Ramblers and was patronized by middle-aged Sierra Leoneans. The Ticklers played highlifes, Latin numbers and meringues which were a bit more polished than Calender's. We also had the female Police Orchestra, a big band with women vocalists, drummers, guitarists, sax and trumpet players. In 1960 rock 'n' roll also started to appear in Sierra Leone through radio and records, and was absorbed into the repertoires of bands like the Ticklers and Police Orchestra. However, the first pop group there was the Heartbeats, formed in 1961-1962 by the young Krio musician Geraldo Pino.

The Heartbeats were modelled on western pop bands with three electric guitars, organ, trap drums and vocals. Inspired by them were a number of other student pop groups in Freetown, such as the Echoes formed in 1964 (this was the band Olu King was in), the Red Stars and the Golden Strings. Akpata Jazz featuring Congo and pop music was another band started at this time that was financed by the Prime Minister, Sir Albert Margai. According to Olu King, the early pop influences were songs like Cliff Richard's 'Devil Woman' and 'Put on Your Dancing Shoes', Elvis Presley's 'Jailhouse Rock', the Beatles 'Hard Day's Night', Sam Cooke's music, Fats Domino's 'Hello Josephine' and Chubby Checker's 'Twist'.

In 1964, the Heartbeats went to Monrovia for two years and returned to Sierra Leone, having learned to play soul. Liberia was the first West African country where the records of James Brown, Ray Charles, Otis Redding and Wilson Pickett became popular. The Heartbeats consequently became West African first soul band and they went to Ghana in 1966 and then Nigerian in 1968, spreading this music as they travelled. Another creative influence on the local pop and jazz music scene in Sierra Leone during the mid-60s was the Yellow Diamond nightclub, owned by a group called the Leone Stars. Olu King comments on it:

> *It was formed by the break-up of two groups. At this time (1964) we had some visiting bands, one called Outer Space from Nigeria, and a Ghanaian band based at the Tijuana nightclub in Freetown. Both bands were in town when they broke up. There were a couple of people from the Outer Space who were very popular in Sierra Leone, for instance Sharp Mike, a Nigerian trumpet player who had been popular in Ghana during the days of the Star Gazers, and Eddie Ewa a sax player. They had a couple of friends from the Ghanaian band such as Tetteh a trumpeter, Archie a drummer and Nat a guitarist. They all teamed up with a Sierra Leonean conga drummer to form the Leone Stars, obtained a loan and renovated a vacant club formerly called the Swazark Club. Progressive music like jazz and pop was played at the Yellow Diamond and on Saturday afternoons, they had jam-sessions featuring prominent musicians. For instance, there was a black American guitarist called Woodie, who was a diplomat. Another was a Ghanaian drummer called Buddy Peep, who had been in the States playing jazz drums and knew Guy Warren. I jammed there, we all jammed there.'*

Instigated by the musicians who congregated around the club, a twelve-hour jam-session was organised at the Juba Barracks just outside Freetown at which fourteen bands played. Most, like the Echoes, Golden Strings, Super Combo, Ticklers and Akpata Jazz came from Sierra Leone (the Heartbeats had left by then). But there was also a band from the Congo, Bembeya Jazz from Guinea and the Formulas pop band from Britain.

A new genenration of dance bands appeared in the 1970s that played maringa music influenced by both foreign Congolese 'soukous' and disco-type Caribbean music – as well as local Temne and Mende folk music. These bands included Patricia Koroma and Sulay Abubakar's Afro Nationals, Super Combo, Vox Afrik, the Daylex Dance Band, Sabbanah 75 and Orchestra Muyah - and they called their new form of maringa 'soca-beat'. The biggest hit in this style was the Afro Nationals 1970s record release 'Money Palaver'.

Despite these developments, many of the young musicians left Sierra Leone, as they found the music scene there too quiet and they wanted to assimilate new ideas. As mentioned, the Heartbeats left the country and ended up in Nigeria where they finally split up in 1971. The founder of the group, Geraldo Pino, recruited some Ghanaian musicians (Lord Lindon's Triffis or Plastic Jims) and took them to Kano, while the other members (including Francis Fuster) remained in Lagos from 1972-8 under the name Baranta. Super Combo took up residence in London where they worked with the Sierra Leonian producer Akie Deen (see next chapter). The Echoes, including Samuel Oju King and bassist Bola left for Ghana in 1967 and formed the Q Masters in Kumasi. Then Maurice Williams, leader of Akpata Jazz also left for Ghana to join the Black Santiagos.He then teamed up with the Q Masters musicians and the Ghanaians Chester Adams and Prince Ali to form the Gee Dee's (Grave Diggers) band in Accra. About the same time the well-known exponent of the palm-wine guitar, Sooliman Ernest Rogie left for the United States Rogie was influenced by American Jimmy Rodgers type country-and-western music and with his Morningstars Band released a number of top West African hits in the early 1960s, such as 'My Lovely Elizabeth'. In 1973 he settled as a teacher in California and was inactive in the palm-wine music scene for a while, but made a come-back in the 1980's with 'World Music' albums like 'The Sixties Sounds of S.E. Rogie'. From then on he regularly toured Europe and the States up until his death in 1994, and I met him on one such trip to the UK.

In 1978 Sierra Leone became a one-party state and, during the 1980s, the country underwent rampant inflation and acquired a huge foreign debt. Not surprisingly the vibrant music scene suffered and many musicians left the country. Sierra Leone's top guitarists, Abdul Tee-Jay and Mwana Musa moved to London in the 1980s to operate their African Connection band. Then the percussionist Ansumana Bangura, whilst on a Germany tour with Miriam Makeba, decided to remain abroad, whilst Jimmy B (James Bangura] left home in the late 1980s for the UK and then South Africa where he became a star in the local 'kwaito' techno-pop music scene.

THE 1991-2002 CIVIL WAR ERA AND AFTER

Up until the eleven year Civil War in Sierra Leone that started in 1991, some of the local dance bands continued to operate, like the Afro Nationals. But after the war had began, night-life suffered and the local popular commercial music scene was only able to continue due to the introduction of new forms or relatively cheap recording technology and cassette production. Between 1991 and 1993, there was the Music and Disco Center that used a Tascam cassette 'portastudio'. In 1992 the Sierra Leone Cassette Sellers Association (CSA) was formed. The young Mende singer Nhoh Gbetuwai, for intstance, managed to operate in the nineties by releasing music on cassette utilising synthesiser backing tracks.

By the mid-1990s, there were five recording studios in Freetown, the most important being the Super Sound Studio that opened in 1992. According to Michael Stasik Michael (2010), this became the mainstay of Sierra Leone's local music industry producing artists such as Johnny M and the Slaves, Jahman and the Sierra Wailers and Sahid Kargbo. Many artists sang about the need for peace. For instance, there was 'Peace For My Native Land' released in 1996 by the blind musician M. B. Attilla and a stream of albums during the late 1990s, like 'Welcome to Democracy Na Salone ' and 'Born For Suffer' by Steady Bongo (Lansana Sherrif) who played an up-tempo form of maringa influenced by West Indian soca and dance-hall reggae. Another was the 2001 'Da System' by the Jungle Leaders hiphop trio that had been formed in one of the refugee camps in Guinea, where many Sierra Leoneans had fled during the Civil War.

Although the Civil War did not officially end until 2002, things began to improve in Freetown from 1999 when there were ceasefires and UN sponsored peace-deals. As a result, the local music scene began to pick up. Radio stations multiplied in Sierra Leone from five in 1999 to twenty five by 2009, by which time there were also around sixty recording studios. Moreover, the Sierra Leone Cassette Sellers Association grew from two thousand members in 2001 to over four thousand in 2007, the same year that the National Association of Sierra Leonean Artists (NASLA) was formed by two hundred musicians.

Not surprisingly, some of the artists who had gone abroad came back home; such as Ansumana Bangura who returned from Germany to establish a recording studio in Freetown. Particularly important was the hiphop artist and recording engineer Jimmy B who returned from South Africa in 1999 to set up his Paradise Records in Freetown through which hundreds of new artists emerged. The Jungle Leaders also came home from Guinea and by 2007 were releasing songs against the ruling Sierra Leone party like 'Pak and Go' and 'Time Don Don.'

Some of the old maringa dance bands, like the Afro-Nationals, Sabannah Internationals (formerly Sabbanah 75) and Super Combo were also able to start operating again. Another case in point is the blind musician Sori Kondi who had lost all his master tapes in one of the rebel attacks on Freetown in the late 1990s, but by 2007 was able to release songs like 'No Money No family' via the Cassette Seller's Association of Sierra Leone.

Local forms of Jamaican reggae and dance-hall ragga also became popular in the post-war era, such as Sisters With Attitude who sing reggae music in Krio. Another is Daddi Cool, a Sierra Leonean who combines reggae and contemporary R&B and who fled to Guinea during the Civil War and still resides there, but releases songs for both the Guinean and his home market. The top reggae/dance-hall artists betweeen 2010 and 2012 were Ragga Spice (Alusine Sesay) and Lady F (Fatmata Tarawally) the 'queen' of dance hall. Another important female artist is 'Lady' Felicia Turaya who, rather than drawing on Caribbean reggae and ragga, falls back on the seventies 'soca-beat' and 'discolypso' forms of up-tempo maringa.

Local hiphop and rap that use Krio and other local languages surfaced in Sierra Leone in the 1990s. This became major genres after the war when many of songs criticized the political class, such as the previously mentioned 'Da System' by the Jungle Leaders. Others are Daddy Saj's rap songs on corruption and lack of basic social amenities like 'E de so', 'Wan Pot Sojas' and 'Ar Vexed', whilst just one month before the 2007 elections the hiphopper Innocent released 'Ijectment Notice' that called for Sierra Leoneans to 'eject' the incumbent party. Some artists combine local forms of hiphop with R&B, one being the 441 rap trio. Another is K Man (Mohamed Saccoh) who began his career in 2004 with fellow Sierra Leonean rappersC-Jay and Camouflag of the Freetown hiphop group Conscious Knowledge, and then began to operate out of Guinea. The most famous Sierra Leonean hiphopper is Kao Denero who began rapping as a schoolboy in the 1990s, but moved with his family to the US in 1997. He is still based in the US but makes regular annual trips to Sierra Leone.

I should finally add that local gospel music also became an important dance music style in Sierra Leone, supplied by local singers like Vicky Formah, Johnny Wisdom, Millicent Rhodes and Alim Sasay. Another gospeller is M.B. Atilla (or Mohamed Bai) who from the late 1970s was a member of the famed Sierra Leonean musical group, the Blind Musical Flames. During the Civil War, he moved to the United States as a refugee where he played recorded with various gospel groups. He then returned home and, in 2010, received a Life Time Achievement Award from Sierra Leone TV. In 2013 he became Deputy Minister of Social Welfare, Gender and Children's Affairs.

Chapter 53

THE SIERRA LEONE MUSIC PRODUCER AKIE DEEN AND HIS DISCO MARINGAS AND DISCOLYPSOS

Sierra Leone's Akie Deen (right) and Bunny Mack (left) around 1980

Akie Deen is a friendly, larger-than-life Sierra Leonean producer based in London who moved in a big way into the Afro-Caribbean disco market that grew up in the 1970s and 80s, and combined this sound with West African music. One of the effects of the international 'disco fever' of the time was the updating of calypsos, meringues, sambas and rumbas by West Indian artists. There was the salsa of Cuba and Puerto Rica, the zook music of the French Antilles and soca (soul calypso) from Trinidadian artists like Ed Watson – as well as old-time calypsonians like Lord Kitchener whose revamped version of 'Sugar Bum Bum' was a major disco success in the late 1970s. Akie Deen simply moved into this field with his disco versions of Sierra Leonean maringas and Ghanaian highlifes, calling his sound disco calypso or simply 'discolypso'.

It should be noted that West Indian music has been popular in Sierra Leone for many years. Indeed, as far back as the 1820s there were regiments of West Indians stationed at Freetown who had marching bands. And in the 1940s to 1960s there were a number of local Freetown artists who played calypsos as well as local maringas; such as Calender, Ali Ganda, Famous Scrubbs and Tejan-Se. So it is no wonder that Akie Deen was easily able to re-combine West Indian and local music together into his discolypso in the 1980s.

Akie was born in Freetown in 1947 and first became interested in music production when he was Social Secretary of the Sierra Leonean Students' Union in England in 1972. In the same year, he helped organise an eight-week tour of Sierra Leone's top guitar-band, the Afro Nationals. He was also involved with their first two singles 'Dem Kick' and 'Wondemuyie'. In 1973, Akie arranged a tour of the United Kingdom for Ghana's top guitar-band, Nana Ampadu's African Brothers, and recorded two songs by them, including the popular 'Maria' based on a Congolese rhythm. Even though his records were popular in West Africa there were problems in England, as he explained to me in the early 1980s at his Clapham house in London.

> *It was with great difficulty that I got the first shop in London to take even ten records. Also I had no car and had to put the records in a friend's car. We used to attend parties and ask the DJ to play them in order to sell them. That was until I convinced Steve Barnard, a DJ on Radio London's Reggae Time, to play them on the air. Then I got requests for boxes of twenty-five from shops who had only taken a single copy. In one week I got through five hundred.*

In 1974, Akie produced two bands. One was the London based Sierra Leone group Super Combo with whom he made the highlife 'Merigueoko'. The other group was the Funkees Afro-rock band from Nigeria and their first album 'Point of No Return' was jointly produced by Akie and Dan Jegede. The following year members of the Afro Nationals, under the name Sabannah 75, came to London again and helped by Akie released three singles: 'Susanna', 'Konko' and 'Carry On', which all became big hits back in Sierra Leone. The band returned yet again in 1977 and Akie released a twelve-inch single version of Rokafil Jazz's 'Sweet Mother' with them, under the registered Afro-Disco name of 'Wagadugu'. Akie continued to release his evolving discolypso sound with Teddy Davies's version of Lord Kitchener's 'Just a Little Bit' and the two singles 'Tumba' and 'Carolina' by Addy Foster Jones of Sierra Leone television. In 1977 Akie also released two traditional songs by the Liberian singer Miatta Fahnbulleh. One in disco style was called 'Amo Sakee Sa' and the other with a reggae beat was 'Kokolioko'. Akie then went on to produce a single by Nigeria's Jake Solo, licensed by Pye. Jake Solo, had been a member of the Hykkers pop group in eastern Nigeria and then formed his Funkees Afro-rock band in 1969.

But the big breakthrough into the Afro-Caribbean disco market for Akie came in 1979 with the release of 'Easy Dancing' by Wagadugu, followed by 'Discolypso' and 'Funny Lady' by Cecil Bunting McCormack (or Bunny Mack). Bunny Mack is from Freetown and had played harmonica and penny-whistle as a child and then moved onto the guitar. In 1966 he formed his Soundmasters band, but used the stage name Kenny Marso due to parental disapproval of his profession. In 1967 the band travelled to Europe and in 1979 began working with Akie Dean. In 1980 Bunny Mack had his first Afro-disco produced entry into the British pop-charts, 'Love Me Love You Forever', which got to number five in the disco charts and number seventy-six in the singles charts. Bunny Mack employed some Ghanaian session musicians on this successful record including Alfred 'Kari' Bannerman, George Lee and Papa Mensah. 'Love Me Forever' was also a hit song in the West Indies and in Africa. In Nairobi it was a number one hit and in Nigeria in 1981 it earned a gold disc, as it sold over one hundred thousand copies there for the Tabansi label.

Akie followed this huge success by even more disco singles like 'Weakness for Your Sweetness' by Jimmy Senyah from Barbados, which reached number twenty-five in the British disco charts and was subsequently released by Scorpion Records in France and got into the French hit parade as well. Other artists whom Akie began producing included the Ghanaian keyboard player Emmanuel Rentoz, the West Indies singer Nina da Costa, Yvonne Mobambo from South Africa, Leon Charles from Barbados and the operatic and folk singer Martha Ulaeto from Nigeria. Akie also organised tours of Nigeria for Bunny Mack to coincide with Mack's second album release, 'Supa Frico'.

So in the 1980s discolypso became popular in Britain, the West Indies and back in Africa radio where stations were constantly playing Akie's productions, especially those of the Cote d'Ivoire Radio Kenya – and Nigeria where one of his records won a gold award in 1981. So the Story of African disco is a circular one. Disco is based on African American soul and funk whose roots go back to Africa; indeed, James Brown admitted that he got some of his beats from Africa. Then funk was computerised by the German groups Kraftwork and Munich Machine, and the resulting disco dance music (at 154 beats per minute) launched the careers of Donna Summers and Boney M. By the mid-seventies, disco-mania was in full swing and, as mentioned above, it influenced the soca (soul calypso) and zook of the Caribbean. When introduced to Africa, it brought in the idea of dancing in dark, enclosed discotheques, quite different from the normal practice of open-air dance spots. For instance, in 1980 the World Disco Championship, which involved fourteen thousand contestants, was won by the creative dancing of the thin and lanky South African Godfrey Raseroka, and in 1985 the Ghanaaian dancer, Adjetey Sowah, won the World Disco Dance Competition in the U.K.

At first, there were many imitations of disco by African musicians, but then in the 1970s and 1980s new types of Africanised disco emerged. A Ghanaian example discussed in Chapter 37 is 'burger highlife'. Likewise, in Sierra Leone, there was the 1970s maringa 'soca-beat' of Freetown-based bands like the Afro Nationals mentioned in the previous chapter and, as discussed in this chapter, Akie Deen's discolypso.

Chapter 54

POP PROFILES OF LIBERIA

Highlife is generally recognised as the first of the modern popular dance-styles to have been created in West Africa. However, it is from Liberia that the guitar techniques of this music originates. For the distinctive highlife guitar picking style (using thumb and first finger) which is related to traditional playing techniques of the African harp-lute, was first developed by the coastal sea-faring Liberian Kru or Kroo people. They were employed on European sailing ships and steamers and spread their distinct fingering style down the West and Central African coast, where it not only became an early influence on Ghanaian guitar highlife, but also on the maringa music of Sierra Leone, the juju music of Nigeria and the makossa of the Cameroon. When I visited Liberia in 1984 and did a radio programme in which I mentioned this important contribution to West African popular music made by the Liberian Kru and related Grebo people, I had a visit the following day from the Minister of Culture. He was surprised by this revelation, as many Liberians are not aware of this piece of Pan West African History that some of their own people were involved with. However, the old-timers do remember – and when I talked to the old Liberian guitarist and accordionist David Kwee Bedell (born in 1907) he told me that modern Liberian music was not only started up by sailors, but also by members of the marching or brass-bands: in both cases mainly in the coastal Maryland County inhabited by Krus and Grebos. The sort of music these early groups played were local quadrilles, folk-songs and the occasional calypso and foxtrot. Indeed, Mr. Bedell recalled the names of two Grebo guitarists of the 1920s, Alfred Collins and Gydate Johnson, who were accompanied by musicians playing banjos, accordions, musical saw, clips and maracas.

In spite of guitar-band music being recorded in Ghana and Nigeria as early as the 1920s, it never was in Liberia, which tended to be swamped by American records. This is not surprising as Liberia itself was set up in the 1822 by African Americans who had been liberated from slavery (thus the name Liberia) with the country becoming independent in 1847. According to the Ghanaian highlife musician E.T. Mensah, who visited the capital city Monrovia in the fifties, "the Liberians had first class night-clubs there, but no bands, only music such as swing and jazz played on hi-fi amplifiers".

In spite of what E.T. saw, there were in actual fact a few local guitar bands in the fifties like those of Hanty Coleman and Tom Brown, but they never played at night-clubs, only at the low class palm-wine bars. Furthermore, they never had a chance to record as there were no recording studios in Liberia until the 1960s. The one exception was some recordings of popular and traditional music done in 1954 on a portable machine by the American Arthur Roberts that included the Greenwood Singers dance band and choral group and the blind pianist Howard Hayes who played local palmwine tunes, calypsos and ragtime. Incidentally, a little earlier Roberts had been in Ghana doing recordings which included the guitar band artists E.K. Nyame and Eupheme Cooper.

By the sixties some recordings were being done in Liberia by the Lebanese record shop owner Mr Shaafi, with the first proper studio being the two-track ABC studio, also set up by a Lebanese man. He recorded top guitar bands like those of Jones Dopoe, Jerome Faye, John Dweh, Anthony Nagbe and Morris Dorley. Later, Studio One was established in Monrovia in which the late South African trumpeter Hugh Maskela was involved. Women also began to make a contribution to the recording business of Liberia during the 1960s. The first was Yatta Zoe in 1964 who went on to release twenty-four singles and six albums over the next twenty years, mostly Gola and Mandinke songs backed by a guitar-band. She represented Liberia at Nigeria's FESTAC in 1977. Another female group of the sixties was the Sherman Sisters who had a big hit with their record 'Bassa Love'. They were followed in the seventies by Hawa Daisy Moore and Christine Clinton who both recorded with Hugh Masekela, and the international Liberian singer Miatta Fahnbulleh.

FAISAL HELWANI'S MONROVIAN STUDIO 99 IN THE MID 1980s

I was invited to Liberia in September 1984 by the Ghanaian-Lebanese music producer Faisal Helwani who had, the previous year, set up Monrovia's third recording studio, Studio 99, after closing his Ghanaian studio due to the economic problems back home. Studio 99 was an eight-track one located near the seaside at Sinkor and recorded Liberian, Guinean, Sierra Leonean and Ghanaian musicians. I was brought over by Faisal to interview some of the thirty-six musicians he had already recorded and whose music he had released on cassette for the Liberian and West African market.

I travelled by plane from Ghana to Monrovia with Faisal's graphic artist Sammy 'Slim' Bentil who, coincidentally, I had worked with in an Achimota school 'Deep Blues Feeling' pop band in the 1969. We landed in a typical Liberian rainstorm and Faisal took us to his studio where we met his twenty-one year old recording-engineer son, Sammy, and the strong-arm assistant Roget Brisson, popularly known as 'Al Capone'. They were in the middle of recording some local hymns by the thirty-two strong Lott Carey Baptist Mission choir led by Rudolph von Ballmoos. After they left I had a chance to talk to some of the musicians around. I met Ciaffa Barclay who was doing a recording with the two Ghanaian session-men Faisal had brought over the previous year, Aweke Glyman (now in Australia) and B.B. Dorwuona-Hammond (now in Germany). I also met my old friend from Ghana, Francis Kenya, whose guitar band and concert party was on an Ivorian tour, and so he was taking the opportunity to extend his trip to neighbouring Liberia to make a master-tape at Studio 99.

Over a period of about two weeks, I interviewed many of the Liberian artists that Faisal had under his production – which I will present here as a series of profiles. It should be noted these are the Liberian recording artists who were popular before the terrible civil war that devastated the country.

MORRIS DORLEY, a Gola man born in 1946 who started playing the congama (giant hand-piano) at sixteen years, until an American bought him a guitar and he moved on to learn palm-wine music. He then formed his Sunset Boys guitar-band which first recorded in 1970 at Mr. Shafi's record shop and then again in 1979 at the ABC studio. His cassette productions done at Faisal's Studio 99 were 'Liberia is my Home' and 'Alive and Well', a mixture of meringues, rumbas and dagomba highlifes sung in his distinctive high pitched voice.

THE MUSIC MAKERS was one of the most popular bands in Liberia. It was set up by Sonny Halawanga and palm-wine guitarist Jerome Paye and started recording with the ABC company in the early seventies. Their production with Studio 99 was a collection of very danceable highlifes, pachangas and traditional songs from Nimba County.

HAWA DAISY MOORE

Liberian singer Hawa Daisy Moore (from www.limupa.com)

Hawa was 29 years old when I met her. Her father had played saxophone for an old Liberian dance band of the fifties called the Greenwood Singers. Daisy started singing on stage from five years and learnt guitar when she was eight. By ten she was appearing on television and did her first album 'Just Daisy' in 1978 at Studio One. On her Studio 99 production, she sang rumbas, meringues and reggaes in the Vai language. She has backed the extraordinary guitar playing of S.N. Thiam, leader of the Africanium band from Guinea. His guitar sound was reminiscent of kora harp-lute of his country.

'KRUBOY' Emmanuel 'Kruboy' Koffa is a vocalist and drummer who played and recorded with the Voices of Liberia guitar-band. He was also the principal exponent of 'Darjze' music that appeared in the sixties and was associated with football matches, played on drums, harmonica, musical saw and sasa (maracas). His Studio 99 releases were meringues and highlifes sung in Kru and Pidgin English.

ROBERT TOE was a warrant officer in the Liberian Army and was born in 1954. His father was also in the Liberian army in which he played trombone in a marching band. Robert learnt guitar by playing with palm-wine guitarist Jones Dopoe, and sings in Pidgin English and Krahn. He joined the army band in 1973.

THE LOFA ZOES (Lofa Wizards). The army man Jimmy Diggs was the leader of this band. On the Studio 99 cassette he sang in the Gbandii language but with a Congo-jazz instrumental touch. He was helped in this by the brilliant soukous-type guitar playing of Old Man Pratt from Sierra Leone.

Fatu Gayflor of Liberia

FATU GAYFLOR is a musician from another section of the government, the cultural ministry's National Cultural Troupe, in which she was lead singer and dancer. She was born in 1966 in Kakata, Central Liberia, began singing in public when she was eight and became known as the 'Golden Voice of Liberia'. She bases her compositions on the traditional music of the Lorma people of north-western Liberia. Faisal's production of her song 'E La Lokpeh' beautifully combines the African pentatonic scale and 6/8 poly-rhythmic time with rock guitar licks supplied by Aweke Glyman. Shortly after I met her, she left for the United States and is still there.

AFRO-POP ARTISTS AT STUDIO 99

The final element in Studio 99's massive musical outpourings came from the western pop influenced sounds that stretch back to the seventies with local bands like the Dynamics, Psychedelic Six (later Afrodelics) and Shades.

OXYGEN: This was the most recent of three Afro-rock outfits that had been formed by the half-Liberian, half-Ghanaian Willie Dee. His Studio 99 recording was called 'Togetherness'.

HUMBLE REBELS was formed by Ox Walker. He was previously with Willie Dee's Oxygen and toured Sierra Leone with them. The Humble Rebels Studio 99 cassette was a collection of funky highlifes and disco-calypsos sung in Kru and Pidgin English, backed by Jehu Brown on bass guitar.

THE MONROVIA BROTHERS This band was jointly led by T. Kpan Nimley and also Donald Cooper who, incidentally, was the musician who introduced me to his grand-father, the seventy-seven year old Mr. Bendell. Donald Cooper's first band was an Afro-rock outfit called Kabassa, run by radio disc-jockey Dougba Caranda. He then joined Alfred Kollie's Kalafadaya band and one of Willie Dee's bands called Third Resurrection. Nimley, on the other hand, started out with a school pop group called the Jesus People. He later joined the late Fred Smith's Dimension, before forming his own group in 1977 called Suhgbaydaytee (Unity), which played at the OAU conference in Monrovia in 1979. The Monrovia Brothers' Studio 99 release were of reggae-highlifes, disco-calypsos and funky meringues, featuring Cooper on keyboards, Nimley on guitar, B.B. Dowuna-Hammond of Ghana on bass-guitar and the African American Salim on saxophone. Sadly, Nimley died in 2005.

CIAFFA BARCLAY was originally the conga player for the Liberian Afro-rock group Kapingbdi run by Ebenezer Kojo Samuels which made three albums in Germany in 1978. Ciaffa's 'Bongos Sound' for Studio 99 consisted of a compilation of highlifes, reggae, makossa style songs and Afro-rock tunes.

O.J. BROWN recorded a cassette for Faisal called 'Music is the Feeling' that comprised rumbas, soca tunes and folk-songs sung in the Kpelle language. O.J. was initially with the Sierra Leonean Godfathers Afro-rock group and then the singer and percussionist with the Ducor Intercontinental Hotel Dance-Band of Monrovia.

FROM THE MID 1980s TO THE TWO CIVIL WARS

Because of the increasing problems in Liberia under the military regime of Samuel Doe who had come to a power in a coup in 1980, Faisal left Liberia in 1985. However, another studio was then set up by the Liberian ex-musician Tonieh Williams who had managed an 'Afro-disco' band from 1978 called Liberian Dreams (that featured Zack Roberts and Gebah Swaray). William's state-of-the-art Hotline Studio was closed just after the first civil broke out in 1989 when the warlord Prince Johnson (who killed Samuel Doe) raided the studio in 1990 and carted off all its $65,000 dollars worth of equipment to his military base. Towards the end of the civil war and when Charles Taylor was elected President in 1997 a number of artists composed songs for peace and stability. In the mid-1990's Zack Roberts released 'Stop the Fighting' and the Swa-Ray Band released 'We Want Peace' and 'Mass Exodus'. Then Miatta Fahnbulleh dedicated her 1997 album 'A Song for Liberia' to the 200,000 Liberians who had been killed in the first civil war. In 2000 Levi Jesse Zenawii released his song 'Suffering'. Then the second Liberian Civil War erupted from 2000 to 2003.

As a result of the two civil wars many of Liberia's musicians quit the country, one of the earliest being Fatu Gayflor who left in the mid-1980's and never returned. Then in 1989, the year the first civil war broke out Ebenezer Kojo Samuels of the Kapingdbi Afro-rock band left for Germany. Hawa Daisy Moore left in 1991 for the United States and is still there. In 1998 the six blind members of the African Gospel Acapella Group obtained political asylum in the States. During the second civil war (2000-3) the Swa-Ray Band members Gebah and Maudline Swaray and their lady singer Naser Sokay settled in the United States. Around the same time Yatta Zoe left for Europe.

The war ended in 2003 and elections were held in 2005 but, except for Yatta Zoe and Miatta Fahnbulleh, few of the exiled musicians returned home. Also some were killed in the wartime conflict, such as Tecumsey Roberts, Robert Toe and Morris Dorley

LIBERIAN MUSICIANS IN GHANA DURING THE CIVIL WARS

Some of the Liberian artists who left or could not stay in Liberia because of the civil wars between 1989 and 2003 settled, or became refugees, in Ghana. Here I will mention four of them.

THE TRUMPETS INTERNATIONAL: This is a group of young Liberian young men who sing spirituals, gospel and popular songs in acappella. They met in 1990 at a refugee camp on the Liberian/Cote d'Ivoire border after the Liberian civil war broke out. They had lost their friends and relatives, some had even seen them murdered, and so they had to flee into exile. An Ivorian radio journalist heard them singing at the camp and arranged for them to appear on television in Abidjan. Then in 1992 they moved to Ghana where they occasionally performed. In 1995 they recorded at Ghana Films (I helped with the mixing), released their first cassette 'Singing Acappella' and went on a West African tour. As the Trumpets put it in the mid-nineties, when peace returns to Liberia, "We'll contribute to the re-building of the country. Now we'll continue to perform and complete what we've started".

THE BOYZ OF BUDUBURAM: At the Buduburam refugee camp for Liberians near Accra, there was a group of young rappers who called themselves the Boyz of Buduburam. They were noticed by the German-Liberian producer Alexander Dworak, who recorded them in a local studio and in 2002 released their album 'Pray for Liberia' (on the German United Sound label). The opening song is 'We Are All Africans' with the message that politicians should stop messing with people's lives.

ESTER MUNA BINTA: Ester came from Liberia to Ghana in the 1990s and joined the Ghana Broadcasting Corporation dance band as trap-drummer. I saw her on many occasions in the late 1990s when the GBC band was playing at its regular Friday night show at the GBC Club-house in Accra. Her precision and stamina are outstanding. I learnt later she had obtained her rhythmic discipline as a member of the Liberian Police Band.

MIATTA FAHNBULLEH

Liberian singer Miattah Fahnbulleh

Miatta is probably Liberia's most well-known star internationally and was recently resident in Ghana for a number of years. In fact, I arranged for her to perform at the Alliance Francaise in Accra for the Feburary 2005 African Amercian History/Heritage Month. I first heard about Miatta way back in 1977 when she began releasing songs on the Afro-Disco label of the Sierra Leone producer Akie Deen. Later, she released the 'The Message of the Revolution' which contained Pan-African ideas. Despite her international upbringing (her father was a diplomat in Sierra Leone, Kenya and Britain), her music is rooted in the Liberian culture. She is in a good position to add an international touch to the local Liberian music, as her travelling continued even after leaving school. For a time, she worked for the Voice of Kenya and then went to the U. S. to study journalism. Whilst in New York, she sang at the famous Apollo Theatre in Harlem, studied at the American Musical and Dramatic Academy and worked with the Negro Ensemble Theatre of New York and with Duke Pearson of Blue Note Records. She returned home in 1973 to appear as a guest artist at President Tolbert's inauguration, and discovered she was a star there. A few years later, she toured West

Africa with Francis Fuster's Sierra Leonean Baranta band (resident in Lagos), and then worked with Hugh Masekela and with the Nigerian artists Jimi Solanke and Remi Kabaka. In 1977, she represented Liberia at the FESTAC Black Arts Festival in Lagos. The same year, she went to England and worked with a number of musicians and producers, including Jab Bunny of Matumbi and Akie Deen. Miatta Fahnbulleh spent some years in Ghana during the mid-2000s, before returning home to Monrovia to establish a school. Coincidentally, I met her on the 17th February 2018 at the Alliance Francaise in Accra, as she and the Nigerian Dede Mabiaku, supported by the West Coast Band, performed at an event in honour of the late South African trumpeter Hugh Masekela, organised by P.K. Holbrook-Smith, Panji Anoff and the Sierra Leone singer Yomo Sower.

THE POST CIVIL WAR ERA

With the 2005 elections Ellen Johnson Sirleaf became Liberia's president and, despite intermittent electricity supplies and rampant music piracy, artists like Zack Roberts and King O'Bryant were able to make their songs available through the local cassette market and FM radio stations, advising people to vote wisely in the 2005 elections. Zack Roberts was also an evangelist and from the late 1990s had also been releasing gospel music cassettes. In fact, danceable gospel became very popular in Liberia, supplied by home-based artists like Sarah Thompson and Twale Geply, as well as Hawa Daisy Moore, Ebenezer Kojo Samuels and the Musical Messiahs who live abroad.

A development in the Liberian music scene that began in the 1990s is a colloquial version of hiphop called 'hip-co' (i.e. hip-colloquial) that is rapped and sung in Liberian English and local languages. It presents the voice of the youth on many matters ranging from politics, human rights, gender issues and social justice. The hip-co rap music scene began in Monrovia in the late 1980s with the groups Hayes & Harvey and the New G-Crew, followed later by Luckay Buckay, Bone Dust and JD Donzo. Another is Takun J (Jonathan Kofa) who, as a child, had spent some years with his parents in Ghanaian and Ivorian refugee camps and began releasing hip-co albums from 2007. More recent hip-co artists are Mighty Blow, Killer-Lu, Noy-Z, King Real, Uncle Shaq, Romeo Lee and the ladies Butterfly and Queen V, all of whose lyrics dwell mainly on personal and romantic matters. But some also rap about social matters, like Pochano's 'Product of a Failed State,' Bentman's 'Lord of War,' Shadow's 'Peace Must Prevail' and Soul Fresh's appeal to 'Lets Come Together.' The success of hip-co was reflected by the two-day hip-co festival held in Monrovia in 2013 that attracted twenty-thousand youth. At the same time Takun J, JD Donzo, Shining Man and others hip-co artists formed the Hip-Co Accountability Network. One member of this Network is the Liberian-Lebanese reggae artist Rabbie Nassrallah, or 'Nasseman' who in 2010 served as an HIV/Aids Ambassador. Some current hipco artists who sing and rap or rather 'toast' in the Jamaican reggae style of dance-hall and ragga, rather than American hiphop, are DJ Cole, J Younkonde, and the ladies M'press One Love and Charlotte.

Quite different from hip-co is a hi-tech Liberian pop genre that uses auto-tuners, is sung in English and focuses on love themes. It is inspired by American contemporary urban/R&B and neo-soul that became popular in West Africa from the 1980s - and African versions are today often referred to as 'Afro-pop.' Some current Liberian 'Afropop' artists are G Rize, Sundaygar Dearboy, Pitty Best, Saga AP, Royal Busta Pain, the soft crooner Benji Cavali and Lady Munnah who sings from a women's point of view. Another is the US-based Jodi Clarke who sings in English and the Liberian Dahn language. Some Liberia Afro-pop artists, like Joe B 2, Marie Nnyenebo and S-Man, draw on the maringa soca-beat style, whilst Benevolence, Santos and Xpolay combine Afropop singing with hipco rapping. . Some Afropop recording artists who have moved beyond personal love themes to socio-political ones, like King Face with his 'Stop Corruption', S-Man and his 'Peace Song' and Piccador's release 'Hail Africa Centre of Civilization.'

The new 'Gbema music' is a quite different electronic mix to the local hip-co and Afro-pop that are inspired by outside influences. Gbema rather draws on traditional Liberian music, although played at a very fast speed. As such it employs syncopated rhythms, uses call-and-response and modal scales and is sung in local languages. Some of the artists that play this up-tempo and 'techno' form of traditional Liberian music are K-Zee, Kingface, Milkman, Crafty K and Blazor.

Chapter 55

THE POPULAR MUSIC OF GHANA'S FRANCOPHONE NEIGHBOURS TOGO, BENIN AND COTE D'IVOIRE

Before turning to some of Ghana's close Francophone neighbours, something must first be said about the fusion of African and Western popular music in the Francophone African countries in general. The earliest evidence of such a trans-cultural music appearing in the French speaking colonies was in the two Congos of Central Africa. An early outside influence came in 1885 when, as mentioned in chapter 23 on Goombay, five thousand or so 'coastmen' from English speaking West Africa were employed as clerks and artisans in the Belgium Congo (now the D.R. Congo) by King Leopold; until 1908 when the Congo was turned over to the Belgium government, who began developing the railways and mining industry of their colony. It was both the 'coastmen' operating on the Congo River and local Congolese miners and railway workers that helped spread Congo's earliest recognised local popular music style, 'maringa' a bar-room music that evolved around 1914[35] in the coastal Matadi-Kinshasa area and spread as far east as the Shaba mining camps in eastern Congo by the 1920s. It was played on frame-drums and likembe hand-piano and later the accordion and guitar. It was danced to in 4/4 time and was sung in the evolving trans-ethnic Lingala trade language of Central Africa. It was also the West African 'coastmen' who taught the two-finger guitar plucking techniques (created by

[35] As mentioned in Chapter 52 Isabela de Aranzadi says maringa was also present in West African Spanish colony of Fernando Po as early as 1910.

Liberian Kru mariners) to the local Congolese sailor-musicians Dondo Daniels and Antoine Wendo who influenced popular music in Kinshasha. Moreover, this West African guitar style reached the Swahili speaking eastern Congo (via the Congo River) in the late 1940s where it was combined with traditional 'ngoma' music and spread through the records of Jean Bosco Mwenda and Losta Abelo. Their 'dry' (or non-amplified) guitar style was an equivalent to West Africa's 'palmwine' guitar music.

During the Second World War, the anti-Nazi Free French Forces of General De Gaulle were based in Congo Brazzaville, where American soldiers introduced jazz and built the most powerful radio transmitter in black Africa for wartime propaganda purposes. After the war, a fusion of local Congolese music with the Afro-Cuban dance music (enjoyed by the French and Belgian colonialists) and the jazz horn-section of American music took place, resulting in the popular dance music style then known as 'Congo Jazz'. This music, sung in Lingala, was pioneered from the late forties in Kinshasha by Antoine Wendo, Kalle's African Jazz, Dr. Nico, Rochereau Tabuley, Franco's O.K Jazz and in neighbouring Congo-Brazzaville by the Orchestre Les Bantous. 'Congo jazz' as it was called was disseminated into every corner of the African continent, via the powerful transmitter of Radio Congo Brazzaville inherited from the Americans. Congo jazz was followed in the 1970s by the more update and guitar driven sound of Zaika Langa Langa and artists like Kanda Bongoman, Papa Wemba and the crooner-voiced Kofi Olomide, all of whom in the 1980s and 1990s became World Music stars.

Whereas the popular music of the two Congos can be traced back to the 1920s, the fusion of local and imported music in Francophone West Africa did not occur until the 1960s. Even up until the 1950s, the popular music scene in cities like Dakar, Bomako, Conakry and Abidjan was dominated by imported Afro-Cuban and Latin-American dance music (son, rumba, chacha, bolero and samba) and ballroom dance bands were set up to play this music sung in Spanish and French. These included La Habanera Jazz of Guinea, the Sor Jazz Band of Senegal, Volta Jazz and Les Imbattables Leopards of Burkina Faso, Alpha Jazz of the Benin Republic, the Melo Togos of Togo, François Lougah's band in Abidjan and Segou Jazz of Mali. The indigenisation of this imported Cuban and Latin dance music only really began after these countries began to become independent from 1958. This is when the Sahelian style of popular music sung in the Manding languages and now so popular worldwide started to appear. Here, I am talking of the Guinean music of Bembeya Jazz, Les

Amazons and Kante Manfila, whose guitar style was influenced by the traditional kora harp-lute of traditional professional musical families known as jalis or griots. Then in Mali there was the similar updated jali music of Salif Keita and Mory Kante who both had their musical training in Latin bands. And from Senegambia since the sixties came the Boabab Band, Ifang Bondi (originally called the Super Eagles) and Youssou N'Dour who moved from Afro-Cuban and Latin dance rhythms to a style driven by local 'mbalax' percussion. Other fusions from Mali are the pentatonic 'woussoulou' music (Oumou Sangare and others) based on hunters' music and the local Sahelian 'desert blues' of the late Ali Faka Toure.

This late development of trans-cultural popular music in French speaking Africa stands in stark contrast to English speaking countries like Ghana, Sierra Leone, Nigeria, Kenya and South Africa where popular music styles can be traced back to the late 19th century. This difference may be partly due to the differing colonial set-ups of the French and British. In the French colonies, there was a system of 'direct rule' from France in which the colonised either became 'évolués' (i.e.black Frenchmen) or remained as 'indigenes'.

This non-assimilationist policy of keeping the two cultures politically separate did not foster cross-cultural exchange, as compared to the British 'indirect rule' system that used traditional chiefs and politico-cultural institutions, which created an atmosphere more conducive to cultural blending. Another reason may be that the Francophone West African countries largely practised Islam which does not focus so strongly as musical worship prayer as did the Christian missions with their hymns harmonies and western instruments. Whatever the colonial differences, the French-speaking countries now have a rich popular dance-music scene and this chapter will look in particular at three of Ghana's close neighbours, starting with the Cote d'Ivoire.

THE POPULAR MUSIC OF COTE D'IVOIRE

To start looking at this country's popular dance music with E.T. Mensah's comments on Abidjan, the capital of Cote d'Ivoire, which he and his Tempos visited in 1955 five years before independence.

The French were treating the country as their own, so you could see European taxi and bus drivers. In the markets were black and white butchers. The French had opened shops side by side with the Africans. They did not leave the town to the blacks so they brought the town up to date. They ran the nightclubs and were importing European musicians and actors. We saw more of the whites in the clubs than the blacks: the whites could afford the nightclub life. The white bands were playing boleros, chachas, tangos and French music. When we played highlife only a few of the Ghanaians there got up and danced; although by the end of the tour some of the whites began to catch on. I never even saw an African dance band.

E. T. also comments about the French territories in general as he also visited Guinea in the 1950s.

On the British side, Africans had gone far ahead socially, but in the French territories there were only a few blacks who were far above everyone else. In 1955 at Abidjan, we were shown the mansion owned by Houphouet-Boigny, it was thirteen storeys high, the first time I had seen such a tall building. A few blacks were very rich but the vast majority were far below the social standard of the Africans in the British areas. The French people dominated the blacks socially and this affected the music as the whites were doing everything. They had white musicians from Paris, but the African musicians were not up to standard; so the dance music from the Africans was small. I should say though, that in Guinea we did meet the leader of one African dance band, but even there we saw mostly white bands, usually small trios of piano, violin and drums. The development, both social and musical in the French territories has occurred mainly since Independence and now they want to catch up.

I should point out that when E.T. says that the music of the Africans is small or below the standard of the French, he is only referring to Western type dance music and not to the indigenous dance music. It is interesting to note, however, that many of the ballroom dances played by these French bands, such as the Brazilian samba and Cuban rumba are, in fact, partially derived from Africa, as they were created by the descendants of African slaves. Another important dance music that began to percolate into the Cote d'Ivoire and other Francophone West Africa countries in the fifties through records and the broadcast of Radio Brazzaville was the Congo jazz of Central Africa. E.T. told me he remembered hearing this music live for the first time in 1957 played by the Melo Togos from Lome.

After independence there were a number of local dance bands in Abidjan in the 1960s still playing imported Afro-Caribbean and Latin music, as well as the rumba influenced Congo Jazz and western pop music: like Yapi Jazz, the Ivoiris Band, Les Souers

Comoe, Francois Lougah's band, Agnebi's Band and the Bozambo band led by guitarist Jimmy Hyacinthe who got his musical training with George Ouedrego's band made up of Bukina Faso musicians resident in Adidjan (other Bukinabe musicians living there were Traoure Saidou Richard, Kabore Oger and Edouard Ouedraogo).

Then, in the seventies, there was a big move towards a more 'rootsy' Ivorian sound, and the first was Amedee Pierre who began using the 'gbete' folk-rhythms of the mid-west Bete people. Then came Ernesto Djedje who created his 'ziglibithy' rhythm and 'nyama nyama' dance based on the music of the Bete people of central Cote d'Ivoire, a style later continued in the 1980s by Jean Baptiste Zibodi. On the other hand, Sery Simplice and Bally Spinto turned to the local 'gbegbe' rhythms of the Baule, an Akan people of south-eastern Cote d'Ivoire. After the Bazambo Band collapsed, Jimmy Hyacinthe moved from rumbas and Congo jazz to the 'goli' beat of the Baule. Another southerner, Freddie Meiway from Grand Bassam, used the local 'abissa' beat of his Appollo people to launch his 'zoblazo' dance in the early 1990s and with it made several tours of Ghana. In fact, he is related to Ghana's Francis Kenya who is an Nzima, as the Nzema and Appollo people are of the same Akan ethnic group, separated from each other during the infamous 1884/5 Berlin Conference and subsequent 'scramble for Africa'. A newer Zoblazo artist on the music scene is Otentchi who, like Meiway, also visits Ghana. With Akans straddling the border it is no wonder that Ghanaian highlife music has always been popular in the Cote d'Ivoire, and the most well-known Ivorian dance band there in the 1970s was Eba Aka Jerome and his Le Sanwi Stars. F. Kenya's guitar band and concert party also went on many tours there from the 1970s and in the early 1980s they settled in Abidjan for some years. More recently, there has been an upsurge of recording releases in the Cote d'Ivoire of old-style Akan palmwine accordion music (that originally came from the Fantis of Ghana) by artists from the south-eastern part of the country like Konan Kouassi Etienne.

Women also began to enter the Ivorian popular music scene in the 1970s, the most famous being Aicha Kone who, at one point, worked with Johnny Hyacinthe. Coming from Odienne in the north of country, she is influenced by local Bambara music. Another was Jane Agnimel from Dabou in the south, who was a member of the RTI Radio Orchestra of Abidjan (then led by by Manu Dibango), and later Nyanka Bell who in the 1980s worked with Kassav, a 'zouk' band from the French Caribbean.

By the mid-1980s, Cote d'Ivoire's popular music scene was so developed that Abidjan boasted a modern record pressing plant, the 32-track JBZ Studio, numerous night-clubs, seventy-five producers and regularly hosted the important international record producers trade fair (MIDEM) that had previously been located in France. Indeed, during the 1980s Abidjan was the recording 'mecca' for Francophone Africa. Non-Ivorian artists who recorded there include the Congolese artists Sam Mangwana and his L'African All Stars (who resided in Abidjan for a while) and Nyaboma Mwandido who made his 'Double Double' hit there. Cameroon's Mone Bile also recorded in Abidjan, as did the Malian singer Salif Keita and his L'Ambassadeurs Internationaux who stayed in Abidjan for a while before leaving for Paris. The Togolese singer and guitarist Agboti Yawo was in Abidjan for two years in the mid-1980s, around the time when the Ghanaian highlife singer and alto sax player Asabea Cropper recorded in Abidjan, after touring Germany with Smart Nkansah's Black Hustlers band. Asabea was given a two-week contract to perform in Abidjan and appeared on TV, but she was so popular and the music scene so lucrative, that her contract was extended to one year which she happily signed, taking into account the low-ebb of Ghana's music industry in the 1980s.

This boom in the Ivorian popular music scene began to wane in the early 1990s with the political and economic problems of the corrupt civilian regime of President Bédié. As a result the music industry collapsed and many Francophone African musicians moved to Paris, which then became the recording centre for Francophone African artists.

As mentioned in Chapter 36 on reggae, it was in the late 1990s that the Ivorian reggae star Alpha Blondy criticized the policies of President Bédié in his album 'Guerre Civile' which was repeatedly played on the radio on the day of General Guei's military coup in 1999. In fact, many of the other Ivorian reggae artists like Jah Tiken Fakoly, Tangara Speed Ghada, Zaga Zigi, Ismael Isaac and Serge Ksassy became politicised in the 1990s, as some were northerners who felt their people were being marginalized. Another response to the political problem was that Ivorian students (particularly Didier Bille) invented, at the end of President Houphet-Boigne's rule in the 1990s, a highly satirical local popular music style called 'zouglou', initially a form of musical 'animation' that high-school students sang and drummed for sports and other school events. The word 'zouglou' referred to the over-crowded and unkempt conditions on the campuses, and it became more political in the late 1990s when the students became radicalised by their opposition to the corrupt civilian regime of President Bedie. After the 1999 army coup of General (later President) Robert Guei, zouglou bands like those of Soum Bill and the Les Salopards were endorsed by the Ministry of Culture. In the late 1990s, zouglou also became associated with a dance craze that swept across West Africa called the 'mapouka' in which women shake the bottoms and many consider indecent. The mapouka was even banned in some African countries, although it is a traditional dance of young people in the western Cote D'Ivoire.

On recordings, zouglou music consist of just vocals, keyboard and local rhythms supplied by a drum-machine and live percussionist. This move away from large bands and towards small 'techno-pop' groups is partly a reflection of the previously mentioned decline in the Ivorian music industry during the 1990s. However, zouglou music has spread far and wide and one particular group had a big impact on Ghana in 2000. This was Magic System formed in 1996 by four students from northern Cote D'Ivoire who released their album 'Premier Gaou' (First Fool), distributed in Ghana by Universal Entertainment. The songs are sung mainly in a distinct minor mode, backed by sparse keyboards and combination of synthetic and live percussion. It was constantly on Ghanaian FM radio stations and the group made several trips to Ghana to perform with accompanying mapouka dancers. It made an impact on the Ghanaian youth as it successfully blended traditional rhythms with computerized drum-machine technology, anticipating what the young 'jama' sound hiplifers are currently doing to their music. Magic System has since become one of the most successful African bands in France.

Local rap also emerged in the Cote d'Ivoire during the mid-1990s with the big names being All Mighty, Angelo and RAS. More recent is a 'coupe-decale' (cut and run) dance-floor music based on computerised Ivorian rhythms and the recent Congolese 'ndombolo' dance, fronted by the DJs Jacob, Douk Saga, Kaloudju, Douk Saga, Serpent Noir, Resistance DJ Collective and DJ Arafat.

Although the song lyrics sometimes dwell on social events this is mainly an escapist dance-floor music that allows young people to have a good time, show off their latest clothes and aspire to wealth, despite the difficult political and economic problems of the times. This attitude is reflected in the name 'cut and run' itself, which means get rich by any means - and then run-away. This music has also become popular in Paris and has spread to many Francophone West and Central African countries.

THE POPULAR MUSIC OF TOGO AND BENIN

Before independence, both Togo and neighbouring Benin Republic (then called Dahomey) had just a few prestigious ballroom dance orchestras playing western quicksteps and waltz, Latin American sambas and tangos, Afro-Cuban music and an occasional Ghanaian highlife. There was the Melo Togos in Lome that E.T. Mensah referred to earlier in this chapter, and Alpha Jazz formed in 1953 in Cotonou, in which the young trumpeter Ignace de Souza obtained his musical training before going to Ghana (see Chapter 15). As de Souza pointed out, the French colonial authorities did not encourage dance bands, but only military bands and brass bands.

During the sixties, and particularly the seventies, more dance bands were created which continued to still play imported ballroom music, but also included western pop music and a heavy dose of Congo jazz. In Togo there was Eryko's Jazz, Orchestre Abass, Lavoix D'Agou and Los Muchchos, whilst Benin had its Orchestre Las Ondas, Gnonnos Pedro's band, the Picoby Band of Abomey, Superstar de Ouida, Les Volcans de la Capital, El Rego and his Los Commandos and the Orchestre Polyrhythmic de Cotonu. The latter released over a hundred singles in the early seventies and specialised in its own rendition of Fela-Kuti's Nigerian Afro-beat. It was also in the 1970s that the Beninoise keyboard player Wally Badarou shot to fame when he worked with the rock stars Grace Jones and the Gibson Brothers and went on to release his own Afro-rock albums in Britain.

During the 1960s and 70s both Togo and Benin were not only enjoying the music of the above mentioned and relatively prestigious urban dance bands, but also that of the more low-class guitar bands that were linked to their two respective neighbours. For instance in the Benin Republic the Yoruba 'juju' guitar band music of its immediate neighbour Nigeria was popular (moreover, the Yoruba and the Fon language of Benin are related). Togo also enjoyed Ghanaian highlife guitar band music and even had its own concert party that performed in Ewe called the Happy Stars of Lome, formed in 1962.

From the late 1960s local women popular artists began to enter the music scene of the two neighbouring countries of Togo and Benin. The first was the Togolese singer Bella Bellow who released a number of Ewe pop tunes, highlifes and folk oriented compositions with a polyrhythmic 6/8 agbadza lilt. Her big hit was 'Rockia' released in

1969 and produced by the Togolese Gerard Akueson. At just twenty years old she represented Togo at 1966 Dakar Arts festival, then worked with Manu Dibango and performed at the famous Paris Olympia Hall. Bella Bellow was seen as West Africa's equivalent to South Africa's Miriam Makeba, until her untimely death in a car accident in 1973. However she influenced and paved the way for other Togolese lady vocalists such as Nimo-Toki Lala in the 1970s, Jourias Mabah and Afia-Mala (who made eleven albums) in the 1980s, and Fifi Rafiatou in 1990s.

Some current Afro-pop stars of neighbouring Benin are Cella Stella, Vivi L'International, Ambroise Coffi Akoha and Bluecky d'Almeida with the most famous being Angelique Kidjo. She was born in the town of Ouida in 1960 and began her singing career as a six year old member of her mother's thirty-strong popular theatre group, the first in the country. In 1979 Angelique went to Holland and France, joined the Pili Pili band and made her first hit. She works with her bass-guitar playing husband Jean Hebrail and in her songs combines Beninoise music with makossa, soukous, zouk and afro-rock. She signed up to Island Records in 1989 and starting with her album 'Parakou' (a town in Benin) she went on to release 'Logoso', 'Aye', Fifi', 'Oremi' 'Black Ivory Soul' and 'Oyaya'. In 2007 she relased 'Djin Djin' that featured international artists like Carlos Santana, Peter Gabriel Ziggy Marley and Branford Marsalis. And in 2010 'Oyo' she won the 2011 Grammy award for Best Contemporary World Music Album. This Beninoise 'world music' star and outspoken social commentator has now settled in New York.

The difference in the commercial music scene of Togo and Benin is quite marked; Togo's has declined whilst that of Benin has expanded. Up until the mid-1980s Togo's music was thriving and its capital city, Lome, boasted the 24-track Studio de la Nouvelle Marche that not only recorded local artists but also other Africans: Nigerians like Nicholas Mbarga, the Congolese female vocalist Abeti – and also numerous Ghanaians as, at that time, the military ruled Ghana and its economy and music scene was at a low ebb. Then in the 1990s things switched around between Togo and Benin as Togo went into crisis during the latter years of President Eyedema, who had been single-handedly running the country since 1967 after the country's first president (Olympio) was assassinated. Consequently many artists left Togo or remained abroad, such as the Afro-rock musician Jimi Hope who worked in Britain, and both Nimo-Toki Lala and King Mensah Ayaovi Papawi (ex Les Dauphins de la Captitale) settled in Paris in the 1990s.

Angelique Kidjo of the Republic of Benin

A more extreme case of exile was that of the Togolese highlife guitarist Agboti Yaw (or Yao) who fled to Ghana in 1990s for political reasons. He was born 1953 in the Southern Togolese town of Have and rose to fame during the late 1970s. According to the music scholar Clement Adom, President Eyedema took an intense dislike to Agbovi's release of 'Ablordee Gbadzaa' (Freedom Unlimited) and that year the musician had to flee to Ghana for fear of his life. He then played with various bands such as Sasamassou and then moved to Germany for many years. In fact, there were rumours in Ghana that he had been killed in Togo for political reasons. To prove these rumours wrong, in 2011 he played many of his old hits at a Ghanaian Independence Celebration at the Woezor Hotel in Ho in the Volta Region, like 'Ablordee Gbadzaa' as well as ' Ele Boto', 'Lorlor fe Sefofo', 'Cherrie je t'aime', 'Akpeda Ha' and 'Tso Wo Dzi'.

In Benin during the 1990, however, things got better after many years of General Kerekou's austere military Marxist regime. Coincidentally, I was in Cotonu in November 1974 just after the military coup and the very day the 'people's revolution' was declared. I was on my way back from playing for a week at Fela-Kuti's Afrika Shrine in Lagos with the Ghanaian Bunzus band. We were meant to be playing in the Cultural Centre of Cotonou but the whole town was deserted, except for a few people

527

waving green fronds. In the end the Ghanaian Ambassador sent a message to us that the whole town had left for Abome to celebrate the 'revolution'. I found this odd, as I wondered why a supposedly atheistic Marxist revolution should be celebrated in the country's traditional religious capital.

After almost twenty years of one-party socialism there were elections in 1997 in Benin, with Kerekou as elected President. Consequently, the country's economy was liberalised, private FM radio and TV stations mushroomed and there was an upsurge in the music industry. Nel Oliver's Studio was going flat-out and in 1997 Angelique Kidjo's brother (Oscar) opened a digital studio. More recently a number of important international festivals have taken place, including the 2002 and 2003 'Gospel and Roots' festivals organised by Magloir Agbali and others, and at which Ghana's Cindy Thompson and the Soul Winners performed. New artists have also appeared on the Benin scene, like the reggae singer Yaya Yaovi and local rap groups such as the Ardiess Posse and Logozo. One band that is doing particularly well is the Gangbe Brass Band that has toured Africa and abroad, including making several trips to Ghana. This dancing and kinetic group of brass band instrumentalists perform a cross-section of Beninoise folksongs and popular tunes, as well as Afro-rock and powerful Afro-beat numbers dedicated to the late Fela Anikulapo-Kuti I should mention that the Orchestre Poly-rythmo has had a revival in recent years. In 2003 some of its old songs have been released on European 'world music' labels like Soundways and Analog. Furthermore, the band regrouped in 2010 for their African Soul Rebels European tour and they recorded a new album entitled 'Cotonu Club' in 2011 for the British Strut Records.

TOGOLESE AND BENINOISE REGGAE AND LOCAL HIP HOP STARS

Togo and Benin boasts several reggae stars, and from Benin comes Yaya Yaovi who released his first roots-reggae album in 1980 that was recorded at Bob Marley's Tuff Gong Studio in Kingston, Jamaica. More recent is Erick Kristal from Porto-Novo who learnt guitar in church and became interested in reggae and rock music. He collaborated with several bands, one of which was Ariya formed in 1998 by Ricos Campos that played music that ranged from high-tech Afro-pop to the traditional mode. Kristal then moved to Italy to study, where he operated his Jungle Fever reggae group and has released album's like 'Ifè Ilé Africa' (Africa, house of love) that attacks the western plundering of Africa. Kezita (Zita Sandrine Ketologo) from Lome is one of the few female reggae artists in Togo. She began singing at the age of fifteen in her church choir, and released her first hit reggae song 'At a Crossroads' in 2011 when she was twenty-six years old. She is a Rastafarian who sports dreadlocks which upset some people in Togo; in fact, on one occasion, she was physically attacked. Nevertheless, she battled on, and in 2014 was involved with a show in Accra to release an album by the Ghanaian reggae/dance hall artist IWAN.

As in other parts of West Africa hiphop, rap and ragga artists appeared in Benin and Togo during the 1990s. Benin had its H2O group and the Ardiess Posse of which one of its members, Logozo, raps in the Fon language. Pioneering Togolese hip hoppers were the Black Syndicate and the rap-ragga man Dzoku-Kay who formed his group in 1998. He sometimes sang in Ewe and employed slow traditional like 6/8 rhythms and the local harp-lute in his electronic mixes. Another pioneering Togolese hiphop act was Djanta Kan, formed by four young men in 1996 whose lyrics dwell on the evils in society. By the early 2000s, they were creating their 'djanta hip' that blended rap with local folk music, such as the Ewe akpesse recreational drum-dance. Also making an appearance in the early 2000s was the MC Eric Ayaovi Mensah (a.k.a. 'Blaak Niggar') who released two albums between 2003 and 2005, became involved in the HIV/AIDS campaign and won two Togo Music Awards. More recent Togolese hiphoppers include RX Patou, Orcyno and Small Poppy.

THE AFRICAN MUSIC BUSINESS AND AFTERTHOUGHTS

10

Highlife TIME 3

This begins with chapters on the West African recording business and the growth of Ghanaian and Nigerian musicians' union. It also includes a look at the rise of the World Music since the 1980s that has helped open up African music to the international community. There are also chapters on five of Ghana's music producers and/or recording studio managers, some of whom have been operating since the 1950s. There is then a chapter that examines the pros and cons of computer technology on highlife and the highlife Imagination. The last chapter surveys the positive musical developments in Ghana since the 1990s when the economy was liberalised and the country returned to civilian government. The developments include the growing commercial music sector, the impact of foreign tourists and Ghanaian returnees, the revival of highlife and live popular performance spots as well as the impact of newer forms of music on the local scene such as jazz, 'world music', revamped folkloric music, 'contemporary highlife' and the Sahelian' or 'Savannah' sounds of Northern/Upper Ghana. The Coda includes updates on the current state of hiplife and Afropop and their associated azonto dance, as well as the activities of MUSIGA and the government's recognition of the Creative Arts Industries.

Chapter 56

WEST AFRICAN MUSIC BUSINESS AND WORLD MUSIC

THE EARLY AFRICAN RECORDING INDUSTRY UP UNTIL THE 1970s

The African record business goes way back to 1907 when records were first sold in South Africa at two shillings each. The main companies were the French-owned Pathe and British-owned Zonophone. By 1914 one hundred thousand records a year were being sold there. In the 1920s other foreign companies came onto the scene like Brunswick, His Master's Voice (HMV) which sold over one million records (including so-called 'native' songs) in South Africa in 1927. During the 1930s black South African-based close-harmony and ragtime groups modelled on African American groups became popular and many of them were sent to England to record for EMI (formed by the merger of HMV, Zonophone and Columbia in 1931). In the 1940s the first African music based record company, Gallo-Africa, was set up which employed the local talent scouts like Griffiths Mosieloa. Gallo established a record pressing plant in the 1950s and had a huge commercial with August Musurugwa's song 'Skokian' (local liquor) which he sold to them for just a few pounds. East Africa was the next African region where the record business opened up, with records in English and Hindi being imported in the early 1920s. But by the late 1920s HMV, Odeon, Columbia, Zonophone and Pathe were recording and releasing local African music sung in Swahili, Luganda and Somali. For instance, in 1939 HMV/Zonophone sold over two hundred thousand records, of which eighty thousand were in the local languages of East Africa.

The West African record business lagged a bit behind, and began in 1925-1927 when the British Zonophone/HMV company first issued West African popular music and local 'spirituals'; particularly after 1928 when the Swizz United Africa Company (UAC) became their distributor. In 1930 the Zonophone/HMV company sold 180,000 shellac 78 rpm records, and between 1930-33 this company and the German Odeon company (working out of Lagos, Nigeria) sold 800,000 records in West Africa. This was all possible as a result of lucrative cash-crops (like cocoa and oil palm) enabling many Ghanaian and Nigerians, even farmers, to buy wind-up gramophones and enjoy local as well as imported music records. In Ghana some of the early Zonophone recording stars were the Fanti guitarist and accordion player George William Aingo who recorded in 1927, and the guitarist Kwame Asare (Jacob Sam) and his Kumasi Trio who recorded at Kingsway Hall in London 1928. The following year Zonophone published a thirty-five page catalogue of recordings by `Native Artists' in eighteen West African languages. Besides Aingo's and Asare's songs, this catalogue included banjo songs, `Negro spirituals', `native jazz orchestras', the Yoruba hymns of Reverend J.J. Ransome-Kuti (Fela-Kuti's grandfather) and foxtrots and turkey- trots in the Akan and Ewe languages. In 1929 Zonophone also released music by the West African Instrumental Quintet that included 'Tin Ka Tin Ka' an instrumental version of the Trinidadian calypso `Sly Mongoose' that later supplied the melody for the popular highlife song 'All for You'.

During the Second World War record production throughout the world was low because of the war effort but by the fifties things were in full swing again. Columbia Records, for instance, released over two thousand different records of African artists in its East Africa series. In 1954, they had a major hit and made a quarter-million pound profit in Britain with Aaron Lerole's South African penny-whistle tune 'Tom Harkc'. Decca launched its West Africa series in 1947 records of top Ghanaian, Nigerian and Sierra Leonean artists. Indeed, Decca West Africa was so successful that a permanent studio was built in Accra. Portable equipment was sent to Lagos twice a year and by the late 1950s they were pressing almost a quarter-million singles a year. The biggest recording company in Africa operating from France during the 1950s was Pathe-Marconi, which had offices in Nigeria, Kenya and South Africa.

The first record pressing plants actually built in Africa by the multi-national record companies were those of EMI and Pathe-Marconi in South Africa, all fully operational in the 1950s. In the early 1960s Phillips/Phonogram (later called Polygram) and EMI built pressing plants in Nigeria ands Phillips built a recording studio in Accra. Then as will be discussed below during the late sixties and seventies the record industry of Ghana and Nigeria became indigenised, However, well until the late 1970s the main international music companies catering to the huge local market in DR Congo (then known as Zaire) and the French-speaking West African countries remained in the hands of the multi-nationals Decca, Polygram and WEA Fillipachi (a subsidiary of Warner Brothers), Pathe-Marconi and the French based companies Safari Ambiance and Sono-Disc. The locally based record business of the French-speaking West African countries was therefore generally lagging behind that of English-speaking ones like Ghana and Nigeria to which we now turn.

THE GHANAIAN RECORD INDUSTRY SINCE THE 1970s AND 1980s

By 1970, Ghana record industry was in full swing as in the mid to late-sixties two record pressing plants (with recording studios) had been set up. The first was the fully Ghanaian owned Ambassador Records built in 1965 by the Kumasi businessman, Mr. A.K. Badu, and capable of pressing 10,000 vinyl records a day. The other was The Record Manufacturers of Ghana Limited jointly owned by Polygram and the local record producer Dick Essilfie-Bondzie (Essiebons label) that was built in Accra in 1969 and which by 1975 was producing a half-million singles and a hundred thousand albums a year. By the mid-1970s there were also four recording studios in Ghana. The eight-track Ghanaian Ambassador Studio near Kumasi; the four-track Phillips/Polygram studio also in Accra, the two track state-owned Ghana Film Corporation's studio in Accra and the eight-track Studio One at Faisal Helwani's Napoleon Club in Accra.

But by the mid to late 1970s the whole of the Ghanaian record business began to meet many difficulties during the Acheampong/Akufo military regime due to the general economic decline of the country and shortages of foreign exchange. Then came the 1978 'indigenisation laws' that made importing vinyl almost impossible. By the late seventies record production dwindled to one-quarter of its former output and this created a bottleneck in the industry that had several serious repercussions. Many of Ghana's top musicians had to go abroad to record. Indeed, in 1979, when I was on the Interim Executive of the Musicians' Union, it was calculated that one quarter of our membership was already overseas or in other African countries (particularly Germany and Nigeria).

The March of the Musicians Union of Ghana to the Castle in May 1979

The late 1970s were so bad that the musicians' union, (MUSIGA), organised a march on the seat of government at the Castle in Accra just a few weeks before the first Rawlings coup. Rawling's new Armed Forces Revolutionary Council (AFRC) government instantly acted and broke the monopoly of the two pressing companies, re-distributed record vinyl to independent producers, reduced the retail price of records and ordered that 75 per cent of all imported vinyl should be used to manufacture local music rather than imported music under licence. Moreover, the Prices and Incomes Board collected over one hundred thousand pounds in unpaid record royalties and passed it on to musicians who were owed money. Yet another project that MUSIGA became involved with was the re-establishing of contact between Ghana and the International Performing Rights Society (PRS), which had broken down a number of years previously. In fact, it was I whom MUSIGA sent to London in the summer of 1979 to contact the then PRS International Affairs

Secretary, an Indian named Mr. Abraham. With pressure from MUSIGA, the government subsequently in its PNDC Law 110 made music copyright infringement and piracy a criminal offence in 1985. MUSIGA helped police the anti-piracy drive, which was made easier in 1992 by the Copyright Administration issuing official or 'banderoles' stamps that were placed on all genuinely produced music cassettes; for since the early 1980s practically the whole of Ghana's commercial music output has been on pre-recorded cassettes that are easy to duplicate and pirate. Nigeria also copied the banderole system for a while, but in both Nigeria and then Ghana the system finally broke down due to counterfeiting of the banderole themselves.

A boost to the Ghanaian music scene during the late 1980s and early 90s came from the Ghanaian musicians who returned from abroad to set up recording studios. Early ones were Nat Fredua Osamanu's Black Note Studio set up in 1986, Oko Ringo's sixteen-track Elephant Walk Studio established in 1988 and Nana Boamah's ARC Studio set up in Tema in 1990. Others that quickly followed were Ralph Casely-Hayford's forty-track Overdrive Studio in Accra, Sidiku Buari's sixteen-track Sid Studio, Danny Blues Combined House of Music and the studios of Gee Man and of the ex-Classic Vibes trumpeter, Arhin. In more recent years studio have gone digital and it is estimated that there are now anywhere from between 200-250 digital studios operating in the country

THE NIGERIAN MUSIC INDUSTRY AND NIGHT-CLUB SCENE SINCE THE 1970s

Whereas Ghana was suffering serious economic problems in the late 1970s and 80s Nigeria was enjoying an oil boom, which boosted the record industry (records are actually made from a by-product of oil). The record business was also helped in 1978 when the government banned imported records. As a result by 1979 Nigeria was pressing twelve million albums a year, which rose to twenty million a year in the 1980s. By the late 1980s, there were many pressing plants in the country, the largest being the Record Manufacturers of Nigerian Limited at Ikeja, a joint local/Decca enterprise which could press up to twenty thousand albums a day. Polygram also had a large pressing plant in Lagos which was 60 per cent Nigerian owned and could manufacture four million records a year. Then there was the Haruna Ishola's (the apala musician) record factory near Ibadan that was opened in 1979 and was pressing thirty thousand records a day; almost a third of Nigerian records. There was also a fully automated plant as well as a twenty-four-track recording studio in Onitsha owned by Prince Tabansi. In fact, there were numerous multi-track studios in Nigerian the 1970s and 80s. The first was the ARC sixteen-track studio set up in Lagos around 1970 with the help of the British rock drummer Ginger Baker. Haruna Ishola had a twenty-four track-studio near Ibadan that was being used by Sunny Ade, Fela-Kuti, Tee Mac and Chris Okotie. Decca had a twenty-four-track studio in Lagos that catered for the artists Ebenezer Obey, the Oriental Brothers, the Ikengas, Kabaka International, Christine Essien and Manu Dibango. Indeed, the 1980s Nigeria's record industry was so far in advance of that of other African countries, that it was the first country in black Africa to have its own pop magazine (Africa Music) and its Top Ten of best-selling records.

Because the Nigeria music profession was so lucrative many clubs, recording studios and record companies were established by musicians over the years. In Lagos in the seventies there were Bobby Benson's Caban Bamboo, Victor Olaiya's Papingo at the Stadium Hotel, Fela's Shrine, Sunny Ade's Ariya Club and record label, Tunde Kuboye's Jazz 38 Club, Art Alade's Place. Others were Haruna Ishola's Phonodisc Company in Ibadan, Victor Uwaifo's Joromi Hotel and Club 400 in Benin City and in eastern Nigeria the hotels-cum-recording studios of Nicholas Mbarga and Stephen Osadabe.

Duing the 1980s disco became the craze in Nigeria and influenced artists such as Sonny Okosun, Jake Solo, Remi Kabaka and Patty Boulaye. Many night-clubs opened in Lagos for imported and local versions of drum-machine driven disco music: like Niteshift, Klass, Lords, Peak, Princess and the Duroof that featured lip-synched shows by artists such as Nigeria's then current heart-throb Mike Okri. In the 1990s and following the disco craze another newer form of 'techno-pop' has developed in Nigeria, which is local hiphop or 'Naija Rap' where the singers 'rap' over the pre-programmed music of beat-boxes. Pioneering Nigerian rap artists were Tony Tertuila, 2 Face Idiba, Weird MC, Zakky, Styl-plus, Trybesman, Plantashun Boyz, and Ruggedman, as well as the British based Nigerian rap groups JJC and the 419 Squad. In the early 1990s the first private FM station (Ray Power) was opened in Nigeria and these quickly expanded to about twenty private stations and forty state ones. However, the music they generally play is imported American and Western music.

Since 1999 there has been a revival of old time highlife. This began with two shows dubbed 'Highlife Party' organised by the late Director of the Goethe Institute in Lagos, Renate Albertson, with the assistance of Benson Idonije and Jahman Anikulapo. There were two main stage bands at these events. One was the Seagulls led by guitarist David Bull who had first played with 'Babyface' Paul Isamade for the Top Spotters band in Lagos in 1958 and then moved to Rex Lawson's Riversmen. The other was the Classic Band of saxophonist Yinusa Akinibosun who had begun his career with Victor Olaiya, Agu Morris and Bongos Ukwue. These two bands provided the music for a host of old-time highlife stars which included E.C Arinze (born 1930) who had operated his Empire Band in Lagos from 1952-65 and then quit the city during the Nigerian Civil War to run his band in Enugu from 1973. The guitarist Alaba Pedro and vocalist Tunde Osofisan who had both played with the late Roy Chicago (until his death in 1989) made an appearance. Also on stage at the Goethe Institute's garden party on Victoria Island was Ralph Amarabem of the Peacocks band. He actually began playing guitar in Ghana with Robert Osuji's Amaraka guitar band in 1950 when he was working there on the railways, then returned to Nigeria to join Lawson's Riversmen in 1963. Others who appeared were Victor Olaiya the so-called 'evil genius of highlife', Nelly Uchenda and Chris Ajilo.

These Goethe Insitute shows were followed by a series of events called 'Highlife Elders Forums' at the O'jez Club in Yaba and the Lagos National Stadium, organised by the O'jez Entertainment Company, MUSON (Musical Society of Nigeria) and CORA (Committee for Relevant Art). These 'Forums' honoured musical highlife giants such as Victor Olaiya, Orlando Julius and Steve Rhodes the one-time director of the Nigerian Broadcasting dance orchestra. Another recently opened venue for old-time highlife in Lagos is the 'Jazz Hole' at the French Cultural Centre in Ikoyi which has featured Fatai Rolling Dollar who, born in 1926, is the oldest living exponent of the Nigerian palm-wine guitar style. Another 'Highlife Party/Elders Forum was held in Lagos on the 1st October 2006 (Nigeria's 46th independence anniversary) to honour Fela-Kuti's sidemen, Lekan Animashahun and Duro Ikujenyo and in 2007 a Great Highlife Party was held at the Hexagon Hotel in Benin City Edo state at which Tunde Osofisan's Highlife Messengers played as did the octagenerian palmwine music artist Fatai Rolling Dollar. Then, in 2008, Rolling Dollar collaborated on the 'Miliki Music' album made by Biodun Ayinde Bakare, the son of the juju pioneer Ayinde Bakare. For a few years after this Rolling Dollar featured regularly at O'jez Club in Lagos, but in 2013 this veteran passed away.

Another ace musician who featured on several occasions for these highlife revivals was Victor Olaiya the so-called 'evil genius of highlife'. Although on semi-retirement Olaiya still occasionally played at his Stadium Hotel, although now-a-days it is Olaiya's trumpeter son, Bayode, who usually leads his father's band at the Club. Incidentally, Olaiya's grand-daughter Wunmi (Omotayo Olufunke Olaiya) is a UK based Afro-beat singer.

Besides these live shows of old-time Nigerian musicians, their classic highlifes are being re-released on CD by companies such as Femi Eso's Evergreen Music and Premier Music, and also being aired on some specialist highlife radio programs of the Ray Power and Radio Nigeria Metro FM stations.

LATE 1970s-1980s COLLAPSE OF THE GHANAIAN LIVE-MUSIC SCENE

As mentioned in chapter 37, the Ghanaian live popular music declined in the seventies and eighties for a number of economic and political reasons during the military governments of Acheampong, Akufo and the early Rawlings period. Yet another reason was the changing technology first apparent in the mushrooming of the mobile sound systems or 'spinners' whose DJ's, strobes and laser lights moved out of indoor discos like Virgins, Keteke, Blow-Up and Black Caesar and onto the nightclub dance floors. This had a disastrous effect on the live-music scene, especially on open-air clubs such as the Tip Toe, Silver Cup, Metropole, Lido and Apollo Theatre in Accra which up then had catered for live dance bands and pop groups. Some musicians even wanted to send the spinners back to the discos, and a petition to this effect was sent to the Musicians' Union of Ghana. However a compromise was made and one of the best suggestions appeared in Ghana's weekly music magazine, the 'Hit Parade', of August 10, 1988:

> *The Musicians' Union must get the mobile disco operators to agree to involve the live bands in their shows. By allowing the bands to use their heavy sound and lighting equipment the mobile discos would be giving the bands a better chance to promote themselves.*

This did not have much impact on the spinning groups operating in the Accra-Tema area that multiplied to ten or so and included Willie Chii, Skyhawks, Mobisco and Studio 44. However, the negative impact of the spinners was mainly felt in the cities and at the time did not much effect the rural oriented guitar-bands and concert parties, like the African Brothers and City Boys. As a result some urban dance bands like Sunsum, A.B. Crentsil's Ahenfo and Jewel Ackah's Butterfly Six, teamed up with concert parties and toured the countryside.

Yet another technological blow to live performance in Ghana was the introduction in the late 1980's of drum-machines and music synthesisers that quickly replaced percussionists, horn players and even bass guitarists; particularly in recording studios. On many local releases the whole instrumental background became pre-programmed by a single studio engineer and as a result many studio musicians became un-employed. Furthermore the bands that recorded in this way, like burgerhighlife ones, could often not reproduce live what they recorded, and therefore had to resort to miming or 'lip synching' their music on television and even on stage. The advantage of these hi-tech recordings is, of course, that they made recording easier and cheaper, an important consideration taking into account the massive import duties on musical instruments at the time.

THE UPSURGE IN GHANA'S MUSIC INDUSTRY SINCE THE MID-1990s

Since the 1990s the music scene has picked up for a whole variety of reasons since its low ebb in the late 1970s and 80s. In the mid-1990s the airwaves were de-regulated and there was a proliferation of private FM radio and television stations whose broadcasts include specialist highlife music programs and live band performances. Currently, there are about eighty TV channels and almost four hundred commercial and community based FM stations in the country. As noted in Section Six the increasing numbers of tourists and World Music fans coming to Ghana since the 1990s has resulted in a proliferation of private drum and dance schools and helped in the revival of live bands. Furthermore, there are now around two hundred digital recording studios in the country that record gospel music, highlife and hiplife for the local market. Indeed, in 1999 and according to the International Federation of Phonogram Industries (IFPI), Ghana's internal cassette and CD sales generated the equivalent of twenty-five million dollars per year, second only to South Africa on the African continent

As listed in chapter 38 there are dozens of companies recording, producing and promoting hiplife music; such as Hush Hush, Goodies, the Combined House of Music, Kays Frequency, Nana Quame's NG Promotions, Panji Anoff's Pidgin Music and the Media Whizz Kids. However by far the biggest sector (around 60%) of the current local music market in terms of cassette and CD sales is of local gospel, and as a result there is a huge infrastructure of studios and production companies catering for this danceable church music.

Many new recording studios have been set up in Ghana since the 1990s and some of the church based ones were mentioned in chapter 43. Here I will name a few of these studios (and their engineers) which cater for highlife, hiplife as well as church and other local music. In Accra there is Quantum Studio (engineer Morris), Vision Audio Laboratory (T.V.O. Lamptey), Panji Anoff's Pidgen studio, Francis Kwakye's Rhythmist Studio, TLL Studio (Zapp Mallet), Brain Studio (Roland Best), Oparah Mensah's Digital Studio, PSI Studio (Sammy I and Faiz) and Despite Studio. In Tema there is Master Mix (Sammy Helwani), Crystal Bay (Steve) and ARC (Boamah), and in Kumasi Nana Yaw Owoahene's Audio Logic Studio and Garth Studio. Some of the important local music producers are JMS Records, Stana Music Productions, Big Ben Productions, Ankobeahene Records, the Winneba based Kampsite Studio, Agiecoat Music, Frimprince, U Name It, Despite Music, Megastar, Hammer Productions, Slip Enterprises, Tree Entertainment, Alexiboat and Lumba Productions and also Kaakyire that won the Ghana Music Awards best gospel producer in 2002. Mention must also be made of Chris Ankrah who in 1986 began City Rock business in Accra, which by 2000 was duplicating three million cassettes a year and supplying about seventy percent of the local music that was played on radio.

Another critical factor in boosting Ghana's music industry has been the influx of foreign tourists and world music fans visiting the country since the 1990 – and by 2009 800,000 visitors were coming to Ghana. The foreign exchange they have been bringing has stimulated the local entertainment industry particularly areas connected with cultural music and live bands, as world music fans are looking for what they consider to be 'authentic' African music rather than African versions of techno-pop. For instance, numerous private cultural centres have been opened up and also venues that put on show of folkloric music, Afro-fusion music, reggae and highlife. As the rise of World Music is one of the factors that has led to Ghanaian governments recently re-assessing the role of the music sector in the economy I will say something more on this topic

THE RISE OF 'WORLD MUSIC'

Of course the word 'World Music' has been around for a long time, but in connection with the international recording trade it emerged as a distinct music marketing category in the mid-1980s. It began with the growing world-wide interest in the early 1980's of 'Afro-Pop' styles like Nigerian juju-music and Afro-beat, Southern African township jazz and chimurenga, Central African soukous and, of course, Ghanaian highlife. Prior to this African music had been limited to a small number of specialists shops and records companies (like Folkways) that catered for ethnomusicologists, foreigners who had visited Africa or African students living abroad. The word 'World Music' itself was coined in 1987 at two meeting in South and then North London, by a group of independent recording companies and music journalists who wished to broaden the marketing potential of African popular music or 'Afro-pop' as it was originally called. In fact, I was at the first meeting in South London and, together with the Ghanaian music promoter Charles Eassmon, objected to the change of name, as at that time it was quiet clear that it was African popular music or 'Afro-pop' that had broken through into this new global musical marketing-slot. Nevertheless, the name 'World Music' came to stay, and although today it includes Cuban, Latin-American, Arabic, eastern European and Asian music styles, the African popular music component represents roughly one quarter of all the sales of World Music. In 2000 I put forward an estimate for a World Bank meeting in Washington on the African music industry, that World Music sales and royalties in 1999 had generated around 6 billion dollars, which means the African component was 1.5 billion dollars. I will refer to this World Bank meeting again below, as its interest in African music has also helped tone-up the Ghanaian music industry. But first let me present five of the main reasons for the commercial explosion of Afro-pop on the international market since the early 1980s.

FIRSTLY: AFRO-POP IS PART OF A LONG-TERM GLOBAL BLACK MUSIC EXPLOSION. The world-wide acceptance of African popular music today is a logical continuation of the global emergence of Black American and Caribbean dance-music that began in the late 19th century: from jazz, blues and the samba right up to today's reggae, rap and salsa. Put the other way round, the gradual internationalisation of the black popular music of the Americas ultimately paved the way for the popular music of Africa itself going global.

SECONDLY: AFRO-POP IS INTRINSICALLY INTERNATIONAL. Unlike traditional ethnic African music that is located in a specific local culture, contemporary African popular music is a fusion of African, Western, Black American and in some cases Arabic and even Indian influences. It is therefore inherently an international idiom.

THIRDLY: THE GROWING AFRICAN MUSIC INTEREST BY JAZZMEN, ROCK STARS AND D.J.'S. From the 1960's jazz musicians like John Coltrane, Max Roach, Sun Ra and Randy Weston became interested in African music. During the seventies some rock stars became interested in African music. Ginger Baker and Paul McCartney recorded in Nigeria, the Rolling Stones worked with the U.K. based Nigerian percussionist Ginger Johnson whilst in the US the Grateful Dead often opened its shows with the Nigerian drummer Babatunde Olutunje. In the 1980's more British and American pop stars visited Africa, like Brian Eno, Mick Fleetwood (of Fleetwood Mac), Sting and Stuart Coplan (of the Police) and Paul Simon. In 1982 Peter Gabriel of the British Genesis rock-band established the annual WOMAD (World Festival of Music and Dance) that features African bands and then set up his Real World record label which records African artists (including Ghana's Pan African Orchestra). More recent visits to Africa by UK pop musicians include those of Damon Alban (of Buzz and Gorilla) and of Jamie Cato and Duncan Bridgeman (of Faithless and One Giant Leap). The Rock musicians Bono and Bob Geldof who are involved with Third World developmental projects have also visited Africa and/or work with African musicians. The most recent turn towards African music has been by the international fans of 'house music', whose D.J.'s use the Afro-funk and Afro-beat of artists such as Nigeria's Fela-Kuti to create their electronic dance-floor grooves.

FOURTHLY: REGGAE AS A STEPPING-STONE BACK TO AFRICA. The Rastafarian theme in Jamaican reggae since the seventies encouraged many West Indian to look towards Africa music for inspiration. Some artists actually visited African: Jimmy Cliff, Greg Isaacs, Misty and Roots, Steel Pulse, Aswad and Bob Marley. When Bob Marley died in 1981 his record company, Island Records, decided to look for their next super-star in Africa rather than the Caribbean. In 1983 this independent reggae label chose Nigeria's top juju-music star, Sunny Ade. His success was a trigger for the current interest in World Music by foreign music fans and independent record companies

FIFTHLY: THE GROWTH OF BRITISH AND FRENCH INDEPENDENT LABELS. The success of Island Records move into African popular music encouraged other British independent labels to do the same. These included Sterns African Records, Earthworks, Oval, Real World and Globestyle – which by 1992 numbered fourteen – and catered for the growing number of western Afro-pop fans. These British independent labels initially signed up artists coming from English speaking Africa, but later added Francophone African material coming out of independent record companies in France, as by the late 1980's Paris had become a recording 'mecca' for musicians from French-speaking African countries. One reason for this was that in France by the late 1970's there were four million black immigrants and so there were hundreds of African musicians in Paris. Another was in 1981 there was the multi-cultural policy of the Mitterand government and its Minister of Culture, Jack Lang, who helped fund and organise tours by African bands. As a result many new independent French companies appeared (like Syllart, Celluloid, Gefraco and Cobal) that began releasing Francophone African material. It was only after the success of these British and French independent African/World Music record labels that the big record companies such as HMV, EMI, and Virgin began to move into African music. One notable example is Warner Brothers who, in 1986, released Paul Simon's South African inspired 'Gracelands' album which sold fourteen million copies. Subsequently, the big distributors began to set up World Music sections in their mega-music stores – and as they say, the rest is history.

THE WORLD BANK INTEREST IN AFRICAN MUSIC

Because of increasing World Music sales in the 1990's the World Bank organised a one day workshop in Washington DC in June 2000 (to which I was invited) to discuss the commercial growth potential of the music industry in Africa; focusing at first on South Africa, Zimbabwe, Ghana, Nigeria, Senegal and Mali. At the meeting the World Bank was represented by Ms. Kreszentia Duer of its Social Development Section and the economist Michael Finger of its Poverty Reduction and Economic Network Department. Others involved were Gerald Seligman of EMI, Coenrad Visser the WIPO (World Intellectual Property Organisation) representative for South Africa, Jerome Reichman of the Vanderbilt University in Nashville (an expert on folkloric copyright) Phillip Hardy editor of the UK Music and Copyright magazine, Frank Penna Director of the Yale based Science Policy Centre, Scott Burnett of the media marketing section of IBM and the economist Keith Maskus of the University of Colorado. Others were the Nigerian WIPO representative Funkasi Koroye-Crooks,

Jayashree Watal of the Institute for International Economics, and the economist and Nobel prize-winner Amartya Sen of Cambridge University. An indication of the World Bank's interest was that the Bank's Director, James Wolfensohn, attended the pre-workshop lunch. Areas discussed were micro-credit loans for musicians, bands, clubs and recording studios in the six African countries; the setting up of digital studio-cum-websites in Africa for distributing and monitoring locally produced music (by MP3 files) and assisting African royalty collecting organisations. The main point I made at the meeting concerning Ghana was that even though it produced Africa's first distinctive genre of popular music, its current music was almost completely absent from the lucrative World Music market, which resulted from the collapse the local music industry and live music scene in the late 1970s and 80s. I suggested what Ghana needed therefore was to create an exportable form of highlife, which the World Bank could assist with by enhancing the live music industry, supplying musical equipment to schools and providing micro-credit loans to bands. As a result of this meeting, Senegal received $5 million in 2002 in soft loans, investments and outright grants for its music industry.

In Ghana things have taken a bit longer and although no money has yet been received, the World Bank's interest in the African music industry is most certainly one of the factors that led President Kuffour's NPP government in 2004 to reduce the massive import duties on musical instruments that has so crippled local live popular music scene since the 1980s. And this was followed in 2005 by the NDC government integrating the music and entertainment sector into its Poverty Reduction Scheme. This was done around the time that a series of meeting in Ho and elsewhere were being organised by the Institute of Music and Development (an NGO run by Korkor Amarteifio and the late Professor Komla Amoaku) and endorsed by the then World Bank Country Director in Ghana, Mats Karlsson, himself a musician.

This integration of music into national policy has been continued by the NDC government when the National Development Planning Commission (NDPC) published in December 2010 its 'Ghana Shared Growth and Development' document that is part of its 'Medium-Term Development Policy Framework on Enhancing Competitiveness in Ghana's Private Sector' MUSIGA and other stakeholder in the music industry are currently working on creating a Music Council that will work with the government on this. This Council was finally set up in 2017 as the Creative Arts Council by the NPP government.

Chapter **57**

THE GHANAIAN AND NIGERIAN MUSIC UNIONS

MUSIC UNIONS IN GHANA SINCE THE 1950s

The late 1970s were so bad that the musicians' union, (MUSIGA), organised a march on the seat of government at the Castle in Accra just a few weeks before the first Rawlings coup. Rawling's new Armed Forces Revolutionary Council (AFRC) government instantly acted and broke the monopoly of the two pressing companies, re-distributed record vinyl to independent producers, reduced the retail price of records and ordered that 75 per cent of all imported vinyl should be used to manufacture local music rather than imported music under licence. Moreover, the Prices and Incomes Board collected over one hundred thousand pounds in unpaid record royalties and passed it on to musicians who were owed money. Yet another project that MUSIGA became involved with was the re-establishing of contact between Ghana and the International Performing Rights Society (PRS), which had broken down a number of years previously. In fact, it was I whom MUSIGA sent to London in the summer of 1979 to contact the then PRS International Affairs Secretary, an Indian named Mr. Abraham. With pressure from MUSIGA, the government subsequently in its PNDC Law 110 made music copyright infringement and piracy a criminal offence in 1985. MUSIGA helped police the anti-piracy drive, which was made easier in 1992 by the Copyright Administration issuing official or 'banderoles' stamps that were placed on all genuinely produced music cassettes; for since the early 1980s practically the whole of Ghana's commercial music output has been on pre-recorded cassettes that are easy to duplicate and pirate. Nigeria also copied the banderole system for a while, but in both Nigeria and then Ghana the system finally broke down due to counterfeiting of the banderole themselves.

A boost to the Ghanaian music scene during the late 1980s and early 90s came from the Ghanaian musicians who returned from abroad to set up recording studios. Early ones were Nat Fredua Osamanu's Black Note Studio set up in 1986, Oko Ringo's sixteen-track Elephant Walk Studio established in 1988 and Nana Boamah's ARC Studio set up in Tema in 1990. Others that quickly followed were Ralph Casely-Hayford's forty-track Overdrive Studio in Accra, Sidiku Buari's sixteen-track Sid Studio, Danny Blues Combined House of Music and the studios of Gee Man and of the ex-Classic Vibes trumpeter, Arhin. In more recent years studio have gone digital and it is estimated that there are now anywhere from between 200-250 digital studios operating in the country

THE NIGERIAN MUSIC INDUSTRY AND NIGHT-CLUB SCENE SINCE THE 1970s

Whereas Ghana was suffering serious economic problems in the late 1970s and 80s Nigeria was enjoying an oil boom, which boosted the record industry (records are actually made from a by-product of oil). The record business was also helped in 1978 when the government banned imported records. As a result by 1979 Nigeria was pressing twelve million albums a year, which rose to twenty million a year in the 1980s. By the late 1980s, there were many pressing plants in the country, the largest being the Record Manufacturers of Nigerian Limited at Ikeja, a joint local/Decca enterprise which could press up to twenty thousand albums a day. Polygram also had a large pressing plant in Lagos which was 60 per cent Nigerian owned and could manufacture four million records a year. Then there was the Haruna Ishola's (the apala musician) record factory near Ibadan that was opened in 1979 and was pressing thirty thousand records a day; almost a third of Nigerian records. There was also a fully automated plant as well as a twenty-four-track recording studio in Onitsha owned by Prince Tabansi. In fact, there were numerous multi-track studios in Nigerian the 1970s and 80s. The first was the ARC sixteen-track studio set up in Lagos around 1970 with the help of the British rock drummer Ginger Baker. Haruna Ishola had a twenty-four track-studio near Ibadan that was being used by Sunny Ade, Fela-Kuti, Tee Mac and

Chris Okotie. Decca had a twenty-four-track studio in Lagos that catered for the artists Ebenezer Obey, the Oriental Brothers, the Ikengas, Kabaka International, Christine Essien and Manu Dibango. Indeed, the 1980s Nigeria's record industry was so far in advance of that of other African countries, that it was the first country in black Africa to have its own pop magazine (Africa Music) and its Top Ten of best-selling records.

Because the Nigeria music profession was so lucrative many clubs, recording studios and record companies were established by musicians over the years. In Lagos in the seventies there were Bobby Benson's Caban Bamboo, Victor Olaiya's Papingo at the Stadium Hotel, Fela's Shrine, Sunny Ade's Ariya Club and record label, Tunde Kuboye's Jazz 38 Club, Art Alade's Place. Others were Haruna Ishola's Phonodisc Company in Ibadan, Victor Uwaifo's Joromi Hotel and Club 400 in Benin City and in eastern Nigeria the hotels-cum-recording studios of Nicholas Mbarga and Stephen Osadabe.

Duing the 1980s disco became the craze in Nigeria and influenced artists such as Sonny Okosun, Jake Solo, Remi Kabaka and Patty Boulaye. Many night-clubs opened in Lagos for imported and local versions of drum-machine driven disco music: like Niteshift, Klass, Lords, Peak, Princess and the Duroof that featured lip-synched shows by artists such as Nigeria's then current heart-throb Mike Okri. In the 1990s and following the disco craze another newer form of 'techno-pop' has developed in Nigeria, which is local hiphop or 'Naija Rap' where the singers 'rap' over the pre-programmed music of beat-boxes. Pioneering Nigerian rap artists were Tony Tertuila, 2 Face Idiba, Weird MC, Zakky, Styl-plus, Trybesman, Plantashun Boyz, and Ruggedman, as well as the British based Nigerian rap groups JJC and the 419 Squad. In the early 1990s the first private FM station (Ray Power) was opened in Nigeria and these quickly expanded to about twenty private stations and forty state ones. However, the music they generally play is imported American and Western music.

Since 1999 there has been a revival of old time highlife. This began with two shows dubbed 'Highlife Party' organised by the late Director of the Goethe Institute in Lagos, Renate Albertson, with the assistance of Benson Idonije and Jahman Anikulapo. There were two main stage bands at these events. One was the Seagulls led by guitarist David Bull who had first played with 'Babyface' Paul Isamade for the Top Spotters band in Lagos in 1958 and then moved to Rex Lawson's Riversmen. The other was the Classic Band of saxophonist Yinusa Akinibosun who had begun his career with Victor Olaiya, Agu Morris and Bongos Ukwue. These two bands provided the music for a host of old-time highlife stars which included E.C Arinze (born 1930) who had operated his Empire Band in Lagos from 1952-65 and then quit the city during the Nigerian Civil War to run his band in Enugu from 1973. The guitarist Alaba Pedro and vocalist Tunde Osofisan who had both played with the late Roy Chicago (until his death in 1989) made an appearance. Also on stage at the Goethe Institute's garden party on Victoria Island was Ralph Amarabem of the Peacocks band. He actually began playing guitar in Ghana with Robert Osuji's Amaraka guitar band in 1950 when he was working there on the railways, then returned to Nigeria to join Lawson's Riversmen in 1963. Others who appeared were Victor Olaiya the so-called 'evil genius of highlife', Nelly Uchenda and Chris Ajilo.

These Goethe Insitute shows were followed by a series of events called 'Highlife Elders Forums' at the O'jez Club in Yaba and the Lagos National Stadium, organised by the O'jez Entertainment Company, MUSON (Musical Society of Nigeria) and CORA (Committee for Relevant Art). These 'Forums' honoured musical highlife giants such as Victor Olaiya, Orlando Julius and Steve Rhodes the one-time director of the Nigerian Broadcasting dance orchestra. Another recently opened venue for old-time highlife in Lagos is the 'Jazz Hole' at the French Cultural Centre in Ikoyi which has featured Fatai Rolling Dollar who, born in 1926, is the oldest living exponent of the Nigerian palm-wine guitar style. Another 'Highlife Party/Elders Forum was held in Lagos on the 1st October 2006 (Nigeria's 46th independence anniversary) to honour Fela-Kuti's sidemen, Lekan Animashahun and Duro Ikujenyo and in 2007 a Great Highlife Party was held at the Hexagon Hotel in Benin City Edo state at which Tunde Osofisan's Highlife Messengers played as did the octagenerian palmwine music artist Fatai Rolling Dollar. Then, in 2008, Rolling Dollar collaborated on the 'Miliki Music' album made by Biodun Ayinde Bakare, the son of the juju pioneer Ayinde Bakare. For a few years after this Rolling Dollar featured regularly at O'jez Club in Lagos, but in 2013 this veteran passed away.

Another ace musician who featured on several occasions for these highlife revivals was Victor Olaiya the so-called 'evil genius of highlife'. Although on semi-retirement Olaiya still occasionally played at his Stadium Hotel, although now-a-days it is Olaiya's trumpeter son, Bayode, who usually leads his father's band at the Club. Incidentally, Olaiya's grand-daughter Wunmi (Omọtayo Olufunke Olaiya) is a UK based Afro-beat singer.

Besides these live shows of old-time Nigerian musicians, their classic highlifes are being re-released on CD by companies such as Femi Eso's Evergreen Music and Premier Music, and also being aired on some specialist highlife radio programs of the Ray Power and Radio Nigeria Metro FM stations.

LATE 1970s-1980s COLLAPSE OF THE GHANAIAN LIVE-MUSIC SCENE

As mentioned in chapter 37, the Ghanaian live popular music declined in the seventies and eighties for a number of economic and political reasons during the military governments of Acheampong, Akufo and the early Rawlings period. Yet another reason was the changing technology first apparent in the mushrooming of the mobile sound systems or 'spinners' whose DJ's, strobes and laser lights moved out of indoor discos like Virgins, Keteke, Blow-Up and Black Caesar and onto the nightclub dance floors. This had a disastrous effect on the live-music scene, especially on open-air clubs such as the Tip Toe, Silver Cup, Metropole, Lido and Apollo Theatre in Accra which up then had catered for live dance bands and pop groups. Some musicians even wanted to send the spinners back to the discos, and a petition to this effect was sent to the Musicians' Union of Ghana. However a compromise was made and one of the best suggestions appeared in Ghana's weekly music magazine, the 'Hit Parade', of August 10, 1988:

> *The Musicians' Union must get the mobile disco operators to agree to involve the live bands in their shows. By allowing the bands to use their heavy sound and lighting equipment the mobile discos would be giving the bands a better chance to promote themselves.*

This did not have much impact on the spinning groups operating in the Accra-Tema area that multiplied to ten or so and included Willie Chii, Skyhawks, Mobisco and Studio 44. However, the negative impact of the spinners was mainly felt in the cities and at the time did not much effect the rural oriented guitar-bands and concert parties, like the African Brothers and City Boys. As a result some urban dance bands like Sunsum, A.B. Crentsil's Ahenfo and Jewel Ackah's Butterfly Six, teamed up with concert parties and toured the countryside.

Yet another technological blow to live performance in Ghana was the introduction in the late 1980's of drum-machines and music synthesisers that quickly replaced percussionists, horn players and even bass guitarists; particularly in recording studios. On many local releases the whole instrumental background became pre-programmed by a single studio engineer and as a result many studio musicians became un-employed. Furthermore the bands that recorded in this way, like burgerhighlife ones, could often not reproduce live what they recorded, and therefore had to resort to miming or 'lip synching' their music on television and even on stage. The advantage of these hi-tech recordings is, of course, that they made recording easier and cheaper, an important consideration taking into account the massive import duties on musical instruments at the time.

THE UPSURGE IN GHANA'S MUSIC INDUSTRY SINCE THE MID-1990s

Since the 1990s the music scene has picked up for a whole variety of reasons since its low ebb in the late 1970s and 80s. In the mid-1990s the airwaves were de-regulated and there was a proliferation of private FM radio and television stations whose broadcasts include specialist highlife music programs and live band performances. Currently, there are about eighty TV channels and almost four hundred commercial and community based FM stations in the country. As noted in Section Six the increasing numbers of tourists and World Music fans coming to Ghana since the 1990s has resulted in a proliferation of private drum and dance schools and helped in the revival of live bands. Furthermore, there are now around two hundred digital recording studios in the country that record gospel music, highlife and hiplife for the local market. Indeed, in 1999 and according to the International Federation of Phonogram Industries (IFPI), Ghana's internal cassette and CD sales generated the equivalent of twenty-five million dollars per year, second only to South Africa on the African continent

As listed in chapter 38 there are dozens of companies recording, producing and promoting hiplife music; such as Hush Hush, Goodies, the Combined House of Music, Kays Frequency, Nana Quame's NG Promotions, Panji Anoff's Pidgin Music and the Media Whizz Kids. However by far the biggest sector (around 60%) of the current local music market in terms of cassette and CD sales is of local gospel, and as a result there is a huge infrastructure of studios and production companies catering for this danceable church music.

Many new recording studios have been set up in Ghana since the 1990s and some of the church based ones were mentioned in chapter 43. Here I will name a few of these studios (and their engineers) which cater for highlife, hiplife as well as church and other local music. In Accra there is Quantum Studio (engineer Morris), Vision Audio Laboratory (T.V.O. Lamptey), Panji Anoff's Pidgen studio, Francis Kwakye's Rhythmist Studio, TLL Studio (Zapp Mallet), Brain Studio (Roland Best), Oparah Mensah's Digital Studio, PSI Studio (Sammy I and Faiz) and Despite Studio. In Tema there is Master Mix (Sammy Helwani), Crystal Bay (Steve) and ARC (Boamah), and in Kumasi Nana Yaw Owoahene's Audio Logic Studio and Garth Studio. Some of the important local music producers are JMS Records, Stana Music Productions, Big Ben Productions, Ankobeahene Records, the Winneba based Kampsite Studio, Agiecoat Music, Frimprince, U Name It, Despite Music, Megastar, Hammer Productions, Slip Enterprises, Tree Entertainment, Alexiboat and Lumba Productions and also Kaakyire that won the Ghana Music Awards best gospel producer in 2002. Mention must also be made of Chris Ankrah who in 1986 began City Rock business in Accra, which by 2000 was duplicating three million cassettes a year and supplying about seventy percent of the local music that was played on radio.

Another critical factor in boosting Ghana's music industry has been the influx of foreign tourists and world music fans visiting the country since the 1990 – and by 2009 800,000 visitors were coming to Ghana. The foreign exchange they have been bringing has stimulated the local entertainment industry particularly areas connected with cultural music and live bands, as world music fans are looking for what they consider to be 'authentic' African music rather than African versions of techno-pop. For instance, numerous private cultural centres have been opened up and also venues that put on show of folkloric music, Afro-fusion music, reggae and highlife. As the rise of World Music is one of the factors that has led to Ghanaian governments recently re-assessing the role of the music sector in the economy I will say something more on this topic

THE RISE OF 'WORLD MUSIC'

Of course the word 'World Music' has been around for a long time, but in connection with the international recording trade it emerged as a distinct music marketing category in the mid-1980s. It began with the growing world-wide interest in the early 1980's of 'Afro-Pop' styles like Nigerian juju-music and Afro-beat, Southern African township jazz and chimurenga, Central African soukous and, of course, Ghanaian highlife. Prior to this African music had been limited to a small number of specialists shops and records companies (like Folkways) that catered for ethnomusicologists, foreigners who had visited Africa or African students living abroad. The word 'World Music' itself was coined in 1987 at two meeting in South and then North London, by a group of independent recording companies and music journalists who wished to broaden the marketing potential of African popular music or 'Afro-pop' as it was originally called. In fact, I was at the first meeting in South London and, together with the Ghanaian music promoter Charles Eassmon, objected to the change of name, as at that time it was quiet clear that it was African popular music or 'Afro-pop' that had broken through into this new global musical marketing-slot. Nevertheless, the name 'World Music' came to stay, and although today it includes Cuban, Latin-American, Arabic, eastern European and Asian music styles, the African popular music component represents roughly one quarter of all the sales of World Music. In 2000 I put forward an estimate for a World Bank meeting in Washington on the African music industry, that World Music sales and royalties in 1999 had generated around 6 billion dollars, which means the African component was 1.5 billion dollars. I will refer to this World Bank meeting again below, as its interest in African music has also helped tone-up the Ghanaian music industry. But first let me present five of the main reasons for the commercial explosion of Afro-pop on the international market since the early 1980s.

FIRSTLY: AFRO-POP IS PART OF A LONG-TERM GLOBAL BLACK MUSIC EXPLOSION. The world-wide acceptance of African popular music today is a logical continuation of the global emergence of Black American and Caribbean dance-music that began in the late 19th century: from jazz, blues and the samba right up to today's reggae, rap and salsa. Put the other way round, the gradual internationalisation of the black popular music of the Americas ultimately paved the way for the popular music of Africa itself going global.

SECONDLY: AFRO-POP IS INTRINSICALLY INTERNATIONAL. Unlike traditional ethnic African music that is located in a specific local culture, contemporary African popular music is a fusion of African, Western, Black American and in some cases Arabic and even Indian influences. It is therefore inherently an international idiom.

THIRDLY: THE GROWING AFRICAN MUSIC INTEREST BY JAZZMEN, ROCK STARS AND D.J.'S. From the 1960's jazz musicians like John Coltrane, Max Roach, Sun Ra and Randy Weston became interested in African music. During the seventies some rock stars became interested in African music. Ginger Baker and Paul McCartney recorded in Nigeria, the Rolling Stones worked with the U.K. based

Nigerian percussionist Ginger Johnson whilst in the US the Grateful Dead often opened its shows with the Nigerian drummer Babatunde Olutunje. In the 1980's more British and American pop stars visited Africa, like Brian Eno, Mick Fleetwood (of Fleetwood Mac), Sting and Stuart Coplan (of the Police) and Paul Simon. In 1982 Peter Gabriel of the British Genesis rock-band established the annual WOMAD (World Festival of Music and Dance) that features African bands and then set up his Real World record label which records African artists (including Ghana's Pan African Orchestra). More recent visits to Africa by UK pop musicians include those of Damon Alban (of Buzz and Gorilla) and of Jamie Cato and Duncan Bridgeman (of Faithless and One Giant Leap). The Rock musicians Bono and Bob Geldof who are involved with Third World developmental projects have also visited Africa and/or work with African musicians. The most recent turn towards African music has been by the international fans of 'house music', whose D.J.'s use the Afro-funk and Afro-beat of artists such as Nigeria's Fela-Kuti to create their electronic dance-floor grooves.

FOURTHLY: REGGAE AS A STEPPING-STONE BACK TO AFRICA. The Rastafarian theme in Jamaican reggae since the seventies encouraged many West Indian to look towards Africa music for inspiration. Some artists actually visited African: Jimmy Cliff, Greg Isaacs, Misty and Roots, Steel Pulse, Aswad and Bob Marley. When Bob Marley died in 1981 his record company, Island Records, decided to look for their next super-star in Africa rather than the Caribbean. In 1983 this independent reggae label chose Nigeria's top juju-music star, Sunny Ade. His success was a trigger for the current interest in World Music by foreign music fans and independent record companies

FIFTHLY: THE GROWTH OF BRITISH AND FRENCH INDEPENDENT LABELS. The success of Island Records move into African popular music encouraged other British independent labels to do the same. These included Sterns African Records, Earthworks, Oval, Real World and Globestyle – which by 1992 numbered fourteen – and catered for the growing number of western Afro-pop fans. These British independent labels initially signed up artists coming from English speaking Africa, but later added Francophone African material coming out of independent record companies in France, as by the late 1980's Paris had become a recording 'mecca' for musicians from French-speaking African countries. One reason for this was that in France by the late 1970's there were four million black immigrants and so there were hundreds of African musicians in Paris. Another was in 1981 there was the multi-cultural policy of the Mitterand government and its Minister of Culture, Jack Lang, who helped fund and organise tours by African bands. As a result many new independent French companies appeared (like Syllart, Celluloid, Gefraco and Cobal) that began releasing Francophone African material. It was only after the success of these British and French independent African/World Music record labels that the big record companies such as HMV, EMI, and Virgin began to move into African music. One notable example is Warner Brothers who, in 1986, released Paul Simon's South African inspired 'Gracelands' album which sold fourteen million copies. Subsequently, the big distributors began to set up World Music sections in their mega-music stores – and as they say, the rest is history.

THE WORLD BANK INTEREST IN AFRICAN MUSIC

Because of increasing World Music sales in the 1990's the World Bank organised a one day workshop in Washington DC in June 2000 (to which I was invited) to discuss the commercial growth potential of the music industry in Africa; focusing at first on South Africa, Zimbabwe, Ghana, Nigeria, Senegal and Mali. At the meeting the World Bank was represented by Ms. Kreszentia Duer of its Social Development Section and the economist Michael Finger of its Poverty Reduction and Economic Network Department. Others involved were Gerald Seligman of EMI, Coenrad Visser the WIPO (World Intellectual Property Organisation) representative for South Africa, Jerome Reichman of the Vanderbilt University in Nashville (an expert on folkloric copyright) Phillip Hardy editor of the UK Music and Copyright magazine, Frank Penna Director of the Yale based Science Policy Centre, Scott Burnett of the media marketing section of IBM and the economist Keith Maskus of the University of Colorado. Others were the Nigerian WIPO representative Funkasi Koroye-Crooks, Jayashree Watal of the Institute for International Economics, and the economist and Nobel prize-winner Amartya Sen of Cambridge University. An indication of the World Bank's interest was that the Bank's Director, James Wolfensohn, attended the pre-workshop lunch. Areas discussed were micro credit loans for musicians, bands, clubs and recording studios in the six African countries; the setting up of digital studio-cum-websites in Africa for distributing and monitoring locally produced music (by MP3 files) and assisting African royalty collecting organisations. The main point I made at the meeting concerning Ghana was that even though it produced Africa's first distinctive genre of popular music, its current music was almost completely absent from the lucrative World Music market, which resulted from the collapse the local music industry and live music scene in the late 1970s and 80s. I suggested what Ghana needed therefore was to create an exportable form of highlife, which the World Bank could assist with by enhancing the live music industry, supplying musical equipment to schools and providing micro-credit loans to bands. As a result of this meeting, Senegal received $5 million in 2002 in soft loans, investments and outright grants for its music industry.

In Ghana things have taken a bit longer and although no money has yet been received, the World Bank's interest in the African music industry is most certainly one of the factors that led President Kuffour's NPP government in 2004 to reduce the massive import duties on musical instruments that has so crippled local live popular music scene since the 1980s. And this was followed in 2005 by the NDC government integrating the music and entertainment sector into its Poverty Reduction Scheme. This was done around the time that a series of meeting in Ho and elsewhere were being organised by the Institute of Music and Development (an NGO run by Korkor Amarteifio and the late Professor Komla Amoaku) and endorsed by the then World Bank Country Director in Ghana, Mats Karlsson, himself a musician.

This integration of music into national policy has been continued by the NDC government when the National Development Planning Commission (NDPC) published in December 2010 its 'Ghana Shared Growth and Development' document that is part of its 'Medium-Term Development Policy Framework on Enhancing Competitiveness in Ghana's Private Sector' MUSIGA and other stakeholder in the music industry are currently working on creating a Music Council that will work with the government on this. This Council was finally set up in 2017 as the Creative Arts Council by the NPP government.

The Musicians Union of Ghana (MUSIGA) Executive in 1979

555

Two weeks after the musicians' march, there was a coup in Ghana, led by Jerry John Rawlings and other young army officers. Part of their three month 'house-cleaning' operation included sorting out some of the musicians' grievances mentioned in the previous chapter, such as sharing out vinyl, reducing the price of records and distributing back-royalties owed to musicians. After three months, the young officers of the AFRC government handed back power to a civilian government. During this time, MUSIGA expanded its membership to five thousand and Ghana hosted two famous foreign musicians. One was Mick Fleetwood (of Fleetwood Mac) who, together with MUSIGA and the Ghana Film Corporation, made a film called 'The Visitor'. The other was Brian Eno, who produced an album for the Accra-based Edikanfo band after being invited to Ghana by MUSIGA.

On December 31, 1981, Jerry Rawlings and the young officers overthrew the civilian government of President Limann. Once in power, they imposed two years of curfew which instantly curtailed the night-life scene. The new Provisional National Defence Council (PNDC) government, however, recognised the plight of the arts and entertainment business and undertook a series of measures. In April 1982, the new Secretary (Minister) of Culture and Tourism, Asiedu Yirenkye, launched the 'cultural revolution'. This programme included making traditional music and dance an integral part of the school curriculum, the recognition of the Ghanaian concert party as a national art form and the playing of more local music by the Ghana Broadcasting Corporation. In addition, young men were brought in to run the various arts institutions in the country. The Ghana Film Corporation (and its recording studio) went under the management by thirty-one-year-old Harruna Attah and after the three top directors of the Ghana Arts Council were transferred, the institution was run by thirty-two-year-old Audrey Homeku. This shake-up of the Arts Council went even further a few years later, after Ben Mohammed Abdallah took over from Mr. Yirenkyi, and the whole national organisation was decentralised into nine and, later, ten Centres for National Culture.

It was during the PNDC period that MUSIGA finally obtained official recognition and its membership expanded further. For instance, in November 1983, an organisation affiliated with MUSIGA was set up, called the Greater Accra Musicians' Welfare Association that catered for old-time and retired musicians. Moreover, a special branch of MUSIGA was formed especially for highlife gospel-bands of the local African Christian churches. Branches of MUSIGA were also established up and down the country. In Kumasi, an office was set up at the Cultural Centre, and, in the Volta Region, a branch was started in the regional capital of Ho under Acting Chairman, Edinam Ansah.

One of the most important things the PNDC did, after it launched its 'cultural revolution' programme, was to bring out the new copyright law (PNDC Law 110) in April 1985, which made copyright infringement a criminal rather than a civil offence. The Copyright Administration of the Ministry of Information (later the National Commission on Culture) also began collecting air-play royalties for the first time from the Ghana Broadcasting Corporation, as well as performance royalties from clubs, restaurants, discos and spinners. This was followed in April 1992 by their introduction of the banderole system of sticking registered stamps to all genuinely-produced recordings, mainly cassettes. This was fully endorsed by MUSIGA and the union became involved in the anti-piracy battle, on many occasions actually apprehending music kiosks owners who were doing illegal duplicating. MUSIGA was also involved in the establishment of COSGA, the Ghanaian royalty-collecting body composed of musicians, poets, writers, photographers, choreographers, painters and other creative artists. However, the banderole collapsed in the late 1990s due to counterfeiting. Although there were attempts to replace these with 'holograms' and then 'gamugrams', as of now no fool-proof and fully comprehensive system has been put into place that has the agreement of all the country's artists.

In 1992, MUSIGA was reorganised with the older executives like Koo Nimo and Kofi Ghanaba stepping down. The new President was the late Joe Mensah who had sung with the Downbeats, Broadway and Uhuru highlife dance-bands in the 1960s and was well-known as the populariser of the highlife song 'Bosoe' and inventor of the 'African Hustle' dance. MUSIGA's new General Secretary was Nana Ampadu and its Vice-President was Sidiku Buari.

As mentioned in Chapter 37, Sidiku had had a big hit with his American record 'Disco Soccer' and, when he returned to Ghana in 1978, he set up his Funky Town Disco in Dzorwulu, Accra. This was where, in the mid-1980s, he also built his Sid Recording Studio which over the years has produced fifteen record albums and ten local videos. Then, in 1987, Sidiku organized a musical charity concert to help handicapped schoolchildren called 'Africa's Response to the World' that echoed the 1985 'We are the World' album of world stars concerned with the famine in Ethiopia. For this Ghanaian song, Buari received a national ECRAG award in 1988. All this, undoubtedly, helped him become MUSIGA Vice-President. In August 1994, Sidiku released the cassette 'Zaman Lafia' made in his studio, which in Hausa means peaceful co-existence. It was released in Tamale and was a plea for peace in the Northern Region, after the previous year's Dagomba-Konkomba War that had resulted in the death of two thousand people.

Not surprisingly, in 1999, Sidiku Buari become President MUSIGA (for two terms). During his long tenure, he established the union's headquarters at the Old Passport Office near Black Star Square. Under Sidiku's leadership, MUSIGA also released a number of highlife, gospel and hiplife CD's/cassettes on social topics, such as 'AIDS Awareness', 'Our Dear Women' concerning the mysterious murders of women around 2000 and 'Peace in the North' about the Yendi Chieftaincy dispute. In September 2000, MUSIGA released another cassette/CD recorded in Sid Studio called 'Land of Peace' to coincide with that year's forthcoming general elections. In 2004, Sidiku was instrumental in getting the government to reduce the import duties on musical instruments that had so crippled the Ghanaian music industry over the previous twenty years. I had the pleasure of going over the final draft of the petition with him, before he sent it to the President. Due to Sidiku international travels as MUSIGA head, he was elected as Vice-President of the International Federation of Musicians in 2005. The membership of MUSIGA by 2005/2006 stood at around seven thousand; it included a gospel wing under the gospel singer Diana Hopeson (formerly Akiwumi) and a hiplife section for the young generation of Ghanaian rappers. Incidentally, in 2008/2009, Diana Hopeson took over the Presidency of MUSIGA from Sidiku Buari. Diana herself was born in Accra and studied Theatre Arts of the University of Ghana (I was one of her teachers). From the early 1990s, she began releasing a string of gospel albums, including her big hit 'Onyame Asem Su'. She was also coordinator of the Gospel Musicians in Ghana and, during Sidiku Buari's tenure, was the Vice-President of MUSIGA.

Besides MUSIGA (which is a trade union), there are also some other smaller bodies and associations active in the current Ghanaian music scene. There is an Actors Guild and a Concert Party Union that used to meet regularly at the Greater Accra Community Centre. Then there is the National Association of Dance that caters for semi-professional dance companies of which there are about twenty in Accra alone. The Ghanaian royalty-collecting and distributing organisation COSGA was still operating up until around 2010 when, due to its lack of transparency, it was replaced by the Ghana Music Rights Association, GHAMRO. There is also the Ghana Association of Composers, Authors and Performers (GHASCAP), the Ghana Songwriters and Composers Association (GSCA) and the Ghana Association of Phonogram Industries (GHAPI).

In 2004, a new copyright bill was put to Parliament supported by the governmental Copyright Administration, COSGA and MUSIGA. Ninety-nine percent of the new bill concerning protection of copyright was fine with everyone. However, in 2005, members of GHASCAP formed the Coalition of Concerned Copyright Advocates (COCA), as they were opposed to some of the clauses in the new copyright bill. In particular, they objected to the idea the COSGA should have a state monopoly for gathering Ghanaian copyright, that there should be a paying public domain, and that Ghanaians would have to obtain and pay for a permit from the government to commercially use Ghanaian folklore, or go to prison for three years. Some of the contentious clauses were removed, but the folkloric copyright tax was not, even though a number of performing artists were against it. They argued that there would be confusion arising from the fact that some forms of folklore straddle Ghana and its neighbours, that it would interfere with artistic creativity, and that it would be a disincentive for the use of folklore by the Ghanaian youth whom many complain are already saturated with too much foreign music. Despite objections, the new copyright law went into operation around 2010 and included the contentious clauses concerning folkoric copyright and a paying public domain

Despite the conundrums and disagreements over some of the clauses in the new copyright bill, it does strengthen the laws protecting copyright owners from music pirates. Furthermore, it includes sections on internet copyright. Indeed internet sales, if properly monitored, offer a potential hi-tech digital solution to musical piracy which is still rampant in Ghana. This could be done through the use of barcodes for commercial musical works and their distribution on secure websites, which means commercial recordings can be automatically logged and musicians can directly collect their royalties, cutting out the middlemen. Several Scandinavian organisations have visited Ghana in recent years (such as Artpages and DiGiDi) to help Ghanaians set up such a system.

With a possible solution for music piracy on the horizon, Ghana's music industry and entertainment scene is generally in good shape. There is a big internal music market around gospel, hiplife and contemporary highlife, many World Music tourists are visiting the country, there are hundreds of recording studios and radio stations, live clubs are opening for those interested in folkloric performances, jazz and highlife, and there is an interest in the local music industry by the Ghanaian government, the World Bank and some of the foreign Diplomatic Missions.

As the President of MUSIGA, Diana Hopeson did not run for a second term, new elections were held for MUSIGA in August 2011. Contestors for the position included the two veteran highlife musicians Gyedu Blay Ambolley and Nana Tuffour; the hiplifer Obour (Bice Osei Kuffour) and the singer-songwiter and inventor of the 24-note octave scale, Willie Roi (Kwase Wilson). As will be discussed in this book's concluding Coda, it was the hiplife muscian Obour who won the position.

NIGERIA: MUSIC UNIONS, PMAN AND THE ANTI-PIRACY STRUGGLE

The first Nigerian Musicians Union (NUM) was formed in 1958 with Bobby Benson as its President, and it was affiliated with the Nigerian Trade Union Congress. After a year, Bobby Benson left to form a rival union with Victor Olaiya, so Chris Ajilo of the Afro-Cubanos band became President of NUM with the trumpeter Zeal Onyia as its Vice-President, the Ghanaian Stan Plange its Treasurer and Amaefule Ikoro its Secretary.

One of the first things the NUM did was to organise a demonstration. As Stan Plange told me:

> *It was in 1960 when the preparations for Nigeria's Independence were going on. The Nigerian government was intending to invite Edmundo Ros to come and play at the National Independence Dance, as Princess Margaret was coming and we understood she liked Edmundo Ros. Victor Olaiya's band was to play second. So the Nigerian Musicians' Union organised a demonstration to protest against the bringing of a foreign group. About eight or nine hundred of us marched with placards from the Empire Hotel, Idioro, to Government House to petition the Prime Minister, Tafawa Balewa. Myself, Zeal, Chris and Amaefule went inside and told him that the contract should be given to the union, who would then form a mass band and select musicians to form a national orchestra for the Independence Dance. He agreed.*

Stan Plange left Nigeria in 1961, Zeal Onyia left for Germany in 1964 and by the mid-1960s NUM was defunct. But, by this time, the drummer Bayo Martins had set up the Musicians Foundation with Bobby Benson and Fela Kuti. However, splits continued, and so, in the 1970s, there was the Music Foundation on one side and Victor Olaiya, Eddie Okunta and I.K. Dairo's Association of Nigerian Musicians on the other. The November 1974 issue of Lagos music paper Gong noted that "Nigerian musicians are at war with themselves, the two major bodies are at daggers drawn, each accusing the other of vices ranging from imposition and misrepresentation to lack of organisation and ignorance." Ultimately, the Nigerian musical unions divided into four factions and the Musicians Foundation folded up when Bayo Martins left the country for Germany.

In 1981, a new constellation of artists organised themselves into the Performing Artists Association of Nigeria (PMAN), patronised by many of the country's top musicians: Sunny Ade, Ebenezer Obey, Sonny Okosun, Christian Essien, Nicholas Mbarga, Victor Uwaifo, Bobby Benson (who died in 1983) and Laoulu Akins. PMAN was out-doored at Sunny Ade's Ariya Club and the main aim of this organisation was to put an end to pirating, then constituting sixty per cent of the Nigerian market. In fact, there was so little control that pirate companies were openly giving their names and addresses on the cassettes they copied. PMAN obtained official recognition and gained wide support. According to the Variety Entertainment Magazine of Nigeria (October 1982), even the then Head of the Association of Nigerian Musicians, Eddie Okunta, joined PMAN and claimed his old association was dead.

PMAN, under the leadership of Tony Okoroji, held a peaceful demonstration in the streets of Lagos in 1988 to get the government to replace the 1971 copyright law. And, in December that year, the Nigerian government issued Decree 47 which gave musicians ten per cent royalty on the producer price of a record or cassette, and made piracy a criminal offence. In 1993, Nigeria copied Ghana's anti-piracy 'banderole' system, and, as in Ghana, the Nigerians were assisted in this initiative by the International Federation of Phonogram Industries (IFPI). However, due to the high degree of open counterfeiting, this was not very successful and quickly collapsed, and piracy in Nigeria reverted to very high levels, some estimating it as high as 90%.

Despite this blow, PMAN continued its anti-piracy struggle. For instance, in 2002, it launched its 'No More Free Music' movement that picketed FM radio stations, hotels and shops that play music for customers. Furthermore, in 2004, and due to the saturation of most Nigerian FM radio stations with western music, PMAN advocated that eighty percent of airplay should be of local music and began seeking a license for their own FM radio station that would only play Nigerian music. In 2007, the flotist and leader of the famous 1970s Afro Collection band, Tee Mac Omatshola Iseli, became president of PMAN and, in that capacity, I met him when he came to Ghana in 2009 to set up a collaboration with the Ghana Musicians Union, MUSIGA. In 2009, 'Admiral' Dele Abiodun became PMAN President. This juju music star formed formed his Top Hitters way back in 1969, which went on to release numerous albums of his 'Adawa System' that blended highlife and juju music. Incidently, Abiodun became familiar with highlife when he ran away from home to Ghana in the early sixties, enrolled in the Young Pioneers School of Music established by Kwame Nkrumah and played bass guitar for several Ghanaian bands.

Chapter 58

ESSIEBONS PRODUCTIONS IN THE EARLY 1980s AND THE FILM 'ROOTS TO FRUITS'

Dick Essilfie-Bondzie of the Essiebons record label has been operating in the local Ghanaian music business since the late 1950s. He started off as a chartered accountant for State Housing Corporation and also a record distributer for Phillips West African Records. Essilfie-Bondzie began music production in 1959 when he launched his Yee Bee label with three 78 records of highlifes by Oscar More Ofori, followed by his opening a record shop in Accra. Then came a break in his musical career when, in 1968, after doing further studies in accountancy in England, he persuaded his businessman father (who ran a bookshop in Accra) to take up half shares with Phillips (Polygram) of Holland to establish a recording studio and pressing plant called the Record Manufacturers of Ghana Limited (RMGL). This enabled Essilfie-Bondzie to set up his own Essiebons label in 1969 which, over the years produced, an astounding 800 singles and 200 albums, scoring many hits. One early one was the All Brothers song 'Yaa Boahema', which became Ghana's first Golden Single in 1969 (sales of 50,000 or more). Another was 'Sikyi Highlife' by Dr. Gyasi and his Noble Kings that was released by Essiebons in 1975 and went on to became a Golden Album. Other artists Essiebons recorded were F. Kenya, C.K. Mann, the Melodic Singers, Agyenim Boateng and the Apagya Show Band that included Ebo Taylor, Gyedu Blay Ambolley and Bob Pinodo. Later, in the early 1980s, he hired the Ghana Film Industry crew to make a seventy-five minute feature film 'Roots to Fruits'.

In 1983, I talked to him at his house in Osu about this film. But first I asked him how he was able to maintain his enormous musical output during the severe economic difficulties that Ghana was going through from the late 1970s.

> *We couldn't bring out a sufficient quantity of what we recorded. For instance, C.K. Mann's first album 'Party Time' should have been a Golden Album, but due to the economic pinch, we couldn't get licences to order sufficient material (i.e. vinyl) – so we couldn't supply popular demand. The artists couldn't get their full royalties and we got poorer as we weren't getting our investments back. Everything became stagnant and locked up in the music industry, especially after 1978 when the import of vinyl virtually stopped. Yet another problem faced by RMGL was a shortage of stereo matrixes (for pressing records). Formerly, we got these stamps from Polygram of Nigeria, as stereo album matrixes cannot be manufactured in Ghana. But, in 1978, when the government there enacted the indigenisation law, Polygram had to sell off 60 per cent of its shares to Nigerians, who decided they could not afford to supply Ghana free.*

I asked Essilfie-Bondzie how, with limited production, he was still able to manage.

> *People bring in their own vinyl and we do custom pressing. Sometimes, we manage to get a matrix made by RMGL's associate, Polygram of Kenya. In 1960, we managed to get an import license for twenty tons of vinyl which arrived last year (1982) and we are stretching this out. A not so difficult task, as now only one of our pressing machines is fully operational due to lack of spare parts.*

Turning to a more positive side, I asked Essilfie-Bondzie about the 'Roots to Fruits' film which was based around a show of that name that took place at the State House in Accra in 1979. I wanted to know the concept behind this film.

> *I wanted to stage my Essiebons artists on film. But, rather than have just a string of artists, I wanted to build a story around the different types of music that I produce, like guitar-band music, choirs, gospel groups, and those modern people who still play in the highlife vein but in a polished form, like C.K. Mann and Bob Pinodo who is Europeanised but draws heavily on the Ghanaian background to evolve something unique. I felt the story*

had to start with the music and dance of the old days; then go on to the advent of the Europeans and the dynamic influences they had on our contemporary music and dance. Nana Bosompra (a famous Ghanaian TV playwright) actually wrote the screen play.

The film was released in Ghana the Christmas of 1982 and it opens up with a breath-taking perusal of roots music from all the regions, performed by the Dance Ensemble of the Institute of African Studies of the University of Ghana. Then, during a traditional religious dance, the entrance of colonialism is symbolised by an African Christian congregation led by a European appearing in the picture. As a result of this musical confrontation, the hymns gradually become syncopated and we begin to hear the creative sounds of the Western Melodic Singers, an Essiebons band that enacted the congregation in the film. The hymns become even more Africanised with the congregation's dancing and drumming being whipped up into a fervour by Super O.D. (Asonoba Kweku Darko), was popular in the 'Osofo Dadzie' television concert party series and in the Essiebons film played the role of an independent African Christian priest. A much more sedate scene is the session by Kakaiku, playing some laid-back palm-wine folk guitar in a style that goes back eighty years or more. Ghana's brass-band music is supplied in the film by Yamoah's band from Winneba, another of Essilfie-Bondzie's groups, which is accompanied by stilted masqueraders.

In part two of the film, we come to the modern sounds, starting with the electric guitar-band music of C.K. Mann's Carousel Seven who made seven albums of funky highlifes for Essiebons. According to Essilfie-Bondzie, they had quite a problem re-dubbing C.K.'s voice for the film, as he never sings songs exactly the same twice! Several of Ghana's top female vocalists sing in the film, like the Ewe singer Efua Dorkenoo and Joana Okang backed by the Uhuru Band. Afua Agyepong also supplies a catchy reggae song from her 'Chaker' album released by Essiebons. The last performance is by Bob Pinodo who began fusing pop, highlifes and the traditional rhythms of the Efutu people (Guan speakers) of his home-town of Winneba back in the late sixties, out of which which he created his 'sonobete' dance and hand-jive. Another number he sings is 'Give Way to Traffic' that refers to Ghana changing over to the right in 1974. The whole film show ends with all the artists singing a hymn on stage – that generates so much feeling that the studio audience erupts onto the dance floor.

The following are some some remarks made in 1983 by Essilfie-Bondzie on his future plans.

The singer Joana Okang who appears in the Roots to Fruits film

I have a strong belief that, provided we can present our music in a way palatable to non-Africans, we can market abroad and make a break through. The right presentation is the thing. Such as my new album I'm planning of compositions by Ebo Taylor with vocalist Pat Thomas. I have also prepared demo-tapes with Amartey Hedzoleh (Lash Laryea) and some songs by Ghana's ace saxophonist Teddy Owusu (both recorded at my Bokoor Studio). Multi-instrumentalist Amartey and bassist Jagger Botchway want to release some material combining Western instruments with traditional percussion, flutes and xylophone. Teddy Owusu is a fantastic sax player if only we could get him to settle down to play (he sadly died in the mid-1980s).

566

To try and sum up, I would say that we have to make our music international and sell it outside the country, as we cannot produce much here at the moment.

Years after this interview, Dick Essilfie-Bondzie was still going strong and, in 2010, he reissued some of his company's 1960s-1980s hits as a double volume CD pack entitled 'Golden Hits of Ghana'. Some of the artists and songs on it are Afua Agyempong ('Chaker'), Houghas Soronko ('Anosonsoma'), Golden All Brothers ('Yaa Boahema'), El Dorados ('Huhuuhu'), Bob Pinodo ('Dance with me'), F. Kenya ('Ewiele'), Ebo Taylor ('Abenkwan Puchaa'), Paapa Yankson ('Spiritual Ghana') as well as tracks by Lola and Pat (ie. Thomas), the 4th Dimension Band, the Diplomats Dance band, the Apagya Showband and the Western Melodic Singers, originaly a part of Sekondi Methodist choir. The same year, Dick celebrated his 80th birthday at a party at the Wangara Hotel in Accra at which many artists played. These included those who released music on his label as well as others who wanted to pay tribute – like Amartey Hedzoleh, Osie Tutu, Mustapha Tetteh Addy, Chi Kin Chee and Ralph Karikari (who sadly died in 2018).

Chapter 59

FAISAL HELWANI, 'F' PROMOTIONS AND THE NAPOLEON CLUB

The Ghanaian-Lebanese music promoter Faisal Helwani was born in Sekondi in 1946 and, by eighteen years old, he was in the music promoting field. As he told me in 1980:

> *I got a dance at the Lido nightclub in 1964 with five bands: the Shambros, Black Santiagos, Ramblers, African Rhythmaires and Ghana Armed Forces Band. Until then, every night there were the same monotonous dances with one band playing for six hours from nine to three in the morning. I wanted to introduce show business competition. Like at the second Lido show, I made Rim Obeng from the Armed Forces Band sit on one side of his drum and Mac Hammond sit on the other, and each would take a solo in turn. Also I used to put up beauty contests and fashion shows. A lot of my activities then were covered on TV.*

By 1966, Faisal and his 'F' promotions was organising student 'pop chains' and promoting school-boy bands like the Thunderbirds and, a little later, his own group the EI Sombreros led by Johnny Opoku-Acheampong and Alfred 'Kari' Bannerman. It was in 1967 that Faisal first met Fela Anikulapo-Kuti, and below explains how it happened.

I then had an electrical hardware shop and, as I had started promoting, I went down to Nigeria to look for some good bands to bring to Ghana. My first time in Lagos was with Chris Ukoli of the West African magazine New Breed. *He came to Ghana and watched one of my shows and invited me to his show in Lagos, and there I went out visiting clubs. Then Fela was at a place called the Kakadu playing Afro-jazz songs like 'Yeshe Yeshe' with Yoruba words but with a jazzy beat. I was introduced to Fela by Chris and I talked to Fela about coming to Ghana. The next day I went to his house where his mother-in-law and wife were staying (later this became the first Kalakuta Republic). He agreed to come for £150 a week and I paid for all accommodation. He did not have any amplification so, when he came, I also hired the equipment for him. I took him all over Ghana: Koforidua, Cape Coast, Swedru, Takoradi, Kumasi, Akim Oda, everywhere. Nobody knew him at that time, He was then playing trumpet and his band was called the Koola Lobitos. I promoted 'Yeshe Yeshe' and went into business with Fela. With Fela, I never made any money, but he liked Ghana and kept coming.*

Fela returned again in 1968 for another tour organised by 'F' Promotions. According to Johnny Opoku-Acheampong, whose EI Sombreros (formed 1968) toured with Fela on that trip, Fela had already started experimenting with the new Afro-beat sound he then called 'Afro-soul'. It is interesting to note that this new music became popular in Ghana before it caught on in Nigeria.

In 1968, Faisal organised 'F' Promotion's most ambitious tour, a six-week tour of East Africa by the Uhuru dance band (led by Stan Plange), the Rolling Beats dance troupe and the ace drummer Kofi Ghanaba. After this, Faisal opened a nightclub he called the Pagoda (renamed the Napoleon in 1973). Instead of simply turning it into a discotheque, as so many other nightclub owners were doing, he took the imaginative step of also setting up an resident Afro-pop band there in October 1973, called Hedzoleh which means 'peace' or 'freedom' in the Ga language. As mentioned in Chapter 42, this group was originally fomed in 1972 by Amartey Laryea, Jagger Botchway, Leepuma and others with the assistance of the Director of the Arts Council Saka Acquaye. But a few months later, Amartey Lash Laryea left after a misunderstading with Faisal who recruited some new musicians. The line-up of the band then became as follows:

1. The late Stanley Kwesi Todd (ex El Pollos pop group) was the leader, bass guitarist and xylophone player. He replaced Lash Laryea who left for the UK.
2. Stanley's brother Frank on trap-drums

3. Isaac 'Okyerema' Asante on talking drums
4. Acheampong Welbeck on cow-bells and calabash
5. Samuel Oko Nortey on calabash and local drums.
6. Jagger Botchway (ex Magic Aliens band) lead guitar
7. James Kwaku Morton from the Arts Council on bass congas
8. Nii Lee Ampoumah (a.k.a. Nat Hammond Leepuma), also from the Arts Council, on antenteben bamboo flute.

Hedzoleh in 1973. Okyerema Asante is playing maracas.
The late Stanley Todd is on bass guitar

This band was 'out-doored' at the Orion Cinema in November 1973, played for the Asantehene in December, won the Arts Council's small dance-band competition the same month and played at the Ga Mantse's palace in January 1974. They also supplied seventy per cent of the soundtrack for the film 'Contact', a joint production of the Ghana Film Corporation and the Ital-Victoria Company of Italy.

The South African trumpeter Hugh Masekela joined the band and in December 1973 they all went to EMI studios in Lagos to record the LP 'Introducing Hedzoleh'. One of most popular numbers on the album was 'Rekpete', an old Liberian Kru song that was released as a single. Early in 1974, the band left with Faisal for the United States but, as Faisal explains in an interview with the Ghanaian Mirror (February 7, 1975), things did not turn out so well.

Hedzoleh's Stanley Todd with Hugh Masekela at the Napoleon Club in 1973

I founded, created, financed, managed, produced and arranged them for recording. On top, I organised the Masekela-Hedzoleh tour of the United States. In all, I broke through the universal market with Hedzoleh within the short period of one-and-a-half years. Hugh Masekela showed up in Accra and was introduced to me by my friend Fela Ransome-Kuti. At that time, Hedzoleh was already a champion band of Ghana and, in fact, the group was ready to launch into the world market, with or without Masekela. I never dreamed that Hugh Masekela, with the political awareness from the South African experience, would ever try to do this to his fellow black men. So we decided to go on the United States trip together. The whole outfit was financed by me, including the booster show we put up for Masekela in Accra. After the Ghanaian Ambassador to the United States had given us a reception at the Kennedy Arts Centre, the way had been paved for full houses wherever we went. We got to Philadelphia and the poster at the entrance of the club where we were playing read 'Hugh Masekela'. There was no mention of Hedzoleh at all. The American pressmen had been brainwashed to believe that the one hit record Hedzoleh cut with Masekela was actually recorded in South Africa. It was bad! I decided to come back.

The Hedzoleh musicians remained in the States and, in 1975, released the Afro-rock album 'The Boys Doing It' that included Hugh Maskela and the Nigerian saxist Orlando Julius (aka O.J. Ekemode). These Ghanaian musicians also appeared on several of Hugh Masekela's mid-1970s albums such as 'Colonial Man' and 'Ojah.'

Hedzoleh in 1974. Photo courtesy Ghana Review Vol No 2 '74

Just before Hedzoleh left Ghana in 1974, Faisal had decided to form another band to play at the Napoleon. This was Basa-Basa (means 'pandemonium' in Ga) and it specialised in a combination of rock music and local rhythms like the Ewe agbadza. The membership was as follows:

1. Francis 'Wallace' Eyeye from the Volta Region was leader and lead guitarist
2. The Ewe identical twins Joseph (Ringo) and Charles Nyarko played cow-bells and congas (They are now in the United States)
3. Nii Edmund Ayitey II (ex Kukurudu and Adam's Apple) was bass guitar player (He is now in Germany)
4. Jerry James Lartey (ex of the Caprice Hotel's Expensive Diamonds) on conga drums (He replaced Basa-Basa's original congaist Slim, a merchant seaman)
5. Ballo Apotey Tabahum on indigenous Ewe agbadza drums
6. Amoa Azangeo from Bolgatanga in northern Ghana on the Frafra calabash. He was originally with the Arts Council and had played at the 1971 'Soul to Soul' concert with

Eddie Harris and Les McCann. The fusion of the Ewe Agbadza with Amoah's Frafra rhythms was one of the most exciting features of Basa-Basa.

Basa Basa as the Napoleon Club in Osu in 1974

In April 1974, Faisal formed yet another band for his club, which concentrated on highlifes and Afro-beats. He called this band the Bunzus but, in fact, the bandsmen had been together for some years playing with concert guitar-bands from Kumasi; such as Kwakye's Music Mayors, the Happy Brothers, Oko's band, Mike Ofori's Dominos and also K. Frempong's Cubanos Fiesta with whom they had a made one-year tour of Ghana, Cote d'Ivoire and Burkina Faso. The composition of the band was:

1. Cliff Eck from Larteh was the leader and lead guitarist (now plays with various jazz groups in Accra)
2. Kojo Eck, Cliff's brother was the alto congaist
3. The late Eddie Agyepong from Koforidua played trap-drums and tuned cowbells
4. Paul from the Volta Region was the bass guitarist.
5. Yram 'Spancky' Hussoo, from the Volta Region was on flute, calabash and organ (in 1976 he moved to Cote D'Ivoire and France where he played keyboards and sax; later moved to the US where he now resides)

6. Jerry Ofori from Accra was the bass congaist

7. From June 1974, I joined the band playing harmonica and sometimes guitar.

During 1974 and 1975, these two bands played almost every night at the Napoleon, with the Bunzus starting at eleven o'clock and Basa-Basa from one in the morning until three. Sometimes, a floor show was done by the comedian Ajax Bukana, or the musical midget Tawia Brown who did a take on James Brown. After the live acts, the club remained open as a discotheque until the early morning. As can be expected, this club became the focus for night people and musicians from Ghana and abroad.

Basa-Basa and the Bunzus also played at a number of charity shows. For example, in September 1974, they played at Nsawam Prison, Kumasi Central Prison and Ussher Fort Prison. To take one specific example, we played at the prison located in the 16th century Ussher Fort to about four hundred male prisoners, all wearing drab white shorts and smocks, or blue cloths. At first the audience was rather subdued, for this was the first time a live band had played in a Ghanaian prison; but by the time we had finished, they were dancing 'bone to bone' (man to man) and were roaring with laughter at the Nigerian comedian Ajax Bukana with his top-hat, tails, odd socks and long pointed shoes. Two of the prisoners even jammed on the drums. To go from one extreme to the other, in December the same year we played for the Head of State, Colonel Acheampong, at a Christmas party in Christiansburg Castle. Although the audience was more sedate than those at the prison, the music finally got to them when two officers started careering around the lawn to the amusement of all. In late 1974, Basa-Basa also played at a concert organised by the Black Brothers International in memory of Kwame Nkrumah and to raise money for the African Liberation Fund; and then again at the Featherweight Commonwealth Boxing Championship held in the Accra Sports Stadium.

The Napoleon Club also became the initial headquarters of the Muscians Union of Ghana (MUSIGA) in 1974, with its first executives being Faisal, King Bruce, Sammy Odoh, Stan Plange, Koo Nimo, E.T. Mensah, Eddie Quansah, Joe Eyison and others. In fact, the muscians who constituted the seven 'B.B.' bands of King Bruce and Faisal's two current bands Basa Basa and the Bunzu constituted the first one hundred members of the union. I was in this first batch of one hundred union members.

One of the Banzu Sounds line-ups at Napoleon Club 1974

In November 1974, the Basa Basa and the Bunzus went to the eight-track EMI studios in Lagos to record LPs and play at Fela's Afrika Shrine, and the following is a journalistic account of the eleven-day trip I wrote for the Ghanaian press on returning.

After a sixteen-hour journey to Lagos, a session at Victor Olaiya's Papingo night club at the Stadium Hotel and finally sleep at the Empire Hotel (Afrika Shrine) in Mushin, we were woken up on our first morning (the 23rd) by the roar of an angry crowd. From our hotel balcony, we could see about sixty riot police axing down Fela's front door, just a hundred yards away. Fela's people fought back, so then came the teargas; and we Ghanaian musicians were down-wind! We discovered later that Fela had refused to allow the police to make a routine search of his place and consequently received nine stitches in the head for his trouble. According to the Nigerian Daily Times of November 27, the 'Afro-beat King Fela Ransome-Kuti stepped into freedom from confinement again yesterday when the police granted him bail following his arrest after last Saturday's police raid on his home'. The very same day he was released he had to appear in court, and the Times continued its report: 'Fela was this morning discharged and acquitted by an Apapa Chief Magistrate's Court on a three-count charge of unlawful possession of Indian hemp'. That day we saw a happier demonstration from our balcony than the one on Saturday, for after the court-case a huge crowd followed Fela's cavalcade to the Shrine, causing a massive 'go slow' of traffic. The same night he played alongside Basa-Basa and the Bunzus, with one arm in a sling and wearing a skull-cap bandage which he humorously called a 'Pope's hat'. For the days Fela had been away, his lawyer sang the vocals and subsequently became known as 'Feelings Lawyer', as he made such a good substitute.

Faisal most certainly did the right thing when he decided to lodge us at the Shrine, the centre of the modern West African music scene. There we met Johnny Haastrup of Mono-Mono, Berkeley Jones of BLO, Big Joe Olodele who used to be with the Black Santiagos in Ghana and is now with the Granadians, and Albert Jones from the Heartbeats '72 who was down from his base in Kano. And we had live juju music every night from the Lido Nightclub opposite the hotel. Our bands went down very well at the Papingo where we played four nights alongside the resident All Stars (ex Cool Cats). We spent two days in the recording studio where Faisal and Fela were co-producing the session. On November 30th we all departed, leaving Fela and Faisal to mix the recordings. We were meant to play at the Cultural Centre in Cotonou on our way back home, but arrived the day the 'People's Revolution' was declared in Dahomey and found Cotonou deserted; everyone had gone to Abome. We did, however, play the following night at the Centre Communitaire in Lome. We all learned lot from our short stay in Nigeria. Fela is the top musician there, much more popular than foreign artists such as James Brown or Jimmy Cliff who was barely able to pull in a crowd of six thousand at the sixty-thousand capacity football stadium at Surulere on the 28th. A lesson for Ghanaian pop fans, I think!

The Basa-Basa LP was released in 1975, followed by that of the Bunzus, both on the New York Makossa label. As the Hedzoleh musicians had dropped the name when they stayed in America, Faisal decided to reform Hedzoleh. He called in the young ace guitarist from Akwapim, Joe Miller as leader, with Ashela and Willie Quist from Accra on bass, maracas and vocals. They were backed by four Akan musicians: Richard Croffie on cowbells, Nortey on lead congas, Abeku on bass congas and Johnny Glover on talking drums. In June 1975, Basa Basa, the Bunzus and New Hedzoleh went to the sixteen-track A.R.C. studio in Lagos (partly owned by Ginger Baker) and recorded more LPs, with Fela Kuti jamming on some of them.

During that year, the Napoleon Club itself underwent major renovation and so the club activities had to stop for a time. When it re-opened, Faisal instituted the successful Monday-night jazz sessions at which popular musicians jammed, like Fela, Victor

Uwaifo, Jerry Hansen, Sammy Odoh, Pat Thomas, E.T. Mensah and the Ghanaian blues harmonica player Henry Mills, all backed by the Alex Kotey Quintet from the Ghana Broadcasting Service Orchestra – and also the New Hedzoleh.

In 1977, Faisal started a regular Friday night programme on Ghana Broadcasting which he called 'Afro-disia Hour' as he was then working with the Decca Afro-disia label in Nigeria. He also started a regular Wednesday night 'Afro-disia Night' at the Tip-Toe Gardens in Accra at which he featured his three bands, plus groups like the Uhuru, Abladei, Kwaa Mensah, Adjo, E.T. Mensah and my own Bokoor guitar band. Also that year he took many of these groups, plus the visiting Black Angels singing sisters, to Lagos to record. Unfortunately, a misunderstanding arose between Faisal and Decca and the eleven master-tapes were never released. Around 1980, Faisal set up his fourth band, Edikanfo, led by trumpeter Osei Tutu. This large dance group (with Chi-Kin-Chi on bass) concentrated on local melodies with a funky touch.

Many international stars visited the Napoleon during the early 1980s. One was the famous British New Wave rock star Brian Eno of the Talking Heads band who flew in from New York and stayed at the Napoleon as Faisal's guest for three weeks (also stayed with me for a few days over the Christmas of 1980). On this trip, Brian worked with Edikanfo at Faisal's just-opened Studio One at the Napoleon Club and released an album for them on his EG record label.

The way Brian Eno was invited to Ghana is interesting. I was on a trip to the UK and saw a copy of the Amercian Rolling Stones pop magazine in which Brian was talking about his and David Byrnes' new interest in African music. I got this information to Faisal. Later, Brian told me that Faisal and the Ghanaian Musicians Union (MUSIGA, of which Faisal was a founder) routed his invitation to Ghana through the United Nations in New York; which really impressed the English rock composer.

Faisal was also involved in the trip to Ghana by Mick Fleetwood, the English leader and drummer of the Los Angeles-based rock group Fleetwood Mac. In early 1981, Mick Fleetwood, George Hawkins and Todd Sharpe flew from California to Ghana for a six-week safari, complete with recording engineers, bodyguards and twelve tons of equipment and a sixteen-track studio. They were expecting to trek around in the bush and even brought mosquito nets and portable latrines with them. Instead, everything was laid on for them by MUSIGA and Faisal, and they were lodged at the Star Hotel in

Accra. So instead of chasing the musicians, the musicians rather came to them, and so they were able to spend their whole time recording on their equipment which they set up at the Ghana Film studio. An album was later released by them called 'The Visitor' that featured the three American musicians, plus local groups and artists like the Super Brains, Koo Nimo and the children's Ebaahi cultural group.

In the early 1980s, the Napoleon Club closed down. But Faisal continued to run his Studio One from there and made local releases of the highlife singer Kobina Okai and the blind Frafra musician Onipa Nua; and later Akompi and Kofi Sammy. Because of the problems in Ghana's music industry at the time, he moved his studio to Liberia for a while in the mid-1980s (see Chapter 54). On his return to Ghana, he became involved in MUSIGA's anti-piracy crusade. In the early 1990s, Faisal left the music business to concentrate on his other businesses but then, in 2000, he opened his Bibini Studio at the the old Napoleon Club. He went on to organise a series of Pop Star Talent Hunts in 2005 at which five hundred youngsters were auditioned to locate a new generation of up-and-coming artists.

Faisal's own daughter Yasmin has also released some albums recorded in her father's studio, whilst Faisal's sons Sammy, Waseem and Bassam were trained as recording engineers. Faisal was also involved with the 'Made in Germany' event on 'burger' (i.e. Hamburg) highlife that was organised by the German Goethe Institute in Accra in 2007 as part of the year-long Ghana celebrations marking Ghana's fiftieth independence anniversary.

So all of us involved in the Ghanaian music scene were sad to hear of his death in Lebanon on 27 July 2008, as this man's musical career went all the way back to 1964 when he was just eighteen years old. Faisal's body was brought back from Lebanon to Ghana and was buried at Osu Cemetary in Accra on 6 August 2008. He was survived by his six children, six grandchildren and his wife Victoria.

Faisal, with his enormous energy, his outspoken voice and his huge contribution to Ghanaian music is sorely missed.

Chapter 60

KING BRUCE'S VIEWS ON THE POPULAR MUSIC BUSINESS

In the late 1980s, I did a number of long interviews with King Bruce of the Black Beats that we were planning to use for his biography. The following is a portion of these interviews that I organised as one of the book's chapters entitled 'Present and Future Plans'

I began by asking King about some of the changes he had noticed as a band leader over the last thirty years or so.

KING: In the old days, when a band had a composition, they rehearsed it and used it at live performances before the public. So, by the time the group went into the studio, all the musicians would have mastered the music and instrumental solos and have a full idea of the public reaction to it. It was also better then, as recording contracts went to bands. It was rare to get a composer going into a studio with picked-up musicians as in those days there were no session-men.

Nowadays, the studio fees are all paid by producers, which is also why we have quite a crop of session-men who don't belong to any particular band and who are always nosing around recording studios. The producers engage these musicians who come

King Bruce at piano working on a composition. (Photo Souza Photo Works Christiansborg)

from all over the place and because producers have little time, they are in a hurry to finish everything off. It may be that the session musician's first contact with the composition will be the first day they meet at the studio. They may not know the songs at all. Also, because of the costs, the producers have to limit the number of instruments to the barest minimum. That doesn't do much good for the music.

Compared to now, the period up to the sixties was fairly free of these problems. Those that existed at the time were, in my opinion, due to poor recording facilities and the total lack of educational institutions for musicians to uplift the quality of their musicianship. But, since the 1960s, with the foreign exchange strangulation, there have been difficulties about importing musical equipment. Also, by the 1970s, there was hardly any foreign exchange to import vinyl for records and what little there was was used by recording companies, like Phillips, to press reggae and foreign music under licence, which they could sell outside Ghana to get foreign exchange. So the problems in the seventies were ten times what they used to be in the sixties and before. As a matter of fact, somebody in the record producing business told me, in 1972 or 1973, that only five per cent of recorded tapes of local Ghanaian music was eventually emerging on disc as finished products. I have had dozens of boys who have made recordings that never came out. And if you have a song and for a long time it doesn't come out, it dies a natural death because the topicality of the thing loses its effect. Ghanaian artists really suffered and many had to go out of the country to finish off their recording ventures. Today, we've been forced to put things on cassette, firstly because cassettes are more easily brought into the country than vinyl. Secondly, for quite a while, you couldn't get a record changer for love of money, and there are more cassette players around than record turntables. But I must say that I find it odd, in the old days we could record and have a disc out within a month. Yet these days with all the better technology, things should go faster, but they don't.

Another reason for the decline in the music industry is that private people don't invest in Ghanaian music, because local businessmen who have invested in it failed or have been disappointed. Those who have persisted have only done so out of love of highlife music, rather than the fact that it could earn them a quick return. In fact, since independence, no Ghanaian musician, producer or promoter has made money on a handsome scale solely in this country. Those that have succeeded in any musical enterprise have done so because they have operated jointly with a concert group where it's not the music as such that is the main source of income, but the drama side. Over the years we've got so many bands, like C.K. Mann's, A.B. Crentsil's Ahenfo, Big Mouth, and Smart Nkansah's Sunsum who were initially all straightforward bands, but have had to go into the concert field.

JC: What is your attitude to the spinners (mobile sound systems)?

KING: The spinners are having an adverse effect on the live music scene. We have had a series of meetings on this current problem and many MUSIGA members thought that the government should ban them in order to protect live music and bandsmen. But I said, how can the government ban them and what law have they broken, for the spinners have legally bought all their equipment and are paying all their income tax and so on. I tried to explain to the MUSIGA members that the only circumstance under which the government could impose a ban on spinners was if they were having a harmful effect on the cultural aspects of music. So I suggested that there shouldn't be an outright ban on them, rather controls on them. For instance, they should always have to play alongside a live group, for we cannot stand in the way of technology.

JC: What are your feelings about the new (1985) copyright law?

KING: It is working. But the very sad death of the Copyright Administrator, Mr. Adoi-Anim, in September 1987, has not helped things. However, since the new copyright law, the GBC (Ghana Broadcasting Corporation) has begun to pay out royalties to musicians. The first of these local payments was made at the beginning of 1987 when three million cedis was given out to Ghanaian musicians. Some people got fifty thousand cedis, some thirty, some twenty and some rather less.

As no accurate monitoring of music has been made previously by the GBC (i.e. logging whose music had been used and how many times), this particular payment was, just for the meantime, based on the particular musician's popularity. Long ago, I believe, there was an accurate system of monitoring music on the radio but, with the ever-increasing difficulties with our foreign exchange, this collapsed. Also another aspect of the new copyright law was that an agreement was made with the PRS (Performing Rights Society) in London as to what should be paid for the use of foreign music on our radio. All these changes occurred after a series of meetings we musicians had with the GBC and the Copyright Administration at the Ministry of Information offices. We in MUSIGA pointed out that ours (i.e. music) was a marketable product which had to be monitored and paid for, and that it wasn't a question of how much the GBC could spare to give us. But even though GBC is short of money we got them to agree that the payment should go up from three million to six million cedis.

JC: What about the live popular music scene?

KING: The future of live bands is very doubtful as the young people like masses of electronic equipment. A live band uses maybe four hundred watts of power and about ten P.A. (public address) systems and instrument speaker cabinets. Whereas, an electronic spinner may use two thousand watts and as many as forty huge speaker cabinets. So, there is no comparison between the sound of live and electronic bands. And electronic bands (spinners) can play from seven o'clock p.m. to two in the morning. No band can play like that. Also the spinners have strobe lights, disco lights, soap bubbles and other weird effects that drive the kids crazy. At the moment, live bands mainly play at hotels where grown-up people go, and there aren't enough of those places for all the dance bands. So our dance band course of action is to go extensively into recordings. That too is not easy because to record and press at least five thousand LPs would cost at least a million cedis (then approximately £1,600), and people here aren't prepared to invest, as no local musician or producer has ever become rich in Ghana from music.

In August 1994, I talked to King about the use of drum-machines at Elephant Walk Studios which he managed for two years in the early 1990s. In his usual methodical way, he gave me a list of the pros and cons of using them.

POSITIVE ASPECTS OF DRUM MACHINES

1. Hastens work and so is economical.
2. The drumulator imposes a certain discipline or tempo on the band.
3. Electronic drums do now drown out the rest of the instruments when played with these instruments.

NEGATIVE ASPECTS

1. With a pre-programmed drum beat, there can be no last minute (percussive) ideas or afterthoughts incorporated into the music.
2. Often mistakes made by a musician (e.g. live drummer) can be a blessing in disguise as he may, on-the-spot, come up with a better idea.
3. The musicians inspire one another to do their best. This is not something done by the arranger. This is especially true with free form music like jazz.

King ended this conversation by telling me about a gospel group he recorded with a drumulator. The leader sent the tape to his brother in the United States. The Americans did not like the drum-machine and so the brother had to return the tape to Ghana to have a new mix done, with the drumulator track replaced by an experienced live drummer.

Chapter 61

MOHAMMED MALCOLM-BEN'S AFRICAN FEELINGS PRODUCTIONS

The late Mohammed Malcolm-Ben was born in the country's Eastern Region and first came into the music business as a practising musician when, between 1960 and 1968, he played as drummer with the Messengers Dance Band, T.O. Jazz and the Fabulous Stars. He was also a session-drummer at Ghana Films Recording Studio and on one occasion recalls he recorded forty-eight songs with the K.K. Masters guitar-band in one sitting!

In 1970, and after a lot of research into current musical trends, he decided to go into music production and later opened a record shop. He produced a string of successful releases and I met him in 1982 when he brought his Yaa Nom Professional Band to my Bokoor Recording Studio, featuring Okyerema Asante on xylophone and percussion. I later interviewed him at his office in Tudu, Accra and the first question I put to him was how he got his name.

MOHAMMED: I took my name from the great Afro-American Malcolm X and I wrote to him telling him that I wanted to take his name. Then, when he came to Ghana in 1963, I went to a lecture by him and met him afterwards. He is one of my heroes and I include him on my list of 'African Warriors' in my latest Yaa Nom recordings that I've just produced.

JC: Can you tell me something about your earlier productions?

MOHAMMED: It was in 1970 that I did my very first. It was two singles by T.O. Jazz led by T.O. Ampoumah that I released on my Ohianiwa Label. The word 'ohianiwa' means a cautious or reserved man. I pressed the records at Ambassador Records in Kumasi and one of them sold as much as eighteen thousand copies, for in those days we had a lot of vinyl and plenty of import licences were being given. After that I produced an album with T.O. Jazz on the same label. Later on, I began to write romantic books like the 'Guile of Man', 'Hidden Truth' and 'Pregnant Virgin' and set up a publishing house in 1979 called African Feeling Associates. All this time, I was the PRO for Nana Ampadu's African Brothers Band, managed and produced by D.K. Nyarko. After Nyarko's death, Ampadu and I decided to do our own recordings and, in 1980, we released an album called 'Agatha' after Ampadu's wife. Then we did one as a tribute to D.K. and another called 'Owua Aye Me Bi' (death has given me a deadly blow). They were recorded at Ghana Films, pressed in Ghana, Ivory Coast, the U.S.A. and Nigeria and were released on my African Feelings Label. I also produced an album of funk and reggae by the Twanky Blacks, the African Brothers second band, which I recorded at the now-closed Phillips two-track studio in Ghana. It was released by Makossa in New York, a company run by two Afro-American brothers, Fred and Roger Frances who I had been in contact with since 1977. In 1981, I helped a friend produce a City Boys album, a guitar-band run by the 'Black Chinese' Obuoba J.A. Adofo. It was recorded at Faisal Helwani's eight-track studio and was called 'Ankwan Obi', a nickname for a lover.

JC: How did you come to change the name of your record label to African Feeling?

MOHAMMED: In 1973, I went to the OAU conference at Addis Ababa, the tenth anniversary of its founding, in fact. It was there that I got the impression that Africans are being forced to unite because of the OAU Charter. Whereas the first thing the founding fathers should have done is to let them feel that they are Africans. Then the political unity would come by itself, for if we don't all feel we are Africans, how can we unite? That's why after the conference I formed my organisation to project the African Feeling.

JC: What changes have you seen in record production here over the years?

MOHAMMED: In 1970, when I started, studios were two-track but quite adequate for the times. Also, there was plenty of vinyl in the country. Nowadays, I have to import my own. Then studio charges have jumped from around forty cedis a day to between 2,500 and 5,000 a day; and with the control price of records being only sixty cedis per album I am forced to market abroad. Then there's the problem that, although we have got multi-track studios here now which have all the basics, they lack supporting equipment like phasers, graphic equalisers, rhythm boxes and so on; which is necessary for success in the international field. This is what makes our music dry compared to, say, Nigeria.

JC: In fact, the problems have led to the formation of a Music Producers Association recently?

MOHAMMED: Yes, it was formed in 1979 by independent local producers to protect their profession. I am the General Secretary, George Prah of Gapophone is President and John Nyarko is our PRO. There's about twenty five of us altogether. You see, in Ghana, we have to sell about ten thousand records to break even, and it's very difficult to do this due to cassette pirating. In May this year (1982), we had a meeting with the Musicians' Union (MUSIGA), the Tape Recordists Association (the TRA was an association of kiosk cassette duplicators), Mr. Asiedu Yirenkyi (then Minister of Culture), Mr. Ato Austin (then Minister of Information) and a legal expert on copyright. Our case to them was that we have the professional equipment to flood the market with cassettes but the TRA says we can't satisfy all the demand, as they know all the nooks and corners of the country. But the crux is that they find the business so profitable as they don't have to produce anything, only copy what we have produced, and so don't pay anything at all to the artists. For example, when Kwabena Okai (E.K. Nyame's vocalist) was sick, he came to us for help and not the tape recorder people. At the meeting, MUSIGA wanted to go on the rampage and close down the tape recordists by direct action. For us (the Producers' Union), we want to produce the cassettes ourselves as we have the duplicating equipment, and then the TRA could simply distribute for us.

JC: What are your future plans?

MOHAMMED: I have just set up a label in London and the Ivory Coast, in addition to my outlet in America through Makossa. So anything I produce here, I can send abroad.

Reggae is selling worldwide and I don't see why highlife shouldn't sell too. The only thing preventing this, as far as I can see, is our own mental slavery and lack of appreciation of our own music. Our minds are always being too tuned to Western ideas. I have even been selling my music to Hong Kong and Taiwan and very soon will be sending a cultural group there to show them how to dance the highlife. The other problem is, of course, the inadequate recording facilities here in Ghana, so I am also trying to build a 24-track studio here, as they have in Abidjan, Togo and several in Nigeria. If we had such studios, our musicians would come back to record. It is because of this lack that Ghanaians are going to Nigeria and other places. The production I'm currently working on is with the Yaa Nom Professionals. It's pure highlife music with words in English dedicated to the black leaders Marcus Garvey, Malcolm X, Martin Luther King, Bob Marley, Kwame Nkrumah and Patrice Lumumba. I'm also doing some other songs about Zimbabwe and will combine them all in one Pan-African album that will be released by Makossa. My intention is to pay tribute to all black warriors, both African and Afro-American, who have suffered and died in the struggle to liberate black people.

Chapter 62

BOKOOR BAND, MUSIC COMPANY AND HIGHLIFE INSTITUTE

THE FORMATION AND RUNNING OF BOKOOR BAND

Although I had been playing with the Jaguar Jokers, F. Kenya's, Happy Stars and the Achimota School pop-band Deep Blue Feelings from 1969, I got more seriously into band life when I formed Bokoor (meaning coolness) band in 1971 with the Ghanaian guitarist Robert Beckley. This was the second band to the Uhuru band at the time and Bokoor then played the music of Jimmy Hendrix, Carlos Santana, James Brown as well as local highlifes. The group folded up when several of the members, who were University of Ghana students (including myself and English musician Peter Wilks) had to take exams. For a number of years I then played guitar, harmonica and percussion with a number of Accra-based groups, such as F. Kenya's guitar band, Szaabu Sounds (with Bob Pinodo, Nat Osamanu, Leslie Tex and Bob Fiscian), the resident Bunzus band at Faisal Helwani's Napoleon Club, the Army Recce Brigade's Black Berets, the Abladei Ga cultural group and Koo Nimo's 'palmwine' guitar group with whom I also recorded.

In 1975, I re-formed Bokoor when I was living at Temple House in James Town Accra, initially as a 'cultural' band with guitar and plenty of percussion, including the giant bass gome frame-drum. By 1977, it had expanded to a full guitar band with the addition of rhythm and bass guitars and, on occasions, trap-drums. The music we played were highlifes, folksongs, congo jazz (soukous and bouche), Afro-beats, reggae-highlifes and songs that used the local agbadja, adowa and kpanlogo rhythms. The band's show also included a session of fire-eating and snake-dancing by the group's lady singers Gifty Naa Dodowa and Brown Sugar. With me on guitar and harmonica, Bokoor became a 12-14 piece group and many musicians played with the band between 1975 and 1979. These included the percussionist and bass player Jones Horatio Attuquayefio and Sammy Brown (originally gome player and guitarist with the Agbafoi 'Ga cultural group'), the Ewe master-drummer Dan 'Bokovi' Banini, the conga players Jerry James Lartey (who later formed Saka Saka) and Bob 'Ajanka' Tawia (a fisherman and brother of dancer Francis Nii Yartey), the bass players George 'Junior' Quarcoo and Joe Kelly Junior (son of the famous 1950s highlife trumpeter), rhythm guitarists James Nanka-Bruce and James Antwi, and percussionists John Odartey Lamptey, Isaac Aban Amarteifio, Foster, Kalala, B. Peters, Kpakpo Allotey and John 'Jeano' Othman. Two other Bokoor percussionists were Kpani 'Gasper' and Emmanuel who belonged to the Ga drumming 'Addy' family (includes Mustapha Tettey, Obo and Yacob Addy). Two Americans also briefly passed through Bokoor: trap-drummer Big Joe Galeota and guitarist Tony Green.

John Collins and his Bokoor band at the Seaview Hotel, Accra, mid-1970s

Bokoor became affiliated to Ghana Arts Council, the Ghana Co-operative Indigenous Musicians Society (that catered for guitar bands and concert parties) and the Musicians Union of Ghana (MUSIGA – of which I was an executive member) in 1979. Between 1977 and late 1979, Bokoor played extensively in the Greater Accra Area, the Volta Region and Togo. In 1977, we played at a private party for the African American heavyweight champion Floyd Paterson, arranged by the Ghanaian boxing promoter Sammy Captan. As Sammy's family ran some local cinemas, we also played at these with the concert party stage-magician Professor De-Ago. The same year, we also performed at the Tip Toe Gardens alongside Kwaa Mensah, Uhuru, E.T. Mensah and Basa Basa at the 'Afro-disia Nights' organised by Decca and Faisal Helwani's 'F' Promotions. We also did regular shows in Accra at the Labadi Tourist Rendez-vous, Fair Gardens, Penthouse, Sea-View Hotel (round the corner from Temple House), Achimota Staff Club and Dome Spot. Moreover, we often played at Sunday afternoon shows (alongside the Ga cultural groups Wulomei and Suku Troupe) organised by Castle Santana Promotions for Ga fishermen and their families in James Town and La.

Sometimes we met problems. At a club in the Togolese town of Kpalime, there was no earth wire and the amplifier humming was so great that I had to stick the wire into my belt and act as a human earth. On another occasion, when we were on a Christmas tour of the Volta Region with Kris Bediako's Afro-rock band, the audience in Denu rioted when there was a technical hitch and our band faltered. Fortunately the problem was solved, despite some dancers having jumped on stage threatening us. Afterwards, some of the rioters, including military personnel, apologised and explained it was just a spontaneous reaction to the dance groove being interrupted. At the Ga fishing village of Bortianor, our bass player 'Junior' didn't turn up and we tried to cover up by getting our rhythm guitarist James to play only bass notes, which didn't satisfy the local fishermen who were expecting a dance-band with a heavy bass sound. Some even produced knives. But our quick-thinking singer-dancer, Gifty, saved the situation when she threw our two pythons at the advancing crowd of men, who instantly scattered to the sides of the venue. Gifty then jumped off stage and did an impromptu dance and went around shaking the snakes in front of the noses of the young fishermen, particularly those whose eyes had gone red with anger. This burnt out the crowd's aggression and adrenalin, so that the show was able to continue and come to a satisfactory conclusion. Later, at the Tabela Night Club in Accra, we lost one of our pythons which wriggled its way into the bamboo decorations.

In 1978, Bokoor appeared on the Mike Eghan television show and released a record and two commercial cassettes in Ghana that were often played on the radio. A demo-tape was first made in 1977 at the Macarthy Hill recording studio of highlife trumpeter Eddie Quansah (who later settled in Australia), followed by two commercial recordings of twenty-two songs done at the two-track Ghana Film Corporation studio in Accra in 1978, with the ace engineers John Kofi Archer, Bossman and Mr. Kwakye.

Bokoor finally broke up in September 1979, largely due to the economic problems and shortages that had developed during the military government of Colonel Acheampong and General Akuffo. I remember many times I had to use pumice-stone to scrape the rust from old guitar strings, as new ones were simply unobtainable. The 1979 devaluation of the currency hit us particularly hard. Bokoor, together with the Grass Roots Music Company (of John Carmichael and Prince George Annan), had just invested a lot of money organising a series of twelve shows at the Sea-View Hotel in Accra. After the third one, there was a sudden withdrawal of some currency notes, which finished off the nightlife scene in Ghana for many months, and our project with it.

After the 1978 Ghana Film Studio recordings, Bokoor released two commercial cassetes and then (with the assistance of a Lebanese patron Michel Bou-Chedid) paid Ambassador Records in Kumasi to press one thousand record albums. For some reason or other, Ambassador Records delayed the pressing, and we only got some action when Jones Attuquayefio and I (after several wasted trips by night-train) went to the pressing factory with a mat, food, water and a charcoal stove and threatened to camp in the foyer. The company saw we really meant business that day and we got results. But we had to make do with a thousand extended play singles instead of albums, as the 1979 currency depreciation had reduced the value of the money we had earlier given Mr. Badu of Ambassador Records. Unfortunately, by then, singles were going out of fashion in Ghana and so we lost heavily. Finally, in September 1979, Bokoor had to sell its instruments to a local Apostolic Church.

By coincidence, the UK-based Ghanaian master drummer Ben Badoo was then in Accra looking for a guitar-band to teach contemporary African music to unemployed West Indian youth at the Wolverhampton Council for Community Relations in the UK. Ben had already set up a successful traditional drumming group with them called Lanzel (Unity). So Jones, Gifty and I spent a year in the British Midlands teaching electric guitar to West Indian youngsters, who at first did not believe that there were any electric guitars in Africa, or even electricity. We solved this problem by bringing in my Nigerian friend Rufus Onishayomi, who showed the youth photo-slides of power-stations, skyscrapers and flyovers in Lagos. These youth then went on to form their own reggae band called the 'Twelve Tribesman', whilst the two other Bokoor members and I teamed up with the Nigerian-Brazilian guitarist Theo Pareira and Guyanan drummer Dino Washington to form the New Bokoor Band. This band performed in London and the Midlands, recorded at Peter Kunzler's Crow Studio and released a 'Cross-over' 12 inch single which combined Jamaican ska music with Ghanaian highlife. This idea was triggered by the Two Tone bands of the times (like the Specials and the Beat) that were combining ska with rock.

BOKOOR MUSIC RECORDING STUDIO

The three of us of the Bokoor band returned to Ghana in 1980 and I brought with me a small portable studio (a TEAC 144 and later a 244) with which I planned to record our group after we had reformed. However, on 31st December 1981, Flight Lt. J. J. Rawlings overthrew the civilian government and, as an immediate result, there was a strict night curfew. I decided it was impossible to run a band, and began experimenting with the porta-studio in my father's farmhouse (later called Bokoor House) which he had built from his retirement pension for working for thirty years at the Philosophy Department of the University of Ghana. After a year of experimenting with the porta-studio and using my old band equipment, I formally opened Bokoor Music Studio as a recording and rehearsal studio in September 1981. And, from my own experience of having worked in studios in Ghana, Nigeria and London, I made two decisions about my own studio. As the studio was located on a farm, I made the studio a semi-open air one of mud or adobi and did away with the need for expensive air-conditioners. Secondly, I decided to have no clock on the premises and not charge by the hour. Instead, I charged by the product (i.e. one album length recording) which took anything from two to four days. This, together with the rustic surroundings, provided a more relaxed recording atmosphere, as music and haste don't mix.

In the years that I ran Bokoor Music Studio (up until the late 1990s), I recorded over two hundred and fifty bands, and hundreds of musicians of all sorts. In the 1980s, some of these works appeared on nine records and over sixty commercial cassettes, mainly produced by the bands themselves. I recorded many traditional drumming groups. One of the earliest was the Nyemoaniwaa Kpanlogo group from Ofankor (the

Bokoor Recording Studio in South Ofankor, Accra, in late 1980s

Ga village from whom Bokoor land was bought in the 1960s). In 1984, I recorded the Guna Efee Noko band from Nungua, Accra, who that year won the Children's Cultural Group Competition organised by the Ghana Art Council. This was a free session I did for this institution, now called the Greater Accra Regional Community Centre. I did two analytical recordings of the drum-ensemble at the School of Performing Arts in Legon, for the Ghanaian musicologists Professor Nketia and Dr. Willie Anku. I also recorded several Ewe borborbor neo-traditional groups. The first was Agbeyeye, brought from Tsito in the Volta Region by guitarist Edinam Ansah who had already made several highlife recordings with me. Two others were the Mehiawo group of Abebe and the Bantus. The Ewe master-drummer Michael Kojo Ganyoh also recorded in my studio and was my own main drum teacher. Others were Colonel Amuzu's Tegbe Dodovee Ewe cultural group, Nii Tetteh's gome group, the Ebaahi children's group and several sessions with Mustapha Tettey Addy's Royal Obonu Drummers at his AMAA Hotel in Kokrobite.

Several palmwine guitarists recorded at Bokoor. One song by by Kwaa Mensah called 'Kalabule' was often played on local radio in the early 1980s (in 2003 released on the Dutch 'world music' Otrabanda label). In 1987, I took some mobile equipment to Kumasi to record Koo Nimo for a session organised by the late Beattie Casely-Hayford, to supply background music for a United Nations film by John Powell on the

593

local industrial Suame Magazine area of Kumasi. The film was called 'The Secret of Wealth: A Study of Grassroots Technology Transfer'. A year later, Koo Nimo came down from Kumasi to record for Sean Barlow's Afro-pop series for American Public Radio. Another acoustic guitarist I recorded was the Ga rasta-man Ellis Salaam whose Cultural Imani Band played local reggae songs, two of which ('Mama Shile Oga' and 'Moko Baba') appeared on the Guitar and Gun I and II compilation albums produced in the mid-1980s by Cherry Red's Africagram label in London (re-released in 2003 by Sterns African Reocord Centre).

I also recorded many of my old friends from the bands of the Napoleon Club where I had been a musician in the mid-1970s. There were the ex-Hedzoleh members Lash Laryea and Jagger Botchway who formed a band called Amartey Hedzoleh. Oko Nortey brought a string of local groups for me to record, and drummer Okyerema Asante was involved with Yaa Nom's Pan-African songs produced by Malcolm-Ben (see previous Chapter). Other Napoleon Club musicians who recorded with me were Jerry James Lartey of Basa-Basa, who went on to run his own Saka Saka group, and Chi-Kin-Chi of the Edikanfo band who is now in Holland.

Among the many highlife dance band and concert party guitar bands that came to my studio and appeared on the mid-eighties Guitar and Gun compilation albums were Francis Kenya, Wofa Rockson (Koo Nimo's younger brother), Kwesi Menu, Blind Dzissan and his Morkpolawo band, and Sloopy Mike Gyamfi's Adinkra Band. One of my Adinkra recordings was featured on the BBC Channel Four's black music television series 'Repercussions'. Guitarist and singer Sloopy and drummer Captain Moro (both ex-Senior Eddie Donkor's band) then moved on to Amsterdam to run a group called Sankofa. Other highlife bands and artists I recorded were King Bruce's Black Beats, Anthony Entsie's Beach Scorpion, Guyoyo, the Happy Boys, T.O. Jazz, the Warriors, Nii Tei's Ashikotones, Desmond Ababio, George Adu's band, Eric Agyeman (a demo tape), Nana Dick's Osagyefo, Kwadwo Donkor, the Oyikwan Internationals, the Ghana Prison's band (with the apt name 'Inside Out'), the Mangwana Stars and the John Teye School brass band. I also recorded several burger highlife artists/bands, like Danny Quist, Papa Charles's Lover Boys (producer Shegerege), the keyboard player Abbie Mensah and Lloyd Mamphey who released an album dedicated to the Ghanaian boxer Azumah Nelson in 1995.

Many concert parties also came to Bokoor Studio, the first being Mr. Bampoe's Jaguar Jokers whom Mr. Bampoe kindly allowed me to record on an experimental basis. In 1985, some member of his group came back as Guyoyo to do a commercial recording. At the time, because the conditions in Ghana were so economically harsh, Guyoyo had gone collectively into farming together to keep their band going (a similar survival tactic that was also pursued around then by Nana Danso's Pan African Orchestra). Much later, I arranged for one of Guyayo's tracks ('Atamfo') to be released on the Naxos 'world music' label. From the mid-1980s, I also began to record musical plays or so-called 'dialogue' cassettes by concert parties and concert comedians like Waterproof, Kojo Brake, Ruby Darling, Nkomede, Super O.D, Ntoboase and the City Kings. The Adehyeman Group (ex-Kusum Agoromma) concert party also did a session at Bokoor Studio for the educational 'Stage Shakers' film on local popular theatre, directed by Kwame Braun.

Some of the experimental and 'Afro' fusion bands I recorded (besides those of ex-Napoleon club musicians) were Kojo Dadson's Talents, Nii Noi Nortey's Mau Mau Muziki, Smart Arpeh's Nokoko, and Morfi 'Jigga' Ative and Eddie Cee's Blekete that featured the keyboardist Lord Lindon's of the 1970s Big Beats band. Another experimental outfit was Nana Danso Abiam's Pan African Orchestra that was quite tricky to record on a four-track machine, as it employed a huge number of instruments consisting of two wooden xylophones, ten bamboo flutes, three gonje-fiddles, four massive Ashanti fontomfrom-drums and assorted percussion.

I also recorded many local pop and reggae bands, such as the Kojo Antwi and the Classic Vibes reggae outfit (later based in Denmark), B. B. Sheriff's See Breeze that included the young Felix Bell, Wassa Ray from the Volta Region and the Achimota school-boy band Kindred whose members later joined Fred Dred's Kente band. Another was Prince George's Anan's Grass Roots band whose line-up included Knox Lokko, Norbert, Jackson and Felix Dada (Charlotte Dada's brother) and played everything from reggae and funk to soca and highlife. In June 1985, I also recorded the reggae band of Yaw Ansah who had employed the Vas Angels to back him together with a young singer from Cote d'Ivoire whom at the time I had never heard of. This was Alpha Blondy and, on this recording, he was singing in Twi.

In November 1986, Mr. Kwakye of Ghana Film Studio, Sammy Helwani of Studio One, and I combined our equipment and efforts to record 'Revofest' (Revolution

Festival), a twelve-hour cross-section of Ghanaian bands organised for fund-raising purposes by Faisal Helwani working with the National Secretariat of the Committees for the Defence of the Revolution (CDR). Some thirty thousand people came to Revofest at the Accra football stadium to hear government and army bands such as the Pink Five, the Police Band, the Prisons Band, the Sweet Beans (of the Cocoa Marketing Board), the Beautiful Creations and the Sappers. Representing the Ga cultural groups were Wulomei, Naa Amanua's Suku group and Kyirem. Highlife bands and artists included the African Brothers, A. B. Crentsil's Ahenfo, Koo Nimo, Onyina, Gyedu-Blay Ambolley, Paa Bobo, Joe Mensah, Abebe, Paapa Yankson, the Kumapim Royals, and Safohene Djeni. This richly-varied programme also featured the reggae groups of Felix Bell and Nframa, Smart Arpeh's Nokoko Afro-rock group, the gospel music of Ola Williams and Professor Abraham as well as the female artists Lady Talata and Lady Lartey. A particularly memorable moment of the show was by the blind minstrel Onipa Nua (Brother Man) who sang his own gravel-voiced version of James Brown's 'Say It Loud', accompanying himself on a small hand-piano made from a sardine can. Another was a moving rendition of 'We Are The World' in various Ghanaian languages by sportsman-turned-musician Sidiku Buari. Then, there was an emotionally-moving act by the physically-disabled singer Pozo Hayes, which brought such a spontaneous rush forward by the audience that the stage nearly collapsed and stopped the show for a while. American audiences were able to share some of the excitement of Revofest when a selection from this marathon live recording was featured as one of the programmes of Sean Barlow's and George Collinet's Afro-Pop series on American Public Radio (programme number 20).

There are several blind musicians and even whole bands in Ghana and, because of their handicap, they face more than the usual hardships of musicians. Blind musicians I recorded included Onipa Nua, who played at Revofest, Nana Kwese Amoako-Attah who ran the Warriors highlife band, and Barima Nti Agyeman who is leader of the Nsoroma Show Band. I also recorded an all-blind band from the Volta Region of Ghana called Morkporlawo, led by the Ewe singer Christian Dzizzan (two of these recordings are featured on Guitar and Gun II).

Later, I worked with the Adom Professionals that, as mentioned in Chapter 9, was a guitar-band whose nine musicians came together at a school for the blind at Akropong. In the middle of one of the songs they were recording at Bokoor Studio a pale-coloured snake came into the recording room and circled the drums. I was the only sighted person in the room and, as I did not want anyone to panic or frighten the snake, I just kept going. After what seemed a long time, the snake reared its head, looked at us and disappeared out of the door. Afterwards, when I told the musicians about our reptilian visitor, they said it was good to have left the snake alone as it was blessing us.

Still on the topic of blindness, in the late 1990s, I recorded three songs on water-borne diseases (which includes River Blindness) for the university's Volta River Basin Project, sung in Ewe and Adangme by Martha Annan, which were disseminated around the schools in the area affected by these diseases.

Some other musicians who passed though my Bokoor Recording Studio during the '80s and '90s were Simmons, Shegerege, Talal Fattal, Shasha Marley, Oko Nortey, Abebe and the Bantus, K.K. Kabobo, Edmund Mensah, Rob Roy, Lady Talata, Pozo Hayes, bassist Marshall, Joe Eyison (with the Metallic Singers), Stephen Kontor, Ray Ellis, Yaw Glyman, trumpeter Patrick Akrakye and Nii Tettey Tetteh. Numerous session-artists were also involved in these recordings who were recruited from bands like the GBC band, Powerful Mercury, City Boys, Jaguar Jokers, Sappers, Uppers International, Quelque Chose, Boom Talents, Black Generation, Eddie Donkor's Ashiko band, the Prisons and Fire Service dance bands, Sweet Beans, Uhuru, Ambassadors and Funky Millionaires. In fact, the total number of muscians who passed though my studio may reach around two thousand, as, in all, I did two hundred and fifty recording sessions (sometimes two albums at a time) that involved one hundred and fifty different highlife, pop, gospel and cultural bands.

BOKOOR STUDIO: TRIBUTE TO THOSE WHO HAVE PASSED ON

TEDDY OWUSU was one of Ghana's greatest sax players and I first met him in the mid-1970s on one of my trips to Nigeria with the Bunzus band. Teddy was in the habit of going everywhere, however far it was, on foot. We met him in Togo walking from Accra to Lagos, as Fela Anikulapo-Kuti wanted him to play for his group. I recall we had great difficulty persuading Teddy to get into our bus, even though we were going to the same place. Teddy was a determined fellow and devoted to his music. I remember that in 1982 when he was recording in my studio (actually in my kitchen, as that was where my studio was first located), Teddy collapsed after a sax solo and continued to direct the session lying on his back in bed. Despite a serious illness and doctor's warnings, Teddy continued playing until his death in the mid-eighties.

NII KOI: When I first met this wizard Hawaiian guitarist he was already elderly. He had come to play with Christian Dzizzan's band and played on the two Morkpolawo songs on Guitar and Gun II. Later, Nii Koi brought his own Ghana Minstrels for a recording session but died shortly afterwards.

KWESI ABEKA: Another sad loss was this pastor of the Christo Asafo Mission and leader of that church's Genesis Gospel Singers, whose music is featured on the Cherry Red label's 'Guitar and Gun' and 'Ntutu' albums (later re-released on CD by Sterns). It was he who introduced me to the church's leader Prophet Kwadwo Safo. By the time of his death in a car crash, Kwesi and I had become very good friends.

SAMUEL PAA GYIMAH was one of the top session-guitarists in Ghana and played in several bands I recorded, including Genesis, Adinkra, Francis Kenya's and Kwese Menu's. He died in 1987 after returning from Nigeria. A massive funeral was held for him at the house of Eddie Donkor for whom Gyimah also played. As at that time I was involved with organising a conference for the International Association for the Study of Popular Music (IASPM), I brought with me a bus-load of foreign musicians and musicologists, which was much appreciated by Gyimah's family and friends.

DAN 'BOKOVI' BANINI played the bongos for many dance bands in the 1950s and 1960s and was an active member of MUSIGA. I first met him when we were both members of the Bunzus, and he later joined my Bokoor Band as a percussionist. Dan was a great teacher of traditional percussion. In this capacity, he worked with Philip Cobson's Aklowa organisation in London and I remember seeing Dan play at the Albert Hall then. Later he taught at the Kokrobite drumming school near Accra, run by Mustapha Tettey-Addy and his Italian-German partner Heidi. Dan recorded at my studio on numerous occasions and was one of my drum teachers. He died quite suddenly in 1989.

KWAA MENSAH (see Chapter 1): The palmwine guitarist Kwaa Mensah, who sadly died in 1991, also recorded with me in the early 1980s. I met Kwaa in 1975 when I visited him on my motorbike at Mankesim. At that time he was so broke that he only had two strings on his guitar. His wife had left him and his best friend was a tiny man called M. Adjei who had the structure of a boy and a razor sharp mind. I arranged for Kwaa to stay with me from time to time at Temple House in Accra and managed to get him hooked up with Faisal Helwani's Afro-disia recording and promotion project. In the late 1980s, Kwaa got a part-time job teaching highlife guitar at the University of Cape Coast and then at Legon near Accra. Anytime he came to teach in Accra, he stayed with me at Bokoor House, as by then I had relocated. It was then that he taught me how to play local palmwine guitar.

LORD LINDON was a keyboard player who recorded at my studio in 1992 with Morfi 'Jigga' Atave's Blekete group. In the 1970s, Lindon had been the leader of the Triffis pop band, which settled in Nigeria as the 'Plastic Jims'. Later, the members of this group became the resident band of the Airport Hotel set up in Port Harcourt in eastern Nigeria by the Sierra Leonian musician Geraldo Pino. The Ghanaian group then returned from Nigeria as the Big Beats and, being influenced by Fela Kuti's music, released their hit Afro-beat in Ghana in 1971 called 'Kyen Kyema Osi Akwan', which warns the old to make way for the young. Sadly, Lord Lindon and the Blekete drummer Eddie Cee were killed in a road accident in 1992, shortly after completing their Bokoor recording.

T.O. JAZZ (see Chapter 10): This wizard guitarist recorded several times at my studio and, later on, I got him a job as guitar tutor at the Music Department of the University of Ghana. From 1996 until his death in 2001, he also worked with Aaron Bebe Sukrua and I in the Local Dimension highlife band.

Even as musical styles and tastes change, these musicians must be remembered for their unique contributions to the development of Ghana's music and their influence on other musicians.

BOKOOR STUDIO: A WITNESS TO CHANGE

From my studio vantage point, I was able to see how the music scene changed from 1981. The greatest proportion of bands that I recorded then were highlife guitar and concert party bands. By the late 1980s, local gospel guitar-bands were in the forefront. They still played danceable highlifes but with Christian lyrics, and in many cases employed the very same musicians who previously were with concert bands. Beside the three bands of the Kristo Asafo Mission (see Chapter 45), some of the many other church bands that I have recorded were the Advent Heralds, the UNIPRA band of the Universal Prayer Fellowship Church (whose leader, Reverend J.M. Odonkor, released an album in London), the King's Stewards, Nungua Minstrel Choir (see photo in Chapter 44), Golden Gates, Sons and Daughters, Gospel Sowers, James Antwi's band (an ex-Bokoor Band member), Compassion Inspiration (that featured Ray Ellis on keyboard), Metallic Singers, George Akimenyi's Ajumako Kromain 12, Blessed Elim Singers, Saint Michael's group, Brother George Kankam's El Shaddai, Sam Ntiamoah's Living Gospel Band, Moses Dwamena's Nkwantabisa Gospel Singers, Rebecca Martin's Glorified Singers, Reverand Stephen Domlevo's Catholic Joyful Singers, Christian Amoah's Christian Messengers and the groups of Brother Frank Agyengo and Prince Boateng. I also did a mobile recording at Faisal Helwani's Nalopeon club of the choir of the the Afrikania Church whose leader, the Reverend Father Dr. Vincent Kwabena Damuah (later assuming the traditional priesthood titles 'Osofo Komfo') was, for a time, a member of Rawlings's PNDC government. Some of the popular gospel releases done in my studio include the Legon Catholic Charismatic Renewal Band 'Give Us Power', the Catholic Joyful Singers 'Mewo Adamfo Pa Bi', Javes Addo's "Jesus' Power", the Christian Messengers Charismatic Renewal's 'Gye W'Ayeyi', Sam Osei Ntiamoah's 'Kae Nyame' and 'Rebecca Martin's 'Nyonmo Hiekaalo'.

Rebecca Martin's cassette brings me to another change I have noticed—the increasing number of women who recorded at my studio. At first, and because I was mainly recording concert guitar bands, there were practically no women coming to the studio. One of the first was the very young Heidi Talata who was a session-singer for a pop band. Others were the women who sang with traditional groups that played kpanlogo and borborbor. However, a large number of women passed through my studio as alto and treble singers with the seventy or so local gospel bands. So, during the 1980s, women became a larger and larger component of the singers that I recorded.

Finally, a change that I noticed from around 1990, and one which disturbed me a lot, is the replacement of musicians by drum-machines and keyboard synthesisers operated by engineers. For a long time I refused to use a drumulator, but was told by many musicians that they would boycott my studio if I did not get one. I finally acquiesced and reluctantly began using a programmable digital drum-machine (Korg DDM-110) in 1990. As a result, of the eighty recordings of pop, gospel and guitar-bands that I did after 1992 in my Bokoor Studio at Ofankor, I used live percussion on only eleven occasions. Because of this, and also because of increasing industrial noise pollution in the Bokoor House areas, I bought the equipment (batteries, trickle chargers, inverters) to make my studio mobile. So I jumped when Edinam Ansah and the Volta Region branch of MUSIGA invited me to base my studio once a month in the Ho-Tsito area of the Volta Region and primarily do live mobile recording sessions there of local borborbor groups, cultural groups, choirs and gospel bands. Between 1995 and 1998, some of these recordings were released in the Volta Region on cassette: by the Trinita Traditional Choir, Mr. Ahegbebu's Nobody's Drumming Group, Kofi Yegbe's Gospel Band, Foster Nkami's Eleme borborbor group, Ben Nyadzi and the AWUSCO School Choir, the Vakpo Choir, the Anfoega Djana E.P. Church Choir and the Voice Across the Volta band led by Dela Fumador and Eddie Ansah. In recognition of my pioneering work in the Volta Region (where there had never previously been a recording studio), I was awarded an honour at the Volta Region MUSIGA show held at the Ho Pleasure Gardens in July 1998 and graced by the Ho District Executive Captain George Njodzo and the Honourable Member of Parliament Kofi Attor. Several of the bands and groups I had recorded played at this function, as did the Supreme Canon's army motor-regiment dance band at Ho whose Music Director was Eddie Ansah.

IMPORTANCE OF LIVE FEEL IN MULTI-TRACK RECORDING STUDIOS

It is amazing to think that all those old wonderful evergreen hits by Louis Armstrong, Ella Fitzgerald, Frank Sinatra, Nat King Cole, Sarah Vaughan and others were done in one-track studios using a few microphones. With multi-track recording equipment, one-take live recordings should be even easier, but in Ghana it has led to practically all recordings being done as a series of overdubs starting with the percussion, then bass, then chordal instruments, then lead instruments and finally voices. Just because one has multi-track facilities, it does not mean one has to record all music in this spread out way so that the whole band never plays as a unit in the studio. Rather, with multi-track facilities, all the singers and instruments can be miked-up to different tracks and so the main recording done in one take, with maybe some minor embellishments being added later. I believe that the live approach to recording will in the long run bring out the most creative aspects of both Ghanaian traditional and popular music. This will make the local music lively, rather than mechanical, enhance immediacy and spontaneity and foster a spirit of collective group enterprise. Furthermore, Ghanaian music with a live feel will be more appreciated by World Music fans who have become saturated with their own computerised techno-pop. Even the international fans of dance-floor 'house music' (that evolved out of drums-machine driven disco music) now insist that their electronic club sounds and electronic dance music are based or built around music that has a live groove; for instance loops of analogue recording made in the 1970s (before digital technology) by funk artists like James Brown, the Afrobeat of Fela Kuti and the Afro-funk of numerous African musicans.

THE BOKOOR AFRICAN POPULAR MUSIC ARCHIVES FOUNDATION (BAPMAF)[36]

The decline of old-time 'classical' highlife and live popular music in the late seventies and eighties convinced me and some other musicians and musicologists of the need to preserve highlife music. So, in the late 1980s, we discussed the setting up of an organisation dedicated to highlife, as well as other forms of Ghanaian and African popular performance. As a result, I officially established BAPMAF as a Ghanaian NGO in 1990, encouraged and assisted by King Bruce, E.T. Mensah, Koo Nimo and Kwaa Mensah. Beattie Casely-Hayford also gave me huge initial encouragement in the late 1980s, as he had always wanted to establish an institute for highlife in Ghana, but died unexpectedly in 1989 before BAPMAF was officially launched. Beattie was involved with the Louis Armstrong trips to Ghana, was one-time head of the Ghana Broadcasting Corporation, gave occasional public lectures on highlife and, at the time of his death, was running a video company called Televid.

The core of the BAPMAF holdings are my own extensive music archives that I began collecting from the late 1960s, with archival contributions from Y.B 'Opia' Bampoe (Jaguar Jokers leader), Professor Atta Annan Mensah (Music Department, Legon), Jimmy Moxon (Ghana's first Minister of Information), Professor Mawere Opoku (Dance Department, Legon), my own father E. F. Collins (Philosophy Department, Legon), Robert Sprigge (History Department, Legon and pianist in 1950s with the Red Spots Band), Oscarmore Ofori (highlife composer) and veteran guitarist T.O. 'Jazz' Ampoumah. Other BAPMAF members/affiliates are Edinam Ansah (Votla Region MUSIGA Executive), Jimmy Beckley (Afro-jazz Combo), Joseph Aduoko (translator), guitarist Anthony 'Scorpion' Entsie, African American jazz percussionist Juma Santos (Jim Riley), multi-instrumentalist Aaron Bebe Sukura, music engineer Panji Anoff, actor Ben Ahorlu Ajokpa and the university lecturers Peter Arthur and Dr. Zabana Kongo.

In its first years, BAPMAF donated materials to the Dubois Centre, the Padmore Library, the University of Ghana's Institute of African Studies, Professor J.H.K. Nketia's International Centre for Music and Dance, Achimota School, Saint John's Grammar School, the British Council, the American USIS Library, the Ghana Broadcasting Corporation and the Ghana Folklore Board.

---

[36]BAPMAF: Ghana Voluntary Organisation Certificate no. 402, 16th April 1991. Ghana Certificate of Incorporation no. 41,108, 20th November 1990. Member of the UNESCO Global Alliance for Cultural Diversity ID no. GHA/AG/185.

In February 1996, BAPMAF and the German Goethe Institute in Accra (under its then Director Sabine Hentzch) organised a Highlife Month that included seminars, highlife films, performances (Ankobra, Grassroots, Mau Mau Musiki and Kofi Ghanaba), with the central focus being the BAPMAF Golden Years of Highlife Music Photographic Exhibition. Organizations who were involved or supported the event included the Dubois Centre (Ebo Hawkson, Director), the National Theatre (Dr. Komla Amuoko, Director), MUSIGA (Joe Mensah, President), the University of Ghana (Professors Kofi Agovi and Kwesi Yankah), the Ghana Copyright Administration (Betty Mould-Iddrisu, Director), the Ghana National Folklore Boards (Colonel Amuzu, Chairman), the Ghana Concert Party Union (Mr. S.K. Oppong and Mr. Mensah, Executives) and the Ghana Record Producers Union (Dick Essilfie-Bondzie and Kojo Donkoh, Executives). The Padmore Library also supplied some materials from its archives.

In collaboration with the French Embassy, the BAPMAF Highlife Photo Exhibition was displayed in Accra as part of the Alliance Francaise 'Story of Highlife' event in May/June 2001 (some photos also being supplied by Mr. Vanderpuie). In January 2002, BAPMAF and the Swiss Embassy organized the launch at the Dubois Centre of the CD 'Ghana Popular Music 1931-57' (released by Arion Disques). This was a collection of old recordings made by the Basel Mission/UTC, rediscovered and digitised by the researchers Viet Arlt and Serena Dankwa. In February/March 2002, BAPMAF organized a series of seven lectures-performances at the National Theatre for the US Embassy Public Affairs Section's 'Black History Month'. In 2004, BAPMAF was involved in with the Presence musical youth talent-scout organization and the Pan African Arts NGO (a highlife photo exhibition at the British Council). BAPMAF was co-organiser of the US Embassy Public Affairs 'African American Heritage/History Month' of February 2005. In August that year, BAPMAF was a facilitator for a workshop on 'Researching Ghanaian Theatre' held at the University of Ghana's Institute of African Studies and, in September 2005, BAPMAF was involved with the opening of percussionist Kofi Ghanaba's (Guy Warren's) African Heritage Library at Medie. In March 2006, BAPMAF provided photos for the Rocky Dawuni/Africa Live 'Independence Splash: Ghana Music Revival Explosion' at the Accra International Conference Centre. In 2007, BAPMAF curated the Ghana Music Exhibition held at the Greenwich Heritage Centre in London in October organised by the African Image Alliance as part of Ghana's 50th independence celebrations.

After the 1996 BAPMAF/Goethe Highlife Month, the BAPMAF Highlife Photo Exhibition was moved to my Bokoor House premises in South Ofankor at Mile 8, Accra-Nsawam Road (near Taifa Junction and next to the MUUS sawmills). There, from 1996 to 2001, it was opened to the general public. During that period, it was televised twice: for Ghana Broadcasting in 1996 (producer Cynthia Jikpani) and, in 2000, by the London Shai Shai company (producer Martine Stone). After extensive re-building, the new BAPMAF premises was re-opened at Bokoor House in 2007 as the 'BAPMAF Highlife Institute'. This was done in conjunction with the Goethe Institute's 'Made in Germany' music festival that was part of Ghana's 50th independence anniversary celebration. Subsequently the Goethe Insitute, through its Director Eleonore Sylla, supplied BAPMAF from 2008/9 with the funds to begin digitising its archives and to set up its www.bapmaf.com website. In 2010, BAPMAF helped organise the Ghana segment of a trip to Ghana by the Cuban writer Carlos Moore, his family and an Afro-Brazilian film crew. Carlos was on a trip to Ghana and Nigeria to re-launch his 1982 book 'Fela: This Bitch of a Life' with the Nigerian company Cassava Republic Press. Then, in March 2011, John Collins, using BAPMAF slides, gave a presentation at the Golden Tulip Hotel at the the sixth of a series of 'Adventurers in the Diaspora' organised by Archi-Afrika, which deals with creativity in the Ghanaian arts, business, agriculture and architecture.

In 2012, the BAPMAF premises recieved assistance from the Dutch 'Prince Claus Cultural Emergency Response' for flood protection control. And, in 2013, John Collins and the BAPMAF archives were involved with 'The Concert Party in Ghana' seminar (part of the International World Theatre Day Celebration) held at Accra's National Theatre, with research by Alison Okuda of New York University into calypso music in Ghana

Materials at the BAPMAF Highlife Insitute currently includes 1,200 photographs, 50 videos, 800 books and journals and hundreds of rare and old documents, speeches, brochures, posters and record sleeves. The BAPMAF holding also includes 1,600 hours of recorded music, including 780 old highlife songs on shellac 78rpm and vinyl 45 rpm records. In 2016 digitised copies of these were been sent to the J.H.K Nketia Archives at the Insititute of African Studies of the University of Ghana currently directed by Judith Opoku-Boateng: both as safety copies and enable students to gain easy access to the materials.

The BAPMAF premises today has a library, digital documentation room and a seminar/exhibition space that holds a Highlife Photographic Exhibition. This is organised into fifteen separate categories, each accompanied by an information sheet. These categories present a pictorial history of all the major forms of highlife since the late 19th century, as well as special sections on musicians unions, women artists, neo-traditional music and local reggae. There is a constant stream of local and foreign students, tourists, musicans, academics and media people coming to this archives – and for the BAPMAF activities, since 2013, the reader can go to its website at www.bapmaf.com.

Chapter 63

COMPUTERISED HIGHLIFE AND THE 'HIGHLIFE IMAGINATION'

THIS CHAPTER IS IN TWO SECTIONS, AS FOLLOWS:

PART A: 'The Musical Ghost in the Machine' deals with the positive and negative impact of computers, drum-machines, synthesisers and the electronic media on live Ghanaian popular musical performance and recordings. It is adapted from a paper I gave at the Composers' Forum of the International Centre for African Music and Dance (ICAMD) held at the School of Performing Arts, University of Ghana, Legon, in August 1994.

PART B: 'The Highlife Imagination' questions the notion that the contemporary computerised burger highlife and hiplife 'techno-pop' trend amongst Ghanaian youth is leading to the demise of highlife; for music is a culturally-transmitted mental attitude or 'imagination' that is not totally tied to the changing material media. Highlife has survived and thrived with the invention of records, radio, television, electic instruments and electronic recording, and is likely to survive the current hi-tech music fashion. This section is based on a talk I gave at the BAPMAF/Goethe Institute's 'Highlife Month' held in Accra in February 1996.

PART A: THE MUSICAL GHOST IN THE MACHINE

I use the title 'The Musical Ghost in the Machine' as it concerns the replacement of musicians operating in a live performance context with electronically-synthesised music, reaching the public through indirect forms like cassettes, CDs, radio, television, music videos, as well as through the use of 'lip-syncing' or miming onstage. Maybe I should add that this expression 'ghost in the machine' was originally coined[37] to decribe the dualistic mind-body concept of the famous 17th century philosopher Descartes who saw the mind as totally separate from the mechanistic body and physical matter. I have taken the liberty of using this expression to describe the state of musicians who get lost in the electronic machine and mix.

The thoughts I want to share come from my experience of running a studio in Ghana from 1981 to the late 1990s. As mentioned in the previous chapter, during this time I have noticed many changes. I have seen the demise of the record and its replacement with cassettes and compact discs. I have seen the gradual disappearance of concert party bands, but also the emergence of 'dialogue' concert cassettes and local video. I have seen the multiplication of gospel groups that record religious dance-music. Partly linked to this is the entrance of many female artists into the popular music field.

One change that I found very worrying, which began in the late 1980s, was the replacement of drummers by drum-machines, horn sections by single keyboard players, guitars by synthesisers; and, in some cases, the whole instrumentation of a band being provided by just one instrument, such as the Yamaha PSR 5700 computerised keyboard.

Before turning to some of the negative aspects of this development, I would first like to point out five advantages of using hi-tech equipment for music.

- Computers make things cheaper for a composer to record, as one only needs a few or even just one musician.

- The drumulator and other metronomic-like machines provide a rhythmic discipline for the recording session.

[37] An expression concerning western mind-body dualism coined by the mid 20th century philosopher Gilbert Ryle.

- Computers are perfect for a musician putting together a musical sketch or working on a composition.

- Electronics helps 'democratise' music by making it easy for anyone, even those without musical skills, to have a go at music production. For instance, in Holland some years ago, it was possible for budding pop stars to pay around fifty dollars to special 'instant music' studios for a couple of hours, buy a ready-made rhythm from them, do a voice-over and walk out with a record or commercial cassette.

-

- For the purely analytical reasons of studying the minute details of complex rhythms, the computer is very useful, as standard notation is often not precise enough to deal with the tiny spaces between the quavers.

I would now like to turn to four main problems that arise for African musicians and composers when machines replace performers.

Firstly, there is a loss of African content. If one listens to the local pop music on FM radio today, one mostly hears vernacular love lyrics sung over a synthesised background, with no local rhythmic content and with little relation between the song-melody and the tonal movement of the language. As a result, although this music is patronised by the youth here, it is unexportable, as no one abroad wants to hear the African variety of World Music without African dance-rhythms. As mentioned in chapter 60, King Bruce told me that when he managed Elephant Walk studio in the 1990s, a tape they had made using a drumulator was returned from the States and the band had to come back to the studio to replace the drum-machine track with a live drummer.

Secondly, the introduction of machines interferes with the flow of creative energy that takes place between musicians in a live context, whether in the studio or onstage. Musicians inspire one another and create new ideas during performance. For instance, many jazz musicians prefer to be recorded in one take and not go through the spread-out process of overdubbing a few musicians at time over a number of days, so that the whole band never plays as a unit. Indeed, the very vocabulary of jazz musicians shows their antipathy towards the excessive use of drum-machines and over-dubbing, for they prefer improvisation, and talk of the music having 'swing', 'play', 'looseness', 'feel', 'soul' and 'groove'. Musicologists also refer to this subjective and flexible side of jazz playing. Thomas Owens has observed that the measures of the jazz saxist, Charlie Parker, fluctuated through his performances. Richard Waterman saw it as a result of the musician's own 'internalised metronome sense'. Charles Keil and Joe Progler call minute and subtle offbeatings 'participatory discrepancies', whilst Peter Reinholdsson has used a fixed metronome to demonstrate the anticipation ('push') and delay ('laidbackness') of the beat by various jazz bassists. Paul Berliner has recently written a full book on the topic called 'Thinking Jazz: The Infinite Art of Improvisation'.

The same need for 'feel' also applies to symphonic orchestras for, in spite of written scores, the subtle interpretations of the composition are done on the spot, by the conductor and virtuoso musicians. This is why classical art music recordings are always made of the whole orchestra in one take, and not by a series of overdubs with the violinists coming on one day, the brass on another and so on. Furthermore, at public performances, classical orchestras never mime their works on stage. In short, although Euoropeans developed technology and mechanics during the industrial revolution, they never allowed machines to overshadow the 'heart' or 'soul' of their own classical music – which right up to the present day is performed and recorded as live performances. For many Ghanaian pop artists, however, overdubbing and miming are the order of the day as they are overwhlemed by the latest fashionable electronic gadget and digital machine. As a result, some bands cannot reproduce on stage what they record in a multi-track studio. For example, a synthesised trumpet may appear on a recording but the band has no trumpeter—a situation which is particulary problematic when the band has to mime its work on TV or on stage.

This brings us to a third major problem arising from the modern tendency of bands to be just recording group or 'studio bands' that distribute their music through sound recording or broadcasting; which results in little or no direct contact between the performers and their audience. Many older musicians will tell you that some of their ideas have been drawn from the immediate response of their audiences. For instance, singers may respond to comments from their audience or a rhythmic dialogue may take place between the percussionists and dancers—both age-old folk traditions in Africa and elsewhere in the world. Likewise, in the old days, one could always hear a highlife band playing live as well as listening to its records. Now, with modern hi-tech popular music styles like burger highlife and later hiplife, this is hardly possible.

A fourth negative consequence of machine music in Ghana is that the clear human voice is becoming compromised by electronic gadgets such as harmonisers, phasers, vocoders, auto-tuners and double tracking. At the same time, the sound level of the singers is often very low as compared to the instrumental background. Literally, the ghostly voice is getting lost in the electronic mix.

All these hi-tech problems that we are facing now in Ghana began to effect the West in the early 1980s, when the computer-generated disco music of groups like Kraftwork, Munich Machine and Donna Summers, playing at exactly 154 beats per minute, became all the rage. However, in the West, there was a counter-reaction to machine music. One is a sort of Western musical 'sankofa' or 'roots' movement in which European and American youth partially turned away from mechanical sounds towards folk-music, non-western World Music and the recycling of old pop songs from the 1960s and 70s. Part of this recycling of the past paradoxically uses the most advanced techniques, which is the electronic sampling of the sounds of old stars, like James Brown and Jimmy Hendrix – and grafting their phrases, shouts, guitar-licks and musical loops into current works. This, incidentally, creates enormous copyright problems, for how many seconds must there be of a sample for it to be copyrightable? And will imitative artistic parody or praise become a copyright offence?

Another response by western artists to over-saturation with techno-pop is that some pop stars, like Neil Young and Eric Clapton, became 'unplugged': that is unplugged from their electric instruments and going acoustic. Moreover, nowadays and even when a drum machine is used, live percussion (such as hi-hats, timbales, congas, etc) are now usually also added. We can take the case of Michael Jackson as an early instance. In the early 1980s, his songs were percussively backed by drum-machines alone, whereas later he used a drum-machine on one track and an actual drummer on another, carefully blending them together to produce a live feel.

This brings us to the third response by western musicians to electronic music: the attempt to humanise it. I will provide a few examples from leading computer music experts who are livening up their sound. Ironically, this humanisation involve the use of the most sophisticated hi-tech digital equipment that increases the music's rhythmic quantization; that is the division of the measure into incredibly tiny metronomic beats, pulses or kicks. Michael Stewart has devised a 'feel spectrum' for livening up digitally-sequenced music. If the drummer plays a few milliseconds ahead of the digital pulse, he calls it 'snappy'; if behind, he calls it 'groovy'. David Jaffe uses 'tempo pertubations' that stagger the attack of the played note in relation to the exact metronomic pulse or kick. Kalle Nemvalts creates degrees of 'swing' by allowing the duration of the placed drum-note to fill differing percentages of the spaces between digital pulses. Travis Charbeneaue utilises 'time shifting adjustments' to strike the hi-hat a 64th note ahead of, or behind, the electronic pulse. All these rhythmic displacement tricks are attempts to simulate human, ambiguity, leeway and creative inaccuracies, and generally put spirit and breathe into mechanically precise electronic rhythms.

So, despite the West's initial fascination with hi-tech sounds, there have been moves by some musicians and composers to re-assert themselves in the three ways just discussed: that is the western 'sankofa' or 'back to-roots' trend, 'unplugged' pop-stars and the 'humanising' of music software programs.

Ghanaians popular musicians and composers can learn something from this, as at the moment they are being swept off their feet by new electronic developments. What is needed is for musicians and other concerned people to raise the issue in the media and get a public discussion going on the matter. I think organisations like the International Centre for African Music and Dance could help in this, as it embraces three categories of musicians and composers who, up to recently, have always operated in the live performance context and who are or will all be directly affected by the new musical technology. These are traditional performers, art-music composers and popular artists. These three groups constitute a common front that can discuss the pros and cons of the new musical technology, find ways of balancing musical performance with computer programs, and prevent the musical spirit or ghost from completely evaporating away in the musical machine.

PART B: THE 'HIGHLIFE IMAGINATION'

Here I want to look at the reason why modern youth insist on calling their computerised dance-music 'highlife' – for instance burger 'highlife' and the later hiphop 'highlife' or 'hiplife'. The older generation, on the other hand, claim this new music is not highlife as it does not contain any recognisable rhythmic or melodic highlife traits. These differences of view between the young and old can be partly explained by introducing another factor into this generational dispute – which I call the 'highlife imagination'.

To examine this, and concentrating on the rhythmic side of things, we can first take the example of Jamaican music. When reggae began in the 1960s (then called ska), it was strongly influenced by western popular dance music with its four beats to the bar. Now when Europeans play their pop tunes, they usually strike their guitars and bass-line in time with the four onbeats of the bar, particularly emphasising the first and third beats. This western rhythm is sometimes called 'oom-pah, oom-pah'. Jamaicans changed all this. Instead of striking down on their rhythm guitars with the four on-beats, they rather struck upwards during the four gaps or offbeats between them. They called this guitar offbeating 'skanking'—thus the name 'ska'. Moreover, Jamaicans emphasised their bass and drum on the second and fourth beat of the bar: the so-called 'back-beat' which is totally the reverse of most standard European music. Using these off-beating techniques, West Indians are able 'reggify' any peice of four-time music. In fact, the Jamaican 'reggae imagination' is so strong that when reggae fans listen to even imported onbeat four-time music, they can automatically hear and dance to it in an off-beat reggae way.

This off-beating 'reggae imagination' is, of course, partly a result of the rich rhythmic heritage they brought from Africa. And this rhythmic sensibility is naturally still part of Ghanaian culture – and is therefore still in Ghanaian minds. Indeed, the traditional Ghanaian rhythmic imagination is so strong that musicians do not need to play all the rhythms out loud. This is why that when a person not familiar with indigenous Ghanaian rhythms listens to an audio-recording of local drum music such as the agbadza (discussed in Chapter 27), they will not get the whole rhythmic picture. It will not include the silent rhythms, such as the agbadza's four non-articulated onbeats, that are nevertheless present in the performer's inward mind or audience's dancing body. Thus, in an audio recording, a whole extra kinetic dimension of silent pulses in the performance is missing: such as hand gestures and rhythmic footwork.

Even though highlife contains foreign ingredients, it is basically a continuation of traditional music. As a result, highlife too has various extra internalised rhythms that are not necessarily played out loud by the musicians, but are supplied by active and participating audiences, like their hand-clap rhythms. Then, there are specific dance movements – such as the two double-steps on the four beats of the bar, and the hip movement on beat three. As in the case of traditional music, highlife dancers supply rhythms that do not actually have to be sounded to be appreciated. They are already in the mental and bodily imaginations of highlife fans.

This 'Highlife Imagination' explains why contemporary Ghanaian youth insist on calling their modern music 'highlife', even though it may not contain any obvious highlife features. The youth were brought up in a highlife culture and, therefore, imaginatively insert highlife percussion and body rhythms into any four-time dance-music, even of foreign disco or hip hop influenced music that uses computers and beat-boxes. So, just as Jamaicans can 'reggify', Ghanaians can 'highlife' (or 'highlify') any piece of imported four-time music. This is exactly what adaha-playing Fanti musicians did to European brass band music a hundred years ago, or E. T. Mensah did to swing sixty years ago. So now we have to give the youth a chance to 'highlife' computer music.

So I end on a note of optimism. As long as traditional music is alive and the 'highlife imagination' is around, Ghanaians will retain their unique rhythmic orientation and always be able to creatively develop their own music and contribute a unique perspective to world music. Moreover, I doubt that in five or ten years, the youth will still be playing today's brand of over-processed computer music. There's always an even younger generation coming up who may get fed-up with too much technological pop and want or demand change. We've already seen this happen in the West with computer-music saturation resulting in many musicians going acoustic, getting unplugged, moving back to live performances and returning to ethnic and roots music.

In fact, there have been signs since the 1990s that this sort of reaction is beginning to occur here in Ghana. There has been the appearance of a new generation of highlife and Afro-fusion dance bands that cater for live gigs – and also numerous re-releases of CDs of old highlife evergreens. Moroever, some hiplifers have collaborated with old-time highlife stars or sampled from old highlife tunes. It was also in the 1990s that highlife courses were integrated into the university syllabus, and several private music archives that include highlife were established, such as Kwame Sarpong's Gramophone Museum in Cape Coast, Kofi Ghanaba's National Heritage Library at Medie, the Bokoor African Popular Music Archives Foundation (BAPMAF) in Accra and Professor Nketia's International Centre for African Music and Dance (ICAMD) based at Legon.

And it is the new developments, including the live music and highlife revival, going on in Ghana since the mid 1990s that is the topic of the last chapter.

Chapter 64

AFTER-THOUGHTS: THE TOURIST BOOM, SAHELIAN GHANAIAN MUSIC, THE HIGHLIFE REVIVAL AND OTHER DEVELOPMENTS SINCE THE MID-1990s

Turning first to the music itself, we have already seen in Chapter 38 that a younger generation of 'jama' style hiplifers have appeared who have moved away from a reliance on imported hiphop beats. They are returning to their roots by utilising the rhythms of traditional music, highlife and Afro-beat, and also beginning to add some local percussion and other instruments in their recordings and stage appearances. These 'new-wave' hiplifers are also beginning to give live performances and are singing as well as rapping. This has resulted to a new genre emerging from the hiplifer generation known as 'contemporary highlife'. In short, the younger generation raised on hiplife is beginning to re-connect with tradition.

And Ghana is lucky in that its rich traditional performance culture was never as severely interrupted by the economic problems of the 1970s and 1980s as was the popular music field. For, whereas popular music depended on foreign imports and an infra-structure of commercial night-clubs, traditional music-making just kept going through those difficult years. The reason is simple: traditional music uses local resources and operates within the non-commercial context of funerals, out-doorings and other customary events.

The situation of gospel music is also very bright as it has trained a whole generation of instrumentalists as well as male and female vocalists who, as the music industry expands, can move into secular music. This would create a situation very similar to what happened in the United States when church-trained 'hot gospel' singers moved into American popular music in the 1950s and 1960s to create soul music. Indeed, if one considers the rise of Ghanaian gospel as being partly a product of the economic collapse of the country in the '70s and '80s, then the similarity between Ghana and the States is even more striking. America had its economic collapse or 'Great Crash' way back in 1929 when record production almost ceased and many unemployed African American jazz and blues musicians moved into the black store-front churches that had multiplied in the poorer areas of cities like Chicago. This produced a fusion of religious and popular music. For instance, the blues pianist Georgia Tom became the composer Dr. Thomas Dorsey of 'hot gospel' fame. With the economic boom that followed the Second World War, church-trained 'hot-gospel' artists like James Brown, Diana Ross and Aretha Franklin went into secular soul, motown music and doo-wop. Ghanaian gospel could be on the verge of a similar transition.

THE TOURIST AND RETURNEES FACTOR

As mentioned in previous chapters, hiplife, contemporary highlife and gospel has created a thriving internal music industry that is catered by literally hundreds of local production companies, digital recording studios and FM radio stations. The local music industry has also been boosted by dramatically increasing numbers of tourists, including World Music fans, coming to Ghana since the 1990s. In 2003, over half a million tourists visited Ghana, bringing with them 600 million dollars, a substantial amount of which was spent on music and entertainment[38]. By 2009, this figure was 800,000 tourists, bringing with them 1.62 billion dollars in foreign exchange and in 2012 over a million visitors bringing in 2.30 billion dollars. As about 9% of this foreign exchange is spent on music and entertainment, the tourist factor is naturally enhancing the local music scene.

[38]Figures from various sources including the Heritage newspaper 28th February, 2005, page 5; Ghanaweb.com Business News 23rd. June 2010 and Graphic Business 30th October, Number 211, 2012 pages 1-3

Also important is the influx of Ghanaians returning from long stays abroad, who bring new musical ideas, with some setting up recording studios, media houses and night clubs. As a result of these Ghanaian returnees, as well as the foreign tourists and World Music fans, there has been a boom in folkloric programs, private drum and dance schools, live music spots and jazz clubs. Venues that have sprung up in the Greater Accra area since the 1990s that feature live highlife, reggae, jazz or Afro-fusion music include the Afrikiko, La Beach, the +233 Club[39], Paloma, Village Inn, Abrantie Spot, Balm Tavern, Chester's, Coco Beach, His Majesty's, Quelquechose, Boomerang, Sunrise, Champs Sports Bar, Osekan, the Golden Tulip, La Palm, Labadi Beach Hotel, Shangri-La Hotel, Asanka Locals, Bywels, Next Door, Cabane Bamboo, Chez Afrique, Odo Jazz Club, Taverna Tropiciana, Tony Maneison's Jazz-Tone Club and Francis Fuster's Kunta Kinte Hotel.

Another group of tourist who are stimulating the local music scene, particualry in the Cape Coast and Elmina area, are the African American and Black Caribbean visitors have been attracted to Ghana since 1992 by PANAFEST. This black diasporic was strengthened from the late 1990s when Ghana began to celebrate Emancipation Day every 31st July, to commemorate the freeing of slaves in the Caribbean in 1838.

Also patronised by tourists and locals alike are the new form of urban street festivals. There is the Osu Street Carnival, initiated in the early 2000s by some of the local FM radio stations in Accra. Then, as part of the Celebration of World Music Rhythms organised in June 2010 by the Accra Culture and Arts Network, the French Embassy and MUSIGA, local brass bands paraded around the Nima area of Accra. The following year (July 2011), the first 'Chale Wote Street Arts Festival' was held in Jamestown Accra, in which 250 artists were involved, with theatrical productions, poetry reading, painting exhibitions and, of course, music and dance. It was sponsored by the French Embassy, the Ga Mashie Development Agency, Pidgen Music and other local art organisations.

THE GROWTH OF SAHELIAN POPULAR MUSIC OF GHANA'S NORTHERN AND UPPER REGIONS MUSIC

Yet another recent development in the Ghanaian music scene is what I call the 'Ghanaian Sahelian' factor. Well-known popular music artists from Ghana's northern and upper regions were less than a handful in the 1970s – like Onipa Nua, Amoa

[39]Located at the old Bass Line/Jazz Optimist Club premises

Azangeo, Prince Ali and Christie Azuma of the Uppers Internationals band. In the 1990s, a few others came onto the scene like Atongo Zimba, Captain Yaba, the African Show Boys, Lady Talata and Aaron Bebe Sukura. But, in the 2000s, and with the opening of numerous music NGOs, promotions, festivals and recording studios in Ghana's Northern, Upper East and West Regions, there has come a flood of new sahelian or savannah artists. These include King Ayisoba, Kawastone (Muhammed Abdul-Rashid), Sheriff Ghale (Mohammed Sheriff Yamusah), Blakk Rasta (Abubakar Ahmed), Abu 'Policeman' Sidiq, Jah Bone (Prince Karim from Wa) and northern

The Ghanaian sahelian sound of Atongo Zimba from the Upper West

hiplifers like D Flex (Abubakar Sadiq from Tamale), KKC, 2Rbees, Lord Wumpini, George Cliff and Lil Malik. Sahelian lady artists include Zina Bizey, Mama Rams, Sirina Issah, Salamata Yakubu ('Sala'), Noella Wiyaala from near Wa and Sherifatu Gunu from Tamale whose 2011 album 'Kanji' combines highlife and traditional rhythms.

According to the Tamale-based reggae artist and recording engineer Sheriff Ghale[40], the music industry in the Tamale and Northern Region took off around 1989, just after the Rawling's PNDC government put Tamale onto the electrical grid and the Depsocom recording studio was set up. Today, there is a small but thriving music industry of studios, producers and retailers that cater for the various music styles of the area. These include traditional and neo-traditional music styles like takai, simpa and jingeling (local fiddle), as well as newer local styles of highlife, hiplife, reggae, Afropop and Bollywood-inspired dance music. Sheriff Ghale mentions more than thirty recording artists from the Tamale area alone that include Lik-K, Don Sigli, Ras Kalimu, Rafio Dachar, Fatawu One-One, Yesu Dagomba, Gordon Lari, Prince Okla, Zacuss, Ahmed Adam, Alfa Tuferu, Kassim Gazor, B-Flesh, Abu Sadio, Bikuraba and Sherifata Issah.

The strength of Tamale as an emerging music centres is also demonstrated by the fact that the New Music Ghana Festival was held there in July 2013, organised by the Insitute of Music and Development. The festival featured bands that fused tradional northern savannah and southern Ghanaian rhythms with highlife and jazz, such as the Bizung Band (of the Tamale Bizung School of Music and Dance), the Bright Stars, North Wings and the Youth Home Band.

THE GOVERNMENT RE-APRAISES THE VALUE OF THE MUSIC SECTOR
All these changes and developments in the Ghanaian music scene, as well as the tourist factor and the World Bank's interest in the African music industry, have made the government re-appraise the music sector. For it is becoming increasing clear that Ghana's musical wealth is, unlike timber, gold and diamonds, a renewable and everlasting source of foreign exchange. As a result, not only did the government reduce import duties on musical instruments in the mid-2000s, it also set up a full Ministry of Culture (and Chieftaincy Affairs), the first time the cultural sector has had this status since the late 1980s. Morevover, in 2005, the music industry was integrated into the NPP government's Poverty Reduction Strategy. Likewise in 2010, this sector

[40] I supervised his M.Phil on 'The Contemporary Popular Artists of Tamale' that he completed in 2015 for the Music Department of the University of Ghana.

*MUSIGA Conference in April 2011. At front (R-L) the Union President Diana Hopeson,
Professor Nketia and John Collins*

was incorporated into the NDC's government Medium Term National Developement
Framework. There were also moves in 2011, supported by musical bodies like
MUSIGA, to set up a Creative Industry Council to give that arts and entertainment
sector a voice at the national level. This was finally established as the 'Creative Arts
Council' in 2017 by the NPP government of President Akuffo-Addo. The recognition
of the Creative Arts industry by musicians and government alike is picked up again in
the concluding Coda of the book.

THE HIGHLIFE REVIVAL

I will end this chapter by looking at what might be called revival of 'classical' highlife
that has been going on for some years now through shows, radio programs and record
re-releases, as well as archives and other music associations being formed that are
dedicated to it. As mentioned in Chapter 56, a similar highlife revival has also been
taking place in Nigeria since 1999, with re-releases of old-time highlife hits by
Evergreen Music and Premier Music, and the various 'Highlife Parties' and 'Highlife
Elders Forums' being put on in Lagos by local and foreign cultural bodies, including
the Goethe Institute.

As noted already Chapter 62, it was the Goethe Institute in Accra that (together with BAPMAF) helped spark off the current Ghanaian highlife revival when they organised a Highlife Month and Photographic Exhibition in 1996. Then, in 2001, the French Embassy, BAPMAF and Paa K. Holbrook-Smith's Harmattan Music Company organised the two-week 'Story of Highlife' event at the Alliance Francaise that included highlife exhibitions, performances and workshops run by Ebo Taylor. The following year, the Swiss Embassy and BAPMAF launched the 'Ghana Popular Music 1931-57' CD at the Dubois Centre in Accra. In 2005, the joint US Embassy Public Affairs/BAPMAF 'African American Heritage/History Month', recognising the link between jazz and highlife, gave Lifetime/Cultural Ambassador Awards to the highlife pioneers Jerry Hansen, Oscarmore Ofori, Stan Plange, Otoo Lincoln, Ebo Taylor, Mac Tontoh, Saka Acquaye and Kwadwo Donkor.

Then, in 2004 and initiated by the Nigerian Professor Awam Amkpa, the New York University in Ghana Akonu Dake's Heritage Development Foundation put on a 'Celebration of Highlife' at the National Theatre with seminars and concert performances by the Sappers, Ramblers, C.K. Mann, Wulomei, Mac Tontoh and Castro.

In 2005, the Citi FM Radio Station set up their Music of Ghanaian Origin (MOGO) organisation that has been regularly hosting shows since 2005. MOGO featured featured Osibisa in the maiden edition in 2005. And, in 2006, the seventy-year-old veteran highlife composer, Ebo Taylor, formed the Ghana Music Foundation together with other highlife musicians and fans (Stan Plange, Dr. Eddie Soga, Paa K., Cox Tamakloe, Mr. Goody and myself). The Foundation was formally launched in October 2006 at a 'Highlife Extravaganza' garden party held at the house of the then World Bank Country Director Mats Karlsson (himself a cello player) and his wife Irena Kunovska. At the event, Ebo Taylor's University highlife dance band and the Local Dimension palmwine group played, and highlife stars were featured, like C.K. Mann, Paapa Yankson, Stan Plange, Jewel Ackah, Kwadwo Donkor, Eddie Soga (ex-Ramblers) and Kojo Menu. The Minister of Health, the late Colonel Quashigah, also surprised the audience when he jammed on drums, after telling the crowd that he had once played for the Hot Barrels army band.

For the country's 50th independence anniversary in 2007, a number of highlife concerts took place, followed by two 'Made in Germany' celebrations of burger highlife in 2007 and 2008 as well as the French-sponsored Cultural Caravan in 2009. The same year, a conference on the future of highlife was held at Cape Coast, financed by the EU Cultural Initiative Support Programme and organised by the musicians Ben Brako and Ato Scott Bennin with Kofi Tsikita of the World Bank. Shortly after this, Ben Brako launched his Highlife Institute project.

New spots, venues and programs have also opened that cater for highlife and live music. Some of these include Guitars in the Park, Hypnotic, Bless the Mike, the New Morning Club, Chelsea Place, Baze Lounge, Famous Five, High Vibes Festival, the +233 Jazz Grill, the Taverna Tropicana, 'Saturday Night Live' at the Africa Regent Hotel and the various 'Hilife Festivals' being organised at the Alisa Hotel and National Theatre by Mark Okraku Mantey. The Danish Embassy, Goethe Institute and Alliance Francaise have also become interested in spotting and sponsoring artistic talent through the 'New Music Ghana' competition, which was won in 2009 by the Wind Afrique Afro-rock band and in 2010 by the Royal Echoes that combines jazz, highlife and the rhythms of the Volta Region. This competition has also featured up-and-coming university bands that combine jazz, highlife and local rhythms, such the Big Shots from Legon, the Eden Vibes from Kumasi and the Afringo band from Cape Coast. Futhermore, there have been in recent years a number of television and radio shows that foster live performances, like Music Music, TV3 Mentor House, Bands Alive, Cover Version, Stars of the Future, Vodofon Icon and Citi FM's Voice Factory.

I should mention that the film director Kwesi Owusu of the Creative Storm music company made a full-length local film on highlife called 'Singing for Freedom: The Influence of Hilife on Popular Music'. It was released in 2010 and contains interviews and performance with/by Kojo Antwi, Gyedu Blay Ambolley, Paulina Oduro, Ebo Taylor, Kari Bannerman, Mac Tonto, John Collins, Kofi Ghanaba, Reggae Rockston, Faisal Helwani, Asem and 4x4.

TEN CURRENT GHANAIAN MUSICAL POTS

To close, I will provide a list of ten types of current Ghanaian musical styles that are like pots simmering on a musical stove – and which will provide the ingredients for future local music developments and music genres.

1. The first is the musical pot that contains old time highlife, as many of the veteran highlife stars and bands have survived the ravages of the 1970s and

80s: Koo Nimo, the new Ramblers, C.K. Mann, the late Paapa Yankson, Ambolley, Jackson A. Ampofo and his City Boys, Pat Thomas, Amakye Dede, Nana Tuffour, Kofi Sammy and many more.

2.   Then we have the disco-influenced 'made in Germany' burger highlife of George Darko, Daddy Lumba and Nana Acheampong.

3.   There also many current highlife artists, like Rex Omar, Amandzeba, Bessa Simons, Ben Brako, Ackah Blay, Kwame Yeboah, Paulina Oduro, K.K. Kabobo and Lucky Mensah.

4.   Another pot simmering on our musical stove is hiplife – now moving away from miming onstage to live performance. Some use local 'jama' rhythms and others sing in 'contemporary' highlife mode: the late Daasebre, Adane Best, K.K. Fosu, Ofori Amponsah, Kofi B, 2Rbees, Kwabena Kwabena and Oheneba Kissi. Some also collaborate with old highlife stars, like Obour with A.B. Crentsil.

5.   Since the 1980s, there has been a 'gospel explosion'. Indeed, danceable highlife gospel now constitutes around 60% of locally-produced music. Moreover, church bands have become the training grounds for band instrumentalists and a venue for women singers.

6.   Yet another pot simmering on the musical stove is 'folkloric' or 'neo-tradional' music, being given a huge commercial boost through the interest of foreign tourists and World Music fans. Some examples of groups that perform updated traditional music include Hewaleh, Kusum Gboo, the Kusun Ensemble, Gauda, Gonje, the Sensational Wulomei, the Royal Obonu Drummers and and Azonko Simpi's Synchro Cultural Band.

7.   Yet another musical pot is a result of the input of some of the three or four million Ghanaian returnees coming to settle back home after many years abroad. This has not only resulted in a proliferation of jazz clubs but also of jazz, Afro-jazz and Afro-fusion bands like Takashie, Bawasaaba, Big Wellington's group, the Sound Factory and Nii Noi Nortey's most recent group, the African Sound Project.

8. Furthermore, the younger Ghanaian returnees who were born abroad are stimulating the growth of venues where live performance of music, poetry and free styling rap take place – like Guitars in the Park and also Bless the Mike that has now developed (sponsored by the French Embassy) into a regular full-blown festival.

9. As mentioned earlier in this chapter, another new development is the rise of Ghanaian 'sahelian' music from Ghana's Northern and Upper Regions. This has been particularly noticeable since the 1990s.

10. The last of these pots simmering on our musical stove is the oldest of all –traditional communal and ceremonial Ghanaian music associated particularly with those living in the rural areas. Luckily, this age-old traditional music was not severly affected by the military regimes the 1970s and 1980s. One reason was that the curfews and shortages of those days did not effect the rural communites as much as it did the towns and cities. Another is that traditional musicians use home-grown natural products like wood and animal skins, so could go on playing despite the lack of imported goods like western musical instruments. So, today, ethnic traditional music still kicking and can still interact with popular music forms. Indeed, traditional music has always been the backbone of Ghanaian popular music and will continue to be so.

The reader should note that in the the Prologue of this book I have expanded the number of musical pots from ten to seventeen.

How all these different musical ingredients – local and imported, cultural and techno, male and female, northern and southern – presently cooking away will actually be blended, brewed and cooked together remains to be seen. But, with so many musical pots on the boil, the future for Ghanaian highlife and other forms of local popular music looks bright.

Coda

HIPLIFE, AZONTO, TWI POP, MUSIGA AND THE CREATIVE ARTS INDUSTRY

This coda updates things to include developments in the music scene that occurred up to the middle of 2013. Events after this are covered in the Prologue of this book.

As mentioned in Chapter 38, since around 2005, a distinct split in the hiplife scene has developed. There is the 'underground 'GH Rap of freestyling' artists like 50 Cedis, Hammer, Okyeame Kwame, Motia, Sarkodie, Scientific, Tinniequaye and D. Black. Then, there are other young hiplifers who sing in highlife or raga/dancehall style (or incorporate local 'jama' rhythms), use some live instruments and perform live. These include Batman-Samini, X-Doe, Castro, Wutah, Praye, Tic Tac, Wanluv the Kubolor, M.anifest and the 2Rbees. Whilst others who passed through hiplife have become 'contemporary highlife' artists, like Ofori Amponsah, K.K. Fosu, Lucky Mensah, Oheneba Kissi, Nana Fynn, Nana Quame, Kwabena Kwabena, Daasebre Gyamenah and Adane Best.

A new development in the hiplife scene is that, after so many years since its inception, a specific dance form has become associated with it that is called 'Azonto' (let's erotically touch). Although danced to electronic beats, this new dance uses some of the moves of older Ghanaian dance styles like the Ga kpanlogo and, according to the dancer/scholar Terry Bright Ofosu, Ga 'apa' work movements. Indeed, the azonto dance has become so internationally fashionable that Nigerians are trying to claim it as their own, by renaming it 'alingo'.

Yet another development in the area of hiplife is that there is now a convergence going on between this Ghanaian version of American hiphop, and American 'contemporary R&B/urban'. This use of the R&B singing mode by hiplifers, in fact, goes way back to the Ghanaian artists Ded Buddy (Eric Turkson) and Nana Quame (Henry De-Mensah) in the 1990s. However, nowadays more and more artists are using this singing style, and some of the current ones who switch between or combine hiplife and R&B include the soft crooner voiced Fianco 'Chase' Bossman, Nii (Jospeh Nii Otu Ankrah), Samini, DJ Black (Kwadwo Ampofo), Nana Kwabena, K. K. Fosu, Kofi Nti, DJ Ashmen, Madzone and Richie (Richard Mensah). At the same time, a crop of artists have moved more into the new 'Twi-pop' style that combines R&B with Akan highlife, singing more than hiplife rapping.

This 'Twi-pop' fusion of Akan singing, hiplife and R&B is similar to the trend that took place in the US from the late 1980s when hip hop and contemporary R&B fed into the 'new jack swing', 'hiphop soul' and 'neo soul' styles of artists like Boys II Men, Mos Def, Jennifer Lopez, Beyonce, Lauryn Hill, Erykah Badu and D'Angelo. In both the American and Ghanaian cases, hiphop music moved away from being used to back rappers to being absorbed into new sung genres of music in America hiphop, fused with contemporary R&B. On the other hand, in Ghana, it was rather hiplife beats that fused with modern R&B sung in local languages. And as popular singing in Ghana is generally in the highlife style and the Akan languages, this blend of R&B has become known as 'Twi pop'. Incidentally, when using other Ghanaian and Nigerian popular music modes and languages, this hiphop/R&B influenced music is called 'Afropop', or even sometimes 'Afrobeats' (with an 's' to distinguish it from Fela Kuti's Afrobeat).

Exponents of the new Ghanaian hiphop/hiplife/R&B 'Twi-pop' style includes the lady singers Becca (Rebecca Akosua Acheampong), Jane 'Efya' Awindor, Mildred 'Eazzy' Ashong, the Liberian-born Jane Logan and Sala Yacubu. On the male side, there is Chico Dawuni, 5Five, Jay Ghartey, Wutah, Nana Boroo (Osei Bonsu), Morris 'Babyface' de Voice, 4X4, Chase (Fianco Bossman) and the Bradez duo of Kunta Kinte and Stone. Henry Dr. Cryme actually calls his hiplife/highlife/R&B fusion 'Twi Pop', whilst Boy Wadon and Henry 'Chemphe' Agyekum call their respective styles

'Komdigi' and 'urbanlife'. Yet another exponent of Twi pop is R2Bees (Refuse to Be Broke), a rap duo consisting of Rashid Mugeez and Faisal Hakeem who collaborated with Nigerian R&B/Afropop star Wande Coal. Coal himself shot to fame with his love song 'Ololufe' on his 'Hustling' album (Mo' Hits label) and won the Ghana Music Awards' Best African Artist of the year in 2007. Indeed, in recent years, a growing number of Nigerian Naija rap and Afropop artists have visited Ghana. These include P-Square, M.I. (Mr. Incredible), 2face Idibia, Tony Tetuila, J. Martins, 9ice, Naeto C, Bracket, Flavour and Midnight Crew.

Despite all these developments in hiplife, it would still be true to say the 'jama' and 'contemporary highlife' styles dominate the youthful hiplife scene at present – with an increasing trend towards live performance, 'freestyling', the use of indigenous musical and rhythmic resources, and singing in an R&B-influenced 'Twi pop' or 'Afropop' mode. As noted in Chapter 38, Barima Sydney (or Sidney) was one of the pioneers of live performance hiplifers. Some others are Kwaw Kese, Mensah, Wanluv the Kubolor and M.anifest. A very recent example is Okyeame Kwame who is now putting on 'Versatile Shows' that stage dramatic concerts that involves dance and combines hiplife music with fontomfrom and other traditional drumming.

Here, I will turn from new hiplife developments to Ghana's music industry, starting with the Musicians Union of Ghana which now, for the first time, includes large numbers of hiplifers. As mentioned earlier in the book, the gospel singer Diana Hopeson took over the presidency of MUSIGA in 2008 and was in charge there until 2011 when new elections were held in Tamale. At this conference, the hiplfe artist Obour (Bice Ofei Kuffour) was elected President, supported by executive members Bessa Simons, Rex Omar, Ahuma Bosco Ocansey, Della Hayes, Debbie Freeman and also fellow hiplifers Kaykire Kwame Appiah, Tic Tac and Appiatus.

One of the first moves by MUSIGA was to twin itself with its UK counterpart, the British Musicians Union. Then, in late 2012, MUSIGA began organising a series of research forums on the Ghanaian music industry to establish the economic contribution of the music sector to Ghana's National Growth Domestic Product (GDP). As a result, the union contracted the KPMG – the Audit, Tax and Advisory Services Company – as consultant and I was attached to the KPMG team The ultimate aim of this research project was to encourage the Ghanaian government to appreciate the importance of the commercial music industry, formulate state policies and legislation that will assist its growth, deal with music piracy and re-introduce music into the school curriculum.

As part of this MUSIGA-KPMG project, on January 15, 2013, MUSIGA held a Stakeholders' Forum at the British Council entitled, 'Revitalizing the Creative Art Industry: the Contribution of the Music Sector to the Socio-Economic Development of Ghana'. This focused on the Ghanaian music industry and its impact on society. The participants were broken up into four groups: the creators, the policymakers, the business people, and the marketing and packaging people.

The results of the MUSIGA-KPMG project came out in 2015 and provided an input into the various governmental iniatives to recognise and boost the countries Creative Arts Industries. This was in line with Ghanaian government Shared Growth and Development Agenda (GSGDA) of 2010-2013. One result of this was that the Cultural and Tourist sectors were removed from the Ministry of Chieftaincy Affairs and rather attached to the brand new Ministery of Tourism, Culture and Creative Arts. The formation of this new Ministry was a result of the government realising the commercial importance of the Creative Arts Industries. Indeed, during the MUSIGA Ghana Music Week held in March 2013 at at the National Theatre, the Minister of this new Ministry, Mrs Elizabeth Ofusu-Agyare, was hosted by the union. Another sign of this government's interest in the creative arts was that, in May 2013, the Ghana Cultural Forum organised a conference on 'Transforming the Cultural and Creative Arts Sector' at the National Theatre, with its guest of honour being P.V. Obeng, the Presidential Advisor and Chairman of the National Development Planning Committee. As mentioned earlier, a Creative Art Council was finally set up by the NPP government in 2017.

This convergence of musicians, cultural workers, tax experts and government agencies – combined with the simmering musical pots mentioned in the previous chapter – all bode well for the Ghanaian music industry.

REFERENCES AND SELECTED BIBLIOGRAPHY

ADEMOWO Paul Wale (1993) History of Fuji Music in Nigeria. Effective Publishers Ibadan.

AGAWU Kofi (1986) 'Gi Dunu "Nyekpadudo" and the Study of West African Rhythm'. Ethnomusicology, Vol. 30, No.1, Winter.

AGOVI K. E. (1989) 'The Political Relevance of Ghanaian Highlife Songs Since 1957'. Research in African Literatures, Vol. 20 (3).

ANKU Willie (2002) Structural Set Analysis of African Music. Soundstage Production, Ghana.

ARANZADI Isabela de. 2010 'A Drum's Trans-Atlantic Journey from Africa to the Americas and Back After the End of Slavery: Annobonese and Fernandino Musical Cultures'. African Sociological Review 14 (1) pages 20-47.

AROM Simha. (1991) African Polyphony and Polyrhythm. Cambridge University Press.

BAME K.N. (1985) Come To Laugh: African Traditional Theatre in Ghana. Lilian Barber Press New York.

BARBER Karin, COLLINS John & RICARD Alain (1997) West African Popular Theatre. Indiana University Press/James Currey.

BEBE Francis. (1975) African Music: A People's Art. Lawrence Hill, New York.

BENDER Wolfgang. (1985) Sweet Mother. Trickster Verlag, Germany

BERLINER Paul. (1994) Thinking in Jazz: The Infinite Art of Improvisation, University. of Chicago Press.

BOONZAJER- FLAES Rob. (2000) Brass Unbound. Royal Tropical Institute, The Netherlands.

BREMPONG Owusu (1984) Akan Highlife in Ghana: Songs of Cultural Transition. PhD Thesis, Indiana University.

CAPROF Fritjof (1975) The Tao of Physics. Shambhala Press.

CHARBENEAUE Travis. (1989) 'Rehumanise Your Sequence,.Part 5', Music Technology, June.

CHERNOFF John Miller (1979) African Rhythms and African Sensibilities, University. of Chicago Press.

CLARK Ebun (1979) Hubert Ogunde: The Making of NigerianTheatre. Oxford Univ. Press.

COLE Cathy. (2001) Ghana's Concert Party Theatre. Indiana University Press, Bloomington US

COLLINS John (1985) Music Makers of West Africa. Three Continents Press/Passeggiata Press, Pueblo, Colorado, USA..

COLLINS John. (1992) West African Pop Roots. Temple University Press, USA.

COLLINS John. (1996) E.T. Mensah the King of Highlife. Anansesem Press, Accra.

COLLINS John. (2000) 'Hi-technology, Individual Copyright and Ghanaian Music'. Ghana: Changing Values/Changing Technologies. Helen Lauer (ed), Council for Research in Values and Philosophy, U.S.

COLLINS John. (2004) Entry on West African "Highlife" African Folklore: An Encyclopaedia, (eds.) Phillip Peek and Kwesi Yankah. Routledge, New York and London.

COLLINS John. (2004).'Ghanaian Popular Performance and the Urbanisation Process: 1900-1980'. Transactions: Journal of the Historical Society of Ghana (eds. Irene Odotey & Per Hernaes) New Series, No. 8.

COLLINS John. (2005) African Musical Symbolism in Contemporary Perspective: Roots Rhythms and Relativity. Pro-Business Book on Demand, Schwedenstr.14, 13357 Berlin.

COLLINS John. (2005) A Social History of Ghanaian Popular Entertainment since Independence. Transactions: Journal of the Ghana Historical Society (eds: Irene Odotey & Per Hernaes) New Series 9, University of Ghana.

COLLINS John (2006) 'Entry on Ghana'. The Rough Guide to World Music: Africa and the Middle East, (eds.) Simon Broughton, Mark Ellington and Jon Lusk. Rough Guide, London.

COLLINS John (2006) 'African Guitarism: 100 Years of West African Highlife'. Legon Journal of the Humanities, Vol. XVII, pp. 173-196, (eds. Gordon Adika & Kofi Ackah). Published by the Faculty of Arts, University of Ghana, Legon.

COLLINS John (2007) 'The Pan-African Goombay Drum-Dance: Its Ramifications and Development in Ghana'. Legon Journal of the Humanities, Vol. XVIII, pp. 179-200, (eds. Gordon Adika & Kofi Ackah). Published by the Faculty of Arts, University of Ghana Legon.

COLLINS John (2007) 'The Entrance of Women into Ghanaian Popular Entertainment'. The Legacy of Efua Sutherland: Pan African Cultural Activism, edited by Anne V. Adams and Efua Sutherland-Addy, published Ayebia Clark Publishing Ltd, UK, 2007 pp. 47-54

COLLINS John (2009) 'Popular Dance Music and the Media'. Media and Identity in Africa (eds. Kimani Njogu and John Middleton) Edinburgh University Press for the International African Institute.

COLLINS John. (2009) Fela: Kalakuta Notes Dutch Royal Tropical Insitute. Republished in expanded form in 2015 by Wesleyan University Press, USA

COLLINS John (2009) 'Ghana and the World Music Boom'. World Music: Roots and Routes, Helsinki Collegium for Advanced Studies, Vol, 6 ed., Tuulikki Pietila
http://www.helsinki.fi/collegium/e-series/volumes/volume_6/index.htm

COLLINS John (2009/10) 'Highlife and Nkrumah's Independence Ethos'. Journal of Performing Arts, Vol. 4, No. 1, pp. 93-104 Published by the School of Performing Arts, University of Ghana,

Legon,

COLLINS John (2010) 'Popularmusikens Generationsvaxling – Exemplet Ghana'. Kultur I Africa (ed Mai Palmberg & Carita Backstrom of the Nordikiska Afrikainstutet), published by Bokforlaget Tranan AB, Stockholm, Sweden pp. 44-53.

COLLINS John (2011) 'World Music: A Stimulus to Ghanaian Tourism. Education & 'Cross-Over'' Musical Collaborations'. Journal of Performing Arts, Univ. of Ghana Vol. 4, No. 2, pp. 71-80.

COLLINS John (2012) 'Some Reasons for Teaching African Popular Music in University'. Reclaiming the Human Sciences and Humanities Through African Perspectives, Vol. 2, (ed. Helen Lauer & Kofi Anyidoho). Sub-Saharan Publishers, Ghana, pp. 1412-1423.

COLLINS John & AGYEMAN Ivor (2013) The Protestants from Abeokuta: Fela Kuti and His Cousin'. Crucible of the Ages - Wole Soyinka at 80: Essays in Honour of African Literary and Cultural Studies. Agyeman-Duah Ivor and Ogochukwu Promise. (eds) Published by Bookcraft (Nigeria) and Ayebia Clarke Publishers (UK), pp. 177-185.

COLLINS John (2013) 'A Historical Review of Popular Entertainment in Sub-Saharan Africa'. Africa in Contemporary Perspective: A Textbook for Undergraduate Students, eds. Takyiwaa Manuh and Esi Sutherland Addy, published by Sub Saharan Publishers, pp. 445-466.

COLLINS John (2014) 'The Ghanaian and Nigerian Gospel Music Explosion'. Journal of Performing Arts, (ed E. J. Collins) University of Ghana School of Performing Arts, Vol. 4, No. 4, pp. 115-132

COLLINS John (2014,) 'Ghanaian Popular Performance: A Century of Changing Urban Spaces, Venues and Identities'. The Performing Arts in Africa: Ghanaian Perspectives (eds. A. Asiedu, E.J.Collins, F.Gbormittah and F. Nii-Yartey). Ayebia Clarke Publishing, Oxford, UK, pp. 43-57

COLLINS John [MUSIGA/KPMG consultant.] (2015) Comprehensive Study of the Music Sector:Abridged Final Report, By MUSIGA in consultation with KPMG. Published by MUSIGA, Accra

COLLINS John ((2016) Highlife Giants: West African Dance Band Pioneers, Cassava Republic Press, Abuja, Nigeria

COLLINS John (2017) 'Popular Performance and Culture in Ghana: Past 50 Years'. Ghana Studies, University of Wisconsin, USA, Vol. 20, Issue, 1 , pp. 175-219

COLLINS John (forthcoming) West African Popular Music: Textbook for African Schools and Colleges, Council for the Development of Social Science Research in Africa (CODESRIA), Dakar, Senegal COPLAN David. (1975) 'Go to my Town Cape Coast: The Social History of Ghanaian Highlife'. Eight Urban Musical Cultures, (ed) B. Nettl, University of Indiana Press.

EMIELU, Austin 'Maro. (2013). Nigerian Highlife Music. Centre for Black African Arts and Civilisation, Lagos, Nigeria

EWENS Graeme. (1991) Africa Oh Ye: A Celebration of African Music. Guinness Books, UK.

GRAHAM Ronnie. (1998/9) Stern's /De Capo's Guide to Contemporary African Music (Vols. 1 and 2). Zwan/Off The Record Press and Pluto Press, London.

JAFFE David: 'Ensemble Timing in Computer Music'. Computer Music Journal, Vol.9, No.4.

Jones A.M. (1959) Studies in African Music. Oxford University Press.

KERR David. (1995) African Popular Theatre. James Currey/East African Educational Books.

KEIL, Charles.. (1966). 'Motion and Feeling Through Music': Journal of Aesthetics and Art Criticism, No. 24. Also a chapter in Rappin' and Sylin' Out: Communication in Black Urban America (ed) T. Kochman. University of Illinois Press, Urbana, 1972.

KOO NIMO and LATHAN J. L. (1969) Ashanti Ballads. Published by the authors.

KUBIK Gerhard (1962) 'The Phenomenon of Inherent Rhythms in East and Central African Instrumental Music'. African Music, Vol. 3, No. 1.

MAZZOLENI Florent & OWUSU Kwesi (2012). Ghana Highlife Music, Institut Francaise, Ghana.

MENSAH A. A. (1971/72) 'Jazz the Round Trip'. Jazz Research, No.3/4, Graz. Germany.

MOORE Carlos. (1982). Fela Fela, This Bitch of a Life'. Allison and Busby, London.

NEMVALTS Kalle (1988) 'Sequence the Swings with Performer'. Electronic Musician, March.

NKETIA J.H.K (1971) 'History and organisation of Music in West Africa'. Chapter One of Essays on Music and History in West Africa, (ed) K. Wachsmann. Published North-western Univ. Press.

NKETIA J.H.K. (1973) Folksongs of Ghana. Ghana University Press.

NKETIA J.H.K. (1981) 'On the Historicity of Music in West Africa'. African Cultures, Bayreuth University Papers.

OWENS, Thomas (1974) 'Applying the Melograph to `Parker's Mood'. Selected Reports in Ethnomusicology, Vol. 2, No.1.

OSUMARE Halifu (2012). Hiplife in Ghana, Palgrave Macmillan

PLAGEMAN Nate, (2013) Highlife Saturday Night. Indiana University Press, USA,

REINHOLDSON Peter (1987). 'Approaching Jazz Performances Empirically': Action and Perception in Rhythm and Music (ed) A. Gabrielsson, Royal Swedish Academy of Music, No. 55.

SACKEY Chrys. (1995) Highlife. Lit Verlag, Munster, Germany.

SCHOONMAKER Trevor: editor. (2003) Fela: From West Africa to West Broadway. Palgrave/MacMillan. Includes a chapter by John Collins called 'The Black President'.

SHIPLEY Jesse, (2013) Living the Hiplife. Duke University Press, USA,

STEWART, Michael (1987) 'The Feel Factor: Music with Soul'. Electronic Musician, October.

SPRIGGE Robert. (1961). 'The Ghanaian Highlife: Notation and Sources'. Music in Ghana, Institute of African Studies, University of Ghana, Legon.

STASIK Michael. (2010). DISCOnnections: Popular Music Audiences in Freetown, Sierra Leone. M.A. Thesis, African Studies Centre, University of Leiden.

SUTHERLAND Efua (1970) The Original Bob: The Story of Bob Johnson Ghana's Ace Comedian. Anowuo Educational Publications, Accra, Ghana.

VAN DER GEEST S. and ASANTE-DARKO N. K. 1982. 'The Political Meaning of Highlife Songs in Ghana'. American Studies Review, Vol. XXV (1), March.

VAN OVEN Cootje. 1981/2. An Introduction to the Music of Sierra Leone. Published by the Ministry of Development Cooperation of the Netherlands.

VEAL Michael. (2000) Fela: An African Musical Icon. Temple University Press, US.

WARD W. E. (1927) 'Music in the Gold Coast'. Gold Coast Review, Volume 3.

WATERMAN Chris. (1990) Juju: A Social History and Ethnography of an African Popular Music. University of Chicago Press.

WATERMAN Richard. (1952) 'African Influence in the Americas. Acculturation in the Americas, (ed) Sol Tax, University of Chicago Press, 207-218.

YANKAH Kwese. (1984) 'The Akan Highlife Song: A Medium for Cultural Reflection or Deflection?' Research in African Literatures, Vol 15 (4), Winter, University of Texas Press.

YOUNG Neil. (1992) 'Digital is a Huge Rip Off'. Guitar Player, May.